The Inventi
of the White

V

THE HAYMARKET SERIES

Editors: Mike Davis and Michael Sprinker

The Haymarket Series offers original studies in politics, history and culture, with a focus on North America. Representing views across the American left on a wide range of subjects, the series will be of interest to socialists both in the USA and throughout the world. A century after the first May Day, the American left remains in the shadow of those martyrs whom the Haymarket Series honors and commemorates. These studies testify to the living legacy of political activism and commitment for which they gave their lives.

The Invention
of the White Race

Volume Two:
The Origin of Racial Oppression
in Anglo-America

THEODORE W. ALLEN

VERSO

London · New York

First published by Verso 1997
© Theodore W. Allen 1997
All rights reserved

Verso
UK: 6 Meard Street, London W1V 3HR
USA: 180 Varick Street, New York NY 10014–4606

Verso is the imprint of New Left Books

ISBN 1–85984–981–4
ISBN 1–85984–076–0 (pbk)

British Library Cataloguing in Publication Data
A catalogue record for this book is available from the British Library

Library of Congress Cataloging-in-Publication Data
A catalog record for this book is available from the Library of Congress

Typeset by CentraCet Ltd, Cambridge
Printed by Biddles Ltd, Guildford and King's Lynn

"There is a sacred veil to be drawn over the beginnings of all government." (Edmund Burke, 16 February 1788, on the impeachment trial of Warren Hastings for maladministration of British rule in India)

"The origin of states gets lost in a myth, in which one may believe, but which one may not discuss." (Karl Marx, *The Civil War in France, 1848–1850*)

Contents

List of Figures

List of Tables

A Note on Dates

Prior to 1750, the legal year began on 25 March. Therefore, dates from 1 January through 24 March are often rendered with a double-year notation. For example, 24 March 1749 would be written as 24 March 1748/9, but the next day would be given as 25 March 1749. But a year later the dates for those March days would be, in the normal modern way, 24 March 1750 and 25 March 1750. Where one year only is indicated, it is to be understood to accord with the modern calendar.

PART ONE
Labor Problems of the European Colonizing Powers

The Labor Supply Problem:
England a Special Case

In 1497, within half a decade of Columbus's first return to Spain from America, the Anglo-Italian Giovanni Caboto, or John Cabot as he was known in his adopted country, made a discovery of North America, and claimed it for King Henry VII, the first Tudor monarch of England. The English westering impulse, after then lying dormant for half a century, gradually revived in a variety of projects, schemes and false starts. By the first decade of the seventeenth century, an interval of peace with Spain having arrived with the accession of James I to the throne, English colonization was an idea whose time had come.[1] In 1607 the first permanent English settlement in America was founded at Jamestown, Virginia. By the end of the first third of the century four more permanent Anglo-American colonies had been established: Somers Islands (the Bermudas), 1612; Plymouth (Massachusetts), 1620; Barbados, 1627; and Maryland, 1634.[2]

The English were confronted with the common twofold problem crucial to success in the Americas: (1) how to secure an adequate supply of labor; and (2) how to establish and maintain the degree of social control necessary to assure the rapid and continuous expansion of their capital by the exploitation of that labor. In each of these respects, however, the English case differed from those of other European colonizing powers in the Americas, in ways that have a decisive bearing on the origin of the "peculiar institution" – white racial oppression, most particularly racial slavery – in continental Anglo-America.

European Continental Powers and the Colonial Labor Supply

The continental European colonizing powers, for economic, military and political reasons, and in some cases because of access to external sources, did not employ Europeans as basic plantation laborers.

Spain and Portugal

The accession in 1516 of Francis I of France and in 1517 of Charles I of Spain, and the installation of the latter as Charles V, Emperor of the Holy Roman

Empire, in 1519, set off a round of warring that would involve almost every country in Europe, from Sweden to Portugal, from the Low Countries to Hungary, for a century and a quarter. The Spanish-headed Holy Roman Empire was at the same time heavily engaged in war with the Ottoman Turks until after the defeat of the latter in the Mediterranean naval battle of Lepanto in 1571. Portugal, with a population of fewer than 1.4 million,[3] was involved in protecting its world-circling empire against opposition from both Christian and Moslem rivals. France was Spain's main adversary in the struggle over Italy, the Netherlands and smaller European principalities.

These wars imposed great manpower demands on every one of the continental governments seeking at the same time to establish colonial ventures. Belligerents who could afford them sought to hire soldiers from other countries. The bulk of Spain's armies, for example, were made up of foreign mercenaries.[4] Portugal, however, lacking Spain's access to American silver and gold to maintain armies of foreign mercenaries, had to rely on its own resources.[5] So critical was the resulting manpower situation in 1648 that Antonio Vieira, the chief adviser to King John IV, felt obliged to advocate the temporary surrender of Brazil to Protestant Holland as the best way out of the sea of troubles besetting the Portuguese interest in Africa, Asia, America, and, indeed, vis-à-vis Portugal's Iberian neighbor. Portugal was so depleted of men for defense, he said, that "every alarm" took "laborers from the plough."[6] Even if, despite this circumstance, a ploughman did manage to get to Brazil, he was not to be expected to do any manual labor there: "the Portuguese who emigrated to Brazil, even if they were peasants from the tail of the plough, had no intention of doing any manual work."[7]

Bartolomé de Las Casas, concerned with the genocidal exploitation of the native population by the Christian colonizers in the West Indies, suggested that, "If necessary, white and black slaves be brought from Castile [Spain] to keep herds, build sugar mills, wash gold," and otherwise be of service to the colonists. In 1518, Las Casas briefly secured favorable consideration from King Carlos for a detailed proposal designed to recruit "quiet peasants" in Spain for emigration to the West Indies. The emigrants were to be transported free of charge from their Spanish homes to the colonies. Once there, they were to be "provided with land, animals, and farming tools, and also granted a year's supply of food from the royal granaries." But, again, these emigrant peasants were not expected to do much labor. Rather they were to be provided with slaves from Spain. It was specified that any emigrant who offered to build a sugar mill in the Indies was to be licensed to take twenty Negro slaves with him. With his assistants, Las Casas toured Spain on behalf of the plan and received a favorable response from the peasants he wanted to recruit for the project. But as a result mainly of the opposition of great landowners who feared the loss of their tenants in such a venture, the plan was quickly defeated.[8] Thus was defined official emigration policy; it assured that Spaniards going to the American colonies were not to be laborers, but such as lawyers and clerks, and men (women emigrants were extremely few) of the nobility or knighthood, who were "forbidden by force of custom even to think of industry or commerce."[9] A few Spanish and Portuguese convicts, presumably of satisfactory Christian ancestry, were transported to the colonies early on, but they were not intended and themselves did not intend to serve in the basic colonial labor force.[10]

The single instance in which basic plantation labor needs were supplied from the Iberian population occurred in 1493. In that year, two thousand Jewish children, eight years old and younger, were taken from their parents, baptized as Christians, and shipped to the newly founded Portuguese island sugar colony of São Tomé, where fewer than one-third were to be counted thirteen years later.[11]

In Spain, seven years of plague and famine from 1596 to 1602, followed by the expulsion of 275,000 Christianized Moors in a six-year period beginning in 1602,[12] reduced the population by 600,000 or 700,000, one-tenth of all the inhabitants.[13] Thus began a course of absolute population decline that lasted throughout the seventeenth century.[14] As it had been with the Jews before, the expelled *moriscos* were officially ineligible for emigration to the Americas, since émigrés were required to prove several generations of Catholic ancestry.[15]

Holland

For the better part of a century up to the 1660s, Holland, in the process of winning her independence from Spain in the Eighty Years' War (1568–1648), was the leading commercial and trading country of Europe. Holland's 10,000 ships exceeded the total number held by the rest of northern Europe combined.[16] On this basis the new Dutch Republic developed a thriving and expanding internal economy. Large areas were diked and drained to increase the amount of cultivable land.[17] Up until 1622, Dutch cities grew, some at a phenomenal rate; in that year, half of Holland's population lived in cities of more than 10,000 inhabitants.[18] The population of Amsterdam alone had grown to 105,000, three and a half times its size in 1585.[19] These cities were expanding not from an influx of displaced Dutch peasants, but because urban needs were growing faster than those of rural areas,[20] and because Holland's "obvious prosperity ... acted as a lodestar to the unemployed and the under-employed of neighboring countries."[21]

Although the casual laborer in Holland was frequently out of work, "unemployment ... was never sufficiently severe to induce industrial and agricultural workers to emigrate on an adequate scale to the overseas possessions of the Dutch East and West India Companies."[22] Those who did decide to emigrate to find work "preferred to seek their fortune in countries nearer home."[23] Plans for enlisting Dutch peasant families for colonizing purposes came to little, outside of the small settlement at the Cape of Good Hope, which in the seventeenth century was mainly a way station for ships passing to and from the Dutch East Indies.[24] As far as the East Indies were concerned, it was never contemplated "that the European peasant should cultivate the soil himself." Rather, he would supervise the labor of others.[25]

France

In seventeenth-century France the great majority of the peasants were holders of small plots scarcely large enough to provide the minimum essentials for survival. The almost interminable religious wars that culminated in the Thirty Years' War (1618–48) had ravaged much of the country, and epidemic disease had greatly reduced the population.[26] But while French poor peasants groaned under the burden of feudal exactions, they were still bound by feudal ties to the land;[27] they had not been "surplussed" by sheep, as many peasants had been in Spain and England.

The first successful French colonization efforts were undertaken on the Bay of Fundy (1604) and at Quebec (1608). The laborers for the colony's upbuilding and development were to be wage workers, transported at the expense of the French government or other sponsoring entity, and employed under three to five year contracts. But New France was not destined to become a plantation colony, indeed not even a primarily agricultural colony.[28] A century after these first Canadian settlements were established, their population was only ten thousand, including a few persons representing a soon-abandoned notion of supplying the labor needs of Canadian colonies from African sources.[29] Some time before the end of the seventeenth century, the French government turned to the idea of Christianizing and Gallicizing the Indians as a means of peopling New France and developing a labor force for it; that plan also failed, however, because the Indians did not perceive sufficient advantage in such a change in their way of living,[30] and they had the resources and abilities to be able to fend off French pressure on the tribal order. Indeed, until the establishment of the Louisiana colony early in the eighteenth century, the entire question of supplying labor for French agricultural undertakings became irrelevant for North America.

French participation in the development of plantation colonies was to occur in the West Indies and, as mentioned, in Louisiana. Having begun with Martinique and Guadeloupe in 1635, in 1697 the French capped a series of Caribbean acquisitions by taking control from Spain of the previously French-invested western half of Hispaniola under the terms of the Treaty of Ryswick.[31] In the beginning, wage laborers called *engagés*, hired under three-year contracts at rates four or five times those prevailing in France, were shipped to serve the labor needs of these colonies.[32] The supply of labor in this form seems to have reached its peak, however, well before 1697. Although the total number of *engagés* is not known, some 5,200 were shipped from La Rochelle, the chief embarkation point, in the period 1660–1710, a rate of around one hundred per year.[33] This was numerically miniscule compared to the total number of imported laborers, which was running at a rate of 25,000 to 30,000 per year in the latter half of this period.

The reasons for the relegation of *engagé* labor to economic insignificance were both economic and political.[34] The mortality rate among plantation laborers on St Domingue, whatever their nativity, was such that most did not survive three years.[35] However, the obligation to pay relatively high wages to the *engagés*, be their numbers large or small, coupled with the fact that the French colonies had ready access to African labor supplies, first through the Dutch and later from French businessmen, made *engagé* labor relatively less profitable, provided that the costs of social control of the laboring population drawn from African sources could be kept satisfactorily low.[36]

Moreover, the need to recruit large French armies for the wars first with Spain and then with England, and the drain on revenues entailed in their support, rendered politically inappropriate the export of *engagés* to the French West Indies. Louis XIV finally forbade even the forcible transportation of indigent persons to the American colonies. His chief minister from 1661 to 1683, Jean Baptiste Colbert, declared that he had no intention of depopulating France in order to populate the colonies.[37]

Other sources of labor

The Spanish and the Portuguese first looked to the native populations to solve their colonial labor problem. The Spanish did so with such spirit that, in the course of a century and a half from 1503 to 1660, they tripled Europe's silver resources and added one-fifth to Europe's supply of gold.[38] In the process, the fire-armed and steel-bladed Conquistadors almost completely destroyed the indigenous population by introducing exotic diseases, and by the merciless imposition of forced labor in gold mining and in the fields. The native population of Hispaniola was thus reduced from 1 million in 1492 to around twenty-six thousand in 1514, and to virtual extinction by the end of the sixteenth century.[39] The same genocidal labor regime in mines and fields simultaneously destroyed the native population of Cuba at a comparable rate.[40]

Epidemic European diseases – smallpox, measles, and typhus – and forced labor under a system of *encomienda* and *repartimiento*[41] reduced the population of central Mexico from 13.9 million in 1492 to 1.1 million in 1605.[42] The impact of disease and of the *mita*,[43] the equivalent of the Mexican *repartimiento*, was equally devastating to the Indian population of Peru, which was reduced from 9 million to 670,000 in 1620.[44]

In Brazil, the Portuguese (and the Dutch as well, during the life of the New Holland colony, 1630–54) also sought to recruit their labor force from the native population. However, they found that, while the people "were prepared to work intermittently for such tools and trinkets as they fancied," they were unwilling to work for them as long-term agricultural laborers, or as bound-servants.[45] In the test of wills that lasted until late in the seventeenth century, the indigenous population was largely successful in avoiding reduction to slavery.[46]

Thus for two opposite reasons – the accessibility of a native labor force that eventually led to its destruction, and the inaccessibility due to resistance by the native population ensconced in dense continental forests – the Iberians turned to Africa as a source of labor for colonial America. This was a labor reserve with which they, as part of medieval Europe and as colonizers of Atlantic islands, were already somewhat familiar.[47] Medieval Europe secured its slaves by trade with southern Russia, Turkey, the Levant and the eastern coast of the Adriatic Sea (the ethnic name Slav is the root of the various Western European variations of the word "slave"), as well as by purchasing Negroes supplied by North African Arab merchants.[48] Spain enslaved Moslem "Moors" in border regions during the "reconquista" wars against the Arab regime on the Iberian peninsula.[49] In the middle of the fifteenth century, the Portuguese established direct access to African labor sources by successfully executing a maritime end run around the North African Arabs.[50] By the end of that century Portuguese enterprise, with papal blessing,[51] had supplied twenty-five thousand Africans as unpaid laborers to Europe, plus one thousand to São Tomé, and seven and a half thousand to islands in the Atlantic.[52] In the sixteenth century the African proportion of the slave population increased in Portugal and Spain. In Lisbon, a city of 100,000 people in 1551, there were 9,950 slaves, most of them Africans. In Seville (1565), Cadiz (1616), and Madrid (up to about 1660), the slave population included Turks and Moors, but the largest number were Africans.[53] During the very early days of American colonization, a number of American Indians were shipped to be sold at a profit in Spain.[54]

In 1518, King Charles I of Spain, acting with papal sanction, authorized the supply to Spanish America of four thousand Africans as bond-laborers, for which project he awarded the contract to a favorite of his.[55] This was the origin of the infamous *Asiento de negros* (or simply *Asiento*, as it came generally to be called), a license giving the holder the exclusive right to supply African laborers to Spanish colonies in the Americas (and to Portuguese Brazil as well during the sixty years, 1580–1640, when Portugal was united with Spain in a single kingdom). At various times it was directly awarded by the Spanish crown to individuals or to governments by state treaty. The *Asiento* was the object of fierce competition among European powers, especially in the last half of the seventeenth century. Allowing for brief periods of suspension, it was held successively by Portugal, Holland, and France, and passed finally to Britain as a part of the spoils of the War of Spanish Succession (1702–14).[56] The *Asiento* was finally ransomed from Britain for £100,000 in 1750.[57]

Scholars' estimates of the total number of Africans shipped for bond-servitude in the Americas under the *Asiento* and otherwise range from 11 to 15 million.[58] Of the 2,966,000 who disembarked in Anglo-America, 2,443,000 went to the British West Indies and 523,000 to continental Anglo-America (including the United States).[59] Two other aspects of the matter seem to have been slighted in previous scholarship: first, the significance of this movement of labor in the "peopling" of the Americas; and, second, the implications to be found in the story of this massive transplantation of laborers for the history of class struggle and social control in general in the Americas.

I am not qualified to treat these subjects in any comprehensive way, but I venture to comment briefly, prompted by an observation made by James A. Rawley, whose work I have cited a number of times:

> The Atlantic slave trade was a great migration long ignored by historians. Euro-centered, historians have lavished attention upon the transplanting of Europeans. Every European ethnic group has had an abundance of historians investigating its roots and manner of migration. The transplanting of Africans is another matter ... [that] belongs to the future.[60]

As to the first of the questions – the African migration and the "peopling" of the Americas – it is to be hoped that among subjects that belong to the future historiography invoked by Rawley, emphasis may be given to the degree to which the migration (forced though it was) of 10 or 11 million Africans shaped the demographics of the Americas as a whole. It is certain that more Africans than Europeans came to the Americas between 1500 and 1800.[61] It would seem that such a demographic assessment might add strength to arguments that place the African-American and the "Indian" in the center of the economic history of the hemisphere, and in so doing sustain and promote the cause of the dignity of labor in general. Such a demographic assessment might be of service in responding to the cry for justice for the Indians from Chiapas (from Las Casas to Subcómmandante Marcos), or to an African-American demand for reparations for unpaid bond-servitude; or in assessing the claim of the "Unknown Proletarian," in a possibly wider sense than even he intended:

> We have fed you all for a thousand years –
> For that was our doom you know,
> From the days when you chained us in your fields
> To the strike of a week ago
> You have taken our lives, and our babies and wives,
> And we're told it's your legal share;
> But if blood be the price of your lawful wealth,
> Good God! We have bought it fair.[62]

Second, with regard to the class struggle and social control in general in the Americas, attention will need to be given to the resistance and rebellion practiced by the African bond-laborers and their descendants, from the moment of embarkation from the shores of Africa[63] to the years of maroon defiance in the mountains and forests of America;[64] from the quarry's first start of alarm[65] to the merger of the emancipation struggle with movements for national independence and democracy four hundred years later.[66]

Historically most significant of all was the Haitian Revolution – an abolition and a national liberation rolled into one: it was the destruction of French rule in Haiti that convinced Emperor Napoleon to see and cede the Louisiana territory (encompassing roughly all the territory between the Mississippi River and the Rocky Mountains) to the United States, without which there would have been no United States west of the Mississippi. By defeating Napoleon's plan to keep St Domingue in sugar plantation slavery, the Haitian Revolution ushered in an era of emancipation that in eighty-five years broke forever the chains of chattel bondage in the Western Hemisphere – from the British West Indies (1833–48), to the United States (1865), to Cuba (1868–78), to Brazil (1871–78). It was in Haiti that the Great Liberator, Simón Bolívar, twice found refuge and assistance when he had been driven from Venezuela. Pledging to the Haitian president, Pétion, that he would fight to abolish slavery, Bolívar sailed from Haiti at the end of 1816 to break the colonial rule of Spain in Latin America.[67]

England and the Colonial Labor Supply

English colonialists were to share the motives and aspirations felt by their counterparts looking westward from the European continent: the search for uncontested access to the fabled treasures of the East; the hope of finding rich gold and silver mines; an eagerness to find alternate sources of more mundane products such as hides, timber, fish and salt; and the furtherance of strategic interests *vis-à-vis* rival military and commercial powers in the development of this new field of activity.[68] Much would be said and proposed also in the name of the defense of one Christian faith (of the Protestant variety in the English case of course). But all endeavors, holy and profane, were to be held in orbit by the gravitational field of capital accumulation.[69]

In regard to the problem of a colonial labor supply, however, the situation of the English bourgeoisie was unique; this was as a result of developments that are so familiar to students of English history that a brief summary will suffice in the present context. With the end of the Wars of the Roses (1450–85), a convergence of circumstances – some old, some new – launched the cloth-making industry into its historic role as the transformer of English economic life to the capitalist basis.[70] Principal among these circumstances were: (1) the emergence of a strong monarchy; (2) England's relative isolation, compared to the countries of continental Europe;[71] (3) improved means of navigation, especially benefiting the coastal shipping so well suited to the needs of an island nation; (4) improved and extended use of water power for cloth-fulling mills, and for other industrial purposes; and (5) the rural setting of the cloth industry, outside the range of the regulations of the urban-centred guilds.

The price of wool rose faster than the price of grain, and the rent on pasture rose to several times the rent on crop land.[72] The owners increased the proportion of pasture at the expense of arable land. One shepherd and flock occupied as much land as a dozen or score of peasants could cultivate with the plough. Ploughmen were therefore replaced by sheep and hired shepherds; peasants were deprived of their copyhold and common-land rights, while laborers on the lords' demesne lands found their services in reduced demand. Rack-rents and impoverishing leasehold entry fees were imposed with increasing severity on laboring peasants competing with sheep for land. At the beginning of the sixteenth century, somewhere between one sixth and one third of all the land in England belonged to abbeys, monasteries, nunneries and other church enterprises. In the process of the dissolution of the monasteries, most of the estimated 44,000 religious and lay persons attached to these institutions were cast adrift among the growing unemployed, homeless population.[73] As these lands were expropriated, under Henry VIII the process of conversion to pasture was promoted more vigorously than it had been by their former owners.[74] Henry VIII's return of 48,000 English soldiers in 1546 from a two-year turn in Boulogne tended further to the creation of a surplus proletariat.[75] The effect was only partially offset by the participation of regular and volunteer English soldiers in the Dutch war for the independence of Holland from Spain later in the century, and by the Tyrone War in Ireland.[76] Generally speaking, the sixteenth century was relatively free of war and plague.[77] The population of England is estimated to have grown by 1.3 million in the last six decades of the sixteenth century, to 4.1 million, but by only another 0.9 million in the entire seventeenth century.[78] Occurring at a time when employment in cultivation was being reduced more rapidly than it was being increased in sheep raising and industry, this demographic factor added substantially to the swelling surplus of the semi-proletarian and vagrant population.[79] During the early decades of the seventeenth century, the oppressive effects of this catastrophic general tendency to increasing unemployment and vagrancy were exacerbated by purely political and cyclical factors, and by market disruptions occasioned by continental wars. In 1614–17, James I – enticed by Alderman Cockayne's scheme whereby the Crown coffers were to be enriched by five shillings on each of 36,000 pieces of finished and dyed cloth to be exported annually – imposed extremely strict limitations on the export of unfinished cloth.[80] The effect was a serious dislocation of trade, and mass unemployment in the cloth industry. English cloth exports fell until in 1620 they were only half the pre-1614 level.[81]

The man who had been serving for some time as treasurer and chief officer of the Virginia Company, Edwin Sandys, urged the colony's cause by pointing out that in Britain, "Looms are laid down. Every loom maintains forty persons. The farmer is not able to pay his rent. The fairs and markets stand still . . ."[82] Recovery was slow. In 1624, an investigating committee of the House of Commons reported that there were still twelve thousand unemployed cloth workers.[83] A modern scholar has concluded that the next decade did not mark much improvement, noting that the proportion of the people receiving poor relief was greater in the 1631–40 period than at any other time before or since.[84] East Anglia, the native region of most of the emigrants to Anglo-America in those years, was at that time especially hard hit by a depression in the cloth trade.[85]

The English case for colonization came thus to be distinguished from those of Spain, Portugal, France, and Holland in its advocacy of colonization as a means of "venting" the nation's surplus of "necessitous people" into New World plantations.[86] Francis Bacon (1561–1626) favored colonization as a way to "disburthen the land of such inhabitants as may well be spared." Just who those were who could be spared had been identified some time before by the premier advocate of overseas exploration and settlement, Richard Hakluyt (1552?–1616): it was the surplus proletarians who should be sent. Contrasting England with the continental countries interminably devouring their man-power in wars and their train of disease and pestilence, Hakluyt pointed out that "[t]hrough our long peace and seldom sickness wee are growen more populous ... (and) there are of every arte and science so many, that they can hardly lyve by one another." Richard Johnson, in his promotional pamphlet *Nova Britannia*, noted that England abounded "with swarmes of idle persons ... having no meanes of labour to releeve their misery." He went on to prescribe that there be provided "some waies for their forreine employment" as English colonists in America.[87] Commenting on the peasant uprising in the English Midlands in 1607, the House of Lords expressed the belief that unless war or colonization "vent" the daily increase of the population, "there must break out yearly tumours and impostures as did of late."[88]

The English Variation and the "Peculiar Institution"

The conjunction of the matured colonizing impulse, the momentarily favorable geopolitical constellation of powers, the English surplus of unemployed and underemployed labor, coupled with the particular native demographic and social factors as the English found them in Virginia, and the lack of direct English access to African labor sources, produced that most portentous and distinctive factor of English colonialism: of all the European colonizing powers in the Americas, only England used European workers as basic plantation workers. This truly "unthinking decision,"[89] or, more properly, historical accident, was of incidental importance in the ultimate deliberate Anglo-American ruling class option for racial oppression. Except for this peculiarity, racial slavery as it was finally and fully established in continental America, with all of its tragic historical consequences, would never have been brought into being.

Essential as this variation in the English plantation labor supply proved to be for the emergence of the Anglo-American system of racial slavery, however, it was not the cause of racial oppression in Anglo-America. The peculiarity of the "peculiar institution" did not derive from the fact that the labor needs of Anglo-American plantation colonies came to the colonies in the chattel-labor form. Nor did it inhere in the fact that the supply of lifetime, hereditary bond-laborers was made up of non-Europeans exclusively. These were common characteristics throughout the plantation Americas.

The peculiarity of the "peculiar institution" derived, rather, from the *control* aspect; yet not merely in its reliance upon the support of the free non-owners of bond-labor, as buffer and enforcer against the unfree proletariat; for that again was a general characteristic of plantation societies in America.

The peculiarity of the system of social control which came to be established in continental Anglo-America lay in the following two characteristics: (1) all persons of any degree of non-European ancestry were excluded from the buffer social control stratum; and (2) a major, indispensable, and decisive factor of the buffer social control stratum maintained against the unfree proletarians was that it was itself made up of free proletarians and semi-proletarians.

How did this monstrous social mutation begin, evolve, survive and finally prevail in continental Anglo-America? That is the question to be examined in the chapters that follow.

2

English Background, with Anglo-American Variations Noted

The same economic, social, and technological developments in sixteenth-century England that supplied the material means for the final overthrow of Celtic Ireland in the Tyrone War (1594–1603) provided the impetus that launched England on its career as a world colonial power. The capitalist overthrow of the English peasantry in the first half of the sixteenth century was the forerunner of the destruction of the Celtic tribal system in the seventeenth. The expropriated and uprooted sixteenth-century English copy-holders had their counterparts in the "kin-wrecked" remnants of broken Irish tribes reduced to tenantry-at-will and made aliens in their own country.

But while the adventitious factor of the English Protestant Reformation in the sixteenth century was a decisive condition for the seventeenth-century English option for racial oppression in Ireland, it was not the force that shaped the events that culminated in the establishment of racial oppression in continental Anglo-America.[1]

Rather, the system of class relations and social control that emerged in the colonies in the seventeenth century rested on the rejection in fundamental respects of the pattern established in England in the sixteenth century. With few exceptions, historians of the origin of racial slavery have generally ignored, or inferentially denied, the significance of this oceanic disjunction in social patterns.[2] The "social control" approach which the present work takes to the origin and nature of "the peculiar institution" makes it necessary to revisit the epoch of English history that produced the founders of Jamestown.

On the Matter of "Transitions"

Many economic historians, taking the long view, have agreed with Adam Smith that the transition to capitalist agriculture in England in the sixteenth century was "a revolution of the greatest importance to public happiness."[3] At the threshold of the sixteenth century, however, the English copyholder, plowing the same land that his grandfather had plowed with the same plow,[4] had little feeling for "transitions." If it had been given to him to speak in such terms, he might well have made his case on historical grounds. It was the

14

laboring people – the copyholders, freeholders, serfs, artisans and wage earners – and not the bourgeoisie, who had swept away the feudal system. Out of the workings of the general fall in agricultural prices in the period between the third quarters of the fourteenth and fifteenth centuries as a result of which landlords preferred to get cash rents rather than rents in produce; out of the shortage of labor induced by the worst-ever onset of plague in England, which, within a space of sixteen months in 1349–50 carried off from one-fifth to one-half of the population;[5] out of the constant round of bloody and treacherous baronial wars for state hegemony (ended only with the Wars of the Roses, 1450–85), and the desultory Hundred Years' War with France, 1336–1453; and, above all, out of the Peasant Revolt of 1381, Wat Tyler's Rebellion,[6] which drew a line in the ancient soil beyond which feudal claims would never be reasserted – thus had been wrought the end of the feudal order in England. And so occurred the English peasant's Golden Age,[7] wherein the self-employed laboring peasant, as freeholder, leaseholder, or copyholder, held ascendancy in English agriculture.[8]

Our copyholder might then go on to say that now the bourgeoisie, burgesses, landlords, merchants and such were apparently attempting to destroy the peasantry; and if that was what was meant by transition to capitalism, the price was too high.[9] And he would conclude with a reminder and a warning: he – his kith and kin – had fought once, and would fight again, to maintain their place on the land and in it.[10]

Fight they did. Between 1500 and 1650, "hardly a generation ... elapsed without a peasant uprising." In local fence-destroying escapades, in large riots, and in rebellions of armed forces of thousands which "at intervals between 1530 and 1560 set half the counties of England in a blaze,"[11] the English "commons" fought. In some cases they were allies of the anti-Reformation, sensing the connection between the Reformation and the agrarian changes that threatened the majority of the peasantry. Even then, the peasants still forwarded their own demands regarding land ownership and use, enclosures, rack-rents, etc. Years that their revolts have made memorable include 1536, 1549, 1554, 1569 and 1607.

In these struggles the peasants made clear their sense of the great heart of the matter; in the words of Tawney:

> Reduced to its elements their complaint is a very simple one, very ancient and very modern. It is that ... their property is being taken away from them ... [and] to them it seems that all the trouble arises because the rich have been stealing the property of the poor.[12]

For this they fought in the northern rebellion of 1536, known as the Pilgrimage of Grace.[13] This revolt, set off by Henry VIII's suppression of monasteries, confronted that king with the greatest crisis of his reign.[14] Although ecclesiastical issues united the movement, "the first demands of the peasants were social and not religious"; for them it was a class struggle "of the poor against the rich," and their demands "against raised rents and enclosures" were included in the program of the movement.[15]

The peasants fought again in 1549, climaxing a three-year period of "the greatest popular outcry against enclosing."[16] In that year, peasant revolts spread to more than half the counties of England. Led by Robert Ket, himself a landowner, a rebel army of sixteen thousand peasants captured Norwich, England's second-largest city. They set up their "court" on Mousehold Heath outside the city, where they maintained their cause for six weeks.[17] They demanded that "lords, knights, esquires, and gentlemen" be stopped from commercial stock-raising, and rent-gouging, and from privatizing common lands. We can agree with Bindoff that this was "a radical programme, indeed, which would have clipped the wings of rural capitalism."[18]

The peasants fought also in 1607, the very year of the founding of Jamestown. These were the peasants of the Midland counties. Thousands, armed with bows and arrows, with pikes and bills, and with stones, sought justice by their own direct action. The later use of the term "Levellers," though more figurative, still was socially congruent with the literal sense in which these Midland rebels applied it to themselves as "levellers" of fences and hedges set up by the landlords to bar peasants from their ancient rights of common land. To the royal demand that they disperse, they defiantly replied that they would do so only if the king "wolde promis to reforme those abuses."[19]

The peasants fought, but in the end they could not stop the "rich . . . stealing the property of the poor." Small landholders constituted the majority of the laboring population in English agriculture at the end of the fifteenth century,[20] but by the end of the seventeenth century more than four-fifths of the land was held by capitalist employers of wage-labor.[21] Well before that time, the majority of the English people were no longer self-employed peasants but laborers dependent upon wages.[22]

Not only were they to be dependent upon wages, making crops and cloth that they would never own, but at wages lower than they had ever been. In the course of the sixteenth century the real wages of English laborers fell into an abyss from which they would not emerge until the end of the nineteenth century.[23] As a typical peasant, "Day labourer was now [his or her] full description . . . and the poor cottager[s] could expect only seasonal employment at a wage fixed by the justice of the peace."[24] One-fourth of the people of England in the 1640s were but "housed beggars," the term used by Francis Bacon to distinguish them from wandering roadside mendicants.[25]

"Why No Upheaval?"

"Why did it not cause an upheaval?" That is a logically compelling question which some historians have posed in light of their findings regarding the general deterioration wrought upon the lives of the laboring population during the "long" sixteenth century, 1500–1640.[26] The same question, but in a form more particularly suited to this present study, is, "How did the English bourgeoisie maintain social control?"

In establishing its dominance over the pillaged and outraged peasantry, the English bourgeoisie did, of course, meet rebellion with armed repression (generally after deceitful "negotiations" designed to divide the opposition and to buy time for the mobilization of government military forces). Having traditionally no standing army, the government employed German and Italian mercenaries on some occasions, along with men recruited from the personal retinues of the nobility. But foreign mercenaries, however important they might have been in certain critical moments, for fiscal and political reasons could not supply the basic control functions on a regular basis. And the very economic transformation that brought the laboring masses of the countryside to revolt was simultaneously reducing the ranks of the retainers whom the nobility might profitably maintain for such ongoing repressive services.

Saving a portion of the yeomanry

The solution was found by deliberately fostering a lower-middle-class stratum. It was in the nature of the capitalist Agrarian Revolution that non-aristocrats rose out of the ranks of the bourgeoisie into the highest councils and organs of power, to serve side by side with the increasingly bourgeoisified old-line aristocrats. Likewise, lower and local functions at the shire level were filled by men from the ranks of the lesser bourgeois country gentlemen and exceptionally upwardly mobile peasants turned capitalist farmers, who might buy into a knighthood. But yet another layer was needed, which would be of sufficient number to stand steadfast between the gentry and the peasants and laborers.

But the juggernaut of the Agrarian Revolution threatened the land titles of the laboring peasants of all categories, from those with hereditary freeholds through all the gradations of tenants to the "customary" tenant-at-will.[27] The state therefore made a political decision to preserve a sufficient proportion of peasants – preference going naturally, but not exclusively, to hereditary freehold tenants – as a petit bourgeois yeomanry (typified by the classic "forty-shilling freeholder"[28]) to serve in militia and police functions.[29]

The case has not been better understood or stated than it was by Francis Bacon, looking back at close range in 1625 to write his *History of the Reign of King Henry VII* (1485–1509):

Another statute was made for the ... soldiery and militar[y] forces of the realm....
That all houses of husbandry, that were used with twenty acres of ground and upwards, should be maintained and kept up for ever; together with a competent proportion of land to be used and occupied by them; and in no wise severed from them (as by another statute in his successor's [Henry VIII's] time was more fully declared).... This did wonderfully concern the might and mannerhood of the kingdom, to have farms of a standard, sufficient to maintain an able body out of penury, and did in effect amortise a great part of the lands of the kingdom unto the

hold and occupation of the yeomanry or middle people, of a condition between gentlemen and cottagers or peasants.... For to make good infantry, it requireth men bred not in a servile or indigent fashion, but in some free and plentiful manner. Therefore if a state run most to noblemen and gentlemen, and that the husbandmen and ploughmen be but as their work folks and labourers, or else mere cottagers (which are but housed beggars), you may have a good cavalry, but never good stable bands of foot [soldiers].... Thus did the King secretly sow Hydra's teeth whereupon (according to the poet's fiction) should rise up armed men for the service of this kingdom.[30]

Bacon likened the process of expropriation of the peasants to the necessary thinning of a stand of timber, whereby all but a few trees are cleared away to allow sound growth of the rest for future needs. By this policy, he said, England would escape certain ills besetting the governments of other countries such as France and Italy

[w]here in effect all is noblesse or peasantry (I speak of people out of towns), and therefore no middle people; and therefore no good forces of foot; in so much as they are enforced to employ mercenary bands of Switzers and the like for their foot [soldiers].[31]

Here was the recognition of the curbs that policy must sometimes impose on blind economic forces, restraining "the invisible hand" in order to avoid promoting "an end which was no part of [the] intention" of the ruling class.[32] It was in the nature of the transformation powered by the capitalist Agrarian Revolution that the non-aristocratic bourgeois gentry should move increasingly into the control of affairs. On the other hand, the deliberate preservation of a portion of economically independent self-employed and laboring small property-owners was not an economic necessity but rather a first derivative of the economic necessities, a political necessity for the maintenance of bourgeois social control, upon which the conduct of the normal process of capitalist accumulation depended. (Even so, it was not a total loss economically, since the yeoman was a self-provider and a principal source of tax revenue.)[33]

The inner conflicts of the bourgeoisie, the conflicts with self in its own various parts – now the governors of a strife-torn nation among striving nations; and, again, as land-grabbing, rack-renting landlords, gentry, merchants, squires, and occasional interloping peasant upstarts, "like tame hawks for their master, and like wild hawks for themselves," as Bacon put it[34] – caused this basic policy to evolve by vicissitudes. But the center held: the same guiding principle obtained when Bacon wrote his history of Henry VII's reign that been in force more than a century before.

The successful day-to-day operation of the social order of the newly ascendant bourgeoisie depended upon the supervisory and enforcement functions performed at the parish level by yeoman constables, church wardens, Overseers of the Poor, jailers, directors of houses of correction, etc.[35] They were charged with serving legal orders and enforcing warrants issued by magistrates or higher courts. They arrested vagrants, administered the prescribed whippings on these vagrants' naked backs, and conveyed them to the boundary of the next parish, enforcing their return to their home parishes. As Overseers of the Poor, they ordered unemployed men and women to the workhouses and apprenticed poor children without their parents' leave. Trial juries were generally composed of yeomen, and they largely constituted the foot soldiery of the militia, the so-called "trained bands." They discharged most of these unpaid obligations unenthusiastically, but with a sense of duty appropriate to their social station.[36] Nevertheless, prior to the Great Rebellion and Civil War of the mid-seventeenth century, yeomen militiamen showed themselves less than reliable for major armed clashes with peasants. In Ket's Rebellion they were left behind when the final assault was made by the king's forces of cavalry and one thousand foreign mercenaries.[37] And, on account of the "great backwardness in the trained bands," the king's commanders were constrained to rely exclusively on the gentlemen cavalry and their own personal employees in the battle against one thousand peasant rebels at Newton in the Midlands in 1607.[38]

Yeomen did enjoy certain special privileges. For one, they were entitled to vote for their shire's member of Parliament. Of far more substantial importance was their right to apprentice their sons to lucrative trades and commerce, and to send their sons to schools and universities.[39] But like the civic duties to which they were assigned, these privileges were theirs because, and only because, of their property status. It never occurred to the ruling classes of England that they could enlist such a cheap yet effective social control force from the ranks of the propertyless classes, the housed beggars, laborers and cottagers, or the vagabonds. That notion would await the coming of the Anglo-American continental colonies.

The "Labor Question": Conflict and Resolution

The ruling class effected the same balance of class policy and the blind instinctual drive for maximum immediate profits by its individual parts in regard to the costs of employment of propertyless laborers.[40]

In the century and a half, 1350–1500, following the great plague, it had been seen that no amount of legislation could keep down labor costs where labor was in short supply. Laws designed to prevent laborers from moving about in search of higher wages, and laws fixing penalties for paying or receiving wages in excess of statutory maximums, were equally ineffective in restraining wages. Half a dozen such laws were passed in that period,[41] but by its end the laborer's real wage was nearly thrice what it had been at its beginning.[42] The objective might have been accomplished if it had been possible to reimpose serfdom, but the landlord class no longer had the power to do so.[43]

But the emergence of a massive labor surplus in the early decades of the sixteenth century presented the employing classes with an opportunity which they were quick to exploit for regulating labor costs. At a certain point it occurred to the government to redress the imbalance by instituting slave labor. Parliament accordingly in 1547 enacted a law, 1 Edw. VI 3, which would have had the effect of creating a marginal, yet substantial, body of unpaid bond-labor, to serve as an anchor on the costs of paid labor. Refusing to recognize the legitimacy of the offspring of their own agrarian revolution, the ruling class presumed that every unemployed person was merely another "vagabond," willfully refusing to work and thus frustrating the proper establishment of fair wages. The 1547 law sought remedy along the following lines:

> who so ever ... man or woman [being able-bodied and not provided with the prescribed property income exemption] shall either like a serving man wanting [lacking] a maister or lyke a Begger or after anny other such sorte be lurking in anny howse or howses or loytringe or Idelye wander[ing] by the high waies syde or in stretes, not applying them self to soem honnest and allowed art, Scyence, service or Labour, and so do contynew by the space of three dayes or more to gither and offer them self to Labour with anny that will take them according to their facultie, And yf no man otherwise will take them, doe not offer themself to work for meate and drynk ... shall be taken for a Vagabonde ...[44]

Any person found to be transgressing the provisions of the law, upon information provided to a magistrate by any man, was upon conviction to be formally declared a "vagabond," branded with a *V*, and made a slave for a period of two years to the informant. The slave was to be fed only bread and water and, at the owner's discretion, such scraps as the owner might choose to throw to the slave. The law specified that the slave was to be driven to work by beating, and held to the task by chaining, no matter how vile the work assignment might be. Such a two-year slave who failed in a runaway attempt was to be branded with an *S* and made a slave for life to the same owner from whom he or she had tried to escape. A second unsuccessful attempt to escape was to be punished by death.

This was not just one of the many anti-vagabond laws enacted by the English Parliament in the sixteenth century;[45] it was distinguished from others by three features: (1) the definition of "vagrancy" was extended to cover any unemployed worker refusing to work for mere board; (2) the beneficiary of the penalty was not the state in any of its parts, but private individual owners of those who were enslaved; (3) the enslaved persons were reduced to chattels of the owners, like cattle or sheep, and as such they could be bought, sold, rented, given away, and inherited ("as any other movable goodes or Catelles").[46] With this 1547 law, the quest for wage control had passed its limits in a double sense, by going to zero wages, and by exceeding the limits of practicability. In 1550, Parliament repealed the law, citing as a reason the fact that "the good and wholesome laws of the realm have not been put in execution because of the extremity of some of them."[47]

Many contemporary observers perceived the causal connection of the officially deplored depopulating enclosures of arable land and the growth of vagrancy, and they viewed the case of the displaced peasants and laborers with sympathy. "Whither shall they go?" asked one anguished commentary. "Forth from shire to shire, and to be scattered thus abroad ... and for lack of masters, by compulsion driven, some of them to beg and to steal."[48] During the life of the slave law, bold, honest preacher Bernard Gilpin made the point in a sermon in the presence of Edward VI himself: "Thousands in England beg now from door to door who have kept honest houses."[49]

There were those who considered such facts a justification for slavery as a means of saving these victims of expropriation from running further risks to their very souls, by the sin of idleness. But a widespread reluctance to attempt slavery as the answer seems to have had much to do with the paralysis of the will that kept the law from being "put in execution."[50]

The interval between the passage and the repeal of this slave law was also the period of "the greatest popular outcry against enclosing,"[51] which, as we have noted, took the form of mass peasant revolts, culminating in Ket's Rebellion. John Cheke, scholar, member of Parliament and former tutor of Edward VI, lectured the Norfolk rebels on "The Hurt of Sedition," linking their contumacy with the spirit of lawless vagabondage plaguing the country.[52] Certainly the rebels were as aware as anyone else of the connection between the threat they were facing, that of depopulating enclosures, and the rise of vagrancy. But there seem to be no reports as to the attitude, if any, that the rebels may have held towards vagrancy in general, or toward the slave law of 1547 in particular. Perhaps we may agree with Davies in seeing this fact as evidence that the law was effectively defunct in 1549.[53] In any case, the Ket rebels evinced no disposition to clear their skirts of the splatters of John Cheke's vagabond-baiting.

What they did say, touching bondage, was this: "We pray that all bondmen may be made free, for God hath made all free with his precious bloodshedding."[54] There has been some conjecture about the significance of the inclusion of this demand in the program issued from Mousehold Heath.[55] Whatever scholars may finally conclude on the point, it was a demand that sounded in sharp dissonance to the cruel clanking of chains in the 1547 slave law. The rebels were, furthermore, voicing the main moral scruple which contributed so much to the nullification of the law: namely that it was wrong "to have any Christen man bound to another."[56]

"Doubtless, moral scruples could have been overcome," Davies says, "if slavery had been practical and profitable."[57] He explains that "dealing with a single slave or a small number ... slavery would have been utterly uneconomic; the constant driving, the continuous need to check into the work done, the ease of flight, the difficulty of recapture, easily outweigh any advantage which might have accrued from 'cheap labor.'" He then takes note of a fact that is of particular relevance for the understanding of racial slavery and social control. He contrasts the situation as it would have obtained under the 1547 law in England and the slavery system in continental Anglo-America, which was operable only because "half the population of the South [was] employed in seeing that the other half do their work."[58] The maintenance of such a system of social control was neither an economically valid option nor a necessary resort of bourgeois social control in sixteenth-century England. In this attempt to turn "anti-vagabondism" into a paying proposition by enslaving laborers, the bourgeoisie found that its reach exceeded its grasp. When in 1558–59 diehards proposed that the old slave law be reinstated, even with amendments to lessen its "extremity," the idea failed of adoption.[59]

Wages had to be paid, low though they were

The slave-law experiment had revealed to the English employing classes a limit beyond which they could not go, but they were not disposed to miss the opportunity to validate their prerogative to control labor costs by state intervention.[60] The result was the Statute of Artificers,[61] which was made law on 10 April 1563.[62] Whether the aim of controlling labor costs was achieved by this act, and, if so to what degree, is a subject beyond the concern of this present work.[63] What is significant is that it remained the basic English master–servant law for more than two and a half centuries until its repeal in 1813.[64] It represented the achievement of an historic equilibrium – after two centuries of class struggle, blow and counter-blow – between high wages and unpaid bondage, between freedom and compulsion, in the disposition of alienable labor power.[65]

English historians of the liberal, labor and socialist tendencies have correctly emphasized the compulsion aspect of the Statute of Artificers.[66] This emphasis would seem to be altogether appropriate for the study of the continuum of English national development. But when one comes to consider Anglo-American history, particularly during the crucial seventeenth century, special concern needs to be directed to the limits of compulsion under the Statute of Artificers, to that counter-balancing residue of freedom of labor which experience had shown to be necessary for the maintenance of social control in England in order that the process of normal capitalist accumulation might go forward. Consider briefly the relevant provisions of the Statute of Artificers in terms of a compulsion-versus-freedom analysis.

Any unpropertied, unemployed, unapprenticed man between the ages of twelve and sixty was obliged to work at farm labor by the year in his locality for any farmer requiring his services. But he had to be paid the established wages. Equally significant, recalling the law of 1547, the 1563 Statute of Artificers put the onus on the employers to offer employment, rather than on the workers to find employment, before the penalties of vagrancy could be imposed upon the worker.

Workers who entered into contract to perform specific works were compelled to continue in them, without leaving to seek other employment, until that job was finished, on penalty of a month in jail and, in some cases, being liable to a suit (in "Action of Debt") by the employer for damages amounting to five pounds sterling. But the punishment entailed no extension of service to the private employer, and the employer had no further recourse than the debt action.[67]

Workers bound to serve by the year were subject to a penalty of thirty days in jail for leaving their employers' service before the completion of their terms. But they could terminate their employment legally by giving three months' notice prior to the scheduled completion of their terms. If a person wished to go outside his own parish or town to take a job, he had first to secure from the authorities a formal written testimonial from the town authorities. If such a worker failed to present such a testimonial when taking a job outside his own town or parish, he was to be given twenty-one days to obtain the needed testimonial, being held in jail the while. Upon failure to secure the testimonial within that time, he was "to be whipped and used as a Vagabond."[68]

Male youths were indentured as apprentices to employers, usually for seven years, but sometimes for longer periods. No person might, without prohibitive penalty, practice any trade without having completed the appropriate apprenticeship. Therefore, the more lucrative the prospective trade, the greater was the incentive and the less the compulsion involved in the recruitment of apprentices. In the more remunerative occupations, apprenticeship was restricted to sons of men already in the trade, or to owners of property yielding an annual revenue of two or three pounds. For more common trades, there were no property or family qualifications, but the number of apprentices might be limited to a quota of one apprentice to one journeyman, after an initial quota of three to one. For "Apprenticeship to Husbandry [farming]," however, there were no restrictions except as to age, and it had generally more the aspect of impressment than selection of a career. Under a policy conceived "for the better Advancement of Husbandry and Tillage," any male between the ages of ten and eighteen and "fit" for such employment was obliged to enter into an "indenture" to serve as a "husbandry apprentice" to any farmer who required him for that purpose, for a term lasting until the youth reached twenty-one years of age at least, and possibly until he was twenty-four, depending upon the terms of the individual arrangement.

Refusal to serve as an apprentice was punishable by commitment to jail until the culprit was placed under bond to assure compliance. An apprentice was forbidden to marry without the employer's consent. He was a member of the employer's household and was obliged to obey the employer in any legal command.

It would seem therefore that, observing the limits of the law of 1547, the English bourgeoisie had decided – as far as male workers were concerned – to venture no further in that direction than the terms prescribed for Apprenticeship to Husbandry. Whatever the apprentice's infractions of the terms of the apprenticeship, his punishment for them entailed no extension of his time of service. If the proper authorities approved, in special circumstances and if the apprentice consented, he might be assigned to another master.[69] The apprentice could be freed from his service before the end of his term upon a validated complaint made to the authorities (magistrates, mayors, etc.) of ill-treatment or of misuse, including failure to provide instruction in the trade as agreed upon in the indenture.

Finally, any woman of the laboring class, between the ages of twelve and forty, being unmarried and "forth of work" (unemployed) was compellable to serve by the year, week, or day in any "reasonable" sort of work and at such wage rates as any two magistrates or aldermen, or the mayor, having local jurisdiction might assign for her. Upon refusal so to serve, the woman was to be held in jail "until she shall be bounded to serve." Even if impressed for labor, she was to be paid wages. At least as far as this law was concerned, there was no impediment to her marrying and chancing thereby whatever better escape such a course might afford.

The oppressive intent of the Statute of Artificers was obvious on the face of it. In a situation made especially difficult by the oversupply of labor, workers were compelled to work for whatever the employing class, through the magistrates, chose to offer, and to forgo any improvement through individual or collective bargaining. By both its general and its apprenticeship provisions, the statute consigned the generality of the wage-earning population to agricultural labor. Women workers were excluded from apprenticeship and made to serve in the lowest-paid drudgery. The severest censures of the anti-vagabond laws were threatened against the worker who sought to move from one place to another to improve his lot, unless he bore the magistrate's certificate of permission. Yet oppressive as that law was, neither its contrivers nor its victims would have believed that within several short generations, in a "New Albion,"[70] English workers would be worked as unpaid chattel bondmen and bondwomen, bought and sold from hand to hand for long terms of years, subject, for infraction, to extensions of that servitude for private owners; denied the right to marry, their children "bastards" by definition – and that such would be the common lot (not a real apprentice in a hundred) under "the custom of the country!"

The Poor Law as Social Control

A third major problem of social control – after the peasant revolts and labor relations – arose out of the mass pauperization wrought by the Agrarian Revolution. The presence of a set of persons having no fixed abode was not a new phenomenon in England. But prior to the sixteenth century it was more likely to be associated with a shortage of labor, leading laborers to slip their villein bonds to take better offers from new employers. The vagrancy problem of the sixteenth century, by contrast, was associated with a protracted general decline of wages, and with a stubborn struggle by laboring people to maintain their rights to stay on their land.

The extent of this "structural unemployment," as it would be called today, is not statistically verifiable,[71] but it cannot be doubted that its appearance presented the state with serious difficulties. It was fundamental; a by-product of the vitality of ascendant capitalism. It was intimately linked with the resistance of the copyholders to expropriation of their lands. In the words of Queen Elizabeth's chief adviser, Lord Burghley, the problem arose from "the depopulating of whole towns ... and keeping of a shepherd only, whereby many subjects are turned without habitation and fill the country with rogues and idle persons."[72]

The repeal of the 1547 slave law (1 Edw. VI 3), after three years of ineffectualness, marked the first glimmer of official acknowledgement that unemployment was not synonymous with willful idleness, vagabondage and roguery. A series of laws still sought to draw a significant distinction between the "impotent poor," who were to be relieved, and the "sturdy beggars."[73] The former were to be certified and provided for by propertied persons of their parishes. But the "sturdy beggars" were still to be subject to whipping, to transportation to their home parishes, and, in some cases, to exile or hanging as felons.

But the threat to the orderly transaction of affairs continued. "All parts of this realm of England and Wales," said Parliament in 1572, "be presently with rogues, vagabonds, and sturdy beggars exceedingly pestered ... to the great annoyance of the common weal."[74] They had become so emboldened by their desperate plight that in 1580 they even pressed their clamor upon the Queen personally "one evening as she was riding abroad to take the air."[75]

"Many thousands of idle persons are within this realm," warned Hakluyt in 1584, "which, haveing no way to be sett on worke, be either mutinous and seeke alteration in the state, or at least [are] very burthensome to the commonwealthe."[76] Two years later, another observer expressed fear that a surfeit of paupers must lead to "divers kinds of wrongs, mutinies, sedition, commotion, & rebellion."[77]

A royal decree of 1593 demanded stricter enforcement of the laws against the multitudes of rootless people who were wandering the highways, begging and extorting relief from the more prosperous persons they encountered. It was said that many of the predators were military and naval veterans "exacting money on pretense of service in the wars."[78]

In time the government came to see, as Nicholls, the pre-eminent student of the Poor Law, puts it, that "severe punishment loses its terrors in the presence of actual want – that a man will beg, or steal, or resort to violence rather than starve;" and that it was not wise to force the unemployed into that hard choice.[79] In 1601 Parliament accordingly made the law (43 Eliz. 2) that was to govern English poor relief for more than three centuries.[80] It provided for a system of guaranteed work to be maintained under the supervision of the Overseers of the Poor of each parish, comprised of the church wardens and from two to four other property owners. In central locations, called work-houses, or in their own abodes, the otherwise unemployed persons were to be set to work on materials such as hemp, wool, iron and thread. The proceeds from their products were to defray the costs incurred and to provide for payment for the workers "according to the desert of their work." Refusal to work on such terms was a legal offense, punishable by a term in the house of correction or common jail. Funds needed for furtherance of work and relief programs were to be raised by the Poor Rate, a regular tax periodically assessed against the property holders of each parish.[81]

In practice this formal relief was supplemented by illegal or semi-legal resort by the pauperized population to unauthorized infiltration into supposedly guild-protected trades, or by "squatting" on wastelands to eke out enough of an existence to escape the ministrations of the Overseers of the Poor.[82] But to the extent that such diversions were attempted, they were but supplementary to the workings of 43 Eliz. 2, the Poor Law, the ultimate monumental "attempt on the part of the powerful Tudor state to prevent the social disorder caused by economic changes, which in spite of its efforts it had not been strong enough to control."[83]

Notorious as the operation of the English system of Poor Relief was ever to be for its parsimony and sanctimony, the right of workers to be paid wages for the work done under its program, and the right to leave that employment if and when a turn of fortune – a legacy, a good apprenticeship opportunity, a decent job, or, for a woman, a marriage prospect – occurred, were matters never questioned by those who first established the system in 1601. Yet within a few decades, irreducible rights and privileges of the most condemned ward of the parish were to be denied to the general run of English workers performing the most essential labor in Anglo-America. To those contrivers of the Poor Rate, it would have seemed unthinkable that the support of the poor might, even in the slightest degree, be derived from impositions on other propertyless laborers.[84]

Oppression of Women

The social transformation wrought by the Agrarian Revolution and the rise of capitalism in England was indeed great. But the class coming to power found no need to amend common or statute law with regard to the subordination of women; it found male domination to be no less congenial to the functioning of the new order than it had been to the old.[85]

Given the absence of a women's rights movement – the first concerted cries for justice would not be heard for another two centuries; and, given the quick bourgeois appetite for wealth accumulation, making their historical ruling-class antecedents dilettantes by comparison – the brutal treatment of women in the new era proceeded unchecked.

As it was in man's record of the beginning, and had since been, the non-person civil status of women should ever be, so far as the bourgeoisie of England was concerned.[86] Classed with children in matters of civil rights, women continued to be classed with heretics when punishment for treason was prescribed; only women were to be burned at the stake for that offense.[87] And, like servants who killed their masters, women who killed their husbands were guilty of petty treason. By law, persons convicted of a felony were subject to the death penalty. But priests so convicted could be pardoned for the first offense by claiming "benefit of clergy," a relic of a former time when cleric felons were dealt with by ecclesiastical courts. (Persons granted this privilege were to be branded in the meat of the thumb to prevent their claiming that right a second time.) From the eve of the sixteenth century onwards, increasing categories of non-clerical men were admitted to this privilege. But women, barred by gender from being priests, were excluded from this mercy. They were granted full access to the benefit-of-clergy plea only in 1692.

The men of the ruling classes had immemorially exercised sex–class privileges at the expense of the women of the laboring classes. In feudal times in England the custom said to have been most hated by the serfs was that of "merchet," which required payment in kind or in money by the serf to the lord when the serf's daughter was to be married.[88] This was considered the most degrading and certain mark of servile status, since it forced the serfs to acknowledge possessory claims of one degree or another by the lord to every female virgin among his "family" of "dependants." The same theme was evident in the fact that a woman serf who married a free man and was later divorced by him again became a serf of her former lord. On the other hand, a woman who had originally been free but who married a serf herself, fell to the status of serfdom, which she could not escape by being divorced; instead she remained a serf, at least during the lifetime of her husband. The widow of a serf was designated by the special term "widewe," meaning the lord's widow.[89] She was obliged to guarantee production sufficient to meet the lord's due. Failing in that, a woman was required to surrender her holding, or else to make arrangements (with the lord's sanction) for the proper performance of her duties, as the ward of some man.

In the new order, women of the propertied classes continued to be hostages to the property to which they were linked through inheritance laws. As before, the cult of female chastity, with all its concomitant social and legal repression and sanctions imposed on women, remained an essential of the process of fortune-building through inheritances and marriage portions.[90] When the most important decisions were to be made concerning a woman's life, her personal interests or preferences carried less weight than the property and power interests of the men with whom her life was involved.[91] As of old, but with possibly greater cynicism, fatherless under-age daughters were, as "wards," dealt about like commodities. A man well regarded by the Court of Wards stood to gain when such a girl or woman was made his ward, for that brought him control of her property with all the opportunity for self-advancement it might make possible for him.[92]

There was to be for women no reformation in the Reformation. The notorious 1547 slave law, even in its general extremity, found a special disability to impose on the woman. If a man slave, by coming into an inheritance or otherwise, secured a "convenient living" he was to be freed. If, for instance, such a possibility presented itself in the form of marriage, a male slave had the unimpeded right to free himself by that course. But the female slave, if she were under twenty years of age, could avail herself of such an opportunity only if she could secure the permission of her owner to do so.[93] And, as we have seen, the Statute of Artificers of 1563 assigned unmarried, unpropertied women to the lowest labor status. If they were unemployed and between the ages of twelve and forty, they could be compelled to serve in any employment to which the magistrates might assign them. Furthermore, their wages were set at only about half of those paid to men doing comparable services.[94]

Above all, there were the reasons of state. The "ancient rights and liberties" of the small-propertied and propertyless classes were, as noted, subject to heavy assault in the sixteenth century. But the new order brought no threat to their rights and liberties as English men vis-à-vis English women.

Sir Francis Bacon voiced official sanction of this limitation on interference with traditional ways, saying that male domination and patriarchy were "natural and more ancient than the law." Addressing "The Lord Chancellor and all the Judges of England" in his capacity as Solicitor-General in 1608, Bacon set forth the premise that monarchy was the best form of rule because its authority was first of all based on the "platform" of male domination and patriarchy.

> The first [platform], he submitted, "is that of a father or chief of a family; who governing over his wife by prerogative of sex, over his children by prerogative of age, and because he is author to them of being, and over his servants by prerogative of virtue and providence (for he that is able of body and improvident of mind is natura servus), is the very model of a king.[95]

But before the king is every man, every man must be a king.[96] In feudal England, in the exercise of male domination over the wife, the serf's claims had priority over those of the feudal lord. The wife was a "feme covert," against whom the lord had no process of claim except through the husband. And in the new day, after the repression of the Pilgrimage of Grace, Henry VIII did not venture to pursue vengeance against the persons of a number of women who had been active rebels. The definitive work on this event explains that royal discretion as follows:

> Henry knew that in the excited state of public opinion it would be dangerous to meddle with them. His reign was not by any means the age of chivalry, but there still remained a good deal of the old tribal feeling about women, that they were the most valuable possessions of the clan, and that if any stranger, even the King, touched them all the men were disgraced.[97]

In the "new age", a man's home was still to be his castle and, if the matter were forced to an issue, a woman's prison. Men could divorce women; women could not divorce men. Some time late in the sixteenth century, Joan Wynstone ran away from her husband John, a man of humble station.[98] Taken up as a vagrant, she was sentenced under the law to work as a servant of the husband she had fled. Finding that life intolerable, Joan again escaped, but she was again recaptured. For this second offense she was hanged on the gallows.

The poor and laboring people of England might not prevail over their kings, or their queens, or their lords and masters, but the man of these classes could be king and lord and master to his wife. Male domination in this way served as a link between the beaten-down peasants and proletarians and the very authority that was beating them down. As such it operated as another instrument of ruling-class social control, disguised as the natural outcome of the sexual differentiation occurring in the population.

No English man of that day, from Lord Chancellor Francis Bacon to lowly John Wynstone, would have imagined that propertyless, yet non-apprenticed, English men would ever be so degraded (as they would have considered it) that under the law they might not have their own "castles" and the male privileges appertaining to their gender status.[99] Nor would Bacon or Wynstone have thought to find in "nature" an apology for the assertion of a general sexual privilege by one set of men – propertied and unpropertied – over all women of another set of the propertyless population. Yet the first of these inconceivable ideas would not only be thought of, it would become an essential operating principle of the Anglo-American plantation economy.[100] And, more amazing, the second, thought of and instituted, would become an indispensable element in the maintenance of bourgeois social control in continental plantation Anglo-America.[101]

3

Euro-Indian Relations and the Problem of Social Control

For all the talk of using colonies as vents for proletarian discontent, the first group of English to arrive in Virginia in 1607 included a disproportionate number of aristocrats and gentlemen, and their personal attendants, for whom productive labor was as unthinkable as it was for any Spanish *hidalgo* bound for New Spain.[1] Like Cortés, they were prepared to find ready access to gold and silver rather than to start cultivation of the soil.[2] By 1622,[3] however, the Virginia Company investors, realizing that Virginia was to be no El Dorado, rationalized their abandonment of dreams of emulating the treasure hunts of the Spanish in Mexico and Peru. "[T]o thinke that Gold and Silver mynes in a Country [Virginia] (otherwise most rich and fruitful) the greatest wealth of a Plantation is but popular error," wrote Edward Waterhouse in a long letter of advice to fellow members of the Virginia Company. He now saw the Spanish case in a different light. The law of diminishing returns had set in for silver and gold mining in Spanish America, he said, and Spain had turned to agricultural products, such as sugar, cotton, indigo, and brazil wood, to offset the decline of mining output.[4] He left no doubt that, in his opinion, the future prosperity of the Virginia plantation likewise lay in exploiting the country's natural potential for commodity production.

Why, he thought, could not the English do as the Spanish had done and recruit a labor force from the native population for that purpose? True, the colony was intended as a vent for the "troublesome poor" of England, but why should they not serve in the English plantation as an intermediate stratum, as overseers and tradesmen, such as had been formed by a certain portion of Spanish immigrants and Spanish creoles in Mexico and Peru?[5] Why should not the Virginia Indians be

> compelled to servitude and drudgery, and supply the roome of men that labour, whereby even the meanest [Englishmen] of the Plantation may imploy themselves more entirely in their Arts and Occupations, which are more generous, whilest Savages perform their inferior workes of digging in mynes and the like, of whom also some may be sent for the service of the Sommer Ilands [Bermuda Islands].[6]

Old planter John Martin likewise suggested that the Indians be "brought into subjection," they being "apter for worke then yet our English are ... and fitt to rowe in Gallies & friggetts and many other pregnant uses."[7] Captain John Smith (1580–1631), the most famous leader of the early Jamestown settlers, retrospectively regretted that the English had not from the beginning done as the Spanish had done, namely "forced the ... [Indians] to do all manner of drudgery worke and slavery for them, themselves [the Spanish] living like Souldiers upon the fruit of their [the Indians'] labours."[8] The Spanish option was not to be dismissed out of hand. Indeed Captain John Smith reasoned that, *vis-à-vis* the respective native populations, the English in Virginia and New England were better situated than the Spanish had been in the West Indies. The Spanish, outnumbered by the West Indies Indians by fifty or more to one, had "no other remedy" but mass extermination of the natives. "Ours," said Smith, referring possessively to Virginia and New England Indians, were "such a few, and so dispersed, it were nothing in a short time to bring them to labour and obedience."[9]

If the English had subdued and forced "their" Indians into "drudgery and slavery," they would have had to confront, as the Iberians had had to do, the problem of establishing a system of social control over the native population that would be, as the phrase is nowadays, "cost-effective."

Social Control: Haiti (Hispaniola), Cuba and Puerto Rico

When European colonization of the so-called New World began in Hispaniola in 1492, the population density of that island was about the same as that of Portugal (around 33 and 38 inhabitants per square mile, respectively), but the society of the island was not highly stratified.[10] Speaking of the Indians of the West Indies, Las Casas said, "They are very poor folk, which possess little ... they are accustomed to have no more store than they ordinarily have need of and that such as they get with little travail [labor]." He elaborated with notations of the people's diet, apparel, and shelter.[11] There was no distinct native social stratum that could act as a buffer between the laboring people and the Spanish conquerors in the administration of a normal, orderly, colony. Hence the *encomienda* system, whereby the King of Spain "commended" the natives to "the care" of individual Spanish colonists as laborers,[12] was conducted "in an irregular, uncontrolled, and highly exploitative form.... Spaniards raided Indian communities, took captives, and, in order to prevent escape or to ensure the full measure of work, practiced large-scale enslavement."[13]

The native population did not willingly submit to such brutal administration. In Hispaniola the Maguana people rose in revolt after the treacherous Spanish killing of the captive Maguana chief Canaobo.[14] In 1511 in Puerto Rico, the Borinqueños under the leadership of a *cacique* named Guaybana mounted a major rebellion against the imposition of the Spanish system of forced labor. A second Borinquen uprising was led by another *cacique*, Humacao, four years later.[15] Other Borinqueños, possibly one-third of the population, sought refuge in remote mountainous areas, or fled by boat to other islands.[16] But in

Haiti (Hispaniola/Santo Domingo) and Cuba, the Spanish advantage of overwhelming military strength exerted without restraint, in the context of the even more devastating toll of epidemic European diseases, resulted in almost complete extermination of the native population. There it was a mathematical certainty that without an intermediate social stratum, "social control" by mere unbridled military force would be self-defeating because it exceeded the limits that had to be observed to preserve an exploitable labor force.

Social Control: Mexico and Peru

At the time of the Spanish invasion in 1519, the population of central Mexico,[17] an area of about 200,000 square miles, was an estimated 13.9 million,[18] representing a density of almost 70 people per square mile. Of this population, 2.5 million, concentrated more than 350 per square mile, lived in the 8,000-square-mile area in and near the Basin of Mexico.[19] Tenochitlan (Mexico City), in the heart of this area, had a population of 300,000.

The invaders found already in place "an elaborate system of levy providing products of all kinds, slaves, and services for the three capitals of the so-called Aztec Empire," and a similar system in other large states outside the Aztec territory. In each case it was organized to support its central government ruling group.[20] Originally a three-layered stratum,[21] the ruling group came to be designated by the Spanish under the general name of *caciques*.[22]

The Spanish were able to adapt this pre-existing form of social organization to extort labor and tribute from the Indians, even in the most rapacious manner,[23] using "Indian office-holders ... at the subordinate levels of the hierarchy for the enforcement of Spanish rules."[24] In the opinion of the well-known historian of colonial Mexico Charles Gibson, it was "[t]he power and prestige of the pre-Spanish states, and their continuing traditions of popular subservience, [that] made it possible for the Spaniards to exact labor and tribute with little opposition." Summarizing, Gibson writes that in both Mexico and Peru, "Spaniards took charge of an established society, substituting themselves for the rulers they had deposed or killed."[25]

But such a displacement at the top would not have been effective in gaining the Spaniards' purposes without the preservation of a buffer social control function for the socially demoted *caciques*.

> The ease with which the first Spaniards manipulated huge numbers of native peoples, even the ease with which the first missionaries induced huge numbers of conversions, depended upon the intermediate position of the caciques. ... Caciques were in the vanguard in the adoption of Spanish dress, foods, language, and styles of house construction. They were excused from tribute and labor exactions and given special privileges, such as permission to ride horses and carry arms. ... Indian caciques and Spanish *corregidores* [Spanish officers in charge of local districts] joined forces to extract from the mass of the Indian population whatever wealth it possessed over and above the subsistence level of its economy.[26]

Considered in terms of social control and resistance, the story of the Spanish defeat of and rule over the Inca civilization of Peru in the sixteenth century closely corresponds to the pattern set in Mexico. The Inca word for chiefs, *kurakas*, was by Spanish decree in 1572 changed to *cacique*,[27] appropriately enough it would seem, since the buffer social control function of that office in Peru was identical with its function in Mexico. The hereditary Peruvian *caciques* were exempt from paying tribute or labor service. They were the collectors of tribute to be paid to the Spanish by Indians between the ages of eighteen and fifty. They were responsible also for furnishing the *mita* laborers for service to Spanish masters in industries, in farming and, worst of all, in the silver and mercury mines of Potosi and Huancavelica.[28]

In Peru, the *caciques* "exercised considerable power over Indians, even within the borders of Spanish towns."[29] In 1558, supreme Inca chief Sayri Tupac struck a sort of surrender-and-regrant "bargain" with the Spanish – as O'Neill and other Irish chieftains had done a few year earlier in Ireland (see Volume One).[30]

For at least a century and a half, the *caciques* of Mexico and Peru served as the principal buffer social control stratum in the Spanish system of social control in those domains.[31] But in Mexico, the relatively class-undifferentiated Chichimecs drew a line, and long maintained it, beyond which the Spanish *encomienda* could not be established.[32] In Peru, the Incas defended the remnants of their independent state in two open rebellions. In 1536, Inca Manco and his uncle Titu Yupanqui, taking advantage of a momentary political and military division among the Spanish, rose in revolt to end the desecration of their lands and temples. Manco led a five-month siege of Cuzco, and Titu headed a large army in an assault on Lima.[33] Thirty-five years later, Tupac Amaru, youngest son of Inca Sayri Tupac, served as a rallying symbol for a last great uprising to throw off the Spanish yoke.[34]

The Social Control Problem in Brazil

Brazil, like Hispaniola, presented no previously established social stratum adaptable to the colonizing power's social control purposes, and Catholic religious orders, most notably the Jesuits and Franciscans, largely succeeded in substituting themselves in that function. It was the Jesuit Bartolomé de Las Casas who first raised the standard of battle for "protection of the Indians" of the West Indies in the sixteenth century, but his pleas were brushed aside by the gold-crazed colonists. A basic factor in the genocide of the native peoples of the West Indies in the early sixteenth century was the difficulty of their making a mass flight by sea. The Indians of Brazil, on the other hand, would serve to establish a general principle of social control in European colonies in the Americas: dominance was less easily established and maintained over continental colonies than over insular colonies.[35]

In the continental expanse of Brazil, there was space, and therefore time, for development of an effective class struggle of the Indian laborers and the Portuguese plantation bourgeoisie (the *moradores*). The Indians, as we have noted, were successful in making the point in the sixteenth century that they had no desire to become long-term sugar plantation bond-laborers (see page 7). Indeed, in the sixteenth century a number of projected areas of Portuguese settlement had to be abandoned in the face of Indian attacks.[36] More generally, the Indians resisted plantation servitude by removing themselves to the continental interior.[37] The Portuguese plantation owners countered by conducting armed expeditions (*entradas*) into the interior in order to "entice or force" Indians into Portuguese-controlled villages (*aldeias*),[38] which were located to provide easy access to a supply of Indian plantation laborers, to be used under conditions that were, for all practical purposes, mere slavery.[39] Just as elsewhere in the plantation Americas, super-exploitation of labor and the spread of epidemic European diseases took a heavy toll on the indigenous labor supply in Brazil.[40] In any case, since Indians, having the continental advantage, "deserted their *aldeias* in large numbers,"[41] the colonists were unable to solve the labor-supply problem by resort to raw force through the *entradas*.

It was in the Amazon region of Brazil during the seventeenth century that the Franciscans and then the Jesuits, led most prominently by António Vieira, after a campaign lasting from 1624 to 1686, were able to win a royal decree outlawing enslavement of Indians and bestowing custody of the *aldeia* Indians on the religious orders. These Indians were then to be assigned by the religious authorities as free laborers to plantation owners for a limited part of each year.[42] In terms of social control, the religious orders were filling in relation to a class-undifferentiated native population a role similar to that performed by the *caciques* in relation to the native class-differentiated societies of Mexico and Peru.[43]

In the Amazon region, Portuguese plantation owners rebelled against the idea of non-enslavability of Indians as government interference with free enterprise; they insisted that the free play of market forces required slave labor. Vieira met the objection by proposing the extension to the Amazon region of the practice that had been in operation in more southern coastal regions of Brazil since the middle of the sixteenth century, namely, by the enslavement of Angolans "of both sexes to assure their propagation." The principle was to be "The Negroes to the colonists, the Indians to the Jesuits." A suitable religious exegetical rationale was contrived. The Angolans, by being baptized Christians, were afforded an opportunity to escape the everlasting torment to which they had been certainly doomed as "pagans." Their souls were to be redeemed by the Calvary-like suffering of lifetime hereditary servitude in the sugar industry. The Indians, having been made wards of a Christian order, could not be consigned to slavery.[44] For an indication of the widespread failure of Afro-Brazilian bond-laborers to find comfort in this thesis, see the note on the Palmares *guilombo* in Appendix II-A.

The Powhatans of Virginia

Of all the Ibero-American cases, Brazil was the one that most resembled Anglo-American Virginia with respect to the problem of establishing that degree of social control essential for basing the colonial economy on the forced labor of the indigenous population. Like Brazil, Virginia was a continental colony, not an insular one. Like the indigenous society of Brazil,[45] Powhatan society exhibited little significant stratification, lacking a strong rulership[46] and concomitant intermediate stratum[47] adaptable to the social control purposes of the conquerors. Storage facilities were insufficient to permit long-term accumulation in the hands of the ruling element of products upon which the people were dependent. There was no wealth in the form of domesticated animals, nor did wealth exist in any other form such as to permit accumulations adequate for the support of a permanent leisure class or a non-productive politico-military bureaucracy. The people derived three-fourths of their living from hunting, fishing and gathering, one-fourth from cultivation. With a population density of only one or two persons per square mile,[48] the Powhatan Indians for most of the year were on the whole well-provisioned, so that they could even share with the starving English colonists on occasion.[49]

There was a degree of social stratification; a chief (Powhatan, the person himself, when the English first arrived) lived on the tribute assessed on the people and had privileged access to the best hunting grounds. He received labor tribute by having his fields planted for him, and tended by a multiplicity of women bound to him. But social distinction was insufficient to produce a permanent category "intermediate between rulers and ruled,"[50] or any politico-military bureaucracy. Powhatan had authority to make alliances and war, and to control trade with other tribes and the English. But he was not always able to enforce his will on all his subjects, nor was he always able to enforce it upon the supposedly tributary tribes. The result was to limit the intensity of the exploitation of the laborers; indeed, the chief himself did productive labor at "men's work" such as hunting and hand crafts.

Any attempt by the English plantation bourgeoisie to subjugate the Indians to "drudgery and slavery" would have to face the "Brazilian" problem, but without the agency of the Catholic religious orders; they had been banned in the sixteenth-century English Reformation.[51] More immediately to the point, at the time that Smith and others were fantasizing about emulating the Spanish Conquistadors, the English simply did not have the preponderance of military force such as that which the Spanish unleashed against the indigenous peoples upon whom they made war.[52] The weakness of the English colony in the early period was such that in the three years 1620–22 the colony was dependent upon *trade* with neighboring Indians to save itself from "absolute starvation."[53]

In these respects, the Powhatan social order was essentially the same as those found among the Pequots, Narragansetts, Wampanoags, and other peoples in New England, and the Yamassees, Creeks, Tuscororas, Cherokees, Choctaws, Chickasaws, and other peoples confronting the colonists of the southernmost region, the Carolinas. With regard to establishing social control, the Anglo-American continental bourgeoisie faced the "Brazilian" problem: a continental people without a *cacique* class.

Despite their early difficulties, the English from the beginning had a fundamental potential advantage over the Indians due to the discrepancy in the development of productive forces and productivity of labor. This advantage was enhanced by the fact that the Indians could not possibly have known what the appearance of the first handfuls of settlers portended for the land.[54] Yet, even if they had foreseen from Powhatan to Powder River, and had been able to mobilize a united resistance to the taking of the Trail of Tears, the Indians probably could not have prevented eventual European colonization in North America,[55] although by such a united effort they might have given American history a more humane course than the one it took.

English Buying and Selling of Indian Captives

The actual strength of the English colony in relation to the Virginia Indians changed markedly to the disadvantage of the latter in the period between 1622 and 1644, the dates of two concerted Indian attacks on the colony. By 1644, the relative superiority of the forces at the disposal of the colony was well established, and all Indian hope of ousting the settlers from the Chesapeake region was lost. The treaty of 1646[56] that ended the Indian war begun by Opechancanough, Chief Powhatan's brother and successor, marked the beginning of Anglo-American "Indian policy." At first that policy contemplated only the displacement of the Indian tribes obstructing the advance of the Anglo-American "frontier," but ultimately it would challenge the legitimacy of Indian tribal society itself.[57] In the context of this chapter, consideration is limited to the relationship of that policy to the general labor supply and social control problem faced by the continental colonial bourgeoisie. The basic considerations that shaped the policy, the optimizing of the combination of the rate of capital accumulation and social control,[58] were essentially the same in Virginia as elsewhere, although in one respect, namely the commerce in Indian chattel bond-laborers, the grossest development occurred in South Carolina and secondarily in New England.

Fourteen years after the 1646 treaty, the Virginia General Assembly declared that if the Indians of Northumberland County failed to pay the damages to be assessed by the court of that county for damages done by the Indians to a colonist there, then "soe many off them as the court shall determine shall be apprehended and sold into a forraigne country to satisfie the award."[59] Although in that particular instance no legal justification was cited, it appears to have been under the principle of *lex talionis*, simple retaliation. In general, however, the Anglo-Americans throughout the continental colonies drew on the ancient principle that victors in "just" wars who spared the lives of "heathen" captives thereby gained the right to hold them as slaves, which Europeans used to justify the forced transportation of Africans to perpetual servitude in the Americas. The Virginia Assembly gave this principle the force of law regarding Indians during Bacon's Rebellion in 1676. It was reasserted in 1677 following the defeat of Bacon's Rebellion, and subsequently in 1679, 1682, 1711 and 1722.[60] Enslavement of Indian captives – children and women as well as men – was general in Massachusetts following the Pequot War of 1636–37, and again after King Philip's War of 1675–76.[61] In Carolina province (both before and after its division into South and North Carolina, first called Albemarle, in 1691), the Anglo-Americans made direct war on Indians and enslaved the captives.

But the chief means of securing Indian bond-laborers was by trade with Indian tribes, in the course of which captives of intertribal warfare, along with deer skins and beaver pelts, were exchanged for English commodities such as firearms and ammunition, metal tools and containers, woven fabrics and garments, mirrors and rum.[62] It was English policy to foment "just wars" between tribes for the particular purpose of securing Indian captives as chattel bond-laborers.[63] As tribes became increasingly dependent upon the English for trade goods, some, out of narrow considerations of tribal interests, made war on other tribes in order to maintain their trade with the English.[64] Nash states for a certainty that "the number [of Indians] enslaved reached into the tens of thousands in the half-century after Carolina was settled by Europeans."[65]

The Abandonment of the Native Sources of Plantation Bond-labor

Yet the fantasy of an Anglo-America based on Indian drudgery and slavery was not to be realized. Why not? The standard reference work in the field is still Almon Wheeler Lauber's *Indian Slavery in Colonial Times within the Present Limits of the United States*, published more than eighty years ago.[66] Lauber presents four theses to explain "the decline of Indian slavery." First, depopulation caused by a combination of European diseases, a declining Indian birth rate, and internecine wars in considerable degree fomented by the English interested in trading for the captives whom they would then use in commercial transactions, principally with other English colonies, most often those in the West Indies. Second, Indians "disappeared" as a result of "the amalgamation of red and black slaves." Third, Indians were "unfitted for servitude," being "unable to endure sustained labor," incapable of developing to a "civilized" social level, and bred and reared to be "opposed to all restraint ... by an exterior force." Fourth, if kept in the capturing colony, Indian bond-laborers were possibly even more likely than other bond-laborers to run away, because of the Indians' hope of "returning to their own people."[67]

It is argued here, from a somewhat different perspective, that the failure of the European power to establish a plantation system based on the bond-labor of the native population in the Anglo-American continental colonies was analogous to that of the Portuguese colonizers in Brazil. The decisive factors in each case were two: each colonization was enacted on a continental land mass, as distinct from insular areas such as those in the West Indies; and, second, the indigenous society was not stratified, in any case not stratified enough to produce a separate and distinct social class of *caciques*, accustomed to command and adaptable for colonialist social control purposes, particularly as mobilizers of forced labor for the European capitalist investors.

From those premises I venture a criticism of Lauber's first and third theses about "the decline of Indian slavery."[68] I take them in reverse order because the third directly confronts the one assumption for which I crave indulgence in the first paragraph of the Introduction of this work.

The "unfitness" sour-grapes rationale

Some historians whose approach to the subject is informed with the spirit of the civil rights movement, and whose citations of Lauber have been quite appropriate, have perhaps thought it redundant to take note of the white-supremacist assumptions encountered in a work conceived in what Rayford W. Logan called the "nadir" of the struggle for civil rights in the United States. One latter-day scholar even endorses the Lauber view of this issue, "despite the racist implications of arguments about the relative adaptability of one people over another to tropical labor."[69]

In my view, if being "constitutionally unfitted" for servitude could explain the "decline of slavery," then it should have led to the extinction of bond-servitude in such places as the following:

- Virginia, where for four or five early decades, not one in five of the English chattel laborers survived the period of "indenture." (Governor William Berkeley in reply to queries of the Lords of Trade and Plantations, in 1671 [Hening 2:511.])

- St Domingue, where the average French *engagé* or African bond-laborer survived only three years. See note 35 of Chapter 1.

- Barbados, where in 1680 an annual supply of five thousand African laborers was required to maintain a Negro population of forty thousand (Vincent T. Harlow, *A History of Barbados, 1625–1685* [1926; Negro Universities reprint, 1969], pp. 323–4); where from 1680 to 1800 hundreds of thousands of African bond-laborers arrived, but the population increased by less than ten thousand. (David Lowenthal, "The Population of Barbados," *Social and Economic Studies*, 6:445–501.)

- The British West Indies as a whole which, between 1700 and 1780, absorbed about 850,000 African bond-laborers, yet the Negro population increased only 350,000. (Gary B. Nash, *Red, White, and Black* [Englewood Cliffs, New Jersey, 1974] p. 178.)

• Mexico and Peru, where in the first centuries after the beginning of Spanish rule, the *repartimiento* and *mita* recruitment by the *caciques* contributed so heavily to the reduction of the Mexican and Peruvian native populations. (See page 7.)

Why were the Spanish so slow to learn what the Portuguese capitalists, with whom they shared a common realm for much of the time, had learned: "the unfitness" of Indians for sustained labor? Was it perhaps because they were laughing so hard all the way to the counting house in Seville? Or could it have been that they felt satisfied that the total value of the gold and silver produced by the Indians of Mexico and Peru was probably as great as, if not greater than, that of the sugar produced by Angolans in colonial Brazil?

Did forced labor itself exact a greater toll among Indians than it did among Africans and their descendants? Despite pious protestations in religious quarters and in occasional formal governmental expressions of sympathy, neither the *encomenderos* of Mexico and Peru, nor the *moradores* of Brazil, nor the "planters" of Anglo-America cared a fig about the unfitness of the labor as long as they could be assured of an affordable functioning supply. Time and again in the seventeenth century the Portuguese *moradores* in northern Brazil rebelled against royal and religious authority in order to keep the Indians enslaved, driving out the religious troublemakers, who themselves were forced to admit that "without the Indians the inhabitants [meaning the Portuguese settlers] would die."[70] In South Carolina, for fifty years, the English colonists ridiculed and evaded the strictures of the London proprietors against trading in captive Indian laborers, the profits of which went to the locals rather than to London.[71]

On the other hand, as the record shows, laborers throughout the Americas considered forced labor "unfit" for *themselves*, and resisted servitude as well as they could. In the *cacique*-habituated countries of Mexico and Peru they could not prevail. But the tribal Indians in continental situations did resist enslavement successfully, and in the process provided the frustrated colonialists with the sour-grapes argument about the "unfitness" of Indians for plantation labor.

It would seem that little time needs be spent in this post–World War Two era on Lauber's notion that the North American Indians were not enslavable because of their inability to become "civilized." Are we to believe that, to paraphrase Chairman Mao, "civilization grows out of the barrel of a gun"? Without that one advantage, the work of the Anglo-American "blessings-of-civilization trust," as Mark Twain called it, would surely have been brought to an end before it ever got to South Carolina. In reacting to Lauber's doubt about the "capacity of the Indian for civilization," because "the dominant idea of Indian life was the love of liberty," one can only ask, "What price civilization?" Looking at the figures on the depopulation of the indigenous Americas, one might better ask: If "civilization" is assumed to correlate with increased well-being, did the age of colonization of the Americas demonstrate a "capacity for civilization"? Finally, how was it that Lauber could ignore that precisely the opposite premise was the mainstay of slaveholder ideology, namely that slavery was the only possible normal basis for "civilized" people like themselves to relate to the "uncivilized"?[72]

Enslavement of Indian labor not a problem of supply, but of social control

Lauber's first thesis, namely that European colonization had a devastating depopulating effect through infections of smallpox, tuberculosis, and other exotic diseases, is undoubtedly true. So also did the intensification of warfare, both against the English and between Indian tribes. These general conditions, coupled with the English policy of trading away a disproportionate number of male captives, would certainly tend to lower the birth rate among the Indians. Before South Carolina came to be chiefly a producer of rice and cotton early in the eighteenth century, the colony was primarily dependent upon commerce with the Indian tribes. It was in that colony's trading sphere, therefore, that the depopulating effect of enslavement was most in evidence. In 1708, the Spanish governor of Florida charged that some 10,000 to 12,000 Florida Indians, chiefly Apalachee people, had been taken as slaves by Creek and Yamassee Indians, directed by English Carolinians; only 300 Florida Indians survived, by finding refuge in St Augustine.[73] The extension of slave-trading into the interior in that same year was justified by South Carolina businessmen on the ground that "it serves to lessen their [the Indians'] number before the French can arm them."[74] The shipment of Indian captives from Carolina to bond-servitude in other English colonies, particularly those in the West Indies,[75] was, while it lasted, a major cause of Indian depopulation. The practice was also a factor in New England in the wake of the defeat of the forces commanded by the Wampanoag chieftain Metacom (called King Philip by the English) in 1675–76. An undetermined number of the captives were sent as bond-laborers "to various parts," namely the Spanish West Indies, Spain, Portugal, Bermuda, Virginia, and the Azores.[76] The Virginia colony Indian trade was primarily for beaver pelts and deer skins in the seventeenth century;[77] the labor supply was mainly English, together with a number of other European bond-laborers, and, to an increasing extent at the end of the seventeenth century, Afro-Caribbean and African.[78] Consequently, in Virginia the employment of and trade in Indian labor was comparatively limited.[79] But whatever the degree of involvement of the respective colonies, it is certain that depopulating wars were, paradoxically, the necessary condition for the beginning and continuation of Indian slavery, while it lasted, in the continental Anglo-American colonies. I know of no study, however, which concludes that the ending of enslavement of Indians within the capturing colony, or for trading abroad, was the result of the depopulating effect of that practice.[80] It was not the "supply' aspect, but rather the "control" aspect that was decisive in ending the labor policy of Indian enslavement in continental Anglo-America.

It was the common rule that enslaved Indian war captives, most particularly the men, be shipped out of the colony, sometimes to other continental colonies, even to England or Spain, but most commonly to England's West Indian sugar plantation colonies.[81] The proportion of Indian bond-laborers was by far the highest in South Carolina. There it peaked in about 1708, when 1,400 Indians (500 men, 600 women and 300 children) constituted one-fourth of the total lifetime hereditary bond-labor force.[82] Yet "only a small proportion of the whole number of Indians enslaved were kept in the [South Carolina] colony."[83] The total numbers of Indians enslaved in the Massachusetts and Plymouth colonies was far less, but it was policy to send male captives "outside the colonies."[84] Shipping value-producing Indian labor out of the colony was not what policy advisers to the Virginia Company had in mind in the early 1620s. Why was it, then, that the great majority were transported by sea to other colonies or countries?[85]

It was not that Indian laborers were unemployable in plantation labor; after all, that is why they were wanted in the West Indies. Nor was it that those colonies were oversupplied with plantation laborers; indeed, the Indians shipped to the West Indies were traded for Afro-Caribbean plantation laborers to be employed in the continental colonies.[86] It was not that Indians could not learn trades; actual instances of Indian craftsmen working within the colonies showed that they could, even as chattel bondmen.[87] Rather, the reasons were rooted in three intractable problems of "white race" social control: (1) resistance by the Indian bond-laborers, principally by running away, which merged sometimes with the same form of resistance of African and European bond-laborers; (2) the necessity to maintain nearby friendly, or "treaty," Indians in the buffer role,[88] in the first instance between the Anglo-American colonies and the more remote "hostile," or foreign-allied, tribes; and then against the escape of African-American bond-laborers beyond the Anglo-American "frontier"; and (3) with the institution of the "white race" system of social control, the key necessity of preserving "white skin" privileges of laboring-class European-Americans vis-à-vis all non-European-Americans.

Indian resistance to being reduced to plantation bond-labor

In the absence of a *cacique* class[89] that from positions of traditional upper-class authority could be co-opted as recruiters of plantation bond-labor, the Anglo-American bourgeoisie adapted the phenomenon of inter-tribal rivalries for their purposes. This was a basic element of the colonialist "Indian policy," and it was made to dovetail with the strategy according to which Indian "allies" were to serve as a protective buffer for the colony against the generally more remote tribes.

But if the English colonizers had the advantage of firearms and the buffer of dependent tribes, the victim tribes had a continental space at their backs.[90] This "continental factor" made possible Indian resistance by migration. When the Savannah Indians of South Carolina migrated north in 1707, "[t]he Iroquois themselves received [them] as brothers and the Delaware called them grandsons."[91] Sometimes migration would enable a tribe largely to avoid the enslaving onslaught;[92] sometimes victim tribes retained sufficient cohesion to be able to maintain their identity even as they migrated; and in other cases broken remnants found refuge with other tribes into which they were adopted.[93]

Unlike the African bond-laborers displaced from home by thousands of ocean miles into an utterly strange land, those relatively few Indian captives retained in a given colony were not so "completely broken from their tribal stems,"[94] and were still in at least somewhat familiar terrain, facing a familiar enemy whom they had already met in open battle. South Carolina Provincial policy was focused on the constant danger of Indian bond-laborers escaping into the woods, or conspiring with enemy tribes, or mounting insurrections, such as the one suspected in 1700.[95]

Colonialist concern was heightened by fears of Indians joining with African-Americans in resistance to their common bondage. In 1729, the French governor of Louisiana expressed his concern that "Indian slaves being mixed with our negroes may induce them to desert."[96] That same year he abandoned a mission of revenge against one Indian tribe, the Nabanez (Natchez?), lest Choctaws and Negroes seize the opportunity to attack New Orleans "to free themselves from slavery."[97] In South Carolina, precautions were advised to prevent "intimacy" between Indians and Negroes, "any Intercourse between Indians and Negroes" being seen as a threat to the colony.[98] In his signal study of the relationship of the Indians and African-Americans in the southeastern Anglo-American colonies, William S. Willis found that "[t]he determination [on the part of the English colonial authorities] to prevent Indian–Negro contacts within the White settlements was a main cause for curtailing the enslavement of Indians."[99]

The threat was made more acute by the constant efforts of the Spanish in Florida and the French in Louisiana to encourage resistance to and flight from the English colonies.[100] In 1716 and for some years thereafter, Yamassees and some Creeks, as well as numbers of Negroes, deserted English Carolina for Spanish Florida; from there Yamassees and Negroes carried on raids against the English colony, spreading the word to the South Carolina Indians and Negroes that freedom was theirs for the having in Florida.[101] When the English commanded by General Oglethorpe invaded Spanish Florida in 1740–42, they were opposed there by joint forces of Indians, Negroes, and Spanish.[102]

As time went on, Indian peoples grew less inclined to engage in internecine wars simply to provide slaves for the trade and exploitation of English "planters" who were intruding on villages of "friendly" and "hostile" Indians alike.[103] This trend matured in the great Indian revolt in 1715, called the

Yamassee War (see page 44), which marked the beginning of the irreversible discontinuation of enslavement of Indians in South Carolina, the province where it had been most extensively practiced.[104]

The inherent ambivalence of the "buffer" role

The buffer tribes had a dual role in the English colonial system of social control.[105] They served as a shield for the English against hostile tribes, including those linked to French and Spanish colonial rivals. Prior to 1715, South Carolina colonial policy "sought to consolidate a double bulwark of Indian allies in the zone of the Savannah and Altamaha Rivers" (present-day east–central Georgia). In the northwestern region, it was the mountain-dwelling Overhill Cherokee who long "bore the brunt of the French Indians." In 1723 the South Carolina Assembly solemnly affirmed, "The safety of this Province does, under God, depend on the friendship of the Cherokees."[106] In England the Commissioners of Trade and Plantations communicated to the King their concern that this dependence had even wider ramifications: if the Cherokees were to desert "your Majesty's interest," then "not only Carolina, but Virginia likewise would be exposed to their excursions."[107]

The buffer tribes were also a buffer between the runaway African-American bond-laborer and refuge beyond the boundaries of the Anglo-American colony.[108] This function was a regular provision in every treaty or memorandum of understanding between the colonies and their "tributary," "friendly," or newly "subject" tribes. Nash notes the "persistent inclusion in Indian treaties of a clause providing for the return of escaped slaves."[109] "Most treaties," Willis writes of the southeastern region in the eighteenth century, "stipulated that Indians surrender all Negroes and return all future runaways at an agreed price."[110] But the pattern had been set more than half a century earlier in the 1646 treaty between the Virginia colony and "Necotowance, King of the Indians."[111] Under the terms of the treaty made in 1700 between the Maryland colonial government and the chief of the Piscataway Indians, "[i]n case any servants or slaves runaway from their masters" to any Piscataway town, "the Indians shall be bound to apprehend them and bring them to the next English Plantation," or be subject to the penalties of Maryland law for the harborers of fugitives.[112]

By definition, "buffer" tribes were those located nearer to,[113] more accessible to, and, above all, economically more dependent upon the English colonists than were other tribes. But by the same token they were therefore more vulnerable to the predations of colonists who were ready to risk, to some degree, the buffer's protective function. It was precisely this sort of undermining of the buffer understanding that led to the Westo War of 1708. For the same reason, in the 1701–8 period the Savannah Indians acted out their resentment by emigrating northward out of South Carolina, "much to the annoyance of the white government, which found them useful as a bulwark against other tribes, and what was probably more important, as slave raiders."[114] As mentioned above, the aggravation of Indian grievances culminated in the Yamassee War (1715–17). The fate of southeast Anglo-America hung by a single thread, namely the loyalty of the Cherokees to the English, and that linkage was itself gravely weakened. But the tie held, and as a result the rebellion was defeated.[115] But it was, nevertheless, a historic victory over Indian enslavement, which immediately went into decline. "Justice to the Indians," Crane writes, "and, in particular the suppression of the traffic in Indian slavery, these were injunctions to successive [South Carolina Provincial] governors and councils," from 1680 to 1715.[116] In the wake of the Yamassee War, the issue could no longer be avoided. South Carolina was becoming a rice, cotton and indigo plantation enterprise for which were wanted African bond-laborers, such as many of the colony elite had been exploiting in the Barbadian sugar plantations. In 1690 the Lords Proprietors had sent an urgent instruction to the Carolina authorities:

> We hear that Indians are still being shipped away underhand. . . . You will do your best to prevent this. . . . [W]ithout them you cannot recover runaway Negroes.[117]

Twenty-five years later, the logic of their lordships' warning finally struck home. That logic was fundamentally dictated by the "continental factor" – providing the vast area for bond-labor escape that no army could patrol, and no navy could surround – and by the absence of an Indian *cacique* class.

Indian Labor and the Invention of the White Race

If not by compulsion, if not as "drudges" for the English colonists of every class, what were the possibilities of voluntary enlistment by Indians in the work of the colony, alongside the "surplus" English men and women who were brought to Anglo-America? In the period ending in 1622, there were instances of Indians who did work voluntarily within the Virginia colony.[118] In 1709 Robin, an Indian shoemaker, was granted leave to practice his trade among the English colonists "wherever he shall find encouragement."[119] But in general the Indians found their tribal life more comfortable and better supplied than the life offered by the English community so sore beset with starvation and disease. The English laboring people after 1622 worked as bond-laborers for terms which most of them did not survive, for debts they should not have had to owe for the trip to America. The Indians, as natives of the country, could not be bound by any such "transportation charges." It was hardly to be expected that Indians would submit voluntarily to the oppressive life endured by the English bond-laborers. Nor would the English employers be willing to spend more for Indian laborers than they had to spend for English laborers in such plentiful supply.

Was there another way? Despite the general inaccessibility of Indians as plantation laborers and the continual displacement of the tribal settlements, could they not, as groups or individuals, still have abandoned the Indian way of life for the English way? Although by far the greater number of the European immigrants arriving in the southern colonies came as bond-laborers, there were some who were able to make the trip from Europe at their own expense, and who began their lives in Anglo-America as independent farmers or artisans. Why might not Indians have opted for the same sort of enterprise within the colony? The English homeland itself was mainly a nation of immigrants, Saxons, Angles, Danes, Normans, Flemings, consolidating with the ancient Angles, Celts and Scots. True, the Indians' tribal lands were being taken away, but might not the inducements for individual Indians entering into the Anglo-American common economic life well have outweighed the disinclining factors, just as it did for some Scots-Irish, for example? Such inducements included credit from capitalist land speculators and freedom from taxes for as much as ten years.[120] With access to English-made iron implements and utensils, and other manufactured goods and supplies, the prospects might well have persuaded enterprising Indians to take up the life of the free yeoman farmer or artisan. Evidence of the appeal of Anglo-American commodity culture would become woefully evident in its ability to dissolve Indian society. Why should not at least a few individual Indians be successful in that culture as members of the colony?

This avenue to use of the labor of the Indian was never taken. The policy of special inducements to independent farmers referred to above was not developed until the early eighteenth century. The immigrants to whom this opportunity was opened were counted upon to provide a barrier against external dangers from French and hostile Indian attacks, and against the establishment of maroon centers of freedom and resistance by African-American bond-laborers in the Allegheny Mountains.[121] By that time, by a historical transformation which is the central concern of this volume, the bourgeoisie had drawn the color line between freedom and slavery, and established white supremacy as article one of the Anglo-American constitution. Only European-Americans, as "whites," were thereafter to be entitled to the full rights of the free citizen, Indians being by definition not "white."[122] The presence within the colony of free independent Indian farmers or tenants would have been a constitutionally intolerable anomaly.

The fate of the Indians under the principle of racial slavery and white supremacy was thus in the end controlled by twin parameters: nonenslavability and nonassimilability. These parameters would eventually govern Anglo-American "Indian policy" throughout the continental colonies.

PART TWO
The Plantation of Bondage

4

The Fateful Addiction to
"Present Profit"

The years 1607–24 are known as "the Company period" of Virginia history, when the affairs of the colony were conducted under the aegis of the Virginia Company of London, chartered by James I in 1606, successively re-chartered in 1609 and 1612, and reformed in 1618 under Sir Edwin Sandys. Historians have long noted that the development of the Virginia colony during the Company period falls naturally into three time phases.[1] (1) 1607 to 1610: Virginia as an experimental colony, 24 May 1607 to the granting of a new charter in May 1609 through the "starving time" in the winter of 1609–10. (2) 1610 to 1618: the expansion of the royal territorial grant to the Virginia Company; the establishment of a special royal council for the Virginia Company; the beginning of tobacco cultivation and export, with the widening of the Company's charter in 1612 to cover the Bermuda (Somers) Islands, and authorization of a local Colony Council to function as a legislative body. (3) 1619 to 1624: the installation of George Yeardley as Governor of Virginia under the Sandys instructions (which the colony elite called the "Great Charter"), authorizing the establishment of an elected General Assembly "for the happy guiding and governing of the people there inhabiting;"[2] the growth of independent, non-Company, plantations; the bankruptcy of the Virginia Company; the devastating Indian attack on the colony in March 1622; the revocation of its charter, and the reversion of custody of Virginia affairs to a royal commission in June 1624.[3]

Most historians treat the Company period primarily in terms of the rise of the Virginia Company, its internal and external struggles, and its eventual dissolution, rather than in terms of the counter-revolution in labor relations that it brought. Some among them see in those events a confirmation of their particular strain of the "germ" theory of American history. This theory is summarized by Alexander Brown in his *First Republic* as follows:[4]

[T]his nation was not brought forth in a day.... The evolution had been going on ever since the free air of America inspired the first petitions against a royal form of government in 1608, to the present day [1898]. The germ is still unfolding and so long as it remains true to the seed it will continue to put forth to the glory of the nation and for the betterment of mankind.... The seedling, after being fostered in England under the advanced statesmen of that transition period, continued to grow in the political system of the new nation . . .

Works of this genre interpret the history of the 1606–24 period in Virginia as an aspect of the struggle of the English bourgeoisie in general against the absolutist tendencies of the bourgeois monarchy, which culminated in the English Civil War in the middle of the seventeenth century. This, for example, is the approach taken to consideration of the successive Virginia Company charters of 1609 and 1612; to the instructions to the newly designated colony governor, Francis Yeardley, in 1618, the so-called "Great Charter"; and to the internal factional disputes of the Virginia Company.

Since such scholars find no differences between the contending policy-setting English parties with respect to the status to be imposed on the laboring people, they find it unnecessary to inquire into the anomalous character of labor relations that evolved in the Company period. Nor do they perceive the causal link between that transformation and the later institution of lifetime chattel bond-servitude as the basis of the continental plantation colonies' economy, which the final victory of the Parliamentary bourgeoisie at home "brought forth."[5]

For the present work on the origin of racial slavery as a particular form of racial oppression of African-Americans, the Company period of Virginia history is of crucial significance, even though only a very small number of Africans or African-Americans were then living in Virginia. The findings of historians of seventeenth-century economic development in Virginia, the plantation system, and racial slavery offer a firm foundation for this approach. A century ago, Philip A. Bruce concluded thus:

> But for the introduction of the indented servant into the Colony upon the threshold of settlement. . . . [t]he unique social conditions established at a later period would never have existed, or, indeed, if such had been the case, only in a modified form.[6]

James C. Ballagh made the point more explicitly:

> Servitude not only preceded slavery in the logical development of the principle of subjection, standing midway between freedom and absolute subjection, but it was the historic base upon which slavery, by the expansion and addition of incidents, was constructed.[7]

Eric Williams, though centering his attention on Caribbean history, included colonial Virginia in the generalization that "[w]hite servitude was the historic base upon which slavery was constructed."[8] Lerone Bennett Jr, looking at colonial Virginia, found:

> [W]hite servitude was the proving ground. . . . The plantation pass system, the slave trade, the sexual exploitation of servant women, the whipping-post and slave chain and branding iron, the overseer, the house servant, the Uncle Tom: all these mechanisms were tried out and perfected on white men and women. . . . [I]t is plain that nothing substantial can be said about the mechanisms of black bondage in

America except against the background and within the perspective of white bondage in America.[9]

Of English "Liberties, Franchises and Immunities"

As profound as the implication of this general premise is, it has never been confuted, although it has been ignored and implicitly rejected by many,[10] and expressly challenged by two.[11]

But when it is accepted, attention is immediately drawn to a basic constitutional principle that informed all of these charters and instructions as first stated in the 1606 charter and reaffirmed in the 1609 charter, establishing the Royal intent that all colonists

> shall have and enjoy all liberties, franchises and immunities of free denizens and natural subjects, . . . to all intents and purposes as if they had been abiding and born within this our Realm of England, or any other of our said Domains.[12]

Before the social demotion of the laboring people to chattel bond-servitude could form the basis for the subsequent lifetime hereditary chattel bondage of African-Americans, those "liberties, franchises and immunities" established in England had to be overthrown insofar as they concerned the relations between employer and employee established in the Statute of Artificers of 1563. The parity of colonists' rights with those prevailing in England was stated again in the 1612 charter that established a Virginia Colony Council, with authority to legislate for the colony, provided that the law and ordinances "be not contrary to the laws and statutes of this our realm of England."[13] So how then was it that the plantation bourgeoisie was able to overthrow basic English constitutional principles and reduce the laboring-class in colonial Virginia to a general condition of chattel bond-servitude? Following the lead of Edmund S. Morgan, I will examine this question by emphasizing the transformation of the relations of production, the relations between laborer and employer.

The 1607–1610 Years

The conditions of life were unimaginably difficult for the English colonists during much of the 1607–1610 period. One statistic will suffice: nine out of ten of the emigrants who came in that period died, an annual death rate of almost 50 percent.[14] The winter of 1609–10, the "starving time," reduced the population of the colony "from 500 to about sixty as a result of disease, sickness, Indian arrows, and malnutrition."[15] In June 1610, Governor Thomas Gates ordered the abandonment of the premises by a demoralized remnant of colonists, and on 17 June the entire company embarked for England. Much to the dismay of the abandoners, they were intercepted by newcomers under the command of Governor de la Warre, at whose order the old settlers returned to Jamestown.[16]

The records of the sufferings of these earliest of Virginia colonists have been extensively reprinted and discussed in the sources noted. I wish, however, to direct special attention to two aspects of the story that are of special relevance for the thesis I am presenting.

First, however appalling the situation was in other regards, the labor, whatever it was, conformed to the traditional English system; none of the laboring people was a chattel bond-servant. In 1607, the Virginia Colony Council complained of English sailors diverting colony laborers from their proper work to pursue a sideline in the sassafras trade. Referring to these men, the council said, "they be all our waged men."[17] It has been questioned whether this use of the term "waged men" should be understood in the modern sense.[18] But the Colony Council was composed of persons who were familiar with the wages system of labor, and who had no experience at all with chattel bond-servitude of English workers. Furthermore, in later years, when the chattel-labor relation of production was established for English workers in Virginia, those workers were never referred to as "waged" workers. Finally, in 1624 when his advice was sought, the famous Captain John Smith, who was a member of the Colony council from 1608 to 1610 and its president for most of that time, firmly believed English workers in Virginia should be "hyred good labourers and mechanical men." He explicitly denounced the buying and selling of workers as an un-English practice.[19]

Second, the sex ratio in this first period was extremely high. The total number of women in the colony was raised to two on the arrival of the second supply ship on about 1 October 1608. Some one hundred women were among the four or five hundred passengers who arrived in Virginia in the nine ships of the so-called Great Supply in 1609. But the death toll of the following winter's "starving time" canceled the sex ratio as a meaningful statistic. English women continued to arrive; still, in the middle of the 1610–1618 period, women and children together constituted less than a one-fifth of the 351-member colony.[20] Whether the scarcity of women contributed to the demoralizing death toll that led to the aborted decision to abandon the colony is speculative. Some of the men were veterans of European armies, accustomed to the ready services of women camp followers. Perhaps even then complaints were heard like one made a decade later, that men were dying for the lack of women to tend them in their sickness.[21] This attention to the sex ratio could perhaps be omitted, if it were not for the fact that it was not a transitory phenomenon soon to be eroded as a result of the normal process of natural reproduction. (See pp. 69–70, below.)

The Middle Years, 1610–1618

The middle period, 1610–1618, began under the new charter of 1609.[22] It was the interlude between the fade-out of the "gold fever" and the beginning of the "tobacco fever"; between the factional president-and-council conduct of the colony's affairs and the establishment of the Virginia Assembly under the "Great Charter" of 1618. It was a period of military dictatorship in the colony headed by a succession of veteran officers of the wars in Ireland and the Netherlands;[23] it saw the creation of the privately organized, separate plantations and the beginning of increasing difficulties for the Company. It ended with the frustration of the social control efforts of the military regime, whose attempts to enforce the progam for balanced economic development wilted in the heat of the "tobacco fever."[24]

The author of the standard study of the Virginia Company regards this 1610–1618 period as primarily an ebb tide in the life of the colony.[25] Nevertheless, it was a time of great significance with regard to the development of the status of labor. The English had, as noted, realized that the Indians were not going to labor for them; therefore,

[a]fter 1609 the chief attention of all concerned was concentrated on the task of sending a sufficient labor supply to produce in Virginia the commodities that would find a ready and profitable market at home.[26]

Under the new administration, production relations were to be those of a producer's cooperative type of enterprise. The projected arrangement was outlined in the pamphlet *Nova Britannia*, published in 1609:

All charges [expenses] of settling and maintaining the plantation, and of making supplies shall be borne in a joint stock of the adventurers [stockholders], for seven yeares after the date of our new enlargement [1609]: during which time there shall be no adventure, nor goods returned in private from thence, neyther by Master [ship's captain], Marriner, Planter, nor Passenger, they shall be restrained by bond and search, that as we supplie from hence to the Planters at our own charge all necessaries for food and apparel, for fortifying and building of houses in a joynt stock, so they are to returne from thence the encrease and fruits of their labours, for the use and advancement of the same joynt stocke, till the end of seven years.[27]

The joint stock was made up of shares purchased by investors, the minimum cost of one share being £12 10*d*. A distinction was made between those who invested money but stayed in England, and those who went to Virginia as colonists. The former were called "Adventurers," the latter were called "Planters." Among the colonists, the power-structure personnel, "the extraordinarie men [as distinguished from the 'ordinary man or woman'], Divines, Governors, Ministers of State and Justice, Knights, Gentlemen, Physitions, and such as be men of worth for special services," were not required to labor, but were still counted as Planters and were "to be maintained out of the common store." At the end of seven years a dividend was to be declared which, it was anticipated, would amount to "five hundred acres, at least," for each stockholder. These Adventurers and Planters would then be free and independent Virginia landowners.

In a further quest for settlers, the Company turned its attention to the destitute proletarians of London, charitably described as "a swarme of unnecessary inmates . . . a continual cause of dearth and famine, and the very originall cause of all the Plagues that happen in this Kingdome." In 1609, the Virginia Company, in a letter to the bourgeoisie corporate of London, "The Lord Mayor, Aldermen and Companies," sought to stress the value of ridding "the city and suburbs" of the surplus poor by shipping them to Virginia.[28] The Company proposed that the London bourgeoisie, individually or in organized forms, should purchase shares of Virginia Company stock. For every share thus purchased, the Company would offer to transport one poor London "inmate" to Virginia. Since it was a fundamental right of English men and women that, except by explicit order of the Crown, they might not be sent out of the kingdom without their own consent, the Company suggested persuasive arguments whereby the city fathers might get that consent:

> And if the inmate called before you and enjoined to remove shall alleadge that he hath not place to remove unto, but must lye in the streets; and being offered to go this Journey, shall demaund what may be theire present mayntenance, what maye be their future hopes? it may please you to let them Knowe that for the present they shall have meate, drinke and clothing, and with an howse, orchard and garden, for the meanest [poorest] family, and a possession of lands to them and their posterity, one hundred acres for every man's person that hath a trade, or a body able to endure day labour, as much for his wife, as much for his child, that are of yeres to do service to the Colony, with further particular reward according to theire particular meritts and industry.

The exact terms on which these people were to "have possession" of the allotted land was not stated; as tenants, apparently,[29] with future prospects of becoming independent landowners. They certainly were not to be chattel proletarians.

In 1614, Acting Governor Thomas Dale sought to rouse the labor force of the colony to a more consistent effort. Among the measures he instituted was the allotment of three acres each to a large number of the colonists. These persons were referred to as "farmers," that is, tenants. Their relation to production was described at the time as follows:

> They are not called into any service or labor belonging to the Colony, more than one month in the year, which shall neither be in seed time, or in harvest, for which, doing no other duty to the Colony, they are yearly to pay into the store two barrels and a half of corn.[30]

The rest of the workforce were to be Company laborers. It is not known how the selection of tenants was made, but it is a reasonable conjecture that the expatriated proletarians were found more frequently among the Colony laborers than among tenants. These workers were required to labor eleven months a year for the Company in exchange for supplies and were additionally allowed to work one month's time for their own private accounts. Among this number some were also given a day a week, from May to harvest time, to tend their own crops.[31] The laborers were, like other colonists, subject to the severities of "*Lawes Divine, Morall, and Martiall.*" Offenses against the code could bring down on a worker the harsh cruelty of the military camp, such as pillorying, cutting off of ears, boring through of the tongue, whipping of offenders through the town tied to a cart, banishment from the colony to the wilderness, and inducement of the premature birth and death of an infant by the whipping of a pregnant woman, for offenses such as speaking ill of a master or official, stealing food from a master's store, and failure to complete a work task.[32]

By way of summary of the production relationships as they existed in the period July 1614 to March 1616, we have John Rolfe's account:

> The general mayne body of the planters are divided into ... Officers; Laborers, and Farmors
>
> (1) the officers [soldiers, guards, etc.] have the charge and care as well over the farmors as laborers generallie – that they watch and ward for their preservation, etc.
>
> (2) The Laborers are of two sorts – lst those employed only in the generall works, who are fed and clothed out of the store. 2nd others, specially artificers, as smiths, carpenters, shoemakers, taylors, tanners, etc. do work in their professions for the colony, and maintayne themselves with food and apparrell, having time permitted them to till and manure their ground.
>
> (3) The Farmors live at most ease – yet by their good endeavors bring yearlie much plentie to the plantation. They are bound by covenant, both for themselves and servants, to maintaine your Majestie's right and title in that Kingdom, against all foreign and domestic enemies. To watch and ward in the townes where they are resident. To do thirty one days service for the colony, when they shall be called thereunto – yet not at all times, but when their own business can best spare them. To maintayne themselves and families with food and rayment – and every farmor to pay yearlie into the magazine, for himself and every man servant, wheat [corn], which amounteth to twelve bushells and a halfe of English measure.[33]

There is not one laboring person in this catalogue whose status is that of chattel bond-servant.[34] Even the least favored member of this labor force was working under a bilateral, mutually binding contract which could not legally be dissolved except by common consent of the laborer and the employer. The laborer was not a chattel; the employer, whether it were the Virginia Company or an independent farmer, could not dispose of the laborer as he could of property. Furthermore, these laborers were assured at least a degree of propertied status at the completion of the terms of their contracts.

A prominent English colonist and member of the Virginia Company returned in 1610 from a trip to the colony and published his "Newes from Virginia," enthusiastically setting forth the prospects of the new land. He described the relations of production in verse:

> To such as to Virginia
> Do purpose to repaire;

> And when that they shall hither come
> Each man shall have his share,
> Day wages for the laborer,
> And for his more content,
> A house and garden plot shall have.[35]

In March of 1616 there were, by Colony Secretary John Rolfe's account, 81 tenants and some 140 laborers working for the Company in Virginia, out of a total population of 351.[36] Later that same spring, the servants belonging to the group favored with extra time for tending their own private crops were granted complete freedom from servant status; this was in accordance with the agreement made between them and the Company three years before in England, prior to their signing on for service in Virginia.[37] They now became tenants like those previously mentioned or, possibly, they joined others in the classification of artisans, or they became agricultural laborers for farmers. A year later, in 1617, at the time of Captain Samuel Argall's assumption of his duties as Governor in Virginia, the number of laborers employed by the Company was reduced to only fifty-four.[38] Perhaps 20 percent of the total population of the colony (after making allowance for the death rate) was thus shifted in one year from the status of contract wage-laborer for the Company – not to chattel bond-servitude but upward to a status preferable and more profitable for them.[39]

It was during the latter part of this middle period that the English first cultivated tobacco in Virginia.[40] The discovery of tobacco was "by far the most momentous fact in the history of Virginia in the seventeenth century," writes Bruce, declaring that it shaped the fate of the people of Virginia absolutely.[41] The high profits that the crop soon began to yield drew the labor of the colony like a magnet. The Company and colony authorities offered special inducements and prescribed penalties to stem the tendency, but to no avail. By the spring of 1618, the former food surplus had become a scarcity:

> The lack of corn became so great in consequence of the exclusive attention paid to the culture of tobacco, that there would have been ground for anticipating a severe famine if two hundred quarters of meal had not been imported into the magazine.[42]

Governor Argall at first attempted to enforce limitations on tobacco planting, and to encourage needed attention to food production.[43] But he had come just at the time when separate private plantations outside the Company were beginning to operate, making the task of enforcing controls on production practically impossible by the efforts of colony officials alone. In 1616, the operation of the supply magazine was farmed out to a separate company of merchants.[44] In that same year, the Virginia Company, having no other means of paying the seven-year dividend that was due to its stockholders, awarded land titles to the original investors.[45]

The initial effort at imposing minimum corn cultivation while limiting the planting of tobacco was soon allowed to lapse.[46] In June 1617, the newly arrived Governor, Samuel Argall, proclaimed a fixed price of three shillings per pound of tobacco. In order to secure compliance with this regulation, he decreed a scale of penalties which serve to throw light on the question of production relations. Violators of the price decree were subject to a "penalty [of] 3 years slavery to the colony."[47] To protect the colonists against profiteering by the newly privatized magazine, the same penalty was to be exacted on those who bought tobacco at less than three shillings. Though Argall's interest in controlling tobacco planting diminished sharply, his belief in slavery as punishment for malefactors remained constant. The following year, desiring to encourage piety among the colonists, Argall ordered that persons failing to attend church on Sundays and holidays should suffer corporal punishment, "and be a slave the week following – 2nd offense a month – 3rd, a year and a day."[48]

What did Argall mean here by "slavery"? And what does it tell us of the nature of the production relationships at that time prevailing? Since this slavery was intended as a punishment, it could not have been the normal condition of labor as it then existed in the colony. The culprit under punishment would be unpaid, but would receive maintenance. It can be inferred, therefore, that workers were normally entitled to recompense other than mere maintenance. This penalty-servitude was imposed without regard to the will or consent of the person subject to it. On the other hand, the laborer under this sentence was not a chattel, subject to purchase and sale. It appears that what Argall meant by "slavery" in this instance was a status between that of the "waged man," the colony laborer working for pay under contract, and that of limited-term unpaid servitude.

Further evidence that the typical laborer at this time was a hired wage worker, and not one employed for "meat and drink only," is to be seen in the following two items. In June 1618, Argall complained that he had personally had to pay "sundry debts of the Company,"[49] including "wages ... payde" for Company laborers.[50] The Company denied knowledge of any such debts, but did not deny the possibility of them. Furthermore, Article XIV of the Virginia Charter of 1612 was specifically aimed at checking the practice of workers who, "having received wages etc. [in England] from the company, and agreed to serve the colony, have afterwards refused to go thither," or who, having gone to Virginia, returned before their contracts expired.[51]

Argall occupied a dual position; he was the Governor of the colony, appointed to serve by and for the Company, and he was also the holder of a 400-acre land patent,[52] being therefore a private planter. As time went on, it was said, he showed an increasing tendency to resolve any conflict of interest in favor of his private-planter side rather than his Company-official side. In August 1618, the Company in London addressed a letter to Argall charging him with peculation and other violations of trust, and notifying him that he was to stand trial before the Company Court in England upon his return to that country. Argall, it was alleged, had used the Company's ships and crews for trading for his own private profit; he had forbidden any other person from trading with the Indians for furs, in order that he, Argall, might have the monopoly of that profitable commerce; he had appropriated Company-owned corn for his own private plantation use; and he had disposed of the Company's livestock to private planters, including himself, in violation of explicit orders from the Company.[53] One of the Company's accusations is particularly relevant to the question of the status of the laboring classes in the colony:

> that you take the ancient Planters which ought to be free and likewise those [colony servants] from the common garden to sett them upon your corne to feed your own men as if the Plantacon were onely intended to serve your turne.[54]

Here is the first alleged instance of a worker being treated like a chattel, in that the worker is transferred without his prior consent from one employer (in this instance, the Company) to another (Argall, the private planter). Lastly, and equally significant, these alleged acts were officially condemned as violations of the rights of the laborers under the Virginia charter, for which the violator would have to render account before English authorities.

In the end, Argall was able to avoid trial. His guilt or innocence is of no particular importance today, except for historical scholars.[55] What is of lasting significance is that these charges against Argall anticipated in detail the known course of self-aggrandizement followed by colony governors, and by other strategically advantaged officers, who succeeded Argall, conduct that was to have historical consequences.

Finally, in this listing of innovations in property and production relations in the 1610–1618 period, we come to the establishment of what would in time come to be called the "headright" principle. As has been mentioned, the investors of 1609 were given their dividend in 1616 in the form of land titles, this being the only form in which the financially embarrassed Virginia Company could meet its obligations. Having struck on this device, the Company decided to use it for raising capital.[56]

This new procedure was distinguished from the old in the provisions it contained for facilitating the free flow of capital. These features betokened not only the difficulties facing the Company in securing capital, but also the impending break-up of the Company's monopoly of colonial enterprise. Under the new Company policy, the investor, or group of investors jointly, though remaining in England, could receive immediate title and possession of Virginia land, at the rate of fifty acres for every £12½ sterling paid to the Company; this clearly was a more attractive arrangement than the previous one of having to leave the investment in the parlous environment of the Company treasury for seven years, with dubious prospects of profitable returns, before getting any land title. Or, alternatively, these private investors could get land by means of the headright,[57] which allowed the investors the same portion of fifty acres for each person whose emigration expenses were paid by the investors. No less significant for our present focus, it was specified that this new opening to capitalist investment in Virginia land was to be used for "sending families to manure [work] it for yearely rent, or for halfe the clear profits as many others doe."[58] These enterprises were called "particular plantations." The perspective here being put forward was that of a capitalist agriculture of the English style, with landlord, tenants and wage laborers, distinguished only by the fact that the landlord was an absentee.[59]

Under this provision, by 1618 six such separate companies had been granted patents for land in Virginia,[60] some of really vast extent, including one for 200,000 acres and another for 80,000 acres.[61] These independent capitalists were given, along with the land, beginning in February 1619, legal jurisdiction over the control of their tenants and laborers; in the words of the Company's order: "to make Orders, Ordinances and Constitutions for the better ordering and dyrectinge of their servants." Yet, significantly, they added the stipulation, "provided they be not repugnant to the Lawes of England."[62]

The new departure represented by the issuance of the Virginia charter of 1609 reflected a change in perspective for the colony; the gold fever was abated, and attention was directed toward the establishment and development of agriculture and of extractive enterprises of sea and stream, of forest and mine, as well as to the trade with the Indians for beaver skins. Virginia, under the new direction, was expected to become a supplier of a wide variety of products, supporting and supplementing the profit-making processes of the home country. The author of "Newes from Virginia" had rhapsodized on the prospects foreshadowed in his mind by two ships he had recently seen coming into England from the colony:

> Well fraught, and in the Same
> Two ships, are these commodities
> Furres, sturgeon, caviare,
> Black-walnut-tree, and some deal boards
> With such they laden are;
> Some pearl, some wainscot and clap boards,
> With some sasafras wood,
> And iron promis't for 'tis true
> Their mynes are very good.[63]

As our account has indicated, these hopes were not, in the main, to be realized. On the other hand, the colony's success in achieving self-sufficiency in food production and in developing commerce with the Indians no doubt explains in large part the lowering of the annual death rate in the 1610–1618 period to less than 9 percent, compared with the rate of just under 50 percent in the 1607–1610 period.[64] In 1616, John Rolfe, his term as Secretary of the Colony having ended, returned temporarily to England with his wife, the Indian princess Pocahontas, and their infant son;[65] there he wrote an account of the colony, now at peace with its neighbors. He said:

The great blessings of God have followed this peace, and it next under him, hath bredd our plentie – every man sitting under his fig tree in safety, gathering and reaping the fruits of their labors with much joy and comfort.[66]

But now, at the close of the 1610–1618 period, the system of allocation of land by head-right, and the opportunity for a freer flow of and quicker turnover of capital had cast a shadow over the peace, the land and the laborer. It was to be a capitalist farming system in Virginia.[67] But what kind of capitalist farming – the English type, or some peculiar system? That was the question to which the next and final phase of the Company period would give an answer.

The Final Phase, 1619–24: The Tobacco Price Problem

The 1619–24 period begins with the installation of Sir Edwin Sandys as Treasurer and chief executive of the Virginia Company, and the entrance of George Yeardley upon his duty as the Company's governor in Virginia, in the spring of 1619. Basic lines of policy, however, had been worked out in the latter part of 1618, in discussions that sought to draw lessons from the experiences of the past, and of the Argall regime in particular.[68]

The program that emerged was fashioned along three main lines: (1) the reclamation of Company lands and stock, and the revitalization and extension of various Company enterprises, all to be financed initially by the sale of patents for separate plantations to be organized by individual and group capitalists outside the Company; (2) the promotion of a generalized economy, and avoidance of reliance upon tobacco as the mainstay; (3) the definition and systemization of land tenure in the colony, and the encouragement of emigration of laboring hands to the colony.[69] Integrally and separately, from the beginning the three points of this program bore within themselves latent contradictions which quickly matured.

As a capitalist operation, the Virginia Company was a failure in 1619. For twelve years of effort and the outlay of £75,000 sterling of investors' money and credit, the Company had nothing in Virginia to show for it but – six goats!:

[The] wholl State of the publique [Company property in the Colony] was gone and consumed, there beinge not lefte att that time to the Company either the land ... or any Tennant, Servant, Rent or trybute corne [from the Indians], cowe or salte-worke and but six Goates onely.[70]

Paradoxically, however, the colony was beginning to throb under the first stimulus of "America's first Boom," as Professor Morgan has called it.[71] It was the tobacco boom, of course, and it drew into itself an increasing share of the colony's labor. The shipment of tobacco from Virginia to England in 1615 amounted to less than one-third of a pound for every person in the colony. By 1619, the figure was twenty pounds per person, and by 1622 it had reached forty-eight pounds.[72] The number of separate non-Company plantations showed a parallel growth. Between 1616 and 1619, six patents were issued to separate capitalist plantation groups. Between 1619 and 1623, forty-four such patents were granted by the Company.[73]

Conceived as a means of financing the development of a generalized economy under Company leadership in the colony, the policy of selling land for separate plantations produced the opposite effect. The directors of these new enterprises emerged increasingly as the vital force in the direction of the economic and political affairs of the colony, and in the ever-increasing reliance upon tobacco cultivation.[74] Although they made some gestures toward developing non-tobacco enterprises, they were not interested in risking very far along a path that had proved so costly to the Company. Their eyes were fixed on tobacco, with its quick turnover and profits. From 1619 on, writes Craven, "the chief interest of the Virginia planter was devoted to his tobacco crop."[75]

A competition developed between the Company and the separate plantations for the supplies of labor and capital. In 1619 and 1620, separate planters were already accounting for the transport of 30 percent of the emigrants; after that, the majority were supplied by the separate planters.[76] This competition took its most dramatic and sharpest form in the Argall-like practice of colony officers diverting Company tenants from Company service to these officers' own private exploitation. In its instructions to the new Governor Yeardley, the Company had endowed the colony officers with lands to be cultivated for their support by tenants supplied by the Company. Leading the list was an allotment of 3,000 acres to be attached to the office of the governor. In addition to this substantial perquisite of office, Yeardley was granted outright a personal plantation of 2,200 acres.[77] Yeardley was an especially arrant offender among the colony officers who appropriated tenants for "their own private Lands, not upon land belongeth to their office," and wasted the time of many others by requiring personal services of them.[78] When he surrendered his office at the end of his three-year term, Yeardley kept for himself all but forty-six of his Company complement of one hundred tenants.[79] The Company officers also betrayed their trust and advantaged themselves by hiring out Company-supplied tenants to private non-Company employers.[80]

In the competition for investment capital, the Virginia Company was also being outdone. In 1620 and 1621, the Company was forced on this account to rely mainly on its public lottery as its capital funds source.[81] By the summer of 1621, the par £12½ sterling Virginia Company shares were selling in London at from £2 to £2½.[82]

The definition and systemization of land tenure was elaborated in the instructions for Yeardley, adopted by the Company Court in London in November 1618, prior to Yeardley's coming to Virginia.[83] These instructions represented a further development of the trend to large-capitalist agriculture and a freer flow of capital, both of which were established principles informing the 1616 policy.[84] The tenants who had been brought to Virginia prior to mid-1616 were, upon completion of their term of service, to receive one hundred acres "to be held by them, their Heirs and assigns for ever," paying only two shillings annual rent. But persons transported at Company expense since mid-1616 had a less attractive option. They could remain as tenants for the Company at the completion of their seven-year term, or be "free to move where they will," but with no land guarantee.[85]

Obviously the prospective creation of a permanent class of tenants would be designed to encourage capital investment, as would the reduction of the growth in numbers of self-employed freehold farmers, through the accretion of landless ex-tenants. On the other hand, this was a policy that would increase class differentiations by reducing social mobility from tenant to landowner, and sharpen class contradictions. The same effects were to be expected from the expansion of the headright principle to provide a grant of fifty acres to any investor who would pay for the transportation of "persons ... which shall go into Virginia with intent there to inhabit, if they continue there three years or dye after they are shipped."[86]

Under Sandys's leadership the Company launched a number of projects – iron mining, processing wood for potash and pitch, timbering, fishing, glass making and fur trading – designed to promote a generalization of the Virginia economy, as a market for and a supplier to England, and in the interest of the strength and stability of the colony itself. Lacking capital of its own, the Company farmed out a number of these efforts to subsidiary joint-stock companies. Although one of these projects – shipping women to be sold for wives among the more prosperous men – was profitable, most of the other endeavors were less remunerative for the investors.[87] By the summer of 1621, writes Craven: "The company was for all practical purposes bankrupt."[88]

Crisis of overproduction of tobacco

Most disastrous, however, was the outbreak of a characteristic capitalist crisis of overproduction:

> [T]he Company had not reckoned with the effect of the rapidly expanded supply of Virginia tobacco, nor with the increasing competition from the new British settlements in Barbados and St Christopher. Consequently, during 1620 and 1621, the adventurers who had underwritten the purchase of the product had been compelled to sell much of it at less than they had paid in Virginia.[89]

In the hope of riding out the storm, the Sandys administration joined, indeed put itself at the head of, the tobacco party.[90] Succumbing to what one of Sandys's opponents called the "straunge dream"[91] of salvation through tobacco, the Company decided to stake all on an application for a royal grant of the monopoly of the English tobacco import trade. They got the contract, but the terms dictated by King James were so onerous that it was guaranteed to fail so far as the Company's interests were concerned.[92] Although the insupportable conditions of the contract led the Company to surrender it within a year, it was of momentous historic significance. It expressed the choice of the Anglo-American plantation bourgeoisie as a whole to base the development of Virginia Colony on a monocultural, rather than on a diversified economy. From the time of the forlornly ambitious projects for non-tobacco products plotted by the Virginia Company, the records of seventeenth-century Virginia are filled with instructions, advice, appeals, exhortations and injunctions aimed at diversifying the economy and avoiding dependence upon tobacco.[93] With even greater consistency the colony was fashioned at every turn in the opposite image. In the end it was a victory of blind instinct over articulate wisdom. But not instinct in general: Indian society had mastered the uses of tobacco without letting tobacco master Indian society. It was, rather, the victory of the specifically bourgeois class instinct for their annual rate of profit and quick turnover of capital.

The "Adventurers" Seek Ways to Support the Tobacco Addiction

The drop in tobacco prices fell upon the just and the unjust, the "publique" and the separate private plantation owners, alike. The Virginia Company passed into history in 1624, but the price of tobacco continued a general course of decline; by 1630 it was less than a penny a pound in Virginia.[94] By the middle of the seventeenth century, Barbados and St Christopher had been transformed into sugar plantation colonies in the interest of a higher rate of profit, but the price of Virginia tobacco never again rose to even one-third of what it had been in the day of the "straunge dream." If the losses sustained on other enterprises had dried up the source of capital flowing into the Virginia Company, the decline in the price of tobacco implied a similar effect, if it were not somehow to be averted, upon the flow of English capital into Virginia tobacco cultivation, whether that cultivation were conducted by a royally chartered company or by separate entrepreneurs operating on their own account.

The capitalists would have to find a way to counteract the market-driven tendency of the rate of profit to fall. As we have noted, the Company and the Virginia Assembly in 1619 had indicated their idea of a fair profit, stipulating a limit of 25 percent mark-up on English goods brought for sale in Virginia. Faced with falling tobacco prices in England, the merchants accordingly discounted the tobacco with which the Virginia people paid for English goods. From a contentious exchange of letters between the Virginia Company of London and the Virginia Colony Council in Jamestown in 1623, we learn that a bushel of meal delivered in Virginia and worth thirteen shillings was exchanged for nine or ten pounds of tobacco, officially rated at three shillings the pound, a discount of 55 percent.[95]

Conceivably this deterioration of the Virginia tobacco-seller's position could have been countered by administrative measures. This was not a practical possibility, however, as more than a century of subsequent efforts at "stinting" tobacco, pegging prices, destroying surplus stocks, etcetera, would prove.[96]

Almost the entire cost of production in Virginia was in payment for labor power, and since these payments were made in tobacco, the capitalists' cost of production declined proportionately to the decline in the price of tobacco.[97] Therefore, although the capitalists' profit was being reduced, the decline was not caused by a rise in the absolute or relative wages of the laboring people, but by the fall of tobacco prices. This built-in elasticity of laborer and tenant costs served to reduce the impact of the lowered price of tobacco upon the interests of the capitalists, in Virginia or in England or in both places. However, it did not protect the capitalists against a reduction of their equity or profit rate in terms of their pound-sterling investment. If the adventurer or planter invested one hundred pounds sterling in Virginia tobacco and the price of tobacco declined by half, the rate of profit on the investment would be cut in half. The plantation bourgeoisie accordingly sought ways to raise its share of the net product by an attack on "entitlements," as they would be called by today's "Conservatives," namely the tenants' "moiety" and the laborers' free-market wage levels.

Intermediate Bond-Servitude Forms: Convicts, Apprentices and "Maids-for-wives"

For some time before 1622, the adventurers and planters had taken measures to secure supplies of non-tenant laborers on conditions more favorable than those provided under the Virginia wage scale. For this purpose they turned their attention to those segments of the English population most vulnerable to such superexploitation, namely prisoners, impoverished youth, and women of the laboring classes.

In the spring of 1617, the Privy Council issued a warrant for the transport of a number of "malefactors" then being held in custody; the king specified that they be sent to Virginia and nowhere else.[98] In October 1619, the king supplied the Company with another one hundred "divers dissolute persons," who were to be transported as "servants" to Virginia. The exact terms on which they were to serve in the colony were not specified, but it was anticipated that the conditions would not be agreeable to the prisoners. This feeling was, it has been said, all the stronger on account of the fact that the group of prisoners included a number of Irish persons captured in their own country in the course of the brutal English plantation of Ulster.[99] Their disaffection caused some delay in the execution of the order for their transportation, as Edwin Sandys explained in speaking of the intended shipment of the first fifty of these persons:

> [T]hey could not goe in lesse than fower Shipps, for feare they beinge many together may drawe more unto them and so muteny and carry away the Ship, which would stand [cost] the Company fowre thousand pounds.[100]

The records of the Privy Council proceedings are sprinkled with orders for the surrender of imprisoned convicts to Company authorities for transportation to Virginia as "servants," on the condition that "they retourne not again into England," on pain of death.[101] For instance:

- 13 July 1617: Chris Potley, Roger Powell, Sapcott Molineux and Thomas Chrouchley, prisoners at Oxford jail; and George Harrison, convicted of stealing a horse, prisoner at Hartford jail.

- March and November 1618: William Lambe and James Stringer, respectively, prisoners at Newgate prison.

- May 1622: Daniell Frank,[102] William Beare and John Ireland, prisoners at White Lion jail in Southwark.

- Also in 1622: James Wharton, convicted of picking pockets, in Norfolk; and John Carter of London, convicted of horse-stealing, but for whom injustice was tempered with mercy since it was doubtful "whether the horse was stolen or not."

Still, as Sandys had warned in 1619, there was a critical mass where further congregation of such deportees meant mutiny. Therefore, whilst they might supplement the labor supply, they were not to be the main source of it, and thus were not the means of achieving a general reduction of labor costs in the colony.

The "Duty boys"

In the 1618–22 period, considerable effort was made to recruit "vagrant" children – mainly, but not exclusively, in London – to work in Virginia. In autumn 1618, the London Common Council and the Virginia Company agreed upon the "taking up" of one hundred homeless boys and girls, aged eight to sixteen, for shipment to Virginia.[103] A year later the Company congratulated itself and the city fathers on the successful delivery of the full one hundred, minus "such as dyed on the waie."[104] The Company then proposed a renewal of the collaboration, with the object of sending another one hundred youths, but this time they were to be "twelve years old and upward."[105]

The program encountered opposition on the part of the youth who were its objects. Two months after the second plan was proposed, it was discovered "that among that number there are divers unwilling to be carryed thither [to Virginia]." Special care was taken that the "troublemakers" who sought to obstruct the program were included among those selected for transport, but they were to be taken to jail for punishment before their departure.[106]

Fifty such young persons were delivered in Virginia in May of 1620 on board the ship *Duty*; thereafter, apprentices brought on the same sort of program were called "Duty boys."[107]

From the standpoint of labor costs, the apprentice role for which these "Duty boys" were destined had obvious advantages for the plantation bourgeoisie. Apprentices were bound to serve seven years, the common apprentice term in England. The cost of getting them to Virginia was "Three pounds a peece for the Transportation and forty shillings a peece for their apparrell."[108] In addition to this outlay, the expenditure for their equipment and food for the first year of the term was not likely to amount to more than another £5 sterling, since their own labor provided their own food and most of their other necessities, except clothing, bedding, metal products and other manufactured goods supplied from England. The cost of maintaining the apprentice declined to practically nothing in subsequent years of the term.[109] The apprentice received no wages except his board and keep; thus the cost of the apprentice's labor, assuming the worker survived for the full term, came to less than thirty shillings per year.

The annual output of the apprentice in the period 1619–23 averaged 712 pounds of tobacco,[110] which would yield £44 10s., at 15d.,[111] in Virginia and £106 16s., at 36d.,[112] in London. The Virginia "planter" would thus get for his tobacco in one year thirty times its annualized labor cost. The use of apprentice youth as a labor supply, however, involved certain negative features. The planters expressed a preference for men "such as have been brought up to labor & those between 20 & 30 yeres of age"[113] rather than inexperienced and less muscular teenagers such as the apprentices mostly were.[114]

Yet each of these drawbacks carried its own partial offset. If the youthful apprentice was not so strong as a mature adult, he was perhaps more tractable for that reason. If the apprentice died before the end of his term, then at least he would not be around to raise the cost of labor by becoming first a tenant-at-halves and then a free farm owner.

There remained one unmitigated handicap in the apprentice arrangement, so far as the needs of the capitalist plantation development in Virginia was concerned. Under English custom and law, even the parish or country apprentice was bound to one particular employer in a one-to-one relationship. It was a relationship equally binding on each party and the apprentice could not be sold to or bought from another employer.[115]

A new opportunity for venture capital: "maids-for-wives"

A third direct and indirect source of labor power that was unpaid was sought by the importation of women. As early as 1618, enterprising men were specializing in this labor supply service. This was revealed in two arrests made in the fall of that year. One man, Owen Evans,[116] who was a messenger for the king, ranged over three counties of southeastern England "pressing maidens" for "His Majesty's service for the Bermudas and Virginia." Paying four shillings to one man, five to another, twelve pence to third, and threatening them with hanging for refusal to comply (so they testified), Evans ordered women to be taken up in the king's name and delivered to him at Sherborne in Dorset. He bore a badge of authority from the King's Chamber which, it was later said, was validly his, but which he used illegally in this business. As many as forty women were said to have fled the one parish of Ottery in Devon to escape this frightful form of class and sex oppression. They must have had to flee to points far distant, because young women from adjoining parishes were also taking flight in terror. Jacob Crystie of Ottery sold his daughter to Evans for twelve pence. A member of the local establishment paid Evans ten shillings to dissuade him from further oppression of the Ottery parish. Evans was finally arrested and sent back to London, being treated in due course with the deference reserved for personal agents of the king. What if anything in the way of punishment was given to Evans for this crime, our historians do not tell us.

Another man, named Robinson, forged a commission for himself and used it "to take up rich Yeomen's daughters to serve his majesty for breeders in Virginia" unless they were ransomed by their parents and friends. He was apprehended, tried, hanged, drawn and quartered for counterfeiting the Great Seal.[117]

Subsequently, bourgeois gentlemen and aristocrats made the trade respectable and profitable: respectable, on the ground of "making of the men feel at home in Virginia";[118] and profitable, by operating it as a Virginia Company monopoly. Of 650 persons sent by the Company to Virginia between August 1619 and April 1620 (see Table 4.1 on page 71), ninety were "Young maids to make wives for so many of the former tenants."[119] This item is included in a "Noate of Shipping, Men and Provisions Sent to Virginia"; women, it seems, were counted as "provisions." The Company in June 1620 projected a plan for sending one hundred more "maids-for-wives," in a total of eight hundred emigrants.[120] On 20 December 1621, the *Warwick* arrived in Virginia with a cargo that the Company's accompanying letter advertized as "an extraordinary choice lot of thirty-eight maids for wives."[121] Investors were apparently encouraged by this bright aspect of an otherwise not very promising general business outlook. In November 1621, a subsidiary joint stock for trading in "maids-for-wives" to Virginia was established in the amount of £800 sterling. Virginia Company leaders Edwin Sandys and the Earl of Southampton patriotically headed the list of investors with subscriptions of £200 each. [122]

The shipment of "one widow and eleven maids for wives" on board the *George* in the late summer of 1621 was accompanied by a Company letter to the Colony Council regarding the disposal of the cargo.[123] That letter, when considered together with other records of the time, helps to outline the economic aspects of this branch of business, as well as to suggest inferences regarding the life of the women traded. The *George* women were to be sold at "120 lb waight of the best leafe Tobacco." The price of the *Warwick* women who arrived in Virginia a month later was increased to 150 pounds of tobacco, partially on the grounds of the declining price of tobacco in England.[124] It was provided that the total payment on the *George*'s twelve would have to be equal to 12 times 120 pounds of tobacco, and that, therefore, "if any of them dye (before sale was made) that proportion must be advanced to make it uppon those that survive."[125] Some of the business had to be done on credit, judging by an order of the Virginia General Court of 2 May 1625 requiring "Debtors for Maids" to pay up or face punitive action by the Court.[126]

Such problems arose despite the effort made to limit the purchasing rights to men of substance. While allowing love its dominion, the Company authorities directed that it operate within the limits of sound business practice. Accordingly, the Company kept one eye on the improvement of prospects; it promised the women that they would not be married off to poor men, "for we would have their condition so much better as multitudes will be allured thereby to come unto you."[127] Therefore, a line was drawn on eligible men for wiving: the Company would "not have those maides deterred and married to servants but only to such freemen or tenants as have meanes to maintain them."[128]

There is evidence of resentment on the part of poor men on account of the deprivation they had to endure because of this pounds-shillings-and-pence approach to the woman question. Thomas Niccolls expressed indignation at this discrimination in a letter he sent to England.[129] Women were so "well sold," he said, that a poor man could never get possession of one. Poor tenants, he wrote, desperately needed wives, for "they depart this world in their own dung for want of help in their sickness." Furthermore, Niccolls could not see why women should not

> be bound to serve the Company for a certain number of years whether they married or not, [since] all the multitude of women [do is] nothing but to devour the food of the land without doing any day's deed whereby any benefit [may] arise wither to the company or the Country.

To speed the turnover of their capital, the stockholders offered a special inducement to prospective customers: "you may assure such men as marry those women that the first servants sent over by the Company shall be consigned to them."[130]

Niccolls's comment and Company promises to the contrary notwithstanding, these women were not absolutely insured against becoming "servants." In its instructions, the Company said that they might "be servants . . . in case of extremetie." Extremity of what exact sort is left to our own inferences. Several years later, a case came before the Virginia General Court concerning a woman who had been brought over to the colony to serve as a wife. But the marriage plan had aborted "because of some dislike between them," and "it was agreed" that the woman was to be a servant to her former fiancé for two years.[131] The Virginia census of 1624–25 showed that of the 222 English women in the colony, forty-six were propertyless workers. How many of this unmarried group had originally come to be sold as wives, and how many came as girl apprentices, or by some other particular arrangement, is not known.[132]

The same census showed that there were 107 Virginia-born English children in Virginia. This statistic points up the special contribution to be had from the importation of women in connection with the reduction of labor costs, but Virginia births were not to furnish the quick solution sought by the tobacco plantation bourgeoisie. In fact, there was a contradiction between the woman's role as child-bearer and as laborer. Her pregnancy, child-bearing and childcare responsibilities entailed an uncompensated expense and loss of labor time for the employer. The child would not reach working age during the mother's term of service, and in any case the child was born free and not under any contractual obligation to the mother's employer. For that reason, severe penalties were imposed upon servant women who became pregnant, or who risked becoming pregnant, and upon men (except the particular employer) who were thus involved with servant women.[133] On the other hand, if a landholder wanted to establish an ongoing estate, male heirs must be produced of undoubted paternity. In those cases, one particular woman in the capacity of wife and mother was indispensable, in spite of the added expense at a time of rising labor costs, it being understood that this particular woman would not be available for common labor as a general rule.

A man could buy a wife, but he could not sell her. Once the investment was made, it dropped forever out of the sphere of circulation of capital, by the law of coverture. The investment could not be restored to its original money form by a return to the market; nor could it be used to settle outstanding debts or as collateral to meet needs for credit. This form of "property," whatever the benefits to its possessor, clearly inhibited the free flow of capital. For these several reasons, therefore, the importation of women was not a means for reducing the general cost of labor to any degree commensurate with the fall in tobacco prices, which by 1622 was already a critical problem.

Sex Ratio and Economic Base: Virginia and New England

The maids-for-wives program may have contributed to a reduction of the sex ratio, but in the colony census of 1624–25 the sex ratio among adults was still nearly four men to one woman.[134] Although it is not surprising to learn that the ratio of men to women in the earliest colonial settlements was high, the ratio in Virginia was significantly higher than it was in New England. In the four-year period 1620 to 1623, 212 persons left England for New England. Among the 203 identified by sex, the sex ratio was just over two to one.[135] Among the adults on the first of these ships, the *Mayflower*, there were 56 men, 26 women, and 19 children.[136]

The contrast would prove to be more than momentary. In the years 1634 and 1635, among passengers embarking for Virginia, males outnumbered females by more than six to one. A similarly derived index for English emigrants going to New England in the years 1620 to 1638 indicated a rough ratio of 150, 60 men to 40 women.[137] A tabulation by Russell R. Menard of eleven selected quantifying items, yields a weighted sex ratio of 338 for European immigrants to Maryland and Virginia for the period 1634 to 1707.[138]

This contrast with New England was a function of the differing relations of production in the two regions. Of the 5,190 bond-laborers shipped for continental Anglo-America from the port of Bristol between 1654 and 1686, New England took only 165, while Virginia took 4,924. The relatively insignificant proportion of bond-labor in New England reflected the fact that there the relations of production originally developed in the matrix of the family kinship group.[139] In Virginia, where bond-servitude was the status of the great majority of European immigrants, family formation was inhibited because the laborers, being chattels, were legally barred from marrying. The retarding effect on family formation due to the bond-labor system is seen in the fact that in seventeenth-century Chesapeake the average age of female European immigrants, who were mainly bond-laborers, was 24.9 years at the time of the first marriage; the corresponding figure for native-born European-American women was 16.8 years.[140]

Tenantry, Wage Labor and Captain Nuce's Plan

The laboring people in Virginia in the beginning of 1622 were predominately tenants, not convicts, wives, or apprentice youth. This is a fact of obvious importance in any effort to investigate the beginnings of the system of chattel bond-servitude as the basic form of labor in the Anglo-American plantation colonies. Since it deserves greater attention than most historians of the period have given to it, the matter merits some documentation here.[141]

Prior to 1622, most emigrants to Virginia were transported by the Virginia Company.[142] The proportion of tenants among those sent by the Virginia Company in the 1619–21 period, and for whom we have a categorization in the records, was about 60 percent, that is, 860 out of 1,450 (see Table 4.1 on page 71). If the 190 "maids for wives" are left out of the account, or if they are counted in the category into which they were inducted by marriage, the tenant proportion among these Company emigrants would amount to around 70 percent.

There is much evidence in the records to indicate that in this period the proportion of tenants was as high, or possibly higher, among emigrants dispatched from England by separate, non-Company, enterprisers. The best and most complete, if not the only, substantial record of a non-Company plantation which has come down from that time is that of Berkeley Hundred, in the form of the papers of John Smyth of Nibley, one of the four incorporators of that enterprise.[143] These documents present a picture of the employment relation of those engaged for service in Berkeley Hundred. The terms of employment are written, specific for each individual (or family), and they are formalized before the emigrant leaves England. The contracted arrangement is mutually binding on both parties; the person employed is bound to service to this employer only; his or her contract is not "assignable" to another employer.

The list includes thirty-four men sent to Berkeley Hundred in September 1619 to serve under plantation manager John Woodleefe, apparently as tenants, excepting two men sent apparently to serve only in their trade of joiner.[144] Beside each tenant's name is the term to be served, in years. The shortest term is three years; all of the "assistants" to Woodleefe are in that category, and that term is most common (nine cases) among the other twenty-

Table 4.1 Shipments of persons to Virginia by the Virginia Company
and by separate planters, 1619–21

	Total	Tenants	Servants[a]	Apprentices	Maids
Sent by Company	1,450[b]				
for own use	1,060	860	100	–	100
for former tenants	390	–	100	200	90
for separate plantations	221[c]				
Sent by separate planters					
(estimate)	750[d]				

Source: *Records of the Virginia Company of London* (4 vols. edited by Susan Myra Kingsbury [Washington, DC, 1906–35]), 3: 313.

a. The Company records distinguish between tenants and servants among those shipped by the Company, but not in the case of those shipped for the separate plantations.
b. The Company figures include some persons who were to have gone, but did not; and others who died en route. Yet a comparison with Alexander Brown's figures (*The First Republic in America* [Boston and New York, 1898], pp. 299, 345, 363, 364) shows the proportion sent by the Company and by the separate planters to have been as presented in this table.
c. In the 1619–20 period, of the 611 sent to private plantations 221 were transported by the Company.
d. The ratio of privately shipped to Company-shipped persons remained constant at about 45 per cent during this period. (See Wesley Frank Craven, *The Dissolution of the Virginia Company* [New York, 1932], p. 301.) For the 800 shipped by the Company in 1620–21, 360 thus would have been shipped for private planters. This number plus the 390 sent by separate planters in 1619–20 equals 750.

eight tenants. There was one serving the longest term, of eight years. Four of Woodleefe's five assistants were assigned 50 acres each; the fifth, one of the two non-tenants, was a skilled artisan (one of the two joiners), who was to receive a percentage of the business. Of the twenty-eight rank-and-file tenants, eighteen were assigned 30 acres each, two were assigned 40 acres each, and the single smallest allotment was 15 acres. Five of these persons were put on a supplemental wage (in some cases paid in whole or part in advance, in England), apparently in consideration of special expected services in trades such as sawyer, cooper, gunsmith, etcetera. Thirteen of these men, including five who were tradesmen, were paid individual earnest money and promised family maintenance money before leaving England. They were engaged as tenants for from three to seven years, and were assigned land, most commonly 30 acres.[145]

A year later, in September 1620, seven persons entered into a contract to go to Berkeley Hundred as tenants.[146] This agreement is remarkable in that there is no time set for the expiration of the agreement; indeed, reference is made to a continued arrangement of the "heires" on both sides. Still, two things are clear: (1) these tenants are to have two-thirds of the corn and wheat they raise, and half of everything else they produce; and (2) there is no provision for a "setting over," "assigning," or "selling" of the tenants to another employer.

These papers show the employers as paying the cost of the transportation of the employees; the laboring emigrants are not obligated to "pay back" this expenditure by servitude or otherwise. The contract agreed to by Robert Coopy, a smith, carpenter and turner, in September 1619 is seen by A. E. Smith as the "first genuine servant's indenture."[147] But Coopy's arrangement was obviously quite different from that of the "indentured servant" that was to be. Although the only recompense appears to have been "to maintayne him with convenient [appropriate] diet and apparell meet for such a servant," it is equally provided that, at the end of his three-year term, he is to be given 30 acres of land, and is "to enjoy all the freedomes and privileges of a free man"; that is to say, within three years Coopy would be a self-employed owner of a 30-acre farm.[148] More fundamental, Coopy was not a chattel, alienable to any person to whom his employer might "assign" him; and his right to a land grant was written into the contract.[149]

The significant aspect of the Robert Coopy document is that it is the earliest evidence in the record that rationalizes transferring the burden of a transatlantic transportation costs from the employer to the laborer. It is perhaps also worth noting that Robert Coopy did not actually come to Virginia, but stayed in England.[150] Whether or not he reneged on the arrangement on account of the obnoxious uniqueness of its wageless feature is not revealed in the record.

While the documentation presented here is not exhaustive, there is nothing in the record, or in the argumentation based on it, to negate its clear implication. The typical form of labor in Virginia at the beginning of 1622 was that of the tenant, "the planters being," as Alderman Johnson said in reviewing the period 1619–22, "most of them Tenants at halves."[151]

A new proposal for getting "hands at Cheaper rates"

The relationship of tenant-at-halves interposed limits to the recoupment of profits by the reduction of labor costs. The tenant relationship also involved a relatively important and less reducible cost of the initial installation in Virginia. Tenants transported by the Virginia Company, for instance, were to be provided with "Apparell, Victuall, Armes, Tooles and Household Implements," the cost of which, delivered with the tenants in Virginia, came to a total of £20 sterling, of which only £6 sterling represented the cost of the transportation of the person, the remainder being for the purchase and freight of the equipment and supplies.[152]

A wage worker, on the other hand, was provided only with transportation, a cost amounting, as in the case of the person of the tenant, to £6 sterling.[153] But once in Virginia, the wage worker was entitled to wages set by the Colony Council several times as great as those of England (see Table 4.2). Even as the Colony Council was establishing that schedule of wages, in January 1621/2, it was telling London that the advancement of the work was hindered by a lack of "hands at so Cheape a rate as cannot yett possibly bee."[154] Although Captain Thomas Nuce was one of the council members who signed their names to the proclamation of wages that January, four months later he was

Table 4.2 Comparative day wages in Virginia, January 1622,
and in Rutland County, England, in 1610–1634

	with meals		without meals	
	Virginia	*England*[a]	*Virginia*	*England*
Master carpenter	3s.[b]	8d.	4s.	14d.
Helper[c]	2s. 3d.[d]	4d.	3s.	6d.
Master bricklayer	3s.	5d.	4s.	9d.
Helper	2s. 3d.	3d.	3s.	7d.
Master sawyer	3s.	6d.	4s.	12d.
Helper	2s. 3d.	–	3s.	–
Master mason	3s.	8d.	4s.	12d.
Helper	2s. 3d.	–	3s.	–
Master joiner	4s.	6d.	5s.	12d.
Helper	3s.	4d.	3s. 9d.	8d.
Master tailor	2s.	4d.	3s.	8d.
Helper	1s. 6d.	–	2s. 9d.	–
Farm laborer	2s.	[40s./year]	3s.	8 d.

a. English wages are for spring and summer; fall and winter wages were one-fourth to one-third less.
b. 1s. equals 12d.
c. "Helper" is intended here as a generic for "apprentice" (England) and "labourer in husbandry" (Virginia).
d. The Virginia helper's wage was set at one-fourth less than that of the respective master tradesman.

Sources: For England: James E. Thorold Rogers, *History of Agriculture and Prices in England*, 7 vols. in 8 (London, 1886–1902), 6:691–3. For Virginia: Virginia Colony Council, Settlement of the Wages of Tradesmen in Virginia, 14 January, 1621/22, (*Records of the Virginia Company of London* [4 vols. edited by Susan Myra Kingsbury, Washington, DC, 1906–35], 3: 589–90). See also wages of farm laborers paid by the year, in G. E. Russell, ed., *Robert Loder's Farm Accounts, 1610–1620*, Camden Society Publications, 3rd ser., vol. 53 (London, 1936), pp. xxviii–xxix.

moving for a reconsideration.[155] He had been sent to the colony to superintend the revival of the Company's enterprises, but he found the prevailing wage rates an obstacle. With patriotic discretion, Nuce chose for illustrative contrast not the wage scale of the Mother Country, but that of Catholic lands. Virginia, he said, where "wee pay iii s [three shillings] a day for the labor of a man who hath no other waie but to digg and dealve," must not be confused with "Italie, Spain, or ffraunce: countries plentiful and prosperous: where are thousands of women and children and such ydle people to be hyred for i d [a penny] or ii d [two pence] a day."

Two things were obvious: first, the decisive element in the cost of labor in the colony at that time was the tenant. Second, given the irrevocability of the bourgeois commitment to the tobacco plantation monoculture in the situation of everlastingly low tobacco prices, wage labor was not to be the alternative to the tenant.

In the course of discussions within the Virginia Assembly on the problem of how "yett" to get "hands at so Cheape a rate" as would satisfy the employers,

Captain Thomas Nuce, having these two above-mentioned imperatives in mind, advanced a plan that received enthusiastic endorsement. In January, 1622, the Governor and Council forwarded that proposal to London:

> Wee have heerin closed sent you a project of Capt newces which if you shalbe pleased to take likinge of, it is thought here will yeelde you, a more certain proffitt then [than] your Tenantes to halfes, which beinge proposed to the generall Assemblie, was by them well approved of.[156]

In reply the Company promised to give careful consideration to the "project of Capt Newce concerning the altering of the Condicons with our Tenants," especially because it was recommended by the Virginia Assembly.[157] A few months later the Company returned to the subject, and assured the colony officials that the Company was more than prepared to send Virginia employers "servants instead of tenants" and to do so "in a manner very advantageable to you."[158] A year after the Virginia Governor and Council had initiated the proposal in the interest of "a more certain profitt," the Virginia Council urged the question again:[159]

> Wee conceave that if you would be pleased to Chaunge the Conditione of Tenants into servants for future Supplies, . . . your revenues might be greatly improved.

In the spring of 1623 Alderman Johnson declared that the Colony officers had all desired to reduce their tenants to servants.[160]

5

The Massacre of the Tenantry

English historical experience had shown that the reduction of non-proletarian laboring people to proletarians, and the creation of a large surplus of labor were the conditions necessary for bringing about a general lowering of labor costs. The essence of the matter was shown to be the placing of the laborers in a position of great and growing dependency upon capitalist employment under conditions in which many workers compete for relatively few jobs. The English bourgeoisie had accomplished both these steps in one operation, the enclosures, during the late fourteenth and the fifteenth centuries. In Virginia in the 1620s the starting point was to be the destruction of tenancy. But whereas the enclosures involved the replacement of one hundred peasant tillers of the soil with one shepherd, the mere transformation of tenants into non-tenants did not involve any increase in labor productivity. Therefore, the Anglo-American plantation bourgeoisie, unable to create a labor surplus above labor demand, sought by other means to achieve a condition of extreme dependency of the laboring people.

The first requisite for the successful completion of the general offensive against the rights of the laboring classes that reduced them to chattels in Virginia was the maintenance of social control. The Anglo-American bourgeoisie did not need to be told that they were dealing with people who were not to be taken for granted in such a matter. The rebellious resistance of the English freehold and copyhold tenants in the sixteenth century had produced a large peasant revolt in the Midlands in the very year Jamestown was founded. Fresher in the minds of the rulers was the meltdown of the regime of *Lawes Divine, Morall and Martiall* in the face of colonists determined to defy attempts to restrict the planting of tobacco.[1]

Open military dictatorship was over; the colony was now governed by the newly created General Assembly, the Colony Council and General Court. Reliance would still be placed on English mercenary veterans of wars in Ireland and the Netherlands, not only to command in warfare against the native population but also for the maintenance of social control in the interest of the tobacco bourgeoisie. The fulfillment of this social control function was favored by four special conditions prevailing in the colony at this time.

Four Special Conditions

First of these was the appalling death rate. The record is filled with testimony of the dying, the doomed and the fearful, about the insufficiency of food, clothing and housing; and about the perils of the period of "seasoning," the first year of acclimatization. Half of the six hundred colonists living in Virginia at the beginning of 1619 were still living in March 1625. But only one out of every six of the new immigrants who came during that period was alive at the end of it. An influx of nearly five thousand persons increased the population by less than five hundred (see Table 5.1). By modern standards, the death rate in England in these years was very high, being about 2.7 percent per year;[2] but it was not such as to interfere with the continuity of the social pattern, as happened at the time of the great plague of the fourteenth century. In the Virginia colony, however, the death rate in this period was seven times that of England. In such a small, far-distant colony, the sheer physical annihilation of property owners implicit in these figures inevitably overwhelmed the orderly procedures of property transfers and afforded exceptional opportunities for illegal expropriations, including the "expropriation" of laboring people.[3] From the standpoint of social control, mere survival in these circumstances became the overriding concern for many of the working people, and the question of rebellion or social rights came to be of lesser concern for the moment.

The second special condition affecting the bourgeoisie's ability to maintain

Table 5.1 Approximate number of English emigrants to Virginia
and the death rate among them in the Company period
(omitting May 1618 to November 1619)

	1607–10[a]	1610–18[b]	1619–24[c]
Shipped from England	640	1,125	5,009
Survivors in Virginia		65	900
Total in Virginia, start of period		1,191	5,909
Alive at end of period	65	600	1,218
Dead *en route* or in Virginia	575	591	4,691
Death toll	90%	45%	80%
Annual death rate	49.5%	8.2%	26.4%
Death rate in England	2.5%	2.6%	2.1%

Sources: Alexander Brown, *The First Republic in America* (Boston and New York, 1898), pp. 129, 285, 612; Charles E. Hatch, *The First Seventeen Years: Virginia, 1607–1624* (Williamsburg, 1957), pp. 3, 7, 5; Irene W. D. Hecht, 'The Virginia Muster of 1624/5 as a Source for Demographic History,' *William and Mary Quarterly* 30:65–92 (1973), p. 70; E. A. Wrigley and R. S. Schofield, *The Population History of England, 1541–1871*, (Cambridge, MA, 1981), p. 532. Cf. Evarts B. Greene and Virginia D. Harrington, *American Population Before the Federal Census of 1790* (New York, 1932), pp. 134–6.

a. December 1606 to prior to May 23, 1610, 3.42 years.
b. May 34, 1610 to May 1618, 8 years.
c. November 1619 to February 1624/25, 5.17 years.

social control was the external contradiction represented by the Indians' resistance to massive, rapid and aggressive English encroachment upon the land. On the one hand, this contradiction made ruling-class social control more difficult, since it presented the laboring people of the colony with a means of frustrating the bourgeois pressure on their living standards and social rights, by abandoning the colony and joining one or the other of the nearby Indian communities. This was more than an abstract possibility. Instances of English colonists fleeing to the Indians are found throughout the records of the early colonial period. They went despite the fact that recapture could mean death "by hanginge, shootinge and breakinge uppon the wheele."[4] The death penalty was not always imposed, however, as the following entries in the record for 20 October 1617 seem to show:

Geo White pardoned [by Governor Argall] for running away to the Indians with his arms & ammunition which facts deserve death according to the express articles & laws of this colony in that case provided and established and for which offenses he stands liable to censure of a marchalls Court.[5]

Henry Potter for Stealing a Calf & running to Indians death [blank space in manuscript].

On the other hand, the increase of immigration worked to the advantage of the plantation bourgeoisie in dealing with the flight of laborers. Expansion of the colony permitted the development of an English institutional superstructure as an inhibitor to self-banishment in a strange country. A second factor was more immediate. While the Indians had been able to absorb a score or so of English left at Roanoke in 1587, the level of development of the productive forces among the Indians, and the need to avoid the strange epidemic diseases of the English, set rather close limits on the numbers of English defectors who could be absorbed into the Indian settlements. English national consciousness aside, the great inpouring of colonists made impossible a general resort to escape from bourgeois oppression by going to the Indians.

Third among these special conditions facilitating the attack by the Anglo-American plantation bourgeoisie against the social status of the laboring people in the colony was the intensified economic pressure on the laboring people in England that occurred just at this time, and that might be assumed to predispose more workers to consider emigration than would have been the case at other times. As I have previously noted,[6] in England real wages had pursued a generally downward course since the close of the fifteenth century. The situation became particularlay acute with the onset of the severe depression in England's chief industry, cloth making, in the period 1620–25. In 1624 there were still twelve thousand cloth workers out of work in England.[7]

Finally, there was the fact of the complete and utter dependence of the colony upon England for supplies, especially of clothing and metal products but also, to a considerable extent, of food and beverages. Not a nail, let alone a plow or a saw, but had to be brought a long sea voyage from England. Not a requested ball of yarn, let alone a coat, a shirt, or a bit of bedding, not a hoe, axe or pail, but must be waited for for six months at least to come from England. This was a major factor in the maintenance of social control, even when the greatest provocation to revolt was being brought to bear on the working people. If they were to succeed, the situation would not be as in England, where there were means of production to be taken over in the form of manufacturing facilities. This dependence upon English supplies enhanced the power of the bourgeoisie, the governor and Colony Council members, the plantation owners, the Cape Merchant in charge of the Company's "maga-zine," and free-trading ship captains relative to the "dependent classes."

The Emergent Colony Elite

The basis for the rise of an elite of rich Virginia planters was laid at the very outset of the Edwin Sandys regime, in 1619; it is seen outlined in the famous "Instructions" issued to George Yeardley upon his appointment as Governor of Virginia that April.[8] For every £12½ share of Virginia stock, "separate planter" capitalists were granted free title to one hundred acres of land, and when that land was "sufficiently peopled," an additional amount was to be given to the stockholder equal to the original amount. The term "sufficiently peopled" is not defined. The four incorporators of Berkeley Hundred, for example, jointly purchased forty-five shares and were given a patent for 4,500 acres of Virginia land, the price being equivalent to 2½ shillings per acre.[9] Furthermore, the separate planters were to benefit from the "headright" principle under which they were to be compensated for transporting laboring people to Virginia at the rate of fifty acres per "head." Later, when the next sections of land were surveyed, the planters were to receive an equal additional amount, provided they had sufficiently peopled the first grant. The capitalist was entitled to the headright land even if the person whose passage he had paid died before the ship ever reached Virginia, or starved or died of disease in Virginia, as most of them did before their three-year term was completed. Such a provision would seem designed to exacerbate the shortage of food and other supplies in the colony. Six pounds sterling invested in supplies and the freight for them to be used by laborers in Virginia could yield a return only if the laborers lived and produced commodities for the capitalist, which were then sold at a profit. But the same amount invested in getting a laborer on board a ship bound for Virginia brought the capitalist a patent on fifty acres of Virginia land. Of course, land needed laborers, and laborers needed provisions, and there was a point beyond which a stinting of supplies would prove counterproductive. But the "headright" privilege tended to push the contradic-tion to the limit in terms of maximum profit for the capitalist and minimum provisions for the laboring people.

The new governor, Yeardley, who had served as Acting Governor in 1616–17 and was already, before his appointment, the owner of two hundred acres by virtue of his two Company shares, was granted two thousand more acres in appreciation of his "long and faithful service." Those lands were to be held by him, his heirs and assigns forever. Three thousand acres, to be called "the Governor's Land," were set aside "in the best and most convenient place," and one-fourth of the produce of them was to belong to the Governor in his official capacity. A similar one-fourth share of the output on twelve thousand acres, called "Company lands," was to be apportioned among four or five other colony officers,[10] such as the Treasurer, the Secretary, and the Vice-Admiral, and for payments to lesser functionaries. One-twentieth of the total product of the Company lands was to be provided for the services of overseers of the Company tenants and other laboring people, and for compensating those who were responsible for dividing the product according to the proper shares.

While concentration of land ownership at this time was less than it would become by the end of the seventeenth century,[11] it was still significant. The land patent rolls for the year 1626 in Virginia show that 20 percent of the patents, comprising those of two hundred acres and more, accounted for 50 percent of the patented acreage. More than half the patents were for one hundred acres or less, but they accounted for only one-fourth of the total acreage.

This phenomenon was by no means merely the working out of the natural processes of capitalist competition whereby the advantage generally accrues to those who are operating with the largest resources of capital, or who benefit from the development of new techniques or instruments of labor. Those favorably placed in the colony government used their legal authority to secure special advantages for themselves.[12] They were able to succeed each other in various high offices, including that of Governor; acting as the Colony Council, they determined the local laws and controlled the public stores of food, arms and gunpowder. They also commanded the special bodies of armed men who enforced "order," and they controlled the colony's relations with the mother country and with the Indians. Acting as the Virginia General Court, Colony Council members dispensed judgments as harsh as they pleased.[13] In these ways, the special difficulties of colonial life, coupled with the crass partiality of the Colony Council and the Virginia General Court, placed the tenants at an extreme disadvantage in contending with the bourgeois attack upon their rights and status.

"Renting Out" of Tenants

The operative principle for using the shortage of supplies, whether absolute or relative, to undermine the position of the tenants is perfectly exemplified by the cases of the one hundred tenants sent at the Company's expense on the *Bona Nova*, who arrived in Virginia on 4 November 1619 to work "under the Comand" of Captain Weldon and Lieutenant Whitaker. The terms under which these men had been engaged to come to Virginia as tenants were explicitly and emphatically published by the King's Council for Virginia:

> Every man transported into Virginia, with intent there to inhabit, as Tenants to the Common land of the Company, or to the publike land, shall be freely landed there at the charge of the Company: And shall be furnished with provisions of victual for one whole year next after his arrival, as also of Cattle: And with apparell, weapons, tooles and implements, both of house and labour, for his necessary use. He shall enjoy the ratable moytie [half] of all the profits that shall be raised of the land on which he shall be Planted, as well Corne and Cattle, as other commodities whatsoever: the other halfe being due to the Owners of the land.[14]

But a week after their arrival in Virginia, the Governor and Colony Council wrote the authorities in London of a different arrangement that had been made:

> It was thought expedient by the governor and Counsell to advise the said two gentlemen [Weldon and Whitaker] to rent out the greatest part of their people to some honest and sufficient men of the Colonie till Christmas Come twelve month for iij [three] barrels of Indian Corne and 55 [pounds] waight of tobacco a man.[15]

This manner of proceeding occasioned, as Weldon reported, "no small discontent among my whole Company [of tenants].[16] Not only did it involve the chattel-like transfer of tenants from one employer to another without the consent of the persons transferred, it also carried with it a drastic reduction of their prospective income from that which they had been promised as tenants-at-halves. According to contemporary authorities,[17] these tenants might normally be expected to produce by the end of that year of service from twelve to thirty-two barrels of corn and 250 to 1,000 pounds of tobacco, of which they would be entitled to a half-share. To be required to labor the full year for three barrels of corn and 55 pounds of tobacco was clearly oppressive.

As to who the lucky "sufficient men" were who were to have the services of these tenants assigned to them, there is no doubt that colony officials were prime beneficiaries of the policy, and of similar appropriations of tenants subsequently. John Rolfe, writing to England,[18] called attention to the

> many complaints against the Governors, Captaines and Officers in Virginia: for buying and selling or to be set over from one to another for yearly rent, was held in England a thing most intolerable, or that tenants or servants should be put from their places, or abridged their Covenants, was so odious that the very report thereof brought a great scandall to the generall action.

The colony authorities justified the "renting out" of the tenants on the ground that they had come ill-provisioned, having only meal for food, and of that only enough for five and a half months, possibly less.[19] Captain Weldon defended his compliance with the arrangement on the same grounds, inadequate food supplies, and added that instead of the promised three suits of apparel for each of his tenants, there were only two, of which one was unserviceable for winter wear.[20] Furthermore, he said, there were only "5 iron pots & 1 small kettle for 50 men." Of "butter Cheese rice oatmeale or any other English victuall" there was none at all.

Yet, the record shows that there was no shortage of food in Virginia in that year. Colony Secretary John Pory wrote to Sir Dudley Carleton in September 1619 that Virginia was enjoying "a marvelous plenty, suche as hath not bene since our first coming into the land."[21] The ground was so fertile, he said, that with less cultivation than was required in Europe, "we shall produce miracles out of this earth." Cattle, hogs and goats, he said, grew larger in Virginia than in England, and they multiplied rapidly. He spoke of the general prosperity based on tobacco, noting that Governor Yeardley was the most prosperous person of all. The labor of the tenants, Pory said, was the most valuable asset of the colony, but he noted that the employer had to pay for the tenants' "armes, apparell, & bedding; and for their transportation, and casuall both at sea & for their first year comonly at lande also."

In an exchange of charge and countercharge with Captain Weldon two years later, the Virginia Company in London condemned the captain for his "renting out" of the tenants, and said that contrary to the claims of Weldon and the colony authorities, the *Bona Nova* invoices showed that the tenants had been supplied with one pound of meat a day for the first year.[22]

John Rolfe, who had preceded Pory as Colony Secretary, remained an active correspondent with persons in England specially interested in Virginia affairs. In January 1620 he reported to Edwin Sandys that toward the end of the previous August, Yeardley had exchanged victuals for "20 and odd" African laborers, men and women, who had been brought to Virginia in a "Dutch man of Warr."[23] The readiness to trade victuals for these workers, as Professor Morgan first pointed out, cannot be squared with the plea of a food shortage being advanced by the Governor and Colony Council, but it would be consistent with a policy of reducing labor costs by inducing an oversupply of laborers relative to the amount of food that would be available to them.[24]

Great significance attaches to the reaction of the Company to this "renting out" of its tenants, the violation of their contract rights, and their consequent impoverishment and deprivation of status. In order to appreciate that significance, it is helpful to contrast the Company's reaction in 1618 when Governor Argall expropriated Company tenants to his own private use, and committed other abuses of authority. The very violations of public trust for private gain that the company charged against Argall were practiced on a greatly expanded scale by the governors and Council of Virginia in the 1619–24 period. They included appropriating "the Indian trade to yourselfe";[25] using the Company boats and sailors to conduct private affairs; taking tenants from Company service, and using them for private plantations of colony officials.[26]

The message sent to Argall regarding his alleged peculations ended with the stern promise that he would be called to account: "either you must think highly of yourselfe or very meanely of us ... to do what you list [wish] ... without being called to account."[27] They then acted; they dispatched a special set of instructions to the Governor designate, Lord Delaware, then *en route* to Virginia, to "cause him [Argall] to be shipped home in this ship ... to satisfy the Adventurers by answering everything as shall be layde to his chardge."

Furthermore, to secure their interest in these proceedings, the Company instructed Delaware to "ceaze upon his [Argall's] goods, as Tobacko and Furrs, whereof it is reported he hath gotten together great stoare to the Colonies prejudice, and so sendinge them to us to be in deposite till all matters be satisfyed."[28]

The Company had the same authority to recall Governor Yeardley or his successor, Francis Wyatt, or any of the other "Captaines and Officers" denounced by Rolfe for violating tenants' contracts. The grounds for such action were certainly present. Captain Weldon, however, was merely reprimanded for his complicity in the matter. He continued his Virginia career, being granted a large land patent there in 1622.[29] Yeardley and the members of the Colony Council who had forced the transfer of the tenants were the recipients of no more rebuke than might be gleaned from the following paragraph in a letter from the Company to the Governor and Council, dated 25 July 1621:[30]

We cannot conceale from youe, that it is heare reported that contrary to the public faith given, not the sicke but the ablest men are lett out to hire and theire provisions converted to private uses. And where it is pretended this planting them with old planters is for theire health, they are so unmercifully used that it is the greatest cause of our tennant's discontent; and though we hope this is not in all parts true, yet we cannot conceive such unwillingness to proceed in this worke should they not have some other grounds than is alledged: lett it therefore be your worke at the first general session of the Counsell to effect this business, and it shall be our care to provide for the well orderinge and furnishinge of them.

As that letter was being delivered to the Virginia colony, George Yeardley's term in office was coming to an end. As Governor, Yeardley had had one hundred tenants assigned to him. When his successor, Wyatt, counted the tenants turned over to him, he could find only forty-six. The Colony Council inquired about the other fifty-four. Yeardley coolly declined to supply the missing number.[31] To have done so would have required him either to return those he had taken or else to pay for the installation of a new supply from England. Seizure of Argall's property had been ordered in a similar situation, but now things were different. In reporting on the Yeardley matter in January 1622, the Colony Council showed no disposition to press the issue. "Sir George Yeardley denieth to make them good," it wrote to London, "[and] we have foreborne to Compell him thereunto, until we Receave your further directiones therein."[32] Apparently, these were not forthcoming. Yeardley remained a member of the Colony Council, restored no tenants to the Company, and continued to thrive in fortune and honors. Having come to the colony in 1610 with nothing but his sword, he lived sumptuously, and died in the second year of his second term as governor, possessed of a very large fortune.[33]

In the contrasting treatment of Argall and Yeardley, we can see measured the progress of the Company's conversion to the cause of tobacco monoculture, to the liquidation of its own productive enterprises in the colony, and to its own transmutation into merely a monopolist of English tobacco imports. It further reveals the essential concord that had been reached by the Anglo-American plantation bourgeoisie for the overthrow of the tenantry.

Another way of bringing pressure on the Company tenant was found in the restriction of tobacco planting. Although official policy was generally ineffective and pursued with steadily diminished vigor,[34] it none the less presented the employing class with opportunities for increasing the tenants' dependency and making tenants more vulnerable to degradation of their status.

When Captain Weldon informed his tenants, those remaining to him after the "renting out" of half their original number, that their tobacco planting was to be restricted, they denounced the policy. They well understood that, completely dependent upon supplies from England as they were, a lack of the medium of exchange, tobacco, would render them destitute. In a report to London, Captain Weldon described the angry mood of these tenants:

> [T]hey will with no patience endure to heare of it bitterly Complayninge that they have no other meanes to furnish themselves with aparell for the insuinge yeare but are likely as they say (and for ought I Cann see) to be starved if they be debarred of it.[35]

As a result of the tenants' strong resistance, the Governor consented to an easing of the restriction, although not to its outright and formal revocation.

When Yeardley was succeeded by Francis Wyatt as governor in 1621, the policy of restricting tobacco planting was officially continued, with output to be limited to 112 pounds per year per laboring hand.[36] To the extent that such a policy was effective, the burden fell with much greater impact upon the laboring tenants than upon the land-owning employer of a number of tenants; the tenant had only one half-share, but the employer would receive as many half-shares as he had tenants. The employer had an additional advantage since he, not the tenant, had the dividing of the product into the employer's and the tenant's shares.[37]

An altercation, involving corn not tobacco, occurred between tenant William Moch (variously spelled) and John Harvey, later to be governor, who was sent by the king and Privy Council to conduct an inquiry into Virginia affairs in 1624–25. Harvey summoned Moch and demanded to see his covenant papers, that is, the agreement under which Moch had been engaged as a tenant. The court minutes continue:

> To which he [Moch] replyed, first lett me see my Corne[.] Capt. Harvey told him he scorned to keep back his Corne, Mutch replyed againe he would have his corne before he should see them. Then Capt. Harvey told him he was an idle knave, and that he could find in his heart to Cudgell his Coate. To which Mutch answered scornefully, alas Sir it is not in you.[38]

Although according to testimony Harvey then struck Moch a blow across the head with a truncheon, Moch continued to "give other provoking speeches" to the king's appointed commissioner. Tenant Moch appears to have been a man of courage, and the record shows that he could have drawn strength from knowing that his stand represented the basic sentiments of the tenants generally.

The majority of the colonists were tenants, and, although they too were as hooked on tobacco as anyone else, they were determined to have their "moiety" of the crop, whatever the particular crop happened to be, and not to be "set over" from one landlord to another without their consent, nor to have their tenant status degraded to one of servitude. Like Captain Weldon's tenants they would "with no patience endure to hear of it." The tradition of Tyler and Ket was bred in their bones, and they had a deep sense of chartered "liberties, rights, and immunities" as their English birthright. Like tenant Moch in his retort to Commissioner Harvey, they could not believe that the landowners had the power to "cudgel the Coates" of the tenantry in a land where labor was destined to be in short supply for a long time to come.

Making One Crisis Serve Another

It was the external contradiction that precipitated the consummating crisis.[39] On 22 March 1622, the Indians of the Powhatan Confederacy mounted what was to be in relative terms the strongest effort ever made after the founding of Virginia to halt the Anglo-American occupation of Indian lands, with the possible exception of the Yamassee War of 1715 in South Carolina. Powhatan had died in 1618, on the eve of the period of accelerated English colonization.[40] His kinsman and successor Opechancanough watched the inpouring of immigrants – more in the next four years than had come during the four decades of Powhatan's time. Yet the Indian guests who had accompanied the ill-fated Pocahontas to England had found the natives too numerous to count.[41] Opechancanough saw them come and die like fish out of water; yet in greater numbers than ever they came, in ships carried by the winds. Tobacco had made them mad. They had guns and they took the land.

We cannot, of course, know the terms in which the discussion was carried on that united thirty-two tribes,[42] but clearly there was much discussion of

[T]he dayly feare that posseste them that in time (the English) by ... growing continually upon them, would dispossess them of this Country, as they had been formerly of the West Indies by the Spaniards.[43]

As Powhatan had succeeded in doing at Roanoke forty years before, and as O'Donnell and O'Neill had tried to do in the Tyrone War (1594–1603), Opechancanough and the Powhatan allies would strike to root out the English plantation.

The strategy against this enemy armed with guns and with cannon-bearing ships was to be that of the single massive blow and subsequent attrition. The English would later congratulate themselves on the partiality of their Divine Providence which, they said, stayed the hands of the Indian attackers;[44] but limited success may simply have been the most that Opechancanough or any other general could have achieved in the circumstances. Even his enemies' historians would concede that the attack was "planned by a master mind."[45] To hold together the alliance of thirty-two tribes for a long war against English firepower and the barrage of cheap commodities[46] was an improbable prospect. On the other hand, the obvious ineptitude of the English colonists gave reasonable grounds to expect that from the single catastrophe they might be moved to abandon the colony[47] and merge with the people of the country, as those of Roanoke had done, and a number of frequent defectors had done since the founding of the colony.[48]

The blow would be aimed at the colony's most vulnerable point, its food supply. It was the time for planting corn, not harvesting it. Even when they had planted corn, the colonists had begrudged each acre and day taken from "their darling tobacco."[49] Close observers perhaps saw the corn shortage as a particular, rather than a general, one, with the haves exploiting the have-nots by virtue of the haves' access to corn among the Indians.[50] If so, the situation presented an opportunity to take advantage of class divisions within the colony. Finally, the day chosen for the attack was, as English preachers and defectors had informed them, the most solemn moment of the Christian calendar, when perhaps their mountainous guilts would sit most heavily on their English souls – the day they called Good Friday.

Viewed from history's elevated ground, the strategy seems to have been foredoomed as far as the achievement of its maximum objective was concerned, even had the English not (as they claimed) received a last-minute warning from a Christianized Indian.[51] The difference in the level of development of productive forces would give the English the ultimate, fundamental advantage. It seems probable, too, that Opechancanough underestimated the persistence of the English promoters of colonization, who scrupled not at a 25 percent death rate if a 25 percent profit could be made in the process.[52] Whatever may have been the possibilities of strategic victory, the attack dealt the death blow to the Virginia Company, although the Company's charter was not formally revoked until 1624. More important was the fact that the attack struck to the very foundation of the life of the colony. It intensified to an extreme degree the uncertainties of existence that resulted from economic dislocation, epidemic disease, the heavy assignments of watching and warding, the dependence upon trans-ocean supplies, and the vulnerability of property and production relations.[53]

Four hundred English colonists died on that day, one-third of the total population.[54] All but a few of the settlements were abandoned, a major portion of the livestock was lost, and there was little prospect of growing corn in the colony during the remainder of the year. Only one-third of the survivors were men fit for work, and a large part of that potential labor was diverted to "watching and warding." The colony authorities forbade the planting of corn near dwellings on the grounds that it provided a lurking place for hostile Indians. They added that, even if corn were planted, it was liable to be cut down or harvested by Indians.[55] A similar problem was cited as a reason for forbidding individual colonists to hunt wild game in the woods; the hunter, it was claimed, would risk death or capture by Indians.[56] However, the colony officials were equally concerned with preventing hungry and overworked English laborers from fleeing the colony to join the Indians. In March 1623, George Sandys reported on a group of eleven Company tenants for whom the Company had no provisions. Seven were sold or relocated. Of the disposition of the other four, Sandys wrote: "two of these . . . ran away (I am afraide to the Indians) and no doubt the other two would have consorted with their companions if sickness had not fettered them."[57] Without food supplies from the outside, the colony would famish.[58] Widespread undernourishment rendered many colonists especially susceptible to the diseases brought from England by the eight hundred immigrants who came to Virginia in the year following the attack of 22 March 1622. According to the Company, six hundred of the emigrants themselves died in Virginia before the year was out.[59]

The dependence upon English supplies was made even more critical under these deprived circumstances. The record is filled with urgent, even anguished, appeals, public and private, for food to be sent from the Mother country. In their first letter to England after the Indian attack, the Virginia Governor and Colony Council asked for enough grain to sustain the colony for a year.[60] Lady Wyatt, wife of the Governor, despite her favored position was not above writing to her sister in England requesting a bit of butter, bacon, cheese and malt, explaining that "since we & the Indians fell out we dare not send a hunting but with so many men as it is not worth their labour."[61]

We may assume that the means and opportunity for writing letters to England describing the sufferings of the colonists, and appealing for assistance, were inversely proportional to the actual privations of the individual letter writers, and directly proportional to their prospects for special assistance from England. Letters by members of the laboring population of the colony are much more rare in the record than those written by members of the owning classes. The great majority of the laboring people could not write; and even if they could have written and had the means and opportunity to do so, they had no friends of substance in England to whom they might have appealed. Laboring people whose letters have been preserved seem to have been persons of "respectable" backgrounds, with significant connections in the middle class of the home country. Yet it is to these latter that we are indebted for what we have of an "inside" picture of the conditions of life as they pressed down on the laboring people of the colony. Frequent citations from these letters have given their authors a sort of immortality, which they doubtless would have traded for a little cheese had the choice been offered.

If the frequency of these letters in the record is indicative, the spring of 1623 was especially hard for the working people of the colony. Richard Frethorne was one of a group of men who arrived as laborers in Virginia about Christmas 1622.[62] Young Frethorne had been sent under an arrangement concluded between his father and Robert Bateman, London merchant, member of Parliament, and prominent member of the Virginia Company.[63]

What Richard Frethorne wished for more than anything else was just about what Opechancanough wanted for him – a swift return to England. Even an utterly incapacitated person, begging from door to door, was better off in England, said Frethorne, than a plantation laborer in Virginia. And this, he wrote, was the feeling of all his fellow workers. What with the Indians' hostility, the pervasive despondency, the scurvy and the "bloody fluxe," the population of Martin's Hundred, he said, had been reduced from 140 to only 22 in the past year. The surviving laborers were subsisting on one-third of a pint of meal per day.[64] It was only ten weeks after his arrival in Virginia, and he was writing to Bateman asking to "be freed out of this Egypt." Frethorne seemed to sense that his "right worshipfull" merchant sponsor might be unable to find it in his purse simply to pay for his immediate release from Virginia service and return passage to England. He sought, therefore, to appeal to Bateman's business instincts. In lieu of immediate deliverance, Frethorne would be satisfied, he said, if Bateman could send him some beef, cheese, butter or other victuals, which Frethorne could sell for a profit. Frethorne would send all the profit back to Bateman to cover the costs of termination of his contract and his return home. Frethorne suggested further that the people of his parish in England might be willing to contribute toward the cost.[65]

In his letter to Bateman, the young plantation worker discreetly refrained from complaints about the oppressive conditions of labor. But to his mother and father he spoke more freely. He had eaten more in a day in England than he had in Virginia in a week, he said. There were wild fowl in the woods, he wrote, but "We are not allowed to goe and get it, but must Worke hard both earlie and late for a messe of water gruell, and a mouthfull of bread and biefe." A part of his time was spent in hauling the employer's goods from ships anchored at Jamestown, ten miles from Martin's Hundred. On those occasions, he had to work until midnight, loading, rowing and unloading. He had had to sleep in an open boat, even on rainy nights, when on this duty, until a gunsmith named Jackson befriended him and built a cabin in which Richard could shelter when in Jamestown at night. There was only three weeks' supply of meal remaining on their plantation. Frethorne speculated with dread on the approaching day when: "My Master ... is not able to keepe us all, then wee shalbe turned up to the land and eat barkes of trees, or mouldes of the Ground." Richard Frethorne's last recorded words have become familiar by quotation: "I thought no head had been able to hold so much water as hath and doth dailie flow from my eyes."[66]

Another laboring man, Henry Brigg, wrote to his brother, a merchant at the Customs House in London, in that April of 1623, "to lett you understand how I live it is very miserable, for here we have but a wyne quart of Corne for a day and nothing else but Water, and worke hard from Sun rising to Sun sett at felling of Trees and we have not victuall not past xx [20] dayes."[67] He asked the London brother to send him provisions for a year, and a gun with ammunition "for I goe in danger of my life every day for lack of one."

Brigg also had a business proposition to make. If his brother would care to invest in a stock of trade goods, Henry would undertake to secure for him a clear profit of 100 percent. The list of items he thought might move well is especially interesting as evidence of the degree of dependence of the colonists upon English manufactured and processed supplies. Understandably, it was made up mainly of food and apparel: oatmeal, peas, butter, cheese, oil, vinegar, aquavita, linen or woolen cloth or apparel for men or women, shoes, stockings, metal-tipped laces, gloves, and garters. Knives and other metal utensils were also recommended.[68]

Thomas Nicolls wrote to England in March and April, saying that each laborer should be allowed "a pound of butter and a pound of cheese weekly, as there was no food in sickness or health but oatmeal and pease, and bread and water." Nineteen men had been captured by the Indians, he said, and conflict, disease and starvation had in the last eighteen months reduced the complement of men on one plantation from fifty-six to fourteen, and from ninety-seven to twenty on another.[69]

Perhaps nothing symbolized more clearly the colony's extreme dependence upon supplies of English commodities than did the waiting for the *Seaflower* in the spring and early summer of 1623. A ship of 140 tons,[70] the *Seaflower* left England around 1 January that year, Virginia-bound, with a cargo of meal and other provisions valued at £500 sterling,[71] to relieve the famine there, at the usual rate of 25 percent profit for the investors in the voyage.[72]

Governor Wyatt and chief councillor George Yeardley told the colonists "that except the Seaflower come in," or they could get corn from the Indians, more than half the colony would starve to death.[73] The people watched the sea, and wrote those letters; Colony Treasurer George Sandys, Colony Secretary Christopher Davison, plantation servant Richard Frethorne all prayed with small planter and silk-raiser Peter Arundell for "the speedie arrivall of the Seaflower."[74] Even as they prayed, the *Seaflower* lay at the bottom of a Bermuda harbor, sunk *en route* by the explosion of its powder magazine.[75] Two ships did come into Jamestown in April, but they lacked even adequate provisions for the people they brought with them.[76] It would be five months before the Company's next supply would arrive on the ninety-ton *Bonnie Bess* in September.[77]

The *Seaflower* sank, and the colonists starved, sickened and died. In self-defense against Company censure, George Sandys begged for understanding in England: "[W]ho is ignorant," he asked, "how the heavie hand of God hath suppressed us? The lyveying being hardlie able to bury the dead."[78] The annual March census was not sent to England, or, if sent, was concealed from public disclosure.[79]

Captain Nathaniel Butler had come from Bermuda and made an investigation of the conditions in Virginia in the winter of 1622–23. At the king's request, Butler wrote a report which came to be known popularly as "The

Unmasking of Virginia."[80] The dominion of death was so established in Virginia, he reported, that people "are not onely seen dying under hedges and in the woods, but beinge dead ly some of them for many dayes unregarded and unburied."[81] Not until 1625 would the population of the colony regain the level it had attained in March 1622.[82]

The difference in the suffering of the owning and the laboring classes apparent in Virginia at this time was, to a degree, normal for a society based on class exploitation. The same phenomenon was observable in England. But the special conditions of colony life presented unusual opportunities for profiteering by the merchant and planter bourgeoisie.

As I have noted, the Virginia Company of London expected investors to make a 25 percent profit on the food that was sent to the starving colony. Because of the continuing decline in the price of the overproduced tobacco,[83] this profit margin was a constant point of contention between the colony buyers and the Company, and in turn between the Company and the king in the tobacco contract negotiations. English colony tobacco, which had sold in England at from 3 to 4½ shillings, and more, the pound in 1619, was selling for 18 to 20 pence in March 1622/3.[84] A year later, it had fallen further to 18d. or less per pound.[85] In April 1624, a group representing "the poore Planters in Virginia" petitioned for a reduction of the combined 12d. per pound royal impost and import custom on tobacco. The price of tobacco in England was at that time so low, it was said, that such charges left insufficient return to continue production.[86] In January 1626, the Virginia Colony authorities reported that their efforts to maintain tobacco at 18d. had failed, and that it was then selling at less than 12d. per pound in the colony.[87]

Profit-making pressure on the colonists was intensified by the presence of the trading ships that anchored at Jamestown. They were laden with cargoes of delectable English commodities and they conducted their offshore business with colonists able and willing to give tobacco for wines, liquors, cider, salad oil, vinegar, butter, candies, cheese and Canadian fish.[88] Trading was so heavy, it was said, that almost the entire 60,000-pound crop of Virginia tobacco produced in 1622 was taken by these private traders.[89] Business was brisk despite the increasingly "excessive and unconscionable" rates of profit extorted by the merchants.[90]

The customers were people who had some tobacco above what they might have needed for purchasing corn. Undoubtedly, they were in the main the poor but free planters, such as constituted something less than half the population of the colony.[91] This aspect of profiteering must have impoverished many small planters and reduced some to proletarians. Certainly, after dealing with the trading ships they had little tobacco left for shipment to England for their own accounts. As the Company stated in March 1623:

[C]oncerning the poor Planters ... the quantitie of Tobacco brought home in right of their proprietie is for the most part verie smale it beinge expended in the Plantacons amongst the Marchantes trading thither with their several necessarie Commodities."[92]

Profiteering, official and otherwise, was coupled with outright expropriation, legal and illegal, on a grand scale, without any color of exchange. Given the special circumstances of colony existence, and given the continuing supply of laborers from England, this profiteering and expropriation were basic factors in the reduction of colony plantation laborers to chattels.

As the remark of Wyatt and Yeardley had indicated, the rulers of the colony had only one active policy for feeding the colony, namely to get corn from the Indians. Two general methods were employed to implement this policy. One was to make war against Opechancanough and his allies. The other was that of peaceful trade with the more distant, friendly Indians on the eastern shore of Chesapeake Bay.[93] But the main method seems to have been the former; when in doubt, or perhaps merely low on English trade goods,[94] the English would allege "treachery" against the Indians and attack them, taking corn without payment and destroying the growing corn of the Indians, a method of warfare that some of the English officers in Virginia had practiced under Mountjoy in Ireland.[95]

As noted above, shortly after the Indian attack of 22 March 1622 the colony authorities ordered drastic restrictions on the planting of corn, as a safeguard against lurking Indian enemies it was said.[96] Many colonists considered the "national defense" rationale for this policy to be spurious, and complained bitterly about it. Later they declared that if they had been allowed to plant corn as they wished, they could have provided for their own needs adequately,[97] even though little food, or none at all, was coming from England. The restriction on corn planting was also challenged in the meetings of the Court of the Virginia Company of London.[98] Nevertheless, the policy was enforced, although the temper of the colonists was so unruly by April 1623 that the governor asked London to institute martial law, as he said to terrorize the people.[99] The ban on hunting for food in the forests, and the abandonment of half the plantations and the withdrawal of the colony into a restricted perimeter, compounded the food supply problem.

It was a recipe for famine; but it was also a recipe for capitalist profiteering, by those equipped and opportunely positioned to exploit the situation. Captain Nathaniel Butler was only reporting, and in terms of understatement, what was an open scandal, when in the spring of 1623, regarding the hardship of the corn famines, he said:

> howesoever itt lay heavy uppon the shoulders of the Generallytie itt may be suspected not to be unaffected by some of the chiefe; for they onely haveing the means in these extremeties to Trade for Corn w[i]th the Natives doe hereby engrosse all into their hands and soe sell it att their owne prizes [prices].[100]

The means for trading for corn with the Indians were boats and small ships. Those who possessed or could secure the use of such vessels had a monopoly of the trade, since there was absolutely no other way of bringing corn into the colony from the Indians of the eastern shore of Chesapeake Bay. Having made it practically impossible for the people to trade simply and directly with their immediate Indian neighbors, the Colony Council and the Governor in the winter and spring of 1622–23 issued corn-trading licenses to owners and operators of cargo-carrying capital equipment. Not surprisingly, George Yeardley appears a foremost actor in this group. On 3 January, Governor Wyatt licensed Yeardley to send Captain William Tucker, an experienced officer and trader, on a corn-getting voyage, using "such shipps, pinnaces boates as hee the s[ai]d Sir George shall thinke fitt to appoint unto him & that doe in any way belong or are in service to him the said George."[101]

Tucker was authorized, on Yeardley's behalf, to "trade or take by force of Armes" in order to secure the Indians' corn. He was instructed to deliver the corn to Yeardley "by him to be disposed as hee in his best discretion shall thinke fitt."[102]

Seven corn-getting ventures were made in that same month, by George Sandys, Colony Secretary, and by a number of "Captains." Four of the six men engaged in these separate voyages in the privileged trade were members of the Colony Council.[103] Yeardley was the largest of the operators; of the four thousand bushels of corn brought into the colony by 20 March, Yeardley, in only one voyage, accounted for one-fourth of the total.[104] The oft-quoted old planter William Capps called Yeardley "[a] worthie statesman for his owne profit," who was willing to prolong the colony's distress in order to gain by it personally.[105] It is reasonable to infer, and it was so implied by Nathaniel Rich, that corn profiteering was the motive of the merchants in the Colony Council generally, when they advised the London authorities in January 1623 that they were "Confident there wilbe noe cause to intreat your helpe for supplie of corne or any other provisions," provided incoming colonists were accompanied by adequate food.[106]

Under ordinary conditions, the colony at its current size needed at least eleven thousand bushels of corn to get through to the next harvest from planting time.[107] The normal price of corn was $2\frac{1}{2}s.$ per bushel.[108] Under normal conditions, the five largest possessors of corn in the colony held 12 percent of the total supply.[109]

In March 1623, there were certainly less than four thousand bushels of corn on hand of that brought in during the previous three or four months. Very little corn had been harvested in 1622; the same would be true of 1623. At the same time a group of not more than a dozen of the colony elite held practically the entire corn supply of the colony. The supply was not distributed according to need; rather it was sold for the highest prices that could be extorted. The price of corn had risen to ten, and then fifteen, shillings a bushel in the winter of 1622. By the spring of 1623, the price was octupled, at twenty shillings per bushel.[110] And within a month after the *Seaflower* went down in Bermuda, Edward Hill was writing to his brother in England that the price of corn in Virginia had reached thirty shillings, and that the land faced "the greatest famine that ever was."[111] As the price of corn was rising to eight times its normal level, the price of tobacco was falling due to overproduction. We have already noted that the commodity-trading ships were said to have taken almost the entire sixty-thousand-pound tobacco crop of 1622.[112] While that estimate may have been exaggerated somewhat, the fact still contributed to the pressure of indebtedness bearing down on the people as a result of profiteering by the plantation bourgeois elite.

In 1623, the Governor and Colony Council sought to fix the exchange rate of tobacco in Virginia at 18*d*. per pound in order to discourage trade with the private ship-merchants.[113] This was only half the three-shilling rate that had been set before the crisis. If the price of corn rose eight times and the price of tobacco fell by half, then the four thousand pounds of corn secured in the winter of 1622–23 would, even at a price of fifteen shillings the bushel, be equal in exchange-value to forty thousand pounds of tobacco at 18*d*. per pound. If the total 1622 tobacco crop of sixty thousand pounds had nearly all been spent with the commodity-trading ships (see page 89), then the indicated indebtedness to the corn elite must have approached something like forty thousand pounds of tobacco. The crushing weight of such debt was enough to drive the tenants into long-term debt servitude. The same pressure was felt, perhaps only slightly less forcefully, by the freemen, the rank-and-file small landholders.

The uprooting of the inhabitants of many English settlements, combined with the extremely high death rate, simultaneously presented the plantation bourgeoisie with opportunities for direct capitalist expropriation of land and labor power in the furtherance of the alteration of labor relations to that of chattel-servitude.

In the aftermath of the 22 March 1622 attack, the boundaries of the colony were drawn back by deliberate decision to Jamestown and Newport-News and points on the north side of James River, and to a few plantation above and opposite Jamestown. In its report to London at the end of April, the Colony Council revealed that "halfe the people" had been uprooted and "enforced . . . to unite with" the other half, along with as much of their livestock as could be salvaged, within the confines of an area less than half that occupied by the colony before 22 March.[114] Two months later, the Colony Council advised London that "[w]e have been forced to quitt most of our habitations, so that many of our people are unsettled."[115]

One-third of the landholders had died in the attack of 22 March. Half of the surviving landholders were those who were displaced from the outlying settlements; and half of that number died within the ensuing year. Chaos in property relations was the result, especially in the common case in which there was no clearly entitled Virginia-dwelling heir-apparent. Three years after the attack, only twenty-eight of the seventy non-corporate landholders were still living of those who had been granted land patents in Charles City prior to 22 March 1622. Most revealing of the chaotic quality of the situation is the fact that sixteen of the seventy are listed as "probably" or "possibly" dead. It was difficult enough to straighten out the lines and portions of inheritance when the patent holder was known to be dead; it was impossible to do so where it was not certain that the original holder was dead. Still, the land "lived," and would yield tobacco for somebody, if "planted" with laborers. The corporate group that operated under the name Southampton Hundred was the holder of title to 100,000 acres in Charles City. In 1625, this land was still "virtually abandoned." In Henrico settlement, only nine of the pre-March 1622 patent holders remained alive in 1625; of these, only two were living in Henrico.[116]

It was a field rich with opportunity for land-grabbing.[117] Immediately after the March 1622 attack, the gentlemen of the Colony Council noted that in the straitened circumstances it would be necessary for colonists to be "contented with smale quantities of Land," and asked London for authority to assign planters "the place and proportions of Land" that the Council in Virginia should think proper.[118] Under cover of a reference to the settling of new planters, the Colony Council asked that the patent-granting authority be transferred from the Virginia Company Court in London to the Virginia Governor and Colony Council.

The Company's reply indicated that, in any case of divergence of interest among claimants, control should be unambiguously located in England. The Company categorically rejected the suggestion of the Virginia Colony council, immediately established a special committee of Londonders to receive claims of Virginia land heirs living in England, and enjoined the Virginia authorities to process these claims as they were forwarded, expeditiously and justly.[119] In November 1622, the Company's committee on Virginia land claims declared as follows:

> The Companie knoweth not what land is Due to men and every Day unjust and false claimes are put up especially upon pretences of beinge heires to persons [in Virginia].[120]

Aside from the individually held lands, around thirty thousand acres of Company lands reverted to the Crown in 1625,[121] to be distributed in time on its terms.

In consequence of this double process of death and displacement, one-third, at least,[122] of the surviving tenants, laborers and apprentices in the entire colony were left without employers or means of employing themselves. The moment had come to put into execution the proposal of Captain Nuce, which had been so ardently embraced by the Virginia Governor, Colony Council and House of Burgesses in January 1622 – to "turn the tenants into pencons."[123] The optimum conditions were conjoined for realizing the intention of the plantation bourgeoisie to reduce the general condition of the plantation laboring classes to that of unpaid bond-labor, working without wages, for board and lodging only.

As of the spring of 1622, there were five officially recognized social classes in Virginia Colony. Two of them were the owning classes: gentlemen (the bourgeoisie) and the freemen, small independent farmers and self-employed artisans (the petty bourgeoisie). The other three were the dependent laboring classes: the tenants-at-halves, the hired servants, and the apprentices.[124]

In the long crisis that followed the Indian attack of March 1622, however, the significant distinctions of status among the three laboring-class elements were deeply eroded by pervasive hunger and sickness, by economic dislocation, and by the general precariousness of existence.[125]

Theoretically, the average tenant could, under normal conditions, raise some five hundred or more pounds of tobacco in a year,[126] half of which was his, plus the corn, of which his share would supply him and his family (if he had a family in Virginia) for the year ahead. But the crisis had confronted the tenants with a far different reality. They were forced into debt by the restriction on tobacco planting, coupled with a fixed rate of rent. Forbidden to plant corn, they were compelled to pay extortionate prices for it from the corn-profiteering elite, and to the shipboard hucksters down at the river. Alderman Johnson, a critic of the Sandys administration in the Virginia Company, said in June 1623: "the planters, most of them being Tenants at halves ... for twelve moneths bread paye 2 years labor and for cloths and tooles he hath not wherewith to furnish himself.[127] Yet friends of the Sandys administration judged the proportion of the tenants' resources to be even less. In January the Virginia Colony Council had said that tenants could not feed themselves three months out of the year.[128] In March, Colony Secretary George Sandys would write that most tenants-at-halves "die of Melancholye, the rest running so farre in debt as keepes them still behind hand," and many too hungry to continue at their works or to wait for the harvest were hunting wild game to keep from starving.[129] And in April, those of Governor Wyatt's twenty-four tenants who still survived were sinking hopelessly into debt merely for corn to get them through the year, because their families would otherwise starve waiting for the year-end division of the crop. Eight of Wyatt's tenants were obliged to submit to being "rented out" to private planters, who paid Wyatt one hundred pounds of tobacco and three barrels of corns for each.[130]

In the case of the hired laborer, what did it matter that, even at the reduced official rate of 18d. per pound, his wage of a pound of tobacco per day was by the numbers equal to three times as much as the wages of a laborer in England? Corn, the basic food, cost four or five times as much in Virginia as grain in England.[131] Two-thirds of the possible employers of hired labor had died or been displaced from their lands in the space of a year. The opportunities for being hired were thus cut in half, while the number of hands available for hired labor was doubled by the displacement of half the tenants from their holdings. January letters from Jamestown described the laborer's situation in such terms as these:

> by occasion of the last massacre ... every man of meaner sort, who before lived well by their labour upon their owne land, being forced to foresake their houses (which were very farre scattered) & to join themselves to some great mans plantation; where having spent what before they had gotten, they are ready to perish for want of necessaries.[132]

The tendency to concentration of land ownership has been noted above. But the most significant index of wealth concentration in Virginia at that time was in numbers of laborers; as Secretary Pory had said, 'our principal wealth ... consisteth in servants.[133] Edmund S. Morgan lists the fifteen "winners" in the servant "sweepstakes," who by the winter of 1624–25 had accumulated a total of 302 "servants."[134] That was 60 percent of all those categorized as "servants" in the Colony.[135] Some significant portion of them had been forced by sheer want "to join ... great men's plantations." The individual holding of the grandees ranged from ten to thirty-nine "servants." Morgan emphasizes the extreme degree of concentration of this engrossment of the laborers in the hands of the colony elite by noting that contemporary Gloucestershire in England, with a labor force nearly forty times as great as that of Virginia Colony, had only slightly more employers of ten or more persons than Virginia's favored fifteen.[136] The concentration of "servants" in the colony was guaranteed for the future by the headright system of land acquisition and tenure; and the arrangement of political power based on it was certain to intensify the already apparent degree of concentration of land ownership in Virginia.

Now completely in the labor market were such ex-tenants as John Radish, one of the "rented-out" tenants-at-halves, who found himself so destitute late in 1622 that he was compelled by necessity to work for his master for food and clothing only, or die of starvation.[137] Such being the lot of the tenants-at-halves and the wage workers, what but despair would come to the apprentices, lacking a master, land and tools, unskilled in labor, possibly displaced from lodging, and three thousand miles from home? It need only be said that their situation was the most precarious of all, and to note that in April 1622 Edwin Sandys in England had come to the opinion that what Virginia needed most was "multitude of apprentices."[138]

A time came, in June 1623, when in labor-scarce Virginia food was proportionately even more scarce than laborers. Writing to his brother Edward in London, Virginia gentleman planter Robert Bennett acknowledged recent receipt of a shipment of "19 buttes of excelent good wyne, 700 jarse of oylle, 16 Barelles of Rysse, tooe halfe hoghedes of Allmonds, 3 half hoghedes of wheate ..., 18 hoghedes of Olives and some 5 ferkenes of butter and one Chesse."[139] Concerning general conditions in the colony, he added in a postscript: "Vittiles being scarce in the countrye noe man will tacke servantes."

Laboring People's Difficulty, Colony Elite's Opportunity

The extreme economic pressure on the laboring people created an opportunity for the abuse of their rights that was deliberately exploited by the official policy and actions of the Virginia Colony Council and General Court. Men on wages were sold after their employers died.[140] Poor planter William Tyler declared that "neither the Governor nor Counsell could or would doe any poor man right." Even if he were a man of means, Tyler said, he wouldn't be a member of the Colony Council, because as such he could not do right as his conscience would dictate, adding that the great men all hold together.[141] Laborer Elizabeth Abbot was whipped to death with 500 lashes, and Elyas Hinton was beaten to death with a rake by his employer, Mr Procter.[142] In the first recorded instance of the un-English practice of punishing a runaway laborer by adding years to his servitude, John Joyce was sentenced by the General Court to thirty lashes and a total of five and a half years' extra labor service.[143] Henry Carman, who had been shipped to Virginia as one of the "Duty boys" in 1619, was the first laborer sentenced to an added time (seven years) of unpaid labor for a criminal offense ("fornication").[144] Company tenants, who had been promised promotion to landowner upon completion of their contracts, were instead merely to serve again as tenants of the colony authorities for "terme of yeares." "Duty boys" who in 1626 completed their seven-year terms, were not promoted to tenants-at-halves, but were divided up among the Governor and members of the Colony Council, with whom they were to "make composition," that is, negotiate terms from their utterly dependent position.[145] Bruce's "explanation" of why the plantation bourgeoisie reneged on the conditions under which these laboring people were originally brought to Virginia seems cold-bloodedly true. If they had been granted land, he says, "the ability of the planters who had been their masters to secure laborers in place of them would have been diminished to a serious extent."[146]

For the laboring classes, it was as if Virginia had been visited with a combination of the plague of the fourteenth century – but without the chance to walk away to higher-paying employment – and the enclosures of the sixteenth century – but without a Pilgrimage of Grace of powerful allies, or their native Mousehold Heath to rally on. They could not escape from Virginia. Rebellion was, at that moment, practically impossible, even if the subjective element for revolt had been prepared. They were dependent upon the bourgeoisie for every peck of corn for their starved bellies. They were thus compelled to submit to the condition dictated by the plantation bourgeoisie: the status of unpaid labor, that is, bond-laborers.

Yet the tenants' desperate situation which had made it possible for the employing class to reduce labor costs to mere "vittles" would certainly end with new corn harvests,[147] although the price of tobacco was bound in shallows from which it would never return to its early high levels. How then would it be possible for the plantation bourgeoisie to make this momentary system of unpaid labor permanent, instead of being forced to return to "that absurd condition of tenants at halves,"[148] or to paying wages higher than those paid in England?[149]

6

Bricks without Straw: Bondage, but No Intermediate Stratum

Bond-labor was not new; in surplus-producing societies, in England and elsewhere, lifetime bondage had been the common condition of labor prior to capitalism. But the social structure of those times was based on production relationships in which each person was socially, occupationally and domestically fixed in place. Pre-capitalist bond-labor was tied by a two-way bond: the workers could not go away, but equally the master could not send them away. However, this relationship, which was essential to feudalism for instance, was inimical to capitalism. The historical mission of the bourgeoisie was to replace the two-way bondage of feudalism with the two-way freedom of the capitalist relation of production. The capitalist was free to fire the workers, and the workers were free to quit the job. The political corollary was that the bourgeoisie was the only propertied class ever to find advantage in proclaiming freedom as a human right.

Capitalism is a system whose normal operation is necessarily predicated upon the continuing presence of a mass of unattached labor-power of sufficient proportions that each capitalist can have access to exploitable labor-power, in season and out, in city or in countryside, and at a minimum labor cost. In newly settled territories, such a necessary reserve army of labor, though at first absent, would eventually be created[1] in the normal process of capitalist development, as a result of: immigration induced by higher wages caused by the shortage of wage labor; increased productivity of labor, resulting from the use of improved techniques and instruments of labor; the normal process of squeezing out the small or less efficient owners and making wage laborers of them by force of circumstance; and the natural increase of the dependent laboring population.[2]

But the situation in which the Anglo-American plantation bourgeoisie found itself in the 1620s, seeking to preserve its profitable tobacco monoculture in the face of the declining price of tobacco, did not permit – so far as its narrow class objectives were concerned – waiting for longer-term solutions.

Since the freedom of the capitalist to fire the workers is predicated on the freedom of the worker to leave the employer, the plantation bourgeoisie created a peculiar contradiction with respect to the free flow of capital within its system by reducing plantation laborers to bondage. The plantations, being capitalist enterprises, were subject to the normal crises of overproduction. As capitalist monocultural enterprises, they were furthermore subject in an extraordinary degree to the vagaries of the world market. Even in times of a generally satisfactory market, natural calamities, wars, or inimical governmental administration inevitably brought business failures and the abandonment or dissolution of individual enterprises in their wake. In the normal course of capitalist events, individual reverses of fortune require liquidation of enterprises, and the normal procedure in such circumstances is to "let the workers go," that is, to discharge them. But the very purpose of bond-servitude is to see to it that the workers are not "let go"; and a system of laws, courts, prosecutions, constabulary, punishments, etcetera, is instituted to enforce that principle. The plantation bourgeoisie dealt with this contradiction by establishing a one-way bondage, in which the laborer could not end the tie to the capitalist simply by his own volition; but the capitalist could end the tie with the worker. In the solution imposed by the plantation bourgeoisie, the unpaid aspect was designed to meet the need to lower labor costs, the long-term bondage was the surrogate for the nonexistent unemployed labor reserve, and the chattel aspect of the new system of labor relations made it operable by satisfying the functional necessity for the free flow of capital.

An Ominous New Word Appears – "Assign"

In attempting to fix the point in time at which the unambiguous commitment to chattelization began, it is helpful to take note of the first appearance of the term "assign" in relation to laborers. To "assign" means, in law, "to make over to another; to transfer a claim, right or property." The appearance of this term in relation to the change of a laborer from the service of one employer, or master, to another betokens the chattel status of the laborer. No longer is the contract for labor an agreement entered into between the laborer and the employer; it is rather a transacation between two employers, in which the laborer transferred, "assigned," has no more participation than would be had by an ear-cropped hog, or a hundredweight of tobacco, sold by one owner to another.

Between January and June 1622, the Virginia Company established a standard patent form.[3] The form carried a provision that the laborers transported under the patent could not be appropriated by the colony authorities for any purpose except the armed defense of the colony. What is significant in the context of the present discussion is that the Company guaranteed this protection not only to the original patentee but to his "heires and Assigns." Implicit here, and as would become explicit within less than four years, is the formal establishment of the legal right of masters to "assign" laborers, or to bequeath them. Already, of course, as early as 1616, a system had been established under which any private investor was entitled to fifty acres of Virginia land for himself for every worker whose transportation costs the investor paid.[4]

The case of Robert Coopy's indenture, dated September 1619, is the first recorded instance of a worker being obligated to work for a specified length of time without wages in order to pay off the cost of his transportation to Virginia.[5] Two years later, Miles Pricket, a skilled English tradesman, while still in England agreed with the Virginia Company to work at his salt-making trade in Virginia for one year "without any reward at all, which is here before paid him by his passage and apparell given him."[6] The one-year term was normal for England, but the worker's paying for his own passage was innovative. Prickett did come to Virginia, and in March 1625 was the holder of a 150-acre land patent in Elizabeth City.[7]

Retrospectively, these early incidents appear as preconditioning the reduction of laborers to chattels. But it was not until 1622 and 1623 that this portentous custom was established as the general condition for immigrant workers, formalizing their status as chattels. An analysis of a score of entries in the records of the time shows how the chattel aspect of bond-servitude was designed to adapt that contradictory form to capitalist categories of commodity exchange and free flow of capital.

Saving harmless the creditors of decedent. William Nuce, brother of Thomas Nuce and member of the Colony Council, died in late 1623. His estate was encumbered with debts, including one of £50 owed to George Sandys, and another of £30 to William Capps. Both debts were settled by the assignment of bond-laborers to the creditors.[8]

Disposal of unclaimed estate. William Nuce left eleven destitute laborers who had been in his charge as company employees, "some bound for 3 yeares, and few for 5, and most upon wages."[9] They were sold for two hundred pounds of tobacco each (not counting those four with whom George Sandys reported having such bad luck).[10]

Avoidance of bankruptcy. Mr Atkins, in order to relieve his straitened circumstances, sold all his bond-laborers.[11]

Option to buy. Thomas Flower was assigned to Henry Horner for three years. But it was stipulated by the Virginia General Court that if Horner decided to sell the man, John Procter would have first refusal.[12]

Capital market operations. In the prelude to the case cited immediately above, John Procter assured Henry Horner that he, Procter, would procure a servant for Horner, saying that "[H]ee [Procter] had daly Choice of men offered him." (Procter told Horner not to let the servant know he had been sold until they were embarked from England.)[13]

In January 1625, three servants of William Gauntlett were sold to Captain Tucker. The sale was recorded in the Minutes of the Virginia General Court.[14]

Velocity of circulation. Abraham Pelterre, sixteen-year-old apprentice, arrived in Virginia in 1624; within two years he had been sold hand to hand four times.[15]

Contract for delivery; penalty for failure to perform. Humphrey Rastill, merchant of London, contracted to deliver "one boye aged about fowerteene yeers ... To serve [Captain] Basse [in Virginia] or his assignes seaven Years," and bound himself "in the penaltye of forfeiture of five hundred pownd of Tobacco." On 3 January 1626, six weeks after the order had been due for delivery, on Basse's petition the Court ordered Rastill to make delivery by 31 January or pay the forfeit.[16]

Property loss: damages assessed. Thomas Savage, a young servant, was drowned in consequence of negligence on the part of a man who had use of him but was not his owner. The culprit was ordered to pay the owner three hundred pounds of tobacco as indemnity.[17]

Exploiting sudden entrepreneurial opportunities. John Robinson sailed from England in the winter of 1622–23, bringing bond-laborers with him, to settle in Virginia. He died *en route*. The ship's captain seized Robinson's property, including the bond-laborers, with the intention of selling all for his own account.[18]

The Privy Council in England in 1623 confirmed the gift to Governor Yeardley, of twenty tenants and twelve boys that had been left by the Company at its liquidation. Yeardley was authorized to "dispose of the said tenants and boys to his best advantage and benefit."[19]

The Colony Council in January 1627 divided up former Company tenants among the Council members themselves: eighteen to Yeardley; three each to five others; two to another; one to each of two others (including the Surveyor, Mr Claiborne, who was given William Joyce and two hundred pounds of tobacco).[20]

Liquidation of an estate. George Yeardley died in November 1627; at the time he was one of the richest men in the country, if not the very richest.[21] He left a will providing that, aside from his house and its contents, which was to go to his wife as it stood,

> the rest of my estate consisting of debts, servants [and African and African-American bond-laborers], cattle, or any other thing or things, commodities or profits whatsoever to me belonging or appertaining ... together with my plantation of one thousand acres of land at Warwicke River ... all and every part and parcell thereof [to be] sold to the best advantage for tobacco and the same to be transported as soon as may be ... into England, and there to be sold or turned into money.[22]

History's False Apologetics for Chattel Bond-servitude

The bourgeoisie, of whom the investors of capital in colonial schemes were a representative section,[23] could have had no more real hope of imposing in

England the kind of chattel bond-servitude they were to impose on English workers in Virginia than they had of finding the China Sea by sailing up the Potomac River.[24] The matter of labor relations was a settled question before the landing at Jamestown. But the Anglo-American plantation bourgeoisie seized on the devastation brought about by the Powhatan attack of 22 March 1622 to execute a plan for the chattelization of labor in Virginia Colony. There had been dark prophecy, indeed, in the London Company's response to the news of the 22 March assault on the colony. "[T]he shedding of this blood," the Company said, "wilbe the Seed of the Plantation," and it pledged "for the future . . . instead of Tenants[,] sending you servants."[25] For from that seeding came the plantation of bondage, in the form known to history as "indentured servitude."

Early in Chapter 4, it was argued from authority that the monstrous social mutation in English class relations instituted in that tiny cell of Anglo-American society was a precondition for the subsequent variation of hereditary chattel bond-servitude imposed on African-Americans in Virginia.[26] Historical interpretations of the institution of "indentured servitude" in the Virginia Company period generally anticipate Winthrop D. Jordan's "unthinking decision" theory of the origin of racial slavery.[27] The initial imposition of chattel bond-servitude in continental Anglo-America is justified by its apologists using three propositions:

First proposition: There was a shortage of poor laborers in Virginia, and an abundance of them in England, so that between English laborers, who wanted employment, and plantation investors, who wanted to get rid of prohibitively costly tenantry and wage labor, a quid pro quo was agreed, according to which the employer paid the £6 cost of transportation from England and in exchange the worker agreed to be a chattel bond-laborer for a term of five years or so.[28]

Second proposition: This form of labor relations was not a sharp disjuncture, but was merely an unreflecting adaptation of some pre-existing form of master–servant relations prevailing in England.

Third proposition: Quid pro quo and English precedents aside, the imposition of chattel bond-servitude was "indispensable" for the "Colony's progress," a step opposed only by the "delicate-minded."[29]

The "quid pro quo" rationale

The argument for shifting the cost of immigrant transportation from the employer to the worker was in some ways analogous to the rationale advanced by the English ruling classes in the late fourteenth century.[30] Because of the plague-induced labor shortage, labor costs rose, and the ruling feudal class and the nascent bourgeoisie sought to recoup as much as possible of the increased cost by introducing a poll tax and increasing feudal dues exacted from the laboring people. Their rationale was that laborers "will not serve unless they receive excessive wages," and that as a result "[t]he wealth of the nation is in the hands of the workmen and labourers."[31] As rationales go, this was fully as valid as that advanced for indebting the laborers themselves for the cost of their delivery to Virginia. The English feudal lords in the fourteenth century used similar "logic" in trying to persuade "their people" of the impossibility of organizing production if the serf were freed. The great difference in the two cases was that the English laboring classes by the Great Rebellion of 1381 showed that the "impossible arrangement" was, after all, not impossible, while in Virgina rebellion, when it came, would fail.

Given the state of English economic and social development as it was at the beginning of the seventeenth century, under the Elizabethan Statute of Artificers (5 Eliz. 4), the "inevitable" thing would have been to employ free labor – tenants and wage laborers – in the continental colonies, not chattel bond-servitude. If the "inevitable" did not happen in Virginia Colony, it was because the ruling class was favored in the seventeenth-century Chesapeake tobacco colonies by a balance of class forces enabling them to promote their interests in a way they could not have done in England. And they could do so in spite of, rather than because of, the shortage of labor in the colonies. The "payment of passage" was simply a convenient excuse for a policy aimed at reducing labor costs and doing so in a way that was consistent with the free flow of capital. Incidentally, as Abbot Smith concluded, the "four or five years bondage was far more than they [the laborers] justly owed for the privilege of transport."[32] Indeed, producing at the average rate of around 712 pounds of tobacco a year, priced at 18d. per pound, even if the laborer survived only one year, he or she would have repaid more than seven times his or her £6 transportation cost.[33] The real consideration was therefore not the recovery by the employer of the cost of the laborer's transportation, but rather the fastening of a multi-year unpaid bondage on the worker by the fiction of the "debt" for passage.

The contrast of labor-supply situations in Holland and England has been discussed in Chapter 1. There appears to be an instructive corresponding contrast in the Dutch attitude toward binding immigrant workers to long periods of unpaid servitude for the cost of their transportation. On 10 July 1638, Hans Hansen Norman and Andreis Hudde entered into a partnership to raise tobacco "upon the flatland of the Island of Manhates" in New Amsterdam. Hudde was to return to Holland and from there to send to Hudde in New Amsterdam "six or eight persons with implements required" for their plantation. It was agreed that the partners would share the expense of "transportation and engaging them" and of providing them with dwellings and victuals.[34] Dutch ship's captain David Pieterzoon de Vries, who was engaged in the American trade at that same time, despised the bond-labor trade of the English, "a villainous people . . . [who] would sell their own fathers for servants in the Islands."[35]

Bond-servitude was not an adaptation of English practice

The imposition of chattel bondage cannot be regarded as an unreflecting adaptation of English precedents. The oppressiveness of the social and legal conditions of the English workers was outlined in Chapter 2 of this volume.[36] But laborers were not to be made unpaid chattels. Except for vagabonds, they had the legal presumption of liberty, a point they themselves had made by rebellion. Except for apprentices and the parish poor, workers were presumed to be self-supporting and bound by yearly contracts, with the provision for three months' notice of non-renewal. The contract was legally enforceable by civil sanctions, including the requirement of posting bond.[37]

Under the bond-labor system of Virginia Colony, the worker was presumed to be non-self-supporting; if taken up outside his or her owner's plantation without the owner's permission, the laborer, already bound to four or five years of unpaid bondage, was returned to that master and subjected to a further extension of his or her servitude. Above all, the Virginia labor system repudiated the English master–servant law by reducing laborers to chattels.

Nor can the origin of plantation chattel bond-servitude be explained by reference to English apprenticeship.[38] Confirmation on this point is to be found in a opinion (citing precedents) written in 1769 by George Mason as a member of the Virginia General Court: "[W]herever there was a trust it could not be transferred ... [as in] the case of an apprentice."[39] Under English law, "The binding was to the *man*, to learn *his* art, and serve *him*" and therefore the apprentice was not assignable to a third party, not even the executor of the will of a master who had died.[40]

Rather than being "a natural outgrowth"[41] of English tradition, chattel bond-servitude in Virginia Colony was as strange to the social order in England after the middle of the sixteenth century as *Nicotiniana tabacum* was to the soil of England before that time;[42] and as inimical to democratic development in continental Anglo-America as smoking tobacco is to the healthy human organism.

Was it inevitable? Was it progress?

Just as historians of the eighteenth century have chosen to see the hereditary chattel bondage of African-Americans as a paradoxical requisite for the emergence of the United States Constitutional liberties,[43] historians of seventeenth-century Virginia almost unanimously, so far as I have discovered, regard the "innovation" of "indentured servitude" as an indispensable condition for the progressive development of that first Anglo-American colony. It is most remarkable that of the interpreters of seventeenth-century Virginian history only one – Philip Alexander Bruce – has ever undertaken a systematic substantiation of that concept.

Here is a summary of Bruce's argument:[44]

The survival of the colony depended upon its being able to supply exports for the English market of sufficient value to pay for the colony's needs for English goods. The economy of the colony was necessarily shaped by its immediate economic interests. Tobacco alone would serve both of those purposes. Since maize – Indian corn – was not then appealing to the European palate, wheat was the nearest possible export rival to tobacco. But wheat required more land for the employment of a given amount of labor for the production of equal exchange-value in tobacco, and much more labor for clearing of the forested land for its profitable exploitation; furthermore, wheat in storage was much more vulnerable to rat and other infestation and required much larger ship tonnage for delivery than did tobacco of equal value.

In order to make profitable use of land acquired by multiple headrights or the equivalent by other means, the owner had to employ more labor than that of his immediate family. Tenantry was not adaptable for this purpose because landowners were not eager to rent out newly cleared land whose fertility would be exhausted in three years, and tenants were not willing to lease land that was already overworked when they could take out patents on land of their own at a nominal quit-rent of two shillings per hundred acres.[45] Labor being in short supply, wage laborers commanded such high wages that they too would have good prospects of acquiring land of their own, and thus of ceasing to be available for proletarian service.

Chattel bondage as the basic general form of production relations was therefore indispensable for the progress of the colony of Virginia.

It seems reasonable to believe that Bruce was aware that tenantry became a significant part of the agricultural economy in eighteenth-century Chesapeake. Allan Kulikoff's study indicates that in southern Maryland and the Northern Neck and Fairfax County in Virginia one-third to half of the land was occupied by tenants.[46] In Virginia, on new ground the first tenant was excused from paying rent for the first two years of the lease. This exemption for payment of fees and rent was "a most advantageous arrangement," writes Willard Bliss, so that, far from being unfeasible, "tenancy was a logical solution" to planters' problems.[47] The rise of tenancy that began in Virginia early in the eighteenth century, particularly in the Northern Neck, was a function of plantation capitalism, which was by then recruiting its main productive labor from African and African-American bond-laborers.[48] The most directly profitable exploitation of their labor was in the production of tobacco, not in clearing new ground, pulling stumps, ditching, fencing, etcetera. For that work, rent-paying tenants were to be employed.

In Maryland, English and other European laborers who survived their servitude were formally entitled to a fifty-acre headright, but to acquire the promised land was "simply impracticable."[49] They generally became tenants of landlords who needed to have their land cleared and otherwise improved for use as tobacco plantation land, or to build up their equity for speculative purposes.[50] In Prince George's County one-third of the householders were tenants by 1705.[51]

These facts would seem to cast doubt on Bruce's argument that the clearing of land could not have been done on the basis of tenancy. The key in both the seventeenth and eighteenth centuries was neither technical difficulty nor any economic impossibility of getting tenants to clear the land, but the owners' calculation of the rate of profit. In the seventeenth century the cheapest way to clear land was not by using tenants, but by using bond-laborers; in the eighteenth century, the cheapest way to clear land was not by using bond-laborers, but by using tenants. It was the work of Adam Smith's "invisible hand,"[52] and, in today's popular phrase, the logic of the "bottom line."

But what was the "bottom line" to the people on the bottom, who were being degraded from tenants and wage laborers to chattels? What good to them was an "invisible hand" systematically dealing from the bottom of the deck against the laboring class? Bruce answers with one word, "progress"; yet even as he does so, he concedes that after all bond-servitude was not inevitable, although he contends the alternative would have been undesirable. Without chattel bondage, he says:

> [t]he surface of the colony would have been covered with a succession of small estates, many of which would have fallen into a condition of absolute neglect as soon as their fertility had disappeared, their owners having sued out patents to virgin lands in other localities as likely to yield large returns to the cultivator. ... [The] Colony's progress would have been slow. Virginia without [chattel bond-] laborers from England and without slaves would have become a community of peasant proprietors, each clearing and working his ground with his own hands and with the aid of his immediate family.[53]

However unpalatable such an alternative may have seemed to Bruce, there were others who showed by word and deed over a span of two and a half centuries in Virginia that they would have assessed the matter differently, had they been given the choice between the life of peasant proprietors and that of unpaid chattel bond-laborers.[54] In New England an alternative practice was followed, as will be discussed in Chapter 9.

Francis Bacon's Alternative Vision: "Of Plantations"

Bruce takes note of Sir Francis Bacon's essay "Of Plantations," dated 1625, the year after the dissolution of the Virginia Company;[55] but while he does not attempt to discuss it in detail, he obviously does not find it persuasive.[56]

> Planting of countries is like planting of woods [wrote Sir Francis]; for you must take into account to lose almost twenty years profit, and expect your recompense in the end; for the principal thing that hath been the destruction of most plantations, has been the hasty drawing of profit in the first years. It is true, speedy profit is not to be neglected, as may stand with the good of the plantation, but not farther.

To this end, it was essential, Bacon said, to keep control out of the hands of the merchants, the most typical form of bourgeois life at that time, "for they look ever to the present gain."[57] The labor of the colonists should be first turned to the cultivation of native plants (among other things, Bacon mentions maize) in order to assure the colony's food supply. Bacon further advised, "Let the main part of the ground employed to gardens or corn be a common stock; and to be laid in and stored up, and then delivered out in proportions." Next, native products should be developed as commodities to be exchanged for goods that must be imported by the colony – but not, Bacon warned, "to the untimely prejudice of the main business; as it hath fared with tobacco in Virginia."[58]

Bacon's thesis seems to have anticipated Bruce's argument, and to refute in advance any attempt to justify the dominance of "immediate needs" and the plantation monocultural base of colonial development.

The record itself – the public and private correspondence, the Company and colony policy statements, laws and regulations, the court proceedings and decrees – presents much evidence of contradictory views within the ruling councils during the Company period. The Company and colony officials inveigh against the inordinate attention given to tobacco growing, while presiding over the ineradicable establishment of the tobacco monoculture, using tobacco for money, squabbling over its exchange-value, staking all on the "tobacco contract." The Company expresses concern over the abuse of the rights of servants while pressing helpless young people in England for service in the plantation. The Company in London continues to send boatloads of emigrants to Virginia without the proper complement of supplies to tide them over till their first crops can be harvested, while the Colony Council in Virginia demands that settlers not be sent without provisions. The colony officials complain that too many ill-provisioned laborers are being sent, and yet at the same time, they deplore the scarcity of "servants ... our principal wealth," and the high wages due to that scarcity.

In puzzling out such apparent antinomies of sentiment, one must make due allowance for the effect of partisan conflicts within the Virginia Company. But as Craven points out, indictments of the treatment of laborers and tenants, or criticism of the tobacco contract with the king,[59] may have been to some extent inspired by factional interests, but that does not invalidate them.[60] When the dust had settled, the transformation of production relations by "changing tenants to servants" had developed from a proposal by the Virginia Colony Council into the prevailing policy of the Anglo-American plantation bourgeoisie as a whole, London "adventurers" as well as Virginia "planters." In all the documents involved in the transfer of the affairs of the colony to royal control, no trace remains of the urgent concern with registration of contracts, abuse of servants, etcetera, ideas that the worried friends and kindred of those gone to Virginia had pressed on the Company Court.

Some Knew It Was Wrong

Nevertheless, the substantial opposition within the Company to the chatteli-zation of labor provides strong evidence that the options for monoculture and bond-servitude were not "unthinking decisions." The "quid pro quo" rationale for chattel bond-servitude was denounced as repugnant to English constitu-tional liberties and common law,[61] and to the explicit terms of the Royal Charter for the Virginia colony.[62] This concern was reflected in the "exceeding discontent and griefe [of] divers persons coming daylie from the farthest partes of England to enquire of friends and Kindred gonn to Virginia."[63] In October 1622, the Virginia Company established a Committee on Petitions, one of whose tasks was to consider wrongs done to "servants" sent to Virginia,[64]

> It beinge observed here that divers old Planters and others did allure and beguile divers younge persons and others (ignorant and unskillfull in such matters) to serve them upon intollerable and unchristianlike conditions upon promises of such rewardes and recompense, as they were in no wayes able to performe nor ever meant.

First among the "abuses in Carriing over of Servants into Virginia" was the following:[65]

> divers ungodly people that have onely respect of their owne profitt do allure and entice younge and simple people to be at the whole charge of transportinge themselves and yet for divers years to binde themselves Servants to them . . .

The remedy was not to be found at that time by strict regulation and control of emigration to Virginia, with a written contract for every worker of which a copy would be kept in Company files.[66] If, in those famine years, 1622–23, laborers had come to Virginia with a contract sealed with seven seals, they would still have surely starved if they could not pay twenty shillings for a bushel of corn, unless they were able to find a master who would *let* them work for mere corn diet and, perhaps, a place to sleep.

It was not the way it was supposed to be. Even those who had never heard of the Statute of Artificers knew as much. "Sold . . . like a damd slave!" raged Thomas Best, cursing his lot.[67] Henry Brigg had come to Virginia having Mr Atkins's promise that Brigg would never serve any other master. But now, in the spring of 1623, he wrote his brother, who had been witness to the promise, "my Master Atkins hath sold me & the rest of my Fellowes."[68]

Young Abraham Pelterre was favored to have a mother in England with some influence with her aldermen. They protested with some effect when they learned that Abraham was being sold from hand to hand in Virginia contrary to the proper conditions of apprenticeship.[69] They knew it was wrong.

Jane Dickinson knew that it was not a thing that could happen in England, and she asked the General Court to see it her way. She had come to Virginia in 1620 with her husband Ralph, a seven-year tenant-at-halves for Nicholas

Hide. Her husband was killed in the attack of 22 March 1622, and she was taken captive by the Indians. After ten months, she and a number of other captives were released for small ransoms. Jane's master had died in the meantime. Dr John Pott, who paid her ransom, two pounds of glass beads, demanded that she serve him as a bond-laborer for the unexpired time of her husband's engagement, saying that she was doubly bound to his service by the two pounds of glass laid out for her ransom. The only alternative, he told her, was to buy herself from him with 150 pounds of tobacco[70] (at the prevailing price of 18d. per pound, this would have been worth nearly twice the £6 cost of her transportation from England).

John Loyde knew that in England if a master died his apprentice was freed, or, perhaps, remained bound to the master's widow. After paying his master £30 to be taken on as an apprentice, and receiving his copy of the appropriate papers for the arrangement, Loyde embarked for Virginia with his master, taking with him the terms of his apprenticeship in writing. His master died *en route*, but the ship's captain had taken his papers that would have established his free status. Without them, Loyde was subject to being sold by the ship's captain into chattel bondage. Loyde sued in court to recover the papers.[71]

William Weston knew it was wrong. In November 1625, he was fined 250 pounds of good merchantable tobacco for failing to bring a servant into Virginia for Robert Thresher. The next month Weston was before the General Court again, and it was testified that, when again asked to bring servants to Virginia

> Mr Weston replied he would bring none, if he would give him a hundred pownde. Mr Newman [who wanted to place an order] asked him why. And Mr Weston replied that ... servants were sold here upp and down like horses, and therefore he held it not lawfull to carry any.[72]

John Joyce, bond-laborer, knew in his aching bones that it was not right; and in August 1626 he sought to reestablish by direct action the capitalist principle of two-way freedom of labor relations. He did not take his case to the General Court, however, preferring the mercy of the wilderness. (Captured by the colony authorities, as noted in Chapter 5, he had the distinction of being the first such fugitive bond-laborer who is recorded as being sentenced to an extension of his servitude time as punishment for his offense. He had six months added to his term with his master, and at the completion of that extended term he was to serve five years more as bond-servant to the colony authorities. It was all to begin with a brutal lashing of thirty stripes.)[73]

And so it came to pass that seventy-five years after the institution of the labor relations principles of the Statute of Artificers, when the good ship *Tristram and Jane* arrived in Virginia in 1637, all but two of its seventy-six passengers were bond-laborers to be offered for sale.[74] The following year, Colony Secretary Richard Kemp reported to the English government, "Of hundreds of people who arrive in the colony yearly, scarce any but are brought in as merchandize for sale."[75]

The Problem of Social Control Enters a New Context

There was another side to the coin of the option by the tobacco bourgeoisie for the anomalous system of bond-servitude as the basis of capitalist production in Virginia Colony. In the sixteenth century, as has been discussed, the English governing classes made a deliberate decision to preserve a section of the peasantry from dispossession by enclosures, in order to maintain the yeomanry as a major element in the intermediate social control stratum essential to a society without an expensive large standing army.[76] The military regime that the Virginia Company first installed under governors Gates and Dale, for all its severity, proved ultimately ineffective. That particular variant of social control had to be superseded because of defiance of the limitations on tobacco cultivation by laboring-class tenants – Rolfe's "Farmors" – who represented the potential yeoman-like recruits for an intermediate social control stratum for the colony.[77]

Following their instinct for "present profit," the plantation bourgeoisie on the Tobacco Coast forgot or disregarded the lesson taught by the history of the reign of Henry VII and the deliberate decision to preserve a forty-shilling freehold yeomanry.[78] Instead, convinced that the tenant class was an "absurdity"[79] from the standpoint of profit making in a declining tobacco market, the Adventurers and Planters decided to destroy the tenantry as a luxury they could not afford.

Perhaps there was special significance in the fact that it was a son of the yeoman class, Captain John Smith, who sounded the warning for those who were forsaking the wisdom of insuring the existence of an adequate yeomanry. Condemning the traders in bond-labor, he said, "it were better they were made such merchandize themselves, [than] suffered any longer to use that trade." That practice, said Smith prophetically, was a defect "sufficient to bring a well setled Common-wealth to misery, much more *Virginia*."[80]

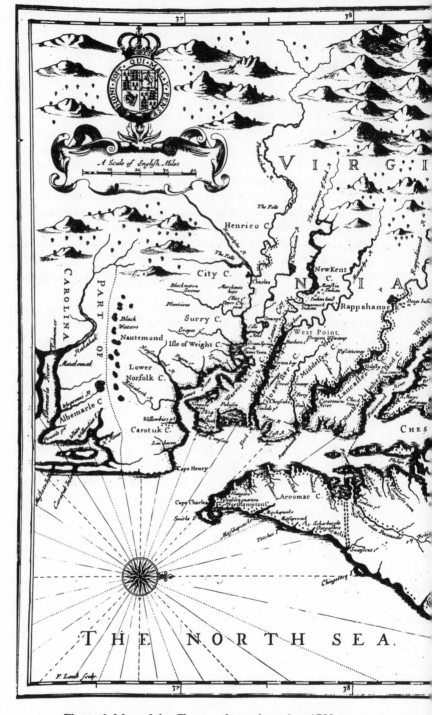

Figure 1 Map of the Chesapeake region, *circa* 1700

This map of Virginia and Maryland was graciously copied for me by the Map Division of the New York 1629). This engraving of the map by Francis Lamb, although not dated, would seem to represent an "up- abbreviated as "C."). Virginia was not divided into counties (first called "shires") until 1634. The New York formed in 1669, and does not mention any of the next three counties, which were formed in 1691, it seems parallel to the lines of almost all of the printed text), it shows details with great clarity. The Atlantic Ocean came to the Chesapeake by sailing north from the West Indies. I myself have labeled West Point, the region slavery" in 1676 (see Chapter 11).

Public Library Research Libraries, whose map catalog identifies the cartographer as John Speed (1542–
dated" version of Speed's work, to judge, for instance, from its identification of counties ("County" being
Public Library catalog tentatively assigns "1666?" to this version. But since it includes Middlesex County,
that this map should be dated sometime in the 1669–91 period. Despite its orientation (the North arrow is
s here called "The North Sea," the designation presumably given to these waters by the English who first
n which "four hundred English and Negroes in Armes" joined in the demand for "freedom from their

Figure 2 List of governors of Colonial Virginia

An attempt has been made to give as nearly as possible the dates of actual service of each of the men who acted as colonial governor in Virginia. The date of commission is usually much earlier.

President of the Council in Virginia

Edward-Maria Wingfield, May 14–September 10, 1607.
John Ratcliffe, September 10, 1607–September 10?, 1608.
John Smith, September 10, 1608–September 10?, 1609.
George Percy, September 10?, 1609–May 23, 1610.

The Virginia Company

Thomas West, Third Lord De La Warr, Governor. February 28, 1610–June 7, 1618.
Sir Thomas Gates, Lieutenant-Governor. May 23–June 10, 1610.
Thomas West, Lord De La Warr, Governor. June 10, 1610–March 28, 1611.
George Percy, Deputy-Governor. March 28–May 19, 1611.
Sir Thomas Dale, Deputy-Governor. May 19–August 2?, 1611.
Sir Thomas Gates, Lieutenant-Governor. August 2?, 1611–c. March 1, 1614.
Sir Thomas Dale, Deputy-Governor, c. March 1, 1614–April?, 1616.
George Yeardley, Deputy-Governor. April?, 1616–May 15, 1617.
Samuel Argall, *Present* Governor. May 15, 1617–c. April 10, 1619.
Nathaniel Powell, Deputy-Governor. c. April 10–18, 1619.
Sir George Yeardley, Governor. April 18, 1619–November 18, 1621.
Sir Francis Wyatt, Governor. November 18, 1621–c. May 17, 1626.

Royal Province

Sir George Yeardley. May?, 1626–November 13, 1627.
Francis West. November 14, 1627–c. March, 1629.
Doctor John Pott. March 5, 1629–March?, 1630.
Sir John Harvey. March?, 1630–April 28, 1635.
John West. May 7, 1635–January 18, 1637.
Sir John Harvey. January 18, 1637–November?, 1639.
Sir Francis Wyatt. November?, 1639–February, 1642.
Sir William Berkeley. February, 1642–March 12, 1652.
(Richard Kemp, Deputy-Governor. June, 1644–June 7, 1645.)

The Commonwealth

Richard Bennett. April 30, 1652–March 31, 1655.
Edward Digges. March 31, 1655–December, 1656.
Samuel Mathews. December, 1656–January, 1660.
Sir William Berkeley. March, 1660.

Royal Province

Sir William Berkeley. March, 1660–April 27, 1677.
(Francis Moryson, Deputy-Governor. April 30, 1661–November or December, 1662.)
Colonel Herbert Jeffreys, Lieutenant-Governor. April 27, 1677–December 17, 1678.
Thomas Lord Culpeper, Governor. July 20, 1677–August, 1683.

(Sir Henry Chicheley, Deputy-Governor. December 30, 1678–May 10, 1680; August 11, 1680–December 1, 1682.)

(Nicholas Spencer, Deputy-Governor. May 22, 1683–February 21, 1684.)

Francis, Lord Howard, Fifth Baron of Effingham, Governor. February 21, 1684–March 1, 1692.

(Nathaniel Bacon, Sr., Deputy-Governor. June 19–c. September, 1684; July 1,–c. September 1, 1687; February 27?, 1689–June 3, 1690.)

Francis Nicholson, Lieutenant-Governor. June 3, 1690–September 20, 1692.

Sir Edmund Andros, Governor. September 20, 1692–December 9?, 1698.

(Ralph Wormeley, Deputy-Governor. September 25–c. October 6, 1693.)

Francis Nicholson, Governor. December 9, 1698–August 15, 1705.

(William Byrd, Deputy-Governor. September 4–October 24, 1700; April 26–June, 1703; August 9–September 12–28, 1704.)

Lord George Hamilton, Earl of Orkney, Governor. 1704–January 29, 1737.

Edward Nott, Lieutenant-Governor. August 15, 1705–August 23, 1706.

(Edmund Jenings, Deputy-Governor. August 27, 1706–June 23, 1710.)

(Robert Hunter was made Lieutenant-Governor April 22, 1707, but never took his office.)

Alexander Spotswood, Lieutenant-Governor. June 23, 1710–September 25?, 1722.

Hugh Drysdale, Lieutenant-Governor. September 25, 1722–July 22, 1726.

(Robert Carter, Deputy-Governor. July, 1726–September 11, 1727.)

William Gooch, Lieutenant-Governor. September 11, 1727–June 20, 1749.

(Reverend James Blair, Deputy-Governor. October 15, 1740–July?, 1741.)

William Anne Keppel, Second Earl of Albemarle, Governor. October 6, 1737–December 22, 1754.

(John Robinson, Sr., Deputy-Governor. June 20–September 5, 1749.)

(Thomas Lee, Deputy-Governor. September 5, 1749–November 14, 1750.)

(Lewis Burwell, Deputy-Governor. November 14, 1750–November 21, 1751.)

Robert Dinwiddie, Lieutenant-Governor. November 21, 1751–January 2–12, 1758.

(John Blair, Deputy-Governor. January–June 7, 1758.)

John Campbell, Fourth Earl of Loudoun, Governor. March 8, 1756–December 30, 1757.

Sir Jeffrey Amherst, Governor. September 25, 1759–1768.

Francis Fauquier, Lieutenant-Governor. June 7, 1758–March 3, 1768.

(John Blair, Acting-Governor. March 4–October 26, 1768.)

Norborne Berkeley, Baron de Botetourt, Governor. October 26, 1768–October 15, 1770.

(William Nelson, Acting-Governor. October 15, 1770–September 25, 1771.)

John Murray, Fourth Earl of Dunmore, Governor. September 25, 1771–May 6, 1776.

The State

Patrick Henry. July 5, 1776–June 1, 1779.

Thomas Jefferson. June 1, 1779–June 12, 1781.

Thomas Nelson. June 12, 1781–November 30, 1781.

Benjamin Harrison. November 30, 1781–November 30, 1784.

Source: William W. Abbot, *A Virginia Chronology, 1585–1783*, Richmond, 1957, pp. 74–6

Figure 3 Virginia counties, and dates of their formation

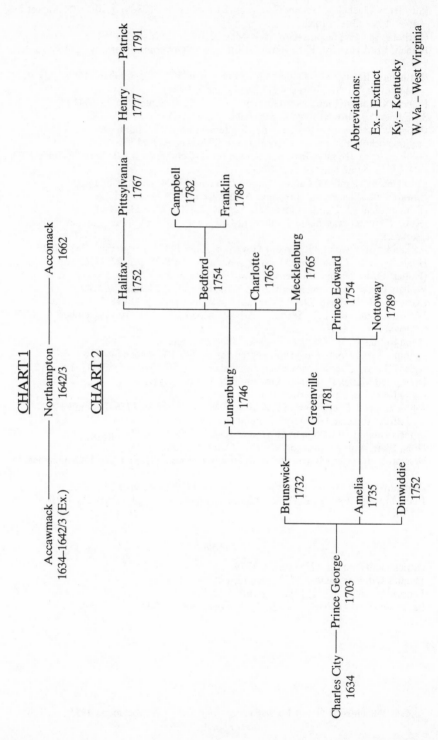

CHART 1

Accawmack
1634–1642/3 (Ex.) ——— Northampton
1642/3 ——— Accomack
1662

CHART 2

Charles City
1634 ——— Prince George
1703

Brunswick
1732

Amelia
1735

Dinwiddie
1752

Lunenburg
1746

Greenville
1781

Prince Edward
1754

Nottoway
1789

Halifax
1752

Bedford
1754

Charlotte
1765

Mecklenburg
1765

Pittsylvania
1767

Campbell
1782

Franklin
1786

Henry
1777

Patrick
1791

Abbreviations:

Ex. – Extinct

Ky. – Kentucky

W. Va. – West Virginia

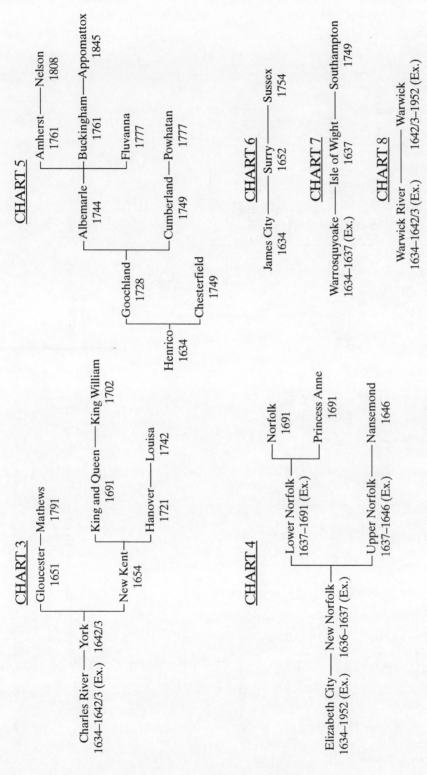

CHART 3

Charles River — York
1634–1642/3 (Ex.)   1642/3

Gloucester — Mathews
1651   1791

King and Queen — King William
1691   1702

New Kent
1654

Hanover — Louisa
1721   1742

CHART 5

Amherst — Nelson
1761   1808

Albemarle
1744

Buckingham — Appomattox
1761   1845

Fluvanna
1777

Goochland
1728

Cumberland — Powhatan
1749   1777

Henrico
1634

Chesterfield
1749

CHART 6

James City — Surry — Sussex
1634   1652   1754

CHART 7

Warrosquyoake — Isle of Wight — Southampton
1634–1637 (Ex.)   1637   1749

CHART 8

Warwick River — Warwick — Warwick
1634–1642/3 (Ex.)   1642/3–1952 (Ex.)

CHART 4

Norfolk
1691

Princess Anne
1691

Lower Norfolk (Ex.)
1637–1691

Upper Norfolk (Ex.)
1637–1646

Nansemond
1646

Elizabeth City — New Norfolk (Ex.)
1634–1952 (Ex.)   1636–1637

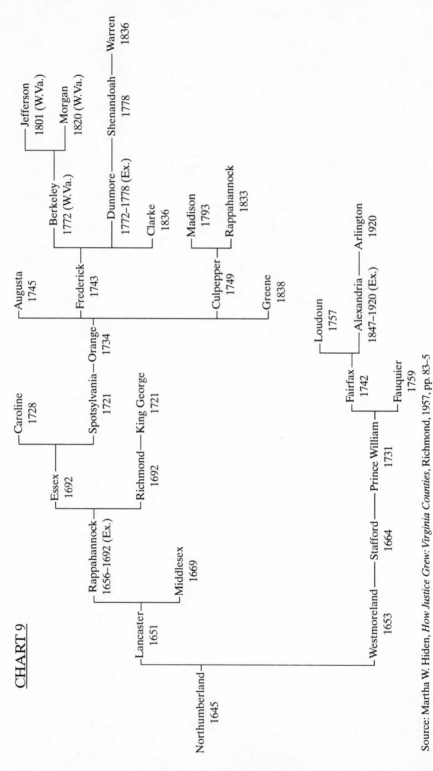

CHART 9

Northumberland
1645

Lancaster
1651

Rappahannock
1656–1692 (Ex.)

Middlesex
1669

Essex
1692

Caroline
1728

Richmond
1692

King George
1721

Spotsylvania——Orange
1721   1734

Augusta
1745

Frederick
1743

Berkeley
1772 (W.Va.)

Jefferson
1801 (W.Va.)

Morgan
1820 (W.Va.)

Dunmore
1772–1778 (Ex.)

Shenandoah——Warren
1778   1836

Clarke
1836

Madison
1793

Rappahannock
1833

Culpepper
1749

Greene
1838

Westmoreland
1653

Stafford
1664

Prince William
1731

Fairfax
1742

Loudoun
1757

Alexandria
1847–1920 (Ex.)

Arlington
1920

Fauquier
1759

Source: Martha W. Hiden, *How Justice Grew: Virginia Counties*, Richmond, 1957, pp. 83–5

116

PART THREE
Road to Rebellion

7

Bond-labor: Enduring . . .

Together with the insubstantiality of the intermediate stratum, the oppressive conditions of the bond-laborers and their resistance to those conditions constitute the most significant social factors that contributed to that pivotal historic event called Bacon's Rebellion. That resistance was a challenge to the very economic basis of the society: the chattel bond-labor form of master–servant relations. Equally significant from the standpoint of the study of the origin of racial slavery is the fact that the record of this period of labor history shows no "white worker" component.

The "Servant Trade": a New Branch of Free Enterprise

The "servant trade," as it came to be called, that is, the export of chattel laborers from Europe, sprang up as a response to the profit-making needs of the tobacco business, and it soon became a special branch of commerce; these bond-laborers "provided a convenient cargo for ships going to the plantations to fetch tobacco, sugar, and the other raw products available,' writes A. E. Smith: "[T]he real stimulus to emigration was not the desire of servants to go to America, but the desire of merchants to secure them as cargo."[1] Investors found the trade attractive. In England, votaries of what today is euphemized as "market principles" sold English men and women for £2 per head (or even less, sometimes) if they had them already in captivity as convicts[2] or workhouse inmates.[3]

In all, some 92,000 European immigrants were brought to Virginia and Maryland between 1607 and 1682, the great majority being sent to Virginia. More than three-quarters of them were chattel bond-laborers, the great majority of them English.[4] In 1676, it was Governor Berkeley's estimate that about 1,500 European chattel bond-laborers were then arriving in Virginia yearly, "the majority English, with a few Scots and fewer Irish."[5] Others were brought to the Chesapeake after the defeat of the Catholic cause in 1689, and they were for a time especially worrisome to the colonial authorities for fear that they might "confederate with the Negroes," as Francis Nicholson warned when he was Governor of Maryland.[6]

Volunteer emigrant bond-laborers were those who boarded ship for America of their own conscious will, although in most cases that will was shaped by extreme hardship and defeat at home, or by self-delusion about the prospect of prospering in the new land. Of those who came thus voluntarily in the seventeenth century, some arrived with written contracts, called "indentures," setting forth the names of their owners, the duration of their periods of servitude, and perhaps some "consideration," or "freedom dues," that their owners were to give the laborers upon the completion of their terms. In some cases the indenture was between the worker and the particular plantation owner whom he or she was to serve in the colony. More frequently, the indenture was arranged with a merchant, ship's captain, or other middleman, who sold the laborer to the highest bidder and then signed over the indenture to the new owner.[7] As early as 1635 a standard indenture form was in use with blank spaces to be filled in with the names of the parties and witnesses.[8]

The involuntary immigrant bond-laborers who came from Europe may also be considered in two categories. There were those who came under sentence as convicted felons and political prisoners, including captives taken in civil war or rebellion in England, Scotland[9] and Ireland.[10] In 1664 a committee on plantation labor supply problems urged the Council for Trade and Plantations (subsequently to be known by various names, and ultimately as the Board of Trade) to have more systematic resort to this and other forms of recruitment of plantation bond-labor. Convicts should be sent to serve seven or fourteen years, said the Committee, according to the seriousness of their offenses. "Sturdy Beggers and Gipsies and other Wanderers" who could not be forced into a settled way of life should "be sent to the plantations for five years under the conditions of Servants." From among the unemployed poor of the towns, villages and parishes of England, some should be "invited or compelled" to emigrate to serve as unpaid bond-laborers "in Jamaica."[11]

The involuntary shipment of still others to the Anglo-Americans colonies, lacking even the color of law, depended on crimps and "Spirits" (so called because they "spirited" their victims away from their native places) who obtained their unwitting victims either by kidnapping or by gross and deliberate deception.[12] The latter and more common method was noted in an English pamphlet published in 1649:

> The usual way of getting servants, hath been by a sort of men nick-named Spirits, who take up all the idle, lazie, simple people they can intice ... who are persuaded by these Spirits, they shall goe into a place where food shall drop into their mouthes. ... The servants are taken up ... and by them [the Spirits] put in Cookes houses about Saint Katherines, where being once entered, [they] are kept as Prisoners until a Master fetches them off.[13]

The Council for Trade and Plantations report to which reference is made above acknowledged the leading part played by the "Spirits," who "receive a reward from the persons who employed them."[14] Like the beaver and deer skin trade that was proving so profitable in the colonies, the English bond-labor supply system in the seventeenth century had its subdivisions. William Haverland was a hunter and trapper, and was accounted a most aggressive one.[15] His role was that of initial seducer and captor of the laborer. Thomas Stone, one of Haverland's prey, told of the experience. One day late in November 1670, he was accosted in a London street by Haverland whom he did not know, but who represented himself to be a native of Stone's own county. By deceit coupled with brute force, Haverland delivered the besotted Thomas to a ship's captain to be taken and sold as a plantation laborer in America. [16]

John Steward and William Thiew, on the other hand, were traders. Since the late 1650s Steward had been buying from such men as Haverland such kidnap victims as Stone, at a price of twenty-five shillings a head. Thiew, another of Haverland's customers during this period, in just one year "spirited away" 840 persons.[17]

Besides the acquisition costs, there were other expenses, for storage, maintenance and transportation, which had to be borne by the entrepreneurs at various stages of the supply process. The cost of holding and maintaining a person for five or six weeks pending shipment came to £3.[18] Clothes provided for the prospective bond-laborer might cost £4, or possibly a little more.[19] But in 1649 this item was reckoned at £3 7s. 10d.;[20] and in 1631 the Essex overseers of the Poor "layd out in parill for two boys that were sent to Virginia, four pownde seven shillings three pence," which averages only £2 2s. 9½d. each.[21] In cases where the merchant and shipowner were one, the cost of transporting a bond-laborer came to about £3; otherwise, the owner of the laborer paid £5 or £6 for each worker's passage.[22]

The price per head of bond-labor delivered live in the plantation colonies varied considerably in response to fluctuations of supply and demand, but merchants could generally count on a profit of from 50 to 200 percent on the transaction.[23] Until 1683, captains of ships delivering European bond-laborers received an additional bonus, a fifty-acre head-right on each one, a claim that the shippers almost invariably sold rather than entering into the cultivation of tobacco themselves.[24] After that, the Virginia practice was followed, limiting such awards to those who used the bond-laborers to improve the land for which they had received patents within a limited period of time.[25]

Besides those regularly engaged in the servant trade, persons of means traveling to the colonies for any reason might be advised to take a few bond-laborers with them for use or sale, according to best advantage. The parents of young Thomas Verney, whom they were dispatching to Virginia, were assured by a supplier that such highly saleable human chattels could easily be secured. "If I were to send forty servants," he boasted, "I could have them here at a dayes warning." (Was he perhaps connected with such suppliers as the Essex Overseer of the Poor?) The cost would be £12 per head, presumably including the agent's own fee. If Verney decided not to stay in Virginia and use the head-rights to start up as a "planter," he could dispose of these chattels at a good profit to be applied against his own expenses.[26]

The shipment of convicts, as "His Majesty's passengers," to be plantation bond-laborers was an especially profitable branch of the trade since it was subsidized by the authorities in England. Although this practice proceeded systematically on a national scale under a law passed by Parliament in 1717, convicts were sent to the Chesapeake colonies in the seventeenth century. Those convicts who survived the voyage were sold by the ship's captain for his own or his employer's account. James Revel arrived in Virginia some time before 1680 at eighteen years of age, having been sentenced to fourteen years' bond-servitude. He later wrote recollections of his experiences, which began with the dockside marketing process. After a seven-week trip, the convicts were put ashore, where they were cleaned up to be made presentable to the prospective customers. The men and women were displayed separately, for "Examening like Horses."

> Some view'd our teeth, to see if they were good,
> Or fit to chew our hard and homely Food.
> If any like our look, our limbs, our trade,
> the Captain then good advantage made.[27]

As was sure to happen, the workings of "the invisible hand" of market forces led to the idea of further specialization. In 1683, Virginia capitalist William Fitzhugh proposed the establishment of a Virginia wholesale enterprise dealing in retailing ships' cargoes as a way of saving English shippers the loss of time and the expense of selling cargoes in the colony. Writing to business associates in London, Fitzhugh stressed the importance of the rate of turnover of capital in the formation of the annual rate of profit, saying, "a certain & sure Market, and easie charge & a quick Dispatch . . . is the life and profit of every trade."[28]

Domestic Sources of Bond-labor

Throughout the colonial period the maintenance of the plantation bond-labor supply was supplemented from domestic sources. For reasons already examined, the early notions of basing English colonial development on the labor of the Indians was short-lived.[29] Nevertheless, some Indians were employed on seventeenth-century tobacco plantations. In the early decades the Indian bond-laborers were mainly children, employed under rather strict limitations involving parental consent.[30] But beginning about 1660, Indian bond-laborers were drawn from the general population, although the Virginia Assembly decreed that they were not to serve "for any longer time than English of like ages should serve."[31] Their condition was worsened under a law passed in 1670 which required Indian bond-laborers to serve for twelve years, more than twice the term of English bond-laborers, and which required the Indian children to be bound until they reached the age of thirty, that is, six years longer than the usual servitude of underage English bond-laborers.[32] Early in

the period of Bacon's Rebellion, in June 1676, the Virginia Assembly authorized that "enemy Indians taken in war be held and accounted slaves dureing
life."[33] This policy was renewed the following year, after the defeat of the
rebellion, in order, it was said, to give the colonial soldiers "better encouragement to such service."[34] Six years later, planters were authorized to hold as
slaves for life Indians purchased from Indian tribes.[35]

For a brief period, Indian bond-laborers played "a considerable role" in the
economy of the tobacco colonies, but this was a phenomenon limited to the
eighth and ninth decades of the seventeenth century.[36] In 1691, the Virginia
Assembly passed a law that from that time forward "there be a free and open
trade for all persons at all times and at all places with all Indians whatsoever."[37]
This same law was re-enacted in 1705 and again in 1733.[38] But it was only after
more than a century of hereditary bondage of the descendants of Indian
women bond-laborers that Virginia courts suddenly discovered that this law,
which made no distinction between friendly and hostile Indians, as previous
laws had always done, and which made no exception as to social rank, was a
formal legal bar to enslavement of Indians in Virginia.[39]

Virginia-born African-Americans as a source of bond-labor

The main domestic source of bond-labor in the plantation colonies was by way
of the imposition of hereditary bond-servitude on African-Americans under
the system of racial slavery and white supremacy. Well before the end of the
colonial period the great majority of the bond-laborers in the plantation
colonies were American-born. In 1790, there were more than twice as many
African-American bond-laborers in the continental plantation colonies as had
come there from overseas in the entire colonial period.[40]

The plantation bourgeoisie had not achieved this condition, however, in the
seventeenth century; at that time most of the plantation laborers were limited-
term bond-laborers, a category composed in its great majority of European-
American immigrants. As far as the difference between limited-term and
lifetime bondage is concerned, that is a question that would have had no
practical significance in the early decades, when most of the bond-laborers did
not survive even their first year in Virginia.[41] Furthermore, the maintenance of
what some historians see fit to call a "dual [that is, black/white] labor
market,"[42] assuming it could have been done, would not have been (as the
phrase is) "cost-effective" in the early decades. One thing is certain: in the
census of 1624/25, taken at the end of the Company period, the colony's total
population of some 1,218 adults listed 507 "servants," of whom 23 were
"Negroes."[43]

Nevertheless, even before the yearning was made explicit in laws of the
early 1660s,[44] there was evidence of a desire on the part of some employers to
develop this source of added unpaid labor time by subjecting African-
Americans to lifetime hereditary bond-servitude. There were also early
instances of legislative and judicial inclinations in this direction.[45] After 1662

under Virginia law and after 1664 under Maryland law, the plantation bourgeoisie could begin to realize profits on the sale and exploitation of laborers born in the tobacco colonies.[46]

The production of a tobacco crop was a most labor-intensive process. Draft animals were not in general use during the seventeenth century.[47] At mid-seventeenth century, when the number of productive workers in Virginia was approaching 7,000,[48] there were no more than 150 plows in the colony.[49] The implements were the human hand[50] for sowing the seedbed and covering it, and for transplanting the seedling to the "hills," spaced at four-foot intervals, and dug with a long-bladed hilling hoe; the wide, sharp weeding hoe for keeping clear the ground between the plants; the tobacco knife for cutting off the top of the plant when the desired number of leaves had put forth; the human hand for pulling the horn worms from the plant, and for breaking the small shoots from the stalk to conserve the plant's energy and food uptake for the nine or so leaves that would mature; the tobacco knife for cutting the stalk at the appropriate time; the human back to bear the cut stalks to the tobacco barn; a knife to cut the pegs driven by hand-held tools into the stalks, before the stalks were hung aloft to allow the leaves to cure in the air for five or six weeks; the human hand again for stripping the cured leaves from the stalks, and removing the stems of the leaves, which had to be delicately handled to preserve their marketability; hand tools and the cooper's skill for the making of hogsheads to specifications to be fit to withstand the stresses of being rolled by workers down to the dock for shipment. The process began with seeding the beds in, say, mid-January, whence they were transplanted to the tobacco field early in May. Continuous attentive labor was required to bring the plant to perfection; in August the stalks were cut down. During the intervals between seeding and transplanting, during the five or six weeks of air curing, and in the months of November and December, there were other sometimes more laborious tasks to be done, such as clearing new fields, cutting down trees and pulling the stumps, burning brush, etcetera.[51] Due to the primitive technique of the process, in the fifty years between the dissolution of the Virginia Company and Bacon's Rebellion the capitalist plantation owners relied almost totally upon increased exertion by the laborers to more than double the annual tobacco output per laborer, from 712 to 1,653 pounds.[52]

Main Forms of the Oppression of Plantation Bond-laborers

The characteristic dependency of the proletarian under capitalism took the most extreme form in chattel bond-servitude. The ancient principle that "A man's home is his castle" had no meaning for the bond-laborers. The woman was denied whatever protection she might otherwise have had as a "feme covert." The limited-term bond-laborers were forbidden the comfort and release of sexual relationships, under heavy penalty. The owner was not only their employer, but their landlord and victualer as well. The extreme rural isolation of their situation, in colonies devoid of the civilizing influences of village and urban centers, limited to an extraordinary degree their ability to appeal their grievances to public conscience and legal remedy.

Edmund S. Morgan's study of colonial Virginia found little basis for the "kindly master" thesis. Nor is he so ready to place the blame for the bond-laborers' bad conditions on objective factors of climate and frontier, as some historians have done. Morgan largely blames capitalist cupidity for the hardships of bond-laborers' lives.[53] This impression is confirmed by the exhaustive studies of the record presented by Richard B. Morris's *Government and Labor in Early America*, and in the *Archives of Maryland* under the illustrious successive editorships of W. H. Browne, C. C. Hall, B. C. Steiner, J. H. Pleasants and Aubrey C. Land.

Most of the evidence of abuse of bond-laborers by their owners is taken from court proceedings wherein certain individual owners of bond-laborers are shown to have carried matters beyond what would seem to be the bounds of sound proprietorship. At the same time the depositions taken, decisions rendered, and orders issued in such cases also serve to illuminate the day-to-day life of the bond-laborers. That which in itself may have constituted a seemingly self-defeating excess of rigor in particular instances, served the general capitalist interest of stimulating the bond-laborers to be more diligent at their tasks, and to stifle their grievances. Such was the declared intention of Captain Bradnox, himself a Kent County Commissioner, who beat bond-laborer Sarah Taylor with extreme force, then reviewed the lesson, saying, "Now spoyle me a batch of bread again!'[54] Courts and legislatures occasionally found it expedient and proper to order some amelioration. Regardless of the degree to which the courts may have been moved by feelings of humanity in such instances, however, it seems certain that they had in mind the overriding interests of the plantation bourgeoisie as a whole in discouraging the wanton destruction of the labor force, and in minimizing the reductions in the labor supply resulting when accounts reached England of brutal treatment of bond-laborers.

The following brief sampling from the court records is not intended to improve on Professor Morris's presentation or to substitute for a reading in the *Archives of Maryland*, but merely to document the theme of social tension in the tobacco colonies arising out of the bond-labor relation of production.

Increasing the length of servitude

Given an adequate supply of labor power, the maximizing of capitalist profit, then as now, depended on raising the productivity of labor per unit of labor cost. In the tobacco colonies the owners did this by (1) extending the labor time of each worker, and (2) intensifying the effort of each worker.

A small minority of the bond-laborers arrived in the tobacco colonies with written indentures specifying the duration of their servitude. By far the greater number who arrived in Virginia in the seventeenth century came without indentures; the duration of their bondage was specified by law under the rubric "custom of the country." At first the custom of the country was set at four years for adult bond-laborers arriving in Virginia and Maryland; then, in 1661 and 1666, respectively, the colony Assemblies increased the custom of the country from four to five years, and made it applicable to all "christian" bond-laborers.[55] The Maryland Assembly in 1666 justified its action by criticizing the former law for

> providing but foure yeares service in which tyme itt is considered the Master and owners of such Servants cannot receive that reasonable satisfaction for the charges trouble & greate hazard which all masters and Owners of Servants are and must of necessity be att with their Servants.[56]

In that same year, the Virginia Assembly acted to eliminate what it saw as an "inequality" in the law, doing so in a way that turned the owner's possible loss into a gain. Under the old law, if a bond-laborer was under sixteen he or she was bound to serve until the age of twenty-four; but if sixteen or over, the term was to be five years. The Assembly, happily from the employers' point of view, raised the critical age to nineteen. Since all those under nineteen were now to serve until they were twenty-four, the masters by this law had claim to from one to three more years of unpaid bond-labor than before from those in the sixteen-to-eighteen-year range, while still retaining the service until twenty-four of those "never so little under sixteene" for whom they expressed such concern.[57]

Special opportunities for securing extra servitude

Besides such steps toward the general extension of the laborers' terms of servitude, the bond-labor relation of production afforded a number of legal opportunities for securing extended service in particular cases, in the form of penalties for a variety of infractions of the principles of the system. These were special opportunities available to the plantation bourgeoisie, which were not open to capitalists operating in England. There, under that normal capitalist labor system, the laborer who violated his or her contract could not be compelled to a specific performance, but could only be held liable for "pecuniary damages as in the case of a breach of any other contract."[58]

As already noted, the Virginia General Court, as early as 1626, imposed an extension of the term of bond-servitude upon a recaptured runaway bond-laborer.[59] Courts continued to apply this principle on a case-by-case basis[60] until it was given the form of legislative enactment that proportioned the extension of servitude to the length of the laborer's absence. In Virginia, the penalty was fixed at two days for every one day of absence.[61] For a repetition of the offense the runaway was to be branded on the shoulder with a hot-iron *R*. In Maryland in 1641, the death penalty was provided, but mercy and profit considerations coinciding, this penalty was made commutable to seven years' added servitude.[62] In 1649, the Maryland penalty was set at two days for each day of absence, but with the additional penalty of payment for all costs and damages, for which the employer might be compensated by a deduction from the freedom dues, and by a further extension of the time of servitude, or by a combination of the two.[63] In 1666, Maryland set the penalty at ten days' extension of servitude for each day of absence.[64] It is somehow not surprising that, with such an incentive, masters frequently sought to extend the period of servitude by alleging that the bond-laborer had been illegally asbent from service, a charge that the laborer was in a weak position to dispute before magistrates who were themselves actual or potential beneficiaries of that same law.[65]

Three cases from the record will illustrate how the employers were able to make such laws serve capital accumulation or, as the modern term has it, "economic growth."

George Beckwith owned Henry Everitt, who had been delivered to Maryland in 1666 at the age of thirteen.[66] Everitt, because of his age, was legally bound to serve nine years, that is, until he was twenty-two. The young worker proved to be a valuable piece of property, despite having at various times "failed to serve" for a total of six weeks. Beckwith, understandably reluctant to part with such an experienced laborer, made timely application to the Provincial Court, on the eve of what was to have been Everitt's last year of servitude, and secured an extension of Everitt's time by ten times six weeks beyond the end of the ninth year. The labor gained would bring Beckwith sufficient return to pay the freedom dues of three bond-laborers (who might perhaps prove more faithful than Everitt), or enough to pay three-fourths the cost of purchasing another thirteen-year-old bond-laborer.[67]

In April 1673, David Driver brought into court two men he owned, James Cade and Timothy Hummerstone, alleging that they had run away for thirty-six days. The court awarded Driver a year of the life and labor of each of the bond-laborers in compensation for the five weeks lost. For Driver this meant a net gain of almost one-fifth of the total labor time originally due him.[68]

On St Valentine's Day 1679, the court showed where its affections lay as between Thomas Doxey and Katherine Canneday:

> Came Thomas Doxey of St Maryes County & made Oath that his servant Katherine Canneday rann away & and unlawfully absented herselfe from his service att severall tymes One hundred and seven dayes, whereupon itt is ordered that shee the said Katherine serve the said Thomas for running away from him as aforesaid, tenn dayes for every one dayes absence according to Act of Assembly in that case made and provided, which amounts to One thousand and seventy dayes.[69]

The costs of recapture, prosecution and corporal punishment

Such proceedings involved costs, of course, as did subsequent execution of court judgments on bond-laborers. Among such costs were the fees paid to the "takers-up" of runaways.[70] Under a Maryland law of 1676, a payment of a matchcoat or the value thereof was provided for "any Indian or Indians which shall seize or take up any Runaway Servant & bring him before some magistrate of any County within this Province."[71] In the middle decades of the seventeenth century the legally established Virginia schedule of fees for sheriff and clerk services included the following items: for sheriffs, twenty pounds of tobacco for each arrest, pillorying and whipping;[72] for clerks, eight pounds of tobacco for writing or copying a court order; and for secretaries, fifteen pounds of tobacco for the same services.[73] In Maryland, sheriffs were paid fifty pounds of tobacco for whippings, and twenty pounds for each day a prisoner was held in jail. In both Maryland and Virginia such charges were at first paid by the county treasury, but in 1662 and 1670 respectively, the provincial assemblies acted to end the discerned gross inequities in such an arrangement. Not only did it make the public bear the costs of supporting criminals, said the lawmakers, it actually was "an encouragement to offendors" by rewarding their misdeeds with idleness and free room and board.[74] Whether such costs occasioned by the capture and public prosecution of bond-laborers were borne by the public treasury or by the individual owners, they were by law recoverable at the expense of the limited-term bond-laborer in terms of additional servitude.[75]

Denial of family life; women exposed to special oppression

For the purposes of quick capital turnover, the importation of unmarried laborers of working age was preferable: it provided the immediate prospect of full utilization of the maximum labor power of the workers; it was simpler in distribution than family-group bond-labor; and, in production, it maximized the employer's access to the laborer's time, unimpeded by the involvement of laborers in family connections and obligations. In short: marriage was fundamentally incompatible with chattel status.

In normal English capitalist conditions, the right to marry was exercised by persons regardless of social class, except that apprentices needed the permission of their masters. The family was the standard form of maintaining, perpetuating and reproducing the laboring classes in proportion to the requirements of capitalist commodity production at the lowest cost and with the highest returns for investors. The expenses of working-class weddings, births, child-rearing and funerals were provided in the wage costs of the employing classes no less essentially than the costs of the day-to-day maintenance of the economically productive population or of the instruments of production. In the seventeenth-century plantation colonies, however, the peculiar chattel bond-labor relation of production carried with it different implications for the lives of the bond-laborers. For almost the entire duration of the seventeenth century, the plantation bourgeoisie was able to secure a steady supply of bond-labor for which it was obliged to pay only the day-to-day subsistence and "operating" costs. All other charges were subsumed in the purchase price, which the laborer was bound to repay (many times over) by long periods of unpaid labor.

Since bond-laborers were wageless and propertyless (except for the few who brought personal items to America, which in the nature of the case would have been of little exchange-value), and since they had no rightful claim to any portion of the day's time for themselves, parenthood on the part of bond-laborers entailed direct and indirect deductions from capitalist revenues, for child-bearing and child-rearing, costs that the employers regarded as economically unjustifiable. The employing class, as a matter of sound business practice, outlawed family life among limited-term bond-laborers.[76] They were forbidden to marry without the express permission of their owners,[77] since, consistent with the principle of coverture, a woman was subject only to the husband.[78] Still, bond-laborers were granted no exemption from the laws against fornication.[79] While nominally laws against "bastardy" made human reproduction outside of legal wedlock a crime for free women, for them – in contrast to bond-laborers – marriage was an automatic defense against that charge;[80] "fornication" and "adulterie" were punishable by a fine for those who could pay it, or whipping or two or three months' imprisonment.[81]

In providing penalties for bond-laborers who violated the law in these respects, the bourgeoisie was typically underscoring its concern for the maintenance of social mores conforming to its own particular class character. But the peculiar nature of the chattel bondage form of labor relations permitted the plantation bourgeoisie to turn that concern to cash account in very specific and immediate ways, ways not available to employers in England.

When, in 1643, Virginia bond-laborers were first forbidden by law to marry, it was provided that the offending wife's term of servitude should be extended to double the time for which she was bound. The husband's term was to be prolonged only twelve months,[82] it being assumed that the anticipated distractions of child care would divert a minimum of his time from serving his employer. The makers of this law, however, did not find it necessary to mitigate the woman's punishment in cases where no child was born during her period of servitude. Twenty years later, the woman's legal punishment was made the same as the man's, one year of extended servitude just for marriage, childbirth and child-rearing penalties being separately provided.[83] At the same time, it was made a crime for a minister to perform the marriage of a bond-laborer without the owner's prior approval. Violators were subject to a fine of ten thousand pounds of tobacco, the equivalent of about five months of a minister's salary.[84] An important consequence of this new feature of the law was to make children of such marriages "illegitimate," as they would have been if no marriage had taken place.[85] Under the Virginia law of 1662, a free man marrying a woman bond-laborer without her owner's permission was obliged to pay a fine of 1,500 pounds of tobacco, or to serve as a bond-laborer for one year to the woman's owner.[86]

Under English law, fornication was punishable, certainly in the most commonly prosecuted cases, those in which pregnancy resulted.[87] In the plantation colonies, early laws were enacted to the same purpose, providing the penalty of a whipping or payment of a fine, as in this 1639 Maryland statute:[88]

> the offender or offenders shall be publicly whipped, or otherwise pay such fines to some publique use as the lieutenant general shall impose.

Free persons were subject to these laws no less than bond-laborers,[89] and "women and men were whipped indiscriminately, women on the bare back apparently as frequently as men."[90] In due course, laws were made that specified the number of lashes to be administered and the amount of the fine. Although the whipping and the fine were equally available forms of punishment under the law, the whipping was actually inflicted only in cases of non-payment of the fine.[91] But limited-term bond-laborers, as proletarians owning nothing of the goods their labor produced, were unable to pay fines. Owners were thus presented with an opportunity, which they routinely exercised, of establishing a claim to additional unpaid labor time by paying the bond-laborer's fine. The usual ratio was six months' extra service for the payment of a fine of five hundred pounds of tobacco.[92]

How "bastardy" laws compounded gender and class oppression

Under the English common law principle of "coverture," the husband was the legal father of children of his wife.[93] Coverture, as already noted, had no application to women bond-laborers, who by law were not allowed to have husbands; their children were by definition "bastards." In England the first specific mention of "illegitimate" children came in 1575–76, and it constituted the basic English "bastardy" law for at least three centuries. It fixed responsibility upon the parents for reimbursing the parish for the charges of keeping the child, by weekly or other periodic payments, on pain of being sent to jail for default.[94]

In the Anglo-American colonies, however, the employers were made direct beneficiaries of the "bastardy" laws as they applied to bond-laborers, with the labor of the mother accounting for the major share of those benefits. In both Virginia and Maryland in the middle of the seventeenth century, the mother was subject to extended servitude for the owner's "loss of service" on account of the distractions resulting from child-bearing and child-rearing. In 1662 the Virginia Assembly fixed the added period of unpaid labor at two years.[95] The Maryland Assembly enacted a similar law in the same year.[96] In addition to the obligation for "lost time," the mother was subject to be publicly whipped on her bare back. The Virginia statute of 1662 specified that the lashing continue only until the blood flowed,[97] but a Maryland court in 1658 called for it to be continued until the count reached thirty.[98]

If the owner felt it was not to his advantage to risk the incapacitation of his bond-laborer that might result from such punishment, he would typically pay the fine.[99] An equally, or even more, compelling motive to this humanitarian gesture was the reward it brought to the owner, as it did for example to the owner of Katherine Higgins, whose case was typical of hundreds. On 26 January 1685, Higgins was found guilty of having become a mother, and was sentenced to an added two and a half years of servitude to her owner, half a year for the fine that her owner paid to save her from whipping, and two years for his trouble and expense in saving the parish any expense for care of the newborn child.[100] Employers were thus able to turn an anticipated "loss of services" into a net profit.[101]

Examination of surviving seventeenth-century Virginia county court records[102] reveals some three hundred cases of such "bastardy" judgments against limited-term women bond-laborers. At a rate of 1,500 pounds of tobacco per year per worker, such of these women as worked in the field during their added 30 months' servitude would have produced tobacco worth more than three times the cost of their transportation to the colony,[103] that cost being the supposed debt for which they were relegated to a social status wherein they were denied the right to marry.[104]

Occasionally an employer was also able to gain some extra labor time from the father. If, as happened in a small number of cases, the identity of the father was established, he would be obliged to provide security to save the parish harmless, that is, to provide a guarantee that the cost of support of the infant would be repaid to the parish. If the father were a bond-laborer, the church wardens took charge of the child, paying the charges of the child's upkeep until it became of working age, or selling the child to a private individual as a bond-laborer-to-be. At the completion of the father's original term of servitude, he was obligated to make recompense for any charges outstanding for the cost of the child's early care. If he could not pay, he could be taken up by the sheriff to satisfy the debt by a period of bond-servitude.[105] But, unlike the mother, the father could not be made to serve extra time for the "loss of services" directly due to the pregnancy.

In a certain number of cases the owner himself was the father, suggesting the grossest form of sexual exploitation. The notorious Henry Smith of Accomack County fathered children by two of his bond-laborers in the late 1660s. Not long before November 1699, John Waugh of Stafford County sold Catherine Hambleton away across Chesapeake Bay, pregnant with his own child. The same sort of sale of his own progeny had been made by Nicholas Chapman of Norfolk County, in or shortly before 1677.[106] But unproven accusations were severely penalized. When, in March 1650, a "search of her body" led the court to disbelieve Sara Reinold's accusation that her owner had made her pregnant, she was sentenced to "thirty-five Lashes on the bare back."[107]

In Maryland, Lucy Stratton, bond-laborer, was brought before the Charles County, Maryland, Court in November 1671, charged with having borne a child. Stratton said that her owner was the father, but the court credited the denial of the owner, a wealthy planter named Turner. On the grounds of having made a false accusation against her owner, the woman was sentenced to and received thirty lashes at the public whipping post. But Turner was indeed the father, as he admitted shortly thereafter in offering to "make satisfaction by marrying" Stratton. Although it might mean an extended term of servitude to refuse, Stratton spurned the blessings of such a "coverture," calling her owner a "lustful man" whom she "could not love ... much less make him her husband," adding that she "had suffered enough by him."[108] The Charles County, Maryland, Court, upon her petition, ordered Turner either to pay child maintenance or to take the child and raise it as his own. But on appeal to a higher court, Stratton's suit against Turner for support for the child was denied because she had refused the marriage offer.[109]

The social conscience of the plantation bourgeoisie – that is to say, the sense of the general interests of the ruling class as a whole – did exert some influence, even if it might possibly run counter to the desires and interests of some individual planters.[110] The supply of laborers was not so plentiful in the seventeenth-century plantation colonies, nor the number of women so great, nor social control so secure, that men of the owning classes could be allowed unrestricted indulgence of their sexual appetites at the expense of women bond-laborers, even if these owners might thereby gain a bonus of unpaid labor as a result. In their respective sixth decades, therefore, Virginia and Maryland adopted laws attempting to serve the general interests of the owning class, while safeguarding the individual owner against deprivation of his rights. In Virginia a woman in such a case was, by a law of 1662, obliged to complete her term of servitude, thus protecting the owner's right-by-purchase. On the other hand, it was provided that the owner should not have the benefit of the extra servitude which was to be imposed on the bond-laborer for her misconduct. Still, the lawmakers felt, it would be courting trouble to excuse the woman from punishment, as that might tempt others in a similar condition to make false allegations of paternity against their masters as a means of escaping their due in legal penalties. The Assembly found justice in a middle course by providing that upon completion of the mother's original term, she should be taken to the church wardens and sold to some new owner for a term of servitude. The purchase price went to the parish revenues, minus the costs of food and clothing for the child until the child was old enough to become a net producer for a private employer.[111]

In the context of these arrangements, occasional losses had to be accepted as a normal, indeed essential, part of the process as illuminators of possible operational limits of the system. Such appears to have been the case of Isabella Yansley, of Ann Arundell County, Maryland.[112] On 3 March 1671, as it was later charged, Yansley hid herself away, "without the company of any other women," gave birth to a boy, and caused him to die. The Provincial Court found her guilty of murder, and by its sentence she was hanged on 17 April. In England a woman facing motherhood unwed might have resorted to the same desperate course, and suffered the same fate for it. But, in a tobacco colony, where the child of a bond-laborer was to be a bond-laborer of the mother's owner until the child was over twenty years of age, such an outcome represented a loss of investment and possible future profit, negating the benefit of the special "fornication" and "illegitimacy" laws applied against bond-laborers.

The procedure for disposing of the potential and actual labor-power of the children of bond-servants in Anglo-America closely followed the pattern that had been established for dealing with indigent children in Tudor England. That system evolved under a series of laws beginning in 1536 and culminating in the fundamental English Poor Law of 1601.[113] First among the stated purposes of the 1601 law was that of "setting to work the children . . . whose parents shall not be thought able to keep and maintain them."[114] In seventeenth-century Virginia and Maryland, under-age Europeans arriving without indentures were bound to serve according to the law. In 1666 in Virginia if they were under nineteen years of age, they were to serve until they were twenty-four. The Maryland law made a more particular differentiation of age levels, but merely to assure that children would serve at least seven years; those arriving at age twenty-two years old or older were bound for five years.[115]

But the peculiar character of the bond-labor relation of production gave these laws a greater practical scope than laws regarding "indigent" children in England. Since bond-laborers were by definition propertyless and unpaid, as parents they were, under 1666 laws, obliged to serve added time as recompense to the owner or the parish for the cost of maintenance of the child.[116] While the labor of indigent children was programmed for exploitation in both England and in the colonies, the profit to be gained therefrom by the exploiters was of relatively greater importance in the labor-scarce Chesapeake than in England. Perhaps it is significant that in 1632, when the per capita production of tobacco was some 700 pounds per year, two women bond-laborers who became pregnant on the voyage to Virginia were forthwith shipped back again;[117] but four decades later, by which time the output per worker had more than doubled,[118] the arrival of a woman in this predicament was more likely to be regarded as an opportunity to profit not only from the extension of the women's servitude, but also from the option on the labor of her child under the provisions of the 1662 law against "fornication."[119]

Nevertheless, despite the various expedients adopted for recapturing the owner's or the parish's expenses for support of the children of limited-term bond-laborers, those measures provided a relatively unprofitable way of recruiting plantation labor power in the seventeenth-century tobacco colonies.[120] The prospective period of unpaid bond-servitude to be had from such children, whether by their original owners or by other persons to whom they were assigned, was limited. The child might not survive until he reached the workable (tithable) age of sixteen.[121] The bond-laborer father, once his term was completed, could take possession of the child, making settlement with the parish or the owner for the care and maintenance of the child up until that time.[122] "Bastards" who remained with the mother's owner were bound to serve only until they were twenty-one if boys, or eighteen if girls. Bastards of European-American parents were bound out by their parents to other men, but they became free at the age of twenty-four if boys, at eighteen, if girls.[123]

If, however, the period of bastards' unpaid servitude could be increased sufficiently, the mating of bond-laborers might be made into a paying proposition for the owners. That was the principle behind the persistent pressure from the side of the plantation bourgeoisie to impose lifetime hereditary bondage on African-Americans. In 1662, the Virginia Assembly discarded English common law of descent through the father, and instituted the principle of *partus sequitur ventrem*, whereunder the child was declared "bond or free according to the condition of the mother."[124] That law was specifically aimed at giving the plantation bourgeoisie a predefined supply of self-perpetuating unpaid labor. Once the owners had this advantage, the courts no longer concerned themselves with prosecuting African-American bond-laborers for "fornication" or "bastardy." Supplementary sources of unpaid labor were tapped under a Virginia law passed in 1681, requiring a child of a European-American mother and an African-American father to serve until the age of thirty.[125] That was six years of extra unpaid labor beyond what would have been served by a child of two European-American bond-laborers. That extra labor should have yielded the owner 9,000 pounds of tobacco, more than enough to buy another limited-term bond-laborer.

Under a Maryland law in effect from 1664 to 1692, any "freeborne" woman who married an African-American lifetime bond-laborer was bound to serve "the master of such slave during the life or her husband." Presented with such an opportunity, many Maryland owners deliberately fostered marriages of European-American women and African-American men bond-laborers in order to get the benefit of the added unpaid labor time of their descendants.[126] The ruling class understood that the bond-laborers' sex drives were "as irresistible and ardent as those of others ... [and therefore t]here is no danger that the considering of their progeny's condition will stop propagation."[127]

In 1692, the Maryland penalty was modified to seven years' bond servitude. If the woman were a bond-laborer, the added seven years were to begin only after the completion of her original term.[128] The penalty for "fornication" and "bastardy" was especially severe (a double fine in Virginia in 1662) when an African-American/European-American couple was involved.[129] When the double penalty of the 1662 law proved generally ineffective, the Virginia Assembly in 1691 passed another, making any English woman in this circumstance, free or bond, subject to public sale by the churchwardens of the parish into bond-servitude for five years. For those who were bond-laborers, this added servitude was to be postponed until the completion of her current period of bondage.[130]

Why? That was the question implicit in the petition of European-American lifetime bond-laborer Mary Peters, who petitioned for manumission having already served eight years beyond the time she should otherwise have served if she had not "been drawn by her master and mistress into marrying a negro, and so being reckoned a slave."[131] Why, wondered Ann Wall, a free European-American woman who had borne two children of an African-American father, when she was sentenced by the Elizabeth County Court to five years' bond-servitude under "Mr Peter Hobson or his assigns" in Norfolk County, and forbidden ever to return to Elizabeth City County on pain of banishment to Barbados.[132] It was a matter that European-American bond-laborer Jane Salman could not understand; she fled from the jurisdiction of the Accomack County Court that had ordered her to be taken for sale by the church warden to another seven-year term of servitude.[133]

Why, indeed? An attempt will be made in Chapter 13 to suggest an answer to that question.

Exploiting the presumption of bondage

Enterprising employers frequently found it possible to retain laborers in bondage even though by law they were entitled to be free. As far as propertyless persons were concerned the presumption was bondage, as evidenced by the enactment of pass laws, in Virginia in 1643 and in 1663, and in Maryland in 1671.[134] In general, these laws made a laboring person subject to arrest as a fugitive, unless he or she had a pass signed by an owner or other officially designated authority.

Thus a laborer who had completed the full period of servitude still bore the burden of proof of his or her liberty. Without a certificate of freedom issued by the county court, the time-expired laborer was subject to arrest as a fugitive, and thereafter to additional servitude under laws provided in such cases. In order to secure the certificate of freedom, the laborer had to appear before the county court with the owner, or with a written deposition supplied by the owner, to establish the fact of the completion of the term of servitude.[135] If, instead of cooperating, the employer chose to attempt to keep the laborer in bondage, the laborer might well face a daunting prospect.[136] Aside from the many difficulties the laborer confronted in getting a petition for freedom before the court, there were commonly other problems. The bond-laborer who had come to Virginia or Maryland with a formal indenture obligating him or her to serve for a time less than that provided under the "custom of the country" had to produce in court the original paper to prove his or her case. To preserve such a document against destruction, loss or theft through several years of bond-labor was not always easy.[137] Yet without it the laborer would have to remain in bondage according to the "custom of the country." William Rogers came to Virginia under a three-year indenture to Anthony Gosse, who sold Rogers to John Stith, transmitting his half of the indenture paper to Stith. Stith, learning that Rogers had somehow left his half of the indenture contract in England, destroyed the paper Gosse had given him, and claimed Rogers for five years according to the custom of the country.[138]

The ordinary custom-of-the-country bond-laborers would perhaps be even more vulnerable to employers' attempts to extend their servitude beyond the legal limit.[139] If the laborer sought redress from the court, pending the court's decision he or she would remain under the absolute power of the owner, on a plantation from which it was a crime to depart without the owner's permission, a plantation moreover equipped with a whipping post or the equivalent for the administration of "moderate correction" by the master or his agent.[140] The owner thus had strong forces of persuasion at his disposal for inducing the bond-laborer to submit to an extension of unpaid servitude. The employer's chances of gains of this sort were perhaps enhanced where the bond-laborer had been sold from one employer to another, if the frequency of such cases in the court records is any indication.[141] Even if, as in the cases to be cited, the employer were not fully successful, he lost little by trying; he even stood to gain incidental benefits.

The Joseph Griphen and Daniel Ralston cases illustrate the denial of their right to a presumption of liberty in Maryland. In 1659, Joseph Griphen was bought by two Maryland merchants who shortly thereafter sold him to John Hatch. In November 1666, at the end of seven years of servitude, Griphen asserted his freedom by rowing downriver in a canoe. Hatch had him hunted by hue and cry, and brought back, alleging that Griphen had been bought for ten years, not seven.[142] Daniel Ralston came to Maryland in 1663 with a written indenture according to which he was bound for four years, at the end of which time he was to receive £10 sterling, plus a good suit and other clothes, and two hoes and an axe. Three years had passed when he ran away from his owner, Henry Robertson. After several weeks Ralston was recaptured and returned to his owner, and then he was sold again to another owner, David Johnson. After Ralston's indentured term was ended in July 1667, his new owner claimed added service at the rate of ten-to-one for every day that Ralston had run away from his former owner. Since Ralston took action in court before his new owner did, the owner's claim was not allowed, although the principle of the assignability of penalty time was not questioned. Though the decision of the jury favored the bond-laborer's claim, the owner was allowed to keep Ralston in servitude pending disposition of the appeal to the Provinical Court, and the freedom dues allowance was reduced to either £10 or the goods but not both, contrary to the terms of the original indenture.[143] In June 1678, John Hickes[?], identified in the record as a "Dutchman," was taken up as a runaway bond-laborer. Even though there was no "positive proof" of the charge, the court in the Virginia Eastern Shore county of Northampton ordered him to "goe along with Capt. Foxcroft" for thirty days while the court sent for information across the bay regarding Hickes's status. If during that time the man "absent[ed] himselfe" from Foxcroft, he was to be hunted "by Hue and Cry as a Runaway Servant."[144]

The removal of the owner from the scene might complicate the laborer's bondage predicament, as it did in the case that came before the Virginia Colony Council in 1675 on the petition of Phillip Corven, an African-American.[145] Originally, Corven had been an under-age bond-laborer of widow Annie Beazeley of James City County. When Mrs Beazeley died in 1664, she left a will assigning Corven to her cousin, Humphrey Stafford, for a term of eight years, until 1672, at which time Corven "should enjoy his freedom & be paid three barrels of corn and as sute of clothes." Long before that day could dawn, however, Stafford had sold Corven's time to Charles Lucas of Warwick County. In his petition for freedom, Corven charged that he had been forced to accompany Lucas to the Warwick County court and there to acknowledge a formal "agreement" to remain a bond-laborer to Lucas, his heirs and assigns for twenty years. Three years of this extra bond-servitude – beyond the original eight years – were actually secured by Lucas in this way before Corven brought his petition before the Colony Council. Corven's petition asked for his freedom dues, and for compensation for the previous three years of unpaid labor. The record of the final disposition of the case has not been preserved. But even if Lucas lost on every point, he would still have been the gainer in all probability, despite the very low price of tobacco in those years, if, as seems likely, Corven was employed in tobacco and producing over 1,500 pounds of it per year; also to be taken into account is the interest gained by Lucas by the delay of any freedom dues.

It was no more than a normal risk of doing business that such aggressive methods should occasionally miscarry, as in the case of William Whittacre.[146] Whittacre bought an African-American bond-laborer named Manuel from Thomas Bushrod, who himself had previously purchased the laborer from Colonel William Smith. Somewhere along the line, whether by self or others deceived, Whittacre came to believe that Manuel was a lifetime bond-laborer. Thus believing, Whittacre paid £25 for the worker, twice what he would have paid for a male limited-term bond-laborer. To Whittacre's utter dismay, the Virginia Assembly subsequently adjudged Manuel to be "no slave but to serve as other Christian servants do," and he was freed in September 1665. Whittacre maintained his innocence in the affair and asked to be exempted from taxation to compensate him for his loss. But the Assembly, "not knowing any reason why the Public should be answerable for the inadvertency of the Buyer for a Judgment given when justly grounded as that Order was," rejected Whittacre's petition.

Cutting labor costs when no wages were paid

Although the employers of bond-laborers could not hope to increase profits by reducing wages, they did have labor costs that they were always eager to reduce – the cost of acquisition of the laborer (the purchase price); the cost of maintenance during the period of servitude; and, finally, the cost of the freedom dues to be paid to workers who survived to the end of their terms. The first of these aspects, reduction of acquisition costs, has been discussed. The owners were just as diligent in their efforts to reduce the costs of maintenance and freedom dues.

In the seventeenth-century Chesapeake colonies no law was ever enacted to provide a minimum level of food, clothing, drink, bedding, housing, or other necessities.[147] The burden of legal remedy was entirely on the laborer. She or he had to find the courage and means to present a magistrate (who himself was certain to be an owner of bond-laborers) with a bill of particulars against her or his own master, citing evidence of insufficient diet, clothing, or shelter. Ordinarily, the worst that the owner might have to expect from such a proceeding was to be ordered to provide "sufficiently" for the laborer in the future. There was also the chance that the laborer might be sentenced to a lashing at the whipping post if the complaint were judged lacking in merit, as happened to William Evans for "saying that Mrs Stone starved her servants to death," and to Thomas Barnes who was judged to have "complained cause-lessly against his Master Mihill Ricketts."[148] From the standpoint of the employers, this manner of dealing with the question of the maintenance of laborers was preferable to any arrangement involving statutory "mandated expenditures" by legislation.

As for the day-to-day *costs* of maintenance of their workers, the employers of bond-labor were able to reduce that factor to zero. The cost of clothing and housing the bond-laborers was more than compensated by the accumulation of interest on the freedom dues, or even the avoidance of the payment of this terminal allowance in an assured percentage of cases.[149] But the most attractive part of the labor maintenance picture, as viewed by the employer, was the fact that the workers produced their own food. Of course, a portion of the laborers' time had to be given to the work, but that could not be considered a loss of labor, any more than waiting for a wet day to replant seedlings or for stripping the stalks could be considered a loss of tobacco. They were all necessary natural processes occurring in the cycle of reproduction and expansion of the owner's capital.

It was in the owner's interest, however, to reduce such "waiting time," and the expenses and risks incidental to it. This was done by forcing the laborers to subsist on Indian corn, even though the laborers desired the regular inclusion of meat and milk products in their diet.[150] The corn diet was cheaper. The same basic labor-training and the same hand implements were usable in cultivating corn as in cultivating tobacco. Corn was relatively easily stored, and it could be prepared and eaten in several forms.[151] The labor of producing and processing corn was easier to supervise than, for instance, that of rounding up cattle and hogs in the woods and thickets where they ranged, free as the bond-laborer wished to be. Finally, corn was not then a profitable export crop, whilst Virginia meats became increasingly so.[152] In England the prices of consumables rose generally throughout the seventeenth century;[153] but from the 1640s onward, food products in Virginia steadily declined in price.[154] As a result Virginia's exporters were able to secure a part of the trade to the sugar colonies in the West Indies. As early as 1657, oxen worth only £5 in Virginia were being exported to Barbados at a price of £25.[155] For all these reasons, the owners in the tobacco colonies found it sound business practice to feed their bond-laborers on corn, and correspondingly to reduce the amount of meat in the workers' diet.[156] By 1676, it was officially reported that in Virginia "the ordinary sort of people" had beef to eat only in the summer, and then only once or twice a week; in the winter they received "only the corn of the country, beat in a mortar and boiled ... [and] the bread [that] is made of the same corne, but with difficulty by reason of the scarcity of mills."[157] In 1679, two Dutch travelers in the northern Chesapeake tobacco country observed that "for their usual food, the servants have nothing but maize bread to eat and water to drink."[158]

Under normal capitalist conditions the employer makes payments to the employee daily, weekly, or semi-monthly. Under the system of limited-term bond-servitude, the only payment the employer was expected (it was not required by statute) to make to the laborer was in the form of the freedom dues paid upon satisfactory completion of the term of servitude, which usually lasted five years. This gave the employer of bond-labor a special advantage over the employer of wage labor. First, the wage-laborer has to advance his/ her labor to the capitalist on credit, so to speak, for only a day, or at most a couple of weeks. But the bond-laborer was compelled to advance his/her labor to the capitalist for five years. The employer of wage labor has to pay out wages six or eight times before he gets his money (plus profit) back from the sale of the laborer's product. The employer of the limited-term bond-laborer, by contrast, was able to turn over his capital five times before the first penny of freedom dues had to be paid out. The original price paid to purchase the laborer was probably less than £12.[159] By the end of five years the bond-laborer could be expected to have brought the employer an income of nearly £40,[160] while the interest on the deferred freedom dues payment would cover the freedom dues cost, worth no more than £6.

Even at the minimum rate of a five-year return of £40 on the worker's labor, the owner would have recouped his purchase price perhaps within a year and a half. Since the £6 cost of freedom dues was equivalent to the product of about nine months' bond-labor, the last nine months of a bond-laborer's scheduled term might be one of diminishing returns for the employer. Ordinarily the owners were most vigilant to frustrate runaway attempts by their bond-laborers, but in this critical nine-month period it might actually be to the employer's advantage if the bond-laborer ran away, or died, since in such cases no freedom dues would have to be paid. At that point, masters possessing initiative and drive might seek to manage matters to that end, in a sort of timely "downsizing," as it might be called today. This practice was noted in the report submitted by George Larkin to the home government in 1701:

> When their time expired, according to custom they [the bond-laborers] are to have a certain allowance of corn and clothes, which in Maryland I think is to the value of £6, but in Virginia not so much, to save which a Planter about three months before the expiration of a servant's time will use him barbarously, and to gain a month's freedom the poor servant gladly quits his pretensions to that allowance.[161]

There is a normal rate of labor that can be continued by the laborer on a regular schedule without shortening his or her life span to less than what could be expected by an economically secure person in a non-competitive situation.

However, historical experience has shown that capitalist employers tend not to be satisfied by such a performance rate on the part of their workers. The wage-labor relation is specially adaptable to the needs of capital because it links wages to production; and it induces competition among the workers in performance of their tasks. To the extent that improved instruments of production are introduced into the labor process, the intensity of labor is more imposed than elicited because the rate of operations is removed from the workers' control. Under the bond-labor system, however, where the normal incentives to competition among workers was lacking, and where the implements of labor were limited to the human hand and the tools it held, the employers necessarily relied solely on close and constant supervision to secure higher labor productivity.[162] That was so whatever the crop, but such supervision was especially critical in making tobacco. Due to "the complete absence of machine processes, in the transplanting, topping, cutting, curing and sorting [of tobacco] . . . care must be supplied by detailed oversight," wrote Ulrich B. Phillips.[163] Joseph Clarke Robert, in his history of the North American tobacco industry, notes that "The best quality of tobacco was the fruit of only the most diligent supervision. To send to market a profitable 'parcel' required a sober crop master who kept a critical eye on the usual laborer."[164] In addressing his own question, "Why did productivity per worker increase?," Russell Menard concludes from his study of the colonial records that "the weight of the evidence suggests that the increased yield per worker was entirely due to the rise in the number of plants one man could handle."[165] George Fitzhugh was merely recording a bit of ancient bourgeois wisdom in noting that tobacco's profitability depended on the maintenance of a high ratio of supervisory force to laborers employed. "Six hands often make double as much money at tobacco as at cotton or sugar," he wrote, "but a crop of tobacco that employes sixty hands, always brings the farmer in debt."[166]

The monocultural economy added further importance to intense supervision. There was only one money, and its name was tobacco – the sole measure of value, standard of price, medium of exchange, and basis of credit. The one customary money function that tobacco, in consequence of its perishability, was unable to perform, was to serve as a means of hoarding.[167] Bruce cites a letter of William Fitzhugh, written in June 1690, complaining "that he had a large number of hogsheads [of tobacco] which it was impossible for him to export in consequence of the scarcity of shipping, their contents undergoing great damage by the delay, and in some cases falling into ruin."[168]

Although the bond-labor system held no positive incentives for increased effort on the part of the workers, it was peculiarly suitable for exerting "negative incentives." For a failure to perform satisfactorily, the laborer faced the threat of corporal punishment by the owner. To resist "correction" or to flee and be caught might entail even more severe treatment. While the bond-labor form inhibited the development of improved instruments of labor, still, the employer had at his disposal the entire twenty-four hours of the laborer's day, except on Sunday. The owner's power in the exercise of this authority was reinforced by the fact that he was not only the employer but also the laborer's landlord and victualer.

The laborers' "victuals" consisted mainly of hominy, which was prepared in a very laborious way. Shelled corn was placed in a mortar formed by hollowing out the end of a hardwood log cut to a suitable length. Then a laborer wielded a sizable stick, formed as a pestle, to pound the grains into hominy. The pestle might be attached to a low-hanging flexible tree branch by a cord, to even out the stress of the upward and downward motions of the pounder's arm. The pounded corn was then sometimes sifted through a cloth to free it of the inedible husks.[169] This was the one major aspect of plantation labor that perhaps presented the laborers with a positive incentive to produce, for whatever their corn allowance they were able to consume it only if the heavy chore of "pounding at the mortar" were regularly done. Having this incentive at his disposal, the owner of the bond-laborers found it the part of efficient management to reserve this task for the periphery of the work schedule, assigning it as a task to be performed after the day's work in the field or woods was done, or perhaps on Sunday, nominally the laborers' day of rest.

The owners' brutal pursuit of higher output per worker

Evidence of the earnestness with which the employers were able to press their advantage in order to raise output per worker is found throughout the colonial records. Frequently cited instances have by repetition come to constitute a body of esoteric lore among students of this aspect of American history.

Spurred on by the all-or-nothing nature of a monocultural economy, and subject to the vagaries of a generally glutted market, Virginia employers pushed matters to the limit to secure the highest possible return on their investment in laborers.[170] According to a mid-seventeenth-century account:

> the months of June, July, and August, being the very height of the Summer, the poore Servant goes daily through the rowes of Tobacco to worm it, and being over-heated, he is struck with a Calenture or Fever and so perisheth.[171]

Henry Smith of Accomack County Virginia strove to get the maximum effort from his bond-laborers; he tasked his workers heavily and punished them brutally for deficiencies in their performance. He was not disposed to make any allowances just because a worker was a woman fed on a meatless diet. Some of Smith's strongest men had weeded as many as three hundred and fifty cornhills in a day. Jane (at first mention the name is "Annie") Powell had been worked in the snow barefoot, and had got by on hominy and salt ever since coming to Virginia. But Henry Smith, perfectionist that he was, could not be moved by such considerations; one day in 1668, when Powell had weeded three hundred cornhills, Smith beat her severely with his whip fashioned from a bull's penis ("pizzle"), for the deficiency of her work performance.[172]

Increased labor intensity required greater time for rest if the laborer's physical condition were not to deteriorate. But nothing was to be permitted to interfere with the timely completion of the annual tobacco crop. According to the record, the owners often found it a profitable option to work their bond-laborers during time supposedly allowed for rest, even at the risk of some attrition of the labor force. Dankers and Sluyter, whose report on their visit to the northern Chesapeake in 1678–80 has been mentioned, found that the bond-laborers, though poorly maintained, were "compelled to work hard" with too little rest. Both African and European laborers, they wrote,

> after they have worn themselves down the whole day, and gone home to rest, have yet to grind the grain ... For their masters and all their families as well as themselves.[173]

When in 1657 bond-laborer William Ireland sought relief from being required to beat at the mortar at night after working all day in the field for his owner Captain Philip Morgan, the Maryland Provincial Court sided with the owner, although it said that such extra duty should be exacted only "at a Seasonable time in the yeare or in the case of Necessity."[174] The interpretation of these limitations, for practical purposes, was left to the owner. But when it was a matter of limiting bond-laborers' resting time, the law was specific. Despite the inclination of kind-hearted masters and English rural custom the government twenty years earlier had resolved that, "touching the resting of servants on Satturdaies in the afternoon . . . no such custom [is] to be allowed."[175]

Some employers had strong reservations as well about the value of "resting servants," even on Sundays, seeming to think that it was necessary and proper to keep the Sabbath day wholly occupied with bond-labor tasks. Such was the recollection of one disgruntled and literate former employee:

> We and the negroes both alike did fare,
> Of work and food we had an equal share;
> But in a piece of ground we called our own,
> The food we eat first by ourselves were sown.
> No other time to us they would allow,
> But on a Sunday we the same must do:
> Six days we slave for our master's good,
> The seventh day is to produce our food.[176]

The trials to which an employer might be put in attempting to raise per capita production may be seen in the case of John Little of Maryland. In the spring of 1657, no doubt a "Seasonable time" full of "necessity," Little commanded one of his bond-laborers, Henry Billsberry, to pound at the mortar on a Sunday. In close company with an Indian comrade, Billsberry fled out of bondage to Indian country. Possibly the youthful laborers were reacting to what they may have regarded as a compounding of injustice and hypocrisy by their owner. For, when sent for in their refuge, they returned reply that "they had rather live with the Pagans."[177]

Illness among bond-laborers was a frequent problem for employers in their constant pursuit of higher output per laborer. Besides the production loss, the cost of medical treatment for the laborer was likely to be too high, at least so high that, according to Bruce, "masters were tempted to suffer a servant to perish for want of proper advice and medicines rather than to submit to their [the physicians'] exactions."[178] Owners might be reluctant to excuse laborers from work on account of illness, as a former bond-laborer recalled:

> At length, it pleased God I sick did fall
> But I no favor could receive at all,
> For I was forced to work while I could stand,
> Or hold the hoe within my feeble hands.[179]

The temptation of masters to which Bruce referred was hard to resist, judging from the high death rate among bond-laborers in the Chesapeake in the seventeenth century.[180] One Maryland employer surrendered to it with such flawless ledger logic that diarists made special mention of it:

> a master having a sick servant ... and observing from his declining condition, he would finally die, and that there was no probability of his enjoying any more service from him, made him, sick and languishing as he was, dig his own grave, in which he was laid a few days afterwards, the others being too busy to dig it, having their hands full attending to the tobacco.[181]

It must be kept in mind that practically all the cases of physical abuse of bond-laborers by their owners are known to us only because the laborer risked bringing the matter to a magistrate, who as we have noted himself was necessarily an owner of many acres and numbers of bond-laborers. Benedict Talbot and William Walworth charged in court that their owner, Captain Hillary Stringer, had "occasioned the death" of their fellow bond-laborer Ellinor Conner. The Accomack County court finding the petition to be worse than groundless, a malicious concoction, ordered Talbot and Walworth to make satisfaction to their owner (presumably by added time of servitude) for all the expenses to which he had been put as a result of their accusation.[182] There were instances of courts ordering that a bond-laborer be sold away from an abusive master. But even on those extremely rare occasions, the owners were not penalized other than by being fined a relatively small amount of tobacco.[183]

There is no way of knowing how many bond-laborers died as a result of starvation, or overwork, or by physical abuse by their owners or on their owners' orders in seventeenth-century Virginia and Maryland. Morris catalogued descriptively half a dozen murders of bond-laborers by their owners.[184] The law passed by the Virginia Assembly in 1662 forbidding secret burials is clear evidence that such occurrences, glossed with suspect allegations of soul-damning "suicide," or other variations of blaming the victim, were of such frequency that they might interfere with the general overriding interest in maintaining the labor supply from the mother country. The law remarked that

[T]he private burial of servants & others give[s] occasion of much scandall against diverse persons, and sometimes not undeservedly so ... [and] servants are fearful to make discovery if murther were committed ... [all ending in] that barbarous custom of exposing the corps of the dead (by makeing their graves in comon and unfenced places) to the prey of hoggs and other vermine.[185]

Occasionally an owner's zeal for increased productivity verged on counter-productive pathology.[186] In Northampton County, Virginia, in the summer of 1640, Thomas Wood was whipped by two men with rope ends for objecting to being forced to beat at the mortar, an onerous chore from which he claimed his indenture exempted him. The next day he was found dead.[187] Early summer "was not the time of yeare for to be sick," said John Mutton to his bond-laborer Francis Burton, a "seasoned hand" who was complaining of a headache. Accusing Burton of "dissembling," Mutton struck and kicked Burton, who died within a few hours.[188]

In May 1657, John Dandy, a large planter, a smith, and owner of a water mill in Maryland, fractured the skull of his young lame bond-laborer Henry Gouge with an axe for reasons not given in the record. Gouge survived, although the wound did not heal. Dandy angrily rejected his wife's suggestion that he "look after" the matter. One day two months later, Dandy went to check on Gouge's performance of a task he had been assigned, and was disappointed at how little Gouge had accomplished. Fellow laborers nearby then heard Gouge cry out in pain as if he were being beaten. He was never seen alive again, but his body was recovered from Cole Kill a month later. Though Dandy denied guilt, the history of the life-threatening abuse he had dealt to Gouge, the two auditory witnesses, the record of his death sentence for killing a young Indian bond-laborer some ten years before (which had been commuted to seven years' service as the executioner of all corporal correction sentences handed down by the provincial courts), his attempt to flee to Virginia because he said Maryland authorities had treated him severely in the past, but above all the accusing blood from the corpse when he touched it – doomed him. He was convicted of murder and hanged.[189]

Late in August 1664, Ann Arundel County, Maryland, employer Joseph Fincher sought to secure a higher per capita output by increasing the size of the load of tobacco plants to be carried by a bond-laborer. When one of the bearers, Joseph Haggman, protested that the load was too great, Fincher tried to encourage him by threatening him with a beating worse than ever a dog was given. Haggman took up the burden, but he staggered under the weight of it. Fincher, apparently provoked beyond endurance, reacted by striking and kicking Haggman, perhaps by way of making an example of him for the edification of other bond-laborers. As it happened, Haggman died of this treatment. Fincher was found guilty of murder on 22 December 1664 and hanged for it.[190]

On 20 January 1665/6 Francis Carpenter, finding his bond-laborer Samuell Yeoungman to be dilatory about fetching firewood, broke a stick over the back of the worker's head as he bent to his task. Unable to recover,

Yeoungman died three weeks later. At trial, the jury found Carpenter guilty of manslaughter but granted him benefit of clergy.[191]

Henry Smith, whose brutality has already been noted, treated all his many bond-laborers with severity, but especially so John Butt, sixty years old and feeble. "Ould John," as Butt was known to all, could never seem to do his work to Smith's satisfaction, nor was he constituted to withstand the beatings that Smith regularly used in order to urge his workers on, even as he was starving them for food. Butt's condition steadily deteriorated, but he was forced to work, eventually in chains. Still somehow his performance could never come up to Smith's standard, and Smith would accuse Butt of shirking and call him a "dissembling rogue." As fellow bond-laborers testified, Smith "would very often Grievously beat the aforesaid Ould John with a Bulls pizzle because he being aged was unable to work." Finally bone weary, utterly broken in body and spirit, John Butt was left in isolation in the winter-idle tobacco house. It was then that he told his fellow bond-laborer Richard Chambers that "the blowes given by his master would be his death," and so they were; Butt died, cold and alone, on the floor of the tobacco house on 25 November 1666.[192] In the absence of further record it appears that Smith was never brought to court for this fatal mistreatment of bond-laborer Butt.

February was a time for clearing woodland that would soon be needed for new tobacco ground. Much of the work involved carrying logs. One Wednesday early in February 1681, James Lewis went to extreme lengths to impress upon his bond-laborers his determination to have the maximum individual effort from them. He became angered when certain of his laborers volunteered to help Joseph Robinson to carry a log which was too heavy for him to manage, even though, as was later revealed, he had nourished himself on a bit of meat stolen from the employer's closet. According to testimony presented to the Maryland Provincial Court, Lewis seized the feeble bond-laborer, "threw him down and Trampled Upon his Throat with such Violence that within Two hours the said Joseph dyed." Then Lewis threatened Mary Naines, another bond-laborer, "to serve her the Same and Swore Dam him he cared not a straw" for the consequences. The employer's careless attitude was not disappointed in the event; though eventually convicted of the murder, he was merely to be "burnt in the hand," a penalty that was more often a cold formality than an actual hot-branding of the fleshy base of the thumb.[193]

In a number of other horrifying cases the record does not link the brutality to supervisory concerns. In three cases now to be briefly noted, it seems that perhaps pure sadistic pleasure may have been the basic motive of the perpetrators. In the summer of 1660, bond-laborer Margarett Redfearne died after a severe beating by her mistress, Anne Nevell. Nevell was found "not Guylty" despite testimony of witnesses to the abuse, and Redfearne's deathbed accusation of Nevell.[194] That same year, bond-laborer Catherine Lake fell down and died within an hour of being kicked by her owner, Thomas Mertine (or Martine). After considering the evidence, including the failure of the corpse to exude blood when touched by the accused, in those times regarded as an accusation of the killer, the jury of twelve men exonerated Mertine.[195] The Maryland Provincial Court record of 27 October 1663 provides the graphic details of the merciless beatings administered by Pope Alvey to his bond-laborer Alice Sandford, which resulted in her death. Alvey was convicted of murder, but by pleading "benefit of clergy" he escaped punishment except for the ritualistic cold-iron "burning" of the flesh of his thumb.[196]

Some scholars who have examined the same documents that I have been citing in this chapter justify the chattel bond-labor system – despite occasional abuses by the owners – as a rational and on the whole benign adaptation to the colonial environment.[197] They are naturally appalled and horrified by the record left by Henry Smith, Pope Alvey, Joseph Fincher and their like. But they seem to ignore the essential relationship between the system of chattel bond-servitude and the documented brutality and hardship to which the chattels were subjected, whether in the extreme cases of murder and rape or in the routine cases of illicit extension of servitude and deprivation of food and clothing.

Psychopathic cruelty can be found in every historical era, and in the seventeenth-century Chesapeake court records there are occasional references to the mentally incompetent.[198] But in no case of murder or rape or other unspeakable brutality by owners of bond-laborers was it even suggested that the owner was acting irrationally. If Smith, Fincher, Alvey were psychopaths, which is the most generous allowance that may be made for them, one must ask why that defense was never invoked in such cases. The record does not tell us; perhaps it would have struck too closely to the irrationality of the same system that in England a century before had been rejected because of its "extremity."[199]

For, psychopaths aside, the records show that the employers of bond-labor were no more charitable toward their workers than were the "spirits", trepanners, "soul drivers", and run-of-the-mill merchants and ship captains in the "servant trade." Were not the "planters" driven by the same compulsion of their social character as accumulators of capital?[200] Who, then would be more likely to succeed in the tobacco-raising business: the owner who, whatever the climate, made lighter demands upon the "unadaptable" laborer, or the master who made heavier demands? And who could have been more vulnerable to those demands than the chattel bond-laborer?

Finally, of the general historians of the seventeenth-century Chesapeake whom I have encountered, with the exception of Allan Kulikoff, none give due attention to the special oppression of women bond-laborers. These workers were routinely sentenced to two and a half years' additional bond-servitude for becoming mothers. Then as now, patriarchy and male suprema-cism were in the ascendant. But the denial of the right to marriage and family, a unique feature of the Anglo-American bond-labor system, in the context of the plantation bond-labor system was not a social aberration; it was an indispensable condition for the preservation of that particular form of capitalist production and accumulation. The chattel bond-labor system of the continental

Anglo-American plantation colonies was incompatible with the status of "coverture" because "coverture" was an insurmountable barrier to the imposition of chattel status on the laborers. At the same time, by nullifying the "a-man's-home-is-his-castle" principle, it denied the plantation bourgeoisie the benefit of the patriarchy as a system of social control over the laboring people.

This is a matter of more than general humanitarian consideration. The family-barring oppression endured by the chattel bond-laborers contributed in a doubly fundamental way to the social tensions that finally rent the social fabric asunder in Bacon's Rebellion. Not only did it directly sharpen the class antagonism of proletariat and bourgeoisie; the very nature of the chattel bond-labor system made impossible the development of a buffer social control stratum normal to English society.

8

. . . and Resisting

W. E. B. DuBois, in his 1909 address to the American Historical Association on post-Civil War Reconstruction in the South, broke the silence regarding the role of bond-laborers as a self-activating social and political force in American history.[1] In time, thanks largely to the single-minded efforts of Carter G. Woodson, together with his associates in the publication of the *Journal of Negro Life and History*, and then later the studies of revolts of African-American bond-laborers, especially developed by Herbert Aptheker, the attention of a number of other scholars was directed to this aspect of our history. As a result of the consciousness-raising effects of the war against Nazism, and of the civil rights struggles of the 1950s and 1960s, there was an upsurge in interest in the study of the seventeenth-century origin of racial slavery, centering on issues that are noted in the Introduction in Volume One of the present work. That interest has focused on the colonial Chesapeake. But discussion of the bond-laborers as a self-activating social and political force has been almost completely neglected, with the exception of the excellent article by Timothy H. Breen, "A Changing Labor Force and Race Relations in Virginia 1660–1710."[2] Breen's argument is especially distinguished by its correction of the general tendency of historians to rely "too heavily upon statute law as opposed to social practice" in interpreting seventeenth-century Virginia history.[3] Breen was also exemplary in the consistency with which he noted the class character of the struggle of the African-American bond-laborers in the eighteenth century, and the overwhelming disadvantage to their cause "without the support of poorer whites and indentured servants."[4]

The present chapter documents instances of self-activation of bond-laborers as molders of their own fate. In keeping with the basic concern of this work, emphasis will be given to evidence of readiness of European-American bond-laborers to join with African-American bond-laborers in actions and plots of actions against their bondage, and to the readiness of free persons to support the struggles of the bond-laborers, both of which were inconsistent with racial slavery. It is to be hoped that this material will prepare the reader to appreciate the historical significance of the role of bond-laborers in the event called Bacon's Rebellion, and the relation of that event to the invention of the white race.

Where There Is Oppression, There Is Resistance

Where there is oppression, there is resistance, insufficient though it may be. When resistance is enough it becomes rebellion. Where the intermediate buffer social control stratum becomes dysfunctional, rebellion breaks through. So at least the records of the Anglo-American plantation colonies seem to show, particularly those of seventeenth-century Virginia.[5]

Denied a livable life, bond-laborers would commit suicide, hazarding hell's fire; alternatively, they might assault their owners. Starve them and they would steal from their owners, or kill hogs, wild or marked, for clandestine feasts, or on occasion they would rise in defiant mutiny. Bloody their backs with lashes "well laid on," add months or years to their servitude for "stealth of oneself," and they still would run away, singly or "in troops."[6] Double the penalty for European-Americans who ran away with African-Americans; they would do so anyway. Deny them the right to marry and the shield of coverture, lash women's backs; they would seek solace in "fornication," and be damned to ye! Double the penalty for European-American women who mated with African-American men; they would do so anyway. Attenuate the intermediate social control stratum; and at an opportune moment, they would join *en masse* in armed rebellion.

Suicide and assault

One day late in October 1656, a chattel bond-laborer known to the record only as "Thomas, an Irishman" and owned by John Custis, shortened his term of servitude by slashing his own throat and then throwing himself down a well.[7] There is no record of any note left or any notice he may have given for his last decision. Had he been an object in "the Irish slave trade" that thrived in the wake of the English conquest of his country?[8] Or was he perhaps brooding on news, conveyed by his owner, of the "custom-of-the-country" law requiring Irish bond-laborers to serve a year longer than English bond-laborers?[9]

At the height of the 1661 tobacco crop season, a bond-laborer, nameless in the record, "willfully Cast himselfe away" in a creek near his owner's Westmoreland County plantation. That was a year when tobacco prices were falling to their lowest level yet, so that each laborer would have to be made to produce twice as much as he/she had produced a couple of years before, just so the owner might stay even. Perhaps this circumstance added chagrin to the moral outrage of the court's order that this unfaithful worker be "buried at the next cross path . . . with a stake driven through the middle of him."[10] That same year, in York County, where tobacco prices were no higher, Walter Catford with spiteful disregard for the interests of his owner and "for want of Grace tooke a Grind stone and a Roape and tyed it around his Middle and Crosse his thighs and most barbarously went and drowned himselfe contrary to the Laws of the King and this Country."[11]

Bond-laborers of different temperament were disposed to turn their anger outward. They were likely to disappoint ruling-class expectations by individual displays of violence against owners or overseers, and by destruction of their owners' property, despite the whippings and extended bondage that the magistrates were certain to impose when such cases came before them, or even the death sentence that could be imposed by the General Court.

Around the end of 1658, Huntington Ayres, wielding a "lathing hammer," murdered his owner and his owner's wife as they slept.[12] No suggestion as to the particular motive for the murder is recorded; it seems to have been considered simply the extreme denouement of the general master–servant conflict. On 16 January 1671, on an Elke River, Maryland, plantation, owner John Hawkins was slain by axes wielded by a group of three of his bond-laborers – two European-Americans and one African-American – and one European-American former bond-laborer. As servants killing a master, they were charged with "petty treason," as if the motive were thereby sufficiently implied.[13]

The more common form of individual struggle was, in the words of a law passed by the Virginia Assembly in March 1662, "the audacious unruliness of many stubborne and incorridgible servants resisting their masters and overseers."[14] That law prescribed an extra year of servitude for any bond-laborer who should "lay violent hands on his or her master, mistress or overseer."[15]

A hoe was the weapon of choice for Charles Rogers, Norfolk County bond-laborer, in his assault on his owner one August day in 1666.[16] It was the hoe too for bond-laborer William Page in 1671 in Lancaster County in September, a climactic period in the annual round of "making tobacco." Upon some disagreement with his owner, Page struck at him with a hoe and defied him to attempt to correct him. "God damn him," he was reported as saying, "if his master strock him he would beat out his braynes."[17]

A year later in Northampton County, Portuguese Nicholas Silvio apparently was sometimes absent without leave pursuing a love affair with Mary Gale, a bond-laborer on a nearby plantation, with whom he would soon have a child. When his owner, Captain John Savage, sought to call him to account, Silvio declined to respond, saying "hee was not intended to worke night & day too." Thereupon, Captain Savage made the mistake of kicking at Silvio, who then "flew att his master and struck him 4 blowes" and tore the Master's "good holland shirt very much."[18]

Provoked on some account one day in June 1765, bond-laborer Nicholas Paine (or Pane) threw "five or six bricks or brick batts" at his owner, Colonel Thomas Swann of Surry County, who saved himself by ducking behind a gate. A fellow bond-laborer wondered how Paine dared to do such a thing, and expressed awe at the sign of "the depression of three bricks in the gate." Paine's only comment was, "a plague take the damn gate[;] if it had not bin for that [I] would have hit him."[19]

Although John Bradley had served as a bond-laborer for eleven years – at a time when according to law no non-indentured bond-laborer was supposed to serve more than seven years[20] – the Norfolk County Court in November 1654 rejected Bradley's petition for freedom. Perhaps as a payback to the system for such abuse of his rights, Bradley set fire to a cornfield three times in less than a month.[21] A similar flaming farewell was tendered by bond-laborer John Parris before he ran away in the spring of 1687.[22]

Sometimes several bond-laborers would combine to confront the owner or overseer. In February 1648, the bond-laborers owned by John Wilkins told him in a menacing manner and in rudest terms that "they [would] not any longer bee his servants."[23]

In the matter of diet

In 1662 the penalty for hog-stealing was two years' added servitude for each hog, and a law passed in 1679 made the third offense punishable by death.[24] Yet there are many, many cases of bond-laborers, often acting in small groups, stealing and killing hogs to supplement their corn-and-water diet.[25] Several such group efforts were made by three European-Americans – John Fisher, Thomas Hartley, and Roger Crotofte (variously spelled) – and two African-American bond-laborers – Tony and one not named in the record – all the property of John West, who owned more bond-laborers than anyone else in Accomack County in that year, 1684. The five would more often than not dress and cook the stolen meat and feast on it in "the swamp," or other clandestine rendezvous. Usually they were able to make the food last for several days. When a fellow worker asked John Fisher about the possibility of being charged by a court, Fisher replied that in that circumstance he would run away and "send his master a very Loveing Letter that his sheep, his hogg & turkeys were very fatt."[26]

In other instances bond-laborers sought to improve their diet not by stealth, but by confrontation with the owning class. One Thursday in March 1663 in Calvert County, Maryland, Richard Preston's eight bond-laborers "peremptorily and positively refused to goe to their ordinary labour," saying that their diet of "Beanes and Bread" had made them too weak to "performe the imployments [Preston] putts us uppon." Preston asked the court's help, for fear that from the example of this unruly eight, "a worse evill . . . should ensue by encouraging other servants to do the like."[27] In 1670, bond-laborers owned by a Widow Hale got some alimentary relief when, upon their complaint, the Lancaster County Court ordered that Hale provide a milk cow for the use of the bond-laborers.[28]

In 1661, bond-laborers owned by Major Thomas Goodwin in York County had become "refractory" about their work because of their "hard usage" and being fed "nothing but Corne and water."[29] When magistrate Thomas Beale came to Goodwin's plantation to remonstrate with the workers there about their defiance of authority, he found 24-year-old freeman William Clutton, who well remembered his own sufferings as a bond-laborer. Indeed, he had declined to be Major Beale's overseer precisely because Beale fed his workers so poorly. Clutton told Beale in the presence of the aggrieved bond-laborers that they ought to be provided with meat three times a week and with cows for milking. The workers, taking encouragement from Clutton but realizing that their first idea, for sending a petition to the king in England, was not practicable, resolved to do battle for themselves not just for a better diet, but for an end to their bond-servitude. They would

> get a matter of Forty of them together & get Gunnes & . . . cry as they went along who would be for liberty and free from bondage & that there would be enough come to them & they would goe through the Countrey and Kill those that made any opposition that they would be either free or dye for it.[30]

The plot, frustrated by discovery, was investigated by Magistrate Beale. Seeing in the event a tendency to the "Disturbance of the peace of the Country & to the hazard of men's lives," Beale ordered "the Magistrates and Masters to looke into the practices & behaviour of their Servants." William Clutton was so widely respected that after he promised to cease his agitation of the workers, his good-behavior bond was returned to him.

Two years later the largest, most widespread insurrectionary plot of bond-laborers was discovered in Gloucester County, Virginia. Unfortunately, as a result of the total destruction of Gloucester County records in two fires, in 1821 and 1865, only a few scraps of the record remain concerning this event.[31]

The design was hatched by a number of Cromwellian veterans who had been sentenced to be transported to bond-servitude by the restored monarchy of Charles II. On the first weekend in September the plotters gathered in the house of Mr Knight (apparently a sympathetic free man) to discuss "a designe for their freedom"; each and all were pledged to secrecy on pain of death. The revolt was to be launched from their rendezvous at Poplar Spring at midnight on the following Sunday, 14 September. The core group, bringing with them "what Company, armes, and ammunicion [they] could gett," would assemble at Poplar Spring. Then, moving forth with the confidence of veterans, they would seize arms, ammunition and a drum from the militia's store. They would "goe from house to house to house" rallying bond-laborers to join in a grand march to Governor William Berkeley and demand their freedom. If the governor should refuse, they would "march out of the Country."

Their plan was betrayed to the authorities by a bond-laborer named Berkenhead,[32] so that the militia authorities were able to get to the Poplar Spring rendezvous ahead of the rebels and arrest them as they arrived. But word spread of the militia's trap, and only a few of the rebels were apprehended; of those, four were hanged.

The colony authorities were shaken by the revelation of the insurrectionary threat to the rule of the plantation bourgeoisie. The Virginia Assembly made the day of its discovery, 13 September, an annual holy day, and granted Berkenhead his immediate freedom and a reward of 5,000 pounds of tobacco.[33] Two other, more substantial, measures were taken in reaction to this event. One was the passage of a new law requiring owners of bond-laborers to prevent the workers from leaving the plantations to which they belonged without explicit permission, "on Sundayes or any other dayes."[34] The other, which will be further noted in Chapter 9, was a proposal to tax by landholding rather than by poll, thus disfranchising the landless poor.[35] While the record makes no mention of African-Americans in connection with the 1663 plot, it is of interest to the present study that there is no indication of any exclusionary tendency on the part of the plotters; rather, their depositions suggest that they intended to recruit every last bond-laborer to their freedom march.

Flight and "fornication"

Of the various ways that the bond-laborers found for defying and resisting their oppressors, the two most common forms were:[36] (1) continual attempts to free themselves by running away (a common theme of studies of the life and status of laborers in that period); and (2) sexual liaisons – criminalized under the term "fornication" – conducted in defiance of the ruling-class denial of the bond-laborer's right to be married (an aspect that, so far as I know, has not previously been even acknowledged as resistance to the owning class, except by Warren M. Billings and by Joseph Douglas Deal III).[37]

Running away

The official records regarding runaway bond-laborers, with few exceptions, concern cases in which recaptured fugitives are being arraigned or are listed in claims being made for payment to the "takers-up" of such fugitives. Occasionally there are grounds for believing that some of the runaways succeeded in avoiding recapture. Owners might refrain from bringing such cases to official attention because of the distance to be traveled to see the magistrate, or the inconvenient timing of court days, or the incidental fees that might have to be borne by the owner if the runaways were not caught; undoubtedly these factors together were responsible for many flights never being noted in the record.[38] For the great runaway year 1676–77, there is a general hiatus in the records in consequence of Bacon's Rebellion, which was fueled by the adherence to it of great numbers of "runaway" bond-laborers.[39]

In many instances bond-laborers sought to escape the jurisdiction of Virginia authorities by fleeing to the Indians, to Dutch colonial territory, to Pennsylvania, or to the more newly formed neighboring Maryland and North Carolina (known as Albemarle until 1691). Probably fewer than half the runaways traveled alone. Many were in groups of two or three, but there were instances of larger undertakings. In Gloucester County (whose records, as previously noted, have all been lost), the General Assembly noted in 1661 that "servants and other idlers [were] running away in troops."[40] I have tabulated a total of between 880 and 890 individual fugitives who were subject to the attention of the county courts. In addition, an indeterminate number were referred to by terms such as "several" and "groups," or simply as "servants" in the plural without enumeration.

With regard to the central concern of this work – the question of the origin of racial oppression – two facts of transcendent significance are presented by the record of runaways. First, considering the fact that no more than about one out of every four or five bond-laborers was an African-American even as late as the 1670s and 1680s,[41] there was a considerable degree of collaboration of African-Americans and European-Americans in a common endeavor to escape. In the records I have examined, such collaboration was noted in fifteen separate instances involving a total of some seventy or seventy-five persons.[42] Second, there was a readiness of free persons to assist bond-laborers in running away, as recorded in fifteen instances involving fifty-eight people. In this chapter, I accordingly cite principally instances that represent these two aspects of the runaway phenomenon. However, with respect to the subjective or ideological element, these cases do not differ in the least from any of the others; all represented a common front against the chattel bond-labor system, free of any evidence of social distinction or prejudice.

One form of resistance of women bond-laborers to their double yoke of gender and class oppression was to run away, usually in the company of men – bond-laborers or free sympathizers – but in some cases without male support. The generally greater vulnerability of women to the perils faced in leaving the plantation in this new strange country would seem obvious. Nevertheless, despite the fact that they were a relatively minor proportion in the population, among the runaways I have noted from the records there were sixty-nine women, including six African-Americans and two Indians.

By 1640, two years after Colony Secretary Kemp had reported on the predominance of human merchandise among Virginia immigrants, the Virginia General Court was receiving daily complaints about "servants that run away from their masters whereby much loss ... doth ensue to the masters." The problem had reached such proportion that the Colony Council made the recapture of runaway bond-laborers a public concern, and ordered that the expense of recovering fugitives be borne not by the owner, but by the public treasury of the counties involved.[43]

Early in June 1640, three Virginia bond-laborers, "Victor, a dutchman ... a Scotchman called James Gregory ... [and] a negro named John Punch," escaped together to Maryland. Unfortunately they were pursued and, at the insistence of the Virginia Colony Council, they were brought back to face the Virginia General Court.[44] That same month, the Virginia Colony Council and General Court commissioned a Charles City County posse to pursue "certain runaway negroes." The provision that the cost was to be shared by all the counties from which they had run away suggests that the phenomenon was extensive.[45] Since no further record seems to exist regarding this particular undertaking, perhaps these workers avoided recapture.

As if encouraged by such a possibility, seven bond-laborers – Andrew Noxe, Richard Hill, Richard Cookson, Christopher Miller, Peter Wilcocke (presumably English), an African-American, Emanuel, and John Williams ("a dutchman") – set off one Saturday night a month later in a stolen boat, with arms, powder and shot. They, however, were taken up before they could reach open water.[46]

In October of that same year, "a most dangerous conspiracy" was entered into by three free men – John Bradye, John Tomkinson, and Richard West – and six bond-laborers – Margaret Beard, John Winchester, William Wooton, William Drummer, Robert Rouse, and Robert Moseley – "to run out of the country" to "the Dutch plantation."[47] The plan was discovered before it could be executed. The punishments meted out by the authorities appear to reflect an increasing alarm that such escapes would reduce the pressure that employers might bring to bear on laborers in the course of their routine employments. In addition to the thirty-stripe whippings, extended periods of servitude, and the working in shackles imposed in the case of Noxe et al., a number of those charged with extensive conspiracies in this case were to be punished also by being branded on the cheek and the shoulder.[48]

In the fall of 1645, an African-American bond-laborer Phillip, owned by Captain Phillip Hawley, helped runaway European-American bond-laborer Sibble Ford hide from her pursuers for twenty days in a cave on Hawley's plantation. His collaborator was European-American Thomas Parks, who addressed the court defiantly when he was arraigned for going about "to intice and inveigle the mens Servants to runn away . . . out of their masters service."[49]

Two large-scale efforts to escape were made in Accomack County in the mid-1660s. In August 1663, some ten bond-laborers ran away together from Eastern Shore plantations. Making use of a horse named Tom Hall and a "good boat," they headed for points north – "the Dutch plantation," "the Manhatans," "New England." Although John Bloxam and Robert Hodge were retaken within a week, it was four years before Miles Grace was caught; but Thomas Hedrington and Robin Parker, and possibly others, were still free. John Tarr was captured, but as soon as he could he again escaped with three others; though Tarr was again caught, the others succeeded in eluding their pursuers.[50]

An elaborate plot was discovered in 1670 in Accomack County. It began with a group of some half-dozen bond-laborers inspired by the report of four others who had succeeded in escaping from another Eastern shore plantation at Pocomoke. A first attempt was made in October, that time being chosen because men of the local "power elite" would then be in Jamestown for a meeting of the General Assembly. However, because of a strong contrary northwest wind that blew on the night chosen for the escape, the men decided to stow the sails prepared for the escape craft and postpone the effort, although Mary Warren protested that "shee never saw such fooles in her life to loose such a opportunity." A second attempt was to be made, and on a grander scale. A score of bond-laborers from several Eastern Shore plantations, along with three to five free persons,[51] were eventually pledged to the enterprise. They were resolved to make good their purpose "by force against all that should oppose" them, according to one of their number, 25-year-old bond-laborer Renney Sadler. Depositions later given before the magistrate revealed that the runaways had planned to tie up one owner, Devorax Brown, and his wife,[52] disable the horse from pursuing, and carry off a large gun for installation on the small sailing vessel, a sloop, that would carry them to freedom. The sloop was to be well stocked with food prepared by a woman co-conspirator who had access to the necessary provisions. Their aim was to sail up Chesapeake Bay to "the dutch plantation" or "New England," with "black James," reputed "the best pylot in the land," at the helm.[53] Perhaps because the plan involved too many people and the preparation period was too long for the preservation of the necessary secrecy, their purpose was discovered in December and prevented.[54]

In February 1672, European-American bond-laborer William Richardson and an African-American bond-laborer, not named in the record, ran away together. How or why they became separated is not revealed, but only Richardson was recaptured and arraigned eight and a half years later; his partner was apparently never heard of again in those parts.[55] In the summer of 1679, three European-American bond-laborers, Mary Axton, Mary West and William Siller, together with African-American bond-laborer Thomas George, somehow managed to escape from the James River plantation belonging to their owner, Lieutenant-Colonel Thomas Milner, and row or sail across Chesapeake Bay to Hog's Neck on the Eastern Shore.[56] Later that same summer in Lancaster County, European-American bond-laborers William Adams, Robert Bull and John Stookley and an African-American bond-laborer, Tom, coordinated their efforts over three different plantations to run away in a boat belonging to a fourth plantation.[57] An African-American, whose name is not supplied in the record, and his fellow bond-laborer Hugh Callon in April 1683 collaborated in running away from the plantation of their owner, Colonel Thomas Brereton in Northumberland County.[58] European-American Thomas Callen [or Caller] and his African-American comrade William Powell "stole themselves" away from their owner, Aron Spring of Elizabeth River. They managed to get a boat in which they crossed Chesapeake Bay and reached Maggoty Bay in Northampton County; there they apparently became separated. Powell was taken up in May 1687, but a year later Callen still had not been recaptured.[59] Appropriating a boat and two sheep, three laborers, Anthony Jackson and Michael Connell, European-Americans, and Mingo, an African-American, ran away from their owner, Charles Egerton, some time before 5 August 1688.[60]

While it is not possible from the record to fit all the pieces together, there is no doubt that bond-laborers were resolved on escaping from Mr Ralph Wormeley, Esquire, their owner, of Middlesex County. In 1687 "John Nickson ... with divers other ill-disposed servants and others" were charged with having plotted "to procure Gunnes powder and Shott and other Armes and to Assemble themselves together with Design to withstand and Oppose all persons that should endeavour to Suppress them ... tending to the greate disturbance of his Majesties Peace and the terrours of his liege people."[61] Despite the discovery of the scheme, it appears that after a delay of some eighteen months the plotters succeeded to some extent; having taken guns and ammunition, a number of the rebels, including African-Americans Mingoe and Lawrence, and European-American Richard Wilkins, remained free for "a Considerable time," in Wilkins's case some twenty-eight months.[62]

The name of Richard Ayry's African-American friend is unknown to the court record; together they planned and, "in the height of the [1688] crop season," executed their escape from Captain Richard Kenner's plantation in Northumberland County.[63] African-American Thomas Roberts and Portuguese John Sherry, two bond-laborers belonging to William Wise, fled from York County, Virginia, on 18 August 1690 and stuck together all the way to Philadelphia.[64]

Free laboring people aid runaway bond-laborers
In the summer of 1669, the Widow Buckmaster and her son Henry Crow refused to enlist in the hue and cry after a runaway bond-laborer belonging to John Harris; instead, they harbored the fugitive in their own house.[65] Thomas Stephens, a skilled seaman, was arraigned in Lancaster County in March 1675 on the charge of devoting his expertise to being "the chiefe causer promoter and instrumenter" in the escape of three bond-laborers who had not been heard of since.[66] Late in 1675, freeman John Fennell accompanied bond-laborers William Beverly and his wife and Jane Getting in running away from their owner, William Carver.[67] At the June session of the Accomack County Court, freeman Thomas Lehay was found guilty of habitually assisting bond-laborers to run away. He was ordered to post £20 sterling for his future "good behaviour."[68]

Freeman Emanuell Rodriggus, an African-American, was brought before the February 1672 session of the Northampton County Court for having "unlawfully entertayned" two runaway European-American bond-laborers owned by Captain John Custis of Northampton County.[69] In mid-summer 1679, four African-Americans, including one child too young to work, ran away in the company of two free European-Americans, John Watkings and Agness Clerk.[70] In November 1690, freeman Edward Short was arraigned for "helping and assisting" European-American Roger Crotuff [Crotofte] and African-American bond-laborer John Johnson to break out of the Accomack county prison.[71] After Ann Redman, an African-American, took her child and ran away from the plantation of European-American Thomas Loyd in February 1696, she was sought by hue and cry. Some twenty months later Redman was seized from the home of European-American Edwin Thacker, where she had found refuge.[72]

In Henrico County early in 1696, two African-Americans, Betty and a man described only as being a "mulatto," ran away and were sheltered in the home of Henry Turner. Somehow constable Edward Tanner was able to arrest Betty and to confine her in his house. Betty broke out at night, however, and returned to Turner's place. Tanner, with two assistants, came to Turner's house and sought to seize and bind the African-American man (the "mulatto"), who naturally resisted, Tanner called upon Turner to help subdue the man, but Turner

> not only refused to assist [Constable Tanner], but forewarned[?] every body from meddling with the said malotto, and when [Tanner] with Edward Ward [his buddy] had gott the said Malloto fellow down and were going to binde him, Henry Turner caught hold of the Rope and plucket it from them, and threw it out of Doors, and taking up a hoe helve said that the fellow (meaning the mallatto that was seized) should not be tyed there for he [Turner] would defend him; which words so Encouraged the mallatto That he took up a pistoll that lay by him and Kockt it, but Tanner and [one of his helpers] layed hold of him and wrested the pistoll out of his hands, and again endeavoured to binde him; but Henry Turner catching hold of the pistoll that then was in [Tanner's helper's] hand said he would lay him in the face if he did not let goe; and the mallatto recovering his Gun and [standing] upon his Guard [Tanner along with his two buddies] who endeavoured to assist ... [were] forced to desist & goe their ways; all which [Constable Tanner] conceives to be a matter of Evill Consequence.[73]

Defiant solace

Deny them the right to marry and the shield of coverture; they would "fornicate" and be damned to ye. Double the penalty for European-American women who mated with African-American men; they would do so anyway.

As noted in Chapter 7, chattel bond-laborer status was incompatible with marriage. Furthermore, despite the various expedients adopted for recapturing the owner's or the parish's expenses for support of the children of limited-term bond-laborers, natural increase was a relatively unprofitable way of recruiting plantation labor-power in the seventeenth-century tobacco colonies. In these circumstances, it was simply good "bottom line" logic to outlaw sex by limited-term bond-laborers, calling it "fornication," for which cruel penalties were imposed. (See Chapter 7 pages 128–9.)

Male supremacism was a fundamental premise of Anglo-American colonial life as it was in England. The seventeenth-century records present depressing confirmation of that fact. Crimes against and abuse of women by men of all classes sometimes became the subject of judicial notice, in cases including uxoricide, rape, denial or access to food, eviction, sexual abuse, economic exploitation, and battery. Altogether I have noted 367 court cases relating to gender oppression. As has been argued in Chapter 7, chattel bond-servitude, which was the condition of the overwhelming majority of women arriving in the tobacco colonies, gave an added dimension to male supremacism, a distinctive blend of class and gender oppression that accounted for 304 of the cases characterized in the record as "fornication" and "bastardy." These more than three hundred court cases, in which the rigor of the law was visited upon women bond-laborer "fornicators," necessarily involved somewhere around twice that number of persons. If the figure of 850 listed runaway bond-laborers is indicative of widespread bond-laborer resistance to the system of chattel bond-servitude, so must the persistent and pervasive assertion by bond-laborers of the right to the solace of sexual relations be regarded as rejection of the enforced sexual abstinence imposed upon them as an essential characteristic of that very system.

In 140 of those 304 cases, the identity of the male partner is known.[74] In all, 17 were owners, 2 were overseers. Of the remaining 121, 67, including 2 African-Americans, were freemen, the great majority of whom had been bond-laborers.[75] Some 54 were bond-laborers – 31 European-Americans, 22 African-Americans, and 1 American Indian.[76]

Leaving aside the instances of sexual relations involving owners and overseers, in which the feelings of the bond-laborers hardly needed to be consulted, what do the general statistics and the particular case records suggest about the motivations of the bond-laborers in the other cases? The sex instinct of a bond-laborer was a power that the plantation bourgeoisie could only hope to curb by fear of legal retribution, glossed by preachments on the virtue of "abstinence." Abstinence, however, was one thing the bond-laborers had in plenty: "abstinence" from decent food, clothing, and shelter, from possessions, from receiving wages, from marriage and "coverture," from normal home life. At the same time, the record shows what one might assume, namely that sexually exploitative motives were common to persons of all social classes. In the male-supremacist environment, such motives accounted for the seduction, abandonment and sexual exploitation of many women, particularly those most vulnerable, the bond-laborers.

The predominance of freemen as partners in these cases may be significant. Anne Collins's interest in freeman Robert Pierce was particularly based on the hope to escape her bondage by alliance with him. "I should never have yielded to his desyres but hee told me he would free me from my Master, whatsoever it would cost him & that hee had Stocke Cattle Servants & a plantation [and] that I should ride his mare & then your [Collins's] Mistress will think much."[77] Despite the risks such bond-laborers ran in "yielding to the desyres" of freemen, it is reasonable to assume that Anne Collins's motivation was a common one for women bond-laborers. In such cases each woman bond-laborer was conducting her own individual strategy for throwing off chattel bondage, even though to do so risked subjection to a husband. Although liaisons between male bond-laborers and free women were rare, perhaps men in those cases were also motivated by a hope of gaining their freedom through such a connection. Yet truly felt and mutual love and sympathy in resistance to the bond-labor system might still have motivated sexual partners even in cases where those feelings were confused with hope for an improved social status.

We have noted that Lucy Stratton was one who did not invest herself in such confusion. In contrast to Anne Collins, Stratton spurned her owner's offer of marriage because she did not love him, and because his interest in her was mere lust.[78] In making the distinction between mere sexual male exploitation and love, she showed the normal desire to be truly loved and cherished, sexually and otherwise.

Being by law denied the right to dispose of property, as lovers bond-laborers[79] had little to offer each other but comfort and emotional support.[80] In 86 of the 140 male-partner-identified "fornication" cases brought against women bond-laborers, the men were free men, and thus property considerations and social mobility expectations might have been factors. Yet there were 50 instances of such charges against women bond-laborers where the man was a bond-laborer.[81]

One does not find many avowals of romantic love in seventeenth-century court records; love letters written by the bond-laborers and the free poor persons of that place and time must be extremely rare, if indeed any exist at all. But one can imagine the sense of love and fear, elation and despair, the passionate avowals and practical concerns they might have expressed regarding experiences described in court records. What love note could more adequately testify to their mutual devotion, for instance, than the decision of two lovers to risk together the perils and penalties of flight from chattel servitude?

What observations were exchanged on love and bondage between Penelope Sandford and Adam Robinson? In June 1666, for becoming parents, those two bond-laborers were sentenced to added servitude of two and a half years and two years respectively. Yet they persisted in their relationship, and a year later they were ordered to be whipped as "incorrigibble fornicators whom no goodness Mercy & admonition can reforme."[82] What might their diary have said about that day when they first decided that being together was worth the risk?

As the seasons changed in 1685, how did runaway bond-laborers William Lloyd and Mary Seymore cheer and advise each other in those nearly ten months before they were recaptured, still together?[83]

What would the journal of African-American bond-laborer Warner and Mrs Welch have told of adventures they experienced as they fled from Accomack County to Pennsylvania some time before September 1685? What opinions did they offer to each other on husbands and masters? Returned by order of a Pennsylvania justice of the peace, they were put in James City jail, and again escaped briefly, before they were retaken and assigned to be tried by a member of the Virginia Colony Council.[84] What might they have recalled for each other in all that time about their respective backgrounds, and of the universal language of love?

In Essex County, bond-laborer Robert Hughes and free woman Ellinor sought to sanctify their relationship by marriage in 1703. To their dismay, they were prosecuted under the law passed against bond-laborers marrying without their owners' prior consent.[85] Hughes was sentenced to an added year of bondage; Ellinor was ordered to pay Hughes's owner 1,500 pounds of tobacco or else she, too, would have to serve that owner for a full year as a bond-laborer.[86] What might the diary of one or the other disclose to us on the conquering power of love over bondage, and on the importance of defying the hypocrisy of the law?

Among the 54 identified male bond-laborer partners in the "fornication" cases examined, 22 were African-Americans involved with European-American women. This was a much higher percentage than the proportion of African-Americans in the bond-labor force. Although the record does not afford a reason for this disproportion, it is a fact that the plantation bourgeoisie came to regard the mating of European-Americans with African-Americans as a serious problem for themselves.[87] In any case, it appears to have been in keeping with the readiness of European-American and African-American bond-laborers to make common cause in the other respects described in this chapter.

No "White Race"

Through Acts of the General Assembly, the plantation bourgeoisie early on expressed its disposition to deny equal rights to African-Americans.[88] The evidence, however, clearly indicates that this purpose of the ruling class did not represent the desire or attitude of the European-American bond-laborers as a whole, or indeed of the common run of European-Americans in general. At the same time, however, it is not surprising that the explicitly anti-Negro tenor of these laws would find some echo in the attitude of ruled-over European-Americans, bond and free. I have found those instances to have been extremely few, however, in comparison to the record of solidarity of European-American and African-American bond-laborers, and in comparison to the readiness of free laboring-class European-Americans to make common cause with African-American fugitives from bond-labor. Here are the only such exceptional cases that I have turned up.

The General Assembly enacted a series of laws, beginning in 1662,[89] directed specifically against African-American women. In February 1669, bond-laborer Mary Hughes, appealing in vain against being raped by her owner, Henry Smith, said "he would make her worse than a Negroe by whoreing her."[90] In 1694, a deposition in a slander case told of mutual accusations between two European-American women of sexual misalliances with various European-American men, and claimed that one had said that the other was "such a whore that she would lye with a Negro."[91]

In Accomack County one day in 1677, when tavern-keeper George Boies refused credit to Indian bond-laborer James, James promptly invited Boies to "Kiss my Arse." Next, Boies and James exchanged the compliments of "Indian Dog" and "English Dogg." Boies attacked James; another patron, bond-laborer (or possibley former bond-laborer) Alexander Dun urged James to return the blows against Boies, and James did so.[92]

Some time prior to November 1681, European-American bond-laborer David Griffin, avowed in the course of an altercation with his overseer, an Indian named James Revell, that "it should never be said that he did yeild to an Indian Dog."[93]

On 5 November 1681, Frank, the African-American "servant" of Mr Vaulx, was sent by Vaulx to "speak with John Machart [or Macarty] about business." Machart and a friend he was with rebuffed Frank, saying "they were no company for Negroes." The following day at the Vaulx house, where some six or seven men were drinking, fighting occurred between Frank's friend Peter Wells and Machart, and then between Frank and Machart. It began with offense being taken by both Frank and Peter Wells at Machart's pretension of superiority. Just before the fighting began, Wells said to Frank, "God damn them he was as good a man as the best of them."[94]

In 1691, when Hannah Warwick was charged with refusing to do her work, the General Court made extenuation on the grounds that "she was overseen by a negro overseer."[95]

By contrast, in none of the hundreds of cases of the oppression of bond-laborers and the resistance by them have I found any instance in which European-American bond-laborers expressed a desire to dissociate their sufferings and struggle from those of the African-American bond-laborers, the case of Mary Hughes being the exception, and perhaps that of Hannah Warwick. It is to be noted that in three of these six exceptional incidents of hostility directed by non-ruling-class European-Americans at non-European-Americans, European-American bystanders were present; in two cases out of the three, the bystanders actively dissociated themselves from such chauvinism.

In general, as this chapter has illustrated, despite the six exceptions cited, the attitude of the laboring-class European-Americans stood in sharp contrast to the succession of enactments whereby the plantation bourgeoisie pressed for the lifetime, hereditary bond-servitude of African-American bond-laborers, and for the circumscription of the rights, and the ultimate practical proscription of free African-Americans.[96]

Two fair conclusions would seem to follow: First, "the white race" – supra-class unity of European-Americans in opposition to African-Americans – did not and could not have then existed. Second, the invention of the white race at the beginning of the eighteenth century can in no part be ascribed to demands by European-American laboring people for privileges vis-à-vis African-Americans.

9

The Insubstantiality of the
Intermediate Stratum

Virginia Colony evolved under the direct rule of a tiny elite which, in the fifteen years leading up to Bacon's Rebellion, included fewer than four hundred men, probably numbering no more than two hundred at any one time, owners of an average of 4,200 acres of land each.[1] The lowest-ranking members of this stratum were the county[2] commissioners, deliberately limited by Act of Assembly in 1661 to no more than eight per county,[3] who acted collectively as the county court, and served individually as magistrates, justices of the peace, in their respective districts. The members of the county courts, among whom the office of sheriff was rotated annually, were appointed from time to time by the Colony Council and Governor, upon the recommendation of the sitting members of the particular county court.[4] Next came the members of the Virginia House of Burgesses who were invariably elected from among the members of the county courts. Originally the vote was exercised by all freemen but as the ranks of propertyless former bond-laborers increased, in 1670 the General Assembly deliberately excluded these latter from the right to vote.[5] At the top were the Governor (appointed by Charles II, king of England during this period) and the Virginia Colony Council, made up of men appointed by the Governor with the formal approval of the General Assembly, the term used to describe the House of Burgesses and the Colony Council together. The Governor and the Colony Council constituted the General Court.[6]

County court and magistrate orders were enforced by the county sheriffs and constables, and through pursuit by hue and cry. But hue and cry after runaway bond-laborers was so generally neglected that in 1658 the General Assembly ordered the imposition of fines on householders and constables for such lapses in civic responsibility.[7] Two years later the General Assembly again faulted the constables for neglect of their duty to hunt down runaways.[8] In 1669, the General Assembly not only noted the plots made by bond-laborers to escape their owners but also charged that "some planters," instead of arresting the fugitives, "have given them assistance and directions how to escape."[9] The General Assembly then proceeded to provide a reward, not only to encourage constables but to enlist the general public in the capture of runaway bond-laborers, by offering to any person one thousand pounds of tobacco for each runaway recaptured. It was intended that when bond-laborers became aware of "soe many spies upon them," they would "keep within the bounds of their duty."[10] The general subject of runaways has been treated in Chapter 8; the point here is to emphasize the absence of an effective social control stratum.

Every man between the ages of sixteen and sixty was subject to service in the militia. Its organizational structure derived from the political structure of organization of the colony, the militia of each county being officered by local members of the colony elite. An establishing order issued by Governor Francis Moryson in June 1661 required each county to mobilize three militia companies, to be made up of "freemen and Servants of undoubted fidelity." Because the population was so widely dispersed that the entire county regiment could not be mobilized for sudden emergencies, a special unit called the "settled trayned band," was to be formed of one-eighth of the entire regiment and divided into three companies, selected because of the members' proximity to the plantation of the regiment's captain.[11] The Governor and Colony Council were obliged to confess the incompetence of the militia for sustained service, citing two factors: the impossibility of storing sufficient corn to sustain the militia on extended duty, because of the infestation of the grain by vermin; and the strenuous objections of the men against being diverted from making their tobacco crop.[12]

In summary, I quote Professor Morgan:

> There was no trained constabulary. The county commissioners, who annually chose the constables in each county, usually rotated the job among men of small means, who could not afford the fines for refusing to take it. There was no army except the militia, composed of men who would be as unlikely as the constables to make effective instruments for suppressing the insubordination of their own kind.[13]

There was, then, in Virginia no intermediate social control stratum based on a secure yeoman class such as had been preserved in England.

The Deference and Reverence Deficit

In well-ordered class societies, ancient traditions of pomp and circumstance play a vital part in instructing the masses in subservience to "their betters." "[R]everence," wrote Francis Bacon, "is that wherewith princes are girt from God."[14] But the claim to authority of the seventeenth-century planter elite rested on raw acquisitiveness, expressed first of all in their possession of mainly English bond-laborers, and in their large handholdings based not on ancient titles but on headrights purchased by import of human chattels.[15] There were no storied manors in Virginia to which they could say they had been born. Furthermore, the fact that the elite planters were necessarily as involved as the poorest of their neighbors in the cheek-by-jowl competition each for his share in the tobacco market was not calculated to promote a deferential attitude toward the same elite planters as the ruling circle.

Auxiliary institutions, particularly those of established religion, render indispensable service in preserving and protecting the awe in which ruling classes need to be held. But that great pillar of reverence for authority the established Church of England did not travel well to seventeenth-century Virginia, where it enjoyed the status of a mere subdivision of the London bishopric. Whereas in England the parish minister, upon recommendation of some eminent person or of a university, was appointed with life tenure, in Virginia, parish vestries made up of rich local planters had the nomination of the minister who was then formally chosen by the Governor rather than by a clerical authority. The result was that ministers, being no more than hired hands employed from year to year at the pleasure of the vestries, often lapsed into demoralization. In cataloguing the sad conditions prevailing in Virginia in the middle of the seventeenth century, an English clerical critic asserted that the colony's ministers were "for the most part, not only far short of those qualifications required in Ministers ... but men of opposite qualities and tempers ... by their loose lives, and un-Gospel becoming conversation."[16] Such a church "could not play its traditional role of fostering obedient habits" among the colonists.[17]

The Anglican church was enfeebled, and neither was the political climate favorable to Puritans. Quakers were outlawed in the seventeenth century; official hostility towards them did not slacken until early in the eighteenth century.[18] In any case, ministers were so few and far between that even if every one of them had been willing and able to play the social buffer role, they would have been an insufficient leaven for the colony's lump of irreverence. In a colony of forty or fifty thousand widely scattered people, there were only thirty-five Anglican priests in 1680.[19]

What is one to conclude, then, about the state of ruling-class social control in the decade before Bacon's Rebellion, when Colony Secretary Thomas Ludwell was fain to confess that Virginia's small landholders were restrained from rebellion only by "faith in the mercy of God, loyalty to the King, and affection for the Governor"?[20]

A Society Shaped by Monoculture

The basic cause of the failure of the plantation elite to establish a viable system of social control in the seventeenth century was, of course, the tobacco monocultural economy itself. Rainbolt stated the case most clearly:

> A colony where most men pursued the same occupation of tobacco planter seemed ill suited to the emergence of a heirarchical social system. A Province where most men lived in relative isolation on scattered plantations prevented that constant scrutiny of inferiors by their superiors deemed vital to the order of a society.[21]

After the margin of profit had been stabilized by the institution of the new chattel bond-labor relation of production in the 1620s, the farm price of Chesapeake tobacco averaged about 4*d.* per pound in the 1630s.[22] In the next two decades, however, the average price was reduced by almost half, to 2.2*d.* It is impossible to fix the year when the falling tendency of tobacco prices reached the critical level in regard to ruling-class social control, but the decline of tobacco to an average of 1.2*d.* per pound for the entire decade and a half beginning in 1660 was a basic condition for the eruption in 1673 of the social control crisis known to history as Bacon's Rebellion.[23]

Tobacco planters were trapped in a vicious spiral: efforts by each planter to make up in volume for the declining price forced all to do as each; as this drove the price even lower, the planters fell ever deeper into debt. In 1664 the planters of Virginia and Maryland went into debt of £50,000 on their shipments to England.[24] But the burden did not fall uniformly on the planters; indeed, it tended to enrich the planter elite.

Warren M. Billings has analyzed the year-to-year changes in the level of the indebtedness in six Virginia counties for the period 1660–75[25] by tabulating the amounts for which creditors sued for payment.[26] The total debt of all planters in cases decided in the courts of those six counties averaged 3,243,000 pounds of tobacco per year. In those counties, with a total population of several thousand,[27] the thirty or so members of the plantation elite accounted for 35.6 percent of the total credit, with the debts owed *to* members of the elite class amounting to twice as much as the amounts owed *by* them.[28] Social dissolution was especially portended by the fact that the indebtedness gap between the elite and the general run of planters tended to increase as time went on, by an average of 375,000 pounds of tobacco every year during the sixteen-year period.[29] The records suggest that the deteriorating conditions of the non-elite planters in these six counties were typical of Virginia as a whole.

This discrepancy between the elite and non-elite with respect to the debt burden would seem to be a reflection of a marked tendency toward concentration of land in the hands of the former (see Table 9.1). Morgan finds an extreme degree of land engrossment by headright for other counties: in 1658, thirty persons owned most of the land – 100,000 acres – on the south side of the Potomac; in 1664, 33,750 acres of headright land went to only thirteen persons in Accomack County, and 15,050 acres of Rappahannock land was claimed by only six persons. These nineteen patents accounted for 30 percent of all the headright acres patented in Virginia in that year, and averaged over 2,500 acres each; eight patents in Accomack, Isle of Wight and Rappahannock counties, averaging more than 4,300 acres each, accounted for 23 percent of all headright land patented in Virginia in 1666.[30] These figures from various counties appear consistent with and confirm the trend suggested by the comparison of figures for 1626 and 1704 shown in Table 9.1.[31]

The most significant indicator of increasing concentration of capital, however, is the number of laborers per plantation. Kevin P. Kelly's study of the records of Surry County, on the south side of the James River, revealed that

Table 9.1 Increase in concentration of landholdings in Virginia, 1626–1704

Holdings	1626	1704
100 acres or less		
(a) % of total acres	24.9%	4.9%
(b) % of all holdings	54.0%	24.0%
(c) no. of holdings	126	1,316
(d) acres	8,610	112,100
(e) average size	68	85
101 to 499 acres		
(a) % of total acres	41.4%	32.7%
(b) % of all holdings	36.9%	54.3%
(c) no. of holdings	42	2,971
(d) acres	13,140	742,000
(e) average size	313	250
500 to 999 acres		
(a) % of total acres	22.5%	22.3%
(b) % of all holdings	7.7%	13.5%
(c) no. of holdings	14	738
(d) acres	7,800	504,300
(e) average size	557	683
1,000 acres or more		
(a) % of total acres	10.2%	40.1%
(b) % of all holdings	1.6%	8.4%
(c) no. of holdings	3	461
(d) acres	3,582	907,900
(e) average size	1,284	1,969

Sources: John C. Hotten, *The Original Lists*, pp. 266–74, patented land in Virginia in 1626; 1704 Virginia Rent Rolls, printed in T. J. Wertenbaker, *The Planters of Colonial Virginia* (Princeton, 1922).

there, small households dominated throughout the seventeenth century, although "there was a growing divergence between the large planters controlling more than ten laborers, and the small, independent planter."[32] Wertenbaker found that the Surry County ratio of tithables to taxpayers in 1675 and 1685, considered together, was 18 to 10, but by 1704 the comparable ratio, of tithables to freeholders, was 39 to 10.[33] Edward Randolph, Royal Inspector of Customs, reported to the Lords of Trade and Plantations in 1696 that the "chief and only reason" for the retarded development of Virginia colony was that "Members of the Council and others . . . have from time to time procured grants of very large Tracts of Land." By the use of headrights, he said, many of this elite group held "twenty or thirty thousand acres of land apiece" which were left unplanted yet unavailable to prospective planters.[34]

Reflecting the results of such egregious engrossment of headright land by importation of bond-laborers by the plantation bourgeoisie, 60 to 65 per cent of Virginia landholders, according to Wertenbaker's estimate, had no bond-laborers at all in the closing two or two and a half decades of the seventeenth century.[35] A corresponding pattern of differentiation is apparent in Russell R. Menard's comparison of estate inventories on the lower western Maryland shore of Chesapeake Bay, in the 1658–70 and 1700–1705 periods.[36] The proportion having bond-laborers declined by nearly one-tenth (49.4 to 45.2 percent). The proportion of the total bond-labor force represented by estates having only one or two bond-laborers was reduced by more than one-third (18.3 to 11.0 percent). At the other end of the scale, in 1700–1705 the proportion of estates with 21 or more bond-laborers was nearly six times what it had been in the 1658–70 period (rising from 1.1 percent to 6.2 percent of all estates), and their share of the total number of bond-laborers had increased to almost five times what it was in the earlier period (from 6.5 to 31.6 percent of all bond-laborers).

The Dutch Wars and Doubtful Loyalty

Threats of Dutch seaborne incursions during the Second and Third Anglo-Dutch Wars, in 1665–67 and 1672–74, served to underscore the weakness of the elite's social control of the colony. In 1667, a Dutch warship succeeded in entering the James River and capturing the Virginia tobacco fleet of twenty ships. That same year, the Dutch admiral de Ruyter audaciously sailed up the Thames and the Medway, and detroyed or captured some of the finest ships of the English navy. But there was a significant difference in the two situations, so far as the ruling class was concerned. England was in no danger of invasion and occupation by Dutch forces aided by the rank and file of the English people; in Virginia that prospect was perceived as real.

On 11 July 1673, during the Third Anglo-Dutch War, another Dutch naval force of nine ships conducted a raid up the James River, defeated the English in a three-hour battle, and captured eleven merchant ships laden with cargo.[37] Governor Berkeley and the Colony Council, writing to the King and Privy Council in England, asked that a large fort be constructed to command the entrance to the James and the Chesapeake Bay, or else that the home government provide regularly for a strong convoy for the Virginia tobacco fleet, the expense to be recovered through raised merchant freight charges. They based their appeal on the non-functional state of the Virginia militia.

But the social control question, which is a central concern of this work, is brought most starkly into focus by the following passage of their letter, which describes Virginia as

> intersected by Soe many vast Rivers as makes more Miles to Defend, then we have men of trust to Defend them, for by our neerest computacon wee leave at our backs as many Servants (besides Negroes) as there are freemen to defend the Shoare and on all our Frontiers the Indians. Both which gives men fearfull apprehentions of the dainger they Leave their Estates and Families in, Whilst they are drawne from their houses to defend the Borders. Of which number also at least one third are single freemen (whose labor Will hardly maintaine them), or men much in debt, both which

Wee may reasonably expect upon any small advantage the Enemy may gaine upon us, would revolt to them in hopes of bettering their Condicon.[38]

Fourteen such debt-ridden Surry County freemen attempted the following December and January to organize a mutiny against payment of the colony levy. Meeting first at Lawnes Creek Church and next in Devil's Field, they declared their determination to stand together come what might, "burn one, burn all." Their effort was thwarted; four were fined 1,000 pounds of tobacco, one 2,000 pounds, and all were put under bond for their future good behavior.[39]

Although the Lawnes Creek Mutiny was thwarted, it was both a validation of the fears of Berkeley and the Colony Council, and a portent of the general mutiny of 1676, Bacon's Rebellion. Objective "social and economic conditions" themselves "conspired against an effective control of the citizenry by the provincial leadership."[40]

Facing the Problem

Three means were available to the plantation bourgeoisie to combat the economic root of social instability: (1) regulate the production and shipment of tobacco to relieve the ruinous effect of the glut of the market; (2) diversify production in order to escape the desperate dependency on tobacco monoculture; or (3) find a way to lower the cost of labor per unit of output.

It was to be expected that contradictions would develop between English monarchy and mercantilism, on the one hand, and the colonial plantation bourgeoisie, on the other. These clashes of interest, which in time would find fullest expression as part of the American War of Independence, first emerged in the context of the long crisis of tobacco overproduction and low prices that began at the moment of the Stuart Restoration in 1660.

Throughout the seventeenth century, the Anglo-American plantation bourgeoisie preached the virtues of diversification of the Chesapeake economy, while reproducing decade after decade the economic morass of tobacco monoculture. Warnings were sounded by Virginia officials against basing Virginia's economy on tobacco alone; they urged that a variety of products be developed to meet a variety of English market demands. The longest-serving and most famous of Virginia colonial governors, Sir William Berkeley, was himself the most articulate denouncer of tobacco monoculture and the most enthusiastic advocate of diversification. "Our Governors," said Berkeley, in a treatise of the early 1660s, "by the corruption of the times they lived in, laid the Foundation of our wealth and industry on the vices of men ... [particularly] this vicious habit of taking Tobacco."[41] But, with encouragement and instruction from the home government, said Berkeley, Virginia within seven years could supply England with all its needs for "Silk, Flax, Hemp, Pitch, Tar, Iron, Masts, Timber and Pot-ashes," that were then of necessity being imported from other countries at great expense.

Over the years, various suggestions were made for reducing production – by limiting the number of leaves on the plant, or the number of plants, or by limiting the time allowed for transplanting seedlings – and for regulating the time of shipping the crop in orders to maximize favorable seasonal factors. Repeated proposals were advanced for co-ordinating with Maryland and North Carolina in limiting tobacco production, but they came to naught. Merchant shipowners opposed this last idea because, as they said in 1662, it would seriously interfere with the shipment of bond-laborers and thus cause a burdensome increase in the number of unemployed in England.[42]

Other measures aimed at directly shoring up tobacco planters' profits by exemptions from export duties, by a measure of relief from the provisions of the Navigation Law, and by exempting Virginia-owned ships from export duties on their cargoes.

Topographical factors, involving the heavy costs of clearing away the ubiquitous forest, and the decentralizing influence of geography (Virginia being a series of peninsulas formed by navigable rivers), as well as clashes of various economic interests, hampered programs aimed at both diversification and the limiting of tobacco production.[43] With regard to diversification, furthermore, there was a lack of capital in Virginia for ventures into other lines of production, since the Virginia bourgeoisie was chronically in debt to English merchants. The three Dutch wars used up English resources that might theoretically have been available for investment in Virginia; later, the same drain of capital accompanied the first phase (1689–1713) of the Anglo-French wars of colonial rivalry. After the Restoration in 1660, the Crown itself was so desperate for funds that, far from wanting to embark on diversification experiments, it was determined to maximize the tobacco trade, which was its most lucrative source of income; integral with that, there was the interest of the English tax-and-customs "farmers," who contracted to collect the king's customs on tobacco imports. In 1671 the king's share from import customs collections on Virginia tobacco was estimated to be £80,000 per year; in 1682 the royal share of tobacco profits was calculated to be £7 per year for every plantation bond-laborer.[44] English merchants, who did have capital they might have invested, were not interested in taking unnecessary risks with it; and they were adamantly opposed to encouraging the rise of a set of competitive industries in Virginia.[45]

On general principles the English mercantilists were increasingly wary of deviations from the primacy of tobacco production, and especially of those deviations that might lead to the development of competition with goods produced in England and to the consequent economic independence of colonies. In April 1705 the Commissioners of Trade specifically instructed the Governors of Virginia and Maryland to "take care not to suffer the People employed in the making of Tobacco to be Deverted therefrom."[46] In the eyes of English manufacturers, such a development "would be of very ill consequence" to English woolen exports and tobacco shipping and imports, and would jeopardize the relation of dependence in which a colony should be kept.[47]

In 1707 Governor John Seymour warned the Board of Trade that credit-starved Maryland planters, rendered "almost starke naked" for lack of English-made clothing, were turning to making their own linen and woolen goods. He too worried about the "ill consequence to the Revenue arising on tobacco" if people in that colony generally laid aside tobacco-making in order to manufacture such goods as they customarily purchased from England.[48] Governor Gooch was confident that wages were so high in Virginia that Virginia-made linen would cost 20 percent more and woolen cloth 50 percent more than English textiles and therefore would be unable to compete with English-made goods as exports. But since they might reduce the market for British manufactures within the colony, such local industry should be discouraged. Acting on Gooch's information, the Board of Trade in London resolved to find a way to "divert their [the colonists'] thoughts from Undertakings of this nature."[49]

Diversification efforts were not aimed at supplanting the tobacco monoculture, but merely at protecting it. One premise was common to all parties – the Virginia ruling elite, the English Crown, English merchants, and rival provincial governments in Maryland and North Carolina. However much they differed over principles, such as those of the mercantilist Navigation Laws, or details regarding the regulation of production and shipment, or the number and location of centralizing port cities, they all held to one inviolable principle – the priority to be given to the maintenance and enhancement of profit on tobacco.[50] Consequently, schemes for limiting directly the supply of tobacco brought to the market were driven aground by the prevailing winds of competitive pressure for the quickest turnover of capital, coupled with the Crown's determination to resist any diminution of its tobacco revenues, which were based on physical volume rather than selling price.[51]

But even if, by a sudden rush of enlightened self-interest to the heads of all parties, some more than evanescent scheme for "economic reform" could have been instituted, it would have been foredoomed by the insubstantiality of the requisite buffer social control stratum. Virginia's "labor- and capital-scarce economy demanded efficient marshaling of effort and resources," requiring social discipline that could not be imposed by the plantation elite, having "large goals but small capacity to command," and "lacking strong supporting social and religious institutions."[52]

The Third Possibility: Reducing Labor Costs

The English bourgeoisie finally secured direct access to African labor at the end of the Second Dutch War, concluded in the Treaty of Breda in 1667.[53] Five years later, with the establishment of the Royal African Company, England embarked on a career that within less than forty years made English merchants the preeminent suppliers of African bond-labor to the Western Hemisphere. A rise in the demand for labor in England, and a corresponding rise in the wage level there (soon to be coupled with the great demand for cannon fodder for the far-flung battle lines of England's contest with France in Europe and in America), reduced the supply of persons available for bond-labor in the plantation colonies.[54]

As it had been when the source of supply had been in Europe, the African labor trade was a self-motivating capital interest. Virginia Governor Thomas Lord Culpeper was urged by King Charles II "to give all due encouragement and invitation to Merchants and others ... and in particular to the Royal African Company of England." Culpeper was further instructed to be on guard against any "interlopers" in that trade, which was intended to be a monopoly of the Royal African Company.[55] Replying a year later, Culpeper asserted that the king alone made at least £6 per year from the labor of each Negro bond-laborer in Virginia.[56]

Now, finally, the plantation bourgeoisie was brought within reach of the realization of the vision foreshadowed in a number of laws already enacted, of enrichment through the imposition of lifetime, hereditary bond-servitude of Africans and African-Americans. In seventeenth-century Virginia the buyer paid an average of £14 and £13 respectively for men and women five-year bond-laborers. The investment in "seasoned" hands depreciated, however, and at an increasing rate; at the end of three years its value would be only £7 for males and £4 for females. The buyer of an adult lifetime bond-laborer was making an average investment of £18 to £20, an amount that depreciated over the remaining years of the laborer's life. Thus the retained value of the investment at the end of three years would run in favor of the option for lifetime bond-labor. If that lifetime lasted ten years, the annual amortization on the investment would have been less than £2, about 30 percent less than on two five-year bond-laborers. There were ancillary benefits of investment in lifetime bond-labor since there was no outlay for freedom dues, and even at birth a child of a lifetime bond-laborer was of some capital value.[57] The anticipated reduction in labor costs would have been desirable for the employing class at any time, but as the end of the seventeenth century neared it appeared to offer the bourgeoisie both a way of evading the unresolvable contradictions between monoculture and diversity, and a significant easing of the contention between English and continental branches of the business with respect to profits from low-priced tobacco. Culpeper stressed this latter consideration in urging the Royal African Company to moderate its prices for the sale of lifetime bond-laborers in Virginia. "[I]n regard to the infinite profit that comes to the King by every Black (far beyond any other Plantation) ... and that Blacks can make [tobacco] cheaper than Whites, I conceive it is for his Majesty's Interest full as much as the Countrys, or rather much more, to have Blacks as cheap as possible in Virginia."[58]

But if a lack of "capacity to command" had made it impossible for the plantation bourgeoisie to impose the necessary social discipline on free and middle-rank tobacco farmers, what hope could there be for imposing social control on a society when masses of kidnapped Africans were added to the ranks of the disaffected bond-laborers already at the bottom of the heap?

A Reflective Postscript

With that question, the narrative portion of this chapter is complete, but a reflective postscript is in order. For the reader's indulgence, I appeal to the example of Philip Alexander Bruce's speculation on the possibility of an alternative path of development for the Old Dominion.[59]

Those historians who intend not only to record and interpret history, but also in so doing to affect its future course are impelled to offer judgments that for them seem to light the path ahead,[60] even though sooner or later other historians are sure to find the light misdirected or insufficient in one or more respects. Having studied the record of the travail of the common people of seventeenth-century Virginia, "The Ordeal of Colonial Virginia," as Professor Morgan has called it, I cannot but ponder if it was possible for history to have followed a different, happier course and, if so, what Virginia by such a course would have become. It is a speculation, but I hope not an idle one.

In 1625 Sir Francis Bacon cited Virginia as an example to be avoided in establishing plantations, arguing that "the base and hasty drawing of profit" from tobacco worked to "the untimely prejudice of the main business."[61] John Smith, son of the English yeomanry, soon warned that to base production on chattel bond-labor was a disastrous course.[62]

Received historiographical doctrine argues to the contrary as follows. Virginia colony could only survive by exports; tobacco was not only the most profitable prospect for that role, but the only practicable one. Because of the low price of tobacco and the high prevailing wages, chattel bond-servitude was indispensable. The alternative was "slow progress" as "a community of small peasant properitors." Such a course would (the thesis concludes) have been "utopian"; Virginia, indeed, was by nature designed to be "A commonwealth of tobacco plantations."[63]

Who is right? If the question were merely a historiographical one, it would be as well to let it rest with the dead past. But the issue is not dead; it is as vital today as it was those nearly four centuries ago. The equating of economic growth with the most rapid accumulation of capital, which led Virginia to misery just as John Smith predicted, has continued to this day to guide the ruling class of the USA, who subordinate to that principle all other interests, heedless of the misery that it may leave in its wake.

"Two roads diverged . . . And that made all the difference"

As Virginia was first getting high on tobacco, the Pilgrims landed at Plymouth Rock to begin in New England a form of internal economic organization that largely embodied the principles advanced by Francis Bacon in that respect.[64] In an appraisal of the condition of Virginia at the close of the seventeenth century, James Blair, the founder of William and Mary College lamented the fact that "No care was taken at the beginning to seat that Country [Virginia] in Townshipps, as in New England." The result, he continued, was that

Virginia was "deprived of the great Company of Citizens and Tradesmen that are in other Countryes."[65]

Although both colonies were products of bourgeois England, four sets of contrasting factors would determine their respective patterns of social development:

1. the domination of landholding by large plantations in Virginia versus the predominance of small farms in New England;

2. the Virginia monoculture, with its utter dependence upon export markets, versus the mainly non-market-centered, and definitely non-capitalist, basic New England economy;

3. the chattel bond-labor force of the Virginia Plantation system versus the non-bond-labor of the small New England farms;

4. the Virginia "family," which included all the persons belonging to one plantation even if most of them were not kin of each other, versus that typical New England family of a mother and father and their children.

The character of seventeenth-century Virginia society in these respects has been adequately described here; however, a brief elaboration of the New England case is in order. The statistics cited by Moller regarding contrasting seventeenth-century sex ratios in Anglo-American continental colonies[66] are explained in terms of the contrasting labor bases:

While in the New England immigration males outnumbered females three to two, the ratio was six to one in the Virginia immigration. The Puritans, broadly speaking, arrived by families ... The movement to Virginia, on the contrary, consisted predominantly of male workers [i.e., chattel bond-laborers].[67]

As we have seen, for every person brought into Virginia in the seventeenth century, a patent on fifty acres of land was bestowed on whomever had paid the cost of the immigrant's transportation. This custom, supplemented by special land grants to favored individuals, was the basis of the high degree of concentration of landownership in that colony. In the very earliest days in New England, the headright form of land grant was observed, but over the colonial period as a whole "by far the greater part of the land disposed of was granted to communities of settlers."[68] Thus was formed in New England the very "township" form of settlement whose absence in Virginia was so much lamented by Commissary Blair. Under the New England system of settlement by families, "Great pains were taken to guard against excessive grants and accumulation of large estates," writes Egleston. "Land, however abundant, was to be given by the community authorities to those who could use it."[69] New England settlement was in the form of communities initiated by a group of families securing, usually from the colony general court, an allotment of land not occupied by other settlers. These "proprietors" then distributed the land to colonists by plots of ground, proportioned to their payment for expenses of surveying, and other incidentals.[70] A tendency toward concentration of land ownership did occur in New England "[t]hrough purchase, marriage, inheritance, [and] proprietary rights ... with the result that later distributions of land, particularly those of the eighteenth century, showed more inequality;"[71] but it was relatively insignificant as compared to that in plantation Virginia.[72]

Schemes and hopes of diversification of the Virginia economy were frustrated, as has been noted, by a shortage of capital for investment. Caught as the planters were between a low-ranging elasticity of tobacco prices and the inelasticity of royal customs and shipping charges, they could not escape the discipline of the next year's indebted crop. Seventeenth-century New England settlers were not faced with that difficulty because "the household mode of production remained the dominant form of existence."[73] By the middle of the eighteenth century, when a degree of market development had occurred,[74] the New England farmer might profit from a cash crop, perhaps wheat. But where does a self-employed person, propertyless except for an ax, possibily a plow, two or three animals, and enough grain to get the family through to his first harvest – where, without credit resources, does such a self-employed person get the capital for clearing land, building shelter for the family and the animals, and storage sheds or barns, and cutting new road?

> [Such a] farmer may be compared to a business corporation which pursues a conservative dividend policy. Instead of paying out all of current income to stockholders, it puts a large share back into the business, thus increasing the value of his capital . . . [thus] literally ploughing in his profits.[75]

Such farmers made up the "communities of peasant proprietors" that Bruce argued were necessarily excluded from the march of "progress" in Virginia. Yet in New England they proved from their seventeenth-century beginnings to be perfectly viable and capable of eventual evolution from natural (subsistence) production to simple commodity production (the commodity beginning as the property of the producer) to capitalist production (wherein the product is never the property of the producer, but of the capitalist employer).[76]

Colonial Virginia has been assessed as "dynamic" and New England as the "least dynamic" of the continental colonies. By the eighteenth century, when Virginia and New England were about equal in population size, Virginia's exports and imports were six to ten times as large as New England's.[77] It is obvious that New England's climate and soil characteristics made the general employment of bond-labor impracticable, even if the land distribution system had formed plantations of a size suitable for profitable capitalist operation, and some staple had been struck upon that would not offend competitors in Old England. But it does not follow that Virginia's climate and soil could not have been settled on the basis of communities of small farmsteads. For New England it was not a matter of choice; for Virginia it was. So it was that New England, more than anywhere else in North America, re-created rural England, while the Virginia plantation bourgeoisie "cast away restraining ideologies and institutions [and] developed a labor process unknown in England."[78]

It was a conscious decision, not an unthinking one. In opting for the "dynamics" of monoculture and chattel bond-labor, the members of the

Virginia plantation bourgeoisie knew they were rejecting the counsel of perhaps the most illustrious member of the Virginia Company. "It is true," Bacon had said, "speedy profit is not to be neglected as far as it may stand with the good of the plantation, but no further."[79] It was simply what preacher Lionel Gatford warned them against in 1657 – the triumph of "Private Interest" over "Publick Good." Now fifty years after the fateful option was made, having ignored Sir Francis's precept and New England's example, the Virginia ruling elite found itself three thousand miles from home with no yeoman buffer between it and a people of whom "six parts of seaven at least, are Poore, Endebted, Discontented and Armed."[80]

10

The Status of African-Americans

For more than a century now, scholars have studied the records regarding the status of African-Americans in Virginia and Maryland in the seventeenth century.[1] Although I in turn have made my own independent study of these materials, persons familiar with the field will recognize the majority of my references to the records. What they and other readers will be challenged to do is to test my interpretation of the facts. Therefore, it seems appropriate at this point to review the basic definition of racial oppression and to enumerate the particular forms of that oppression as they were set forth in Volume One of this work.[2] The hallmark of racial oppression in its colonial origins and as it has persisted in subsequent historical contexts is the reduction of all members of the oppressed group to one undifferentiated social status, a status beneath that of any member of any social class within the oppressor group.[3] It is a system of rule designed to deny, disregard, delegitimate previous or potential social distinctions that may have existed or that might tend to emerge in the normal course of development of a class society.

In Chapter 8 and again in Chapter 9, I have argued inferentially that "the white race," and thus a system of racial oppression, did not exist and could not have existed in the seventeenth-century tobacco colonies. In Chapter 8 that conclusion was based on evidence of class solidarity of laboring-class European-Americans with African-Americans, and the consequent absence of an all-class coalition of European-Americans directed against African-Americans. In Chapter 9 the thesis was linked with the lack of a substantial intermediate buffer social control stratum. In the present chapter a third ply of the argument is to be developed primarily from the Virginia records, directly bearing on the actual social status of African-Americans in those decades. Since, so far as I know, this analytical approach to the study of racial oppression is different from that taken by other historians, I offer the following brief elaboration in justification of it.

Some scholars concerned with the problem of the origin of racial slavery have emphasized that the status of the African-Americans in the seventeenth-century Chesapeake cannot be fully determined because of a deficiency in the records for the early decades.[4] Others, by reference to Virginia statutes, assert that the differentiation of the status of African-Americans and European-

Americans can be determined as beginning only about 1660.[5] I would propose to dissolve this aspect of the debate over the origin of racial slavery by recognizing that the historical records of seventeenth-century Virginia compel the conclusion that the relative social status of African-Americans and European-Americans in that "Volatile Society" can be determined to have been indeterminate. It was indeterminate because it was being fought out:[6] fought out in the context of the great social stresses of high mortality, the vicissitudes of a monocultural economy, impoverishment, and an extremely high sex ratio – all of which were based on or derived from the abnormal system of chattel bond-servitude. The critical moment of that social struggle arrived with Bacon's Rebellion of 1676 which posed the question of who should rule. The answer, which would be contrived over the next several decades, would not only determine the status of African-Americans but would install the monorail of Anglo-American historical development, white supremacy.

The reduction of the almost totally English labor force from tenants and wage-laborers to chattel bond-servitude in Virginia in the 1620s was indeed a negation of previously existing laws and customs, but it was imposed by one set of colonists on another set of colonists. It was not, therefore, an act of racial oppression (no more than was the 1547 slave law in England[7]), but merely an extremely reactionary sort of class oppression. As for seeking to establish two distinct categories of servitude – limited-term and lifetime servitude – the death rate was so high for several decades[8] that there would have been no practical advantage for employers in such a distinction.[9]

In 1640, however, just such a distinction was anticipated when the Virginia General Court, in a singular instance, imposed lifetime bond-servitude on John Punch. Punch, an African-American, and two European-American fellow bond-laborers were arraigned for having run away.[10] But why did the appetite for profit not lead the court to sentence John Punch's European-American comrades to lifetime servitude also?[11]

Winthrop D. Jordan directs particular attention to this decree, and cites it as evidence for his belief that the enslavement of Negroes was the result of an "unthinking decision," arising out of a prejudice against Negroes.[12] It may be true that the court in this case was motivated by such feelings, although any such conclusion rests totally on inference; it is not a fact of the record. Other inferences are possible. Under English common law, Christians could not be enslaved by Christians; presumably, Scots and Dutchmen were Christians; but Africans were not. As a practical matter, England's relations with Scotland and Holland were critical to English interests, so that there might well have been a reluctance to offend those countries to whom English concerns were in hostage, whereas no such complication was likely to arise from imposing lifetime bondage on an African or African-American. The court members in all probability were aware of the project then under way to establish an English plantation colony, using African lifetime bond-laborers, on Providence

Island;[13] and they surely knew that some Africans were already being exploited elsewhere in the Americas on the same terms. They might have been influenced by such examples to pursue the same purpose in Virginia. They were also aware that the African-American bond-laborers arriving in Virginia from the West Indies (or Brazil via Dutch colonies to the north of Maryland[14]) did not come with English-style, term-limiting indentures; the members of the General Court may thus have felt encouraged to impose the ultimate term, a lifetime, in such cases. Whether the decision in this instance was a "thinking" or an "unthinking" one, the court by citing John Punch's "being a negro" in justification of his life sentence was resorting to mere bench law, devoid of reference to English or Virginia precedent.[15] What the record of this case does show, so far as the ideas in people's heads are concerned, is a disposition on the part of some, at least, of the plantation bourgeoisie to reduce African-Americans to lifetime servitude.

As the proportion of bond-laborers who were surviving their terms increased, some employers began to see an appeal in extending the bond-laborers' terms generally. The "custom of the country" for English bond-laborers in Virginia, which had been set at four years in 1658, was increased to five in 1662.[16] With the flourishing of the Irish slave trade in the wake of the Cromwellian conquest,[17] laws were enacted to make Irish bond-laborers (and, after 1658, "all aliens" in that status) serve six years.[18] That provision was eliminated, however, by the post-Cromwell law of 1660, in the interest of "peopling the country."[19]

The 1660 law equalized at five years the length of "the custom of the country" without distinction of "aliens," but that same law *for the first time* restricted term-limiting to those "of what christian nation soever" (the Anglican Church having been established in Ireland, Ireland now qualified as a "christian country"). Since the only "christian nations" were in Europe, this clause was most particularly, though not exclusively, aimed at persons of African origin or descent. This exclusion of African-Americans from the limitation on the length of servitude imposed on bond-laborers reflected and was intended to further the efforts made by some elements of the plantation bourgeoisie to reduce African-American bond-laborers to lifetime servitude. But even that, in and of itself, would have been no more than a form of class oppression of bond-laborers by owners, somewhat like the slavery of Scots miners and saltpan workers from the end of the sixteenth century to the eve of the nineteenth century, a form distinguished however by its categoric denial of social mobility to those in bondage.[20]

This was a long way from the establishment of a system of racial oppression; but its implicit denial to African-Americans of even the lowest range of social mobility, from bond-labor to freedom, contained a seed of a system of racial oppression, although that seed could not be fully developed without a strong intermediate social control stratum.

There are two sides to the coin of the General Court's order relating to John Punch; his sentence to lifetime servitude is equally proof that he was not a lifetime bond-laborer when he ran away. Indeed, by that act he was demonstrating his unwillingness to submit to even limited-term bond-servitude. The John Punch case thus epitomized the status of African-Americans in seventeenth-century Virginia. On the one hand, it showed the readiness of at least some of the plantation elite to equate "being a negro" with being a lifetime bond-laborer. On the other hand, development of social policy along this line was obstructed by several factors. First, there was what might be called institutional inertia presented by English common law, by the historic retreat from the slavery gambit of 1547 in the wake of Ket's Rebellion, and by the deep-rooted principles of Christian fellowship. Second, of course, there was the opposition of African-Americans,[21] both bond-laborers and non-bond-laborers, with the general support – certainly without the concerted opposition – of European-American bond-laborers and other free but poor laboring people, determined by a sense of common class interest.

For the period before 1676, the Virginia and Maryland records, particularly those of Virginia, are rich with examples of how the historically evolved legal, institutional and ideological superstructure of English society presented a countervailing logic to the General Court's equation regarding John Punch – examples of a recognition of normal social standing and mobility for African-Americans that was and is absolutely inconsistent with a system of racial oppression. Illustrative cases are found most frequently, though not exclusively, in the Northampton and Accomack county records.[22] In 1624, the Virginia Colony Court had occasion to consider an admiralty-type case, in the routine course of which the court considered the testimony of John Phillip, a mariner, identified as "a negro Christened in England 12 yeares since."[23] In a separate instance, a Negro named Brase and two companions, a Frenchman and a "Portugall," were brought of their own volition to Jamestown on 11 July 1625. Two months later, Brase was assigned to work for "Lady Yardley" for forty pounds of good merchantable tobacco "monthly for his wages for his service so long as he remayneth with her." In October, Brase was assigned to Governor Francis Wyatt as a "servant"; no particulars are recorded as to his terms of employment with his new employer. There was no suggesting that, "being a Negro," he was to be a lifetime bond-laborer.[24]

African-Americans who were not bond-laborers made contracts for work or for credit, and engaged in commercial as well as land transactions, with European-Americans, and in the related court proceedings they stood on the same footing as European-Americans. At the December 1663 sitting of the Accomack County Court, Richard Johnson and Mihill Bucklands disputed over the amount to be paid to Johnson for building a house for Bucklands. With the consent of both parties the issue was referred to two arbitrators.[25] The Northampton County Court gave conditional assent to the suit of John Gusall, but allowed debtor Gales Judd until the next court to make contrary proof, or pay Gusall "the summe & grant of fore hundred powndes of tobacco due per speciality with court charges."[26] Emannuel Rodriggus[27] arrived in Virginia before 1647, presumably without significant material assets, and was enlisted as a plantation bond-laborer.[28] Rodriggus became a dealer in livestock on the Eastern Shore (as the trans-Chesapeake Bay eastern peninsula of Virginia came to be known). As early as January 1652/3 there was recorded a bill of sale signed with his mark, assigning to merchant John Cornelys "one Cowe collered Blacke, aged about fowre yeares ... being my owne breed."[29] Thereafter, Rodriggus and other African-Americans frequently appear as buyers and sellers, and sometimes as donors, of livestock in court records that reflect the assumption of the right of African-Americans to accumulate and dispose of property, and that also assume the legal parity of buyer and seller.[30]

The Indian king Debeada of the Mussaugs gave to Jone, daughter of Anthony Johnson, 100 acres of land on the south side of Pungoteague Creek on 27 September 1657.[31] In 1657 Emannuell Cambow, "Negro," was granted ownership of fifty acres of land in James City County, part of a tract that had been escheated from the former grantee.[32] In 1669, Robert Jones (or Johns), a York County tailor, acting with the agreement of his wife Marah, "for divers good causes and considerations him thereunto moveing ... bargained & sold unto John Harris Negro all the estate rite [right] title & Inheritance ... in fiftie Acres of Land ... in New Kent County."[33] A series of land transactions – lease, sub-lease, and re-lease – was conducted by Manuell Rodriggus with three separate individuals over a ten-year period from June 1662.[34]

Marriage and Social Mobility

In the colonial Chesapeake in the seventeenth century, marriage might be a significant factor for social mobility. The prevailing high death rate and the high sex ratio resulted in a relative frequency of remarriages of widows in the records.[35] Whatever a widow might own generally became the property of the new husband. Phillip Mongum, though only recently free, had begun an ascent in the social scale that would eventually result in his becoming a relatively prosperous tenant farmer and livestock dealer (in 1672, he was a partner of two European-Americans in a joint lease of a plantation of three hundred acres[36]). When Mary Morris, a widow with children, and Phillip Mongum were contemplating marriage early in 1651, they entered into a prenuptial agreement regarding the property she then owned. Mongum agreed in writing that her property was not to be sold by him but was to remain the joint heritage of Mary and the children from her previous marriage(s): "one Cowe with a calfe by her side & all her increase that shall issue ever after of the said Cowe or calfe[,] moreover Towe featherbeds & what belongs unto them, one Iron Pott, one Kettle, one fryeing pan & towe gunnes & three breeding sowes with their increase." Mongum signed the agreement and bound himself to see to its faithful performance.[37]

Francis Payne's second wife Amy was a European-American. When Payne died late in the summer of 1673, his will made Amy his executrix and the sole heir of his "whole Estate real & personal moveables and immoveables."[38]

Within two years Amy married William Gray, a European-American, whose interest was to stop his own downward social mobility by looting Amy's inheritance from Francis Payne. In August 1675, Amy charged in court that Gray had not only beaten and otherwise abused her but had also "made away almost all her estate" and intended to complete the process and reduce her to being a public charge. The court did not attempt to challenge Gray's disposal of her inherited estate to satisfy his debts; but it did keep him in jail for a month until he satisfied the court that he would return a mare belonging to Amy and promised to support her enough to prevent her being thrown on the charity of the parish.[39] Some time in 1672, an African-American woman named Cocore married Francis Skipper (or Cooper), owner of a 200-acre plantation in Norfolk County. She had been lashed with thirty strokes the year before on the order of the court for having borne a child "out of wedlock." Perhaps there was a social mobility factor in her marrying Skipper. But they apparently lived together amiably for some five years until his death, an event which she survived by less than a year.[40]

Historical Significance of African-American Landholding

Landholding by African-Americans in the seventeenth century was significant both for the extent of it and because much of it, possibly the greater portion, was secured by headright. This particular fact establishes perhaps more forcefully than any other circumstance the normal social status accorded to African-Americans, a status that was practically as well as theoretically incompatible with a system of racial oppression. For the reader coming for the first time to the raw evidence in the Virginia Land Patent Books, or to the abstracts of them done by Nell Nugent, or to the digested accounts presented by historians of our own post-Montgomery boycott era – for such first-time readers the stories carry a stunning impact. Thanks particularly to the brief – but penetrating – emphasis on the subject by Lerone Bennett,[41] and to the special studies made by Deal and by Breen and Innes, the story of the Anthony Johnson family is readily available. Another African-American in this category, Benjamin Dole of Surry County, may yet find biographers. It is especially noteworthy that the persons for whose importation these particular patents were granted were mainly, if not all, bond-laborers brought from Europe.

Since considerable attention has been devoted to these African-Americans in the works referred to above, I will simply list them:

• Land patent granted to Anthony Johnson, on 250 acres for transport of five persons: Tho. Benrose, Peter Bughby, Antho. Cripps, John Gessorol[?], Richard Johnson (Virginia Land Patent Book No. 2, p. 326, 24 July 1651).

- Patent granted to John Johnson, son of Anthony Johnson, on 500 acres, on Great Nassawattocks Creek, adjacent to land granted to Anthony Johnson, for the transportation of eleven persons: John Edwards, Wm. Routh, Thos. Yowell, Fran. Maland, Wm. Price, John Owe, Dorothy Reely, Rich Hamstead, Law[rence] Barnes (Virginia Land Patent Book No. 3, p. 101, 10 May 1652).

- Patent on 100 acres bounded by lands owned by Anthony, Richard's father, and by brother John Johnson, granted by Governor Richard Bennett to Richard Johnson, "Negro," for the transportation of two bond-laborers: William Ames and William Vincent (Virginia Land Patent Book No. 3, p. 21, November 1654).

- Land patent dated 17 December 1656 granted to Benjamin Dole, "Negro," 300 acres in Surry County for the importation of six persons (Virginia Land Patent Book No. 4, p. 71, 17 December 1656).

It has been pointed out that headrights could be sold by the original importers to other persons, and that such a patent might therefore be granted to persons other than the original owners of the bond-laborers. There is no way of knowing whether the Johnsons and Benjamin Dole ever were in possession of the bond-laborers whose headrights they exercised, or whether they bought the headright from other persons. In any case, the point being made here is not affected. There was no suggestion that African-Americans were barred from the privilege of importing bond-laborers. Indeed, the enactment of such a ban in 1670 clearly implied that it was an accepted practice prior to that time.[42]

There is a case which for all of its uniqueness still sheds light on the question of the social mobility of African-Americans in seventeenth-century Virginia. Anthony Johnson acquired, presumably by purchase, a Negro bond-laborer named Casar. Casar stubbornly claimed he was entitled to be free, that he had come to Virginia around 1638, indentured for seven or eight years, but that Johnson was attempting to hold him as a lifetime bond-laborer. Under the threat of a lawsuit for unjustly detaining Casar, and persuaded by members of his family, in November 1653 Anthony Johnson agreed to abandon his claim and set Casar free. Four months later, in March 1654, Johnson, having thought more deeply, secured a court order returning Casar "into the service of his said master Anthony Johnson." Twenty years later the family had moved to Somerset County, Maryland, and Anthony Johnson had died there, but Casar was still living as a "servant" of Anthony's widow Mary.[43]

A Demonstrative Statistical Excursion

We know from the studies made by John H. Russell, Carter G. Woodson, Luther Porter Jackson and others that free Negroes in Virginia in the nineteenth century could acquire land by inheritance, gift, or purchase, and that they had the corresponding rights to dispose of it, although they lived under a system of racial oppression. Seventeenth-century data are not comprehensive.[44] The seventeenth-century Virginia Land Patent Books are available for the colony as a whole, but the preserved court records for Northampton and Accomack are more nearly comprehensive than those of the rest of the counties, and richer in detail than the records of the Virginia Colony Council and the House of Burgesses. The population of these two counties appears to have constituted between 7 and 8 percent of the population of the entire colony during the last third of the century.[45] These counties may not have been typical of the colony as a whole in respect to the prominence of African-Americans in matters that rose to the level of attention in the public records.[46] However, there is no evidence to indicate that other county courts or the central organs of government regarded proceedings in Accomack and Northampton counties as worthy of special notice. Nor have the works dealing with the Eastern Shore suggested that the attitudes of official society and the common run of European-Americans there differed qualitatively from those held in the rest of the colony.

The contrast in the ratios of farm ownership between African-Americans and European-Americans in Northampton County in 1666, and in Virginia as a whole in 1860, documents the difference between normal social class differentiation and a system of racial oppression. In Northampton County in 1666, 10.9 percent of the African-Americans and 17.6 percent of European-Americans were landholders. This disparity is no more than normal considering that 53.4 percent of the European-American landholders, but none of the African-Americans, came as free persons. The concentration of ownership is also normal, indeed an irresistible tendency of capitalist production. It is not surprising, therefore, to find that the ratio of farm ownership among European-Americans was 46 percent less in 1860 than it was in 1666. But the fact that the proportion of the African population owning land was 98 percent less in 1860 than it was in 1666 was the result not of normal capitalist economic development but of racial oppression. Let it be noted in passing that the proportion of European-Americans owning land in Virginia in 1860 was less than the proportion of Africans owning land in 1666. (See Table 10.1.)

If the proportion of land ownership among African-Americans had declined, but only as much as the ratio of land ownership among European-Americans, an indicated 30,000 landholdings would have been in the hands of the 53,000 free rural Virginia African-Americans in 1860. That would have represented an African-American land ownership ratio nearly six times the actual ratio of European-American land ownership in that year. The facts are even more dramatic when put in terms of family units, which averaged 5.6 persons per family in 1860. The operation of 30,000 African-American farms by some 5,400 families would have required a considerable degree of employment of European-American tenants and wage laborers. That would have been

Table 10.1 African-American and European-American land ownership in the entire state of Virginia in 1860 and in Northampton County in 1666

	1666	1860
Landowners, as percentage of:		
African-American rural population	10.93%	0.26%
European-American rural population	17.55%	9.53%
Ratio of the frequency of landownership among African-Americans to that among		
European-Americans	62.23%	2.73%

a. Virginia's population in 1860 was 1,595,906; African-Americans 548,607 (490,565 bond; 58,042 free); and 1,047,299 European-Americans. US Census Office, *Preliminary Report on the Eighth Census, 1860* [Washington, 1862], pp. 134–5. The state's population in 1860 was 91.5 percent rural. (Bureau of the Census, *Sixteenth Census of the United States, 1940*, Vol. I [Washington, 1942], Table 8, p. 23.) The rural/urban ratio is here assumed to be the same for the African-American and European-American populations. This assumption may tend to exaggerate the degree of land ownership among African-Americans, since the rural proportion of the African-American population was higher than that of the European-American population. (See Richard Wade, *Slavery in the Cities* [New York, 1964], pp. 17–19.) A closer approximation, however, would only add force to the point that land ownership by African-Americans was minimal in Virginia in 1860.

b. There were 92,605 farms in Virginia in 1860, of which 1,300 were owned by African-Americans. (Bureau of the Census, *Ninth Census of the United States, 1870. Statistics of Wealth and Industry*, Vol. 3 [Washington, 1872], p. 340. Luther Porter Jackson, *Free Negro Labor and Property Holding in Virginia in 1860* [New York, 1942], p. 134.) The assumption is made here that each farm had a separate owner. Since multiple ownership was less frequent among African-Americans than among European-Americans, a stricter count, if it could be made, would lower the proportion of land ownership among African-Americans less than it would the land ownership ratio among European-Americans. However, the alteration could not significantly affect the argument of this table regarding the difference between the 1666 and 1860 ratios of land ownership.

c. In Northampton County in 1666, seven of the 64 African-Americans were landholders, as were 145 of the 826 European-Americans. There were 422 tithables (54 African-Americans and 368 European-Americans), of whom 152 (7 African-Americans and 145 European-Americans) were landholders. (See the Northampton list of tithables for 1666, in Jennings Cropper Wise, *The Kingdom of Accawmacke, on the Eastern Shore of Virginia in the Seventeenth Century* [Richmond, 1911; Baltimore reprint, 1967], pp. 373–8. Edmund S. Morgan's figures vary slightly – 158 households, 434 tithables, and the African-American proportion of the total population a suggested 13.2 percent [*American Slavery, American Freedom*, New York, 1975, pp. 420, 425.])

My estimate of the total population (all rural, of course) of Northampton County in 1666 is based on the following assumptions: Children under sixteen years of age, the untithable portion of the African-American population, constituted 15 percent of all African-Americans, thus among African-Americans the ratio of total population to tithables would be 1.18. (Morgan uses this 15 percent figure, though he calls it a 'generous' estimate [pp. 421, and 422 n. 46.]. If this is indeed an overestimate of the untithable proportion of the African-American population, it will be on the safe, conservative, side of the argument being presented here concerning the greater dispersion of landholding in 1666 as compared to 1860.) The figure of 2.11 for the ratio of total population to tithables for Virginia is assumed to be true for Northampton County. This figure is an extrapolation based on Morgan's assumed linear rise in the ratio from 1.65 in 1640 to 2.69 in 1699; in 1666, the ratio would be 2.11 to 1. The statistical analysis is as follows: total population (2.11 x 422) 890; total African-American population (1.18 x 54) 64. The figures for the European-American population 368 tithable (men) multiplied by 2.11 makes a total of 826.

incompatible with the anomalies of social class relationships characteristic of a system of social control based on racial oppression.

The same point can be made in terms of social mobility, expressed as the ratio between the number of European-American tithables and those land holders who were former bond-laborers (identifiable through a search of the abstracts of land patents in Nugent's *Cavaliers and Pioneers*). Of the total 145 European-American landholders in Northampton in 1666, 58 are identifiable in these patents. Of these, 27, i.e., 47 percent, had come as bond-laborers. If this ratio is assumed to have been the same for the entire roster of 145 European-American landholders, then 68 were in that category. Since there were 209 European-American (tithable) bond-laborers, the social mobility ratio was 69 to 209, or 32.5 percent; for the African-American tithables the ratio was 7 to 44, or 15.9 percent.

The disparity of the two ratios seems understandable in terms of two main factors. Some of the European-American bond-laborers had family or other personal ties on one side of the Atlantic or the other that afforded them some support in getting started after the end of their terms of servitude. Such ties were less likely to be available to African-Americans, except possibly to those who came to the colony from England. Second, the disposition on the part of plantation owners to extend the bond-laborers' terms of servitude operated to extend the terms of limited-term African-American bond-laborers for periods longer than set by the custom of the country, thus reducing the relative number of African-Americans who survived to become socially mobile.

Yet even this relatively diminished rate of African-American social mobility of 1666 was such as would have been incompatible with a system of racial oppression. In 1860, the African-American proletarian population fifteen years of age and over in Virginia numbered around 330,000. The social mobility rate of 15.9 percent on that base would imply the existence of a class of African-American Virginia landholders of 52,740, a number nearly equal to the total number of free African-Americans (58,000) in Virginia in 1860. That would have meant a rate of landholding among free African-Americans nine or ten times the land-ownership ratio prevailing among European-Americans, a situation incompatible with the character of racial oppression and hence of racial slavery as a form of it. It may be concluded that the social mobility rate among African-Americans in Northampton County, Virginia, in 1666 was inconsistent with racial oppression.

African-American Owners of European-American Bond-laborers

In some cases, African-Americans became owners, buyers and sellers, of European-American bond-laborers. Francis Payne, when still a bond-laborer, was owned by Mrs Jane Eltonhead in right of her children from a previous marriage. In May 1649 the two signed an agreement in their own hands, according to which Payne was to have the usufruct of the land he was working for her for two crops, and then be free. The conditions were that Payne was to pay 1,500 pounds of tobacco and six barrels of corn out of the proceeds of the current crop.[47] Out of the second crop he was to supply Eltonhead with "three sufficient men servants between the age of fifteen & twenty fower & they shall serve for sixe yeares or seaven att the least." Mr Eltonhead made the search for the bond-laborers on behalf of Payne, and in March 1649/50 struck a bargain with "Mr Peter Walker merchant for Towe men Servants which is for the use of Francis Payne Negro towards his free-dome." In April, 1651, Eltonhead acknowledged receipt from "Francis Payne Negro the quantity of sixteen hundred & fifty pownds of Tobacco & two Servants (according Unto the Condition betwixt him & his mistris) also a Bill taken in of his mistris which she passed unto Mr. Edward Davis for a mayd servant Jeany."[48] In November 1656, Mrs Eltonhead, then living in Maryland presumably widowed a second time, acknowledged the receipt of 3,800 pounds of tobacco from Payne, and formally freed Payne and his wife and children "from all hindrance of servitude."[49]

On 28 April 1653 the Northampton County Court ordered John Gussall, "Negro," according to the terms of his contract with Montroze Evellyn, to pay 1,000 pounds of tobacco and "one sufficient able woman servant for four yeares time." If the woman bond-laborers were to die "in seasoning the first yeare," Gussal was to recompense Evellyn with 1,200 pounds of tobacco.[50]

Continuing Bourgeois Pressure for Unpaid Labor Time

All the while the pressure continued to reduce African-American bond-laborers to lifetime servitude. A law passed in March 1661 specifying punishment for runaway bond-laborers referred to "any negroes who are incapable of makeing satisfaction by addition of time."[51] In September 1668, free African-American women were declared tithable on the explicit grounds that "though permitted to enjoy their freedome ... [they] ought not in all respects be admitted to a full fruition of the exemptions and impunities of the English."[52] In October 1669, owners who killed their Negro or Indian lifetime bond-laborers under "correction" were "acquit from molestation" on the grounds that it would not be reasonable that an owner would destroy his own property with malice aforethought.[53] Three years later this immunity from prosecution was extended to any person who killed "any negroe, molatto, Indian slave, or servant for life" who became the object of hue and cry as a runaway.[54] All the laws were especially oppressive in their intentions regarding African-Americans, of course. Insofar as they made reference to African-Americans as lifetime bond-laborers, they were a denial of the possibility of achieving either any social distinction or the enjoyment of the legal rights of marriage and family formation. But it is the 1668 law directed at *free* African-American women that most explicitly anticipates racial oppression.

Contracts and last wills increasingly contemplated raising the number of African-Americans in the category of lifetime bond-laborers. As early as 1649, eleven African-American bond-laborers from Barbados were sold to Argoll Yardley "to have hold possess and quietly enjoy ... [by] him his heirs, or assigns for ever."[55] In 1653, Yardley contracted to provide John Machell "one Negro girle named Dennis Aged 12 yeares next November to serve him . . . his heyres or Assignes for her lifetime."[56] In his will, dated February 1656, Rowland Burnham bequeathed his English bond-laborers to members of his family for the limited terms they had been bought to serve; the African-American bond-laborers were to serve "forever" those to whom they were willed.[57]

At the same time there was a growing desire among owners of bond-laborers to make African-American servitude hereditary, an impulse that found expression in a depraved adaptation of the customary reference to property in animal stock. In September 1647, Stephen Charlton made a gift of a Mare colt, three Cows, and "A Negro girle named Sisley aged about fowre or five years . . . them and their increase both male and female Forever."[58] The settlement of the estate of Edmund Scarburgh in 1656 assigned to Charles Scarburgh "one Negro man called Tom & Masunke his wife with all their issue."[59] In his will dated 12 February 1656, Rowland Burnham distributed some seventeen bond-laborers to various beneficiaries, the ten English ones "for the full terms of tyme they have to serve"; "the negroes forever." Among the African-Americans given to his sons was a "woman called Joane with what Children she shall bear from this date to them and their heirs forever."[60] In December 1657 Captain Francis Pott sold Ann Driggus, nine or ten years old, "with all her increase forever" to John Panell.[61]

African-Americans Challenge Hereditary Bondage

As noted in Chapter 8, African-American bond-laborers joined in direct action with other bond-laborers in resisting their bondage by running away. They also were aware of the need to challenge aspects of the bond-servitude system that were or might be directly aimed against them in particular.

Phillip and Mingo, two African-American bond-laborers whom John Foster bought from Captain William Hawley in January 1649, were trouble from the moment the purchase was made. Concerned about the "fine print" of the Hawley–Foster contract, the workers engaged in what today would be called a "slow-down strike," making Foster "fearfull that [they] would run awaye from him" altogether. Upon their insistence, Captain Hawley was brought into the discussion. Acting as mediator, Hawley "went downe to the seaboard side, And made a wrighting to the Negros," specifying that at the end of four years, "they shalbe free from their servitude & bee free men; & labor for themselves." At some subsequent point the two workers were to pay Hawley 1,700 pounds of tobacco, or "one Man servant."[62]

Resistance might sometimes take the form of the buy-out. In May 1645, Emanuell Dregus (Rodrigues) arranged to purchase from his employer, Captain Francis Pott, the freedom of two children whom he had adopted, eight-year-old Elizabeth and one-year-old Jane, who were bound until the age of twenty-one and thirty respectively.[63] Rogrigues may well have been aware of the sentiment expressed by the General Court in the John Punch case, and of the disposition of some owners to keep Negroes in perpetual servitude, and he might, judging from his name, have had memories of such a regime in some Dutch or Portuguese colony. Although Pott appears to have been personally sympathetic to him, Rodrigues nevertheless preferred to have his children at his own disposal. Indeed, as noted above, the time would come when Pott himself would adopt the notion of hereditary bondage.

Perhaps the most frequent form of challenges to discriminatory terms of servitude in the court records were petitions for freedom presented by African-Americans. Some were submitted by persons who had come into Virginia as limited-term indentured bond-laborers, others were based on promises made by deceased owners' wills or otherwise. The story of the struggle of John Baptista, "a moore of Barbary,"[64] began in 1649, when he was sold by a Dutch merchant, Simon Overzee, to Major Thomas Lambert of Norfolk County, Virginia. But for how long? That was the matter that concerned John Baptista. There came a point at which Baptista refused to continue in servitude saying that "he would serve but fowre yeares" and that he intended to take the matter to the Governor. He did so and in March 1653/4 the General Court ruled that he had not been sold for his lifetime and ordered that Baptista serve Lambert for two more years and then be free. Alternatively Baptista was to buy back the two years by paying Lambert 2,000 pounds of tobacco. Baptista was free of Lambert in less than a year and had departed for Maryland with Overzee.[65]

Dego took his owner, Minor Doodes, to court in Lancaster County in March 1655/6. Apparently Doodes was intending to leave the area and wanted to sell Dego as a lifetime bond-laborer. A paper was presented signed by Doodes, providing that if he sold Dego, it was to be for no more than ten years.[66]

African-American John (or Jack) Kecotan arrived in Virginia as a bond-laborer in about 1635. Eighteen years later his owner, Rice Hoe Senior, promised Kecotan that if he lived a morally irreproachable life, he would be given his freedom – at the end of another eleven years! Sadly, Hoe Senior passed away before the time had elapsed, and the court ordered Kecotan to continue in servitude with Hoe's widow until her death. That mournful event occurred sometime before 10 November 1665, leaving Rice Hoe Junior in possession of the estate, including, he assumed, John Kecotan. But it being then thirty years since Kecotan had started his servitude under the elder Hoe, Kecotan petitioned the court for his freedom. When Junior Hoe opposed the petition on the grounds that some time during the elder Hoe's lifetime Kecotan had had child-producing liaisons with two or more English women, thus violating the good-conduct condition of the original promise of freedom, the Virginia General Court ordered that Kecotan be freed, unless Hoe could prove his charges at the next County Court. There five men, apparently all European-Americans, supported Jack Kecotan's petition with a signed testimonial to his character. Hoe produced two other witnesses for his side.

Apparently Jack Kecotan at some point secured his freedom, at least enough that he and his co-defendant, Robert Short, won a jury verdict in their favor in a suit brought against them by Richard Smith.[67]

In 1654 Anthony Longo was a hard-working farmer living in Northampton County with his wife Mary, two daughters and a son. He had long before demonstrated his mistrust of the intentions of European-American owners of bond-labor regarding the freedom of African-Americans. "For certain considerations" Longo had achieved freedom from his owner in 1635. Suddenly, five years later, in August 1640, two months after the General Court in the John Punch case sought to equate "being a negro" with lifetime bondage, Longo induced his former owner, Commander Nathaniel Littleton, to affirm Longo's freedom in the Northampton County Court record.[68] Longo had a contempt for government interference; and when he was served a warrant to appear in court to answer charges of obstructing a road by building a fence across it, he said he'd go to court when he had got his corn crop in and not before. He called the warrant server an "idle Rascall" adding, dismissively, "shitt of your warrant."[69] When, as mentioned above, in September 1668 the General Assembly made free African-American women liable to taxes, the Longo family was not one to submit quietly. Longo took his grievance directly to Governor Berkeley, petitioning "to be eased of his great charge of children."[70] As the eventual disposition of the petition shows, Longo's purpose was not to have his children taken away but to protest the discriminatory tax on African-American women such as those in his family. The County Court, in apparent retaliation for Longo's having "by his petition complained to the Honorable Governor," charged Longo with being a bad parent, and accordingly sought to deprive him of the children, cynically adding that Longo would be "discharged of publike taxes." The children were ordered bound out to two of Longo's richer neighbors until the children reached the age of twenty-four, the girls to learn "housewifery, knitting and such like;" the boy shoemaking.[71] Longo petitioned the court to be allowed to keep his children, and the order relating to the elder of the daughters was rescinded.[72]

Andrew Moore arrived in Virginia to serve as a limited-term bond-laborer. In October 1673 he petitioned the General Court for his freedom, contending that his owner, Mr George Light, was keeping him in bondage well past his proper time of service. He won a decision ordering Light to free him with the customary allowance of "Corn and Clothes," and to pay Moore 700 pounds of tobacco for his overtime.[73]

Thomas Hagleton, like Moore, came from England.[74] He arrived in Maryland in 1671 with signed indenture papers to serve for four years. In 1676, Hagleton petitioned the Maryland Provincial Court complaining that his owner, Major Thomas Truman, detained him from his freedom. The court, citing the presence of witnesses prepared to testify on Hagleton's behalf, granted Hagleton's request for a trial of the issue.[75]

European-American Nathaniel Bradford had become wary of such challenges. In April 1676 he purchased an African-American woman bond-laborer from Matthew Scarburgh for 3,000 pounds of tobacco, to be paid in two annual installments, presumably from the product of two years' labor. But the purchase agreement carried a protective clause requiring Scarburgh to post bond "to save [Bradford] harmless from ... any claime ... that she hath liv'd in England or Barbados" as a basis for suing for her freedom.[76]

Evangelical Questions and Objections

The obstructive effect of the institutional inertia of common-law principles and Christian religious scruples with respect to racial oppression found both implicit and explicit expression among the owning classes.[77] Three who explicitly addressed the issue were English ministers, Morgan Godwyn (fl. 1685), Richard Baxter (1615–91), and George Fox (1641–91). Godwyn, author of *The Negro's and Indians Advocate* and other works of the same tenor, was an Anglican minister who served in Virginia in Marston parish in the late 1660s.[78] Fox, the first Quaker, wrote and spoke on the subject of the treatment of African-Americans by Anglo-Americans, both before and after his journey to the British West Indies and the Chesapeake in 1671–74.[79] Richard Baxter, also a Puritan, wrote a scathing denunciation of the commerce in human commodities.[80] As they observed the extreme brutality and callousness of the actual practice of enslavement, their core theme of Christian equalitarianism led them to challenge aspects of slavery, the slave trade, the inhumanity of the treatment of the slaves, even to advocate replacing perpetual servitude by limited-term servitude.

The well-known authority Thomas E. Drake has said that these seventeenth-century preachers "sought the liberation of Negroes' souls, not their bodies."[81] They did not demand immediate general emancipation; rather, they preached to the slaves the sanctity of submissiveness. Nevertheless, the doctrine of a common humanity as children of God, and of Christ's blood as the universal solvent of sin, as well as the jubilee tradition of the people of the Book, limiting the time that even strangers might be held in bondage – all that was an obstacle that the plantation bourgeoisie knew it could not ignore.[82]

Such an ideology was unsuited to the superstructure of a colony founded on lifetime hereditary bond-servitude. "[W]e cannot serve Christ and Trade," said Godwyn, in warning to those who sought enrichment through denying the humanity of the plantation bond-laborers.[83] "From this fundamental idea of the brotherhood of men through the sacrifice of Christ," writes Drake, "Fox reasoned that the servitude of Negroes should end in freedom just as it did for whites"[84]; accordingly Fox urged Barbados Quakers to "deal mildly and gently with their negroes ... and that after certain years of servitude they would make them free."[85] These ideas if put into practice would negate the very purpose of lifelong bondage by shortening the period of servitude. Further-more, such a practice would reduce the supply of bond-labor in two ways. First, it would deprive the owners to some degree of property in newborn children. Second, the reduced profitability of bond-labor resulting from shortening the period of servitude, coupled with the moral crusade against the slave trade as "the worst kind of thievery" as Richard Baxter put it, would have reduced the profitability of that branch of free enterprise.[86]

Furthermore, these equalitarian implications were absolutely incompatible with racial oppression, which in Anglo-America would take the form of "white supremacy." Morgan Godwyn, for all his assurances about not prejudicing the interests of the owners of lifetime bond-laborers, justified his campaign for Christianizing African and African-American bond-laborers in terms that had quite different implications. Godwyn denounced plantation owners who opposed the admission of African-American bond-laborers to Christian fellowship by pretending "That the Negro's, though in their figure they carry some resemblance of Manhood, yet are indeed no Men." In terms of pure economic determinism, Godwyn ascribed this denial of the humanity of Africans and African-Americans to "the inducement and instigation of our Planters['] chief Diety, Profit."[87] Calling such ideas "strange to the People in England," Godwyn argued the case for a common humanity:

> How should they [Africans and African-Americans] otherwise be capable of Trades, and other no less Manly imployments, as also of Reading, and Writing; or show so much Discretion in management of Business; eminent in diverse of them; but wherein (we know) that many of our own People are deficient.[88]

The ruling elite in the plantation colonies found such notions so threatening that, despite Quaker disavowal of any intent to incite Negro insurrection, respective colony legislatures enacted stern measures against the sect. In Barbados, where Negroes were a majority of the population by the end of the third quarter of the seventeenth century, elaborate systems of repressive measures were instituted. Laws providing severe penalties were enacted against those who allowed the attendance of Negroes at Quaker meetings and schools.[89] In the Chesapeake, laws were enacted generally proscribing the Quakers, but without making any specific reference to African-Americans or bond-servitude.[90] Although throughout the seventeenth century a majority of the bond-laborers in the Chesapeake were European-Americans, the spread of such doctrines as Quakerism might threaten to unravel bond-servitude altogether, especially in light of the fact that, from its inception in the 1620s, it represented a violation of English master–servant principles. Of course, the equalitarian implications of Christian doctrine were not the invention of seventeenth-century Puritanism.[91] The rebels on Mousehold Heath in 1549 had based their argument against bondage on the grounds of an appeal to Christian fellowship.[92] Later in that same century, Thomas Smith had made the point in his *Republica Anglorum* – that Christians might not hold Christians in slavery, a principle drawn from ancient Hebrew tribal law.[93]

Elements of the Propertied Classes Oppose Racial Oppression

In Virginia in the period before Bacon's Rebellion, actions taken by some of the plantation owners implied a rejection on their part of the principle of racial oppression, although explicit references to English common law and Christian doctrine were omitted. Owners of African-American bond-laborers frequently encouraged them by allowing them to have livestock and small cultivable plots, not just for their subsistence but for disposal by sale. Such a practice was contrary to the conditions of chattel bond-servitude in general, since it implied the legal ability of the worker to make contracts for purchase and sale.[94] Indeed in the instances cited above of African-American cattle dealers, self-purchasers, plantation owners, and tobacco sellers, those persons first achieved social mobility through encouragement by their European-American owners. In other cases African-Americans were assured of places on the first rung of social mobility by the expiration of their limited terms of servitude, or under the terms of wills of owners who died, which frequently provided them with allowances of livestock. In order to resolve any doubts about the ownership of certain "Cattle, Hoggs & poultrey, with their increase" in the possession of African-Americans Emanual Driggs and Bashawe Farnando, two prominent planters, Francis Pott and Stephen Charlton, attested that those animals had been "Lawfully gotten, & purchased" from Pott when Driggs and Farnando were in Pott's employ, and that "they may freely dispose of them either in their life tyme or att their death."[95]

Aside from other cases mentioned incidentally in other parts of this chapter, here are half a dozen instances in which European-American employers acted on the assumption that African-American bond-laborers need not serve for life, nor hereditarily, but only for limited terms.

On 2 December 1648, Stephen Charlton made a legal record of his intention that "John Gemander his servant" was to serve a limited term of ten years, and then "the said Negro is to be a free man." On the same day, Charlton "assigned" Grace-Suzana, a "Negro childe," to serve Mr Richard Vaughan until the age of thirty and then "to be freed from further servitude."[96] On 16 April 1650 Richard Vaughan made a court record of his intention that when they reached the age of thirty, two Negro children owned by him, three-year-old Temperance and two-year-old James, should be free.[97] Stephen Charlton's will, probated on 29 January 1654/5, provided for freedom, on certain conditions, for Jack in four years, and for Bridgett if she paid his daughters 2,500 pounds of tobacco and cask, or otherwise at the end of three more years.[98] When Christopher Stafford died around the end of 1654 his will provided that Mihill Gowen was to be free after serving Stafford's uncle four more years. The executrix of the will, Stafford's sister, Amy Barnhouse, "for divers good causes" (and apparently a year ahead of time) freed Gowen and his baptized infant son William.[99] Francis Pott died before he had a chance to include in his will his intention to free "his Negroe Bashore." His widow and executrix married William Kendall, member of the County Court. On 30 May

1659 Kendall, in accordance with Pott's wishes, "set the said Bashore at Liberty and proclaim[ed] him to be free . . . for Ever."[100]

In the spring of 1660, Thomas Whitehead died; he was survived by two children, Mary Rogers, the elder, and James Rogers. Although Mary was still under age, Whitehead appointed her his chief heir and the executrix of his will. In a further provision he set free his African-American bond-laborer named John to "be his owne man from any person or persons whatsoever," and gave him a cow and a heifer, the house John lived in, and "ground to plant upon . . . and peaceably to injoy it his lifetime.' He also appointed John "to be Mary Rogers['] Guardyan & Overseer of hir & what I have given hir till she is of age." Finally, if Mary and his son James died before coming of age, the entire estate, which at that time included an unnamed boy bond-laborer with two years yet to serve, "shall returne to my Negro [John]." Whitehead correctly anticipated that the court might not accept John as Mary's guardian, and named one Andrew Rider to serve in John's stead. There are indications that Rider was negligent in the execution of the will. In September 1660, possibly on John's petition, the County Court "ordered that John Negro servant to Thomas Whitehead deceased be and hereby is declared Free & that hee have his Cattle & other things belonging to him delivered to him."[101]

One other will seems worth notice here, although it was not left by a member of the propertied classes. English seaman George Williams would never see home again. He died in October 1667 in Virginia, where he had been tended and comforted by Manuel Driggus in his last days. Like Joe Hill, he had little to divide, but that little he bequeathed to Driggus "for his care and trouble in tendinge mee in my sickness," namely, eleven months' back wages due for his service on his ship, *Loves Increase*, whatever tobacco he had laid by, his sea chest and its contents, and all else he owned in Northampton County. In keeping with the custom of the time, he made Driggus, his largest creditor, the executor of his will.[102]

The Case of Elizabeth Key

Elizabeth Key (the name is variously spelled) was born in Virginia around 1631. She was the daughter of Thomas Key, of Northumberland County, and of an African-American woman, not named in the record, but who was a bond-laborer owned by Key.[103] In 1636 the father, intending to return to England to stay, sold his plantation to Humphrey Higginson (the child's godfather and a member of the General Assembly), and bound Elizabeth to him for a term of nine years. Under the terms of this assignment, Higginson was "to use her more respectfully than a Comon servant or slave." Elizabeth was not to be sold to anyone else. If Higginson survived and stayed in Virginia until the end of the nine years, Elizabeth was then to be free. If Higginson were to return to England before that time, he was to take Elizabeth with him at his own expense and return her to her father there. If Higginson died in

Virginia before the end of the nine years, Elizabeth was then to be immediately free.

Thomas Key died before he could embark for England, and Higginson, too, died some time before Elizabeth's nine-year term was completed. Instead of achieving her freedom, however, she was held in servitude by the administrator of the Higginson estate, a planter named John Mottrom. Mottrom also died and in 1656 Elizabeth Key, with the assistance of William Greenstead as her attorney, brought suit for her freedom against those who were now in possession of Mottrom's estate. The grounds taken by the defense imparted a far-reaching significance to the case by claiming Key as a lifetime bond-laborer on the grounds that such had been the condition of her mother.

In January 1656 a jury of twelve men found Elizabeth Key to be rightfully entitled to her freedom. The overseers of the Mottrom estate appealed the decision to the Virginia General Court. The original record of the General Court for that period was destroyed by fire in 1865. But a transcript of it made prior to 1860 has the following entry under the date of 12 March 1656: "Mulatto held to be a slave and appeal taken." Historians may be correct in inferring that this is a reference to Elizabeth Key, and that it indicates that the General Court reversed the decision of the Northumberland County Court. That inference it strengthened by the fact that a week later the General Assembly, the normal court of appeal from General Court decisions at that time, took the case under its consideration. On 20 March a special committee of the General Assembly, chosen to make a determination of the matter, expressed the sense "of the Burgesses of the present Assembly," holding that Key was entitled to freedom on two legal grounds that are of critical importance for the present discussion of the origin of racial slavery as a particular form of racial oppression in continental Anglo-America. First, there was the ancient common law principle of *partus sequitur patrem*, according to which the condition of the child follows the condition of the father. Since Elizabeth was the daughter of John Key,[104] she should be free "by the Comon Law [that] the Child of a Woman slave begotten by a freeman ought to be free." Second, Key should be free based on the Christian principle against holding Christians as slaves. Elizabeth Key "hath bin long since Christened, Colonel Higginson being her God father." The Assembly ordered that the matter be returned for consideration, noting that Key should be given not only freedom dues, but also compensation "for the time shee hath served longer than shee ought to have done."

One of the Mottrom estate overseers, George Colclough, who was later to come into possession of one-third of the estate by marrying Mottrom's widow, appealed to Governor Berkeley. On 11 June the Governor ordered a suspension of further proceedings pending a rehearing of the case by the Fall term of the General Court. There is no record, however, of the General Court ever having taken further notice of the case. The last word in the litigation was had by the Northumberland County Court; in effect it ignored the Governor's order and instead implemented the sense of the General Assembly by ordering that Key be freed and compensated. The fact that the judgment of the General Assembly effectively prevailed is incontestably indicated by the following series of developments. The March sitting of the General Court ruled that, if a woman bond-laborer married a free man with the consent of her owner, she became free thereby. Key and Greenstead had developed a personal as well as a professional relationship. The banns of their marriage were proclaimed in the church, and since no one could "shew any Lawful cause whey they may not be joyned together," they were married. It is apparent that the administrators of the Mottrom estate were tacitly acknowledging that they had no legal grounds to prevent the marriage. The certificate of the marriage was recorded at the same July Northumberland Court that finally ordered Key freed. Lastly, when the Mottrom estate was finally divided the following January, it included one Irish, four English, and three African-American bond-laborers, but Elizabeth Key was not among them.

Lacking further legal recourse, the Mottromites finally let Elizabeth Key go, without, however, conceding the principle involved. Rather, they still asserted their right to "assign and transfer unto William Greenstead a maid servant formerly belonging to the estate of Col. Mottrom commonly called Elizabeth Key being nowe Wife unto the sad Greenstead." Thus the advocates of hereditary bondage covered their embarrassment with the principle of "the feme couvert," according to which the wife is not at her own disposal but at that of her husband, and thus is still not a free individual.

The Critical Importance of the Key Case

The case of Elizabeth Key presented a direct confrontation, played out on a colony-wide scale, between the desire among plantation owners to raise their rate of profit by imposing lifetime hereditary servitude on African-Americans, and an African-American's right to freedom on the basis of Christian principles and English common law.[105] The jury that heard the case and the General Assembly that reviewed it in 1656 acted on the traditional English principle in finding that Elizabeth Key's Christian baptism and rearing barred her from being held as a lifetime bond-laborer. At the same time, they took their stand on the common-law principle that the social status of the child followed that of the father.

If the principles affirmed in the findings of the Northumberland County jury and the special committee of the General Assembly had prevailed, the establishment of racial slavery would have been prevented. If African-Americans were to be reduced to lifetime hereditary bond-servitude and kept in that status, it was essential for the exploiters of bond-labor to establish the principle of descent through the mother. For, as an owner claimed when another woman sued for her freedom a century later: "If, in a case of a dispute about the property of negroes, it is not sufficient to prove the mother to be a slave, there will soon be an end to that kind of property."[106] What was involved here was not a mere matter of ancestry; it represented an attack on the patriarchy, though limited, of course, to the Negro family. In principle it was akin to the attack on the Catholic Irish family under the Penal Laws of the eighteenth century.[107] And, as in the case of that aspect of the Penal Laws, it was not associated with any equalitarian impulse on the part of the ruling class.

It was equally important, for purposes of maximizing profits by reducing labor costs, to cut the knot that tangled Christian baptism with freedom. Already a decade and a half earlier the organizers of the ill-fated English colony on Providence Island had said that only Negroes not yet converted to Christianity could be enslaved, but that those who had been converted could not.[108] The early response of Barbados planters to proposals to Christianize the Negroes there was that it would be the end of their system, because they could no longer be accounted as slaves.[109]

Notice has been taken of the quick reactions of the General Assembly to aspects of the runaway problem, and to the servants' plot of 1663, and of the timely changes in the terms of bond-servitude to be imposed on Irish bond-laborers, which reflected the alteration from the ascendancy of the Puritan Commonwealth to the restoration of the crypto-Catholic Stuarts in England. Each of these cases also involved considerations of labor costs, but they did not impinge on the sacred and constitutional principles of patriarchy and religious conversion, deep-running principles not to be disposed of quickly. It would be six years before the Virginia General Assembly in 1662 resolved "doubts that [had] arisen" about the status of children of English fathers and African-American women, by enacting that "all children borne in this country shalbe held bond or free according to the condition of the mother," establishing the principle of *partus sequitur ventrem*, directly contrary to the English common law principle of *partus sequitur patrem*, descent through the father.[110] In 1667, eleven years after Elizabeth Key had won her fight for freedom as a Christian, the General Assembly again was able to receive "doubts that [had] arisen" by decreeing that "the conferring of baptisme doth not alter the condition of the person as to his bondage"; thus, as it was said, "masters, freed from this doubt, may more carefully endeavour the propagation of christianity."[111]

A widened lens brings significant rough coincidences into focus. In January 1663, the year after the Virginia General Assembly enacted the legal principle of descent through the mother in order to make African-Americans subject to hereditary bond-servitude, the English government re-chartered the Company of Royal Adventurers to Africa, for the first time listing the trade in human chattels among its purposes.[112] In October the English bourgeoisie threw open a challenge to Dutch domination of that trade by sending a naval force to carry out extensive raids on Dutch posts on the coast of West Africa. The issue thus joined was to eventuate in the Second Anglo-Dutch War (1665–67); it ended with the Treaty of Breda which finally gave the Anglo-American plantation colonies secure direct access to African bond-laborers. In 1672, the Royal Adventurers, who had been bankrupted by the long struggle with the Dutch, were succeeded by the Royal African Company, which was granted a monopoly as the supplier of African laborers to Anglo-America.

The 1667 assurance given by the Virginia General Assembly to the plantation bourgeoisie at large that they need no longer fear the liberating effect of Christian baptism coincided with the signing of the Treaty of Breda. Three years later, in 1670, the General Assembly made it illegal for African-American planters to buy "christian" bond-laborers, limiting them to the purchase of persons "of their owne nation."[113] Although the reasoning that led to this enactment is not recorded, except that the issue "hath beene questioned," it was not intended as a way of promoting the sales of African bond-laborers. Rather, it was designed to promote the principle of racial oppression. The purchase price for Africans was half again as much as that for Europeans,[114] prohibitively high for poor planters such as African-American planters generally were. This restriction therefore was an effective bar to advancement to the employer class.

In 1672 the General Assembly enacted a law "for the apprehension and suppression of runawayes, negroes and slaves" because, it said,

> many negroes have lately beene and now are out in rebellion in sundry parts of this country, and ... noe means have yet beene found for the apprehension and suppression of them from whome many mischiefes of very dangerous consequence may arise to the country if either other negroes, Indians or servants should happen to fly forth and joyne with them.[115]

Into this Virginia in 1674 or 1675, some 250 bond-laborers were brought directly from West Africa in ships under contract to the Royal African Company.[116] The tobacco bourgeoisie generally certainly hoped to solve the problem of perennially low-priced tobacco by importing Africans as lifetime hereditary bond-laborers. The tobacco bourgeoisie was also strongly urged by the highest circles in the English government to patronize the African labor trade, "Blacks ... being the principall and most Usefull appurtenances of a plantation."[117]

But as the historian Bruce noted, "Those [bond-laborers] snatched directly from a state of freedom in Africa were doubtless in some measure difficult to manage."[118] If it came to that, who would do the "managing"? If the hopes of the rich planters and of the Royal African Company were to be realized in a rapid increase of the labor supply directly from Africa, how would the ruling elite cope with the attendant increase in problems of social control, of "negroes out in rebellion?" They could, of course, pass more stringent laws, but how effective would they be? Leaving aside the demonstrated moral and humane attitudes that ran counter to such denial of English rights to African-Americans, there were interests belonging to the field of political economy that were directly or indirectly inconsistent with devoted enforcement of repressive measures against African-Americans. In the years 1672 to 1674,

England was engaged in the last of the three Anglo-Dutch wars. Even some of the more prosperous Virginia planters, who might have been able to afford to buy lifetime bond-laborers at £18 to £20 each, were in a treasonous disposition, and were "saying openly, that they are in the nature of slaves" because they were being denied free trade with the Dutch. Their disaffection was so great, it was said, that Virginia was "in danger, with their consent, to fall into the enemy's hands."[119] Of course that war would end, but the English Navigation Acts directed against the Dutch trade would remain; still, these more prosperous planters might be expected to return to their allegiance and perhaps find common interest in acquiring lifetime bond-laborers from Royal African Company contractors. But, at the least, their priorities diverged from those of their government to a degree that was not for that moment propitious for effective administration of laws. The poor majority of the planters, and the landless freemen, could not afford to buy lifetime bond-laborers, who would be forced to compete with additional numbers of African lifetime bond-laborers; they had better things to do than to help the rich planters keep their newly arriving Africans. As for the bond-labor majority of the producing classes, they were so unreliable that of their number African-Americans and all but a few of the European-Americans were denied the right to bear arms even in face of the threat of a Dutch invasion.[120]

Given the English superstructural obstacles and the already marked resistance of African-Americans to lifetime hereditary bondage that have been described in this chapter, a rapid and large addition of African bond-laborers to the population would certainly tend to reduce the effectiveness of the already weak social control stratum in enforcing the laws for the "suppression of rebellious negroes." It might indeed lead to the appearance of *guilombos* in the Blue Ridge or the Allegheny Mountains rivaling in scope the Palmares settlement that withstood the assaults of Portuguese and Dutch colonialists for nearly a century.[121]

PART FOUR
Rebellion and Reaction

11

Rebellion – and Its Aftermath

In 1624, Captain John Smith had warned that basing the colony on chattel bond-servitude was bound to "bring ... [Virginia] to misery."[1] A half-century later, a revolt that had been brewing since about 1660, when the long period of very low tobacco prices began, fulfilled that prophecy.

No other event of Anglo-American colonial history has received so much attention from historians as Bacon's Rebellion, which convulsed the Virginia colony for nearly nine months beginning in May 1676.[2] Over a period of nearly three centuries, they have produced three main lines of interpretation of that event's historic significance. At first, Bacon's Rebellion was regarded as a bad thing because of its lawlessness; "rebel" was *ipso facto* a pejorative term, although extenuations were found by reference to errors of government policy, official corruption, and abuse of power. In the "Nationalist" period, between the American Revolution and the War against Great Britain of 1812, a new look in the light of new events led to a reinterpretation wherein Nathaniel Bacon himself was seen as "the torchbearer of the Revolution" and the rebellion was regarded as a dress rehearsal for the American Revolution; issues raised against George III by the Continental Congress were seen to vindicate Bacon's rebellion against Charles II's Governor, William Berkeley. One well-known variation on this theme eschews such hero worship and glorification of rebellion but nevertheless regards the events as the beginning of the shift in the locus of power from the royal provincial authorities to an aristocracy of the "county families" with a sense of a new Virginia identity that a century later they would assert by enlisting as "rebels."[3] To the extent that Bacon's Rebellion is seen as a reaction against the effects of the Navigation Act and exorbitant duties laid on tobacco sent to England, the parallel with the American Revolution has validity. But that analogy limps when it comes to Governor William Berkeley's role, for he, the villain of the piece, was the most articulate critic of the Navigation Laws. A more fundamental objection is that the comparison is limited to the matter of throwing off English domination and the establishment of an independent republic, and consequently ignores the factor of the extremes of economic inequality that resulted from the system of bond-labor.

When World War Two and then the modern civil rights movement brought the thesis of equal rights and anti-racism to the fore, Bacon's Rebellion was once again seen as a bad thing, but not because to "rebel" was unjustified, but because the rebellion was regarded as not a real rebellion at all, but merely a dramatic early event in the "frontier" phenomenon, whereby the path of white empire took its westward way completely disregardful of the rights of the American Indians. Wilcomb E. Washburn, author of the standard presentation of this point of view, concluded that the failure to take this "frontier aggressiveness" into account was due, at least in part, to "the white historian's immersion in his racial bias."[4]

All these various approaches, as well as that of the present work, share a common disregard of the admonition of the widely respected historian Wesley Frank Craven to avoid attempts to read any lasting significance into Bacon's Rebellion.[5]

My concern with the origin of racial oppression in continental Anglo-America stresses the class struggle dimension of colonial history. At the same time, it is consistently informed by an equalitarian motif.[6] I thus have a transient foot in both the second and the third of the three camps, but only in passing through to a still different interpretation. By the light of a consciousness raised by the modern civil rights movement, I have examined the records of the seventeenth and early eighteenth centuries, with which scholars have long been familiar, and it is on those records that my somewhat iconoclastic assessment of the historical significance of Bacon's Rebellion must stand or fall.[7]

Such being my focus, I have centered my attention on the second, civil war phase of Bacon's Rebellion – April 1676 to January 1677 – rather than the first, anti-Indian, phase – September 1675 to April 1676. In more explicit justification of this emphasis, I offer the following four considerations.

The first of these is that the details of the anti-Indian phase of the rebellion are all taken from accounts of the English; the Pamunkey, the Susquehannocks and the Occaneechee left no record of those events. Although the English accounts do acknowledge particular English faults in the conduct of the colony's relations with the Indians, they all presume that the English were licensed by divine providence, and/or the right of conquest (thinly disguised perhaps by "purchase" or "treaty"), to reduce them to subject, tributary status, and sooner or later to expropriate them.[8]

Second, despite the policy of enslaving Indian war captives, the basic Indian policy of the English ruling elite was motivated not primarily by consideration of social control over exploitable Indian bond-labor in Virginia, but rather by a desire to exclude the Indians from English-occupied territory. (To the English aggressors, the Indians were regarded much as were the "wild Irish", the "Irish enemy" outside the English Pale – the small portion of Ireland that was under English control – prior to the seventeenth century.)

Third, "white-race" identity was not the principle for which freemen were rallied for the anti-Indian phase of Bacon's Rebellion. The "not-white" and "redskin" classification of the Indian in Anglo-America would be the outcome of the invention of the white race, a transmogrification of the European-American that had not yet been accomplished in 1676.[9]

The fourth and final consideration is that Bacon's Rebellion was not primarily an anti-Indian war,[10] although that was the tenor of the first call to arms voiced by frontier plantation owners such as Nathaniel Bacon and William Byrd, capitalists recently arrived in Virginia.[11] An analogy is provided by the American Revolution which was not primarily an anti-Indian war, although Thomas Jefferson, the Virginian author of the Declaration of Independence, did indict George III for having "endeavoured to bring on the inhabitants of our frontiers, the merciless Indian savages" etcetera, etcetera, and Congress arranged for the "extinction" of Indian land claims in order to grant 9,500,000 acres to Revolutionary War veterans.[12]

The "lesson of history" to be drawn from the anti-Indian phase of Bacon's Rebellion is clear and retains its relevance today. The European occupation of Indian lands shows that, from Columbus to Custer, the bourgeois eye looks upon progress and genocide indifferently, as incidental aspects of the process of the accumulation of capital; the anti-Indian phase of Bacon's Rebellion was merely another example of that lesson. Its logic requires that the United States government that brought the American Indians to the verge of extinction make restitution in some form that will at least end the legacy of extreme poverty and discrimination that American white supremacy has imposed on them. The struggle for justice in this respect merges with the general struggle against white-supremacist racial oppression.

Departing from the "Great Men" Interpretation of the Rebellion

The civil war phase of Bacon's Rebellion offers relevant insights into the course of the history of Anglo-America in its colonial and in its regenerate United States form. The usual treatments of the rebellion describe it largely in terms of the contest between the Governor, William Berkeley, and the Rebel, Nathaniel Bacon, even though their differences are seen to involve policy questions of great interest to the free population generally. Bernard Bailyn's analysis avoids the heroic interpretation; he finds the significance of the rebellion in the struggle within the elite, but he ignores the bond-laborers and the poor farmers as well, except for the latter's opposition to unfair taxation and corruption and abuse of power by the Governor and his faction. I do not intend a narrative presentation, but rather merely to center attention on those elements of the rebellion that relate most meaningfully to the origin of racial oppression in continental Anglo-America.

Sir William Berkeley arrived in Virginia in 1642 as Governor and served in that office until January 1677, except for eight Cromwellian interregnum years, 1652 to 1659. To him, and to his appointed Colony Council, was assigned the custody of the imperial interest, and he was given great powers of patronage in establishing and maintaining the provincial bureaucracy for carrying out the appropriate official functions of that responsibility. Beginning in the mid-1640s, in the time of the English Revolution, and continuing during the first half-decade after the restoration of Charles II to the throne in 1660, a number of wealthy and well-connected newcomers reactivated claims descended from Company period "Adventurers". These claims, Bailyn says, were "the most important of a variety of forms of capital that might provide the basis for secure family fortunes."[13] These new planters became established as dominant families in the various counties. The political implications of this decentralization of power, through the ascendancy of the "county families," were at least potentially contradictory to English imperial interests, as represented by the Navigation Acts which required Virginia planters to ship their tobacco in English ships to England, so that the Crown and English merchants, respectively, could rake in the profit from the royal import duty on tobacco or from re-export sales from England mainly to continental Europe.[14]

This tension between the scattered county families and the imperial interest accounts for the English government's proposals for the establishment of a limited number of port towns as the sole authorized sites for shipping tobacco. These would facilitate enforcement of the Navigation Act and assure full collection of the 2s. export duty per hogshead of tobacco that supplied the Governor's salary and unaudited expenditures involved in the operation of the provincial government, including the work of collecting the royal quit-rents of 2s. per hundred acres of patented land. This divergence of interests was also expressed in the establishment in about 1663 of the elected House of Burgesses as a separate section of a bicameral Assembly and in the fact that for more than a decade the Governor did not call a single general election of burgesses. The result was the development of a political differentiation within the colony elite, between the county magnates, on the one hand, and the royally privileged inner circle around the Governor and the Colony Council that came to be called "the Green Spring" faction.[15] In 1676, that divergence would produce a breach in the ranks of the ruling elite through which would erupt profound social upheaval.

Bacon's Rebellion began in that year, not as a new bond-labor plot for flight or rebellion, nor as a mutiny of poor disfranchised freemen sinking hopelessly into debt and the regressive system of taxes by the poll,[16] but rather as a dispute within the ranks of the colony elite over "Indian policy". More specifically it was a dispute between Governor Berkeley and owners of "frontier" plantations where, beginning in June 1675, war had flared between settlers and mainly Susquehannock Indians.[17] Nathaniel Bacon (1647–76)[18] who had been appointed to the Colony Council by Berkeley in March 1675, just a year after Bacon's arrival in Virginia, was chosen by the "frontier" country planters the following April to lead their aggressive anti-Indian cause.[19]

The issue between Berkeley and Bacon was not whether Indians were to be displaced by the advance of English settlement – they were in fundamental agreement on that – but merely the priority to be given to it at a given time, and thus the rate at which it was to be done. There are those historians who feel bound to euphemize Berkeley's "Indian policy," and one of them presents Berkeley as a "champion of the right of the American Indians to hold undisturbed the land they occupied."[20] But such an assessment seems questionable in the light of the record. In October 1648, "upon the humble representation of the Burgesses to the Governour [Berkeley] and Council," it was enacted that, beginning in the following September, English colonists were authorized by the English colonial government to occupy land previously guaranteed to the Indians under the treaty of 1646 "upon the north side of Charles [later called the York] River and Rappahannock river." The justification for this displacement of the native inhabitants was that English planters needed those lands because their lands were overworked and their cattle needed more range.[21] In June 1666, Berkeley urged the Rappahannock militia to "destroy all those Northern Indians." He was particularly keen on the plan as being self-financing, because the militiamen would be paid by capturing "women & children." But, he slyly suggested, if the Rappahannock men did not think they could do the work alone, there were plenty of others from other counties who would be willing to serve in return for their "share of the Booty." The Rappahannock County court members (militia officers ex officio) hastened to reassure the Governor that they could do the job themselves, without outside help – that they needed only the "Incouradgement [of] the spoyles of our Enemies."[22] At the end of June 1676, Bacon led an onslaught on the friendly Pamunkey Indians, killed some of them and took others as captives to be sold as slaves of the English. According to a marginal note in one of the official documents, "The Indian prisoners were some of them sold by Bacon and the rest disposed of by Sir William Berkeley."[23] The tattered remnant of the Pamunkey people fled from the land that the England had assigned as their only legal place in the English scheme of settlement.[24] When requested to return to that "reservation," the Queen of the Pamunkey (a descendant of Opechancanough) replied that she and her people had fled for their lives, and that they would willingly return to their assigned place when the Governor could assure them of protection from murderous assault by the frontiersmen who made no distinction of friendly Indians. Berkeley's cold reply was that he was "resolved not to be soe answered but to reduce her and the other Indians" as soon as he had settled accounts with Bacon.[25]

For historians who have no investment in defending Berkeley's reputation, this aspect of the Governor's behavior should pose no difficult threat; rather it appears to be perfectly of a piece with his "Indian policy." Among the responsibilities of the Governor and the Colony Council was the formulation and maintenance of an "Indian policy" that would assure the minimum diversion from making tobacco. The essence of that policy was to maintain advantageous political and economic relations with the friendly neighbouring tribes, the Doegs, the Pamunkey, the Nottoway and the Meherrin, who were first subdued and then reduced to dependency as "tributary" subjects of the king of England. They were to serve as a two-way buffer, shielding the English from enemy tribes, and capturing and returning runaway bond-laborers who fled from servitude.[26] One such arrangement was designed to frustrate "all Loitering English as [blank in manuscript] which throughs [throws] themselves amongst" the Indians "for harbour or to be conveyed unto remote parts with intent to defraud their masters of their Time of Service." The "King and great men" were to bring any such runaway to the Rappahannock County magistrates and "be immediately payed five armes lenths of Roanoake or the value thereof."[27]

This agreement lends specificity to Governor Berkeley's general policy, which "always and most prudently Indeavored to p[re]serve [the neighbor Indians] as being as necessarie for us as Doggs to hunt wolves."[28] Furthermore, in exchange for English firearms, powder and other goods, the tributary tribes supplied beaver and other pelts that were an easy source of profit for the plantation bourgeoisie, more particularly for those men who were expressly licensed by the colonial authorities to engage in the trade.[29]

Both aspects of this policy found opposition among the newer, "county family" types. Upon observing that much of the best tidewater land was already patented to earlier claimants, some of these new investors saw better prospects for exploiting bond-labor in opening up new areas to settlement. At the same time, the conduct of the fur trade monopoly was regarded as another instance of the use of provincial authority to line the pockets of the Governor and his faction. However, as Bailyn says, "These dissidents ... represented neither the downtrodden masses nor a principle of opposition to privilege as such. Their discontent stemmed to a large extent from their own exclusion from the privileges they sought."[30]

True, some planters were also only too eager to gain the bond-labor of Indian war captives when that opportunity presented itself.[31] Some, "rather than bee Tennants, seate upon the remote barren Land, whereby contentions arrise between them and the Indians."[32] But the fact that one out of every four of the freemen in Virginia were landless seems to indicate that the common run of the people did not see moving to the "frontier" as a viable option for achieving upward social mobility.[33] They indeed "thought it hard to be a Tennant on a Continent,"[34] but they saw that the most direct, preferable, sensible and the safest course out of their straitened circumstances lay not in "Indian policy" but in a change in Virginia land policy.[35] The remedy was, as stated in the proposal of James City County to the English government commissioners sent to investigate Bacon's Rebellion, to tax land, and tax it so heavily that the tidewater-land engrossers would find it prohibitively expensive to hold onto idle land, which would then become available to the land-hungry poor and dispossessed.[36] The validity of their view would be acknowledged many times by those reporting to the home government. William Sherwood deplored the activities of the "Land lopers, some [of whom] take up 2000 acres, some 3000 Acres, others ten thousand Acres, nay many [of whom] have taken up thirty thousand Acres of Land, and never cultivated any part of it."[37] Giles Bland, collector of the King's customs in Virginia, noted that "A poor man who has only his labour to maintain himself and his family, pays as much [taxes] as a man who has 20,000 acres." Bland proposed that "the richest sort" be taxed as a means of getting them to "lay down parte of their Land to bee taken up by such as will Employ it."[38]

This proposal for a land-tax incentive to induce a redistribution of the land represented the popular sense of the unfairness of the tax system. In the name of reducing costs of government, the Governor and Colony Council were authorized to impose annual levies, without consulting even the House of Burgesses.[39] The privilege of trading with the Indians was by law restricted to a few appointees of the Governor. In addition to the colony taxes, each tithable was subject to county and parish levies, and occasional additional levies for particular purposes. In 1673, during the Third Anglo-Dutch War, the Governor and Colony Council imposed a targeted levy for the construction of forts at points susceptible to Dutch shipborne incursions. In 1675, the Governor and Colony Council laid a special levy of 100 pounds of tobacco on each tithable, to be collected in two annual installments, to finance efforts to persuade King Charles to revoke two grants, made in 1669 and 1673, whereby some eight of his England-dwelling friends were endowed with the title to all the remaining unpatented "public" lands in Virginia, including the Eastern Shore.[40] The Governor and the Colony Council perceived these grants as prejudicial to their control over the acquisition of fee-simple land titles (held directly from the Crown) via the head-right system, or otherwise. The men sent to make the case before the government in England noted that the laying of this levy was intensifying the already existent "mutinous discontents" among the planters.[41]

The same class discrimination prevailed in relation to the fur trade with the Indians. Except for a few of the elite no colonists were allowed to have any interest in the fur trade.[42] In 1675, Nathaniel Bacon and William Byrd I, both of whom were Berkeley's cousins by marriage and members of the Colony Council, were given an exclusive license by Governor Berkeley, under terms requiring them to pay Governor Berkeley 800 beaver skins the first year and 600 every year thereafter.[43] Yet popular resentment over the fur monopoly was concentrated against Berkeley, as being a protector of Indians "for the lucre of the Beaver and otter trade &c."[44] The generality of the planters were excluded from this privilege; certainly the one-eighth or more of the adult male population who were freedmen just out of their time, and the half of the tithables who were bond-laborers, knew that they could not expect to become licensed in the fur trade. Richard Lee, a staunch supporter of the Governor and member of the House of Burgesses, was convinced that the zeal of the multitude in the rebellion was due to "hopes of levelling, otherwise all his [Bacon's] specious pretenses would not have persuaded them but that they believe to have equall advantages by success of their design."[45] Thomas Ludwell and Robert Smith advised the king that "the present disorders have their beginning ... from the poverty and uneasyness" of some of the "meanest" colonists.[46]

The quarrel that erupted between factions of the numerically small elite in 1676 over profit-making opportunities did not lead to new conquests of Indian territory for the expansion of English plantations.[47] Instead "the challengers were themselves challenged", says Bailyn, by "ordinary settlers [angered] at the local privileges of the same newly risen county magnates who assailed the privileges of the Green Spring faction."[48] The result was a complete breakdown of ruling-class social control, as the anti-Indian war was transformed into a popular rebellion against the plantation bourgeoisie.

In May 1676, Giles Bland, administrator of his father's plantation interests in Virginia, and collector of the King's customs there, informed Secretary of State Joseph Williamson in England that "Virginia is at this point of time under the greatest Destractions that it hath felt since the year 1622." A war with the Indians was impending; a force of five hundred volunteers had gone forth to war on Indians in general in defiance of the orders of the Governor; and tax collections were threatened with disruption. The main declared grievances of the rebels, however, were directed at unfair taxation and peculation in high places. Most serious of all, unlike the Lawnes Creek Parish mutiny of 1674, which had been "suppressed by a Proclamation, and the advice of some discreet persons," the present uprising was led by "Nathaniel Bacon lately sworne one of the Counsell and many other Gentlemen of good Condition." Bland worried that "the enemie," presumably some rival European power, would "take advantage of these Disorders."[49]

A new House of Burgesses was elected (it was the first election in fourteen years), a sort of official reconciliation was staged with Bacon, and legislation was passed for raising an anti-Indian army of 1,000 men and calling for the Governor to commission Bacon as the "general and commander-in-chief". When Berkeley temporized about signing the commission, several hundred armed men formed in combat array before the Assembly meeting house on 23 June, and by threatening the lives of the members forced Berkeley to sign the commission.[50] Thus, in effect, power had been conceded to the armed rebels, and the militia function had passed out of the hands of the nominal authorities, causing "the Indian design to recoil in a Civil War upon the colony."[51] This last fact was emphasized in July by the abject failure of the Governor's attempt to rally the Gloucester County militia to go against the rebels. Neither Governor nor king could control the situation sufficiently to prevent this extreme crisis.[52] So far from being in control was Colonel Joseph Brigder, chief of the colony militia, that "he could not ride safely on any road for fear of rebels," even six months after the supposed end of the rebellion.[53] So far from being in control was the Governor that from July 1676 to January 1677 "the only shelter for the Governor and his party" was Accomack, "separated Seaven Leagues distance."[54] Francis Moryson, one-time lieutenant governor of the colony and one of Virginia's representatives in England in October 1676, could only express his dismay that "Amongst so many thousand reputed honest men, there should not be one thousand" to fight against the rebellion.[55] Later Moryson and his fellow commissioner John Berry declared positively that of the fifteen thousand possible combatants in Virginia there were "not above five hundred persons untainted in this rebellion."[56]

The majority of the fifteen thousand were bond-laborers – six thousand European-Americans and two thousand African-Americans.[57] In view of the seventeenth-century Chesapeake record of resistance by the bond-laborers to the unconstitutional and oppressive conditions of their lives, how has it happened that, even in the course of invaluable and illuminating research, with very few exceptions,[58] historians have completely ignored this section of the population as a significant, self-activating shaper of history, and have instead relegated it to monographs on "white servitude,"[59] or to treatment as a mere economic category defined exclusively by market choices of the owning class?[60] Call it the bourgeois blindspot, that prevents them from seeing and accepting the capacity for historic self-activation in "people of no property."

My placement of the bond-laborers and the bond-labor relations of production at the center of the history of Bacon's Rebellion is not an exercise in self-indulgent revolutionary romanticism; rather, it proceeds directly from the record-based presentation of the history of Virginia Colony in the preceding chapters. Without bond-labor, there would have been no tobacco monoculture; without tobacco monoculture the economy would not have been dominated by an oligarchy of owners of large plantations gained by headrights on imported chattel bond-laborers.

Freedom for the bond-laborers would have revolutionized colonial Virginia from a plantation monoculture to a diversified smallholder economy.[61] The demand of the smallholders for a more equitable distribution of tidewater land if fully realized would have resulted in a predominance of family-sized farms without capital to import bond-laborers, and a more diversified economy. But, as the king's commissioners said in reply to county grievances, the oligarchy would never agree to that course of action. Indeed, that appears to have been the basis of the divide-and-conquer strategy proposed to the king by Virginia's representatives in England. The rebellion, they said, did not result from any desire of "the better or more industrious sort of people," and the best hope for ending the insurrection lay in "a speedy separation of the sound parts from the rabble."[62]

At the highest levels of government in Virginia and in England, the great question to which all others were secondary concerned the preservation of chattel bond-servitude. Five days after the Governor, Council and Burgesses capitulated to armed threat by Bacon's supporters and made him commander-in-chief of an army to go against the Indians, Philip Ludwell, Assistant Secretary of the colony and member of the Colony Council, wrote to Secretary of State Williamson confiding the possibility of a complete overthrow of the system fashioned by the tobacco bourgeoisie. For fear of having their throats cut by rebels, he said, the Assembly was granting Bacon's demands "as fast as they come." Ludwell also expressed concern about "the Indians on our

Borders." But his greatest fear was "our servants at home, who (if God prevent not their takeing hold of this Great advantage), must carry on beyond Remedy to destruc[ti]on."[63] That was the great danger for, in the words of Governor Berkeley himself, "The very being of the Collony doth consist in the Care and faithfulness, as well as in the number of our servants."[64] For those very reasons, it was the striving of the bond-laborers for freedom from chattel servitude that held the key to liberation of the colony from the misery that proceeded from oligarchic rule and a monocultural economy.

The prospect of freedom for the bond-laborers was more than a colonial concern; it bore heavily on domestic English politics. Charles II was in financial straits, but because he was at loggerheads with Parliament over other issues, he was unwilling to risk calling it into session to authorize revenue-raising measures. The collection of domestic excise taxes, income from Crown lands, and feudal dues, fell far short of the anticipated £1,200,000. In 1672, the government had been forced to repudiate its outstanding debt despite the secret subsidy of £200,000 a year supplied by Louis XIV of France.[65] In short, Charles found himself very much dependent on the £100,000 annual duties he collected on imports of tobacco from Virginia.[66] The losses caused by the Virginia rebellion, which completely disrupted the operation of the tobacco fleet of 140 ships, played a major part in compelling Charles to call for the election of a new parliament in 1678.[67] This domestic crisis no doubt added to the anxiety of the king and Privy Council as they prepared to send a military expedition to quell the rebellion; they wanted to know "[w]hether there be not more servants than Masters, and whether Bacon has not nor will not proclaim freedom to them?"[68]

Throughout Virginia in 1676 the county courts, where refractory bond-laborers were routinely sentenced to extensions of their servitude and lashes well laid on, were grossly disrupted by the rebellion. The same was true of the parishes in many of their functions, including their role in the execution of court orders regarding bond-laborers and their children. In Charles City County "the Courts of Justice [were] totally interrupted, hindered, and neglected" from the spring of 1676 until some time in 1677.[69] Social services (visiting the sick, burying the dead, performing marriages, caring for orphans and the indigent) normally performed by the minister, clerk and vestry of Middlesex County's Christ Church parish were suspended "by meanes and Armed Force of ill Desposed persons then in Rebellion."[70] Westmoreland County Court was adjourned begining in May 1676, and did not conduct business again until the following April or May.[71] The very circumstances that completely broke down the social control system also resulted in the main source of records regarding the day-to-day sufferings and struggles of the bond-laborers lapsing for much of 1676 and 1677. The editor of the colonial Virginia parish records concluded that, "in those parishes directly and fundamentally affected by Bacon's Rebellion it was found advisable the year following the Rebellion to destroy the existing parish records, or at least to render illegible some part of those records."[72]

However, it is not unreasonable to conjecture that bond-laborers in Charles City County would glory in the relaxation of social control.[73] At such a juncture of history, would not a person like Ann Berrey have been glad of her improved chance of a choice in the matter before being "gott with child" by her owner?[74] Might not one such as William Rogers have been tempted to validate his purloined indenture papers by simply walking away to seek better terms of employment, leaving half of his owner's tobacco seedlings untransplanted?[75] In the absence of a functioning Middlesex County Court to order him to "return to his Service," a bond-laborer would surely have gloried in the opportunity to defy Major Robert Smith, who sought to keep him in bondage by denying the validity of his "printed paper."[76] With the whole country in a state of social dissolution, who would have been there to capture a "Mulatto runaway boy" and return him to the parish minister who claimed him and on whose orders he was whipped to death?[77] There would have been no General Court or Charles City Council to order the pursuit of "certain runaway negroes," and nor would there have been any posse to carry that order out.[78] Perhaps among desperately unhappy bond-laborers the improved prospects for the outward expression of anger reduced the inclination to suicide.[79] A few names survive in the records of bond-laborers more disposed to turn their aggression outward. The Governor himself said that his own "servant," a carpenter named Page, had joined the rebellion and "for his violence used against the Royal Party [was] made a Colonel," and that another "servant," named Digby, was a rebel captain.[80] Bond-laborer James Wilson was apparently a rank-and-filer, as were William Baker, a "souldier ... by his own voluntary act," and John Thomas, who served in the rebellion for nearly six months.[82] Bond-laborer Mary Fletcher ran away to the rebel garrison that had taken over the house of Arthur Allen in Surry County.[82]

More significant than this random identification of individual bond-laborers is the fact that nameless-to-history bond-laborers intervened *en masse* in the rebellion for their own particular interest – freedom from chattel servitude. English poet and Parliament member Andrew Marvell reported on 14 November 1676 that a ship had recently arrived from Virginia with the news that Bacon had "proclam'd liberty to all Servants and Negro's."[83] A letter written from Virginia in October seemed to suggest that a class differentiation had occurred among the rebels: "Bacon's followers having deserted him he had proclaimed liberty to the servants and slaves which chiefly formed his army when he burnt James Town."[84] According to another ship's report, "most of the servants flock to [Bacon], and he makes their masters pay their wages."[85] The Virginia Assembly retrospectively declared that "many evill disposed servants in these late tymes of horrid rebellion taking advantage of the loosenes of the tymes, did depart from their service, and followed the rebells in rebellion."[86] The Royal Commissioners noted that "sundry servants and other persons of desperate fortunes in Virginia during the late rebellion deserted from their masters and ran into rebellion on the encouragement of liberty."[87]

Among the captains of merchant ships whom the king and Berkeley recruited for service against the rebellion, perhaps the most active, and certainly the most noteworthy, was Captain Thomas Grantham of the thirty-gun *Concord*. Grantham arrived in York River on 21 November.[88] Governor Berkeley came over from Accomack and, in a shipboard conference, agreed on a strategy whereby Grantham would attempt to go to the rebels and to persuade them to surrender and receive the Governor's pardon. The main concentration of some eight hundred men was around West Point, where the Pamunkey and the Mattaponi rivers meet to form the York. Laurence Ingram, who had assumed the rebel command after the death of Bacon on 26 October, was an old friend of Grantham, on whose ship Ingram had first arrived in Virginia.[89] Whatever the particulars of the conversation, an agreement was reached under the terms of which three hundred of the rebels marched with drums and colors down to Tindall's Point where the Governor was waiting aboard a ship. Through Ingram and the other rebel officers a ceasefire was agreed upon pending the arrival of "his Majesties Shipps." But such blind faith in the benevolence of His Majesty was not to be expected from the rebel rank-and-file; Ingram's arrangement with the Governor "was broke by the Rebells in three dayes time," and it became clear, in the words of one Virginia account, "the name of Authority had but litle power to [w]ring the Sword out of these Mad fellows hands." Authority failing, Grantham "resalved to acoste them with never to be performed promises" of pardon for the freemen and freedom for the bond-laborers, English and Negroes, such as had constituted the rebel army from the time of the burning of Jamestown.[90]

After a secret conference between Berkeley and Ingram and his lieutenant Gregory Walklett, three hundred of the rebels with only small arms at West Point did accept the terms.[91] But three miles further up the country, the chief garrison and magazine remained intact at Colonel West's house, armed with "five hundred Musketts and fowling pieces, and a Chest of Powder, and about a Thousand Weight of Bulletts and shott, and three great Guns." Not only were these rebels heavily armed, they were furious at Grantham for abusing the ceasefire to secure the absolute surrender of West Point. Grantham himself described the historic encounter:

> I went to Colonel West's house about three miles farther, which was their Cheife Garrison and Magazine; I there mett about foure hundred English and Negroes in Armes, who were much dissatisfied at the Surrender of the Point,[92] saying I had betray'd them, and thereupon some were for shooting mee, and others were for cutting mee in peeces: I told them I would willingly surrender myselfe to them, till they were satisfied from his Majestie, and did ingage to the Negroes and Servants, that they were all pardoned and freed from their Slavery: and with faire promises and Rundletts of Brandy, I pacified them, giving them severall Noates under my hand, that what I did was by the Order of His Majestie and the Governor ... Most of them I persuaded to goe to their Homes ... except about Eighty Negroes and Twenty English which would not deliver their Armes.[93]

Grantham's testament has a significance that is beyond exaggeration: in Virginia, 128 years before William Lloyd Garrison was born, laboring-class

African-Americans and European-Americans fought side by side for the abolition of slavery. In so doing they provided the supreme proof that the white race did not then exist.

Virginia was not Ireland, the Atlantic was not the Irish Sea. Reaction time from the burning of Jamestown to knowledge of it in England to the arrival of the royal expeditionary force in Virginia in late January and early February was four and a half months. In the meantime, the rebels having driven Berkeley into refuge on the Eastern Shore, they moved quickly to crush him. They commandeered a ship, installed cannon on it, and sent a force with it to capture Berkeley. If the plan had succeeded, the history of continental colonial America might have taken a much different path. The English expeditionary force of perhaps 1,350 soldiers, about one-third of them raw recruits,[94] might not have been able to win a timely victory. When interviewed by John Good (like Bacon a Henrico plantation owner), Bacon argued that "five hundred Virginians" could defeat 2,000 redcoats, by guerrilla strategy and tactics they had learned from the native fighters, "we having the same advantages against them that the Indians have against us."

> Are we not acquainted with the country, so that we can lay ambuscades?: Can we not hide behind trees so render their discipline of no avail? Are we not as good or better shots than they?

When John Good said that in the end the rebels would not be able to withstand being cut off from the supplies of necessities from the mother country, Bacon countered that the French or the Dutch would be willing to fill the trade vacuum. To Good's doubts on that score, Bacon countered with the prospect of extending the rebellion to North Carolina and Maryland.[95]

Bacon always had hope that if the king could be apprised of the actual state of affairs in Virginia, he would see justice in the rebel cause. Might not Charles II, mired in a state deficit and heavily engaged in his struggle with Parliament, have made a great effort to find some accommodation with the propertied element aligned with Bacon, so long as it could preserve the king's tobacco revenue? How would "Governor Bacon" have sounded, with Berkeley being treated in the same way that Charles's father had dealt with his close friend and advisor, Strafford?[96] Of course, Virginia's fundamental problems would have remained, but the rebel forces would have been divided beyond repair. No such deal would have been conceivable without the casting-off of the bond-laborers and the poor freedmen; their demands were incompatible with "all the principall Men in the Country," as Good termed them, and with the English Crown and merchants as well.

The initiative that the rebels held at the time of the Good interview was lost, however, with fatal consequences, when the attempt to invade Accomack miscarried and Bacon died of illness contracted by exposure to the elements. The Governor then enlisted armed merchantmen, whose strategy was based on the principle that "in this plentiful watered Country, the water commands the Land." The rebels' one bid for maritime strength having failed, the initiative swung to the side of the Governor and the king. By the middle of January, ten days before the first English soldiers arrived, these floating forts, by virtue of their mobility and the cannon they carried, had been decisive in reducing the half-dozen or more of the scattered garrisons.[97] The Royal Commissioners reported, "About the 16th of January [1676/7], the whole country had submitted to the Governor"; a week later he called a meeting of the General Assembly at his own house at Green Spring.[98]

In the Aftermath of Rebellion

By sitting as judges in ordering the death sentences of nine of the total of twenty-three rebels hanged,[99] the Royal Commissioners, Governor-designate Colonel Herbert Jeffreys, Major Francis Moryson,[100] and Captain Sir John Berry, gave countenance to Berkeley's defiance of the King's proclamation of 20 October 1676. That proclamation granted amnesty to rebels who took the oath of obedience within "the space of twenty days," but Berkeley dispatched these enemies without regard to the amnesty.[101] The Royal Commissioners were also at one with Berkeley with regard to repealing the measure, enacted by the "Bacon Assembly" the previous year, that had extended the vote to all freemen, propertied and propertyless. The new General Assembly withdrew the franchise from the propertyless "freemen."[102] But with regard to the most practical policy for capitalizing on their victory, controversy dominated the relations between Governor Berkeley and his most enthusiastic local support-ers, on the one hand, and the Royal Commissioners, on the other.[103]

Berkeley was not willing to make any allowances for the rebellious dispo-sition of the population of the colony, even though he himself had noted it and related it to the critical state of the tobacco monoculture economy. He regarded the rebellion as an intolerable repudiation of his stewardship, made the more infuriating by the king having so cavalierly, so to speak, handed him his hat courtesy of the meddling Royal Commissioners, and brought him home under a cloud of suspicion to render account for the breakdown of order in the colony. The Royal Commissioners and the entire English government, on the other hand, as Charles's proclamation suggests were less interested in vengeance than in the speediest revival of the tobacco trade.[104]

On 10 February 1676/7, commissioners Berry and Moryson addressed a letter to James, Duke of York. They were concerned to find that not one in thirty of the colonists was innocent of involvement in the rebellion. The populace was

> sullen and obstinate and unless they receive timely reddress it is to be feared that they will either abandon their plantations, discharging their servants and disposing of their stock, and go away to other parts, or else most of them will only make corn instead of tobacco, careless of their own estates and the King's customs.

They further warned that if the opportunity of a war presented itself, the people of Virginia "might throw off their yoke and subjugate themselves to a foreign power."[105]

Fundamental Destabilizing Factors Persisted

The social instability noted by the Royal Commissioners was rooted in five long-range fundamental factors.

1. The train of overproduction, mass impoverishment, and indebtedness produced by the tobacco monoculture, which continued to dominate the lives of the great majority of the population

Experienced observers consulted by the Lords of Trade in 1681 concurred in urging the continued presence of regular English troops in Virginia, noting that "Virginia is at present poorer and more populous than ever," and that "extreme poverty may cause the servants to plunder the stores and ships."[106] Colony Secretary Nicholas Spencer ascribed that danger to "the low price of tobacco [having] made them desperate," and he was fearful that mere plant-cutting "will not satiate their rebellious appetites."[107] In another letter on those riots, Spencer specifically alluded to the evil of monoculture: "Tobacco, the sole manufacture of the Country, [has] grown out of esteeme by its over great quantities yearely made."[108] In 1687, the price of tobacco was so low that potential creditors were rejecting it as collateral.[109] The following year Governor Culpeper, noting that everything else was being neglected in favor of tobacco growing, feared that "our great plenty will glutt the market again."[110] In March 1689, during the War of the League of Augsburg (King Billy's War) against the French, 1689–97, Spencer ironically suggested that "our poverty is our best defence, for where ther's noe Carcase, the Eagles will not resort."[111] In 1710, during the War of the Spanish Succession (Queen Anne's War), 1701–1713, the price of tobacco was so low that in Virginia the people were deeply in debt, yet there were few buyers for it.[112] A modern scholar declares that for thirty-five years, from 1680 to 1715, such conditions "recurred with appalling regularity."[113]

2. The plantation bourgeoisie's failure to diversify production, a subject treated in Chapter 9

In the House of Commons in 1671 it was estimated that £80,000 of the annual Crown revenues came from Virginia tobacco; ten years later Governor Culpeper asserted that the King's revenues from Virginia tobacco alone exceeded all the revenues from all the other colonies combined.[114] In 1690, when the price paid for tobacco in Virginia was less than a penny a pound, shipowners sold it in England for 7*d.*, of which 5*d.* was collected as the King's share.[115] Every additional pound sterling of royal tobacco import revenue was an argument for keeping Virginia engaged exclusively in making tobacco. Opposition to diversification was constantly voiced by English capitalists, who (a) were enriched by trading in Virginia tobacco and in bond-labor for the plantation colonies, and (b) were jealous of any colonial productive enterprise that might reduce colonial dependence on English export supplies. Finally it was impossible for chronically indebted Virginia to accumulate capital for the relatively long-term investment needed to develop new lines of production.[116]

3. The increase in the bond-labor population, eager as ever for "an end to their Slavery"

The numbers of bond-laborers grew despite the reduction of the exportable labor supply in England that resulted from the demands for ship crews and cannon fodder in two successive wars with France that lasted from 1689 to 1713 with only a four-year (1698–1702) interruption. It is impossible to construct a statistical table of the numbers of bond-laborers from year to year, but a reasonable estimate can be made for the period.[117]

As previously noted, three out of every four Europeans who came to the Chesapeake in the colonial period were imported as chattel bond-laborers.[118] In 1671, 8,000 of the 15,000 tithables in Virginia were bond-laborers according to Governor Berkeley, who put the total population of Virginia at 40,000.[119] Of the 30,000 Europeans who came to the Chesapeake region between 1680 and 1699,[120] we may assume that 24,000 were bond-laborers. In a roughly equivalent period, 1674–1700, around 6,000 African bond-laborers were imported.[121] In that same period, 1674–1700, the total number of Virginia and Maryland tithables (taxables) rose from about 21,000 to about 34,000,[122] a linear average of 1,600 per year. Europeans were arriving at an average rate of 1,500 per year, 1,125 of them bond-laborers, and Africans were arriving at the rate of 240 a year, presumably as bond-laborers, making an incoming total of 1,365, equal to 85 percent of the increase of the total tithables.[123] Not only was the number of bond-laborers increasing, it was increasing as a proportion of the number of tithables, and doubtless of the total population.[124]

The rebellion was over, but the rebelliousness of bond-laborers was not. In 1698, Francis Nicholas, then Governor of Maryland, reported to the Board of Trade the arrival of 326 "Negro" bond-laborers directly from Africa, and 70 more from Virginia and Pennsylvania. Pending an exact count soon to be made, he estimated that another 600 or 700 bond-laborers had arrived from Europe, "Chiefly Irish ... , most if not all, papists." If that trend were to continue, he said, the two groups might join forces in both Virginia and Maryland to make "great disturbances, if not a rebellion."[125] The following year, 1699, the Virginia House of Burgesses rejected the Board of Trade's idea of arming their "servants" against the possibility of a French invasion should war be renewed. With the signing of the Peace of Ryswick, a lull in the war with France had begun, but a by-product of the peace was that too many ungovernable Irish veterans were being shipped as bond-laborers to the Chesapeake. "If they were armed . . . we have just reason to fear they may rise upon us," said the Burgesses. Although of one mind with the Board of Trade on the possibility of a French invasion, the Burgesses feared the bond-laborers, "from the sake of their freedom and the difference of the religion, a great many of them (especially the Irish) and for other reasons . . . would rather be our enemies than contribute to our assistance."[126]

Apparently deciding to wait no longer for foreign invasion, African-American bond-laborers in two adjacent southside counties, Surry and James River, plotted an Easter rebellion in 1710 which was discovered just on the eve of R-Day.[127] In 1712, Virginia governor Alexander Spotswood declared that "insurrections" by African-American bond-laborers and invasion by Indians were dangers as serious as that of attack by sea had been during the height of the war with France.[128] At a new large plantation near the head of James River, the African-American bond-laborers looked not to rescue by sea, but to escape into the interior. They "formed a design to withdraw from their master and to fix themselves in the fastnesses of the neighboring mountains." They did indeed succeed in establishing briefly a settlement and began planting their crops, and defended it with arms against the militia.[129]

4. The continued lack of an effective intermediate buffer social control stratum

Berkeley's old Green Spring faction had been superseded by the hegemony of the county families, on terms that practically foreclosed the possibility of rebellion within the ruling class and led to a growing consensus against arbitrary administration by royal governors. But the attenuated state of the presumptive buffer stratum was demonstrated by the plant-cutting riots that occurred between May and August 1682, starting in Gloucester and then spreading to New Kent, Middlesex and York counties.

Narratives of the event are familiar fare to students of seventeenth-century Virginia history. The following brief description first published in 1705 has been appropriately cited by generations of historians:[130]

> . . . despairing of succeeding in any Agreement with the Neighbouring Governments [to limit tobacco production, the rioters] resolved on a total Destruction of the Tobacco in that Country [Gloucester, New Kent, Middlesex, and York counties], especially of the Sweet-scented; because that was planted no where else. In pursuance of which Design, they contrived, that all Plants should be destroy'd while they were yet in their Beds, after it was too late to sow more.
>
> Accordingly the Ring-leaders in this Project began with, their own first, and then went to cut up the Plants of such of their Neighbours as were not willing to do it themselves.

The riots did succeed in reducing the glut of tobacco for that year by ten thousand hogsheads.[131] This, however, was not Bacon's Rebellion revisited; it was a spontaneous outburst of small planters[132] over a single issue, and rather than being directed at altering the government, it was merely a form of direct economic action for a season. Since the action was limited to the area specializing in sweet-scented tobacco, it did not become a colony-wide phenomenon. In consequence of that circumstance, indeed, the militias from remote areas were employed to suppress the riots.[133]

But this was no way to run a social control system in a civil society. Edmund S. Morgan makes the point concisely:[134]

> Although the plant-cutting rebellion had been successfully suppressed ... [it] is questionable how long Virginia could have continued on this course, keeping men in servitude for years and then turning them free to be frustrated by the engrossers of land, by the collectors of customs, by the county courts, by the king himself.

It is unfortunate, at least in my opinion, that Professor Morgan here introduces the idea that only desperate free men might rebel, implying what he subsequently states explicitly, namely that bond-laborers did not have rebellion in them.[135]

Virginia Governor Culpeper likened the tobacco-cutting riots to the anti-enclosure riots in sixteenth-century England.[136] Indeed, the high debts and the low price of tobacco were to the laboring-class free people of Virginia like the hedges and fences that had shut out the copyholders from their ancestral lands in England. But this "downsizing" of the poor planters in Virginia contemplated no purposeful and controlled "thinning" of a stand of social timber with the deliberate preservation of a proportion of yeomanry out of social control considerations.[137] The invisible hand of free market forces in seventeenth-century Virginia operated without such conscious allowances, and the devil take the hindmost. The English copyholder was competing with sheep for land; the laboring free poor in Virginia were forced to compete with unpaid chattel bond-labor. Sheep, however, do not rebel, bond-laborers did, and their freedom was a common class interest of the poor and landless free population such as had joined hands with bond-laborers in 1676.[138]

5. The practical unfeasibility of maintaining a system of social control in Virginia by means of the English army

First of all, there were the logistical problems. English government preparations for sending troops to Virginia to suppress Bacon's Rebellion were under way by the first week of October,[139] but the five companies of English troops that were despatched did not sail from England until around the end of November, and it was mid-February 1677 before the last of the troop-carrying merchant ships arrived at Jamestown,[140] a month after the end of the rebellion.

From the beginning the costs were a dominating consideration. The king was to bear the cost of the transportation and of victuals for the first three months. The colony government was supposed to provide quarters, but because Jamestown was in ruins the troops could not be disembarked promptly, and the king had to pay "demurrage" for quartering them on board ship until they could be put ashore. The troops were in the king's pay, but the colony had to pay for their victuals out of the quitrents assigned to them and from a special tax on wines and liquors enacted for that specific purpose.

Three months after the troops reached Virginia, the Lords of Trade and Plantations ordered Governor Jeffreys to send all but one hundred of them back to England as soon as possible. The cost factor was the primary consideration, as indicated by the proviso permitting those who so desired to stay in Virginia as "planters or servants."[141] Although Governor Culpeper wanted three 200-man companies of the king's troops to be kept in Virginia, the Lords of Trade and Plantations decided in August 1678 to allow him only two.[142] Three years later, in October 1681, Culpeper asked that two companies be kept permanently in Virginia, advancing the financial consideration that the presence of such a force in 1676 might have prevented the rebellion that "cost and lost the king above a hundred thousand pounds."[143] But the Privy Council ordered that the two remaining companies be disbanded by Christmas 1681, unless the colony paid the cost of maintaining them.[144] Subsequently the home government advanced money to pay the soldiers until April 1682. In May 1682, colony officials reported to England that the General Assembly, bitter because of the unremedied glut of tobacco, refused to do the one thing it was asked to do, namely to provide money for further maintenance of English soldiers. Because of the irregularity of their pay, some of the soldiers were reduced to selling themselves into servitude in order to survive. Consequently, just when they were expected to put down the plant-cutting riots in Gloucester, "the only time they [had] been needed since they came to Virginia," as Colony Secretary Spencer observed, they were "apter to mutiny than serve His Majestie."[145] The soldiers were finally paid off and disbanded in June 1682 even as the plant-cutting riots were still spreading.[146] In May 1683 the Virginia Colony Council unsuccessfully asked that the Crown pay for the maintenance of a garrison of sixty soldiers in Virginia.[147] In October of that year, however, the Privy Council did approve Governor Effingham's request for the stationing of a man-of-war in Virginia, as a guarantee to prevent "Disorder or Rebellion ... to grow to that head as it did in the year 1676," and to "cure the insolencies" of rioters in the future.[148] Whether such a guard ship was ever sent and, if sent, what role it might have played as a social control measure seems so far to be a blank page of Virginia history.

In January 1677 the Lieutenant Governor of Maryland, Thomas Notley, watching with understandable anxiety the unfolding events in Virginia, had sounded a warning. "There must be an alteration though not of the Government yet in the Government[;] new men should be put in power. The old men will never agree with the common people, and if that not be done, His Majestie will never find a well settled Government in that Colony."[149] Four months later, Notley again made the point in a letter to Lord Baltimore. If a new leader came forward ready to risk his life in the cause, he said, "the Commons of Virginia would Emmire themselves as deep in Rebellion as ever they did in Bacon's time." The plantation bourgeoisie must find a new strategy for social control, for

> if the ould Course be taken, and if Coll. Jeoffreys [Herbert Jeffreys, Berkeley's successor as Royal Governor of Virginia] build his proceedings upon the ould foundation its neither him nor all his Majesties Souldiers in Virginia will either satisfye or Rule those people.[150]

But what sort of "alteration in the Government" could be fashioned that would "agree with the common people" enough that it could rule them?

12

The Abortion of the "White Race" Social Control System in the Anglo-Caribbean

The English plantation bourgeoisie in the continental colonies and in the Caribbean opted to base their ventures on chattel bond-labor, at first European but – sooner in the Caribbean, later in the continental plantation colonies – mainly African bond-labor. Then, in both cases – sooner in the Caribbean, later in the continental plantation colonies – the ruling class sought to establish social control on the principle of racial oppression of non-Europeans.

In the very beginning, it was theorized that the ranks of European bond-laborers who survived their servitude might furnish the Anglo-American equivalent of the Ulster Scots or English-style yeomen as a middle class, with a vested property interest (as fee-simple smallholders or as secure tenants) and be the middle-class buffer between the plantation bourgeoisie and the bond-labor force. But circumstantial differences between the Ulster plantation and those in English colonies in America produced differences in the degree of dependence upon tenantry. In Ireland the English bourgeoisie was faced with the fact of the unassimilability of the Irish Catholic chieftains allied with Spain and the fact that English land claims were predicated on expropriation of those chieftains' tribal lands. In Anglo-America the plantation bourgeoisie was practically immune from successful native challenge to its continued possession of the land, and from an imminent overthrow by African bond-laborers "broken from their tribal stems." The denial of any degree of social mobility of Africans and African-Americans, the hallmark of racial oppression, was an option not rooted in geo-political considerations; rather it was driven simply and directly by the greater rate of profit to be had by the employment of lifetime hereditary bond-laborers – provided a cost-effective system of social control could be established.[1] The result was to give the term "planta-tion" a new meaning, implying monoculture and engrossment of the land by capitalist owners of bond-laborers. This meant that the early prospect for the establishment of an adequate intermediate stratum of European (and European-American), chiefly small freeholders or eviction-proof leaseholders was not to be realized. Consequently, different ways of maintaining ruling-class social control would be required. The class struggle would produce forms of social control in the Anglo-Caribbean colonies, however, that diverged in historically significant ways from that which was adopted in continental Anglo-America.

The Social Control Problem in the British West Indies[2]

In 1627, the English made Barbados a colony, using a labor force at first made up principally of bond-laborers brought from England, Ireland and Scotland.[3] The English also made efforts to reduce natives of the Caribbean to plantation bond-servitude; there are references to such workers in the record.[4] The class-undifferentiated Caribbean Indian tribes were not dominated by "casiques" possessing authority to deliver tribe members into European servitude.[5] Because of the Indians' warlike resistance, the English plans in this regard were by and large frustrated before they could be made operational. A pivotal point was reached in the mid-1660s. An English colony established on St Lucia in 1663 was wiped out by the native Indians by 1667. After retaking the island in March 1668, the English concluded an agreement with these Indians under which they were to be English subjects, but with the right to come and to depart at pleasure in the English islands.[6] "The Barbadians ... held Indian slaves," writes Richard S. Dunn, "but never very many."[7]

Regardless of their nativity, bond-laborers presented the owning class with serious problems of social control. When the *Ark*, bearing the first Maryland-bound colonists, stopped at Barbados on 3 January 1634, this fact of life was starkly dramatized for the voyagers:

> On the very day we arrived there we found the island all in arms, to the number of eight hundred men. The servants on the island had plotted to kill their masters and then handsomely take the first ship that came[,] and go to sea.[8]

After first being used primarily in tobacco cultivation, Barbados by the 1650s had been transformed into a sugar colony.[9] But the switch to sugar had done nothing to sweeten the disposition of the workers. On Barbados by 1648, when around one-fourth of the bond-laborers were Africans, it was reported that "many hundreds of Rebell negro slaves were in the woods."[10] The following year a plot was formed by European chattel bond-laborers to massacre their owners and seize control of the island. Some indication of the extent of the plot may perhaps be inferred from the fact that, after it was betrayed to the authorities, eighteen plotters were executed.[11] In 1655, Barbados received no less than 12,000 prisoners of the War of the Three Kingdoms, in addition to felons and vagabonds. Their numbers, combined with the draining away of artisans from Barbados to Jamaica, caused the authorities to be fearful of imminent mass rebellion by the bond-laborers.[12] Between 1675 and 1701, there were four major revolt plots in Barbados. In 1686, African and European rebel bond-laborers joined forces.[13] In 1692, a "Negro conspiracy" to seize the English fort at Bridgetown was discovered.[14]

Historican Richard S. Dunn identifies "seven separate slave revolts in the

English islands between 1640 and 1713, in which blacks and whites were killed."[15] "Rebellion, or the threat of it, was an almost permanent feature of Jamaican slave society," writes Orlando Patterson; he concludes that, "[W]ith the possible exception of Brazil, no other slave society in the New World experienced such continuous and intensive servile revolts" as Jamaica. Aside from the Second Maroon War (1795–96) Patterson mentions large-scale revolts, or discovered plots, in 1760, 1776, 1784, 1823 and 1824. "The last and most ambitious of all the slave rebellions of the island broke out two days after Christmas 1831," he writes; a roughly estimated 20,000 took part, with wide support, and 207 were killed; over 500 more were executed; 14 whites were killed, and property damage mounted to over £1.1 million; over £161,000 was spent in suppressing the revolt.[16]

The Jamaica maroons

When the Spanish abandoned Jamaica in 1655, some 1,500 Negroes escaped to the mountains. They became the Jamaica maroons who, from that time until 1796, maintained a separate set of independent communities.[17] In 1656 the main part of the maroons, under the leadership of Juan de Bolas, "surrendered to the English on terms of pardon and freedom." The others continued to be a thorn in the side of the English colony, so much so that they "intimidated the whites from venturing to any considerable distance from the coast." According to the account by the English historian of the West Indies, Bryan Edwards, the English governor offered, "full pardon, twenty acres of land, and freedom from all manner of slavery, to each of them who should surrender. But ... they were better pleased with the more ample range they possessed in the woods, where there [their] hunting grounds were not yet encroached upon by settlements." In 1663 the English sent a black regiment under Juan de Bolas, who was now their colonel, but he was killed and the general effort was a failure.

> In this way they continued to distress the island for upwards of forty years, during which time forty-four acts of Assembly were passed, and at least 240,000 *l.* expended for their suppression. In 1736, they were grown so formidable, under a very able general named Cudjoe, that it was found expedient to strengthen the colony against them by two regiments of regular troops, which were afterwards formed unto independent companies, and employed, with other hired parties, and the whole body of the militia, in their reduction.[18]

This struggle, known as the First Maroon War, 1725–40, was concluded under terms of a treaty signed at Trelawney Town on 1 March 1738/9. Under its terms, the maroons were guaranteed freedom, and possession of a region of 15,000 acres in which they might cultivate non-sugar crops and raise livestock, and the right to licenses to trade their products with people of the English colony.[19] The maroons, for their part, agreed "That if any negroes shall hereafter run away from their masters or owners, and fall into Captain

Cudjoe's hands, they shall immediately be sent back to the chief magistrate of the next parish where they are taken; and those that bring them are to be satisfied for their trouble, as the legislature shall appoint."[20] This latter provision is similar to previously mentioned agreements between the English colonial authorities in Virginia, Maryland and Carolina and various tributary Indian tribes, requiring the Indians to return runaway bond-laborers.

Objective Factors that Shaped Social Control Strategy

In relation to the question of social control and the invention of the white race, the British West Indies differed from the continental plantation colonies in five significant ways.[21] First, because of the narrow absolute limits of land area, and the relatively high capital costs of sugar production, the West Indies was especially inhospitable to non-capitalist farmers or tenants. Second, in the West Indies the attempt to establish a "white race" social control system was seriously and critically complicated by the substantial Irish presence. Third, the central role of the English military and naval forces regularly stationed in the West Indies constituted the most important guarantor of social control. Fourth, the predominance of persons of African descent in the population of the West Indies made it impossible to exclude them altogether from the intermediate stratum. Fifth, the reliance upon persons of African descent in the skilled trades and in the conduct of the internal economy of the West Indies colonies led to the emergence of the "free colored" as the predominant element in the middle class. The remainder of this chapter will be mainly an elaboration of these points.

1. Land area limits, capital costs

The plantation system, wherever it existed, was characterized by the engrossment of the land by the bourgeoisie. But the effect of that engrossment on the prospective formation of an intermediate social control stratum was much greater in the island colonies than in continental plantation colonies. In the British West Indies, in addition to the typical economic and political difficulties facing the smallholder in a monocultural economy, the absolute limits of land area played a decisive part. In continental plantation colonies the barrier to the formation of a stable yeoman class was not an absolute scarcity of land, but merely the economic and political disadvantages of competing as non-capitalist entrepreneurs in a monocultural capitalist economy based on bond-labor. At the end of the seventeenth century, some 51,000 people, 88 percent of the total population of Virginia, lived in the Tidewater region, an area of 11,000 miles, representing a population density of 4.6 per square mile.[22] Virginia at large, including the transmontane region (not including Kentucky), had an area of some 64,000 miles. The total area of all patented land in Virginia in 1704 was equal to less than 40 percent of the area of the Tidewater region alone.[23] Even in the most heavily settled Tidewater area, the farms were so remote from each other as to hinder mustering the militia, and to make it difficult to assure effective collection of import and export duties.[24]

Barbados, the second-largest of England's Caribbean colonies, but with an area of only 166 square miles, was inhabited by 70,000 people in 1694 and had a population density of 423 per square mile.[25] By 1717, all but 6 percent of that island's total area was under cultivation; the great houses of the planter estates were not remote from their neighbors but were "within sight of each other."[26]

Jamaica was the exception; its 7,400 square miles made up more than half the land area of the British West Indies and had a population density of only 6.5 per square mile in 1698. Most of Jamaica was unoccupied, even in the early nineteenth century.[28] Only half its land was under patent, and only half of that was under cultivation.[29] At least until the end of the First Maroon War in 1739, the colony's frontiers were "no longer any Sort of Security [and] must be deserted."[30] But the main and sufficient reason for the limited number of smallholders in Jamaica was one that was common to the British West Indies generally – the relatively capital-intensive technology of the principal economic activity, the production of sugar and rum.

Excessive emigration of freemen
In the seventeenth-century Chesapeake, most of the limited-term bond-laborers never succeeded in completing their terms and becoming landowners. Those who did so needed only elementary individual hand-labor implements to engage in the common tobacco economy, poor and indebted though they most likely were destined to be. In the West Indies, the capital requirement for becoming a sugar planter – for buildings, mills, boiling pots, sugar pots, stills and, above all, for bond-labor – were beyond the means of the former bond-laborers.[31] The contrast in estate values in the late seventeenth century in Jamaica and Maryland is indicative. The average estate of the sugar planters of Jamaica in the last quarter of the seventeenth century was appraised at nearly £2,000, and the average value of all estates was £531, of which two-thirds to three-fourths might represent investment in bond-labor. In Maryland in the same period there were no estates appraised at as much as £2,000, and fewer than 4 percent of the estates had a value of more than £500.[32] Separate findings by highly regarded investigators suggest that in the late seventeenth century the prospect of a bond-laborer in Barbados surviving to become a landholder was only one-half as great as that of a bond-laborer in Virginia.[33]

From at least as early as the third quarter of the seventeeth century, many of those who survived their limited-term servitude in the English West Indies only to be confronted by this unpromising prospect were opting to leave their respective islands. Between 1660 and 1682, some 16,000 or 17,000 people emigrated from Barbados, most of them "landless freemen and small farmers."[34] In the last forty years of the seventeenth century the total population of Barbados is estimated to have doubled, from 40,000 to 80,000, but emigration was so great that the European population did not increase at all. Many of such emigrants chose initially to pursue their careers in nearby islands,[35] but it appears that nowhere in the British West Indies did such European migration reverse the long-range reduction of the European proportion of the population. Richard S. Dunn's table "Estimated Population of the English Sugar Islands, 1669–1713" shows a steady decade-to-decade decline in the European proportion of the populations of Barbados, Jamaica, and the Leeward Islands.[36]

Emigration became a major concern of the West Indies colonial authorities, not on account of the loss of labor-power it represented but because of the difficulty in maintaining the militias for defense against rival colonial powers, particularly the French, and for purposes of social control of the bond-laborers. The European population of Barbados in 1640 was around 25,000; of these more than one-third were proprietors and 10,000 were "servants," while the non-European bond-laborers, including a few Amerindians, numbered 6,400. By 1680, the total number of Europeans had fallen to 17,000, and because of the cost of capital and land requirements for sugar planting the number of "considerable proprietors" was less than 500, and the number of European bond-laborers in the island had shrunk to 2,000.[37] In the 1660s, Barbados had a fighting force of only 7,000 men, of whom only the large landholders were interested in the colony enough to be ready to defend it; the rest were concerned only with emigrating to find better prospects than they could have in Barbados.[38] Harlow's conclusion regarding Barbados was generally applicable to the British West Indies: it was "the concentration of land into large estates which was gradually depriving Barbados of her 'yeoman' class, and which eventually put an end to her development as a white community."

Social control was aimed at bond-laborers, whether of European or African descent. But the limited-term bond-laborers who, in the West Indies, were exclusively European, were prospective enlistees in the social control system as members of the militia, provided they survived their terms of servitude. This was a scheme for class collaboration of Europeans that required a new term of social distinction, namely "white," that would include not only laborer and capitalist but also bond-labor as well as free labor.[39] The alternative or redundant term "Christian," was sometimes applied to European bond-laborers, despite complications that arose regarding the Christian conversion of African bond-laborers;[40] or from the belief that some Europeans, namely the Irish, though Europeans had yet to be made Christians.[41] It became customary also to use the term "servants" for the European bond-laborers, potential militiamen, as distinct from African lifetime bond-laborers, called "slaves."[42]

A succession of proposals, schemes and laws were proposed, some of them adopted, that were explicitly aimed at increasing the proportion of the militia-producing European population in the English West Indies, or at least maintaining it. Compulsory measures were undertaken of which the most general type imposed fines on plantation owners who failed to keep in their employ a quota of one European, bond or free, for every so many African bond-laborers; these were the so-called "deficiency laws." The ratio varied from place to place and from time to time. Whatever the particular ratio, the home government constantly expressed its concern that it be met. In 1682 in Jamaica, the quota was one white bond-laborer to the first five lifetime bond-laborers, "for ten slaves two whites, and for every ten slaves over and above the said number one white . . . on penalty of £5 for every servant that shall be wanting."[43] In 1699, the Governor of the Leeward Islands was instructed "to use his utmost endeavor that each Planter keep such a number of white servants as the law directed."[44] The Nevis Assembly in 1701 passed "An Act for encouraging the Importation of white Servants, and that all Persons shall be obliged to keep one white Servant to every Twenty Negroes."[45] Other compulsory measures were designed to limit emigration. For example, English prisoners who had been sentenced to ten years' servitude in Barbados for the 1685 rebellion led by the Duke of Monmouth were ordered to be freed from bond-servitude, but they were forbidden to leave the island without royal permission.[46]

In the 1660s, the usual term of servitude in Barbados was reduced to encourage bond-laborers to come to the island.[47] In order to get and keep European craftsmen in Barbados, the island's Assembly prohibited the employment of Africans and Afro-Barbadians as coopers, smiths, carpenters, tailors, or boatmen.[48] In 1695, Governor Russell of Barbados remarked on the deplorable condition of the European former bond-laborers, who were "domineered over and used like dogs." Such treatment, he believed, would "drive away the commonalty of the white people." There were hundreds of such unfortunates, he declared, that never enjoyed fresh meat nor a dram of rum. That woeful lack could be made up, he suggested, by reducing the property qualification for voting at the annual elections in the expectation that candidates for the Assembly "would sometimes give the miserable creatures a little rum and fresh provisions and such things as would be of nourishment and make their lives more comfortable, in the hopes of getting their votes."[49] In 1709, a merchant trading to Jamaica proposed to the Commissioners of Trade and Plantations the settling of a colony of German Protestants in that island, because the European militia was reduced to 2,500 and there were 40,000 African bond-laborers to be repressed. These settlers were to "be free so soon as they set foot on shore in that island, and enjoy all privileges;" they were to be granted five or six acres of land in fee simple for every member of each family.[50] Six years later, the Lords of Trade and Plantations proposed that all Protestant European immigrants be extended those privileges on arrival in Jamaica.[51]

Suggestions were advanced that, voluntarily or otherwise, the great plantation owners should surrender title to a small portion of their lands to European ex-bond-laborers; but that notion came to naught because of a lack of sufficient support from the prospective donors.[52] Ultimately a compromise was reached; the land would remain in the ownership of the capitalist owners, but they would allow a few acres to be occupied by European tenants without any rent or other obligation except that of service in the militia. Properly called "military tenants," these men represented the ultimate stage in the evolution of "whiteness"; their contribution to the economic life of the colony was neglible to nonexistent, and there was no other rationale for their existence except the political one of serving as a ready reserve for social control over bond-laborers. For especially meritorious service in the war against external or internal enemies, some such men might be given ownership of an African bond-laborer. The result, however, was not an enhancement of their participation in the economic activity of the colony, but merely provided a means of making the "military tenants" more comfortable in their shiftless existence.[53]

In token of their acquired status as "whites," even European bond-laborers were by law protected against "excessive correction" by their owners, but by and large such encouragement failed to convince European laborers to come to and remain in the West Indies in the numbers that were necessary for the establishing of a civil regime of racial oppression.[54] In time the propertyless majority of the European population of the British West Indies would be assigned to a special category, socially and economically *marginalized* as "poor whites."[55]

2. The Irish complication

The policy designed by the plantation bourgeoisie to enlist laboring-class Europeans, as "whites," in a social control stratum against Africans occasionally encountered manifestations of the contrary normal tendency of European and African bond-laborers to make common cause against their owners. Such events were a challenge to the establishment of the new all-class, all-European "white" identity.[56] It was the behavior of many of the Irish bond-laborers that created the greatest breach in that concept.[57]

The Caribbean was a cockpit of European colonial rivalry. Over a period of eighty years from 1667 to 1748, the region was involved in four formal wars, in which England was aligned against one or more Catholic powers, primarily France, but also Spain.[58] This period coincided with much of the tragic English conquest of Ireland and Ireland's subjection under the most extreme period of the racial oppression under the "anti-Popery" Penal Laws.[59] In this period, Catholic Irish bond-laborers, who constituted a major proportion of the European bond-laborers in the British West Indies, were often disposed to ally their cause with any challenge to British authority, whether that challenge were made by African bond-laborers or by a rival colonial power.

In November 1655, following the Cromwellian conquest, when the "Irish slave trade" was at its fullest, the Barbados Colony Council was apprised that "there are several Irish servants and Negroes out in Rebellion in the Thicketts and thereabouts."[60] Two years later, the Barbados General Assembly warned that Irish men and women were wandering about the island pretending to be free, some of whom had "endeavoured to secure with Armes: and others now forth in Rebellion."[61]

During the War of Devolution in which the French captured and held St Kitts for two years, 1666–67, decisive roles were played by "French Negroes," who burned six strong English forts on the island's north coast, and by the Irish on the island, who "rose against the English planters and joined the French."[62] In 1667, Governor William Willoughby of Barbados wrote to King Charles II that of a possible fighting force of 4,000, "what with Blacks[,] Irish & servants, I cannot rely upon more then between 2 and 3000 men."[63]

In March 1668, it was reported that Barbados had contributed so many men to help retake the Leeward Islands from the French that it was "in an ill Condition, in regard to the multitude of Negros & Irish Servants, which is much superior to the rest of the Planters and Inhabitants."[64]

Citing five entries in the Great Britain *Calendar of State Papers, Colonial*, Gwynne documents Irish insurrections against the English in the battles for the Leeward Islands in 1689.[65] Although the law enacted on Nevis forbidding servants and slaves to "company" or to drink together did not specifically mention the Irish,[66] it is reasonable to believe they were among the usual suspects. In the 1692 plot to capture the Barbados fort, Irish bond-laborers undertook a special tactical role: by guile or by force, they were to open the doors of the fort to the Negro rebels.[67] Two laws were enacted by the Nevis Assembly on 21 December 1701: one "to prevent Papists, and reputed Papists, from Settling in the Island," and the second "for encouraging the Importation of white Servants."[68] As late as 1731, Governor Hunter of Jamaica was contesting an act of conciliation of the Irish Catholics, "of which our Servants and Lower Rank of People chiefly consists."[69]

Just as an eventual rapprochement was begun in Ireland between the Catholic bourgeoisie and the British rulers in the middle of the eighteenth century, so in the West Indies the spirit of Protestant Ascendancy and "anti-popery" directed against the Irish abated.[70] But by then it was irrelevant to the solution of the problem of ruling-class social control in the British West Indies. By the end of the seventeenth century "the old system of defence by white servants had broken down," writes military historian John W. Fortescue.[71] What he said with particular reference to defense applies also to the failure of the attempt to establish a system of social control in the Anglo-Caribbean by an English-style yeoman militia of European former bond-laborers.

3. "Sending an army to do it . . ." – English military and naval enforcement of social control

Contemplating the way in which control over the massive bond-labor population was achieved in the British West Indies, one is reminded of Sir John Davies's dictum that the conquest cannot be regarded as complete "if the jurisdiction of . . . ordinary Courts of justice doth not extend" to all parts of the territory ". . . unlesse he send an Army to do it."[72] Because of the breakdown the system of social control by European bond-laborers and former bond-laborers, a new concept and composition for an intermediate social control stratum that included persons of African ancestry was contrived. Nevertheless, social order depended on the constant presence of English military and naval forces. "[I]t was customary," writes our historian, "for British troops to police the slave population, in addition to fighting the soldiers of other colonial powers in the West Indies."[73]

In 1680, Port Royal, Jamaica, with four forts manned by two regular English army companies, was the most strongly fortified place in all of colonial Anglo-America. "Night and day," writes Dunn, "one of the Port Royal companies was always on duty, working twelve-hour shifts." Of the fort's 110 big guns, 16 were located to face any assault by land.[74] Throughout Queen Anne's War, 1701–13, Jamaica was "a garrison colony."[75] For most of the eighteenth century, at least two regular English army regiments were stationed in Jamaica.[76] During the First Maroon War two regiments sent from Gibraltar served effectively to deter bond-laborers from joining the revolt.[77] On its frequent calls in Jamaica ports, the British navy was counted on to assist in putting down revolts of African bond-laborers.[78] Although in 1788 the Jamaica militia of "whites" and "free Negroes and free persons of color" numbered about 7,000 or 8,000, 2,000 regular troops were maintained on the island – to assure control over one-quarter million Negro bond-laborers and 1,400 maroons.[79] A British observer writing in about 1774 believed that the inhabitants of Jamaica relied too much on the protection of the king's troops."[80] In the final Maroon War, 1796–1797, the number of regular British troops was increased to 3,000.[81] In 1793, at the beginning of Britain's war against revolutionary France, the dispatch of 700 soldiers, more than half the Jamaica garrison, "drained the island of troops that were to protect the inhabitants" just at the moment when the alarming news came that the French Assembly had proclaimed freedom for all slaves in French colonies.[82] At that time, "no fewer than nineteen British battalions – out of a total strength of eighty-one – were in the Caribbean or en route."[83]

A regiment of the king's troops was sent from England to protect St Kitts after the island's recapture from the French in 1697.[84] The President of the Council of Barbados in 1738 declared that the emigration from the island had been so great that that island would have to have a naval force to protect it.[85] There no doubt seemed to be good imperial reason for the stationing of a 1,200-man regiment on tiny Antigua, where a European population of 5,000 (not half what it had been forty years before), dwelt together with 45,000 "blacks, Mulattos, and mestees."[86]

4. Afro-Caribbean majorities in the British West Indies

When former bond-laborers in Virginia tried to start farming on their own, or small planters lost out to creditors, they did not embark for another country; they took their hoes and axes and headed for North Carolina or Maryland, or to the Piedmont, or even farther westward. Whatever the extent of migration may have been, the European-American population of every continental plantation colony, according to present best estimates, grew absolutely decade by decade, from a combined total of 71,847 in 1700 to 734,754 in 1780. Although the European-American proportion of the population of the plantation colonies declined from 84 percent to 59 percent, only in South Carolina had it been reduced to less than half, to 46 percent.[87]

In the British West Indies, on the other hand, Euro-Caribbeans were a minority population before the end of the seventeenth century. Barbados had a higher proportion of European-descent inhabitants than any other colony in British West Indies. Yet by 1713 in Barbados, and in the Leeward Islands as well, Europeans made up only one-fourth of the population; in Jamaica the ratio was only one in nine.[88]

In obvious acknowledgement of the absolute impossibility that the militia-providing former bond-laborers would ever become viable yeomen farmers, various laws were enacted to preserve other petit bourgeois opportunities for them, by excluding non-Europeans from engaging in skilled occupations or huckstering.[89] But in the end, the purpose of such measures, which were absolutely essential to the meaning of "white," were nullified by the economic advantage of the use of African bond-laborers in skilled and lower supervisory occupations on the plantations,[90] and by the valuable service to the internal market provided by African bond-laborers, particularly the women.[91]

In time, as a result of emancipation by self-purchase, by testaments of free owner-fathers, and in reward for special service, as well as by natural increase, a population of free persons of some degree of African descent developed throughout the West Indies. The same was true in the continental colonies. There was a critical difference, however, in the resulting proportion of the total free population constituted by persons of some degree of African ancestry. In the continental plantation colonies and in the Upper South and Lower South states of the United States in the period 1700–1860, free African-Americans never constituted as much as 5 percent of the free population. Their proportion reached its high point, 4.8 percent in 1830, but in the two ante-bellum decades it declined appreciably, to 3.1 percent.[92] By contrast in Jamaica, which had more than half the total population of the British West Indies, and of the total free population as well, free persons of color were 18 percent of all free persons in 1768, 36 percent in 1789, and 72 percent in 1834.[93] The proportion in Barbados was 5 percent in 1786, 12 percent in 1801, and 34 percent in 1833–34.[94] In the Leeward Islands toward the end of the eighteenth century, one-fourth of the free population was of some degree of African ancestry.[95]

By the late 1700s, freedmen throughout the West Indies were working in artisan trades. In Barbados the freedman usually began as a hired unskilled worker, but quickly sought skilled work for which there was greater demand, and which had a "higher prestige value."[96] Professor Sheppard notes that by late in the eighteenth century, European freemen in that colony were able to practice their trades only to a decreasing extent, and as hucksters "they faced severe competition, as in other spheres, from the free coloreds."[97] In Jamaica in the first decades of the nineteenth century, most of the freedmen were in skilled trades, as "carpenters, masons, wheelwrights, plumbers, and other artisans,"[98] while the freedwomen in Jamaica usually became shopkeepers and sellers of "provisions, millinery, confectionery, and preserves." In Barbados in 1830, writes Professor Handler, "the Sunday market was ... an institution of fundamental importance to all segments of Barbadian Society"; he cites the contemporary observation that most of the produce sellers were free colored people.[99]

5. Afro-Caribbeans as the middle class of the British West Indies

It seems to me that nothing could have prevented the development of a normal class differentiation within the African and Afro-Caribbean population of the British West Indies as the freedmen came to constitute a substantial proportion of the free population. That was not the original intention when the sugar planters for reasons of present profit began to recruit their skilled labor force from the ranks of African bond-laborers and, by land engrossment, made the flourishing of a European yeomanry impossible. Although from time to time they made legislative gestures toward reversing the trend, the need to make the highest possible rate of profit emptied such gestures of significance.

Just as the Irish Catholic bourgeoisie, disfranchised and barred from owning land, found entrepreneurial outlets for their acquisitive compulsion by becoming graziers and merchants,[100] so in the British West Indies freedman enterprise – both petit bourgeois and capitalist – sprouted through the cracks of "white" exclusionism despite the dogged opposition of the "white" diehards who, like the Orange Order in Britain, saw chaos in any concession to the oppressed majority.

In the British West Indies generally, the free coloreds included "shopkeepers, and ... owners of land and slaves." In the trade in non-sugar commodities with the North American colonies, many free colored merchants traded directly with captains of cargo vessels. In Barbados, the energy and initiative of freedmen hucksters in meeting bond-laborers on the way to market and ships just arriving in the harbor enabled them to control the supply of produce and livestock to the general public. They were likewise involved in supplying the sugar estates with essentials that could not be got from England. Indeed, this proved a route to sugar estate ownership by occasional foreclosure on a bankrupt creditor.[101] Three years after the repeal of the prohibition on freedmen acting as pilots, they had nearly monopolized Jamaica's coastal shipping.[102]

In 1721 the Jamaica Assembly took a positive view of such trends as it turned its attention to the problem of unsettled lands becoming "a receptacle for runaway and rebellious negroes." It occurred to them to establish a buffer zone between coastal sugar plantation regions and the mountainous (and maroon-infested) interior, by offering free homesteads to laboring-class settlers and their families. Among the beneficiaries were to be "every free mulatto, Indian or negro" who would take up the offer and remain on the land for seven years. Each was to have twenty acres of land for himself, and five acres more for each slave he brought with him.[103] Perhaps some of those homesteaders served in the "companies of free Negroes and mulattoes" who were employed effectively in the First Maroon War, ended with the 1739 Treaty of Trelawney Town binding the Maroons to capture and return runaway bond-laborers.[104] By the early 1830s, "free blacks and coloreds" owned 70,000 of the total of around 310,000 bond-laborers in Jamaica.[105]

When the militia system based on the European former bond-laborers proved a failure, the sugar bourgeoisie relied on the British army and navy to guarantee their control, while at the same time recruiting free persons, black and white, into the militias as an auxiliary. In Barbados, as in Jamaica, by the 1720s freedmen were required to serve in the militia, even though they were denied important civil rights.[106] The British army and navy, however, were subject to many demands because of the almost constant worldwide round of wars with France that would last for 127 years, from 1688 to 1815. In the decisive moment – the coming of the French Revolution and the Haitian Revolution – when all hung in the balance, more extreme measures were required, for then the British in the West Indies were confronted with "blacks inspired by the revolutionary doctrine of French republicanism" and were "forced to conduct operations against large numbers of rebellious slaves in the rugged and largely unknown interiors of their own islands" of Grenada, St Vincent and Jamaica.[107]

The internal and external dangers were so critical that the British supreme commander in the Caribbean was forced to conclude that "the army of Great Britain is inadequate to ... defend these colonies" without an army of black soldiers. Eight West India regiments were formed, composed in small part by freedmen, and partly of slaves purchased by the army from plantation owners; but more were acquired directly from Africa.[108] However, "[i]t was clear that the continued existence of the West India Regiments depended upon establishing the black soldier as a freedman"; indeed, in 1807 it was so declared by act of the British Parliament: the bond-laborers who entered the British army by that act became freedmen.[109] But the logic of the policy represented a major violation of the principle of denial of social mobility of the oppressed group.[110] Many of these soldiers when discharged settled on plantations as free persons.[111]

In the meantime, thoughtful observers had begun to advocate the advantages to be had from a positive attitude toward freedmen in general. Consider the advice put forward by four authoritative English writers: Edmund Burke, in 1758; Edward Long, in 1774; the Reverend James Ramsay, in 1784, and George Pinckard in 1803.

Indubitably, [said Burke] the security ... of every nation consists principally in the number of low and middling men of a free condition, and that beautiful gradation from the highest to the lowest, where the transitions all the way are almost imperceptible ... What if in our colonies we should go so far as to find some medium between liberty and absolute slavery, in which we might place all mulattoes ... and such blacks, who ... their masters ... should think proper in some degree to enfranchise. These might have land allotted to them, or where that could not be spared, some sort of fixed employment.... [T]he colony will be strengthened by the addition of so many men, who will have an interest of their own to fight for.[112]

[Mulattos, said Long,] ought to be held in some distinction [over the blacks]. They would then form the centre of connexion between the two extremes, producing a regular establishment of three ranks of men. [If mulatto children were obliged] to serve a regular apprenticeship to artificers and tradesmen [,that] would make them orderly subjects and defenders of the country.... But even if they were to set up for themselves, no disadvantage would probably accrue to the publick, but the contrary: they would oblidge the white artificers to work at more moderate rates.[113]

Reverend Ramsay, too, limited his proposal to mulattos. The girls should be declared free from their birth, or from the time the mother became free. Male mulattos should be placed out as apprentices "to such trade or business as may best agree with their inclination and the demands of the colony," and should be freed at the age of thirty. He was persuaded that, "By these means ... a new rank of citizens, placed between the Black and White races, would be established." They would be an intermediate buffer social control stratum since "they would naturally attach themselves to the White race ... and so become a barrier against the designs of the Black."[114]

George Pinckard had served several years as a surgeon in the British expeditionary forces in the Caribbean, and looked favorably on the prospect of gradual reform leading to abolition of slavery in the West Indies. What Pinckard suggested anticipated Charles James Fox's prescription for social control adaptation in Ireland from racial oppression to national oppression: "Make the besiegers part of the garrison."[115] Pinckard argued for the social promotion of a "considerable proportion of the *people of colour*, between the whites and negroes." The installation of such a middle class "would save Britain a great expenditure of life and treasure. This middle class would soon become possessed of stores and estates; and the garrison might be safely entrusted to them as the best defenders of their own property."[116]

In 1803, John Alleyne Beckles, Anglo-Barbadian member of the Barbados Council, denounced the limitations on property rights of freedmen. Such property ownership, he argued, "will keep them [the free colored] at a greater distance from the slaves, and will keep up that jealousy which seems naturally to exist between them and the slaves . . ."

... it will tend to our security, for should the slaves at any time attempt a revolt, the free-coloured persons for their own safety and the security of their property, must join the whites and resist them. But if we reduce the free coloured people to a level with the slaves, they must unite with them, and will take every occasion of promoting and encouraging a revolt.[117]

Such ruling-class insights recognized the link between concessions to the freedmen and the maintenance of control over the bond-laborers, who in the late 1770s outnumbered the total free population of Barbados by nearly three and a half times, and outnumbered by nine times that of Jamaica.[118] As members of the militia that quelled the 1816 bond-laborer revolt in Barbados, "the free coloureds were reckoned to have conducted themselves 'slightly better' than the whites."[119] In Jamaica in the First and the Second Maroon Wars, the mulatto militia justified the expectation that they would be a "powerful counterpoise ... of men dissimilar from [the Maroons] in complexion and manners, but equal in hardiness and vigour," capable of "scour[ing] the woods on all occasions; a service in which the [British Army] regulars are by no means equal to them."[120] As the struggle to end slavery entered its critical stage, there were freedmen who supported the cause of the bond-laborers, but they were the exceptional few.[121]

By the late 1770s, in Jamaica 36 percent of the free population was composed of persons of some degree of African ancestry; on the eve of emancipation, in 1833, they were a 72 percent majority. In Barbados in 1786, only 5 percent of free persons were persons of African ancestry; in 1833 they were 34 percent.[122] Although this increase in the freedmen population brought added forces to the intermediate social control stratum against the bond-laborers, it conversely became a major factor in the final crisis of the system of chattel bond-servitude, coming as it did in the larger context of the Haitian Revolution (in which the role of the free colored had been decisive) and the rise of the abolitionist movement in England. The "increasing wealth and numbers of the coloreds as well as their importance in the militia made it more difficult for the Assembly to deny them their rights."[123]

Of some 5,200 slaveowners in Barbados in 1822, around 3,600 owned no land; of these the majority were freedmen.[124] But due to "deficiency law" restrictions, the freedmen owners of bond-laborers for the most part exploited their bond-laborers in non-agricultural occupations. These same laws obstructed the employment of freedmen wage workers. In 1830, two persons of color were members of the Jamaican House of Assembly, but they were still barred from giving testimony in court unless they first produced proof of their baptism.

In 1816, a group of the "coloreds" petitioned for admission of all freemen to the "rights and privileges of white subjects."[125] This demand was the fulcrum by which the combined forces on the side of abolition of slavery – the Haitian example, the example of the West India regiments, the increasing rebelliousness of the plantation bond-laborers (expressed in revolts in Barbados in 1816 and Jamaica in 1831), English religious humanitarianism, and abolitionism – were able to leverage the abolition of slavery by act of Parliament in 1833. At the heart of the matter was the fact that every concession made to the freedmen to strengthen social control over the bond-laborers represented an erosion of the rationale of white supremacy upon which the system of plantation bond-servitude was based. Eventually, the essential politics of the

Haitian Revolution had its innings in Jamaica. The plantocracy's resistance to further concession to the "free coloreds" brought probably a majority of the freedmen to the support of abolition, especially when slaveowners among them were assured of being compensated by the British government for the loss of their human chattels.[126]

In continental Anglo-America, only the rivalry between the plantation bourgeoisie and the industrial bourgeoisie for national hegemony provided the civil war possibility of emancipation as a measure for preserving the Union. Emancipation in the West Indies, on the other hand, was forced by the struggle of the bond-laborers and by the demands of the "free colored" bourgeoisie and petty bourgeoisie for full citizenship rights in the wake of the Haitian Revolution.[127] The course of their struggles paralleled events that ended religio-racial oppression in Ireland. A century elapsed from the first recruitment of Irish Catholic soldiers for England's wars with the French for colonial primacy to the disestablishment of the Anglican Church of Ireland in 1869.[128] As in Ireland, so in the British West Indies, it was by no means a smooth steady evolution, but a procession by vicissitudes: from the recruitment of free Afro-Caribbeans into trades, commerce and professions countered by schemes for bestowing privileges on the "poor whites" to induce them to come and stay; from laws explicitly denying Afro-Caribbeans civil rights, and the obstruction of individual petitions for full rights by members of the Afro-Caribbean petty bourgeoisie and bourgeoisie, to the enactment of the "Brown Privilege Bill" in Barbados in 1831.[129] What most distinguishes the story of both the Irish and the Anglo-Caribbean histories, on the one hand, from that of continental Anglo-America, on the other, is that Catholic Emancipation in Ireland, and the admittance of "free colored" to full citizenship rights in the British West Indies were the culmination of the growing economic and political strength of the Catholic bourgeoisie in Ireland, in the one case, and of the "free colored" population of the British West indies, in the other. In the United States, on the other hand, free African-Americans were never acknowledged as a legitimate part of the body politic; quite the contrary, their very right to remain in the United States was officially and unofficially questioned, as, for instance, in the persistent demands for the forced exclusion of free African-Americans from the United States.

What is to explain the dramatic difference in the status achieved by free persons of African descent in the Anglo-Caribbean and in continental Anglo-America? And what larger historical significance is implied in that variation? That question brings us back to the Chesapeake and the problem that faced the plantation bourgeoisie there in the wake of Bacon's Rebellion.

13

The Invention of the White Race
– and the Ordeal of America

What Virginia's laboring-class people, free and bond, were fighting for in Bacon's Rebellion was not the overthrow of capitalism as such, but an end to the version of that system imposed by the plantation elite, based on chattel bond-servitude and engrossment of the land. Their idea regarding a proper social order was about the same as that which would be expressed by Edmund Burke some eighty years later: "the security ... of every nation consists principally in the number of low and middling men of a free condition, and that beautiful gradation from the highest to the lowest, where the transitions all the way are almost imperceptible." [1] If they had succeeded, the outcome of their struggle would have improved opportunities for social mobility within the colony. For the bond-laborers that would have meant an end to unpaid bond-servitude; for them and for the landless freemen, victory would have meant improved opportunity to become independent farmers. Most emphatically, they were not content to be "Tenants to the first Ingrossers, ... to be a Tennant on a Continent." [2]

However, just as the overthrow of the tenantry in the 1620s had cleared the ground for the institution of chattel bond-servitude, so the defeat of Bacon's Rebellion cleared the way for the establishment of the system of lifetime hereditary chattel bond-servitude. The relative position of the plantation elite became more dominant than ever not only because of the continuation of their large landholdings, but also because of their advantage in bidding for lifetime bond-labor.

Virginia's mystic transition from the era of "the volatile society," most dramatically represented in Bacon's Rebellion, to "the Golden Age of the Chesapeake" in the middle quarters of the eighteenth century is a much-studied phenomenon. It was during that period that the ruling plantocracy replaced "the ould foundation" that Governor Notley had warned them of, in order to "build their proceedings" on a new one. Central to this political process was, as John C. Rainbolt described it, "The Alteration in the Relationship between Leadership and Constituents in Virginia, 1660–1720."

In no other period or province did the relationship between rulers and ruled and the role of government alter so markedly as in Virginia between the departure of

Governor William Berkeley in 1676 and the administration of Alexander Spotswood from 1710 to 1722.[3]

The "art of ruling" so manifestly deficient during Bacon's Rebellion was retrieved; the ruling planter elite had learned "to improvise a style of leadership appropriate to the peculiar weakness of authority and the undisciplined and frustrated citizenry of Virginia."[4]

Edmund S. Morgan discusses the transition in a succession of chapters beginning "Toward" – "Toward Slavery," "Toward Racism," "Toward Populism," "Toward the Republic" – and concludes that the subordination of class by "race" at the beginning of the eighteenth century is the key to the emergence of the republic at the end of it.[5] Commentary directed specifically to the relationship of "race" and "class" is particularly relevant to the subject of the invention of the white race.[6] In a paper read before the Virginia Historical Society in December 1894, Lyon G. Tyler, son of President John Tyler, and seventeenth president of William and Mary College and editor of The *William and Mary Quarterly*, noted that "race, and not class, [was] the distinction in social life" in eighteenth-century Virginia.[7] The modern historian Gary B. Nash is more explicit: "In the late seventeenth century," he writes, "southern colonizers were able to forge a consensus among upper- and lower-class whites. . . . Race became the primary badge of status."[8]

Why was social transformation given this particular form; and *how* was it brought about? It will not do to say that this "race, not class" phenomenon was the result of the shift to Africa as the main labor supply source.[9] That same shift occurred in the British West Indies without the obliteration of class by "race". It will not do to ascribe it to the play of free market forces fashioning a "divided labor market" of skilled European-Americans and unskilled African-Americans.[10] The privileges and perquisites accorded to skilled workers do indeed express "free market economy" principles but "race" discrimination, in the form of the "deficiency laws" and prohibitions established in all English plantation colonies in the Americas against employing African workers in skilled occupations, did not. It will not do to say that persons arriving in the Americas already enchained were not good candidates for rebellion.[11] Consider the history of the maroons throughout the Americas, including British Jamaica.[12] Most important of all, it will not do to say that the "race, not class" phenomenon was the *result* of the reduction of African-Americans to lifetime hereditary bond-servitude.[13] One need only recall the solidarity of "the English and Negroes in Armes" in Bacon's Rebellion, at a time when the great majority of African-Americans were held as lifetime bond-laborers; or note the fact that 23 percent of the African bond-laborers in Jamaica on the eve of Emancipation were owned by persons of one degree or other of African ancestry.[14] Rather it was only because "race" consciousness superseded class-consciousness that the continental plantation bourgeoisie was able to achieve and maintain the degree of social control necessary for proceeding with capital accumulation on the basis of chattel bond-labor.

That the plantation bourgeoisie and those engaged in the labor supply trade favored the imposition of perpetual bondage on the plantation labor force can be seen as simply prudent business practice designed, in terms of current jargon, "to keep down inflationary labor costs in order to promote economic growth and to make Anglo-America competitive," by utilizing opportunities in Africa newly opened up by "the expanding global economy." At the same time, it was understood that, as always, success depended on establishing and maintaining an intermediate stratum for social control purposes. Why, then, were free Negroes and "mulattos" to be excluded from that stratum in the pattern-setting continental plantation colony of Virginia?

In September 1723 an African-American wrote from Virginia a letter of protest and appeal to Edmund Gibson, the Bishop of London, whose see included Virginia. On behalf of observant Christians of mixed Anglo-African descent, who were nevertheless bound by "a Law or act which keeps and makes them and there seed slaves forever," the letter asked for the bishop's help and that of the king "and the rest of the Rullers," in ending their cruel bondage.[15]

Aspects of discrimination against African-Americans also bothered British lawyer Richard West, the Attorney-General, who had the responsibility of advising the Lords of Trade and Plantations whether laws passed in colonial legislatures merited approval, or should be rejected in whole or in part as being prejudicial or contradictory to the laws of England.[16] In due course, West had occasion to examine a measure that was passed by the Virginia Assembly in May 1723, entitled "An Act directing the trial of Slaves, committing capital crimes; and for the more effectual punishing conspiracies and insurrections of them; and for the better government of Negros, Mulattos, and Indians, bond or free." Article 23 of that 24-article law provided that:

... no free negro, mulatto, or indian whatsoever, shall have any vote at the election of burgesses, or any other election whatsoever.[17]

The Attorney-General made the following categoric objection:

I cannot see why one freeman should be used worse than another, merely upon account of his complexion . . .; to vote at elections of officers, either for a county, or parish, &c. is incident to every freeman, who is possessed of a certain proportion of property, and, therefore, when several negroes have merited their freedom, and obtained it, and by their industry, have acquired that proportion of property, so that the above-mentioned incidental rights of liberty are actually vested in them, for my own part, I am persuaded, that it cannot be just, by a general law, without any allegation of crime, or other demerit whatsoever, to strip all free persons, of a black complexion (some of whom may, perhaps be of considerable substance,) from those rights, which are so justly valuable to every freeman.[18]

The Lords of Trade and Plantations "had Occasion to look into the said Act, and as it carrie[d] an Appearance of Hardship towards certain Freemen meerely upon Account of their Complection, who would otherwise enjoy every Priviledge belonging to Freemen [they wanted to know] what were the Reasons which induced the Assembly to pass this Act."[19]

Governor William Gooch, to whom the question was ultimately referred, declared that the Virginia Assembly had decided upon this curtailment of the franchise in order "to fix a perpetual Brand upon Free Negros & Mulattos."[20] Surely that was no "unthinking decision"! Rather, it was a deliberate act by the plantation bourgeoisie; it proceeded from a conscious decision in the process of establishing a system of racial oppression, even though it meant repealing an electoral principle that had existed in Virginia for more than a century.

But upon examination, Governor Gooch's explanation of the thinking that led to the decision seems grossly disingenuous. His response to the criticism comprised four points. (1) The immediate cause of the enactment of that law, he said, had been the discovery of a revolt plot among African-American bond-laborers in 1722, "wherein the Free Negros & Mulattos were much suspected to have been concerned (which will for ever be the case) . . . though there could be no legal proof" of it.[21] (2) Another reason, said Gooch approvingly, had been "to make the free Negros sensible that a distinction ought to be made between their offspring and the descendants of an English-man." As we might say today, Gooch felt threatened by "the Pride of a manumitted slave, who looks upon himself immediately on his acquiring his freedom to be as good a man as the best." (3) Gooch's perturbation was all the greater when the prideful offender was "descended from a white Father or Mother," these being mostly, he said, "the worst of our imported Servants and convicts." The law in question, he argued, served as a way of "discouraging that kind of copulation." (4) Anyway, he said, the number of persons disfranchised by the law was "so inconsiderable, that 'tis scarce worth while to take any notice of them in this particular."

Although Gooch's letter has been noticed before by our historians, it has never been subject to analysis. However that neglect is to be explained, let it end here: for such an examination gets to the heart of the motives of the Anglo-American continental plantation bourgeoisie in imposing not just a system of lifetime bond-servitude only on persons of African descent, but a system of *racial oppression*, by denying recognition of, refusing to acknowl-edge, delegitimizing, so far as African-Americans were concerned, the normal social distinctions characteristic of capitalist society. Consider the points of the Gooch thesis in that light.

(1) As noted in Chapter 12, in the Anglo-Caribbean societies the security of the social order based on lifetime bond-servitude of Africans and Afro-Caribbeans was deliberately linked to the making of such a social distinction among persons of African ancestry. In the early 1720s, at the same time that the Virginia Assembly was emphasizing the exclusion of free Negroes from any place in the intermediate social control stratum, in Barbados free Negroes and persons of color, like other free persons, were required to serve in the colony militia, and in Jamaica the Assembly offered free Negroes and persons

of color free homesteads. In both cases the policies were calculated to promote and maintain social control and the security of those colonies.[22] Far from undermining the slave system, the policy in the West Indies proved over and over again to be an effective counterweight to bond-labor revolt. It was correctly feared that to refuse to maintain such distinctions was to court disaster.[23] In Virginia there had been free African-Americans living as land-owners, owners of bond-laborers, livestock breeders, and hired laborers at least three-quarters of a century before Gooch ever left England. Although they sometimes helped bond-laborers to escape, that offense was more often committed by European-American free persons. Yet no proposal was made to reduce the latter to villeins by taking away their franchise.

(2) If poor free persons in England or in Anglo-America displayed delusions of social grandeur in such a degree as to discomfit their neighbors, hot ridicule and cold reality would likely soon disabuse them of the notion. The preser-vation of a civil society would not require the disfranchisement of a whole demographic category in order to preserve good order in such cases. The system of racial oppression is not characterized by the distinction maintained between one of the common run of laboring people and the "best of his neighbors," i.e., the gentlefolk of the leisure class. Rather, its hallmark is the insistence on the social distinction between the *poorest* member of the oppressor group and any member, however propertied, of the oppressed group.

(3) It is to be noted that when Gooch expressed his objection to sexual union between "whites" and African-Americans, he referred only to instances in which the former were "people of . . . mean condition." He passed over in silence the common practice of sexual exploitation of African-American bond-laborers by their owners and their owners' sons.[24]

Why this omission? There was a difference in the two cases so far as the purposes of racial oppression were concerned. In the second case, the mother being a lifetime bond-laborer, the child would also be bound for life. The father, as the owner or heir presumptive of the mother, would not find it in his interest, and very rarely in his heart, to acknowledge his child as his own. The mother and the child were, by the laws forbidding their testimony, incapable of making a claim against the owner. If the owner did acknowledge paternity, he was subject to the penalties for "fornication," which were doubled in cases of sexual congress between European-Americans and African-Americans. If, out of an elementary sense of human decency, he freed his own child, the child was bound by law to leave Virginia within a certain time or to be taken up and sold as a lifetime bond-laborer.[25]

According to Gooch, the majority of the parents of mulatto children were of the laboring class, and most were bond-laborers. Although only those whose mothers were African-Americans were to be bound for life, Gooch vents his hostility towards all mulattos, whether bond or free, whose mere presence presented a cognitive dissonance for the system of racial oppression. But his emphasis is on the laboring-class origin of those who, he says, made up the majority of the mulattos. Was that because he saw in it the seed of a revolutionary class solidarity such as had once been enacted in Virginia by "English and Negroes in Armes"? Whatever weight may be given to that speculation, it is clear that Gooch regarded bonds of mutual affection between African-Americans and European-American laborers as an affront to the "perpetual brand" of racial oppression.

(4) To dismiss the disfranchisement of African-Americans on the grounds that they included few persons who met the property qualifications was to reject the premise set in Attorney-General West's reference to the rights of "every free man." Furthermore, this argument seems inconsistent with Gooch's first point. If the number of substantial African-American propertyholders was so few that their disfranchisement was not worth noticing, then concern over the prospect of their involvement in the freedom-seeking exploits of bond-laborers would be correspondingly diminished.

I have given such prominence to the Gooch letter because it provides rare documentation of a discussion of the issue of white supremacy among the ruling classes in the eighteenth century in Virginia.[26] Although the Board of Trade acknowledged Governor Gooch's reply by saying that it would let the matter rest,[27] historians of the origin of racial oppression in Anglo-America should not be content. I have sought to show that Gooch's argument for "fixing a brand" on the free African-American is illogical, even in its own terms.

How, then, *is* this categoric rejection of the free Negro to be explained? The difference between the English plantation bourgeoisies in the British West Indies and in the continental plantation colonies cannot be ascribed to a difference of degrees of "white" consciousness. Down to the last moment, and past it, the sugar plantocracy resisted any attempt to undermine that consciousness, just as the ruling class did in the continental plantation colonies. The difference was rooted in the objective fact that in the West Indies there were *too few* laboring-class Europeans to embody an adequate petty bourgeoisie, while in the continental colonies there were *too many* to be accommodated in the ranks of that class.

The tobacco bourgeoisie assumed that bond-laborers would resist in every way they could, including marronage and revolt. Note has been made of the anxiety expressed in 1698 by Governor Francis Nicholson, then of Maryland, over the prospect of "great disturbances" in which he believed that the Irish bond-laborers would "confederate with the negroes."[28] In 1710 the Deputy Governor of Virginia reported to the Board of Trade the discovery of "an intended Insurrection of the negros which was to have been put in Execution in Surry and James City Countys on Easter Day." Two of the freedom plotters were hanged in the official hope that "their fate will strike such a Terror in the other Negros, as will keep them from forming such designs for the future."[29] Alexander Spotswood arrived in Virginia in 1710 to begin his ten-year tenure as Governor in June of that same year shortly after the discovery of the plot. Whatever reliance he intended to put upon terror, experience had shown, he said, that "we are not to depend on either their [the Negroes'] stupidity, or that babel of languages among 'em; freedom wears a cap which can, without a tongue, call together all those who long to shake of[f] the fetters of slavery."[30] Although the attempt of African bond-laborers to establish a free settlement at the head of James River in 1729 was defeated,[31] Governor William Gooch feared that "a very small number of negroes once settled in those parts, would very soon be encreased by the accession of other runaways," as had happened with "the negroes in the mountains of Jamaica."[32]

In 1736, William Byrd II, a member of the Virginia Colony Council, wrote to the Earl of Egmont, president of the Trustees of the Georgia colony which had been founded four years earlier on the principle of exclusion of slavery. Byrd expressed his approval of the new colony's policy, and his fear for Virginia's future in view of the rapidly increasing proportion of African-American bond-laborers. He too had Jamaica on his mind, worrying "lest they [the lifetime bond-laborers in Virginia] prove as troublesome and dangerous ... as they have been lately in Jamaica. We have mountains, in Virginia, too, to which they may retire safely, and do as much mischief as they do in Jamaica." Open revolt might occur; there were already 10,000 African-American men capable of bearing arms in Virginia, he noted, and he warned that "in case there should arise a Man amongst us, exasperated by a desperate fortune he might with more advantage than Cataline kindle a Servile War."[33] In 1749, Virginia Council members Thomas Lee and William Fairfax favored discouraging the importation of English convicts as bond-laborers. They cited former Governor Spotswood's allusion to freedom's cap, and warned that increasing the number of convict bond-laborers in Virginia, "who are wicked enough to join our Slaves in any Mischief ... in all Probability will bring sure and sudden Destruction on all His Majesty's good subjects of this colony."[34] Nothing could have been more apparent than that the small cohort of the ruling elite must have a substantial intermediate buffer social control stratum to stand between it and "great disturbances," or even another rebellion. Like the capitalist enclosers of the peasants' land in sixteenth-century England, the men for whom the plantation world was made needed an effective intermediate yeoman-type social control stratum.

Whilst I have made no special effort to check for occasions of the use of the term "yeoman" in the colonial Virginia and Maryland records, I do not recall having seen it there; nor have I seen it in citations from the records in secondary works. Thomas J. Wertenbaker transplanted it from the agrarian history of the mother country – where it meant the laboring-class "forty-shilling freeholder" – even though that designation had little practical significance to a society where freehold farmers paid their debts and taxes not in sterling money, but in pounds of tobacco.[35] Other historians have followed Wertenbaker's lead in synonymizing "yeoman" with "middle class." But that has not been of much help in arriving at a functional definition of either "yeoman" or "middle class."

Various standards of measurement have been used to draw the lines of class distinction in the colonial Chesapeake, such as land ownership, bond-labor ownership, the number of pounds of one's annual tobacco crop, tax lists, and estate inventories.[36] Even within one or the other of these particular parameter systems, one historian's "yeoman" can be another's "poor man." In the midst of the conceptual confusion, one does notice that the yeoman band is wider in the eyes of those who, on the whole, find that eighteenth-century Virginia was a democracy and not an aristocracy; on the other hand, the "yeoman" category tends to wash out in the studies of those who tend to be more sensitive to the prevalence of inequality in the Chesapeake tobacco colonies.

The present study is concerned with the question of ruling-class social control and the choice of a system of racial oppression in the Anglo-American plantation colonies. The concept of "yeoman" or "middle class" in this context is examined as an intermediate social control category. For that reason, I take as the first criterion the degree to which a "planter's" interest was benefited by the system of chattel bond-servitude. The lower boundary of the middle class by this standard would lie between those who owned lifetime bond-laborers (the number being augmented by incidental functionaries of the system, such as overseers, clerks, slave-traders), on the one hand, and those who did not own bond-laborers, on the other.[37]

In relation to the Chesapeake generally, Kulikoff states that by the 1730s the social power structure was dominated by the gentry, a leisure class comprising 5 percent of the Anglo-American men.[38] The "gentry" can be regarded as the ruling class, and it was composed of persons whose wealth, however gained, was such as to relieve them of any economic need to work. From their ranks came those who actually occupied the posts of political authority.[39] "About half the [European-American] men," says Kulikoff, "were yeomen, and many of them owned a slave or two, or hoped to someday."[40] Being dependent on the gentry for credit to tide them over rough spots or to expand their holdings, the yeomen reciprocated by going along with the system of rule by the gentry.[41]

Aubrey C. Land approached the study of class differentiation in the colonial Chesapeake by way of analysis of Maryland estate inventories,[42] which he grouped by a scale of hundreds of pounds sterling: £0–£100, £100–£200; £200–£300, etcetera. In the period 1690 to 1699, three-fourths of the planters were in the £0–£100 category. The typical annual crop of such a planter was from 1,200 to 3,000 pounds of tobacco. "Between investment and consumption he had no choice. . . . He could not invest from savings because he had none." For him to buy either a limited-term or a lifetime bond-laborer was "very difficult." Often, because of his debts, the heirs of such a person were left penniless.[43] More than one-third of the planters in this category were tenants on twenty-one-year or three-lives leases on wild lands.[44] It is interesting to note the contrast between the Scots tenant in Ulster, who retained property claim to the improvements he made on the leasehold,[45] and the Chesapeake tenant, who was obligated to clear the land and make improvements, the entire value of which was claimed by the landlord for expansion of a soil-exhausting monoculture based on bond-labor. Although the proportion of planters in £0–£100 group had declined by 1740, they still made up more than half the total.[46] Such a planter "was not the beneficiary of the planting society of the Chesapeake ... [and] it would stretch the usual meaning of the term to call him a yeoman, particularly if he fell in the lower half of his group."[47]

The £100–£200 category presents a dramatic contrast, in that 80 percent of these estates included bond-labor.[48] Taking this category together with the others up to £500, representing 21.7 percent of all estates in the 1690–99 period, by 1740 their proportion had increased to 35.7 percent. Of this larger, £100–£500 band of estates, lifetime bond-labor accounted for between half and two-thirds of the total value of an estate. In this £100–£500 category, farms without bond-labor had crops of only from 1,200 to 3,000 pounds of tobacco. But with bond-labor the output increased in proportion to the number of laborers.[49]

In the interest of completeness of coverage, Jackson Turner Main based a study on the Virginia tax lists for 1787.[50] But by treating various regions, from east to west, as representative of successive historical stages of plantation development, as well as by drawing to some extent on historical regional data, Main concluded that the general tendency of social evolution in Virginia [within the white population] was toward "a larger landless class and a larger class, too, of those who had almost no property."[51] In conclusion, Main declared:

> ... it is evident in the first place that landowners were in a minority. Excluding the Northern Neck, about 30 percent of the adult [white] males were laborers with very little property. About one tenth of the men had no land but had a fair amount of other property and had access to land owned by relatives. About one eighth were tenants. A little over one third of the men were small farmers with less than five hundred acres.[52]

To summarize, then, somewhat less than 50 percent of the total adult white male population were landowners. Of the total number of landowners, one-fifth were large landholders, those with 500 acres or more. Those with from 100 to 500 acres constituted two-thirds of the total. Of these, one-fourth worked their land without the employment of bond-labor. The one-tenth of the landowners having up to 100 acres were even more likely to do their own work. Thus while at least seven out of eight landowners were also owners of bond-laborers, around 60 percent of the adult white male population were not employers of bond-labor but, rather, were put in competition with employers of bond-labor.[53] Jackson T. Main's study suggests the presence of a "yeoman" or "middle" class in eighteenth-century Virginia of not more than 40 percent of the adult white male population. That seems compatible with Land's conclusions regarding Maryland estate evaluations.

Professor Kulikoff relates these relative class proportions in the population to the central concern of the present work, the question of ruling class social control, by concluding that, "Once the gentry class gained the assent of the yeomanry, it could safely ignore the rest of white society."[54] But, recalling the question raised by Attorney-General West, why should African-Americans "possessed of a certain proportion of property" have been effectively barred from the ranks of this "yeomanry"? I have great respect for Kulikoff's work, from which I have learned much, but I believe that this proscription of the free African-American can be explained best precisely by the fact that, despite its sway over the "yeomanry," the gentry could *not* "safely ignore the rest of white society" because their bond-labor system was antithetical to the interests not only of African-American bond-laborers, but also of all the rest of the population that did not own bond-laborers. In their solidarity with the African-American bond-laborers in Bacon's Rebellion, the laboring-class European-American bond-laborers had demonstrated their understanding of their interests, and bond-laborers had had the sympathy of the laboring poor and propertyless free population.

What was to be done? What was the "alteration in the government, but not of the government"[55] that would exorcise the ghost of Bacon's Rebellion? How was laboring-class solidarity to be undone? Back to first principles, never better enunciated by an English statesman than by Sir Francis Bacon.[56] "[I]t is a certain sign of wise government," Sir Francis advised, ". . . when it can hold men's hearts by hopes, when it cannot by satisfaction." And, with acknowledgment to Machiavelli, Bacon advocated "dividing and breaking of all factions and combinations that are adverse to the state, and setting them at distance, or at least distrust among themselves."[57]

In the world the slaveholders made, however, "hope" depended upon the prospect of social mobility into the ranks of owners of bond-labor, and as we have seen there was little opportunity for the non-owner of bond-labor to make that transition to the "yeoman" class. The cost of lifetime bond-laborers presented a threshold that few non-owners of bond-labor could reach. The monoculture tended to glut the market and leave the small producer who had no bond-labor in debt so that accumulation of the capital necessary for this path to "yeoman" status was drained away.

Instead of social mobility, European-Americans who did not own bond-laborers were to be asked to be satisfied simply with the presumption of liberty, the birthright of the poorest person in England; and with the right of adult males who owned sufficient property to vote for candidates for office who were almost invariably owners of bond-laborers. The prospects for stability of a system of capitalist agriculture based on lifetime hereditary bond-servitude depended on the ability of the ruling elite to induce the non-"yeoman" European-Americans to settle for this counterfeit of social mobility. The solution was to establish a new birthright not only for Anglos but for every Euro-American, the "white" identity that "set them at a distance," to use Sir Francis's phrase, from the laboring-class African-Americans, and enlisted them as active, or at least passive, supporters of lifetime bondage of African-Americans. Edmund S. Morgan introduces a catalogue of these white-skin privilege laws, with the assertion that "The answer to the problem [of preventing a replay of Bacon's Rebellion] . . . was racism, to separate danger- ous free whites from dangerous slave blacks by a screen of racial contempt." In this way, he emphasizes, "the [Virginia] assembly deliberately did what it could to foster contempt of whites for blacks and Indians."[58] Bruce attests that "[t]oward the end of the seventeenth century" there occurred "a marked tendency to promote a pride of race among the members of every class of white people; to be white gave the distinction of color even to the agricultural [European-American bond-]servants, whose condition, in some respects, was not much removed from that of actual slavery; to be white and also to be free, combined the distinction of liberty."[59]

Here, then, is the true answer to the issue raised by the anonymous Virginian to the Bishop of London and by Attorney-General Richard West and the Board of Trade to Governor Gooch. The exclusion of free African-Americans from the intermediate stratum was a corollary of the establishment of "white" identity as a mark of social status. If the mere presumption of liberty was to serve as a mark of social status for masses of European-Americans without real prospects of upward social mobility, and yet induce them to abandon their opposition to the plantocracy and enlist them actively, or at least passively, in keeping down the Negro bond-laborer with whom they had made common cause in the course of Bacon's Rebellion, the presumption of liberty had to be denied to free African-Americans.

H. M. Henry, though writing about South Carolina, posed a question of general relevance.

> The financial interests of the large planters are sufficient to explain why they sought to perpetuate such a system of labor [racial slavery]. But why should the non- slaveholders, who formed the majority of the white population, have assisted in upholding and maintaining the slavery status of the negro with its attendant inconveniences, such as patrol service, when they must have been aware in some measure at least that as an economic regime it was a hindrance to their progress?[60]

The Virginia General Assembly showed how it was to be done; it deliberately stuffed the "racial" distinction with anomalous privileges to make it look like the real thing, promotion to a higher social class. The distinction was even emphasized for European-American chattel bond-laborers, whose presump- tion of liberty was temporarily in suspension.

Any owner of an African-American, practically without hindrance, could legally use or abuse his African-American bond-laborers, or dispose of him or her by gift, bequest, sale, or rental as a matter of course, but by a law enacted in 1691, he was forbidden to set them free.[61] Examples of emancipation of African-Americans by final will and testament have been cited from the record in Chapter 10; never had such a will been challenged. But when in 1712, under the terms of the will of John Fulcher of Norfolk County, sixteen African- American bond-laborers were to be freed and given land in fee simple "to live upon as long as they Shall live or any of there Increase and not to be turned of[f] or not to be Disturbed," the Virginia Colony Council reacted by proposing to bar even this door to freedom.[62]

On the other hand, the revised Virginia code of 1705 took pains to specify unprecedented guarantees for the European "christian white" limited-term bond-laborers. Before, masters had merely been required not to "exceed the bounds of moderation" in beating or whipping or otherwise "correcting" the bond-laborer, it being provided that the victim, if one could get to the Justice of the Peace and then to the next county court, "shall have remedy for his grievances."[63] The new code forbade the master to "whip a christian white servant naked, without an order from the justice of the peace," the offending master to be fined forty shillings payable to the servant.[64] Upon a second offense by a master in treatment of "servants (not being slaves)," the courts could order that the servant be taken from that master and sold at outcry.[65]

Freedom dues for limited-term bond-laborers had never been specified in Virginia law, but were merely referred to in court orders by the loose term "corn and clothes." The 1705 code, however, noting that "nothing in that nature ever [had been] made certain," enumerated them with specificity: "to every male servant, ten bushels of corn, thirty shillings in money (or the equivalent in goods), a gun worth at least twenty shillings; and to every woman servant, fifteen bushels of corn, forty shillings in money (or the equivalent in goods)."[66] Lifetime bond-laborers were not to have freedom dues, of course, but they had been allowed to raise livestock on their own account, and to have them marked as their own. But in 1692, and again in 1705 with greater emphasis, livestock raised by African-American bond-laborers on their own account were ordered to be confiscated.[67]

The act of 1723 that was the subject of the correspondence between Governor Gooch and the Board of Trade was by no means the first evidence, in terms of the law, of ruling-class desire not only to impose lifetime hereditary bond-servitude on African-Americans, but to implement it by a system of *racial oppression*, expressed in laws against *free* African-Americans. Such were the laws (several of which have been previously noted) making free Negro women tithable;[68] forbidding non-Europeans, though baptized Christians, to be owners of "christian," that is, European, bond-laborers;[69] denying free African-Americans the right to hold any office of public trust;[70] barring any Negro from being a witness in any case against a "white" person;[71] making any free Negro subject to thirty lashes at the public whipping post for "lift[ing] his or her hand" against any European-American, (thus to a major extent denying Negroes the elementary right of self-defense);[72] excluding free African-Americans from the armed militia;[73] and forbidding free African-Americans from possessing "any gun, powder, shot, or any club, or any other weapon whatsoever, offensive or defensive."[74]

The denial of the right of self-defense would become a factor in the development of the peculiar American form of male supremacy, white-male supremacy, informed by the principle that any European-American male could assume familiarity with any African-American woman. That principle came to have the sanction of law. We have earlier cited the Maryland Provincial Court decision of 1767 that "a slave had no recourse against the violator of his bed."[75] "The law simply did not criminalize the rape of slave women," writes Philip Schwarz. "No Virginia judge heard [such] a case."[76] Free African-American women had practically no legal protection in this respect, in view of the general exclusion of African-Americans, free or bond, from giving testimony in court.[77]

The ruling class took special pains to be sure that the people they ruled were propagandized in the moral and legal ethos of white-supremacism. Provisions were included for that purpose in the 1705 "Act concerning Servants and Slaves" and in the Act of 1723 "directing the trial of Slaves . . . and for the better government of Negros, Mulattos, and Indians, bond *or free*."[78] For consciousness-raising purposes (to prevent "pretense of ignorance"), the laws mandated that parish clerks or churchwardens, once each spring and fall at the close of Sunday service, should read ("publish") these laws in full to the congregants. Sheriffs were ordered to have the same done at the courthouse door at the June or July term of court. If we presume, in the absence of any contrary record, that this mandate was followed, we must conclude that the general public was regularly and systematically subjected to official white-supremacist agitation. It was to be drummed into the minds of the people that, for the first time, no free African-American was to dare to lift his or her hand against a "Christian, not being a negro, mulatto or Indian" (3:459); that African-American freeholders were no longer to be allowed to vote (4:133–34); that the provision of a previous enactment (3:87 [1691]) was being reinforced against the mating of English and Negroes as producing "abominable mixture" and "spurious issue" (3:453–4); that, as provided in the 1723 law for preventing freedom plots by African-American bond-laborers, "any white person . . . found in company with any [illegally congregated] slaves" was to be fined (along with free African-Americans or Indians so offending) with a fine of fifteen shillings, or to "receive, on his, her, or their bare backs, for every such offense, twenty lashes well laid on." (4:129).

Thus was the "white race" invented as the social control formation whose distinguishing characteristic was not the participation of the slaveholding class, nor even of other elements of the propertied classes; that alone would have been merely a form of the "beautiful gradation" of class differentiation prescribed by Edmund Burke. What distinguished this system of social control, what made it "the white race", was the participation of the laboring classes: non-slaveholders, self-employed smallholders, tenants, and laborers. In time this "white race" social control system begun in Virginia and Maryland would serve as the model of social order to each succeeding plantation region of settlement.[79]

The effort bore fruit so far as danger from the European-American bond-laborers was concerned. "[t]he fear," writes Winthrop D. Jordan, "of white servants and Negroes uniting in servile rebellion, a prospect which made some sense in the 1660s and 70s . . . vanished completely during the following half-century." He continues with a corollary: "Significantly, the only rebellions of white servants in the continental colonies came before the entrenchment of slavery."[80] But that is only half the story: the poor and propertyless European-Americans were the principal element in the day-to-day enforcement of racial oppression not only in the Chesapeake but wherever the plantation system was established. After 1700, according to Wertenbaker, "Every white man, no matter how degraded, could now find pride in his race. . . . Moreover, the immediate control of the negroes fell almost entirely into the hands of white men of humble means."[81] In 1727, special militia detachments known as "the patrol" were instituted "for dispersing all unusual concourse of negroes, or other slaves, and for preventing any dangerous combinations which may be made among them at such meetings."[82] A student of criminal laws in Virginia relating to bond-laborers states that "Patrollers were the ultimate means of preventing insurrection."[83] Historians who analyzed the Virginia militia records of 1757–58 have reported that "the muster rolls were apt to be filled mostly with the lower class." Many, they say, were "former indentured servants."[84] In colonial South Carolina, even the European-American bond-laborers were recruited into the militia and the "slave patrol," where "[their] role in defense against Negro insurrection was more important than as a defense against the enemy from without."[85] At the time of the American Revolution, a number of African-American bond-laborers were freed by their South Carolina Quaker owners. The law subsequently enacted to prevent further emancipations proved ineffective at first because only freeholders were authorized to collect rewards for reporting violations. But in 1788 effectiveness was achieved by extending this civic function to "any freeman." By this means, says our historian, "the State secured the co-operation of the landless whites who were usually strangely willing to have a fling at the slaves and who, no doubt, were anxious to get the reward offered for such information."[86]

In a mode often akin to modern-day "featherbedding," deficiency laws provided jobs for European-American workers simply for being "white." In 1712, the South Carolina Assembly, for example, passed a law stipulating that, at any plantation six miles or more remote from the owner's usual abode, for every "Six Negroes or other Slaves" employed, a quota of "One or more White Person" must be kept there. Ten years later the quota was one to ten, but that applied to the home plantation as well as to those far removed.[87] Job preference for "whites" was to be further guaranteed under a proposal of a committee of the South Carolina House of Assembly in 1750 "That no Handicrafts Man [other than the owner] shall hereafter teach a Negro his Trade."[88]

Georgia colony, founded by its trustees in 1732 on the no-slavery principle, was territory irresistible to the South Carolina plantation bourgeoisie anxious as its members were to "grow the economy," as it might be put today. They soon began to campaign for an end of this government interference with free enterprise. In the course of the controversy, a Savannah man objected that abandonment of the founding principle excluding slavery from Georgia "would take work from white men's hands and impoverish them, as in the case of

Charleston [South Carolina], where the tradesmen are all beggars by that means." The promoters of the slavery cause countered by saying that "the negroes should not be allowed to work at anything but producing rice ... and in felling timber.[89] Accordingly, the 1750 act repealing the ban on slavery in Georgia included a "deficiency" provision requiring the employment of one "white man Servant" on each plantation for every four Negroes employed. It further barred the employment of Negroes except in cultivation and coopering.[90] Although this system of white-skin privileges had not been initiated by the European-American laboring classes but by the plantation bourgeoisie, the European-American workers were claiming them by the middle of the eighteenth century.[91] In South Carolina white workers were demanding the exclusion of Negroes from the skilled trades.[92] Richard B. Morris's monumental study of labor in the continental Anglo-American colonies found that "the effort of white artisans to keep free Negroes and slaves from entering the skilled trades" radiated from Charleston to "every sizeable town on the Atlantic coast."[93] In 1839, "white" mechanics in Culpeper and Petersburg, Virginia, demanded that Negroes be barred from apprenticeship, and from any trade without a "white" overseer. A decade later a similar petition from Norfolk showed a high degree of political sophistication. Barring Negroes from competing for employment, its sponsors said, would guarantee against "jealousy between slaveholders and non-slaveholders."[94] Within two decades slaveholding would end, but the appeal to "white race" solidarity would remain the country's most general form of class-collaborationism.

The White Race and Theories of American History

If the Virginia laws of 1705 represent ruling class manipulation of the rank-and-file, the inescapable implication seems to be that the social transformation that they expressed – to the system of racial slavery, racial oppression, white supremacy – must not have been in the real interests of the majority of the people, the smallholders, the tenants and laborers, those who did not own bond-laborers.

There have been many historians who would not accept this argument. Some would reject the premise, others the conclusion; still others would reject both the premise and the conclusion. There are those, the psycho-cultural cohort in the debate over the origin of racial slavery in continental Anglo-America, who see white supremacy as having been genetically or culturally foreordained before the English settlers sailed into James River.[95] Arguments made by others – based on considerations of demographics, blind market forces, Euro-Afro cultural dissonance, and the fact that only persons of African descent were held in lifetime servitude – along with my brief counterpoints are specified earlier in this chapter at page 240.

But a major theme shared by some who reject the premise and some who accept it concerns not the origin of racial oppression but the assessment of white-supremacism in relation to the foundation of the United States as a republic. That theme may properly be called the "paradox thesis" of American history. The essential element in this argument is that democracy and equality, as represented in the Declaration of Independence and the Constitution of 1789, were, by the logic of history, made possible by racial oppression. The lineage of this thesis goes back at least to 1758, when Edmund Burke argued that "whites" in the southern continental colonies were more "attached to liberty" than were colonists in the North because in the South freedom was a racial privilege.[96] Virginia scholar Thomas Roderick Dew contended that slavery made possible and actual "one common level" of equality "in regard to whites." "The menial and low offices being all performed by the blacks," he continued, "there is at once taken away the greatest cause for distinction and separation of the ranks of society."[97]

Special interest, however, attaches to Edmund S. Morgan's espousal of this rationale. His book *American Slavery, American Freedom* appeared in 1975 in the afterglow of the civil rights struggles, sacrifices and victories of the 1960s. Furthermore, his socio-economic approach to the origin of racial slavery supplied the most substantial response that had yet appeared to the "natural racism" thesis of Carl Degler and of Winthrop D. Jordan. Historian H. M. Henry had asked: "why should the non-slaveholders, who formed the majority of the white population have assisted in upholding and maintaining the slavery status of the negro ...?" Sixty years later, Morgan posed essentially the same question. "How could patricians win in populist politics?" That question, Morgan says, "leads to the paradox ... the union of freedom and slavery in Virginia and America."

The essence of Morgan's paradox, to the extent it is a true paradox, is a renewal of the same euphemism of the system of white-supremacism and lifetime hereditary bond-servitude that characterized the opinions of Burke and Dew. Unconsciously paraphrasing Edmund Burke, Morgan says, "Virginians may have had a special appreciation of the freedom dear to republicans, because they saw every day what life without it could be."[98] T. R. Dew and others are recognized in Morgan's approvingly quoted observation of Sir Augustus John Foster, an English diplomat who traveled in Virginia at the beginning of the nineteenth century: "Owners of slaves among themselves are all for keeping down every kind of superiority." It is pure Dew again when Morgan shares Foster's view that "whites" in Virginia, "can profess an unbounded love of liberty and democracy ... [because] the mass of the people who in other countries might become mobs [in Virginia are] nearly altogether composed of their" African-American lifetime bond-laborers.[99]

The argument rests on the assumption that early in the eighteenth century "the mass of white Virginians were becoming landowners" and the small planters began to prosper, thus giving the large and small planters "a sense of common identity based on common interests."[100] This feeling, says Morgan, was sufficient basis for the small planters to put their trust in the ruling plantation bourgeoisie and thus cease to be a danger to social order.[101] Sources cited by me such as Jackson Turner Main, Gloria Main, T. J. Wertenbaker, Aubrey C. Land, Willard F. Bliss, Russell R. Menard, and Allan Kulikoff show that the economic assumption made here by Morgan is open to serious question. Morgan, in a passing reference to the growth of tenancy, devotes a reference note to Bliss and Jackson Main, but that is the limit of his concern with such studies, although they cast great doubt on his facile conclusion that of European-Americans "[t]here were too few free poor to matter,"[102] a conclusion without which his "paradox" unravels.

Morgan, in passages that I have previously cited with approval, declared that the answer to the problem of social control was a series of deliberate measures taken by the ruling class to "separate dangerous free whites from dangerous slave blacks."[103] But if, as the country moved "Toward the Republic" and after it got there, among "whites" there were "too few free poor to matter," why did the social order not revert to the normal class differentiation, Burke's "beautiful gradation" from rich to the less rich and so on through the scale, in which the free Negroes could take their individual places according to their social class? They could be expected, as James Madison said, to function properly in that social station.[104] The "white race," as a social control formation, would have been a redundancy. Instead, there was a general proscription of the free Negro, laws against emancipation, even by last will and testament, and banishment for those so freed. That, I submit, is unchallengeable evidence of the continued presence of poor whites who had "little but their complexion to console them for being born into a higher caste," yet served as an indispensable element of the "white race," the Peculiar Institution.[105]

Morgan's book was a trenchant contribution to the socio-economic and "deliberate-choice" explanation of the origin of racial slavery. In seeking to understand his adoption of the "paradox" thesis, it seems helpful to consider the following passage from his 1972 presidential address to the Organization of American Historians:

> The temptation is already apparent to argue that slavery and oppression were the dominant features of American history and that efforts to advance liberty and equality were the exception, indeed no more than a device to divert the masses while their chains were being fastened. To dismiss the rise of liberty and equality in American history as a mere sham is not only to ignore hard facts, it is also to evade the problem presented by those facts. The rise of liberty and equality in this country was accompanied by the rise of slavery. That two such contradictory developments were taking place simultaneously over a long period of our history, from the seventeenth century to the nineteenth, is the central paradox of American history.[106]

Morgan set out to meet the "challenge" of those who, in his opinion, overemphasize slavery and oppression in American history. Yet the effect of Morgan's "paradox" thesis seems no less an apology for white supremacy than the "natural racism" argument. At the end of it all, he writes, "Racism made it possible for white Virginians to develop a devotion to ... equality.... Racism became an essential ... ingredient of the republican ideology that enabled Virginians to lead the nation." Then, as if shying at his own conclusion, Morgan suggests the speculation that perhaps "the vision of a nation of equals [was] flawed at the source by contempt for both the poor and the black."[107] But what flaw? If racism was a flaw, then "the rise of liberty" would have been better off without it – a line of reasoning that negates the paradox. On the other hand, if racism made "the rise of liberty possible," as the paradox would have it, then racism was not a flaw of American bourgeois democracy, but its very special essence. Morgan's "paradox" therefore contains in itself the very challenge that he set out to refute. The "Ordeal of Colonial Virginia" was extended as the Ordeal of America, wherein racial oppression and white-supremacism have indeed been the dominant feature, the parametric constant, of United States history.

The white frontier

Being made to compete with unpaid bond-labor "practically destroyed the Virginia yeomanry," writes Wertenbaker. "Some it drove into exile, either to the remote frontiers or to other colonies; some it reduced to extreme poverty; ... some it caused to purchase slaves and so at one step to enter the exclusive class of those who had others to work for them. ... The small freeholder was not destroyed, as was his prototype of ancient Rome, but he was subjected to a change which was by no means fortunate or wholesome."[108]

The tendency toward concentration of capital ownership is a prevailing attribute of capitalism. The social impact of that tendency is illustrated in Wertenbaker's comment on the Virginia colonial economy of the eighteenth century. But this was not the typical case of increased concentration of capital based on the introduction of new instruments of labor requiring increasing relative investments in fixed capital. It was caused by land engrossment in general, and by the diminished supply of good lands in the older, Tidewater area, but even more by the lower labor costs per unit of output of those planters who had means to invest in the high-priced lifetime bond-laborers. By the closing third of the eighteenth century this process had produced a situation in which at least 60 percent of the white adult men in Virginia were non-owners of bond-labor.[109]

Among that 60 percent were those encountered by the Marquis de Chastel-lux as he travelled through Virginia in spring 1782. For the first time in his three years in America, "in the midst of those rich plantations," he often saw "miserable huts ... inhabited by whites, whose wan looks and ragged garments bespeak poverty." It seemed clear to him that the cause of this poverty was the engrossment of land by the plantation bourgeoisie.[110] The impoverished included those landless European-Americans previously noted who stayed in eastern Virginia but with "little but their complexion to console them."[111]

Wertenbaker asserts, however, that the number of such very poor was never large, because anyone with a little drive and ambition "could move to the frontier and start life on more equal terms."[112] Among those who moved and moved frequently were those who opted for being tenants,[113] some on leases but, says Kulikoff, more typically as tenants-at-will, working on shares with tools, buildings and marketing facilities furnished by the landlord. Share tenants moved on after a short tenure. Squatters left land where they could not afford the surveying and patent fees; two-thirds of the original settlers of Amelia County, formed in 1735 – mostly squatters – left the county between 1736 and 1749. In Lunenberg County, formed in 1746, only one-fifth of the laborers were able to establish households, whilst two out of five of the householders left the county between 1750 and 1764.[114] Others moved directly to "new" territories taking out patents as fee-simple owners.

The result was an increasing number of would-be planters moving to "the frontier," wherever that meant at a given time – the Piedmont, the south side of the James, North Carolina, the Shenandoah Valley, or beyond the Cumberland Gap – as tenants, as patentees of "new" land, or as unpatented squatters. Though the squeezing out of such a poor planter to the "frontier" negated the assumption of a common interest with the gentry, he was still "made to fold to his bosom the adder that stings him," the bondage of African-Americans.[115] Denied social mobility, these would-be planters were to have the white-skin privilege of lateral mobility – to the "frontier." By the same token they went as "whites"; resenting Negroes, not their slavery, indeed hating the free Negro most of all; ready now to take the land from the Indians in the name of "a white man's country."[116]

Turner's frontier-as-social-safety-valve theory

In 1893, Frederick Jackson Turner (1861–1932), one of the giants of American historiography, presented a theory, "a hypothesis," of American historical development. He likened it to the career of the ancient Greeks in the Mediterranean world, "breaking the bond of custom, offering new experiences, calling out new institutions and activities."[117]

> Up to our own day American history has been in a large degree the history of the colonization of the Great West. The existence of an area of free land, its continuous recession, and the advance of American settlement westward explain American development.[118]

Turner ended that essay with a portentous epitaph: "[T]he frontier is gone, and with its going has closed the first period of American history."[119] In 1910 he continued his theme: "The solitary backwoodsman wielding his axe at the edge of a measureless forest is replaced by companies capitalized at millions, operating railroads, sawmills, and all the enginery of modern machinery to harvest the remaining trees." He then formulated what came to be called the "safety-valve corollary" of the "frontier" thesis. "A new national development is before us," he said, "without the former safety valve of abundant resources open to him who would take." He delineated the consequent sharpening of class struggle between capital and anti-capital, between those who demand that there be no governmental interference with "the exploitation and the development of the country's wealth" on the one hand, and the reformers – from the Grangers to the Populists, to Bryan to Debs and Theodore Roosevelt – who emphasized "the need of governmental regulation . . . in the interest of the common man; [and] the checking of the power of those business Titans."[120] It is not surprising," he added later that year, "that socialism shows noteworthy gains as elections continue, that parties are forming on new lines. . . . They are efforts to find substitutes for the former safeguard of democracy, the disap-pearing lands. They are the sequence of the disappearing frontier."[121]

It is now more than a century since the disappearance of the "frontier", to which Turner ascribed a sharpening struggle between the "Titans" and "the common people." But his expectation of the emergence of a popular socialist movement of sufficient proportions to "substitute" for the end of the "free-land safety valve" was disappointed. Turner died in the midst of the Great Depression in 1932. Toward the end of his life, he felt "baffled by his contemporary world and [he] had no satisfying answer to the closed-frontier formula in which he found himself involved."[122]

The Great Social Safety Valve of American history

The white laboring people's prospect of lateral mobility to "free land", however unrealizable it was in actuality, did serve in diverting them from struggles with the bourgeoisie.[123] But that was merely one aspect of the Great Safety Valve, the system of racial privileges conferred on laboring-class European-Americans, rural and urban, poor and exploited though they themselves were. That has been the main historical guarantee of the rule of the "Titans," damping down anti-capitalist pressures by making "race, and not class, the distinction in social life." This, more than any other factor, has shaped the "contours of American history"[124] – from the Constitutional Convention of 1787 to the Civil War, to the overthrow of Reconstruction, to the Populist Revolt of the 1890s, to the Great Depression, to the civil rights struggle and "white backlash" of our own day. If Turner had taken note of the Southern Homestead Act and its repeal, and the heroic Negro Exodus of 1879, might he have given his "frontier" theory an added dimension? Would he have then taken into account the social safety-valve function of the two other broad general forms of lateral mobility in the nineteenth century – immigration into the United States and farm-to-factory migration – which like "free land" were also cast in the mold of "racial" preference for Europeans and European-Americans, as "whites"?[125]

The Civil Rights Legacy and the Impending Crisis

Properly interpreted, Turner's reference to the "safety valve" potential in anti-capitalist "reform" movements of his day had its innings in the Keynesian New

Deal which at least some of its supporters hoped might be a road to "socialism," and some of its reactionary enemies regarded as the real thing. The limitations of that line of reform, which had become evident by 1938, were masked by the prosperity of the United States role as the "arsenal of democracy" in World War Two, which ended with the United States being the only industrial power left standing and the possessor of three-fourths of the world's gold reserves. By 1953, other major powers had recovered to pre-war levels; by 1957 the United States was beginning to experience a chronic unfavorable balance of trade; in 1971 the United States formally abandoned the gold standard for settlement of international balances of trade and the "gold cover" for the domestic money supply. Finally, even the party of the New Deal has cast all Keynesian pretense to the winds, proclaiming that "the era of big government is over," and boasting of "ending welfare" in any previously recognizable form.

Now, at the end of the twentieth century, the social gap between the Titans and the common people is at perhaps its historic maximum, real wages have trended downward for nearly two decades. "Entitlements" and "welfare," as they relate to students, the poor and the elderly, have become obscenities in the lexicon of official society. There is less of a "socialist" movement today in the United States than there was in Turner's day, and anti-capitalist class-consciousness is hesitant even to call its name. The bourgeoisie in one of its parts mockingly dons "revolution" like a Halloween mask. "Class struggle" is an epithet cast accusingly at the mildest defenders of social welfare reforms, and the country is loud with the sound of one class struggling.

Yet, there are unmistakable signs of a maturing social conflict, such as that noted by Turner a century ago, because of intensifying efforts to "balance the budget" at the expense of the living standards of non-stockholders. But there is a most significant variation. Unlike in Turner's time, the present-day United States bears the indelible stamp of the African-American civil rights struggle of the 1960s and after, a seal that the "white backlash" has by no means been able to expunge from the nation's consciousness. Perhaps in the impending renewal of the struggle of "the common people" and the "Titans," the Great Safety Valve of white-skin privileges may finally come to be seen and rejected by laboring-class European-Americans as the incubus that for three centuries has paralyzed their will in defense of their class interests *vis-à-vis* those of the ruling class.

Appendix II-A

(*see Chapter 1, note 64*)

"For more than four centuries, the communities formed by ... [African and African-American] runaways dotted the fringes of plantation America, from Brazil to the southeastern United States, from Peru to the American Southwest." Their existence "struck directly at the foundations of the plantation system, presenting military and economic threats that often taxed the colonists to their very limits."[1] Maroon communities, from Jamaica to Cuba, from Brazil to Mexico, were more successful where located in mountainous terrain, and continental mainland situations seem to have been of extra advantage, as in Panama, Colombia and Brazil, as compared to the more limited room of small insular colonies.

"The major concern of the colonial government of Cuba was the persecution of maroons and the destruction of *palenques*, even after the first half of the nineteenth century."[2]

"Mexico experienced its first widespread wave of slave insurrections in the period 1560–80. ... By the 1560s ... [T]he [Spanish colonial] bureaucracy and slave owners, outnumbered by slaves in the mining regions, were helpless in the face of such anarchy," which found Africans "allying with the Indians."[3] The main maroon settlement, in a mountain fastness located not far from Vera Cruz, was led by Yanga, an African reputedly of royal rank in his native Abrong kingdom. He was the first Mexican maroon, having fled to the mountains in about 1580. An expedition sent against the maroons' settlement failed in its search-and-destroy mission. Instead, the encounter resulted in a historically unique agreement, "The only known example of a fully successful attempt by slaves to secure their freedom en masse by revolt and negotiation, and to have it sanctioned and guaranteed in law."[4]

Another former African king, known to Cartagena (the Caribbean coastal region of Colombia) as Domingo Bioho, King Benkos, fled the Spanish plantations at the head of thirty men and women comrades and established a maroon settlement in a forest and marsh area of the interior, where these original maroons were soon being joined by individuals and small groups of runaways. After standing off a posse of slaveholders that came after them, the maroons finally established a *palenque* at a place to be known as San Basilio. The Spanish, after failing in two military expeditions against San Basilio, finally made a pattern-setting peace with the maroons in 1619, based on non-aggression principles.[5]

In the mid-1560s in the Darien province of Panama, maroons led by their elected king, Bayano, reputedly a former African king, secured a peace treaty with the Spanish colonial government.[6] These or such as these were those who allied with Sir Francis Drake against the Spanish as mentioned in *The Invention of the White Race*, Volume One.

As early as 1575 there was a maroon settlement near Bahia in Brazil; by 1597 it was reported that "the principal enemies" of the Portuguese colonists were such mountain-based groups of runaway African bond-laborers.[7] Hundreds of such settlements would come into existence in the seventeenth and eighteenth centuries. The greatest of these settlements, or group of settlements, was Palmares, founded some ninety miles from Pernambuco in northern Brazil, by Africans escaping from plantation slavery around the beginning of the seventeenth century.[8] Palmares was not merely a refuge, a *guilombo* (African word) from which to raid Portuguese and Dutch plantations, but a Negro republic in Brazil, with its own agrarian economy and elected ruler.[9] Despite repeated colonialist military assaults, Palmares grew until by the mid-1670s, by Portuguese report, it embraced some 99,000 square miles, an area about the size of Wyoming or Nevada, with a population of from 15,000 to 20,000 in ten major settlements.[10] The elected king of Palmares, called Ganga Zumba [Great Lord], and most of the ruling element were native Africans, although among the leaders named in a 1677 Portuguese report there was one, Arotirene, presumed to have been an Amerindian.[11] The Ganga Zumba in 1677 claimed to have been a king in Africa.[12] Having endured for almost a century, Palmares finally fell to the colonialist forces in 1694, after a siege of six weeks.[13]

Appendix II-B

(*see Chapter 2, note 6*)

By the beginning of the fourteenth century, expansion of agricultural production in England had led to a general decline of agricultural prices. The landowning class then sought advantage by demanding payment of rent in cash, rather than in a share of the product of the free tenant. In turn, these rent-paying tenants, if they wanted to expand production, were obliged to pay their workers wages, since the latter were under no feudal obligation to the peasant proprietor or tenant. Thus capitalist relations of production began to be introduced in English agriculture.

The bubonic plague that swept Europe between 1348 and 1351 struck England in August 1348, and within sixteen months it had wiped out one-third to half of the population.[1] Inconceivable horror though it was, the plague created such a shortage of labor that it became extremely difficult for landowners to continue to exact feudal labor dues from the villein, or to dictate the wages of labor: "The wages of labour were nearly doubled," writes Thorold Rogers, "and the profits of capitalist agriculture sank from 20 per cent to nearly zero."[2]

The ruling classes sought to reverse this trend by repressive measures, among the earliest of which was the Statute of Laborers of 1350, designed to impose compulsory labor at fixed wages under penalty of jail, hot branding irons, and outlawry. The wage-laborers and villeins struck back. The most common forms of resistance were those of combining for mutual strength and simple flight to other districts. Because this movement was so widespread, and escape so generally successful,[3] repressive measures were insufficient remedy for the landowners; they were forced to pay the higher wages and to reduce rents if they were to prevent their crops from rotting in the fields for lack of hands.

In 1381, the ruling classes sought to filch back part of their higher labor costs by the imposition of a one-shilling poll tax on every person above fifteen years of age (except clerics and licensed beggars). It quickly became apparent that they had misjudged the temper and mettle of the people. The result was the Great Rebellion of 1381, more popularly known as Wat Tyler's Rebellion, in honor of its leader.[4]

The revolt was national in scope. It lasted only one month, June, but in that time "half of England had been in flame."[5] The ranks of the rebels were composed about half of peasants and half of proletarians – rural wage-laborers, and journeymen and apprentices of London and other towns. Most chroniclers estimate their number at from forty to sixty thousand; but the only eyewitness account states that at Blackheath one hundred and ten thousand rebels assembled to confront the king with their demands. They were a disciplined force, and armed; in their ranks were thousands of longbow veterans of the Hundred Years' War, then in its forty-fifth year.

The lines of revolt converged on London, a metropolis with a population of some 23,000 (males of fifteen years of age and over). On 13 June a rebel army of ten thousand entered London through gates opened by the welcoming proletariat within; by that afternoon, "the rebels were in possession of London, without having had to strike a single blow."[6] Combining xenophobia with anti-feudalism, they killed a large number of the Flemish community of weavers whom the former king had imported and installed in London. Young King Richard II took refuge in the Tower of London with his armed guard and his advisers. His position was so desperate that "he was prepared to grant anything" the rebels were demanding.[7]

Through the voices of John Ball, the radical priest, and Wat Tyler, their commander-in-chief, the "commons of England" made their demands known: for an end to bondage of villeins and laborers, the revocation of the poll tax, and no more "outlawry" for resistance to forced labor. Tyler addressed the king as "Brother," and in the royal presence he declared, "there should be equality among all people," adding only courteously, "save the king."[8]

Even as the king parleyed with the rebels and agreed to their demands, he arranged for the assassination of Wat Tyler.[9] But he did not dare to revoke the promises he had made; not, that is, until the rebels had decamped from London and dispersed to their homes. Then the king did revoke his promises and sent forth his armed bands to wreak vengeance on the deceived and demobilized rebels, and to inaugurate a period of "pacification" and punishment.

Some commentators seem disposed to disparage the revolt as a factor in bringing feudalism to an end in England. It is true that there were a number of factors contributing to that end, but surely Wat Tyler's Rebellion was one of them. It barred the way to a raising of the rate of profit by means of feudal dues on the peasantry. Even a prime disparager conceded that in the following century "tenants did not find it impossible to resist pressure from their landlords."[10] Shorter-range goals achieved included the revocation of the attempt to force down wages to the old levels under the provisions of the Statute of Laborers of 1350. These ancient rebels would seem to merit the enthusiasm expressed by Thorold Rogers five centuries after their audacious rising: "The peasant of the fourteenth century struck a blow for freedom ... and he won."[11]

Appendix II-C

(*see Chapter 5, note 46*)

Perhaps the "cheap commodity" strategy for capitalist conquest of foreign countries was never more clearly outlined than by William Bullock in his *Virginia Impartially Examined*, which was published in London in 1649. Expressing the view that the Indians were too numerous and strong to be coerced, and too self-sufficient to be won to easy trust and dependence in their relations with the English, Bullock suggested a subtle strategy, which he defined and discussed as follows:

First, by making them sensible of their nakedness.

Secondly, by taking them off from their confidence upon nature, whereby they may take care for the future.

Thirdly, that they may desire commerce.

Fourthly, that they may be brought to depend. And for themselves, I shall propose that we gently steal through their nature, till we can come to pull off the scale from their eyes, that they may see their own nakednesse; which must be done in manner following.

Either by making them ambitious of Honour, or by making them ambitious of Riches . . .

First, I shall advise that slight Jewells be made at the publique charge of thirty or fourty shillings price, and one better then [than] the rest, of some such toyes as they shall most affect, which fitted with Ribands to weare about their necks of their heads, as their custom amongst them is; shalbe sent from the Governour of the Plantation in his own, and also in the name of the People and the Governor to distinguish them by some pretty titles, which should always after be observed; as also to make some of them favourites, and to sollicite their preferement with their King, & this by degrees will kindle the fire of Ambition, which once in a flame must be fed, and then is the time to work.

For the second I shall advise, that their nature be observed what way it most poynts at, and then to fit them with what they most desire, and if by degrees you can bring some of them to weare slighte loose Garments in Summer, or to keep them warmed in the Winter; which if you can effect, the worke is halfe done . . .

The author acknowledged that his plan would entail certain initial outlays by the English, but he assured his readers that even this cost would be recompensed by taking animal skins and provisions from the Indians in barter. Once having got that far, the English "need not fear the coming of the rest."

> The poore Indian being cloathed, his sight is cleared, he sees himselfe naked, and you'le find him in the snare . . .

Bullock stressed that still the matter must be managed by stages, because "you shall finde that for themselves they will worke, but not for you." Therefore as the English bourgeoisie had done in their owne country, Bullock proposed a sort of contracting system of work to be done by the Indians in their own houses and villages. By steps then they could be introduced as laborers within the English colony. But they were not to be *fully* trusted "until you see them be so sensible of their poverty, that they come necessitated to worke." (*Virginia Impartially Observed*, [London, 1649], pp. 56–9.)

Appendix II-D

(*see Chapter 7, note 197*)

Some scholars are convinced that the bond-labor system, despite acknowledged abuses, represented an improvement for the laborers over the prospects they would have had in Europe. Bruce[1] and Ballagh[2] believe that, except for the axemen noted by Bruce, the work was easier than that of the English wage-laborer. McCormac, lowering his sights a few degrees, says merely that at any rate the lot of the limited-term bond-laborer was "better than languishing in a debtor's cell in England."[3]

Attention is also given to the condition of the European-American bond-laborers in the eighteenth century, when African-Americans came to constitute the majority of the plantation bond-labor force. Gray asserts that in the eighteenth century the conditions of the European bond-laborers were alleviated.[4] On the other hand, Richard B. Morris found that the increased employment of Africans did not bring "any material improvement in the treatment" of immigrant European bond-laborers.[5] McCormac seems to agree on this point with Morris, at least so far as Maryland was concerned. There, he says, the life of the European bond-laborer was better prior to the large-scale arrival of African laborers beginning at the end of the seventeenth century.[6] Despite the high mortality rate of the first years, and although the burdens of the poor were increased if they emigrated to the colonies as bond-laborers, still, says A. E. Smith, both masters and bond-laborers endured "the hardships of pioneer life," and in the end "America presented to the average man a far better chance of attaining decent independence than did Europe."[7] If the bond-laborers' plight was difficult, he declares, the difficulties should not be ascribed to bondage as such, nor to the evil disposition of the masters, but to the general difficulties of the earliest colonial years that made inevitable a harsh regime, in which little allowance could be made for "shiftless or weak servants." Within such limits, he found that the degree of oppressive treatment suffered by the bond-laborers depended largely upon the luck of the draw in the matter of masters to whom they were disposed. There were, Smith says, two basic sources of the sufferings of limited-term bond-laborers, and neither involved any disposition on the part of the plantation bourgeoisie to take advantage of the chattel bond-labor relation of production to exploit their workers in ways which they could not have done free tenants and wage laborers. These two fundamental causes of hardship were, he says: (1) the climate of the plantation colonies; and (2) the non-adaptability of non-farm laborers such as constituted a large part, if not the majority, of the bond-laborers drawn from England.[8] Russell R. Menard's study of early colonial Maryland led him to essentially the same conclusion as that drawn by Smith regarding the general state of master–servant relations. In the course of challenging Edmund S. Morgan's assertion that limited-term bond-servitude prepared the way for the lifetime bond-servitude eventually imposed on African-Americans, Menard is at pains to contrast the two cases. "Indentured servitude ... was not degrading," says Menard. True, their mortality rate was shockingly high, "nor were all servants well treated"; but Menard dismisses the notorious cases such as those of Henry Smith, John Dandy, and other monstrously cruel owners as "not typical." Menard stresses that "master–servant relationships were often friendly and sometimes affectionate and that servitude offered poor men a chance to gain entry into a society that offered great opportunities for advancement."[9]

These apologies for the chattel bond-labor system have not gone unchallenged. As for the contention that the life of the bond-laborers was better than it would have been if they had remained in England, that the work was not so hard in the tobacco plantations as that performed by agricultural laborers in England, there is more of assumption than substance in it. Edmund S. Morgan, on the basis of well-known English works on economic history, effectively maintains that the relatively easy regime of the farm worker in England utterly unsuited the English laborer for the unremitting round of heavy toil on the tobacco plantations.[10] Even McCormac's extreme analogy to the English debtors' prison loses much of its force when it is considered that the situation of the plantation bond-laborers was like a debtors' prison where the inmates of any age were regarded as minors, so far as their rights were concerned.

The more instructive comparison, that between the laborers in New England and those in the tobacco colonies in the seventeenth century, is almost totally ignored by apologists for the chattel bond-labor system.[11] But the late Richard B. Morris, in his exhaustively documented study *Government and Labor in Early America*, found that the treatment of bond-laborers was much more rigorous in the tobacco colonies than in New England. The contrast of the all-or-nothing dependence on the tobacco monoculture of the Chesapeake plantation economy, and the small independent farms of the varied, largely self-sufficient, New England economy was fundamental to the difference in day-to-day social relationships.[12] In the New England and Middle colonies, said Morris, the limited-term bond-laborers, who were relatively few in number, enjoyed close personal relationships with their masters, relationships that were normal to their occupations in crafts and household service; but in the plantation colonies, where the bond-laborers were "employed primarily in field work under the supervision of exacting overseers," master–servant relations were harsh.[13]

Without wanting to indict the entire planter class, Morris concluded: "Maltreatment of servants was most flagrant in the tobacco colonies." Not only did a large number of drunken and dissolute owners treat their bond-laborers with sadistic brutality, members of the Colony Council and county courts "set a poor example to their own communities in ruling with a rod of iron. . . . Such masters preferred to discipline their servants themselves rather than to bring them into court," says Morris. While only the most serious cases of maltreatment came to court, they serve to reveal the "fairly typical" life of the plantation bond laborer.[14]

My own study of the record affords more support to the views of Morris and Morgan cited here than to the apologists of the bond-labor system.

Appendix II-E

(*see Chapter 9, note 54*)

The population of England and Wales, which had grown by one-third in the first half of the seventeenth century, grew by only one-tenth in the second half.[1] In this last half of the century, the expansion of industrial production was based primarily on the increase in the mass of labor employed rather than on improved technology.[2] In consequence of the expansion of industrial employment, the "surplussed" agricultural workers found employment more easily than they had prior to the English Revolution.[3] The English military demand for manpower experienced two great surges at the end of the seventeenth and the beginning of the eighteenth centuries. England, traditionally a land without a large standing army, conscripted scores of thousands of men for military and naval duty in the War of the League of Augsburg (1689–97) and the War of the Spanish Succession (1702–13). Between 1698 and 1708, for instance, the number of English-speaking troops under arms was increased nearly fourfold, and the naval forces were nearly tripled.[4] Thus sectors of the population that had been a ready supply of plantation bond-laborers in England were needed elsewhere, as is made clear by Trevelyan's description of the methods employed to draft recruits for the continental armies of the Duke of Marlborough in the earliest years of the eighteenth century:

> ... armed raids of the press-gang [descended] on the folk of the port towns and neighboring villages.... Criminal gangs were drafted wholesale; bounties sometime amounting to four pounds for each recruit tempted the needy to enlist.... [Since] the country was prosperous and work abundant ... the naval press was abused for the purposes of the land service.... Parish constables were to be given ten shillings for every person suitable for the press gang whom they produced before the authorities. Magistrates were instructed to hand over to recruiting officers persons who could show no means of supporting themselves.[5]

Already in 1667, a member of the House of Commons, Mr Garroway, had warned that emigration to Virginia would "in time drain us of people and will endanger our ruin."[6] In 1673, the author of *The Grand Concern of England*

Explained believed that the drain of emigrants from England had been made even more critical by the "two last great Plagues, the Civil War at Home, and the several wars with Holland, Spain and France [which] have destroyed several hundred thousands of men which lived among us."[7] Roger Coke argued that the drain of bond-laborers and other emigrant workers to the American plantations was seriously weakening England. His treatise, published in 1671, warned, "... we have opened a wide gap, and by all encouragement excited all the growing youth and industry of England which might preserve the trades we had herein, to betake them to those of the Plantations."[8] One of the most eminent voices cautioning against too much emigration of English labor was that of Sir William Petty. The "remote governments" of the American plantation colonies, according to Petty, "instead of being additions are really diminutions" of the national wealth of England. Far from favoring increased English emigration to America, Petty would have had the New England Pilgrims come home. "[A]s for the People of New England," he wrote, "I can but wish they were transplanted into *Old England* or Ireland."[9]

Appendix II-F

(*see Chapter 13, note 26*)

In April 1699, a joint committee of nine – three members of the Colony Council and six members of the House of Burgesses – was ordered to begin a complete revision of the Virginia laws.[1] Seven years later in June 1706, the new code was enacted into law on royal instruction. In the book of laws, however, the code is ascribed to October 1705, the date on which it was first passed by the Assembly.[2] It contains significant provisions relative to the establishment of racial oppression and the "white race," that are further noted in Chapter 13.

The instructions of the Commissioners of Trade and Plantations that first ordered the revision of the laws required that "if there bee anything in them, either in the matter or Stile which may bee fit to be retrenched or altered, you are to represent the same unto us, *with your opinion touching the said Laws.*"[3] Does a record of those opinions exist today? It seems reasonable to believe much light would be shed on that subject by the record of discussions and exchanges of dispatches and enclosures – the existence of which is a matter of record – that occurred within the committee, and in meetings of the Governor and Colony Council as well, and between the Virginia authorities and the government in England – if such records could be found. What was said by members of the Virginia committee or in the meetings held by the Commissioners of Trade and Plantations in England, or in the correspondence regarding those deliberations – some of which are specifically, but cryptically, alluded to in records that do exist?

This entire present work has been a rejection of the "unthinking decision" thesis coined by Winthrop D. Jordan. But where are the "thoughts" in this "revisall of the Lawes"? Somebody in the array of lawmakers and critics must have proposed that, after forty years, it was time to change the requirement that masters not "exceed the bounds of moderation in correcting" servants, and that if a servant were able to get to the justice of the peace and then to the next county court, "the servant shall have remedy for his grievances"; and, instead, to define "moderate correction" to mean that the master was not to "whip a christian white servant naked, without an order from the justice of the peace," the offending master to be fined forty shillings payable to the servant.[4] Some "reviser" must have thought it necessary to provide that upon a second offense by a master in treatment of "servants (not being slaves)," the courts could order that the servant be taken from that master and sold at outcry.[5] Which member of the committee first took notice that in regard to freedom dues, "nothing in that nature ever [had been] made certain," and urged that they be enumerated specifically: "to every male servant, ten bushels of corn, thirty shillings in money (or the equivalent in goods), a gun worth at least twenty shillings; and to every woman servant, fifteen bushels of corn, forty shillings in money (or the equivalent in goods)"? In this case we do have evidence that the revisal was not an exercise in somnambulism. The Virginia Colony Council at the last minute proposed to amend the draft law, by providing a differentiation of the freedom dues to be paid to men and women bond-laborers.[6] But to whom did it occur to raise the question and by what argument? And, incidentally, who was it who successfully moved to strike out the words "at least" as proposed by the Colony Council, before the specification of the freedom dues to be required for women servants? What was the discussion that preceded the decision to include a totally new provision making any free Negro subject to a whipping of thirty lashes if he or she raised a hand against any "white" person?[7]

I shall not intrude here the details of my search for such substantive records, although I will gladly share that information with any scholar who might wish to join the hunt. A number of documents include references to meetings of the Lords of Trade and Plantations convened to consider the draft laws sent from Virginia for approval or disapproval. They note, among other relevant matters, the attendance of Virginia Colony Secretary Edmund Jennings, at their Lordships request, to explain and assist in the review of those proposed laws.[8] On 27 and 29 March 1704, Jennings did attend, and "presented to their Lordships his observations on the Collection of Laws."[9] Sir Sidney Godolphin (later Earl) Lord High Treasurer advised Virginia governor Nicholson on 12 December 1704 that over a period of several months, Jennings had diligently worked with the Lords of Trade and Plantations to complete the work of "Inspecting [and?] amending" the proposed revisions of the Virginia laws.[10] Reference is also found to communications with Virginia governors Andros,[11] Nicholson and Nott, but there are no particulars in those documents that might serve to reveal the thinking processes that produced the new set of laws. Sir Edward Northey first served as English Attorney-General from July 1701 to October 1707. Where are the opinions, if they exist at all, rendered by him regarding the proposed revisal of the Virginia laws? A sizable number of documents relating to the laws carry the notation "a Page inserted in the file to indicate that [the particular document]" had been "removed and filed elsewhere."[12] Where is "elsewhere"? Finally, do answers to some of these questions remain to be discovered in some family papers that my search at the Library of Congress did not turn up?

A collateral matter no less puzzling is this: Why has no historian I have studied even taken notice of this apparent gap in the records of that critical period of Virginia history?

The argument made in the present work – that the invention of the "white race" social control system was a deliberate course taken by the ruling plantation bourgeoisie – would, I suspect, be strengthened by the discovery of such records regarding the process of framing the new Virginia code. But the thesis does not depend upon such discovery.

Notes

Abbreviations of Some Frequently Cited Sources

AHR	*American Historical Review*
Bacon, *Works*	*The Works of Francis Bacon*, edited by James Spedding, Robert Leslie Ellis and Douglas Denon Heath, 14 vols. (London, 1857–74).
Blathwayt Papers	Blathwayt Papers, ca. 1675–1715, 41 vols. on microfilm at Colonial Williamsburg.
CO	Great Britain Public Record Office, Colonial Office records.
County Grievances	"A Repertory of the General County Grievances of Virginia . . . with the humble opinion of His Majesties Commissioners annexed" (October 1677).
County Records	Virginia County Court Records (photocopies, microfilm and abstracts), available at the Virginia State Archives, Richmond.
Coventry Papers	*[Henry] Coventry Papers Relating to Virginia, Barbados and other Colonies*, microfilm prepared by the British Manuscripts Project of the American Council of Learned Societies and available at the Library of Congress (originals at the estate of the Marquis of Bath, Longleat House, Wiltshire, UK).
CSP. Col.	Great Britain Public Record Office, *Calendar of State Papers, Colonial Series: America and the West Indies,* 44 vols. (London, 1860–1969).
CTP	Commissioners of Trade and Plantations. Operated under various official designations: Committee (of the Privy Council) for Trade and Plantations (from 1660); Lords of Trade and Plantations (from 1675); and Board of Trade (from 1696).
Force Tracts	Peter Force, *Tracts and Other Papers, related principally to the Origin, Settlement and Progress of the Colonies in North America, from the discovery of*

	the country to the year 1776, 4 vols. (Washington, 1836).
Gwynne, *Analecta Hibernia*, No. 4	Irish Manuscripts Commission, *Analecta Hibernia*, No. 4 (October 1932), "Documents Relating to the Irish in the West Indies," Aubrey Gwynne SJ, collector, p. 266.
Hening	William Waller Hening, comp. and ed. *The Statutes-at-Large; being a Collection of all the Laws of Virginia, from the First Session of the Legislature in the year 1619,* 13 vols. (Richmond, 1799–1823; Charlottesville, 1969).
Hotten, *Original Lists*	John C. Hotten, *The Original Lists of Persons of Quality; Emigrants; Religious Exiles; Political Rebels; Serving Men Sold for a Term of Years; Apprentices; Children Stolen; Maidens Pressed and Others Who went from Great Britain to the American plantations, 1600–1700* (London, 1874).
Manchester Papers	In *Historical Manuscripts Commission, Eighth Report* (London 1881), Part 1, Appendix.
MCGC	*Minutes of the Council and General Court of Virginia,* edited by H. R. McIlwaine (Richmond, 1924).
Norfolk County Wills	*Volume 3 of Virginia Colonial Abstracts,* 34 vols., compiled by Beverley Fleet (Baltimore, 1961).
RVC	*Records of the Virginia Company of London,* 4 vols. edited by S. M. Kingsbury (Washington, DC, 1906–35).
Smith, *Travels and Works*	*Travels and Works of Captain John Smith, President of Virginia and Admiral of New England,* 2 vols., edited by Edward Arber and A. G. Bradley (Edinburgh, 1910).
VMHB	*Virginia Magazine of History and Biography.*
WMQ	*William and Mary Quarterly.*

1 The Labor Supply Problem: England a Special Case

1. See Klaus E. Knorr, *British Colonial Theories, 1570–1850* (Toronto, 1944), Part I, "Colonial Theories, 1570–1660."

2. As mentioned in Volume One of *The Invention of the White Race* (p. 8), in the early 1630s the English planted a colony on Providence Island, some 350 miles north of Panama and 135 miles from the eastern coast of present-day Nicaragua, but they were forced to abandon it in 1641.

3. E. E. Rich and C. H. Wilson, eds., *The Cambridge Economic History of Europe,* Vol. IV, *The Economy of Expanding Europe in the Sixteenth and Seventeenth Centuries* (New York, 1967), p. 304.

4. J. H. Elliott, *Europe Divided, 1559–98* (New York, 1968), pp. 24, 289.

5. Between 1503 and 1660, according to records kept at Seville, Spain received from America 16 million kilograms of silver and 185,000 kilograms of gold, of which the Spanish Crown's share was 40 percent. (J. H. Elliott, *Imperial Spain, 1469–1716* (New York, 1964), pp. 174–75.) This

treasure quickly passed from Spain to its creditors, most notably the Fugger family of Augsburg and Antwerp, as payments on imperial debts, however. (Immanuel Wallerstein, *The Modern World-System*, Vol. I, *The Modern World-System, Capitalist Agriculture and the Origins of the European World-Economy in the Sixteenth Century* [New York, 1974], pp. 178–85. See also Henri Pirenne, *A History of Europe, From the Invasion to the XVI Century* [New York, 1955], pp. 524–6.)

6. Vieira's *O Papel Forte* is here cited from Robert Southey, *History of Brazil*, 3 vols. (London, 1817); 2:225. "(I)t was men of which Portugal was in want," said Southey, "not extent of territory." (Ibid., p. 224.)

7. Charles R. Boxer, *The Portuguese Seaborne Empire, 1415–1825* (New York, 1969), p. 88.

8. Henry Raup Wagner, *The Life and Writings of Bartolomé de Las Casas* (Alburquerque, 1967), pp. 22, 38–43. Though Las Casas's plan for establishing a Spanish peasant colony in the Americas failed, his proposal for using Negro slaves would soon lead to the royal licensing of the wholesale shipment of African bond-laborers to the Americas, which would come to be known as the Asiento. Some thirty-five years later, Las Casas regretted his role in this development. Even though he felt he had made a well-intentioned mistake that was generally approved by his contemporaries, he feared the divine judgment that he had yet to face for his role in bringing such terrible injustice on the Africans. (Bartolomé de Las Casas, *História de las Indias*, 3 vols, edited by Augustin Millares [Mexico City, 1951]; 3:474 [Capitulo 129].)

9. Charles Edward Chapman, *Colonial Hispanic America* (New York, 1933), p. 109. Special permission of the king or other qualified official had to be obtained before anyone might go to the Indies.

10. In a comment that anticipated Adam Smith and Edmund Burke (See *The Invention of the White Race*, Vol. One, pp. 33 and 71), Las Casas decried the social anomaly of "rabble who had been scourged or clipped of their ears in Castile, lording it over the native chiefs." (Edward Gaylord Bourne, *Spain in America, 1450–1580* [New York, 1907], p. 208.)

11. Luis Ivens Ferraz, "The Creole of São Tomé," *African Studies*, 37:3–68 (1978), p. 16. Most of these survivors married men and women who were brought from the African mainland.

12. John Lynch, *The Hispanic World in Crisis and Change 1598–1700* (Oxford, 1992), p. 8; Elliott, *Imperial Spain*, pp. 300–301.

13. Elliott, *Imperial Spain*, pp. 300–301. Lynch, p. 8. In 1609, the *moriscos* constituted perhaps one-third of the population of Valencia, where they were chiefly agricultural laborers. (Elliott, p. 300.)

14. Ernest John Knapton, *Europe, 1450–1815* (New York, 1958), pp. 238–9.

15. Chapman, pp. 109–10. In an analogous situation, English governments, whether guided by Puritan or Anglican principles, were untroubled by sectarian scruples. Irish Catholics in significant numbers were sent to Anglo-American plantation colonies in the seventeenth century, where their substantial presence caused the plantation owners some anxiety. (See *The Invention of the White Race*, Volume One, p. 74, and chapter 12 and 13 below.)

16. James A. Rawley, *The Transatlantic Slave Trade: A History* (New York, 1981), p. 81.

17. Jan de Vries, *Dutch Rural Economy* (New Haven, 1974), pp. 87–8. Rich and Wilson give the proportion as three-fourths (*Economy of Expanding Europe*, pp. 46–7).

18. De Vries, pp. 120, 184 and 203–34. De Vries concludes this section of his discussion by speculating that the absense of a numerous displaced and unemployed agricultural population retarded Holland's industrial development.

19. Rawley, p. 80.

20. De Vries, pp. 120, 184 and 203–34.

21. Charles R. Boxer, *The Dutch Seaborne Empire: 1600–1800* (New York, 1965), p. 58.

22. Boxer, *Dutch Seaborne Empire*, p. 58.

23. Ibid., p. 218. Although in 1630 the Dutch seized from Portugal the northern region of Brazil and called it New Holland, they were driven out in 1654, in part because "they were never able to induce adequate numbers of Dutchmen to settle in the faraway colony to influence the ethnic makeup of the settlement." (Johannes M. Postma, *The Dutch in the Atlantic Slave Trade, 1600–1815* [Cambridge, 1990], p. 19.)

24. See *The Invention of the White Race*, Volume One, Appendix C, p. 207.

25. Boxer, *Dutch Seaborne Empire*, p. 219.

26. Jean Jacquart, "French Agriculture in the Seventeenth Century," translated by Judy Falkus, in Peter Earle, ed., *Essays in European Economic History, 1500–1800* (Oxford, 1974), pp. 165–84; 165, 177.

27. Ibid., p. 180.

28. The failure of one line of agricultural development is discussed in Sigmund Diamond, "An

Experiment in 'Feudalism': French-Canada in the Seventeenth Century," *WMQ*, series 3, 18:3–34 (1961).

29. W. J. Eccles, *France in America* (New York, 1972), pp. 76–7. Léon Vignols, "La Mise en Valeur du Canada à l'Époque Française,' *La Revue d'Histoire Économique et Sociale*, 16:720–95 (1928); p. 736.

30. Eccles, *France in America* p. 77. In 1680, Robert LaSalle, the noted French explorer, reported that in Canada more trade goods were being converted into beaver pelts than Indians were being converted into Christians. (Vignols, "La Mise en Valeur," p. 724.)

31. Hispaniola was the name first given by the Spanish to the island that the native people called Haiti. At the end of the seventeenth century, France took over the entire island and called it St Domingue. It reassumed the name Haiti when France lost possession as a result of the Haitian Revolution (1800–1804). Spain finally reasserted its claim to the eastern portion of the island in 1844. Since that time the island has remained divided: Haiti in the west, the Dominican Republic in the east.

32. Eccles, *France in America*, p. 148.

33. Ibid., p. 149.

34. For a further discussion of the French reasons for turning away from the idea of supplying plantation labor from among the French population, see W. J. Eccles, *Canada Under Louis XIV* (Toronto, 1964), especially pp. 52–8.

35. Eccles cites a 1681 finding that only one out of every twelve of the *engagé* laborers were surviving three years out of service, and another that in the eighteenth century only one out of every three African laborers were surviving as long as three years of labor in the French West Indies. (Eccles, *France in America*, pp. 149 and 151.)

For a more detailed treatment of the subject of *engagé* labor, see two articles by Léon Vignols: "Les Antilles Françaises sous l'Ancien Régime – aspects économiques et sociaux: l'institution des engagés, 1626–1774," *La Revue d'Histoire Économique et Sociale*, 16:12–45 (1928); and "Une Question mal posée: le travail manuel des blancs et des ésclaves aux Antilles (XVIIe–XVIIIe siècles)," *Revue Historique*, 175:308–15 (Jan.–June 1935); pp. 310–11.

36. Charles Woolsey Cole, *Colbert and a Century of French Mercantilism*, 2 vols. (New York, 1939), 2:19–20.

37. Eccles, *France in America*, pp. 76, 148. See also A. J. Sargent, *The Economic Policy of Colbert* (London, 1899; 1968 reprint), pp. 47–8; and Cole, pp. 21–2.

38. Elliott, *Imperial Spain*, pp. 174–5.

39. William M. Denevan, ed., *The Native Population of the Americas in 1492*, 2nd ed (Madison, 1992), xxiii–xvi, xxviii (Table 1); Noble David Cook, *Demographic Collapse: Indian Peru, 1520–1620* (Cambridge, 1981). Both Denevan (p. xxiii) and Cook (p. 2) note the irreconcilable extremes of the estimates of the 1492 population of Hispaniola, which range from sixty thousand to 8 million. Denevan, taking into account newly reported evidence of a devastating epidemic of swine flu in 1493, agrees with studies that fix the population at about 1 million. The 1514 figure is mid-range of a general consensus. (Cook, p. 2.)

40. In 1574 there remained in Hispaniola only two Indian villages, and in Cuba only nine, comprising 270 married Indian men. (Bourne, pp. 197–8.) Certain countervailing factors operated to limit the degree of destruction of the indigenous population of Puerto Rico in this period. (James L. Dietz, *Economic History of Puerto Rico: Institutional Change and Capitalist Development* [Princeton, 1986], p. 6; Salvador Brau, *Ensayos: Disquicisiones Sociológicas* [Rio Piedras, 1972], p. 15.) I am indebted to Bill Vila Andino for directing me to these sources relative to the history of Puerto Rico.

41. *Encomienda* was the assignment of a given number of Indian laborers to a Spanish employer. *Repartimiento* was the assignment of Indian laborers by an *encomendero* to another employer. Indentured servitude was an alternative form to the forced labor of the *repartimiento*. (See Charles Gibson, *Spain in America* [New York, 1966], pp. 144–7.)

Repartimiento involved movement to workplaces outside of one's village; however, it required twenty men to be travelling to and from the mines, to maintain a supply of ten working in the mine. (T. R. Fehrenbach, *Fire and Blood, A History of Mexico* [New York, 1973], p. 225.) The *repartimiento* miners were forced to labor at a wage one-fourth that of free laborers. (Lynch, pp. 306–7.)

Ultimately, the Indian agricultural laboring class in Mexico, though nominally free, was reduced to peonage, a form of practical bondage by debt to the owner of the *hacienda*. (Gibson, pp. 118–19, 147, 156).

42. Denevan, ed., Table 1, p. xxvii. Woodrow Borah and Sherburne F. Cook, *The Indian*

Population of Central Mexico, 1531–1610 (Berkeley, 1960), p. 48. Cf. Noble David Cook, *Demographic Collapse: Indian Peru, 1520–1620* (Cambridge, 1981), pp. 2–3.

The decline of the indigenous population of Mexico ended in the middle or late seventeenth century, but by the end of the eighteenth century their number was still less than it had been in 1492.

43. Markham, who spells the word *mitta*, identifies the term as a native Peruvian Quichua word meaning "time" or "turn." (Clement R. Markham, *A History of Peru* [1892; reprinted New York, 1968], p. 157.)

44. Cook, pp. 113–14, 246. Compare the slightly higher estimate of 11.7 million for the Indian population of the "Central Andes" at the time of the arrival of the Spanish. (Denevan, p. xxviii.)

45. Boxer, *Portuguese Seaborne Empire*, p. 88. Basic to the difficulties of the Portuguese in Brazil was the fact that the unstratified, non-sedentary, native social structure there – in contrast to the class-differentiated sedentary societies found by the Spanish in Mexico and Peru – did not present opportunities for co-optation of native social forms for colonialist purposes.

46. See Chapter 3 for further discussion of the Portuguese social control problems in Brazil.

47. The Belgian historian Charles Verlinden, a preeminent authority on slavery in medieval Europe, has contributed a series of studies showing the link between medieval European and Ibero-American colonial slavery, noting both parallels and divergences. He emphasizes the historical continuity that existed between slavery in medieval European societies, including the Portuguese plantation gambits in the Atlantic islands, on the one hand, and the labor supply system in colonial Ibero-America, on the other. See Charles Verlinden, *The Beginning of Modern Colonization: Eleven Essays with an Introduction*, translated by Yvonne Feccero (Ithaca, 1970), especially pp. 33–51, Chapter 2, "Medieval Slavery and Colonial Slavery in America."

48. African bondmen and bondwomen, nearly fifty thousand of whom were brought to Europe in the sixteenth century, worked mainly as domestic servants, artisans and farmers, and enjoyed a considerable degree of social mobility. (Verlinden, p. 47; Rawley, pp. 24–5.)

49. Verlinden, p. 38.

50. Basil Davidson, *The African Slave Trade, Precolonial History, 1450–1850* (Boston, 1961), pp. 33–4.

51. A. J. R. Russell-Wood, "Iberian Expansion and the Issue of Black Slavery: Changing Portuguese Attitudes, 1440–1770," *Journal of American History*, 83:16–42; 27.

52. Philip D. Curtin, *The Atlantic Slave Trade: A Census* (Madison, 1969), p. 116. See also Russell-Wood, p. 22; Boxer, *Portuguese Seaborne Empire*, pp. 88–9; Rawley, pp. 24–5.

53. Verlinden, p. 39. It is interesting to note that among these Africans brought to Portugal was the putative great-grandmother of Jesuit priest António Vieira (1608–1697), the famous royal adviser and advocate of sparing the Brazilian Indians of the Maranho region by substituting laborers bought and brought from Angola. ("Não custa a crer tivesse vindo a bisavó de Africa, trazida por escrava a Portugal.") (Lúcio de Azevedo, *História de António Vieira*, multi-volume [Lisbon, 1992–   ], 1:14. See also: the Inquisition documents, ibid., pp. 311–17; Mathias C. Kiemen, *The Indian Policy of Portugal in the Amazon Region, 1614–1693* [Washington, DC, 1954], p. 140.)

54. Verlinden, p. 40.

55. Wagner, p. 40. Chapman, p. 119. Rich Wilson, eds. p. 322.

56. Rawley, pp. 26–27. Postma, p. 31. George Scelle, "The Slave Trade in the Spanish Colonies of America: The Asiento," *American Journal of International Law*, 4:612–61 (1910), pp. 614, 618, 622.

57. Basil Williams, *The Whig Supremacy, 1714–1760*, revised 2nd ed. (Oxford 1962), pp. 265 n. 1, 315.

58. Estimates considered include: W. E. B. DuBois, 10 or 12 million (Herbert Aptheker, ed., *The Correspondence of W. E. B. DuBois*, Volume 1, *Selections, 1877–1934* [Amherst: University of Massachusetts Press], p. 124) and J. D. Fage, 11,360,000 (*A History of West Africa*, 3rd. edition [Cambridge, 1969], pp. 82–3, 225). David Brion Davis puts the number at a minimum of 15 million (*Slavery in Western Culture* [Ithaca, 1966], p. 9). Rawley estimates the number at 11,048,000 (Rawley, pp. 428–9). Philip D. Curtin concludes that more than 8 million and fewer than 10.5 million Africans survived the Middle Passage to arrive as bond-laborers in the Americas. (Curtin, p. 87). Fage bases his estimate on Curtin, adding a percentage for those who lost their lives during the voyage.

Discussing the overall impact of the Atlantic slave trade on Africa, Davidson writes: "it appears reasonable to suggest that one way or another, before and after embarkation, it cost Africa at least fifty million souls" (Davidson, pp. 80–81). See also Walter Rodney, *How Europe Underdeveloped Africa* (Washington, DC: Howard University Press, 1982), pp. 95–8. (This work was originally published in London and Dar es Salaam, 1972.) Compare Rawley, pp. 425–7.

59. Rawley, p. 428.

60. Rawley, p. 424. I hope that my remarks are not inconsistent with Rawley's intention.

61. Curtin, p. 87.

62. The concluding stanza of "We Have Fed You All for a Thousand Years," by "An Unknown Proletarian", in *IWW Songs, Songs of the Workers*, 27th edition (Chicago, 1939), p. 64. IWW stands for Industrial Workers of the World.

63. See "The Enslavement Process in the Portuguese Dominions of King Philip III of Spain in the Early Seventeenth Century" (1612), in Robert Edgar Conrad, *Children of God's Fire: A Documentary History of Black Slavery in Brazil* (Princeton, 1983), pp. 11–15.

English captain Thomas Phillips described the determined resistance of captive Africans being assembled for shipment to Barbados in 1693 in his ship the *Hannibal*. Though shackled two-by-two "to prevent their mutiny, or swimming ashore," ". . . they have often leap'd out of the canoes, boat, and ship, into the sea, and kept under water till they were drowned, to avoid being taken up by our boats, which pursued them; they have more dreadful apprehension of Barbadoes than we can have of hell. ("A Journal of a Voyage in the Hannibal of London, Ann. 1693, 1694 from England to Africa and so Forward to Barbadoes, by Thomas Phillips, Commander of the said Ship," in John and Awsham Churchill, comp., *A Collection of Voyages and Travels* [Churchill's Voyages], 6:171–239; 219.)

Compared with ships in Mediterranean or Baltic commerce, the slave ships required a higher crew-to-tonnage ratio to hold down their rebellious cargoes. (Kenneth L. Davies, *The Royal African Company*, [London, 1957], pp. 193–4.) In this brutal commerce, writes Basil Davidson, "Every ship's captain feared revolt on board, and with good reason, for revolts were many." (Basil Davidson, *Africa in History* [New York, 1968], p. 187.) It was for fear of revolt that 120 Africans were suffocated below decks, in order that the remaining 380 could be delivered to New Spain (Mexico), on a Portuguese ship in about 1612. (Conrad, p. 15.) See, in the same work, pp. 39–40, Document 1.7, "A Slave Revolt at Sea and Brutal Reprisals [1845]".

64. See Appendix II-A.

65. ". . . the Moors, with their women and children were leaving their houses as fast as they could, for they had seen their enemies" (Document 1.1, "The Beginnings of the Portuguese-African Slave Trade in the Fifteenth Century, as Described by Chronicler Gomes Eannes de Azurata," in Conrad, pp. 5–11; p. 6; the name of the chronicler is given as Gomes Eanes de Zurara in biographical encyclopedias.)

66. In the nineteenth century, the liberation struggle tended to merge into the general abolitionist and anti-colonialist struggles, especially in Cuba, Venezuela, Mexico, Brazil and Uruguay. (In Richard Price, ed., *Maroon Societies: Rebel Slave Communities in the Americas* (New York, 1973), see: Jose L. Franco, "Maroons and Slave Rebellions in the Spanish Territories," p. 48; Miguel Acosta Saignes, "Life in a Venezuelan Cumbe," p. 73; David M. Davidson, "Negro Slave Control and Resistance in Colonial Mexico," p. 99; Roger Bastide, "The Other [than Palmares] Palenques," p. 171. In Magnus Mörner, ed., *Race and Glass in Latin America*, (New York, 1970), see: Carlos M. Rama, "The Passing of the Afro-Uruguayans From Caste Society into Class Society," pp. 21, 37–9; Richard Graham, "Action and Ideas in the Abolitionist Movement in Brazil," pp. 62–6.

The maroon settlements in the mountains in eastern Cuba "lasted till the beginning of the first War of Independence in 1868, when the maroons joined en masse the ranks of the Cuban Liberation Army." (Franco, p. 47.)

67. See: C. L. R. James, *Black Jacobins: Toussaint L'Ouverture and the San Domingo Revolution* (New York, 1963), p. 411; Robin Blackburn, *The Overthrow of Colonial Slavery, 1776–1848* (London and New York, 1988), pp. 245–6.

68. Edward D. Neill, *History of the Virginia Company of London* (Albany, NY, 1869), p. 11. Wesley Frank Craven, *The Dissolution of the Virginia Company, the Failure of a Colonial Experiment* (New York, 1932), pp. 28–9. Philip Alexander Bruce, *Economic History of Virginia in the Seventeenth Century: An Inquiry into the Material Conditions of the People, based upon original records*, 2 vols. (New York, 1895; Peter Smith reprint, 1935), 1:10–19. Alexander Brown, *Genesis of the United States*, 2 vols. (Boston and New York, 1890), pp. 562–5.

69. Las Casas denounced his Christian fellow countrymen on this account. Spanish *encomenderos*, given Indians of Hispaniola into their care to teach them the Catholic faith, merely "took care," said Las Casas, to "send the men into the mines, to make them drain them out gold." (Bartolomé de Las Casas, *Brevisima Relación de la Destruicion de las Indias Occidentales*, written in 1539; first printed in 1552, excerpted in George Sanderlin, trans. and ed., *Bartolomé de Las Casas: A Selection of his Writings* (New York, 1971), p. 84.) The Indian *cacique* Hathuey, who had

fled from Hispaniola to Cuba in about 1511, explained to the people what he had learned of the Spanish religion. Pointing to a small chest of gold and jewels, he said: "Behold here the God of the Spaniards." (Ibid., p. 87.)

Francis Bacon, the famous English essayist and statesman and member of the Virginia Company, generalized as follows: "It cannot be affirmed (if one speak ingenuously) that it was the propagation of the Christian faith that was the adamant of that discovery, entry and plantation [of America]; but gold and silver and temporal profit and glory." (Bacon, *Works*, 7:20–21, "An Advertisement Touching An Holy War.")

70. Robert Brenner, "Agrarian Class Structure and Economic Development in Pre-industrial Europe," *Past and Present*, no. 70, pp. 31–73 (February 1976); p. 69. R. H. Tawney, *The Agrarian Problem in the Sixteenth Century* (New York, 1912), p. 195. George M. Trevelyan, *A Shortened History of England* (New York, 1942), pp. 206–8.

71. "This fortress built by Nature for herself/ Against infection and the hand of war . . . / . . . set in the silver sea, / Which serves it in the office of a wall" (Shakespeare, *Richard II*, Act 2, Scene 1). This sentiment perhaps was even more appropriate to Shakespeare's time than in the reign of Richard II (1377–99).

72. J. D. Mackie, *The Earlier Tudors* (Oxford, 1952), p. 450. Tawney, p. 195–6. Eric Kerridge, *Agrarian Problems in the Sixteenth Century* (London, 1969), pp. 120–21, 126–8, 132–3, 201.

73. Mackie, pp. 374–5.

74. See Tawney's discussion of the stimulating effect of the confiscation and redistribution of monastic lands on the pace of the conversion of arable to pasture land (Tawney pp. 379–84).

75. C. S. L. Davies believes that the turbulence of the following couple of years may have been worsened by the tardiness of their reabsorption into civilian life. ("Slavery and the Protector Somerset: the Vagrancy Act of 1547," *Economic History Review*, 2nd series, 19:533–49 (1936); p. 538.)

This retreat from France marked the withdrawal from the alliance with Charles V, as whose ally the English had invaded France in September 1544. It was the beginning of the Tudor "island policy," which relied on the build-up of the Royal Navy rather than on military campaigns in Europe to protect the English position. (Trevelyan, p. 216.)

76. C. G. Cruickshank, *Elizabeth's Armies*, 2nd edition (Oxford, 1966), pp. 14–16. For the number of English soldiers in the Tyrone War (1594–1603), see *The Invention of the White Race*, Volume One, Chapter 5.

77. Demographers' corrected figures, based on London bills of mortality for seven plague years in the period 1563–1665 (three in the sixteenth century and four in the seventeenth century), totalled 292,598, only one-fifth of them in the sixteenth century. (E. A. Wrigley and R. S. Schofield, *The Population History of England, 1541–1871: A Reconstruction* [Cambridge, Mass., 1981], pp. 81–2 [Table 3.9].)

78. Wrigley and Schofield, pp. 531–5 (Table A3.3). The annual rate of natural increase of the English population in the last six decades of the sixteenth century averaged 0.76 percent contrasted with 0.36 and 0.57 percent for the ten decades of the seventeenth and the eighteenth centuries respectively. (Ibid., p. 183 [Table 6.10].)

79. Lawrence Stone, taking issue with Tawney, asserts that, "It was relentless demographic growth . . . rather than the enclosing activities of monopolistic landlords which . . . was responsible for the rise of a landless labourer class, of a semi-employed squatter population eking out a living in cabins in the wastes and heaths, and of a small but conscious body of unemployed vagrants." (Lawrence Stone, Introduction to the 1967 edition of Tawney's *The Agrarian Problem in the Sixteenth Century*.)

80. Joan Thirsk and J. P. Cooper, eds., *Seventeenth-century Economic Documents* (Oxford, 1972), p. 200.

81. Sir John Clapham, *A Concise History of Britain from the Earliest Times to 1750* (Cambridge, 1949; Princeton, 1963), pp. 251–2.

82. Thirsk and Cooper, eds., p. 1 (House of Commons, 26 February 1621).

83. *Journals of the [English] House of Commons*, I:711.

84. E. M. Leonard, *The Early History of English Poor Relief* (Cambridge, 1900), p. 266.

85. John Eastcott Manahan, "The Cavalier Remounted: A Study of the Origins of Virginia's Population, 1607–1700," PhD Dissertation, University of Virginia, 1946; p. 28.

86. Leo Francis Stock, ed., *Proceedings and Debates of the British Parliaments Respecting North America*, 5 vols. (Washington, DC, 1924), 1:64, "Petition of the Virginia Company" (26 April 1624).

87. "A Letter of Advice Written to the Duke of Buckingham" (1616), in Bacon, *Works*, 13: 13–24, 21. Richard Hakluyt, *A Discourse of Western Planting* (1584), in *Collections of the Maine*

Historical Society, 2nd ser., 2:37 (1877). R. I. (Richard Johnson), *Nova Britannia* (1609), p. 19. The original sources are given here, but these quotations, along with twice as many more to the same point, are found in Knorr, pp. 42–4.

The opposing minority did not challenge the colony-makers on the fact of the surplus of common labor. Instead, they argued mainly from the following three principles: (1) that a large population was essential to the strength of the realm; (2) that colonies, once established, might become unwelcome competitors in the markets supplied from England; and (3) that emigration might seriously reduce the home supply of skilled workers.

88. "A Consideration of the Cause in Question before the Lords touching Depopulation," British Museum Mss., Cottonian Mss., Titus F, iv, ff. 322–3 (5 July 1607). Reprinted in Kerridge, pp. 200–203.

89. See *The Invention of the White Race*, Volume One, pp. 8–11, for my criticism of Winthrop Jordan's use of the term "unthinking decision" in his psycho-cultural explanation of the origin of racial slavery.

2 English Background, with Anglo-American Variations Noted

1. The religious issue in England, which culminated in the overthrow of the Catholic King James II, and which paralleled the establishment of the racial oppression of Catholics in Ireland, had its echoes in Maryland, which was founded as a proprietary colony of Catholic convert George Calvert (c. 1580–1632). A number of Protestant rebellions, interlinked with class conflict, were launched in the province, with varying degrees of success, against a succession of Lords Baltimore, until 1715 when the third Lord, Charles Calvert, converted with his family to the Protestant religion. The difference between the fate of Catholics in Maryland and of those in Ireland is betokened by the fact that the land holdings of Maryland Catholics remained intact, even in the 1691–1715 period when the Calvert proprietorship of the colony was revoked on religious grounds. In Ireland, as has been discussed in Volume One, the Catholic landowning class was systematically expropriated by Protestants under the Protestant Ascendancy regime of racial oppression. Irish Catholics brought to Maryland as chattel bond-laborers did become the occasion for expressions of ruling-class alarm, principally because of the worry that they would join the African-American bond-laborers in class solidarity.

2. See Part Two below.

3. Adam Smith, *An Inquiry into the Nature and Causes of the Wealth of Nations* (London: Ward, Lock & Co., n.d.), Book III, Chapter IV, p. 329.

Karl Marx, Thorold Rodgers, R. H. Tawney and Rodney Hilton present a more sober view. Tawney's concluding eloquence on this point should not be missed. (R. H. Tawney, *The Agrarian Problem in the Sixteenth Century* [New York, 1912] pp. 406–8.)

Eric Kerridge (*Agrarian Problems in the Sixteenth Century* [London, 1969], Introduction), however, thinks that Tawney sacrificed scholarship to the social dogma to which Tawney supposedly adhered as a member of the Fabian Society and the Labour Party. By portraying capital as relentless and remorseless, as the violator of common-law rights of peasants, and as the perpetrator of giant exploitation of man by man. Tawney – as Kerridge sees it – led "whole generations of history students into grievous error."

For a sharp counter-criticism of Kerridge, see Lawrence Stone in the *Times Literary Supplement*, 2 October 1970, pp. 1135–6.

4. A paraphrase of Tawney, p. 264.

5. Estimates range from 20 percent mortality (Josiah Cox Russell, "Demographic Patterns in History" *Population Studies*, no. 1, 1948) to possibly half (J. H. Clapham and Eileen Power, eds., *The Agrarian Life of the Middle Ages* [Cambridge, UK, 1944], Volume I of *Cambridge Economic History of Europe*, p. 512).

The preamble of the 1349 Statute of Labourers posed the feudal lords' problem more adequately than the remainder of the law served to assuage it: "Because a great part of the people, and especially workmen and servants, late died of the pestilence, many seeing the necessity of masters and the great scarcity of servants, will not serve unless they may receive excessive wages." (23 Edw. III, *The Statutes at Large from Magna Charta to the forty-first year of the reign of King George, the Third, inclusive* [London, 1786–1800].)

6. See Appendix II-B, on Wat Tyler's Rebellion. Historians such as Charles Dobson (*The*

Peasant Revolt of 1381 [London, 1970], p. 30) question the importance of the revolt as a factor in bringing an end to feudalism in England. Yet Dobson concedes that in the following century "tenants did not find it impossible to resist pressure from their landlords."

Thorold Rogers, on the other hand, declares that, "the gradual emancipation of the serfs [dates] unquestionably from the great Insurrection [of 1381] .... The peasant of the fourteenth century struck a blow for freedom ... and he won." (Thorold Rogers, *Economic Interpretation of History* [London, 1889] pp. 31 and 82.) Rodney Hilton's *Bond Men Made Free: Medieval Peasant Movements and the English Rising of 1381* (London, 1973) presents an equally sympathetic discussion of the revolt, but takes note of fateful shortfalls in its accomplishments.

7. Rogers coined the term (p. 82).

8. W. H. R. Curtler, *The Enclosure and Redistribution of Our Land* (Oxford, 1920), p. 117.

9. "It is not easy to discover any economic reason why the cheap wool required for the development of the cloth manufacturing industry should not have been supplied by the very peasants in whose cottages it was carded and spun and woven" (Tawney, p. 407).

10. The peasants in Ket's Rebellion put forward a program which, had they won, would have given a severe check to the ascendancy of the bourgeoisie. (See S. T. Bindoff, *Ket's Rebellion, 1549* [London, 1949], Historical Association, General Series G. 12.)

11. Tawney, p. 318.

12. Ibid., p. 333.

13. For the most comprehensive treatment of this event, see Madeleine Hope Dodds and Ruth Dodds, *The Pilgrimage of Grace, 1536–1537 and the Exeter Conspiracy, 1538* (Cambridge 1915), 2 vols.

14. J. D. Mackie, *The Earlier Tudors* (Oxford: Clarendon Press, 1952), p. 385.

15. Dodds and Dodds, 1:220 and 2:225–6. Tawney, pp. 334–35.

16. Tawney, p. 11.

17. Gilbert Bernet, *History of the Reformation* (originally published in 1679–81 and 1714; republished Oxford: Clarendon Press, 1865; 3 vols., cited in George L. Craig and Charles Macfarlane, *The Pictorial History of England, being a History of the People as well as a History of the Kingdom*, 4 vols. (New York, 1843), 2:464. Edwin F. Gay, "The Midland Revolt and the Inquisition of Depopulation of 1607," *Transactions of the Royal Historical Society*, Vol. 18 (1904): 195–214; p. 203 n. 2. John Hales, *The Discourse of the Common Weal*, edited by E. Almond (circa 1549) (London, 1893), p. viii. [Raphael] Holinshed, *Chronicles of England, Scotland and Ireland* (originally published 1577; London, 1808; AMES Reprint [New York, n.d.]), 3:963–85 (Holinshed's account of Ket's Rebellion).

18. Tawney, pp. 335–7. Bindoff, *Ket's Rebellion*, p. 9. The quotation is from Bindoff. (Although "privatizing" is my own anachronism, it seems appropriate for this earlier process of "the rich stealing the property of the poor.")

The government did make a notable concession in response to the demands of the rebels, although it proved to be a time-limited and fundamentally ineffectual one. Two years after Ket's Rebellion, Parliament enacted a law (5 & 6 Edw. VI 5) requiring that as much land be established in tillage as was in tillage in the first reign of Henry VIII (1509). This law was repealed a decade later by 5 Eliz. 2. (E. M. Leonard, "The Enclosure of Common Fields in the Seventeenth Century," in E. M. Carus-Wilson, ed., *Essays in Economic History* 3 vols. (New York, 1966), 2:227–56; p. 242 n. 65.)

19. Edwin F. Gay, "The Midland Revolt and the Inquisitions of Depopulations of 1607," *Transactions of the Royal Historical Society*, 18:195–244 (1904); pp. 212, 216 n. 3, and 240.

An interesting example of how in formulating a deliberate policy of social control, ruling-class concessions were weighed against the danger of encouraging rising expectations, is to be noted in a House of Lords commentary following the Midlands anti-enclosure revolt of 1607. If indeed "depopulation" was to be adjudged the cause of the revolt, the House of Lords wondered "Whether time may be fit to give remedy, when such encouragement may move the people to seek redress by the like outrage, and therefore in Edward the sixth his time was not pursued until two years after the rebellion of Kett." (Kerridge, pp. 200–203; p. 200, Document No. 27 [British Museum, Cottonian Manuscripts, Titus F. iv, ff. 322–3, "A Consideration of the Cause in Question before the Lords touching Depopulation," July 6, 1607].)

20. Curtler, p. 117.

21. Robert Brenner, "Agrarian Class Structure and Economic Development in Pre-industrial Europe,' *Past and Present*, 70(1976):31–73; 63 n. 80.

22. D. C. Coleman, "Labour in the English Economy of the Seventeenth Century," in Carus-Wilson, ed., 2:291–308; 295 (originally published in *Economic History Review*, 2nd ser., 8(1956),

no. 3). Sir John Clapham, *A Concise History of Britain from the Earliest Times to 1750* (Cambridge, 1949; Princeton, 1963), pp. 212–13. "By no means the least burden of complaint," writes Kerridge (p. 132), "was that family farmers were deprived of their livings and replaced by wage workers."

23. E. H. Phelps-Brown and Sheila V. Hopkins, "Seven Centuries of Building Wages," in Carus-Wilson, ed. 2:168–78; pp. 177–8 (originally published in *Economica*, vol. 22 [1955]). E. H. Phelps-Brown and Sheila V. Hopkins, "Seven Centuries of the Prices of Consumables compared with Builders' Wage-Rates" in Carus-Wilson, ed., 2:178–96; pp. 194–6. (originally published in *Economica*, vol. 23 [1956]).

24. Peter Laslett, *The World We Have Lost* (New York, 1965), pp. 14–15.

25. Francis Bacon, *The History of the Reign of King Henry Seventh*, in *Works*, 6:124. Laslett, pp. 14–15. Coleman, 2:295.

In 1688, Gregory King estimated that of the total English population of 5,500,000, nearly one-fourth, or 1,300,000, were just such "cottagers and paupers" (Gregory King, "A Scheme of the Income and Expense of the several Families of England calculated for the year 1688," in Jan Thirsk and J. P. Cooper, eds., *Seventeenth-century Economic Documents* [Oxford, 1972], pp. 780–81).

26. Phelps-Brown and Hopkins ("Wage-Rates and Prices: Evidence for Population Pressure in the Sixteenth Century," *Economica*, 24(1957): 289–306) relate this question specifically to the wage earners, but I have taken the liberty of giving it more general reference. The term "upheaval" is not precise, although the peasant revolts of 1536, 1549 and 1607 certainly qualify for that term. But an "upheaval" sufficient to check the ascendance of the bourgeoisie and its heedless and heartless expropriation and impoverishment of the laboring people did not occur. It is in this broader sense that I wish the matter to be understood in the discussion that follows concerning the establishment of bourgeois social control.

Rodney Hilton, a historian who identifies emotionally with the peasant rebels, traces their defeat in the sixteenth century to the fourteenth-century "failure of the rebels [behind John Ball and Wat Tyler in 1381] to end villeinage and to extend the rights of free tenure [as against mere manorial copyhold rights] to all tenants." Such a thorough sweep, he maintains, "would have meant the end of manorial jurisdiction . . . [and] it would have involved the removal of all cases about land to the common law courts. . . . At one stroke the material basis for deference and the respect for the hierarchy which had dogged the English rural masses for centuries would have been removed." (Hilton, pp. 232 and 224).

The "long" sixteenth century might be taken to mean roughly 1500–1640. For a discussion of this concept, see I. W. Wallerstein, *The Modern World-System: Capitalist Agriculture and the Origins of the European World-Economy in the Sixteenth Century* (New York, 1974), pp. 67–9.

27. These gradations related to the degree of security of the tenant's claim to the land. See Tawney, Chapter III; Kerridge, Chapter 2; and Mildred Campbell, *The English Yeoman Under Elizabeth and the Early Stuarts* (New Haven, 1942), Chapter IV.

28. The term "forty-shilling freeholder" was first defined by Thomas Littleton, in his treatise on *Tenures*, near the end of the fifteenth century. Strictly interpreted, it would mean a person free of personal labor obligations to any lord, and holding a hereditary lease on lands yielding at least forty shillings' annual income. While the land-income qualification remained constant, the term came to be not so strictly applied in other respects.

29. See Tawney, pp. 340–44. "It was an essential feature of Tudor policy to foster the prosperity of the yeomanry, from whose ranks were recruited the defenders of the realm" (Ephraim Lipson, *The Economic History of England*, 3 vols. [London, 1926, 1931, 1931]; 1:141).

30. Francis Bacon, *History of the Reign of King Henry VII*, in Francis Bacon, *Works*, 6:28–245; pp. 93–5.

31. Ibid., 6:95.

32. Though the producer "intends only his own security . . . [and] only his own gain, . . . he is . . . led by an invisible hand to promote an end which was no part of his intention" (Smith, *The Wealth of Nations*, Book IV Chapter 2, p. 354). But where does one's self-interest lie? In this yeoman-preserving policy, the English ruling class was drawing a distinction between the self-interest of the individual exploiter and the overriding self-interest of the exploiting class as a whole.

33. Bacon, *History of the Reign of King Henry VII*, in *Works*, 6:94.

34. Ibid., p. 219.

35. Campbell. Chapter IX, "For the Common Weal," is the general basis for this paragraph on the public functions of the yeomen.

36. Thomas Smith, *De Republica Anglorum, Discourse on the Commonwealth of England* (1583; 1906, edited by L. N. Alston; reprint New York, 1974), pp. 43–4.

37. Bindoff, p. 216. Joseph Clayton, *Robert Kett and the Norfolk Rising* (London, 1912), p. 217.

38. Gay, p. 216.

39. The Statute of Artificers, in *The Statutes at Large from Magna Charta to the forty-first Year of the Reign of King Goerge, the Third, inclusive* (London, 1786–1800).

40. The wage level, whether high or low, operates as an essential mechanism of social stability. The limits of its fluctuation, however, are set by the premises of the bourgeois social order itself. The formulation of this basic principle has not been improved upon since Sir Bernard de Mandeville first set it down in his *Fable of the Bees, or, Private Vices, Publick Benefits. With an Essay on Charity and Charity-Schools, and A Search into the Nature of Society*, 6th edition (London, 1732), pp. 193–4: "[T]hose that get their Living by their daily Labour ... have nothing to stir them up to be serviceable but their Wants, which it is Prudence to relieve but Folly to cure. The only thing then that can render [them] industrious, is a moderate quantity of Money; for as too little will ... either dispirit or make [them] Desperate, so too much will make [them] Insolent and Lazy.'

41. 25. Edw. III, Stat. 1, c. 1 (1351); 37 Edw. III, c. 6 (1363); 12 Richard II, c. 3–9 (1388); 13 Richard II, Stat. 1, c. 8 (1390); 6 Henry VI, c. 3 (1427); 8 Henry VI, c. 8 (1429); 23 Henry VI, c. 12 (1445); and 11 Henry VII, c. 72 (1495). In *The Statutes at Large from Magna Charta to the forty-first year of the Reign of King George, the Third, inclusive* (London, 1786–1800). See also W. E. Minchinton, ed. *Wage Regulation in Pre-Industrial England* (republished, New York: Barnes and Noble, 1972). This collection comprises works by R. H. Tawnet originally published in *Vierteljahrschrift fur Sozial- und Wirtschaftsgeschichte*, XI (1914), pp. 307–37 and 533–64; R. Keith Kelsall, "Wage Regulation under the Statute of Artificers" R. Keith Kensall, and, "A Century of Wage Assessment in Hertfordshire, 1662–1772," originally published in *English Historical Review*, vol. 57 (1942):115–19.

42. Phelps-Brown and Hopkins, in Carus-Wilson, ed., pp. 171, 177, and 194.

43. Rodney Hilton, ed., *The Transition from Feudalism to Capitalism* (London, 1978), p. 27.

44. 1 Edw. VI, 3. In *The Statutes at Large from Magna Charta to the forty-first year of the Reign of King George, the Third, inclusive*.

45. C. S. L. Davies, "Slavery and the Protector Somerset: the Vagrancy Act of 1547," *Economic History Review*, 2nd ser., 19:533–49 (1966); 535–6. "The 1547 act," says Davies, "was aimed at a wider target than those bands of wandering beggars which terrorized the Tudor countryside. The latter were a useful excuse to make palatable a policy of enforced employment, and, by implication at least, to reduce still further the worker's limited ability to bargain" (p. 536).

46. 1 Edw. VI, 3, *Statutes at Large from Magna Charta to the forty-first Year of the Reign of King George, the Third*.

47. 3 & 4 Edw. VI, 16, *Statutes at Large from Magna Charta to the forty-first year of the Reign of King George, the Third*.

48. Cited in Lipson, 1:149.

49. Cited in ibid.

50. Davies, pp. 547–8.

51. Tawney, p. 11.

52. John Cheke, "The Hurt of Sedition" (1549; republished, 1569), in Holinshed, 3:987–1011.

53. Davies, p. 546.

54. F. W. Russell, *Kett's Rebellion in Norfolk* (1859), p. 48; cited in Tawney, p. 337.

55. Bindoff, while calling it "the only resounding denunciation of villeinage ever heard in Tudor England," still thinks that it had no reference to the slavery provided by the 1547 law; he considered this rebel programmatic point as merely high-flown symbolic verbiage borrowed from the German peasant uprising of 1512 (*Bindoff*, pp. 12–13).

Diarmuid MacCullogh rejects Bindoff's speculation. He believes that the anti-bondage demand was narrowly directed against Thomas Howard, late Duke of Norfolk, who was much disliked for mistreatment of and refusal to manumit bondmen (villeins) on his East Anglia estates (Diarmuid MacCullogh, "Kett's Rebellion in Context," *Past and Present*, 84(1979):36–59; p. 55).

56. Davies, p. 547. The original voice was that of one Fitzherbert, *Description of England*, which Davies cites from E. R. Cheyney, "The Disappearance of English Serfdom," *Economic History Review*, vol. 15:20–37 (1900); 24.

57. Davies, p. 548.

58. Davies is here citing Charles Lyell, *A Second Visit to the United States*, 2 vols. (New York, 1849), 2:72. Davies's reference is by way of the citation in Kenneth Stampp, *The Peculiar Institution: Slavery in the Ante-bellum South* (New York, 1956), p. 399. I cannot expiain why Stampp's page reference differs from mine.

59. Davies, p. 544, citing ms. *Cecil Papers*, 152/96. But a century after the repeal of the 1547 law, it yet provided the model for the first Barbadian slave code. (Rev. George Wilson Bridges, *The*

Annals of Jamaica, 2 vols. [London, 1827], 1:507. Cited by Lewis Cecil Gray, assisted by Esther Katherine Thompson, *History of Agriculture in the Southern United States to 1860*, 2 vols. [Washington, DC, 1932], 1:347.)

60. R. H. Tawney, "The Assessment of Wages in England by the Justices of the Peace," in Minchinton, ed., *Wage Regulation in Pre-Industrial England*, pp. 47–53.

61. 5 Eliz. 4, "An Act touching the divers Orders for Artificers, Labourers, Servants of Husbandry and Apprentices." Good modern discussions of this statute are to be found in Minchinton, ed. and in S. T. Bindoff, "The Making of the Statute of Artificers," in S. T. Bindoff, J. Hurstfield, and C. H. Williams, eds., *Elizabethan Government and Society* (London, 1961), pp. 56–94.

62. Bindoff, "Making of the Statute of Artificers," p. 72.

63. The studies made by Phelps-Brown and Hopkins would indicate that the statute did not affect the trend in nominal or real wages. (See Carus-Wilson, ed., 2:168–96, especially pp. 177–78 and 193–96.) But Tawney's study of magistrates' records led him to believe that "it is probable that the practice of assessing wages tended to keep them low by setting up a standard to which the master could appeal, [but, he adds] it is also probable that it was evaded without much difficulty by the exceptionally competent journeyman, or by the master who was in difficulties through a shortage of labor" (Tawney, "Assessment of Wages," pp. 92–3).

64. 53 Geo. 3, c. 40, *Statutes of the United Kingdom*, p. 191, "Act to Repeal the Statute of Artificers." Reprinted in Joel H. Wiener, ed., *Great Britain, The Lion at Home, A Documentary History of Domestic Policy, 1689–1973*, 4 vols. (New York: Chelsea House Publishers in association with R. R. Bowker Company, 1974), 1:913.

65. The testimony of Sir Thomas Smith, who had himself been a major architect of the Statute of Artificers (see Davies, pp. 542–3), provides a catalog of degrees of servitude and freedom of labor as they had evolved in the sixteenth century: "Thus necessitie and want of bondmen hath made men to use free men as bondmen to all servile services: but yet more liberally and freely, and with more equalitie and moderation, than ... slaves and bondemen were wont to be used. This first [apprenticeship] and Latter [wage-labor] fashion of temporall [limited-term] servitude, and upon paction [mutual agreement of employer and employee] is used in all such countryes, as have left off the old accustomed man[n]er of servaunts, slaves, bondemen and bondwomen, which was in use before they received the Christian faith." (*De Republica Anglorum*, p. 139 [lib. 3, ch. 9].)

66. For instance Rogers (p. 38); Tawney ("Assessment of Wages," p. 49), and Marxists such as A. L. Morton (*A People's History of England*, 2nd edition [London, 1948], p. 173).

67. Matthew Bacon, *A New Abridgement of the Law*, 5 vols., 5th edition (Dublin 1786), p. 359, paragraphs 46–8. The remedy, "when any Man covenants to do a Thing, ... and that cannot be, then [he is] to render Damages for not doing of it."

68. Michael Dalton, *The Country Justice* (1619); edited, with an appendix, by William Nelson, London, 1727), p. 179.

69. Under certain unusual circumstances – such as the death of a master or the removal of his master to another place – the apprentice, if he were willing, might be put with another master, but the apprentice could not be compelled to accept the assignment against his will. (Dalton, pp. 222, 245; John Strange, *Reports of Adjudged Cases in the Courts of Chancery, King's Bench, Common Pleas and Exchequer*, second edition, 2 vols. [London, 1782], 2:266–7.)

70. In 1648 a promotional pamphlet for colonizing in Virginia was written by Beauchamp Plantagenet entitled, *Description of the Province of New Albion*. It was printed in Peter Force, ed., *Tracts and Other Papers Relating Principally to the Origin, Settlement, and Progress of the Colonies of North America from the Discovery of the Country to the Year 1776*, 4 vols. (Washington, DC, 1836–46); vol. 2, no. 7.

71. A number of modern historians, such as Edwin F. Gay, W. H. R. Curtler, and Eric Kerridge, stoutly maintain that the actual extent of the economic dislocation occasioned by the Agrarian Revolution was exaggerated in the original accounts, and subsequently by uncritical historians. To the present writer these objections seem narrowly based. However that may be, the fact remains that real wages declined from decade to decade throughout the sixteenth century and into the first decade of the seventeenth, when they were only 44 percent of what they had been in the first decade of the sixteenth century (Phelps-Brown and Hopkins, "... Prices of Consumables," 2:194–5). It is impossible to believe that such a catastrophic decline in real wages could have occurred without massive unemployment.

72. Tawney, p. 273, citing Historical Manuscripts Commission, *Marquis of Salisbury*, Part VII (November 1597, "Notes for the present Parliament").

73. These laws included 14 Eliz. 5 (1572) and 39 Eliz. 4, 5 and 17.

74. Preamble to 14 Eliz. 5 (1572), cited in George Nicholls, *A history of the Country and Condition of the People*, 3 vols. (supplementary volume by Thomas Mackay) (1898; 1904; Augustus M. Kelley reprint, 1967), 1:157.

75. Nicholls, 1:178, citing John Stow, *Survey of London and Westminster* (1598), book V, chapter 30.

76. Richard Hakluyt, *A Discourse of Western Planting* (1584), in *Collections of the Maine Historical Society*, 2nd ser., 2:37 (1877).

77. Nicholls, 1:178.

78. Sir Henry Knyvet, *The Defense of the Realme* (1596; Oxford, 1906), p. 11. Cited in Klaus E. Knorr, *British Colonial Theories 1570–1850* (Toronto, 1944), p. 43.

79. Nicholls, 1:188.

80. It was repealed by the National Assistance Act of 1948, Geo. 6, c. 29, Public General Statutes (1948), declaring that "The existing poor law shall cease to exist." Reprinted in Wiener, ed., 4:3553–9.

81. Nicholls, I:189–92.

82. E. M. Leonard, 255–6, citing *State Papers, Domestic*, Vol. 185, No. 86.

83. Tawney, pp. 275–6 and 280.

84. I cite but two examples: First, A Virginia law passed in April 1962 provided that "all horses, cattle, and hoggs" belonging to any African-American or other lifetime bond-laborer were, in default of the claim of the bond-laborer's owner, to be "forfeited to the use of the poore of the parish" through the good offices of the churchwardens. (Hening, 3:103.)

Second, under the provisions of a Maryland law of 1717, any free African-American who married a European-American, or any European-American marrying a free African-American, was to be taken and sold by the county court into a seven-year term of servitude, the proceeds of the sale to be "applied to a [whites only] Public School." (Thomas Bacon, comp., *Laws of Maryland at Large* [Annapolis, 1765], Chapter XIII, Section V.)

85. Male domination – the practice and the doctrine – is a social institution of such immemorial origin that both the makers and the recorders of history may have mistaken it for a natural condition, and thus outside the scope of their concerns. Except for those investigators specifically committed to exposing and abolishing the wrongs that women, as women, have been forced to bear, our historians have generally ignored the function of male supremacy as a basic element of ruling-class social control.

86. The unmarried adult woman ("feme sole") of the propertied classes was a partial exception, she having some limited individual rights with regard to property. But even so, because of the generally subordinate social status of women she would find her position extremely vulnerable if she attempted to capitalize on her property independently.

87. Of the 216 persons executed for treason for participating in the Pilgrimage of Grace, only one, Margaret Cheyne, Lady Bulmer, was burned at the stake. Many women had been involved in the ill-fated rebellion, and some of them more directly and deeply than Cheyne. But Henry VIII preferred to make examples rather than to carry through large-scale executions, and Lady Bulmer was vulnerable. She and her husband were true lovers; some of their children were born before she and John were married; and they remained faithful to each other to the end. According to the Dodds, Henry's aim was "an object lesson to husbands, which should teach them [women] to dread their husband's confidence" (Dodds and Dodds, 2:214 and 226).

Anne Boleyn, convicted of treason on charges instigated by her husband, Henry VIII, in 1636, after she had twice miscarried in an attempt to bear him his much-desired male heir, was treated with greater mercy than that shown to Margaret Cheyne a year later. Instead of being burned alive, Anne Boleyn was beheaded. A specially skilled executioner with his special French sword was brought from Calais for the occasion. Anne Boleyn privately insisted on her innocence to the end, but she abstained from doing so publicly for fear of bringing down the wrath of her husband on her daughter, Elizabeth, the future queen. (William Douglas Hamilton, ed., *A Chronicle of England During the Reign of the Tudors from AD 1485 to 1559, by Charles Wriothesley* [hereafter referred to as *Wriothesley's Chronicle*] 2 vols. [London: Camden Society, 1875 and 1877]).

But Henry's purpose was constant. When Anne Seymour, whom he married the day after Anne Boleyn's execution, pleaded with him to desist from his expropriation of church abbeys, a course that had brought on the beginnings of the Pilgrimage of Grace, Henry warned her against meddling in "his" affairs, and cowed her into silence by a direct reference to the fate of her predecessor (Dodds and Dodds, 1:108).

88. Unless otherwise noted, the comments made here on social relationships under feudalism in England are based on the following readings: (1) Paul Vinogradoff, *Villainage in England* (London,

1927), especially Chapter II, "Rights and Disabilities of the Villain," and Chapter V, "The Servile Peasantry and Manorial Records"; (2) idem, *The Growth of the Manor*, 2nd. edition (London, 1911), especially Book III, Chapter III, "Social Classes"; (3) H. S. Bennett, *Life on the English Manor* (London, 1948), especially pp. 240–44; (4) a legal discussion of the status of the serf *vis-à-vis* that of the lifetime bond-laborer in continental Anglo-America, set forth in a decision by Judge Daniel Dulany, of the Maryland Provincial Court, 16 December 1767; printed in Thomas Harris and John McHenry, *Maryland Reports, being a Series of the Most Important Cases argued and determined in the Provincial Court and the Court of Appeals of the then Province of Maryland from the year 1700 down to the American Revolution* (New York, 1809), 1:559–64, especially 560–61.

89. Once, during the days of the final paroxysms of English feudalism, an agent of the Duke of Norfolk (in order to promote a prosecution of interest to the Duke) entreated a certain widow whose testimony was to be required "to be my Lord's wewe [a form of the Anglo-Saxon word "widewe' (widow)] by the space of an whole year next following, and thereto he made her to be bound in an obligation." ("R. L. to John Paston," 21 October 1471, in John Warrington, ed., *The Paston Letters*, 2 vols. (London: Everyman, 1956), pp. 118–19. The editor notes that, "The widow of a feudal tenant was called the lord's widow."

In Roman times, the Latin term "nativus" was applied to the personally unfree, the born slave. In feudal England, its etymologically evolved form "naif" was reserved for the serf woman, thus emphasizing her doubly servile role, by virtue of class and gender. A man of the laboring classes, whether free or serf, was simply termed "villein."

90. At one point during the Pilgrimage of Grace, in 1536, non-gentlemen rebels sought to put this sort of upper-class concern to their own purposes, but in a way was equally informed with callous and cruel male supremacism. Having the Earl of Cumberland besieged in Skipton Castle in Yorkshire, these rebels threatened to use the Earl's two daughters and his daughter-in-law as shields in assaulting the castle; and if they failed in that, they said, they would "violate and enforce them with knaves unto my Lord's great discomfort" (Dodds and Dodds, 1:210, citing James Gairdner, ed., *Letters and Papers of Henry VIII*, [London, 1888], vol. XII [1], 1186).

91. Henry VIII justified it as a necessity for the "purity of the succession," when he had his second and fifth wives charged with "adultery," and executed. (*Wriothesley's Chronicle*, 1:xxxviii [Hamilton's introduction]). This was but a royal example; the same basic principles applied (though not with the same latitude of remedy) wherever women and inheritable property were present in conjunction.

92. Lawrence Stone, *The Crisis of the Aristocracy, 1558–1641* (London: Oxford University Press, 1967), pp. 200–205.

93. 1 Edw. VI, 3, *The Statutes at Large from Magna Charta to the forty-first year of the Reign of King George, the Third*. See also Davies, p. 534.

94. Documents relating to the assessment of wages for the East Riding of Yorkshire in 1593, Lancaster in 1595, and Rutland in 1610. (James E. Thorold Rogers, *A History of Agriculture and Prices*, 7 vols. in 8 [London, 1886–1902], 6:686–93.

95. Francis Bacon, "The Case of the Post Nati of Scotland" (1608), in *Works*, 7:641–79; pp. 644–6.

96. In "An Advertisement Touching An Holy War," an uncompleted dialogue written about 1618, Bacon has one of his characters pose a case which in his view would justify holy war: "Now let me put a feigned case (and yet antiquity makes it doubtful whether it were fiction or history) of a land of Amazons, where the whole government public and private, yea the militia itself, was in the hands of women. I demand, is not such a preposterous government (against the first order of nature, for women to rule over men) in itself void, and to be suppressed?" The speaker then goes on to link such a government with two others whose very existence would justify holy war for their destruction: ". . . for those cases, of women to govern men, sons the fathers, slaves freemen, are much in the same degree, all being perversions of the laws of nature and nations." (*Works*, 7:33).

Bacon understood: "And therefore Lycurgus [the great Spartan state-builder], when one councelled him to dissolve the kingdom, and to establish another form of estate, answered, 'Sir, begin to do that which you advise first at home in your own house;' noting, that the chief of a family is as a king; and that those that can least endure kings abroad, can be content to be kings at home" ("Case of the Post Nati of Scotland," *Works*, 7:633–4).

97. Dodds and Dodds, 2:216.

98. J. C. Jeafferson, ed., *Middlesex County Records*, 4 vols. (London, 1886–92), 1:lii–liii. Wynstone's social station is inferred from the fact that he is not accorded any distinguishing term of address.

99. I must not commit the error for which I have criticized Jordan and Degler, by making

sweeping assertions about the "English mind." All I mean here is that I have not come across records of any contemporaries of Bacon and Wynstone repudiating male privileges.

100. Virginia laws imposed a year of extra servitude for a male bond-laborer and two years for a woman bond-laborer for marrying without the consent of the owner, and laid a heavy fine on any minister who performed such a marriage. (Hening, 1:252–3 [1643]; 2:114 [1662].)

A Maryland man, together with his wife, was forced by impoverishment to enter into a seven-year term of bond-servitude. One day in 1748 when his wife was bound up to undergo a whipping by her overseer, the husband endeavored to loosen her bonds, avowing that he would untie her "If it cost me my life . . . for she is my lawfull Wife." He himself was severely beaten and the whipping proceeded. When he appealed to the county court for redress, his appeal was rejected. (Prince George's County Court Records, Book HH, 165–8, CR 34717, Maryland Hall of Records.)

101. In a previously mentioned decision (see *The Invention of the White Race*, Volume One, pp. 89, 90) handed down by the Maryland Provincial Court in 1767, Judge Dulany made this point clear in differentiating between the status of the English villein and the lifetime hereditary bond-laborer in Anglo-America. "If a neif married a freeman," he said, "she became free, it being the necessary consequence of her marriage, which placed her in the power of her husband [even though this] without doubt was an injury to the lord." But "slaves are incapable of marriage . . .," he said, and consequently "we do not consider them as the objects of such laws as relate to the commerce between the sexes. A slave has never maintained an action against the violator of his bed." (1 Harris and McHenry, Appendix, pp. 560, 561, 563.)

"To debauch a Negro woman they do not think fornication . . . they still have the feeling that the blacks at large belong to the whites at large." (Statement of Colonel Samuel Thomas, Assistant Commissioner, Bureau of Refugees, Freedmen, and Abandoned Lands for Mississippi, appended to the Report of Major General Carl Schurz to President Andrew Johnson, 27 July 1865, on "Conditions of the South," 39th Congress, 1st Session (1865–66), *Senate Executive Documents*, Vol. 1, p. 81.

As noted in *The Invention of the White Race*, Volume One (p. 148), a major motive of the Negro Exodus of 1879 was the necessity to escape the gross imposition of the white male privilege against black women in the South. See 46th Congress, 2nd Session (1879–80), Senate Report 693, *Report and Testimony of the Select Committee of the US Senate to Investigate the Causes of the Removal of the Negroes from the Southern States to the Northern States*; Part II, pp. 177–8; part III, pp. 382–3.

3 Euro-Indian Relations and the Problem of Social Control

1. Of sixty-eight mentioned by name, thirty-eight were "Council Members," and "Gentlemen" (*Travels and Works of Captain John Smith, President of Virginia and Admiral of New England*, 2 vols., edited by Edward Arber and A. G. Bradley [Edinburgh, 1910], 1:93–4. In subsequent references, this work will be abbreviated Smith, *Travels and Works*.)

2. "I came to get gold, not to till soil like a peasant!" Cortés replied when it was first suggested that he might receive a large grant of land in Cuba. (William H. Prescott, *History of the Conquest of Mexico and History of the Conquest of Peru* [New York: Modern Library, n. d.], p. 130.)

3. "Until 1622 each side [Virginia colonists and Powhatan Indians] tried to gain control over the other one." (Christian F. Feest, "Virginia Algonquians," in Bruce G. Trigger, ed., *Northeast*, Volume 15 of *Handbook of North American Indians*, William C. Sturdevant, General Editor, 20 vols. (Washington, DC: Smithsonian Institution, 1978–), 15:256.)

Waterhouse, Martin and Smith were speaking in the immediate aftermath of the massive attack made by the Powhatan Indians on the English settlement on 22 March 1622. (See Chapter 5.)

4. Edward Waterhouse, "A Declaration of the State of the Colony . . ." [1622], in Susan Myra Kingsbury, ed., *Records of the Virginia Company of London*, 4 vols. (Washington, DC, 1906–35); 3:541–79; 562–3 (hereafter abbreviated *RVC*). Waterhouse appears to have been right about the decline of Spanish silver and gold. The peak of receipts of bullion at Seville was reached in the early 1590s. (See J. H. Elliott, *Imperial Spain, 1469–1716* [New York, 1964], p. 175.)

5. See Gonzalo Aquirre Beltrán, "The Integration of the Negro into the National Society of Mexico," in Magnus Mörner, ed., *Race and Class in Latin America* (New York, 1970), p. 18.

6. *RVC*, 3:558–9.

7. John Martin, "The manner howe to bringe the Indians into subjection without makinge an utter exterpation of them . . ." [1622], in *RVC*, 3:704–7; 706.

8. Smith, *Travels and Works*, 2:579 (1622). A decade before he got to Virginia, Smith had been captured in battle against the Turks in Hungary and served in Turkey as a slave, eventually escaping through Russia. (Ibid., 1:360.)

9. Smith, *Travels and Works*, 2:955–6.

10. Anthropologist William M. Denevan remarks that he and other scholars in that field "more and more find a causal relationship between size of population and cultural change and evolution." (William M. Denevan, ed., *The Native Population of the Americas in 1492*, 2nd edition [New York, 1992], p. 235.) Though I am not an anthropologist, it seems to me that comparisons such as that between Portugal and Hispaniola suggest a more indirect relationship between population density and complexity of social structure; that both increasing population density and class differentiation are functions of the development of the productivity of labor. *If* the productivity of labor is such as to provide a storable surplus, population density may be higher *and*, moreover, a possibility of the seizure of power may exist through control of the surplus product by a segment of the society; then, and only then, is a basis for class differentiation present. Without the wheel and domesticated animals, the level of disposable surplus in Portugal would have made it as impossible as it was in contemporary Haiti for a parasitic leisure class to emerge. This is not meant to be the basis for a wider comparison; Noble David Cook points out that intensive agriculture with terracing and irrigation, like that of ancient Peru and in some places in the modern Far East, makes possible a higher level of labor productivity (generally expressed in calories per unit of cultivated area) than that achieved in some other places cultivated with domesticated animals and wheeled equipment.

11. Bartolomé de Las Casas, *Brevisima relación de la Destrución de las Indias* (written in 1539; first printed in Spain in 1552), edited by André Saint-Lu (Madrid, 1982), p. 72.

12. Las Casas commented sarcastically, that the Spanish *encomenderos*, who were supposed to care for the souls of the island natives, merely took "care ... to send the men into the mines, to make them drain out golde" (ibid., p. 84).

13. Charles Gibson, *Spain in America* (New York, 1966), pp. 51–2.

14. Las Casas, pp. 81–2.

15. Salvador Brau, *La Colonizacion de Puerto Rico, Desde el descumbrimiento de la Isla hasta la reversión a la corona española de los privilegios de Colón*, 4th edition (San Juan de Puerto Rico, 1969), pp. 142–63, 259.

16. Salvador Brau, *Ensayos: Disquicisiones Sociológicas* (Rio Piedras, 1972), p. 15. Dietz, *Economic History of Puerto Rico*, p. 6. Las Casas reported that the natives of Hispaniola also resisted the Spanish by inter-island flight (Las Casas, p. 83).

17. Comprising the present-day Mexican states of Vera Cruz, Oaxaca, Guerrero, Puebla, Tlaxcala, Morelos, Mexico, Hidalgo, Distrito Federal, Michoacán, Jalisco, Colima, and Nayarit, plus small portions of Zacatecas, Querétaro, and San Luis Potosi (William T. Sanders, "The Population of the Central Mexican Region, the Basin of Mexico, and the Teotihuacán Valley in the Sixteenth Century," in Denevan, p. 87.

18. Denevan, p. xxviii, Table 1.

19. "The Central Mexican Symbiotic Region," as it was termed by demographer William T. Sanders, comprises the present-day Distrito Federal and the states of Mexico and Morelos, plus southern Hidalgo, southwestern Tlaxcala, and the western third of Puebla (Sanders, in Denevan ed., p. 87). For population and population density figures, see ibid., pp. 130–31, Table 4.9. To convert square kilometers to square miles, divide by 2.59.

20. Woodrow Borah and S. F. Cook, *The Population of Central Mexico in 1548*, p. 7. The Aztec Empire was an alliance of three city states in the Valley of Mexico, composed of Tenochitlan (Mexico City), Tezcoco, and Tlacopan.

21. Borah and Cook, pp. 57, 66–67.

22. Gibson, p. 149. In another work, Gibson's glossary defines *cacique* as an Aztec "Indian chief or local ruler." (Charles Gibson, *The Aztecs under Spanish Rule: A History of the Indians of the Valley of Mexico, 1519–1810* [Stanford, California, 1964], p. 600). According to the dictionary, *cacique* originated as a Haitian word. Clement R. Markham, writing of the *caciques* of Peru, tends to this view, but he allows the possibility that it derived from the Arabic term for chieftain, *sheikh*, which the Spanish adapted for Hispaniola. (Clement R. Markham, *A History of Peru* [1892; reprinted, New York, 1968], p. 156.)

Socially subordinate to the Aztec *caciques*, but still free, were the commoners, the land-owning but tribute-paying *macegual* class. The social attributes of this class – their relatively substantial numbers, their wide distribution, and their direct contact with the serf-like *mayeques* – were characteristics typical of a buffer social control stratum. But I do not know whether they actually functioned as such. (See Borah and Cook, pp. 8, 60.)

23. Gibson, *Aztecs Under Spanish Rule*, pp. 78–80.

24. Gibson, *Spain in America*, p. 149.

25. Ibid., p. 149.

26. Ibid., pp. 150–51.

27. Markham, p. 156.

28. See ibid., p. 157; Lynch, *The Hispanic World in Crisis and Change*, pp. 330–31.

29. James Lockhart, *Spanish Peru, 1532–1560: A Colonial Society* (Madison, 1968), p. 210.

30. Markham, pp. 145–6, 152. At the ceremonial banquet in Lima, Sayri Tupac fingered the richly fringed table covering, saying, "All this cloth and fringe were mine, and now they give me a thread of it for my sustenance and that of all my house." Returning to his own ancient capital, Cuzco, he languished in melancholy and died not long after. (Ibid., p. 146.)

31. The sheer population decline eventually diminished the importance of these executors of the colonial labor supply system. Between 1650 and 1680, say Borah and Cook, "much of the Indian nobility [in Mexico] . . . vanished into the general mass of commoners which had become too small for supporting an upper [Indian] stratum." (*The Population of Central Mexico in 1548*, p. 65.) I do not intend to pursue the matter of the history of the replacement of this Indian *cacique* class as the intermediate stratum, beyond referring to the finding of T. R. Fehrenbach that in Mexico this role came to be played by descendants of European fathers and non-European mothers. (T. R. Fehrenbach, *Fire and Blood: A History of Mexico* [New York, 1973], pp. 238, 240.)

32. Borah and Cook, pp. 59–60; Lynch, p. 305. One would hope that Fehrenbach intended to allow room for an ironic interpretation of his characterization of the Chichimec resistance as "merely the savage struggles . . . against advancing civilization." (Fehrenbach, p. 217.)

33. Markham, pp. 93–6.

34. After the defeat of the rising, the Spanish beheaded the young Tupac Amaru on 4 October 1571, after instructing him in the Christian religion and baptizing him. (Markham, pp. 152–3.)

35. Five years after Bacon's Rebellion, Virginia Governor Thomas Culpeper made that point in his appeal to the English government for the continued maintenance of two companies of soldiers in Virginia to prevent a renewal of rebellion. "There is a vast difference [he wrote] between Virginia and Jamaica, Barbados and all other Island Plantations, by its situation on the Terra Firma. They have little to fear whilst England is Master of the Sea . . . [In island colonies] there is no shelter or hopes for Rebels to escape long unpunished." (Culpeper to the Lords of Trade and Plantations, 25 October 1681. In Great Britain Public Record Office, Colonial Papers, CO 5/1355, pp. 407–9; 407.)

36. Charles R. Boxer, *The Portuguese Seaborne Empire 1415–1825* (New York, 1969), p. 86.

37. Richard Graham, *The Jesuit Antonio Vieira and his Plans for the Economic Rehabilitation of Seventeenth-century Portugal* (São Paulo, 1978), p. 29.

38. Mathias C. Kieman, *The Indian Policy of Portugal in the Amazon Region, 1614–1693* (Washington, DC, 1954), p. 181.

39. Graham, p. 30. Justification was found for holding still other Indians captured in "just wars" (ibid.).

40. Boxer, p. 88.

41. Kieman, p. 184.

42. See ibid., pp. 181–6.

43. A similar effort was made, but ultimately failed, in Spanish Florida, where, writes Robert L. Gold, "the [Franciscan] mission rather than the *encomienda* became the institutional structure upon which colonial power rested." "The indigenous peoples, and territories of Florida," he continues, "were integrated within a system of missions which offered the Spaniards the typical opportunities of expansion, exploitation and proselytization." Robert L. Gold, *Borderline Empires in Transition: The Triple-Nation Transfer of Florida* [Carbondale and Edwardsville, Illinois, 1969(?)], pp. 6–7.

44. António José Saraiva, *História e Utopia, Estudos sobre Vieira* (Lisbon, 1992), pp. 56–7.

45. See Stuart B. Schwartz, "Indian Labor and New World Plantations: European Demands and Indian Responses in North-eastern Brazil," *Journal of American History*, 83:43–79 (1978); 45–7. It was a society characterized by "[a] communal or reciprocal attitude toward production and consumption, a domestic mode of production, a society on [in?] which status was not derived from economic ability" (p. 47).

46. In the following argument, I have relied upon the analysis by Helen C. Rountree and the criteria she has adapted from Mary R. Haas defining strong rulership (Helen C. Rountree, *Powhatan Indians of Virginia: Their Traditional Culture* [Norman, Oklahoma, 1989], especially Chapter 6, "Social Distinctions"); upon Feest, in *Handbook of North American Indians*, 15:256–62;

and upon Philip Alexander Bruce, *Economic History of Virginia in the Seventeenth Century*, 2 vols. (New York, 1895; reprinted 1935), 1:149, 157, 168, 175, 178.

47. This thesis is anticipated in *The Invention of The White Race*, Volume One, pp. 12–13, 23–4, 69–70, and Appendix G. It must be understood that the distinction made here – between societies with and without the intermediate stratum – is different from that between kinship and non-kinship societies. Kinship societies may in some cases be class-stratified, even though the two patterns of social division – kinship and class – are contradictory to each other. (See the discussion of Irish tribal society in Volume One.)

48. Maurice A. Mook, "The Aboriginal Population of Tidewater Virginia," *American Anthropologist*, 46:193–208 (1944); pp. 206–7. Mook considers valid John Smith's estimate that the indigenous population numbered 5,000 within a sixty-mile radius of Jamestown. (Smith, *Travels and Works*, 1:360.) This was the most densely populated area of the "South Atlantic Slope" region, wherein the total Powhatan Confederacy numbered some 8,000, in an area of 0.89 inhabitants per square mile, compared with 0.43 per square mile for the entire region. Other scholars present somewhat different estimates, on the basis of different population numbers and territorial extent, ranging as high as just over two persons per square mile. (Rountree, p. 143 and Feest, in *Handbook of North American Indians*, 15:256.) The most important primary sources in this regard are John Smith, *Map and Description of Virginia* (1612) and William Strachey, *Historie of Travaile into Virginia Britannia* (c. 1616), in Smith, *Travels and Works*.

It should be noted that, from the vantage of a consciousness raised by the civil rights struggles of the 1960s, anthropologists and historians have critically reexamined the scholarly European-American estimates of the population north of the Rio Grande prior to the contact with the exotic diseases of the Europeans. They have persuasively argued that the actual numbers were some ten times greater than those given by earlier authorities. For examples of the earlier ethnography see: James Mooney, "The Powhatan Confederacy, Past and Present," *American Anthropologist*, 9:128–30; idem, "The Aboriginal Population North of Mexico," in *Smithsonian Miscellaneous Collections, LXXX, No. 7* (1928), edited by J. R. Swanton, pp. 1–40; and A. L. Kroeber, *Cultural and Natural Areas of Native North America*, University of California Publications in American Archaeology and Ethnology, XXXVIII (Berkeley and Los Angeles, 1939). For examples of recent critical examinations of the subject, see: Francis Jennings, *The Invasion of America: Indians, Colonialism and the Cant of Conquest* (Chapel Hill, 1975); Sherburne F. Cook, "The Significance of Disease in the Extinctions of the New England Indians," *Human Biology*, 45:485–506 (1973); and Henry F. Dobyns, "Estimating Aboriginal American Population: An Appraisal of Techniques with a New Hampshire Estimate," *Current Anthropology*, 7:395–416 (1966).

49. "It pleased God, after a while to send those people which were our mortall enemies to releeve us with victuals, as Bread, Corne, Fish, and Flesh in great plentie . . . otherwise wee had all perished. Also wee were frequented by diverse Kings in the Countrie, bringing us store of provision to our great comfort." (George Percy's *Discourse* [1608?], in Philip L. Barbour, *The Jamestown Voyages Under the First Charter, 1606–1609*, 2 vols. [Cambridge, 1969], 1:145.)

50. Rountree, p. 143.

51. The possibility of a Mexican-style *encomienda* and *hacienda* form of sedentary labor reserve never arose. But if it had, it would surely have proved unsuitable for the constant westward-rolling cycle of clearing and transplanting characteristic of the tobacco monoculture to which the Chesapeake colonies were committed almost from the moment, around 1618, when the bourgeoisie got the first whiff of its profitable possibilities. Of Mexico and Peru, Gibson says: "Native agriculture was little affected by European techniques or crop innovations . . ." (*Spain in America*, p. 142.)

52. Though veteran soldiers were important in the Company period of Virginian history which ended in 1624, the colony was by no means primarily a military force. They certainly had no cavalry. When Hernado Cortes sailed from Cuba to invade Mexico, his forces included 110 mariners and 553 soldiers (including 32 crossbowmen and 13 men with firearms) plus 200 Cuban Indian auxiliaries. The force brought 10 heavy guns, four lighter pieces, well furnished with ammunition, and sixteen cavalry horses. (Prescott, pp. 145, 157.)

53. Wesley Frank Craven, *The Dissolution of the Virginia Company, the Failure of a Colonial Experiment* (New York, 1932), pp. 167–8.

"The argument of technological superiority at that time was a weak one; despite guns and large ships, the Europeans could not wrest a living from a terrain which, by English standards, supported an exceptionally large population." (Nancy Oestreich Lurie, "Indian Cultural Adjustment to European Civilization," in James Morton Smith, ed., *Seventeenth-Century America, Essays in Colonial History* [Chapel Hill, 1959] pp. 33–60; 39.)

54. "The appearance of the English was probably far less alarming [to the Indians] than 350 years of hindsight indicate it ought to have been" (Lurie, p. 36).

55. "There was never any real chance of holding the English back after 1646 ..." (Helen C. Rountree, *Pocahontas's People: The Powhatan Indians of Virginia through Four Centuries* [Norman, Oklahoma, 1990], p. 89.)

56. "Treaty of Peace with Necotowance, king of the Indians," 5 October 1646 (Hening, 1:323–6).

57. See *The Invention of The White Race*, Volume One, pp. 36–8.

58. Ibid., pp. 52–3.

59. Hening, 2:15–16 (11 October 1660).

60. Hening, 2:346, 404, 440; Hening, 4:10, 102.

61. Almon Wheeler Lauber, *Indian Slavery in Colonial Times within the Present Limits of the United States* (New York, 1913), pp. 108–9, 123–5.

62. See tabulations of peltry exports from Carolina and Virginia and the prices of various trade goods in the early eighteenth century in Verner W. Crane, *The Southern Frontier, 1670–1732* (Durham, North Carolina, 1928), Appendices A and B.

63. "The native tribes were encouraged [by South Carolina traders] to make war on one another and to sell their prisoners to the colonists." (Lewis C. Gray, assisted by Esther K. Thompson, *History of Agriculture in the Southern United States to 1860* [Washington, DC, 1932; 1958 reprint]. p. 361.) See also: Lauber, pp. 170–71; 183–4; 184 n. 1; 286; Gary B. Nash, *Red, White and Black: The Peoples of Early America* (Englewood Cliffs, New Jersey, 1974), pp. 116–17; Chapman James Milling, *Red Carolinians* (Chapel Hill. 1940), p. 87.

64. A section of the Cherokee Indians complained in 1715 that if they complied with English Yamassee War policy by ceasing to make war on the Creek tribe, "they should have no way in getting Slaves to buy ammunition and Clothing" (Crane, p. 182).

65. Nash, p. 152.

66. See note 61.

67. Ibid., pp. 283–9.

68. No separate comment on the second thesis is attempted; it will be briefly noted in the context of the discussion of the third thesis. (See note 122.) Lauber's fourth thesis seems consistent with the argument I am presenting.

69. Stuart B. Schwartz, "Indian Labor and New World Plantations: European Demands and Indian Responses in Northeastern Brazil," *Journal of American History*, 83:43–79 (1978); pp. 76–8.

70. Kiemen, p. 183. See also Graham, pp. 28–31, 34–35; the quoted phrase, used in a letter written by Vieira to Portugal's King John in May 1653, is at page 28. Charles Edward Chapman, *Colonial Hispanic America: A History* (New York, 1933), p. 80.

71. Lauber, pp. 173–4.

72. The preamble of the first (1712) South Carolina slave law justifies its enactment on the ground of the "barbarous, wild, savage natures" of Negroes and Indians. Richard Hildreth, *The History of the United States of America from the Discovery of the Continent to the Organization of Government under the Federal Constitution, 1497–1789,* 3 vols. (New York, 1848), 2:271–2.

Alexander Stephens, who became the Vice-President of the slaveholders' Confederacy, declared that the Confederacy was founded on "the great truth, that the negro is not equal to the white man; that slavery – subordination to the superior race – is his natural and normal condition." (Savannah Georgia speech, 21 March 1861, quoted in Michael P. Johnson, *Toward a Patriarchal Republic: The Secession of Georgia* [Baton Rouge, 1977] p. 125.) See Volume One of *The Invention of the White Race*, p. 287 n. 15, for other examples.

73. William C. Sturtevant, "Creeks into Seminoles," in Eleanor Burke Leacock and Nancy Oestreich Lurie, eds., *North American Indians in Historical Perspective* (New York, 1971), p. 101. Nash, p. 117.

74. Lauber, p. 171.

75. Ibid., pp. 169, 174.

76. Ibid., pp. 126–7.

77. Bruce, 2:385, 386; Nash, p. 112.

78. Bruce, 1:572–3.

79. Lauber, pp. 108, 187. Governor Berkeley reported that there were 2,000 "black slaves" in Virginia in 1671. (Samuel Wiseman's Book of Record, 1676–77, Magdalene College, Cambridge, Pepysian Library, document 2582.) He did not offer an estimate of the number of Indian slaves. Lauber does not seem to be justified in implying that Berkeley included Indian slaves in the 2,000 figure. (Lauber, p. 108.)

80. Indeed, Lauber says, "it would seem that the supply was sufficient to nourish the system of

Indian slavery indefinitely ...''; he adds, however, that the Indian tribes were "generally remote from the English settlements." (Ibid., p. 283.)

81. Ibid., pp. 124–7.

82. The total population was 9,580, of whom only 41 percent were free persons (1,360 men, 900 women and 1,700 children). In addition to Indians, the bond-labor force included 4,100 Negroes (1,800 men, 1,100 women and 1,200 children), 43 percent of the total population, and 120 "whites", 60 men and 60 women. (Governor and Council of South Carolina to the Commissioners of Trade and Plantations, 17 September 1709. *CSP, Col.,* 24:466–9.)

83. Lauber, p. 106. Crane, pp. 112–13. I have not sought to check their respective sources to account for the substantial discrepancy between Lauber and Crane regarding the number of African-Americans (Lauber 4,100; Crane: 2,900).

84. Lauber, pp. 124–7.

85. Ibid., p. 106. Lauber in this instance was referring to South Carolina but, as has been noted, the same policy was followed in other colonies.

86. Ibid., pp. 169, 174. Crane, p. 113.

87. Crane, p. 113. Lauber, 245.

88. Nash, p. 155.

89. There is at least one record referring to Carolina chiefs as "cassiques" (Crane, p. 137). The cited sources are (1) CO 5/288, p. 100, *Report of the Committee, Appointed to examine into the Proceedings of the People of Georgia* [1737], and (2) Collections of the South Carolina Historical Society, 5:456, n. But in terms of the colonial power social control function, there was a fundamental difference between the Carolina chiefs and the Mexican and Peruvian *caciques*; the Carolina chiefs were in no position to recruit from their own tribes bond-laborers for the colonizing power.

90. The space advantage could be limited in special circumstances, as in the case of the Appalachees and, later, the Seminoles, on the Florida peninsula; and that of the Wampanoags cut off by the English-allied Mohicans of New York in the 1675–76 Metacom War. See Nash, p. 127; and Sturtevant, p. 75.

91. Milling, p. 86. The Delaware were by then under the hegemony of the Iroquois. (Ibid.) See also Nash, p. 118.

92. The Creeks moved away from the English in 1717. (Sturtevant, p. 101.) The Tuscarora plan to migrate to Pennsylvania failed in 1711 because they were not able to get timely approval from the Quakers there. (Nash, p. 147.)

93. A portion of the Wampanoags merged into the Mohicans after defeat in the Metacom War, 1675–76; and the Delaware tribe was formed by a number of remnants of other tribes. (T. J. C. Brasser, "The Coastal Algonkians," in Leacock and Lurie, eds., p. 75; The Natchez, after defeat by the French in the Lower Mississippi in 1730, "in small bands sought refuge with other southeastern tribes." (Nash, p. 109.)

94. The phrase was used by Ulrich Bonnell Phillips in contrasting the situations of Indians and Africans *vis-à-vis* the Anglo-American plantation colonists. (Ulrich Bonnell Phillips, *Life and Labor in the Old South* [Boston, 1929], p. 160)

95. Crane, p. 113.

96. William S. Willis, "Divide and Rule: Red, White and Black in the Southeast," *Journal of Negro History*, 48:157–76 (1963); p. 162.

97. Ibid., p. 161.

98. Ibid.

99. Ibid., p. 162.

100. Lauber, pp. 172, 172 n. 1. Kenneth Wiggins Porter, "Negroes on the Southern Frontier," *Journal of Negro History*, 33:53–18 (1948) pp. 59–62. Sturtevant, pp. 100, 101. Crane, pp. 255–6, 274. Willis, p. 159.

101. Crane, pp. 247–8.

102. Porter, pp. 67–8.

103. Crane, pp. 162–5.

104. Willis, p. 158.

105. For a highly informative dissertation on "Indian policy" of the English colonial governors and legislatures of New York and Maryland, and the involvement of Indian tribes in the rivalries of England, France, Holland and Sweden in the seventeenth century, see Francis Jennings, "Glory, Death, and Transfiguration: The Susquehannock Indians in the Seventeenth Century," *Proceedings of the American Philosophical Society*, 102:5–53 (1968).

106. Crane, pp. 254, 272–3, 275. "[I]t certainly is of the Highest Consequence that they [the Cherokees] should be engaged in Your Majesty's Interest, for should they once take another party,

not only Carolina, but Virginia likewise would be exposed to their invasion" (Commissioners of Trade and Plantations to King George I, 8 September 1721 [CO 324/10, pp. 367–8]).

The thesis that history repeats itself finds expression in the pithy colloquialism "What goes around comes around." History's cruel revisit to the Cherokees, the most "English" of all tribes, is briefly noted in *The Invention of the White Race*, Volume One, pp. 33–4, 37, and 243 n. 44.

107. CO 324/10, pp. 367–8. (8 September 1621).

108. Bruce, 2:115–16. Porter, pp. 59, 63. Willis, p. 169. Sandford Winston, "Indian Slavery in the Carolina Region," *Journal of Negro History*, 19:430–40 (1934); p. 439.

109. Nash, p. 294. He goes on to say, however, that the bounties offered "often evoked little response on the part of the Indians" (ibid.).

110. Willis, p. 163. See also Winston, p. 439.

111. Hening 1:325–6; a similar "agreement" was imposed in South Carolina following the 1711–12 Tuscarora War. (Winston, p. 439.)

An April 1700 treaty between the English colony of Maryland and the Piscataway Indians provided that "[i]n case any servants or slaves run away from their masters to any Indian towne in Oquotomaquah's territory, the Indians shall be bound to apprehend them and bring them to the next English Plantation; any Indian who assists fugitives shall make their masters such compensation as an Englishman ought to do in the like case." (*CSP, Col*, 18:150–52; 9 April 1700 Minutes of the Maryland Colony Council, a treaty between the Governor of Maryland and Oquotomaquah, Emperor of Piscataway.)

112. *CSP, Col.*, 18:150–52.

113. The critical significance of "nearness" informed an order issued by the South Carolina Proprietors in 1680, purposing to prohibit colonists from engaging in the Indian slave trade within 200 miles of Charles Town; two years later the exclusion zone was widened to 400 miles (Crane, pp. 138–9). The settlers on the ground, for whom at that time the Indian slave trade was the principal source of income, were able to evade and nullify such formal restrictions. But their disregard of the "nearness" principle would eventually become a major consideration in the ending of Anglo-American enslavement of Indians.

114. Milling, pp. 86–7.

115. In the extremity of its situation, the South Carolina Provincial government sent emissaries to Virginia to appeal for three hundred "white" volunteers. These recruits were to be paid 22s. 6d. per month. In addition, for each volunteer who came, the South Carolina Provincial government undertook to send one African-American woman to Virginia. (Milling, pp. 144, 146–7, 149.)

South Carolina Governor Charles Craven reported to the English government that he had enlisted about two hundred Afro-American men, "who with a party of white men and Indians are marching toward the enemy," the Yamassees. (*CSP, Col*, 28:228 [23 May 1715].) Noting the irony of the situation, Kenneth Porter commented on its uniqueness: "So far as I can discover, in no other part of the British colonies in North America were slaves so employed." (Porter, p. 55.)

116. Crane, p. 138.

117. *CSP, Col.*, 13: 331–2, Proprietors of Carolina to Governor Colleton, 18 October 1690.

118. Indian employees within the colony played an important part in the surprise Indian attack of Good Friday 1622. At the same time, the English credited an Indian employee with giving the English warning of the attack (*RVC*, 3:555).

119. "Colonial Papers," folder 30, item 29 (27 October 1709), Virginia State Archives, Richmond.

120. Hening 4:78. Morgan Poitiaux Robinson, *Virginia Counties, Those Arising from Virginia Legislation* (Richmond, 1916), p. 95.

121. William Byrd II of Westover to Mr Ochs, ca. 1735. *Virginia Magazine of History and Biography*, 9:225–8 (1902); 226. This periodical will hereafter be abbreviated *VMHB*.

122. Lauber's second thesis regarding the decline of Indian slavery involves not a reduction in the number of slaves but rather an official ethnic reclassification. Upon the birth of a child of an Indian bond-laborer whose other parent was an African-American, the Indian identity ended. Any such child was classified as a Negro, or "mustee," a corruption of the Spanish term *mestizo*. Lauber considers this erasure of the Indian identity simply a matter of the dominance of African genetic traits. (Lauber, p. 287.)

Lauber might better have considered the cases of African-American male bond-laborers who escaped to Indians beyond the boundaries of the colonies, and who "in most cases ... seemed to have disappeared into Indian society where they took Indian wives [and] produced children of mixed blood" (Nash p. 296). Two "disappearances," but in one case the "Indian" identity disappears; in the other, the Negro identity disappears. The disappearance of the Negro identity is by the normal assimilation of the immigrant. But the disappearance of the Indian identity does not involve immigration from one people to another. Rather, the official stripping-away of the Indian identity may be better understood in relation to the following three social control considerations: (1) it was a way of breaking the children from the Indian tribal stems, with the enhanced propensity for running away that such ties entailed; (2) it was a cheap way of formally accommodating the policy of discontinuance of the enslavement of Indians without losing any bond-laborers; and (3) it served to preserve and strengthen the system of white-skin privileges of the European-American colonists, first of all the presumption of liberty.

4 The Fateful Addiction to "Present Profit"

1. The periodicity is noted in Wesley Frank Craven, *The Dissolution of the Virginia Company* (New York, 1932) p. 47; Philip Alexander Bruce, *Institutional History of Virginia*, 2 vols. (New York and London, 1910), 2:229; Philip Alexander Brown, *The First Republic in America* (Boston and New York, 1898), Table of contents; and by others.

2. *RVC*, 3:98–99 (Virginia Company. Instructions to George Yeardley, 18 November 1618, *RVC*, 3:98–109). The document is also available in Jamestown 350th Anniversary Booklet, No. 4, *The Three Charters of the Virginia Company of London, 1606–1624*, with introduction by Samuel M. Bemiss, pp. 95–109, and in *Virginia Magazine of History and Biography*, 2:154–65 (July 1894). The title of this journal will hereafter be abbreviated *VMHB*. See also: Brown, p. 309; Lyman G. Tyler, *Narratives of Early Virginia, 1606–1625* (New York, 1907), "Proceedings of the Virginia Assembly, 1619," pp. 249–78; Craven pp. 52–54.

3. The well-known facts in this introductory paragraph are conveniently presented in William W. Abbot, *A Virginia Chronology, 1585–1783*, Jamestown 350th Anniversary Historical Booklet No. 4 (Williamsburg, 1957), pp. 1–11.

4. Brown, pp. 332 and 650. See also 2:633–6.

5. A corollary of the "germ" theory is found in the idea sometimes advanced that the history of the Company period offers a vindication of the "free enterprise" economic system as against the supposed "collectivism" of the efforts made during the first two phases of the Company period, namely up to 1618. A. E. Smith is one who subscribes to this view. In his standard general work in the field of "white servitude," as it is called, Smith sees the failure of the early efforts of the Virginia Company as due to a "kind of collective farming" approach: "The colony was saved because private individuals took over the activities formerly reserved for the company, and made the profits of the free planters themselves the basis of the settlement's life". (Abbot E. Smith, *Colonists in Bondage: White Servitude and Convict Labor in America, 1607–1776*, [Chapel Hill, 1947; New York, 1971] p. 14.)

Considering the dearth of material on the origin of chattel bondage during the Company period, however, Smith's brief discussion of it (pp. 6–16) is still valuable.

6. Philip A. Bruce, *Economic History of Virginia in the Seventeenth Century*, 2 vols. (New York, 1895), 1:586–7.

7. James C. Ballagh, *A History of Slavery in Virginia* (Baltimore, 1902), pp. 31–2.

8. Eric E. Williams, *Capitalism and Slavery* (Chapel Hill, 1944), p. 19.

9. Lerone Bennett Jr, *The Shaping of Black America* (Chicago, 1975), pp. 40–41.

10. For example: Charles M. Andrews, *The Colonial Period in American History*, 4 vols. (New Haven, 1914–1938); Wesley Frank Craven, *The Southern Colonies in the Seventeenth Century, 1607–1689* (Baton Rouge, 1949); idem, *Colonies in Transition, 1660–1713* (New York, 1967); and idem, *White, Red and Black, The Seventeenth-Century Virginian*; Carl N. Degler, *Out of Our Past* (New York, 1959 and 1970); Winthrop D. Jordan, *White Over Black, American Attitudes Toward the Negro, 1550–1812*, (Chapel Hill, 1968); Richard L. Morton, *Colonial Virginia*, 2 vols. (Chapel Hill, 1960); Edward D. Neill, *Virginia Carolorum* (Albany, NY, 1886); Herbert L. Osgood, *American Colonies in the Seventeenth Century*, 3 vols. (New York, 1904–1907); Thomas J. Wertenbaker *Patrician and Plebeian in Virginia* (Charlottesville, 1910); idem, *Virginia under the Stuarts* (Princeton, 1914); and idem, *The Planters of Colonial Virginia*, (Princeton, 1922).

11. By Russell R. Menard, in his works *Economy and Society in Early Colonial Maryland* (New York, 1985), especially pp. 191–201, 234–5, 268–9, 286, and "From Servants to Slaves: The Transformation of the Chesapeake Labor System," *Southern Studies*, 16:355–90 (1977); and by David W. Galenson in his "White Servitude and the Growth of Black Slavery in Colonial America," *Journal of Economic History*, 41: 39–47 (1981), in his *White Servitude in Colonial America: An*

Economic Analysis (New York, 1981), and in *Traders, Planters and Slaves: Market Behavior in Early English America* (New York, 1986).

As historians, Menard and Galenson are economists rather than political economists. The class struggle between laborers and employers does not enter at all into their discussions; indeed Menard spends a lot of time establishing the absence of class struggle, especially between poor and rich, bond-laborer and owner among European–Americans. They seem to presume that all the employer had to do was to decide that a given category of laborers was more advantageous to employers' interests, and that all else automatically followed. On this basis Menard challenges Edmund S. Morgan's attempt to suggest that racial oppression of the Negro was a deliberate decision by the ruling class. Menard and Galenson offer their presumption under the rubric of "the divided labor market." Job discrimination in early colonial times is rationalized by Menard and Galenson as a function of the common language of the English master and servant and the skills that the English workers brought with them to America. This discrimination was undergirded, Menard says, by "cultural barriers and the depth of racial prejudice." (*Economy and Society*, p. 270).

Menard and Galenson appear not to be disposed to look at the "white" identity objectively.

12. Cited here from Hening, 1:64; 95. This work will hereafter be cited as "Hening, [vol. no.]: [page no.]." See also: Jamestown 350th Anniversary Booklet, No. 4, *The Three Charters of the Virginia Company of London, 1606–1624*, with an introduction by Samuel M. Bemiss; and Brown.

13. Hening, 1:103.

14. See Table 5.1.

15. Charles E. Hatch Jr, *The First Seventeen Years, Virginia, 1607–1624*, Jamestown 350th Anniversary Booklet, No. 6 (Williamsburg, 1957), p. 10.

16. Brown, pp. 126–7.

17. "Coppie of A Letter from Virginia, Dated 22nd of June, 1607. The Councell there to the Councell here in England;" printed in Alexander Brown, *The Genesis of the United States* (Boston, 1890) 1:106–8; 107.

18. Bruce, *Economic History*, 1:588 n. 1.

19. Answers to a 1624 Royal Commission on "the reformation of Virginia" (Smith, *Travels and Works*, pp. 615–20; pp. 616, 618).

20. Brown, *First Republic* ("John Rolfe's Relation," [1616]), pp. 135, 144. Evarts B. Greene and V. D. Harrington, *American Population before the Federal Census of 1790* (New York, 1932), p. 135.

21. See Thomas Niccolls's complaint, p. 68.

22. Referring to the 1609 charter, Alexander Brown says: "this charter, it seems, was drafted by Sir Edwin Sandys, possibly assisted by Lord [Francis] Bacon" *Genesis*, 1:207.

23. Sir Fernando Gorges (1566–1647), an early venturer in American colonization schemes, took note of the predisposition of English mercenaries displaced by the (1603–24) peace with Spain to find employment of their talents in Virginia. The Spanish spy Molina reported from Virginia in 1613 rather disparagingly on the quality of the English soldiers there, while noting "the great assistance they have rendered in Flanders in favor of Holland, where some of them have companies [of soldiers] and castles" (Brown, *Genesis*, 2:649). From 1607 to 1627, from Captain Edward Maria Wingfield to Sir George Yeardley (second term), every head of the Virginia colony government, except Francis Wyatt (a kinsman by marriage of the Sandys clan), was a veteran of mercenary service in the Netherlands. They were, as was said of Yeardley, "truly bred in that university of Warre, and Lowe countries" (Brown, *Genesis*, 2:1065). Some also served against the Turks, and others against the Irish in the brutal plantation of Ulster. (See Brown, *Genesis* vol. 2, "Brief Biographies" of Delaware, Thomas Dale, Thomas Gates, George Percy, John Ratcliffe, John Smith, Winfield and Yeardley.) Gates and Dale each served in Holland, both before and after their terms as governor in Virginia. When Gates went to Virginia, he brought his company from the Netherlands to Virginia (by way of England) under the command of George Yeardley (Brown, *Genesis*, 2:895). Such references leave no doubt that such men constituted the chief supply source for the "Governors and Captaines for peace and war" which the Company was sending to Virginia in this period. (The quoted phrase is from "Briefe Declaration of the State of Things in Virginia," by the King's Council for Virginia [1616] [Brown, *Genesis*, 2:775–9; 775]. As "governors" they would oversee the laboring people; as "captains" they would organize war against the Indians or against Spanish or other European intruders. It would seem that their role corresponded to that of the "Servitors" in the plantation of Ulster. (See *The Invention of the White Race*, Volume One, pp. 118–19.) See especially Darrett B. Rutman, "The Virginia Company and Its Military Regime," in Darrett B. Rutman, ed., *The Old Dominion: Essays for Thomas Perkins Abernathy* (Charlottesville, 1964), pp. 1–20. Sir Richard Moryson, whose participation in the conquest of Ireland by starvation in the Tyrone War (1594–1603) has been noted in Volume One, urged "using Irish

veterans in Virginia." Indeed three veterans of the Tyrone War (see Volume One) did serve successively as governors of Virginia in the 1610–16 period, namely, Acting Governor Sir Thomas Gates (promulgator of the "Laws Divine, Moral, and Martial," a draconian set of laws derived from European military codes in which he was well versed), Governor Lord De La Warre (Delaware) and Acting Governor Sir Thomas Dale. (See: *A Memorial Volume at Virginia Historical Portraiture*, Alexander Willbourne Weddell, ed., [Richmond, 1930], pp. 66, 68, 79, 80; Darrett B. Rutman, "Virginia Company" pp. 6–7; idem, *A Militant New World, 1607–1640* [New York, 1970, a reprint of the author's PhD dissertation, University of Virginia, 1959], pp. 134–9.)

24. "[T]obacco not militarism was to prove the 'sovereign remedy' for Virginia's ills," writes Rutman (*Militant New World*, p. 231).

25. Craven, *Dissolution of the Virginia Company*, p. 33.

26. Ibid., p. 34.

27. "Nova Britannia: Offering Most Excellent fruits by Planting in Virginia. Exciting all such as be well affected to further the same," By R. I. (Robert Johnson probably, London alderman, rich merchant, and Deputy Treasurer of the Virginia Company from 1616 to 1619), London, 1609; printed in *Force Tracts*, Vol. I, No. 6, p. 23.

28. "A Letter from the Councill and Company of the honourable Plantation in Virginia to the Lord Mayor, Aldermen and Companies of London," London, 1609; printed in Brown, *Genesis*, 1:252–3. The term "inmate," as used here, simply means "inhabitant."

In their crusade to "end welfare as we know it," our modern-day conservatives will doubtless find reassurance in this ancient expression of bourgeois "traditional values".

29. See Bruce's comment on the laborers of Charles Hundred: "The probability is that the emancipated laborers of Charles Hundred became tenants" (*Economic History* 1:220).

30. Ralph Hamor, *A True Discourse of the Present Estate of Virginia* (London, 1615); cited in Brown, *First Republic* pp. 205–11; p. 205.

31. Bruce, *Economic History* 1:213–15, 219–20. Bruce says: "It is impossible to give the proportion between those who received and those who did not receive this privilege" (p. 214 n. 2).

32. Deputy-Governor Sir Thomas Dale promulgated this code in mid-1611. It was published in London in 1612. See William Strachey, comp., *For the Colony of Virginian Britannia, Lawes Divine, Morall, and Martiall*, edited by David H. Flaherty (Charlottesville, 1969). See Tyler; H. R. McIlwaine, *Minutes of the Council and General Court of Virginia* pp. 14, 62, 85, 93, 117, 163–64 (hereafter abbreviated *MCGC*; Rutman, *Militant New World*, p. 135.

33. John Rolfe, *Relation of Virginia* (London, 1616), reprinted in part in Brown, *First Republic*, pp. 226–9; p. 227. The bracketed emendations are Brown's. The term "familie," as used here and generally in documents cited in this present work, includes the household of persons, and not merely the blood and marriage kin.

As late as 1622, the official catalogue of social statuses comprised "Gentlemen," "Freemen," "Tenants," "Hired Servants," and "Apprentices" (*RVC*, 3:658 [Governor Francis Wyatt's proclamation against drunkenness, 21 June 1622]). The absence of an "indentured servant" category presumably reflects the fact that the plantation bourgeoisie's option for chattel-bond servitude was just then being made.

34. Speaking specifically of laborers in this middle period, L. D. Scisco states: "they were really hired employees and were treated as such. [P]rivate property in labor was absent." ("The Plantation Type of Colony," *American Historical Review*, Vol. VIII, No. 2 [January 1903], 260–70; pp. 261.) This periodical will hereafter be abbreviated *AHR*.

35. "Newes from Virginia," by Robert Rich (London, 1610), in Brown, *Genesis*, 1:420–26; pp. 425–6. The author of "Newes from Virginia" was an interested party and an enthusiast, of course; but so was the author of another promotional pamphlet, titled "Leah and Rachel," published to the glory of Virginia and Maryland half a century later. In the later tract, however, there is no promise of "day wages for the laborer," but rather the prospect of long-term, unpaid, chattel bond-servitude, at the end of which the worker would find that the right to land was but "an old delusion." ("Leah and Rachel, or, the Two Fruitfull Sisters Virginia and Maryland: Their Present Condition, Impartially Stated and Related," by John Hammond [London 1656]; printed in *Force Tracts*, III, No. 3, esp. pp. 10–11.)

36. Rolfe, p. 229.

37. Bruce, *Economic History*, 1:220.

38. Edwin Sandys, Report to the June 1620 Court of the Virginia Company of London, in Edward D. Neill, *History of the Virginia Company of London* (Albany, NY, 1869), p. 180.

39. Bruce, *Economic History*, 1:221, 227–8.

40. Native Virginia tobacco could not complete with the product of the Spanish colonies in the

world market. John Rolfe induced a friendly ship captain to smuggle Trinidad and Venezuela tobacco seeds into Virginia. When planted in Virginia they produced the "sweet-scented" product that tobacco users found as appealing as the Spanish-American product. The first shipment to England was made in 1615–16. George Arent, "The Seed from which Virginia Grew," *WMQ* second series, 19:123–9 [1939], pp. 125–6.

41. Bruce, *Economic History* 2:566. Here Bruce was assuming the indefeasibility of the capitalist principle of the "bottom line," as it might be called today. When that assumption was brought into question by social upheaval later in the seventeenth century, class struggle was revealed as an even more fundamental determinant of Virginia's fate. However, when considered simply in terms of the historical impact of innovations in capitalist production techniques in Anglo-America, the "discovery" of tobacco as a profitable Virginia crop in 1616 can only be compared with the invention of the cotton gin in 1793 (see *The Invention of the White Race*, Volume One, pp. 160–61).

42. Bruce, *Economic History*, 1:226.

43. Ibid., 1:222–3.

44. Craven, *Dissolution of the Virginia Company*, pp. 33–4.

45. Brown, *Genesis*, 2:776, 777–9.

46. Bruce, *Economic History*, 1:225–6. Bruce comments: "Beginning his control of the affairs of Virginia with the strict enforcement of the regulation that every cultivator of the ground should plant four acres in grain, he [Argall] ended with this regulation in entire abeyance."

47. Brown, *First Republic*, p. 254. A year later Argall was trying to get the price of tobacco raised *vis-à-vis* the magazine supplies (ibid., p. 279).

48. Ibid., p. 278.

49. Ibid., p. 279.

50. Neill, *History of the Virginia Company*, p. 117.

51. Brown, *Genesis*, 2:550–51.

52. Ibid., 2:939; "William Lovelace" biographical note. Argall came to Virginia the possessor of a new patent for 400 acres as the transporter of eight tenants.

53. "Letter of the Virginia Company to Deputy Governor Argall, 22 August 1618"; in Neill, *History of the Virginia Company*, pp. 114–19; p. 115. Argall was liable to criminal prosecution for his acts. In a letter to Lord Delaware regarding Argall, the Company said, "the adventurers . . . are hardly restrayned . . . [,] the Kings Court in progress[,] from going to the Court to make there complaynte and to procure his Majesty's command to fetch him [Argall] home" (ibid, p. 119).

54. Ibid., p. 115.

55. Recent historians have seemed more inclined to suspend judgment regarding Argall's actions. For examples of the earlier condemnatory view, see Brown, *First Republic*, and Bruce, *Economic History*; for the revised view, see Craven, *Dissolution of the Virginia Company*, and Morton.

56. "The Trades Increase," by R. I. (Robert Johnson) (London, 1615); extract in Brown, *Genesis*, 2:766. "Briefe Declaration of the present state of things in Virginia, and of a Division now made of some part of those Lands in our Actuall possession, as well to all such as have adventured their moneyes there, as also to those that are Planters there" (London, 1616) (ibid., 2:775–9).

57. My use of "headright" here is anachronistic, since that laconic term was not in vogue until some time later than 1616.

58. Brown, *Genesis*, 2:779.

59. Events were to show that absentee landlordism was not practicable. Rutman notes that these so-called "'particular plantations' were soon to disappear altogether from Virginia, their owners having first lost money in their undertakings then lost interest" (Rutman, *Militant New World*, pp. 307–8).

60. *RVC*, 2:350 (Virginia Company. A Delcaration of the State of Virginia. 12 April 1623). In the four years 1619 to 1622, the number of "adventurers," London investors in Virginia plantations, increased by ten times the previous number, and each of the ventures involved at least 100 men (ibid.).

61. Bruce, *Economic History*, 1:507–9. The patents lapsed, however, for failure to settle the lands with the required numbers of tenants (ibid., 1:505–6).

62. Minutes of the Quarterly meeting of the General Court of the Virginia Company of London, 2 February 1619; reprinted in Neill, *History of the Virginia Company*, pp. 129–30.

63. "Newes from Virginia," in Brown, *Genesis*, 1:420–26; p. 426.

64. See Table 5.1.

65. Pocahontas's actual native name was Matoaka. She was christened by the English "Rebecca." She and Rolfe were married around the middle of April 1614. Their Virginia-born son was named Thomas. (Brown, *First Republic*, pp. 203, 204, 225).

66. Rolfe, p. 226.

67. The three southern plantation colonies of the seventeenth century were Virginia, founded in 1607; Maryland, founded in 1634; and South Carolina, founded in 1670. Virginia was first also in the volume of exports. Tobacco was first in time and importance, and it held the leading place throughout the colonial period. The commercial cultivation of rice in South Carolina did not begin until the end of the seventeenth century. (Lewis C. Gray, assisted by Esther K. Thompson, *History of Agriculture in the Southern United States to 1860*, 2 vols. [Washington, DC, 1932] 1:57–8.) As in substance, so in form: Virginia was the pattern-setter for the institution of racial slavery in the southern colonies and in the development of the social and legal structure of white supremacy to reinforce the institution. "The discovery of the great resource for profit in raising tobacco," writes Ulrich B. Phillips, "gave the spur to Virginia's large-scale industry and her territorial expansion . . . [and] brought about the methods of life which controlled the history of Virginia through the following centuries and of the many colonies and states which borrowed her plantation system" (in Ulrich Bonnell Phillips, *The Slave Economy of the Old South: Selected Essays in Economic and Social History*, edited by Eugene D. Genovese [Baton Rouge, 1968], p. 8). Emphasizing the pattern-setting role of Virginia in legal institutions of white supremacy and racial slavery, Phillips says: "the legislation of Virginia was copied with more or less modification by all the governments from Delaware to Mississippi and Arkansas" (ibid., pp. 26–7).

Maryland was a proprietary colony of the Catholic Calverts, with "manorial" land ownership, where – in contrast to Virginia – the "headright" principle of land acquisition never applied to the importation of African laborers. These circumstances appear to have been the cause of the "large proportion" of limited-term bond-laborers held by small planters there. (Menard, pp. 129, 189.)

South Carolina was different in that the rice plantation economy did not emerge there until after the pattern of racial slavery (including the system of white-skin privileges of European-American workers) had been firmly established in Virginia and Maryland. The general employment of European-American bond-laborers in plantation field labor in South Carolina came late, was relatively less important than it was in the other two early plantation colonies, and was short-lived.

Unless one accepts the "natural racism" theory of the "psycho-cultural" school, these Maryland and South Carolina distinctions *vis-à-vis* Virginia have no contrary implications for the thesis being developed in the present work, namely that the chattelization of English plantation labor constituted an essential precondition of the emergence of the subsequent lifetime chattel bond-servitude imposed upon African-American laborers in continental Anglo-America under the system of white supremacy and racial slavery.

68. Craven, *Dissolution of the Virginia Company*, pp. 44–6.

69. Ibid., pp. 47–57.

70. Neill, *History of the Virginia Company*, p. 180.

71. Morgan, "The First American Boom," *WMQ* 28:169–98 (1971).

72. For deriving these ratios the following sources were used: export figures from Gray pp. 21–2; population figures from Brown, *First Republic*, pp. 226, 309, 464.

73. Craven, *Dissolution of the Virginia Company*, p. 59. *RVC*, 2:350.

74. Craven, *Dissolution of the Virginia Company* pp. 176–9, 301.

75. Ibid., p. 178. In 1619, the Virginia Assembly was established as the first elected legislative body in Anglo-America. At its first meeting, the Assembly decreed tobacco to be the money of the colony, making it clear in the following order to the Cape Merchant of the Colony: "you are bound to accept the Tobacco of the Colony, either for commodities or upon letters, at three shillings the beste and the second sort at 18d the pund, and this shallbe your sufficient discharge." Tyler, p. 260.

76. Craven, *Dissolution of the Virginia Company*, p. 190 n. 33, 301. See also Table 4.1.

77. *VMHB*, 2:154–65 (1894); pp. 155, 159. *RVC*, 3:99, 104 ("Instructions to Yeardley," *RVC*, 98–109 18 November 1618).

78. Smith, *Travels and Works*, 2:571.

79. *RVC*, 3:584 (Virginia Colony Council letter to Virginia Company in London, January 1621/22).

80. *RVC*, 3:479 (Virginia Company of London Instructions to Virginia Colony Governor and Council, 24 July 1621, 3:468–84); 3:489 (Treasurer and Company in London to Virginia Colony Council, 25 July 1621, 3:485–90).

81. Craven, *Dissolution of the Virginia Company*, pp. 149–50.

82. Ibid., p. 184.

83. *RVC*, 3:98–108.

84. "A Briefe Declaration" (by the Virginia Company), Brown, *Genesis* 2:774–9.

85. *Force Tracts*, III, no. 5, pp. 14–15. Cf. Craven, *Dissolution of the Virginia Company*, p. 56; Bruce, *Economic History*, 1:231.

86. "Instructions to Yeardley," *RVC*, 3:108.

87. Craven, *Dissolution of the Virginia Company*, pp. 100–102, 191.

88. Ibid., p. 189.

89. Gray, 1:259.

90. Craven, *Dissolution of the Virginia Company*, pp, 230–32. "Sandys had accepted the Company's dependence on tobacco" (ibid., p. 178).

91. At a meeting of the Virginia Company Court in July 1621, Samuel Wrote, member of the King's Council for Virginia, called attention to the unreality of the high official price of tobacco in Virginia, and deplored the fact that "It hath not been possible hitherto to awaken out of this straunge dream." (Virginia Company of London, *Court Book* I, cited in Gray, 1:260.)

92. The king got one-third of the crop and that transported to England free of charge, plus a duty of half a shilling on the other two-thirds. Furthermore, at a time when the Virginia crop sent to England would reach just 60,000 pounds the Company was required to agree to the English import of not less than 80,000 pounds of Spanish-produced tobacco, an amount approximatley equal to the crops being sent from Virginia at that time. (Craven, *Dissolution of the Virginia Company*, pp. 233–4. Bruce, *Economic History*, 1:269–70. See Gray, 1:22, for the 1622 Virginia tobacco export figure.)

93. See, for example: King James I, *Counter Blast* (1610); Gray, 1:25, 180–81, 231. "It was easier to decide upon such limitations [on tobacco-growing] than to make them efffective in Virginia." (Craven, *Dissolution of the Virginia Company*, p. 176.)

94. *CSP, Col.*, 1:117, Governor John Harvey's Report to the Privy Council, 29 May 1630. The price recovered to 6 pence a pound in 1635, but from then to 1660 the price averaged no more than $2\frac{1}{4}$ pence. A major crisis of overproduction in 1638 brought prices down to extremely low levels, says Gray, and even with recovery prices ranged between $1\frac{1}{2}$ pence per pound until the mid-1660s. (Gray, 1:26.) See also Russell R. Menard's tabulations of prices paid for tobacco in the Chesapeake (*Economy and Society in Early Colonial Maryland*, pp. 444–50, Tables A-5 and A-6).

In London in 1634, "Virginia tobacco was so low in price that it would no longer bear the old duty of twelve pence a pound; nor even the nine pence to which the duty had been reduced in 1623." (*Aspinwall Papers*, Massachusetts Historical Society Collections, Series 4, IX [Boston, 1871], p. 71.)

95. Brown, *First Republic*, pp. 562–3. See also Bruce, *Economic History*, 1:255.

96. Gray, Vol. 1, Chapter XII. See Chapter 9 of this volume for further treatment of the diversification of the Virginia economy.

97. This is another insight to be had from the frequently quoted comment of the Secretary of the Virginia Colony, John Pory, in 1619: "Our principall wealth consisteth of servants" (Pory to Sir Dudley Carleton, 30 September 1619 [*RVC*, 2:219–22; 221]). In 1618 a method was suggested of airing tobacco leaves by hanging them on strings rather than laying them on loose hay. When they could get the needed string from England, the colonists used this method which, by preserving tobacco, raised the productivity of labor. Aside from this innovation, however, there was to be but little technological advance in tobacco raising, and that would come slowly. (Brown, *First Republic*, p. 260. Craven, *Dissolution of the Virginia Company*, p. 181. See "Pounds of Tobacco Per Laborer, 1619–1699," Menard, *Economy and Society in Early Colonial Maryland*, p. 462.)

98. Brown, *First Republic*, pp. 248–9.

99. Ibid., p. 348.

100. Minutes of the meeting of the Virginia Company Court, 17 November 1619 (*RVC*, 2:271). See *The Invention of the White Race*, Volume One, p. 118, for the shipment into exile of mainly Ulster Irish rebels in 1610. George Hill notes the 1619 proposal of the English Lord Lieutenant of Ireland for shipping away Irish "woodkernes." (George Hill, *An Historical Account of the plantation in Ulster at the Commencement of the Seventeenth Century, 1608–1620* [Belfast 1877], p. iii, n. 2.)

101. They were forbidden to return except by express permission of the Privy Council as provided in a General Order of 24 March 1617. *Acts of the Privy Council of England, Colonial Series*, Vol. I, 1618–1638 (London, 1908), pp. 12–13, 19, 22, 52, 55, 56. See also Bruce, *Economic History* 1:603–4: "At this time, there were three hundred crimes in the calendar from which capital punishment was inflicted. It seemed to be too harsh a punishment to impose deaths for the smallest offense. Transportation was a compromise on the part of the English judges with the more humane feelings of their nature."

102. This man was put to death in Virginia in 1623 for the theft of a cow worth £3 sterling. The cow was the property of the once and future governor Yeardley who himself had stolen with impunity fifty-four men from the Virginia Company, his employer, two years previously. (*MCGC*, 4, 5.)

103. Brown, *First Republic*, pp. 273–4.

104. *RVC*, 2:270–71 (General Court of the Virginia Company of London meeting, 17 November 1619).

105. *RVC*, 2:271.

106. Acts of the Privy Council, Colonial, 1:28–9 (31 January 1619/20). Prior to 1750, the legal year began on 25 March. Therefore dates falling between 1 January and 24 March inclusive appear in the records in the form shown here. Where one year only is indicated, it is to be understood according to the modern calendar.

107. Brown, *First Republic*, p. 375.

108. *RVC*, 2:271.

109. Gray, 1:366. Bruce, *Economic History*, 1:629–30.

110. This is the average of estimates in the record as made by: John Rolfe, in 1619, 250 pounds (Smith, *Travels and Works*, 2:541); John Pory, in 1619, two "rare cases" averaging about 1,054 pounds according the 1619 price of 42*d*. in London (*RVC*, 3:221); William Spencer, recalling his experience in 1620, which works out to an average of 538 pounds (*RVC*, 1:256, 268); William Capps, in 1623, 500 pounds (*RVC*, 4.38); and Richard Brewster, also in 1623, 700 pounds (*RVC*, 2:524). Russell Menard's estimate of 712 pounds per worker for the period 1619–29 appears to be based on his figures for this same five-year 1619–23 period. (Menard, *Economy and Society in Early Colonial Maryland*, pp. 460, 462.) Although my average figure of 712 per pounds per worker is exactly the same as Menard's, they were not derived altogether from the same sources.

111. Menard, *Economy and Society in Early Colonial Maryland*, p. 444, Table A-5, "Chesapeake Tobacco Prices. 1618–1658." The average is calculated from fourteen citations (all but two being for 1619 and 1620) mainly from the *Records of the Virginia Company*; I did not count those tagged as "overstatements." Averaging by the year, the price paid in Virginia for the 1619–23 period was 20*d*. (Ibid. p. 448, Table A-6.)

112. Ibid. This is the average of fifteen instances of London wholesale prices.

113. *RVC*, 3:264 (William Weldon, letter to Sir Edwin Sandys, 6 March 1619/20).

114. Ibid.

115. See discussion and notation in Chapter 6, under the heading "Bond-servitude was not an adaptation of English practice."

116. Records of Magistrate's Court, Netherstone, Somerset, England, 19 October and 13 November 1618, *Correspondence, Domestic, James I*, vol. 103, Nos. 42, 42, I, 87 and 87 I; reprinted in *VMHB*, vi (1898–99), pp. 228–30.

117. Neill, *History of the Virginia Company*, p. 121. Brown, *First Republic*, p. 292.

118. Brown, *First Republic*, p. 376. The late Professor Richard L. Morton made the erroneous statement that "the women who were sent to be wives" in Virginia were not sold like merchandise, and that the enterprisers did not intend to make a profit on the transaction. (*Colonial Virginia*, 1:71.)

119. Virginia Company Court, 22 June 1620, *RVC*, 3:115. See also David Ransome, "Wives for Virginia," *WMQ* 48:3–18 (1991).

120. *RVC*, 3:313.

121. Brown, *First Republic*, pp. 459, 461. Actually a few of these women arrived in January on the pinnace *Tiger*.

122. Craven, *Dissolution of the Virginia Colony*, pp. 191–2. Of these five subsidiary joint-stocks launched in 1621, only the matrimonial business returned a profit (*RVC*, 2:15).

123. Virginia Company in London to the Virginia Colony Council in Virginia, 12 April 1621; in Neill, *History of the Virginia Company*, pp. 233–9; 234–5.

124. Ibid., pp. 241–50.

125. Ibid., p. 235.

126. *MCGC*, p. 54.

127. Neill, *History of the Virginia Company*, p. 235.

128. Ibid.

129. Manchester Papers, in *Historical Manuscripts Commision, Eighth Report* (London, 1881), Part I, Appendix, p. 41 (hereafter referred to as *Manchester Papers*).

130. Ibid.

131. *MCGC*, pp. 154–5 (11 October 1627).

132. Brown, *First Republic*, p. 627.

133. *MCGC*, pp. 117, 142 (11 October 1626 and 4 April 1627).

134. Herbert Moller, "Sex Composition and Correlated Culture: Patterns of Colonia America,"

WMQ 3d ser., 2:113–53 (1945), p. 114. *Historical Statistics of the United States, Colonial Times to 1970* (Washington, DC, 1975), Series Z-121–131 (p. 1171).

135. Moller, p. 115, citing J. A. Goodman, *The Pilgrim Republic* (Boston and New York, 1920), pp. 182–4.

136. Rutman, *Militant New World*, p. 355.

137. Moller, pp. 116–17. John C. Hotten, *The Original Lists of Persons of Quality, Emigrants; Religious Exiles; Political Rebels; Serving Men Sold for a Term of Years; Apprentices; Children Stolen; Maidens Pressed and Others Who went from Great Britain to the American plantations, 1600–1700* (London, 1874), pp. 35–138. Hereafter noted as Hotten, *Original Lists*.

138. Menard, *Economy and Society in Early Colonial Maryland*, p. 145.

139. "The Puritans, broadly speaking, arrived by families, although they had a considerable surplus of men. The movement to Virginia, on the other hand, consisted predominantly of male workers" (Moller, p. 118).

140. Allan Kulikoff, *Tobacco and Slaves: The Development of Southern Cultures in the Chesapeake, 1680–1800* (Chapel Hill, 1986), p. 34.

141. Bruce, *Economic History*, 1:538–89; Morgan, p. 176; A. E. Smith, pp. 14–16.

142. Craven, *Dissolution of the Virginia Colony*, p. 311.

143. John Smyth of Nibley Papers, documents in the New York Public Library, calendared in the New York Public Library *Bulletin*, 1:68–72 (1897), and 3:276–95 (1899).

144. "A Lyste of the men nowe sent for plantacon under Captayne Woodleefe ..." (September 1619), *RVC*, 3:197–8.

145. Ibid. See also "Capt Woodleefes Bill, Setpember, 1619," New York Public Library *Bulletin*, 3:221 (1899), p. 221.

146. "Berkeley, Thorpe, Tracy, and Smith. Agreement with Richard Smyth and Wife and Others" (1 September 1620), *RVC*, 3:393–4.

147. A. E. Smith, p. 14.

148. *RVC*, 3:210–11 (Indenture between the Four Adventurers of Berkeley Hundred and Robert Coopy of North Nibley, 7 September 1619). Among thirteen other men engaged for Berkeley Hundred in that same month, there were two other Coopys – Thomas and Samuell – but I do not know whether they were kin.

149. *RVC*, 3:210–11.

150. A. E. Smith, *Colonists in Bondage*, p. 15.

151. Part of "Drafts of a Statement touching the miserable condition of Virginia [May and June, 1623] by Alderman Robert Johnson" (*RVC*, 4:174). This was the opening blast of the campaign that was to end in the following year in the revocation of the Virginia Company charter. Johnson was a rich London merchant, who had over the years held positions of great authority in both the East India Company and the Virginia Company. See note 27.

152. Broadside published by the Virginia Company in 1622, prior to the receipt of the news of the Indian attack aof 22 March of that year; in Brown, *First Republic*, p. 486.

153. Ibid.

154. Virginia Governor and Council to Virginia Company of London (January 1621/22), *RVC*, 3:585–8; 586.

155. Thomas Nuce to Edwin Sandys, 27 May 1621 (*RVC*, 3:457).

156. *RVC*, 3:588. The actual enclosure seems not to have survived in the records, but the essential substance is clear from references to it in documents that have been preserved. It is curious that historians have chosen to ignore Nuce's proposal, while at the same time noting (Craven, *Dissolution of the Virginia Colony*, p. 173, Morgan, "First American Boom," p. 172) a letter written seven months earlier in which he states that his tenants are depressed by the prospect of a seven-year term of service, "which course, I am of opinion you should alter" (Nuce to Edwin Sandys, 27 May 1621 [*RVC*, 3:456–7]). The facts are that the conditions of the tenants were altered – to those of chattel bond-labor; that Nuce specifically recommended that tenants be replaced by "servants"; and that he was unwilling to pay the wages of free wage workers. Therefore, the imputation of benign motives to Nuce should not divert attention from his apparent role in promoting the change in the conditions of labor that took place in the 1620s in Virginia.

157. Virginia Company of London to the Virginia Governor and Council, 10 June 1622; (*RVC*, 3:646–52; 647).

158. Virginia Company of London to the Virginia Governor and Council, 7 October 1622 (*RVC* 3:683–90; 684).

159. Idem, 20 January 1622/23 (*RVC*, 4:9–17; 16).

160. *RVC* 4:178. The word used in this instance was, "pencons." This word is nowhere else to be

found in the records, but it seems to suggest a servant who lives with the employer, or at least one whose meals are provided by the employer. Indeed, references to this proposed change from tenantry all translate the term as "servant." Although the term "servant" has various applications in the records of the time, it is not necessary to explore that matter here; it is clear that the purpose was to reduce the cost of labor, and to levels below the wages then current in Virginia.

5 The Massacre of the Tenantry

1. See pp. 56, 61.

2. Back projection of the average annual crude death rate, 1619–1625, inclusive of a 4.16 percent spike for 1625. (E. A. Wrigley and R. S. Schofield, *The Population History of England, 1541–1871: A Reconstruction* [Cambridge, Massachusetts, 1981], p. 352.) This modern study confirms the reliability of the estimate of 2.5 percent made by Sir William Petty more than three centuries ago in his *An Essay concerning the Multiplication of Mankind together with another Essay in Political Arithmetick concerning the Growth of the City of London . . .* (London 1686), reprinted in part in Joan Thirsk and J. P. Cooper, eds., *Seventeenth-century Economic Documents*, (Oxford, 1972), pp. 761–4.

3. Edmund S. Morgan, *American Slavery, American Freedom: the Ordeal of Colonial Virginia* (New York, 1975), p. 120. Idem, "First American boom: Virginia 1618 to 1630," *WMQ*, 28: 169–198 (1971), p. 185.

4. "The answere of the Generall Assembly in Virginia to a Declaration of the state of the Colonie in the 12 years of Sir Thomas Smiths Government, exhibited by Alderman Johnson and others" (*RVC*, 4:458, 20 February 1623/40). Edward D. Neill, *History of the Virginia Company of London* (Albany, NY, 1869), pp. 407–11.

5. *RVC*, 3:74.

6. See Chapter 1, pp. 10–11.

7. [House of] Commons Journals, I, p. 711.

8. "Instructions to Yeardley," *VMHB*, 2:154–65.

9. Wesley Frank Craven, *The Dissolution of the Virginia Company* (New York, 1932), p. 60.

10. Alexander Brown, *The First Republic in America* (Boston and New York, 1898), p. 427.

11. This conclusion is based on an analysis of the following two documents: the Virginia Muster of 1624/25 in Annie Lash Jester and Martha Woodruff Hiden, eds., *Adventurers of Purse and Person: Virginia, 1607–1625* (Princeton, 1956); and "The Virginia Rent Rolls of 1704;" in T. J. Wertenbaker, *Planters of Colonial Virginia*. See further in Chapter 9, Table 9.1.

12. See McIlwaine, *MCGC*, pp. 72–3, 83, 136–7, 154.

13. Neill, p. 408.

14. *RVC*, 3:307–40; 313–14 ("A Declaration of the State of the Colony and Affaires of Virginia. By his Majesties Counsell for Virginia," 22 June 1620).

15. *RVC*, 3:226–7 (Virginia Colony Council, 11 November 1619, "The putting out of the Tenants that came over in the B. N. [*Bona Nova*], with other orders of the Councell").

16. Letter of William Weldon to Sir Edwin Sandys, 6 March 1619–20 (*RVC*, 3:262–5; p. 263).

17. See Smith, *Travels and Works*, p. 541. *RVC*, 3:586 and 4:38.

18. Smith, *Travels and Works*, 2:542.

19. *RVC*, 3:226 (The Governor and Council in Virginia "The putting out of the Tenantes that came over in the B. N. [*Bona Nova*] . . .," 11 November 1619).

20. *RVC*, 3:263 (William Weldon. Letter to Edwin Sandys, 6 March 1619/20).

21. *RVC*, 219–22; 220–21 (Letter of Colony Secretary John Pory in Virginia to Sir Dudley Carleton in England, 30 September 1619).

22. *RVC*, 1:584–604 (Record of the Meeting of the Virginia Company of London Court, 30 January 1621/22).

23. *RVC*, 3:241–8; 243 (Letter of John Rolfe to Sir Edwin Sandys, January 1619/20). Rolfe does not describe these new arrivals as "Africans" but as "Negroes." The fact that some of these new workers bore Christian names (Maria and Antonio, for example) and the fact that the ship on which they arrived came to Virginia from the West Indies, suggests that at least some had spent time in the Caribbean, or might even have been born there.

24. Those who read Edmund S. Morgan's "First American Boom" and Chapter 4 of his *American Slavery, American Freedom*, may realize how much I am indebted to his insights. Credit

must go to Morgan for opening the way to a reexamination of the history of the Company period, particularly the critical years 1619–24, from the standpoint of the consideration of the internal contradictions of the colony, those between the few rich and the common run of the people. After a year-by-year review and analysis of colony's food supply situation, Morgan concludes: "Yeardley's complaints, his purchase of the Negroes, and his disposal of the men from the Bona Nova at a time when the colony was reporting an unprecedented abundance, suggest that the problem was not altogether one of whether supplies existed, it was a question of who had them and who could pay for them. In a year of plenty the governor and Council were unable or unwilling to make use of fifty men without supplies when other Virginians were able and willing to do so. The great shortage of supplies, to which we attribute the failure of the Sandys program, was not an absolute shortage in which all Virginians shared and suffered alike. It was a shortage that severely afflicted the Company and its dependants, but it furnished large opportunities for private entrepreneurs and larger ones for Company officials who knew how to turn public distress to private profit." ("First American Boom," p. 175).

25. *RVC*, 2:375; *RVC*, 4:186; 234. Morgan, "First American Boom," p. 182.

26. Smith, *Travels and Works*, 2:571. *RVC*, 3:581–7; 584 (Virginia Colony Council to Virginia Company of London, January 1621/22).

27. Virginia Company of London to Deputy Governor Argall, 22 August 1618 (Neill, *History to the Virginia Company*, pp. 114–17; p. 115).

28. Virginia Company of London to Lord Delaware, 22 August 1618 (Neill, *History of the Virginia Company* pp. 117–29; p. 119). Delaware died *en route* to Virginia. Argall returned to England aboard a ship specially sent by his patron, the Earl of Warwick, not waiting for instruction or permission from the London authorities.

29. *RVC*, 1:601 (13 February 1622). *RVC*, 1:579 (30 January 1622). The Virginia Company Court granted Weldon a patent for the transportation of one hundred persons which, at the allowance of fifty acres each, implied for him a private plantation of five thousand acres.

30. *RVC*, 3:485–9; 489. Virginia Company of London to the Governor and Council in Virginia, 25 July 1621 (Neill, *History of the Virginia Company*, pp. 223–33; p. 230).

31. *RVC*, 3:584–5 (Virginia Colony Council to Virginia Company of London, January 1621/22).

32. *RVC*, 3:219–23; 221 (John Pory to Sir Dudley Carleton, 30 September 1619): "the Governor here [Yeardley], who at his first coming, besides a great deale of worth in his person, brought onely his sworde w[i]th him, was at his late being in London, together with his lady, out of his meer gettings here, able to disburse Very near three thousand pounds to furnish himselfe for his [return] voiage."

33. An incomplete indication of Yeardley's success at self-enrichment is to be found in his Last Will, dated 12 October 1627 (*New England Historical and Genealogical Register*, 28: 69 [1884], p. 69). Yeardley's estate, "consisting of goods debts, servants 'negars,' cattle ..." and including his thousand-acre plantation on Warwicke River, was valued at six thousand pounds by his uncle in a petition to the Privy Council in 1629.

34. Craven, *Dissolution of the Virginia Company*. pp. 176–8.

35. Weldon to Sandys (*RVC*, 3:263).

36. *RVC*, 3:581–8; 586 (Council in Virginia to Virginia Company of London, January 1621/22).

37. In 1622, tenants who had been brought to Bermuda by Captain Nathaniel Butler included in a letter of grievances the charge that they had been "forced to send all their tobacco into England unto their undertakers [employers], undivided," in spite of the fact that their contracts provided that they were to "divide their yearly tobacco" and "to be accountable for the moiety [half] only" (*Manchester Papers*, p. 38).

38. *MCGC*, p. 46 (Last day of January 1624/25).

39. "It was the Powhatan Uprising that both unleashed the company's self-destructive urges and accelerated Virginia's evolution" (J. Frederick Fausz, "The Powhatan Uprising of 1622: A Historical Study of Ethnocentrism and Cultural Conflict," Ph.D Dissertation, College of William and Mary, 1977, p. 547).

40. Alexander Brown, *The Genesis of the United States* (Boston, 1890), 2:971.

41. Neill, *History of the Virginia Company*, pp. 96–105. Philip Barbour, *Pocahontas and Her World: A Chronicle of America's First Settlement in which is Related the Story of the Indians and the Englishmen – Particularly Captain John Smith, Captain Samuel Argall, and Master John Rolfe* (Boston, 1970), pp. 169–70.

42. Richard L. Morton, *Colonial Virginia* 2 vols. (Chapel Hill, 1960), 1:74.

43. *RVC*, 3:556 ("A Declaration of the State of the Colony and ... a Relation of the Barbarous Massacre," after April 1622, 3:541–80).

George Yeardley was accused in England of having provoked the Indian attack of 22 March by treacherously attacking an assembly of the friendly Chickhominy Indians with whom he had asked to parley. Thirty to forty of the Indians were killed. "The perfidious act made them all fly out & seek revenge, they joined with Opichankano" (*RVC*, 4:118 [Sir Nathaniel Rich's Draft of Instruction to the commissioners to investigate Virginia affairs, 4:6–8]).

44. *RVC*, 3:555 (Edward Waterhouse "A Declaration of the state of the Colony and ... a Relation of the Barbarous Massacre, 1622).

45. Brown, *First Republic*, p. 467 n.1.

46. See Appendix II-C.

47. *RVC* 3:613; 4:11–12. In the summer of 1622 the Virginia Governor and Council did contemplate moving out, but to just across the Chesapeake Bay. The Company in London strenuously condemned the notion, and by the following January the Governor and Council were disowning the idea. *RVC*: 3:613 (Virginia Colony Council to Virginia Council in London, 3:609–15, 13 April 1622). *RVC*: 3:366–7 (Treasurer and Council for Virginia to Governor and Colony Council of Virginia, 3:366–73, 1 August 1622). *RVC*, 4:11–12 (Virginia Colony Council to Council for Virginia, 4:9–17, 20 January 1622/23).

48. The first English colony was established in 1587 on Roanoke Island on the North Carolina coast by an expedition organized by Sir Walter Raleigh (a second attempt). When the first relief ship returned to the spot in 1591, there was no trace to be found of the colony, except the eternally mystifying scrawl "Croatan." It is assumed that the colonists were adapted into an Indian tribe of the region. (See Hamilton MacMillan of Robeson County, North Carolina, "Sir Walter Raleigh's Lost Colony, with the traditions of an Indian Tribe in North Carolina indicating the fate of the Colony" (1888), cited in Brown, *Genesis*, 1:189–90. During a military trial in 1864, according to MacMillan, an Indian named John Lowrie asserted he was descended from this merger, and complained that nevertheless "white men have treated us as negroes."

49. *RVC*, 3:146 (Treasurer and Council in Virginia to George Yeardley, 3:146–8, 21 June 1619). *RVC* 3:496 (Virginia Company in London to Virginia Colony Council, 3:492–8, 12 August 1621).

50. See Morgan, "First American Boom," pp. 172–3, 175.

51. *RVC*, 3:555.

52. At the end of October 1618, the Company, in order to reduce overcharging for goods at the colony's supply store (called the "magazine"), forbade any mark-up on goods beyond "the allowance of 25 in the hundred proffitt" (*RVC*, 3:167).

53. The precariousness of property claims in the conditions of epidemic death prevailing at that time in Virginia, and the danger of fraud in disposition of property of deceased persons there is to be seen in the letter addressed by the Company to the Colony Governor and Council, 7 October 1622, in which they noted "greevances for wrongs by unjust factors and partners in Virginia, and of claymes to lands and foods by the late death of friends" (*RVC*, 3:689 [Virginia Company to the Governor and Council of Virginia, 3:683–9]).

54. *RVC*, 3:537 gives the population as 1,240 (Notes from Lists showing Total Number of Emigrants to Virginia [1622]). See also Brown, *First Republic*, pp. 467, 624.

Regarding the number of lives lost in the colony, Brown writes, "The exact number may not be certainly known ... [at first] the company published a list of 347; but it was almost necessary to make the list as small as possible at that time.... The Company afterwards placed the number at 'about 400,' and Edward Hill put it at '400 and odd.'" Hill was a Virginia planter living in Elizabeth City. (Brown, *First Republic*, 467, 624; and Philip A. Bruce, *Economic History of Virginia in the Seventeenth Century*, 2 vols. [New York, 1895] 2:71.)

55. *RVC*, 3:611–15 (Virginia Colony Council to Virginia Company of London, April (after 20) 1622). *RVC*, 4:13 (Virginia Colony Council to Virginia of London, 4:9–17, 20 January 1622/23).

56. *RVC*, 4:58 (Richard Frethorne letters, 4:58–62, Spring 1623).

57. *RVC*, 4:22 (George Sandys to Mr Ferarr).

58. *RVC*, 3:613.

59. *RVC*, 4:525 (Virginia Company of London, Discourse ... April (?) 1625).

60. *RVC*, 3:614

61. *RVC*, 4:233 (Letters arriving in England on the *Abigail*, 4:228–29, 19 June 1623).

62. *RVC*, 4:61 (Richard Frethorne letters to his father and mother, 20 March and 2 and 3 April, 1623, *RVC*, 4:58–63).

63. *RVC*, 4:41, 59. Brown, *Genesis*, 2:802–3, 826.

64. *RVC*, 4:58.

65. *RVC*, 4:41 (Frethorne to Bateman, 5 March 1622/23).

66. *RVC*, 4:62.

67. *RVC*, 4:236.

68. Ibid.

69. *RVC*, 4:231–2. Great Britain Historical Manuscripts Commission Eighth Report and Appendix (London, 1881), Part I; Appendix (Duke of Manchester Papers), p. 41.

70. *RVC*, 3:639.

71. *RVC*, 4:525 (Virginia Company "Discourse of the Old Company," April 1625, 4:519–61).

72. This is an inference drawn from the rate of profit specified to be secured on the supplies subsequently sent on the relief ships the *George*, the *Hopewell*, and the *Marmaduke* (*RVC*, 4:263–4).

73. *RVC*, 4:61–2.

74. *RVC*, 4:107, 116, 230.

75. *RVC*, 4:120 (Letter from Captain Kendall in Somers Islands to Sir Edwin Sandys, 14 April 1623).

76. *RVC*, 4:105 (Sir Francis Wyatt to John Ferrar, 7 April 1623).

77. Brown, *First Republic*, p. 559.

78. *RVC*, 3:639 (28 March 1623).

79. *RVC*, 4:215–16 (Draft for a Report on the Condition of the Colony, June or July 1623).

80. Butler was a leading opponent of the Edwin Sandys headship of the Virginia Company, and might therefore be expected to be biased. But Alexander Brown, an early and staunch historiographical supporter of Sandys, believes that Butler's report was on the whole factual (*First Republic*, p. 506).

81. In seeking to counter this point in Butler's report, Sandys's supporters conceded that such public dying might occur in Virginia. But they were confident that it did not take place under hedges, because, they asserted, "there is no hedge in Virginia" (*RVC*, 2:382). Next case!

82. Brown, *First Republic*, pp. 444, 506, 627. Professor Morgan revises the total population figures upward from those given by the records for 1623–24 and 1624–25, by 20 percent and 10 percent respectively. He does not suggest any revision of the 1622 figure. (*American Slavery, American Freedom*, pp. 101, 404.)

83. Besides the specific references to the record for the period up to 1626 in this paragraph, see Chapter 4, note 94.

84. *RVC*, 4:46 (17 March 1622/23).

85. *RVC*, 2:523. Brown, *First Republic*, p. 563.

86. *RVC*, 2:519–20 (Virginia Company of London Court, 21 April 1624).

87. *RVC*, 4:453 (30 January 1623/24); 4:570 (4 January 1625/26).

88. *RVC*, 4:271–2. ("A proclamation touching the rates of Comodities," 31 August 1623.)

89. *RVC*, 4:14.

90. *RVC*, 4:271.

91. The census of Virginia Colony for 1624–25 (March 1625) showed 432 male adults who were free in a total population of 1,227. Of the non-free adults, 298 were in the service of an elite bourgeois group of fifteen employers. (Hotten, *Original Lists*, pp. 261–5.) See also Morgan's analysis and tabulation in "First American Boom," pp. 188–9.

92. *RVC*, 2:339 (Virginia Company of London Court, 24 March 1622/23).

93. *RVC*, 3:614. Brown, *First Republic*, pp. 474–5.

94. It seems not unlikely that there was a shortage of English trade goods, since the production of glass beads had been halted at this time in the colony for lack of suitable sand (*RVC*, 4:108).

95. RVC, 4:9–10 (Virginia Colony Council to the Virginia Company of London, 20 January 1622/23). For references to Mountjoy's strategy of starvation in the Tyrone War, see Volume One of *The Invention of the White Race*.

96. RVC, 3:614.

97. *RVC*, 4:186 ("Rough Notes in Support of the Preceding Charges of Mismanagement of the Virginia Company, May [after May 9] or June, 1623," 4:183–7); 4:234 (letter of Edward Hill to his brother Mr Jo. Will, 14 April 1623).

98. *RVC*, 4:186.

99. *RVC*, 4:105. Brown, *First Republic*, p. 513.

100. *RVC*, 2:375 ("The Unmasked face of our Colony in Virginia as it was in the Winter of the yeare 1622," 2:374–6).

101. *RVC*, 4:6–7.

102. Ibid.

103. *RVC*, 4:9–10. These Colony Council members were Yeardley, Tucker, George Sandys and Hamor.

104. Ibid.

105. *RVC*, 4:37 (Letter of William Capps to Dr John Wynston, March or April, 1623).

106. *RVC*, 4:14.

107. Brown (*First Republic*, p. 627) says that 11,185 bushels was regarded as a minimum supply in March 1625.

108. Smith, *Travels and Works*, 2:615.

109. Brown, *First Republic*, pp. 625–6, 627.

110. *RVC*, 4:89, 92, 231.

111. *RVC*, 4:234.

112. *RVC*, 4:14.

113. *RVC*, 4:453.

114. *RVC*, 3:612 (Virginia Colony Council to Virginia Company of London, April [after 20 April] 1622, 3:611–15).

115. *RVC*, 3:656 (Sir Francis Wyatt, A commission to Sir George Yeardley, 6 June 1622).

116. Brown, *First Republic*, pp. 617–20.

117. See Morgan, "First American Boom," pp. 189.2.

118. *RVC*, 3:613.

119. *RVC*, 2:94–5 (Virginia Company of London Court, 17 July 1622). *RVC*, 3:689 (Virginia Company of London to Governor and Council in Virginia, 3:683–90, 7 October 1622).

120. *RVC*, 2:124 (Virginia Company of London Preparative Court, 18 November 1622, 2:124–31).

121. Brown, *First Republic*, pp. 617, 618, 620, 623, 627. Brown adds, however, that he does not know the particulars of the disposition of the large corporate holdings such as Southampton Hundred. John C. Rainbolt argues that English heirs of Virginia Company land claims "parlayed [these holdings] into estates of several thousand acres" in the third quarter of the century. ("An Alteration in the Relationship between Leadership and Constitutents in Virginia, 1660–1720," *WMQ*, 27:411–34 [1970]; 413). Bernard Bailyn, in his essay on the evolution of the Virginia social structure, provides the details, showing that mid-seventeenth century claims on Company period inheritances constituted "the most important, of a variety of forms of capital" that provided the fortunes on which were based the oligarchy of slaveholding families of Virginia of the eighteenth century (Bernard Bailyn, "Politics and Social Structure," in James Morton Smith, *Seventeenth-century America, Essays in Colonial History* [Chapel Hill, 1959], p. 99).

122. I have assumed that the death rate was at least as high among workers as among employers.

123. *RVC*, 4:185 (May or June [after 9 May] 1623).

124. *RVC*, 3:658 (Proclamation of Governor Sir Francis Wyatt for the suppression of drunkenness, 21 June 1622). The quintuplex of social classes set forth in this Virginia order perfectly mirrored the categories as established in England at that time: noblemen, freemen, yeomen, artisans, and farm laborers. See Sir Thomas Wilson, *The State of England, Anno Dom. 1600*, Publications of the Camden Society, 3rd ser., Vol. 52, *Camden Miscellany*, Vol. 16 edited by F. J. Fisher (London, 1936), p. 17.

125. See Morgan, "First American Boom," pp. 171–75. The use by Professor Morgan of the "mining camp", boom-town metaphor seems somewhat questionable on the grounds of one-sidedness. Lewis C. Gray used the same argument (see Gray, assisted by Esther K. Thompson, in the *History of Agriculture in the Southern United States to 1860* [Washington, DC, 1932; reprinted 1958], 1:256). I am no student of that aspect of social history, but was it characteristic of the gold and oil boom towns in the American West and in Alaska, for example, to have two-thirds of the people die of starvation and starvation-related disease in a one- or two-year period? In a boom town, do not wages rise, even though the lucky, grasping few may fare better? In Virginia in the 1620s, the position of the laboring people deteriorated not only relatively but absolutely.

126. *RVC*, 4:37–8 (William Capps, Letter to Doctor Thomas Wynston. March or April 1623). But that same April, Governor Wyatt said that on the best ground a pair of tenants could make 2,500 pounds, and that because of guard duty his sixteen tenants produced only 1,000 pounds per capita. (*RVC*, 4:104–6 [Wyatt to John Ferrar, 7 April 1623].)

127. *RVC*, 4:175 ("Alderman Johnson(?), Parts of Drafts of a Statement Touching the Miserable Condition of Virginia," 4:174–87, May or June [after 9 May] 1623).

128. *RVC*, 4:13 (Virginia Colony Council to the Virginia Company of London, 4:9–17).

129. *RVC*, 4:74 (George Sandys to Sir Samuel Sandys, 30 March 1623, 3:73–5).

130. *RVC* 3:105 (Sir Francis Wyatt to John Ferrar, 7 April 1623, 4:104–6).

131. "From 1606 to 1624, the average value of wheat in England was only five shillings a bushel" (Bruce, 1:256). As noted above (page 91), the price of corn in Virginia was twenty shillings per bushel in 1623.

132. *VMHB*, 71:410 (1963), citing Harleian Ms. 389, f. 309, unsigned letter to Joseph Mead, 4 April 1623.

133. *RVC*, 3:221 (John Pory to Sir Dudley Carlton and Edwin Sandys, 30 September 1619).

134. Morgan, *American Slavery, American Freedom*, p. 119.

135. See *Historical Statistics of the United States, Colonial Times to 1970* US Department of Commerce, Bureau of the Census (Washington, DC, 1975), series Z-125-128.

136. Morgan, *American Slavery, American Freedom*, p. 119 n. 50. Morgan refers to A. J. and R. H. Tawney, "An Occupational Census of the Seventeenth Century," *Economic History Review*, 5:25–64 (1934–35). Although Morgan omits page references, his comment seems to be supported by the Gloucestershire figures showing 19,402 men between the ages of twelve and sixty (p. 31), and, in agricultural and domestic occupation, only sixteen employers with ten or more employees (tables VI and VII, pp. 52 and 53).

137. *VMHB*, 71:409 (1963). See also *RVC*, 4:104.

138. *RVC*, 3:618 (Edwin Sandys Letter to John Ferrar, 30 April, 1622 [before news of the 22 March Indian attack had arrived in England]). Historians (Craven, *Dissolution of the Virginia Company*, pp. 152–3, and Morgan, "First American Boom," pp. 171 and 183, for example) have considered it a "blunder" on Edwin Sandys's part to have persisted in the policy of sending thousands of ill-provisioned emigrants to Virginia. If so, it was a blunder that flowed from flawless bourgeois logic: an oversupply of dependent and ill-supplied laborers was an objective necessity for securing a general reduction of labor costs and thus keeping tobacco profitable enough to attract capital investment.

139. *RVC*, 4:220–22 (9 June 1623).

140. Colony Secretary George Sandys was one of the purchasers (*Manchester Papers*, p. 39 Letter from "G. S." [George Sandys?] to "Mr Ferrer" [Ferrar]).

141. *MCGC*, pp. 19–20 (16 August 1623). Tyler's opinions are from testimony against him in the General Court.

142. *MCGC*, pp. 22–4 (10 October 1624).

143. *MCGC*, p. 105 (7 and 8 August 1626).

144. *MCGC*, p. 117 (11 October 1626). For her part, servant Alice Chambers was ordered to receive unspecified "worthy punishment."

145. *MCGC*, pp. 135–7 (13 January 1626/7). "The Order by which the [thirty-six] Tenants of the Company are distributed to the Governor & [8 other members of the] Councill" shows eighteen assigned to Governor Francis Yeardley, and three to most of the others. The Colony Council order regarding the "Duty boys" was issued on 10 October 1627 (p. 154).

146. Bruce, 2:43.

147. By the end of 1624, the Virginia Colony Council was reporting to the Virginia Company that there was much corn in the colony, but that they were short of laborers (*RVC*, 4:507–8, 2 December 1624).

148. So characterized by George Sandys in a letter to his brother Samuel in England, 30 March 1623 (*Manchester Papers*, p. 39).

149. *RVC*, 4:106 (George Sandys to John Ferrar in England, 8 April 1623). See also Bruce, 1:47–8.

6 Bricks without Straw: Bondage, but No Intermediate Stratum

1. See Oliver Ellsworth's comment cited in *The Invention of the White Race*, Volume One, p. 286 n. 3.

2. Labor might also have been recruited from among the native population if terms were made sufficiently attractive, or as a result of the destruction of the original native population's economy of the area by the bombardment of cheap commodities, or by the expropriation of the lands and resources. But this alternative and reasons for its ineffectiveness were discussed in Chapter 3.

3. *RVC*, 3:592–8 (Virginia Company, The Form of a Patent, 30 January 1621/22); 3:629–34 (Virginia Company, The Form of a Patent for a Planter Only, 22 May 1622).

4. This principle of granting land patents at the rate of fifty acres for each person brought into Virginia would later be known as the "headright" system. See Chapter 4, pp. 58–9.

5. See p. 72.

6. *RVC*, 3:507.

7. *RVC*, 3:586; 4:558.

8. *RVC*, 2:105, 3:699, 4:14 (7 October and 2 November 1622; 20 January 1622/23).

9. *RVC*, 4:22 (March 1622/23).

10. See p. 86.

11. *RVC*, 4:235 (12 April 1623).

12. *RVC*, 4:466–7. *MCGC*, p. 12 (9 March 1623).

13. *RVC*, 4:467 (9 March 1622/23).

14. *MCGC*, p. 40 (3 January 1624/25).

15. *MCGC*, p. 109 (28 August 1626). Hotten, *Original Lists*, p. 237.

16. *MCGC*, p. 90 (20 January 1625/26).

17. *MCGC*, pp. 131–2 (20 January 1626/27).

18. *RVC*, 4:5–6 (between January and April 1622/23).

19. *MCGC*, p. 83 (19 December 1625).

20. *MCGC*, pp. 136–7 (13 January 1626/27).

21. Alexander Brown, *The First Republic in America*, (Boston and New York, 1898), p. 627.

22. *New England Historical and Genealogical Register*, 38:69 (January 1884).

23. See Theodore K. Rabb, *Enterprise and Empire* (Cambridge, Massachusetts, 1967).

24. "The liberties of Englishmen – the privileges and immunities of the free-born English subject ... [include] personal liberty ... signifying the freedom to dispose of one's person and powers of body and mind, without control by others who are not representatives of the ultimate supreme authority."(John Codman Hurd, *The Law of Freedom and Bondage in the United States*, 2 vols. [Boston, 1858; Negro Universities Press reprint, 1968] 1:140.)

25. *RVC*, 3:683–4 ("Virginia Company. A Letter to the Governor and the Council in Virginia, October 7, 1622," *RVC*, 3:683–90).

26. In the Gloucestershire occupational census of 1606, the only such existing record for seventeenth-century England, tabulations of employers and their servants in agriculture or domestic employment show that servants constituted 27 percent of the total; 4 percent were of the leisure classes, 11 percent were yeomen, and 58 percent were husbandmen (A. J. Tawney and R. H. Tawney, "An Occupational Census of the Seventeenth Century," *Economic History Review*, 5:25–64 [1934–35]; see Tables VI and VII, pp. 52 and 53). In Virginia in the era that followed the economic massacre of the tenantry, the great majority of the laboring population were to be not even husbandmen, but chattel bond-laborers.

27. The reader is referred particularly to my Introduction to *The Invention of the White Race*, in Volume One.

28. With the honorable exception of Edmund S. Morgan, those historians who have concerned themselves with the origin of chattel bond-labor of European-Americans have repeated this rationale as an article of faith.

See, for example, Marcus W. Jernegan, *Laboring and Dependent Classes in Colonial America* (New York, 1931), p. 46; Lewis C. Gray, assisted by Esther K. Thompson, *History of Agriculture in the Southern United States to 1860* (Washington, DC, 1932; reprinted 1958), 1:342; Philip A. Bruce, *Economic History of Virginia in the Seventeenth Century: An Inquiry into the Material Conditions of the People, based upon original records*, 2 vols. (New York, 1895; reprinted 1935), 1:587. Winthrop D. Jordan is content to say "it was indentured servitude that best met the requirements for settling in America" (*White Over Black: American Attitudes Toward the Negro, 1550–1812* [Chapel Hill, 1968], p. 52].).

29. Abbot E. Smith, *Colonists in Bondage: White Servitude and Convict Labor in America, 1607–1776* (Chapel Hill, 1947; New York, 1971), pp. 8–9. Bruce, *Economic History*, 1:262.

30. It is also analogous to the argument advanced by coalmine owners in the twentieth century, with the support of even United Mine Workers officials in McDowell County, West Virginia in 1940–41. Resolutions passed by several United Mine Workers locals demanding portal-to-portal pay were dismissed as utopian. "What!" opponents cried. "Do you think the coal operators are going to pay you for just sitting in the man-trip?" But in that case the general relationship of class forces was such that after Pearl Harbor we miners got our just due in this matter.

31. *(English) Statutes at Large*, 23 Ed. III (1349).

32. A. E. Smith, p. 305. Smith was here generalizing about the entire history of "white servitude."

33. See pp. 65–6.

34. *Documents relating to the History of the Early Colonial Settlements, principally on Long Island, with a Map of its Western Part, made in 1666, translated and compiled from this Historical Records by B. Fernow* (Albany, 1883).

35. *Voyages from Holland to America, AD 1632–1644*, Collections of the New York Historical

Society, 2nd ser., vol. III, part 1, translated and edited by Henry Murphy (New York, 1857). There is no indication of de Vries's feelings regarding the buying and selling of African bond-laborers in which the Dutch were then principal merchants.

36. See especially pp. 22–4.

37. Under English common and statute law, the failure of a servant to fulfill his or her contract could be remedied by pecuniary damages only, not by "compelling a specific performance." (Hurd, 1:138). The English courts resolved as follows. By 27 Henry VIII, legal compulsion to performance of a contract was ended; failure to perform as contracted could only be remedied by the recovery of damages from the party failing to meet the contractual obligation. (Matthew Bacon, *A New Abridgement of the Law*, 5th edition, 5 vols. [Dublin, 1786], 5:359, "Covenants to stand seized to Uses," paragraphs 46–48).

The distinction between the penalty of adding time to the bond-laborer's term of servitude in colonial Virginia and the provision of English law is underscored in a Virginia manumission agreement requiring a to-be-freed laborer to pay to his emancipator 6,000 pounds of tobacco over a three-year period, but with the proviso that the worker could "not bee restrained of his liberty for default of payment, but is left to the course of the Law as all other free subjects are in case of debt." (*Northampton County Records, 1668–80*, pp. 158–9 [1678]).

38. Paul H. Douglas begins by equating plantation bond-servitude and apprenticeship. But he then honestly presents "the chief differences" until, in spite of his intentions, his premise is in tatters (Paul H. Douglas, *American Apprenticeship and Industrial Education* [New York, 1921], pp. 28–9).

Louis P. Hennighausen says that though "white servitude" was sometimes called "apprenticeship," it was slavery (Louis P. Hennighausen, *The Redemptioners and the German Society of Maryland* [Baltimore, 1888], p. 1. Cheesman Herrick found that in Pennsylvania, "What ordinarily passes as the apprenticeship system differs from that now under discussion . . ." (Cheesman Herrick, *White Servitude in Pennsylvania* [Philadelphia, 1926; Negro Universities Press reprint, 1969], p. 108). There is no reason to think the conditions and status of bond-laborers were more favourable in Virginia in the seventeenth century than they were in Maryland in the eighteenth and nineteenth centuries.

39. Thomas Jefferson, *Reports of Cases Determined in the General Court of Virginia, from 1730 to 1740; and from 1768 to 1772* (Charlottesville, 1829); Gwinn v. Bugg, p. 89.

40. John Strange, *Reports of Adjudged Cases in the Courts of Chancery, King's Bench, Common Pleas and Exchequer*, 2 vols. (London, 1782); 2:1266–7. See also: William Salkeld, *Report of Cases Adjudged in the Court of King's Bench . . .*, (Philadelphia, 1822) 6th edition, 3 vols., 1:67–8; and Michael Dalton, *The Country Justice* (1619; edited with an appendix, by William Nelson London, 1727), p. 191. (I am grateful to Director Frederic Baum and the staff of the Library of the Association of the Bar of the City of New York for making these old books available to me.) In a marginal note, Dalton says that by London custom (allowance for which appears to be made in the Statute of Artificers [5 Eliz. 4] section 40 – T.W.A.) an apprentice "may be turned over to another." But the consent of the apprentice was presumably still required. With regard to such transfers of an apprentice to another master, according to Lipson, only rare exceptions were made, and these involved extraordinary and particular review and agreement by the wardens of the trade (Ephraim Lipson, *Economic History of England*, 3 vols. (London, 1926), 1:285).

The distinction between assignability and non-assignability, between chattel and non-chattel indenture to bond-servitude, was explicitly instanced in an order of the Charles County Maryland Court of 28 January 1661. The court approved an agreement between widow Ane Ges binding out her step-daughter (called "daughter-in-law" in those times) to one man for six years, and her three-year-old son, for fifteen years, to another man, specifying in each case that the child was bound to the man, "his heirs, Executors, administrators but not Assignes"(*Archives of Maryland*, 52:182–3). For Virginia examples of such specific provisions, see: *Rappahannock County Records, 1656–64*, pp. 275–6 (1683); *Northumberland County Records, 1678–1698*, pp. 250, 826 (1685; 1698).

41. This characterization is given by Gray in his *History of Agriculture in the Southern United States to 1860* (1:344), in concluding his discussion of the origin of "indentured servitude" (1:342–4). On this point, Gray appears to have misappropriated the authority whose title he cites but does not quote. Indeed, that authority seems to contradict Gray's assertion most directly, as follows: "[T]he relation of master and servant in indented servitude was unknown to that [English apprenticeship] law, and could neither be derived from nor regulated by its principles. it had to depend entirely for its sanction on special statutes, or on the action of tribunals which had no precedents before them." (James Curtis Ballagh, *White Servitude in the Colony of Virginia: A Study of the System of Indentured Labor in the American Colonies* [Baltimore, 1895; 1969 reprint], p. 46).

Awareness of the distinction between colonial indentured chattel servitude and terms of employment in the home country is revealed in the exceptional indentures that were conditioned upon non-assignability. See, for example, Virginia County Records, *Rappahannock County Records, 1656–64*, pp. 275–6 (18 February 1662/3; *Lancaster County Records*, 1660–80, p. 353 (8 March 1675/6); *Northumberland County Records, 1678–98*, pp. 250, 826 (1 January 1684/5 and 15 June 1698).

42. Tobacco seeds were first planted in England in 1565 (*Encyclopedia Britannica*, 15th edition (Chicago, 1997), 11:812, "Tobacco."). The short-lived 1547 slave law (1 Edw. VI, 3) was repealed in 1550.

43. See *The Invention of the White Race*, Volume One, p. 19, and p. 239 n. 96, for the names of half a dozen champions of the "paradox" thesis.

44. Bruce, *Economic History* 1:52–69; 238–9; 254–62; 411–12; 585–6; 2:43, 48–51, 415–17.

45. The patentee's first seven years in possession were free of quit-rent (Hening, 1:228).

46. Allan Kulikoff, *Tobacco and Slaves: The Development of Southern Cultures in the Chesapeake, 1680–1800* (Chapel Hill 1986), pp. 132–4. Authorities agree that elsewhere in Virginia tenancy was much less practiced, although the tax records provide no category for tenants. (Ibid., p. 134; Jackson Turner Main, "The Distribution of Property in Post-Revolutionary Virginia," *Mississippi Valley Historical Review*, 41:241–58 (1954–55); pp. 245 n. 12; 248 n. 21. The name of this publication was later changed to *Journal of American History*.)

47. Willard F. Bliss, "The Rise of Tenancy in Virginia," *VMHB*, 58:427–41 (1950), p. 429.

48. Ibid., p. 427. Cf. Carville V. Earle, *The Evolution of a Tidewater Settlement System: All Hallow's Parish, Maryland, 1650–1783*, University of Chicago Department of Geography Research Paper No. 170, 1975. "Slaves did not cause tenancy and the decline of the yeomen," says Earle (p. 226).

49. Russell R. Menard, *Economy and Society in Early Colonial Maryland* (New York, 1985), p. 72.

50. Ibid., p. 76; Kulikoff, p. 133; Gregory A. Stiverson, *Poverty in a Land of Plenty: Tenancy in Eighteenth-century Maryland* (Baltimore, 1977), p. 10.

51. Kulikoff, p. 133.

52. Adam Smith, *An Inquiry into the Nature and Causes of the Wealth of Nations* (1812 reprint of 3 vols. in 1 by Ward Lock, & Co., London, n.d. [19th century]), p. 354.

53. Bruce, 1:586. A. E. Smith likewise rejects the possibility of any alternative to chattel bond-servitude, seeing it as being "too expensive," for purposes of colonization "without rearranging society in some utopian fashion" (*Colonists in Bondage*, p. 305). Craven describes the bond-labor system as merely a part of Virginia's being "allowed to follow what was perhaps her most natural development as a commonwealth of tobacco plantations" (Wesley Frank Craven, *The Dissolution of the Virginia Company; the Failure of a Colonial Experiment* (New York, 1932), p. 334).

54. Incidentally, while it is true enough to say, as Bruce does, the "The system of large estates was the result of tobacco culture alone," large estates are by no means necessary for the raising of tobacco. Indeed, tobacco is especially suitable for cultivation on small farms. (Fernando Ortiz, *Contrapunteo Cubano del Tabaco y Azucar* [Havana, 1940], pp. 82–3, 466; Eric Bates, "The 'Tobacco Dividend': Farmers Who are Kicking the Habit," *The Nation*, 13 February 1995, pp. 195–8. Bates quotes a "farm activist" as saying that, "If it weren't for tobacco, we wouldn't have small farms" [p. 196]).

55. Francis Bacon, *Works*, 6:93–5.

John C. Rainbolt (*From Prescription to Persuasion, Manipulation of Eighteenth Century Virginia Economy* [Port Washington, NY, 1974]) examines circumstantial factors that frustrated efforts at diversification of the Virginia economy. Although the title refers to the eighteenth century, Rainbolt's main attention is directed to the 1650–1710 period, well after the commitment to tobacco had become a settled question in practical terms, and the guiding principle of colonial Virginia government had been firmly established: to secure the highest quickest profit for the Virginia planters, shippers, servant-trade merchants, English Crown interests, tax-and-customs farmers.

56. Bruce, *Economic Histroy*, 1:51–2.

57. Being of the aristocracy himself, Bacon favored control by "noblemen and gentlemen." But this would seem to lapse from Bacon's wonted attachment to empirical data. The Earl of Warwick, a prominent member of the Virginia and Bermuda companies, was so passionate for present gain that he directed his main adventurers to piracy (Wesley Frank Craven, "The Earl of Warwick – A Speculator in Piracy," *Hispanic American Historical Review*, 10:457–79 [1930]). And by 1622 the arch-aristocrat King James I had come to a view of the matter quite opposite to that held by Bacon. Said the king: "Merchants were the fittest for the government of that Plantation [Virginia]" (*RVC*, 2:35).

58. In regard to the rate of expansion of the colony's population and the colony's relations with the native population, Bacon's words seem like good advice wasted: "Cram not in people, by sending too fast company after company; but hearken how they waste, and send supplies proportionably; but so as the number may live well in the plantation, and not by surcharge [excess population] be in penury." Then, in logical corollary to this doctrine of slow and controlled population expansion, Bacon urged that: "If you plant where savages are, do not only entertain them with trifles and jingles; but use them justly and graciously, with sufficient guard nevertheless: and do not win their favor by helping them to invade their enemies, but for their defense it is not amiss."

Bacon was successively Solicitor-General, Attorney-General, Lord Keeper of the Seal, and Chancellor during the period of the completion of the plantation of Ulster by the English. In that light, it is especially interesting to find Bacon saying in this essay: "I like a plantation in a pure soil; that is, where people are not displanted to the end to plant in others. For else it is an extirpation than a plantation."

59. James and Charles, father-and-son Stuart kings of England, decreed the encouragement of the sale of Virginia tobacco in England at the expense of English-grown tobacco (royal Proclamations of 29 September 1624 and 9 May 1625: reprinted in Ebenezer Hazard, *Historical Collections*, 1:198ff, 203ff). This act brought a net gain to the English balance of trade, in which English-grown tobacco was a negligible factor.

60. See Craven's comment on Nathaniel Butler's "Unmasking of Virginia" (*Dissolution of the Virginia Company*, p. 255).

61. "The practice was loudly condemned in England and bitterly resented on the part of the servants, but the planters found their justification in the exigencies of the occasion . . .' (Ballagh, p. 43).

62. See p. 51.

63. *RVC*, 2:125.

64. *RVC*, 2:110–13.

65. *RVC*, 2:129.

66. *RVC*, 2:124–5, 128–31 (Report of the Committee on Registering of Contracts between men of the Company and their Servants, 18 November 1622).

67. *RVC*, 4:235 (12 April 1623).

68. *RVC*, 4:235 (12 April 1623). Atkins was also the employer who sold Thomas Best.

69. *MCGC*, p. 109 (28 August 1626).

70. *RVC*, 4:437 (30 March 1624).

71. *RVC*, 4:128–9 (26 April and 3 May 1623).

72. *MCGC*, pp. 75–6, 82.

73. *MCGC*, p. 105 (7 and 8 August 1626).

74. Martha W. Hiden, "Accompts of the Tristram and Jane," *VMHB*, 62:427–47 (1954); p. 437.

75. Richard Kemp, Secretary of Virginia colony to Francis Windebank, English Secretary of State, 6 April 1638; in *CSP. Col.*). Hurd, 1:136, n. 4.

76. See pp. 17–19.

77. See pp. 55–6.

78. See pp. 17–18.

79. See p. 96.

80. Smith, *Travels and Works*, 2:618 (Reply to the questions of the royal commission for inquiring into the state of conditions in Virginia in 1624), emphasis in original. Looking back two and a half centuries later, Scharf, a most eminent historian of his state, seemed to confirm Smith's prediction of "misery" and its root cause: "Unquestionably, tobacco made Maryland a slave State, and much poorer than she would otherwise be" (J. Thomas Scharf, *History of Maryland from the Earliest Period to the Present Day*, 3. vols. [Baltimore, 1879; 1967 reprint], 2:48).

7 Bond-labor: Enduring . . .

1. Abbot E. Smith, *Colonists in Bondage: White Servitude and Convict Labor in America, 1607–1776* (Chapel Hill, 1947), p. 39. Smith makes this generalization for the entire period 1607 to 1776.

2. Smith, pp. 99, 102, and 103.

3. Essex [County, England] Overseers of the Poor, 1631 accounts (extract), Broadside, "Transportation of the Poor to Virginia, 1631," courtesy of Francis L. Berkeley, Manuscripts Division, Alderman Library Manuscripts Division, University of Virginia, Charlottesville.

4. Wesley Frank Craven, *White, Red, and Black: the Seventeenth-century Virginian* (Charlottesville, 1971; New York, 1977), pp. 5, 14–16; 85–86. Craven's count of some 66,000 head-rights granted in Virginia between 1625 and 1682, plus his estimated 6,000 free immigrants for the period prior to 1625, minus some 1,400 head-rights granted for persons of African ancestry, gives a European immigration total for Virginia of between 70,000 and 71,000. A. E. Smith, working with head-right records for Maryland, estimated the European emigrants to that colony in the period 1633 to 1680 at 21,000, practically all of them bond-laborers (*Colonists in Bondage*, pp. 323–4). See also: Russell R. Menard, "Immigration to the Chesapeake Colonies in the Seventeenth Century," *Maryland Historical Magazine*, 68:323–7 (1973); idem, *Economy and Society in Early Colonial Maryland* (New York, 1985), pp. 117, 128; Eugene I. McCormac, *White Servitude in Maryland 1634–1824* (Baltimore, 1904) p. 30; James Horn, "Servant Emigration in the Seventeenth Century," in Thad Tate and David L. Ammerman, eds., *The Chesapeake in the Seventeenth Century: Essays in Anglo-American Society and Politics* (Chapel Hill, 1979), pp. 51–95; p. 54.

5. Governor William Berkeley's answers to questions submitted by the Lords of Trade and Plantations: Hening, 2:511–17; 515 (1671). The same questions, together with answers stated in the third person plural, appear in Peypsian ms. 2582, Magdalene College, England, *Samuel Wiseman's Book of Record, 1676–1677* (available on microfilm of the Virginia Colonial Records Project, survey report 578, pp. 108–11, microfilm reel 6618). They are signed by John Hartwell as being "a true copy." The date of the answers in the Hartwell copy is not given. Since Samuel Wiseman was the Secretary of the Royal Commissioners who arrived in Virginia in January and February 1677 to investigate the causes of Bacon's Rebellion and to propose remedies in its wake, it would appear that the answers were sufficiently current for the Royal Commissioners' purposes.

6. CO 5/714, Nicholson letter to the Lords of Trade and Plantations, 20 August 1698.

7. Robert Powis, a minister of the Church, lost out in the bidding for Eleanor Clure. But "in a drinking merriment," in order to frustrate the high bidder, he married Clure to a third party, Edward Cooper. Months later, by way of penalty against Powis for his abuse of office, the court deducted 300 pounds of tobacco from a judgment of a debt of 3,200 pounds owed him by Cooper. It appears that Clure herself was not asked to testify. (Norfolk County Records, 1656–1666, pp. 125, 151 [16 February 1657/8; 15 June 1658].) As a general note on the marketing process, see also Smith pp. 17–18.

8. *A Relation of Maryland* (London, 1635), Ann Arbor University Microfilms, Inc., March of America Facsimile Series, 22; p. 53.

9. The military force dispatched from England in October 1651 to reduce Virginia to obedience to the Cromwellian Commonwealth also brought "one hundred and fifty Scotch prisoners, taken in the recent battle of Worcester, and sent over to be sold as servants" (John Thomas Scharf, *History of Maryland from the Earliest Period to the Present Day*, 3 vols. [Baltimore, 1879; 1967 reprint], 1:209).

10. Of the total of some 250,000 limited-term bond-laborers that came to the continental colonies from 1607 to 1783, 35,000 to 50,000 were convicts; most of them, however, were sent following passage of a law (4 Geo. I 11) in 1717 "for the further preventing robbery, burglary, and other felonies, and for the more effectual transportation of felons and unlawful exporters of wool," and at the same time supplying the "great want of servants who by their labor and industry might be the means of improving and making more useful the said colonies." By that time the term "servants" was reserved for European-Americans bond-laborers.

A Council of State of the Commonwealth in 1653 authorized Richard Netherway of Bristol "to export one hundred Irish tories who were to be sold as slaves in Virginia." (Philip Alexander Bruce, *Economic History of Virginia in the Seventeenth Century: An Inquiry into the Material Conditions of the People, based upon original records*, 2 vols. (New York, 1895; reprinted 1935), 1:609, citing *Interregnum Entry Book*, vol. 98, p. 405.) Perhaps the order was interpreted to include potential "tories": in October 1654, two Maryland investors bought eight Irish boys, four of whom were so little that it was suggested that the buyers should have "brought cradles to rock them in." (*Archives of Maryland*, 41:478). See also *The Invention of the White Race*, Volume One, p. 74, for reference to "the Irish slave trade." See also John W. Blake, "Transportation from Ireland to America, 1653–60," *Irish Historical Studies*, 3:267–81 (1942–43), especially pp. 271, 273, 280 in relation to Virginia.

11. "Certain propositions for the better accommodating Forreigne Plantations with servants," CO 324/1, ff. 275–83; f. 275.

12. The number of kidnapped British laborers in the entire colonial period has been estimated at between ten thousand and twenty thousand. (Albert Hart Blumenthal, *Brides from Bridewell, Female Felons Sent to Colonial America* [Rutland, Vermont, 1962], p. 76.)

13. William Bullock, *Virginia Impartially Examined* (London, 1649), pp. 14, 47.

14. CO 324/1. "A much larger portion of our colonial population than is generally supposed found itself on American soil because of the wheedlings, deceptions, misrepresentations and other devices of the 'spirits.'" (Smith, p. 86.)

15. CO 389/2, items "I," "J," and "K." These were affidavits taken in proceedings before Justice William Morton in England in January 1671. Haverland's aggressiveness is noted in the testimony given by Thomas Stone and by Mary Collins who, it seems, was also a spirit. According to her, Haverland was reckless and disdainful of the law in the practice of his profession. He replied to hints of possible trouble with the authorities in unrestrained language: "... He did not care a turd for my Lord Chief Justice nor his warrant and that he would wipe his arse with the Warrant." Speaking of a Dorsetshire Justice of the Peace who was said to be seeking Haverland, Haverland "swore God damn him ... He would have the life of ... [the Justice of the Peace] Mr Thomas or hee should have the life of him [Haverland], and shooke his sword and Swore God damn him, his sword should be both Judge and justice for him" (CO 389/2, item "I").

16. CO 389/2, items "I," "J," and "K."

17. CO 389/2, item "K," Haverland affidavit, 30 January 1670/1.

18. Bullock, p. 47.

19. Smith, p. 36.

20. Bullock, pp. 35–6.

21. Francis L. Berkeley (see note 3) cites that entry as evidence that "persons dependent on the parish were transported to the colonies."

22. Smith. In 1668, sixty-nine bond-laborers were shipped from England to Thomas Cooper, Maryland merchant or planter, at a charge of about £3 10s. each.

23. Ibid., p. 36.

24. Ibid., pp. 41–2.

25. The principle was reinforced by Royal Instructions, as in Queen Anne's directions to Francis Nicholson, who was then Governor of Virginia: "[N]one shall acquire a [head] Right meerly by importing or buying servants." The patentee was required to employ the bond-laborers in work on the headright land within three years. (CO 5/1360, p. 268. 16 October 1702.)

26. Apparently young Verney opted for the latter course; he was back in England in less than a year. *Verney Papers*, Camden Society Publications, 56:160–63 (1853).

27. James Revel, 'The Poor Unhappy Transported Felon's Sorrowful Account of His Fourteen Years of Transportation at Virginia in America (circa 1680)," cited by John M. Jennings, *VMHB*, 56:189–94 (1948). There is no way of tracing the lineage of this poem to an actual identifiable author; its first publication was in the form of a chapbook, or popular pamphlet, sold by street peddlers in London in the middle of the eighteenth century. Its authenticity is indicated by certain place names, topographical references and travel routes, that were not familiar in England. Jennings refers to authorities such as Jernegan, Ballagh, and Bruce in concluding that, in any event, the work "presents a realistic picture of conditions in Virginia in the middle of the seventeenth century." Jennings is able to deduce that the author would have had to have come to Virginia somewhere between 1656 and 1671. I would further hazard that, since the poem does not allude to Bacon's Rebellion, Revel would have completed his term of servitude before that unignorable event. That fact would seem to fix the date of his arrival in the colony between 1656 and 1662. The poem is reprinted in Warren M. Billings, ed., *The Old Dominion in the Seventeenth Century, A Documentary History of Virginia, 1606–1689* (Chapel Hill, 1975), pp. 137–42. This particular passage is found there at pp. 138–9.

28. Richard Beale Davis, ed., *William Fitzhugh and his Chesapeake World, 1676–1701* (Chapel Hill, 1963), pp. 128–9.

29. See Chapter 3, especially pp. 40–45.

30. Hening, 1:396 (1656); 1:410 (1655); 1:455–6 (1658); 1:481–2 (1658); 1:546 (1660).

31. Hening, 2:143 (1662).

32. Hening, 2:283.

33. Hening, 2:346.

34. Hening, 2:404 (February 1677).

35. Hening, 2:492–3. This 1682 law resulted in the "importation of many more Indian slaves than has usually been recognized." (Edmund S. Morgan, *American Slavery, American Freedom: The Ordeal of Colonial Virginia* [New York, 1975], p. 330.)

36. Bruce, 2:129. *Economic History.* James C. Ballagh, *A History of Slavery in Virginia* (Baltimore, 1902), pp. 35–6.

37. Hening, 3:69.

38. Hening, 3: 69 n.

39. William W. Hening and William Munford, *Reports of Cases, Relating Chiefly to Points of Practice, Decided by the Supreme Court of Chancery for the Richmond District,* 2nd edn., "Hudgins v. Wrights," (1806), 1:133–43; p. 137. But the court refused to extend the presumption of liberty to African-Americans as Judge George Wythe had urged. That privilege, the court stated, "relates to white persons and native American Indians" but not "to native Africans and their descendants" (pp. 134, 143).

40. Lewis C. Gray, assisted by Esther K. Thompson, *History of Agriculture in the Southern United States to 1860* (Washington, DC, 1932; reprinted 1958), 2:1025; Table 39 gives the number of African-American bond-laborers for four colonies/states (Virginia, Maryland, North Carolina, South Carolina, and Georgia) as 632,000. Philip D. Curtin, *The Atlantic Slave Trade: A Census* (Madison, 1969), p. 72, estimates the number of African bond-laborers brought into the thirteen original colonies to have been around 275,000.

41. Replying to an inquiry about the mortality rate made by the Commissioners for Foreign Plantations in 1676, Governor William Berkeley said that, "whereas previously not one in five escaped the first year," the situation had so improved that "not one in ten unseasoned hands die now." *Samuel Wiseman's Book of Record,* pp. 108–11. Cf. Hening, 2:515.)

The average annual death rate in England in the 1670s was less than 3 percent. (E. A. Wrigley and R. S. Schofield, *The Population History of England, 1541–1871: A Reconstruction* [Cambridge, Mass., 1981], p. 532.)

42. Russell R. Menard: *Economy and Society in Early Colonial Maryland* (New York, 1985), pp. 254, 268–9; idem., "From Servants to Slaves: The Transformation of the Chesapeake Labor System," *Southern Studies,* 16: 355–90 (1977); David W. Galenson, "White Servitude and the Growth of Black Slavery in Colonial America," *Journal of Economic History,* 41:39–47 (1981); idem, *White Servitude in Colonial America: An Economic Analysis* (New York, 1981); idem, *Traders, Planters and Slaves: Market Behavior in Early English America* (New York, 1986), pp. 162–6.

43. Annie Lash Jester, comp. and ed., *Adventurers of Purse and Person: Virginia, 1607–25* (Princeton, 1956; 2nd edition, 1964), pp. 1–70. The discussion of the muster by Irene W. D. Hect, "The Virginia Muster of 1624/25 as a Source for Demographic History" (*WMO,* 30:65–92), is of invaluable help to students of that period. Her use of the phrase "Negro servants or slaves" in the "or slaves" part does not reflect the record that she has produced and discussed.

44. Hening, 2:170 (1662). *Archives of Maryland,* 1:533 (1663–64). See further in Chapter 10.

45. *MCGC,* p. 466 (June 1640). Hening, 2:26 (1661). Helen Tuncliff Catterall, ed., *Judicial Cases Concerning Emerican Slavery and the Negro,* 5 vols. (Washington, DC, 1926–37 Octagon reprint, 1968), 4:189.

46. Hening, 2:170 (1662). *Archives of Maryland,* 1:533 (1663–64). See also: Whittington B. Johnson, "The Origin and Nature of African Slavery in Seventeenth Century Maryland," *Maryland Historical Magazine,* 73:236–45 (1978); p. 237.

47. Gray, 1:203.

48. Morgan, p. 404.

49. "A Perfect Description of Virginia," in *Force Tracts,* Vol. 2, No. 8, p. 14. A study of twenty-two estate inventories recorded in Surry County, Virginia in the years 1686 to 1688, found not one plow listed. (Kevin P. Kelly, "Economic and Social Development of Seventeenth-century Surry County, Virginia," PhD Dissertation, University of Washington, 1972; p. 138.)

50. Tobacco historian Robert says that in order to remove buds more efficiently in order to limit the number of tobacco leaves drawing on the plant's nutrition, "Some of the yeomen who worked their own crops allowed their thumb nails to grow long and then hardened these nails in the flame of a candle." (Joseph Clarke Robert, *The Story of Tobacco in America* [New York, 1940], p. 14 n. 3.) I have not seen any evidence of this practice among bond-laborers; perhaps they did not see any advantage for themselves in such an improvement in "the instruments of production."

51. Gray, 1:215–17. Bruce, 1:439–43. Joseph Clark Robert, *The Tobacco Kingdom: The Plantation, Market, and Factory in Virginia and North Carolina (1800–1860)* (Durham, North Carolina, 1938), pp. 34–55. Ulrich Bonnell Phillips, *Life and Labor in the Old South* (Boston, 1929; 3rd edn., 1967), pp. 112–15.

52. Russell R. Menard, *Economy and Society in Early Colonial Maryland* (New York, 1985), p. 462. Menard's summary of extensive data that he presents on the previous two pages for the

period 1619 to 1698 cites mainly, but not exclusively, Maryland data only from 1635 on. There is no significant discrepancy between the increase of product per worker in Virginia and Maryland. See also Gray, 1:218–19.

53. Morgan, pp. 126–9, 281–2. Morgan also attaches much importance to the "unadaptability" of English laborers for colonial labor. (He seems to imply that Africans were better suited by their previous labor experience.) But whereas Smith attributes the inability to adapt to those who had not been agricultural laborers in England, Morgan finds the typical rural English worker to have been unsuited for plantation labor. He even gives this typical emigrant worker a sobriquet, "The Lazy Englishman," linking his unsuitability for plantation labor to that of "The Idle Indian" (Ibid., Chapter 3, especially, pp. 50–65).

54. *Archives of Maryland*, 54:234.

55. Hening, 1:257; 2:113. *Archives of Maryland*, 2:147–8. I have used the term "adult bond-laborers" to cover the various cases in which the non-youth ages range from sixteen for Irish and "aliens," in 1643 and 1658, respectively, and then for all bond-laborers in 1662 in Virginia, to twenty-two in Maryland in 1666.

56. *Archives of Maryland*, 2:147–48.

57. Hening, 2:240.

58. John Codman Hurd, *The Law of Freedom and Bondage in the United States*, 2 vols. (Boston, 1858; Negro Universities Press reprint, 1968), 1:138–9. Under the Statute of Artificers of 1562, a laborer who failed to fulfill the terms of a contract for a particular job might also be put in jail for one month. (See pp. 22–3.)

59. *MCGC*, p. 105.

60. *MCGC*, pp. 466–8.

61. Hening, 1:440. (1658).

62. *Archives of Maryland*, 1:107–8.

63. McCormac, p. 52.

64. *Archives of Maryland*, 2:524; "Runaway servants were usually rewarded with a severe whipping by their masters ..." (*Proceedings of the County Court of Charles County, 1658–1666, and Manor Court of St Clement's Manor, 1659–72, Archives of Maryland*, 53:xxxiii (editorial comment).

65. *Proceedings of the County Court of Charles County, 1666–1674, Archives of Maryland*, 60:xxxv–xxxvi (editorial comment).

66. Ibid., 2:149; 65:xxxiii.

67. At that time the average product per worker was 1,553 pounds of tobacco per year, and the price of tobacco was exceptionally low at 0.9*d.* per pound. The price of male bond-laborers with four years or more to serve was then 2,100 pounds of tobacco. (Menard, *Economy and Society in Early Colonial Maryland*, pp. 249 (Table VII–2); 448 (Table A–7); 462 (Table A–14). The product of sixty-two weeks of labor would equate to nearly 1,800 pounds of tobacco.

68. *Archives of Maryland*, 65:92

69. *Archives of Maryland*, 69:154–5.

70. For Virginia laws, see Hening, 2:273–4 (1663), 277–8, (1669) and 283 (1672). See also *Archives of Maryland*, 54:502, 527, 524, for examples of court awards to captors of runaway bond-laborers.

71. *Archives of Maryland*, 2:523–8.

72. In authorizing the expenditure of 1,000 pounds of tobacco for construction of the apparatuses for these forms of punishment, the Northumberland County Court gave most particular specifications: "The said pillory is to be supplied with two Locust posts, the plank of which it is made to be white oake two inches and a halfe thick [not recommended for the short-necked], Eight foot in Length, and at least Seaven foot and a halfe high from the holes [for the hands and the head of the victim] in the pillory to the Ground, with a bench of Convenient height to stand upon[.] The stocks to be made of white oake ten foot long and three inches and halfe thick with a bench to sitt upon[.] The whip[p]ing post to be of Sound Locust at least Eight foot above the ground and three foot and halfe within the ground, to be eight-square [octagonal] and at least eight inches in Diameter" (*Northumberland County Records, 1678–98*, p. 424 [15 February 1687/8]).

73. Hening, 1:265–7, 463–5; 2:143–6.

74. Raphael Semmes, *Crime and Punishment in Early Maryland* (Baltimore, 1938), pp. 37–8. Semmes comments: "A man must indeed have been in wretched circumstances if life in one of the jails seemed attractive." See also Hening, 2:278–9.

75. Hening, 2:278–9 (1670). *Archives of Maryland*, 10:292.

76. Good surveys of this aspect of the status of bond-laborers are to be found in: Smith

pp. 270–274; Bruce, 2:35–9; *Economic History* (Baltimore, 1895) and James C. Ballagh, *White Servitude in the Colony of Virginia*, pp. 50–51.

Smith generalizes: "Legal marriage without the consent of the masters was always forbidden" (p. 271). Bruce appears to empathize with the owners: "Secret marriages among the servants of the colony seem to have been a common source of serious loss to masters" (2:37).

77. If a master consented to the marriage of a woman bond-laborer belonging to him, the woman was freed from him (*MCGC*, p. 504 [12 March 1655/56]).

78. The record seems to reflect the fact that defiance of this law was more likely where the bond-laborer was attempting to marry a free person, since it almost necessarily involved absconding from the owner's plantation. In 1656, the Lancaster County Virginia Court judged the marriage of a bond-laborer John Smith to be "no marriage" and ordered him to be returned constable-to-constable to his owner (*Lancaster County Records, 1652–57*, p. 285). The following year, the fine for ministers conducting such marriages was by law increased from 1,000 pounds of tobacco to 10,000 pounds (Hening, 1:332, 433). For other examples of such illegal marriages, see: *Norfolk County Records, 1637–46*, p. 51 (1640); *Norfolk County Records, 1646–51*, ff. 147–147a (1650); and *Essex County Records, 1703–1708*, p. 3 (1703).

79. Hening, 1:252–3 (1643). *Archives of Maryland*, 1:97 (1640). See also John Leeds Bozman, *The History of Maryland from Its First Settlement in 1633 to the Restoration in 1660*, 2 vols. (Baltimore, 1837), 2:135.

80. Forlorn bond-laborer Sarah Hedges was unsuccessful in her invocation of this defense because the man she said was her husband, a seaman, did not return with "the next shipping." (*Norfolk County Records, 1656–66*, f. 423 [17 April 1665]; *Norfolk County Orders, 1666–75*, f. 2 [10 May 1666].) For successful invocations of this immunity, see: *Accomack County Records, 1690–97*, pp. 173–173a (21 November 1695). See Also *Northampton County records, 1657–64*, ff. 163, 166 (23 March 1662/3; 28 April 1663).

81. See Hening, 3:74, 139, 361.

82. Ibid., 1:253.

83. Ibid. 2:114–15.

84. A minister's salary was £80 by law (ibid., 2:45 [1662]). Ten thousand pounds of tobacco would have equated officially to £34 (ibid., 2:55).

85. When the English takeover of New Netherlands began in 1664, the so-called "Laws of the Duke of York" were promulgated for the former Dutch territories. These were compiled from those already in effect in earlier Anglo-American colonies. One paragraph of these laws declared that marriages of bond-laborers done without owner consent "shall be proceeded against as for Adultery or fornication." Children of such unions were to be "reputed as Bastards." (Cheesman A. Herrick, *White Servitude in Pennsylvania Indentured and Pennsylvania Labor in Colony and Commonwealth* [Philadelphia, 1926. Negro Universities reprint, 1969], pp. 28, 287.)

86. Hening, 2:114–15.

87. Bozman, 2:135n.

88. Ibid.

89. The Maryland Provinical Court in 1657 sentenced a free woman and free man to twenty lashes each for "having lived in a notorious and Scandalous Course of life tending to Adultery and Fornication." The man's punishment was remitted upon the payment of a fine of five hundred pounds of tobacco. (*Archives of Maryland*, 1:508–9, 588.)

In April 1649, in an instance that apparently involved no physical punishment, a Virginia county court ordered that "William Watts & Mary, Captain Cornwallis's Negro Woman . . . each of them doe penance by standing in a white sheet with a white Rodd in their hands in the Chapell of Elizabeth Rivers in the face of the congregation on the next Sabbath day that the minister shall reade divine service and the said Watts to pay the court charges." (*Norfolk Wills and Deeds, 1646–51*, p. 113a.) I have noted half a dozen early Norfolk County cases in which this "white sheet, white rod" penance was imposed on fornicators.

90. *Archives of Maryland*, Vol. LIII, *Proceedings of the County Court of Charles County, 1658–66*; editor's comment, p. xxx.

91. Bozman, 2:135n.

92. Hening, 2:115 (1662); 3:139 (1696).

93. For Virginia instances in which the "coverture" defense was used (once unsuccessfully and once successfully) see *Henrico County Record Book No. 1, 1677–92*, p. 164 (1 August 1684); and *Accomack County Records, 1690–97*, f. 153 (18 June 1695).

On the other hand, the Virginia Assembly in 1662 ordered the erection of a ducking-stool for punishment of women whose utterances might make "their poore husbands" subject to law suits under the "coverture" principle. But it appears that there were reasons for which unmarried women as well could be subjected to this sometimes fatal treatment. In 1663, Elizabeth Leveritt, a husbandless bond-laborer, was sentenced to endure the ordeal of watery suffocation for being "impudent" to her owner. In an order that was unique so far as my study of the seventeenth-century Chesapeake records goes, the same court ordered that her owner be similarly tortured for failing to maintain a proper discipline over Leveritt. (*Accomack County Records, 1663–1666*, f. 26.)

94. 18 Eliz. I, c. 3. George Nicholls, *A History of the English Poor Law in Connection with the state of the country and Condition of the People*, 3 vols.; (supplementary volume by Thomas Mackay), (1898; 1904; Augustus M. Kelley reprint, 1967), 1:165–6.

95. Hening, 2:115, 167. In 1691, the added time was reduced to one year when the parents were European-Americans (Hening, 3:139–40).

96. *Archives of Maryland*, 1:373–4.

97. Hening, 2:115. Bruce, 2:35–6.

98. *Archives of Maryland*, 58:28. The editors of this volume (*Proceedings of the County Court of Charles County, 1658–1666 and Manor Court of St Clement's Manor, 1659–1672*) state that "Both men and women were whipped indiscriminately, women on the bare back apparently as frequently as men" (p. xxx).

99. Ballagh, *White Servitude in the Colony of Virginia*, p. 48. Smith, p. 271.

100. *York County Deeds, Orders, Wills Etc., 1684–87*, f. 7 (26 January 1685).

101. Commenting on the common occurrence of sentences of two or three years for mothers in such cases, A. E. Smith notes that the actual time off for child-bearing rarely lasted for more than a month or six weeks. "[I]t is plain that the maidservant generally served far more extra time than she can possibly have lost through her misdeeds [let that judgementalism pass]; sentences of two and even three years are quite common, though childbirth can rarely have incapacitated a woman for more than a month or six weeks." (Smith, p. 271.)

102. See Chapter 8, note 37, regarding the extent of these records.

103. Rating tobacco at 10s. per hundred pounds, and the cost of transportation of European-American bond-laborers at £6 each.

104. Output per worker in pounds of tobacco increased in every decade from 1619 to 1699, and it is estimated to have been more than 1,500 pounds in the 1660s. (Menard, *Economy and Society in Early Colonial Maryland*, p. 426, Table A–14.) Though the price of Chesapeake tobacco fluctuated, it was officially rated at about ten shillings a hundred pounds, 1.2d. per pound, during the last four decades of the seventeenth century. (See Morgan, p. 204 n. 29.)

105. Smith, p. 271. Hening, 2:168.

106. *Accomack County Records, 1666–70*, f. 176, 3 February 1669/70. *Accomack County Records, 1697–1703*, f. 78, 17 November 1699. *Norfolk County Records, 1675–86*, p. 44, 22 November 1677.

107. *Norfolk County Records, 1646–51*, f. 140, 26 March 1650.

108. *Archives of Maryland*,, 53:xxviii–xxix, pp. 28–30.

109. Ibid., 53:xxix, p. 37.

110. For instances of this aspect of gender-class oppression, see: *Norfolk County Records, 1651–1656*, ff. 35 and 46 (1653); *Lancaster County Records, 1655–1666*, p. 82 (1659); *Charles City County Records, 1655–1665*, p. 523 (1664); *Norfolk County Records, 1666–1675 (part 2)*, f. 74a (1671); *Norfolk County Records, 1675–1686*, ff. 44 and 99 (1677, 1679); *Accomack County Records, 1697–1703*, ff. 78–78a, and 129a–130 (1699, 1702); *Surry County Records, 1671–91*, pp. 454–55 (1684). In four of these cases, the owner sold away his own child in the womb of the pregnant bond-laborer.

These acts were treated as "fornication," which entailed a fine of 500 pounds of tobacco on each party. If the woman bond-laborer was unable to pay her fine, she was to suffer 20 or 30 lashes at the whipping post "on her naked back," or alternatively, if the owner paid her fine, she was bound to serve six months for that, and two years more for the expense her pregnancy and the child would be to the master (Hening, 2:115; 3:74, 159). In Virginia after 1662, as is noted below, the extra two years was to be served under a different master, to whom she was to be sold by the churchwardens (Hening, 2:167).

111. Hening, 2:167. In Maryland in 1694 a woman in this situation was required to swear "in her pains of Travaille" that the owner was the father. This oath, which the bond-laborer could swear falsely only at the peril of hell's eternal fire, would be taken as proof only if it seemed to the male judges to be consistent with all other evidence and testimony. (*Archives of Maryland*, 19:47.)

112. *Archives of Maryland*, 60:xxxvi, 9–11. The court record identifies Yansley as a "Spinster," most likely a reference to her occupation, not to her unmarried status. The editor of this volume of the *Archives of Maryland*, says that Yansley was "presumably" a bond-laborer.

113. George Nicholls, 1:114–19, 121–5, 189. The laws were 22 Henry VIII c. 10, 27 Henry VIII c. 25, and 43 Eliz. c. 2.

114. Nicholls, 1:189.

115. Hening, 2:240. *Archives of Maryland*, 2:147–8. See also Semmes, pp. 85–7.

116. Hening, 2:115, 168.

117. Hening, 1:552.

118. Menard, *Economy and Society in Early Colonial Maryland*, pp. 460–61, 462. It is to be noted that European-American women were not tithable unless they were "working in the ground"; but the records indicate that many, perhaps most, were engaged directly in the cultivation of tobacco fields.

119. See the cases of Bridgett (last name omitted in the record) and Wilking (?) Jones: *Norfolk County Records (part 2, Orders), 1666–75*, pp. 94, 101 (June and August 1673); *Norfolk County Order Book, 1675–86*, p. 108 (2 March 1679/80). For the 1662 law, see Hening, 2:114–15.

120. When the plantation bourgeoisie was able to reduce its labor force to mainly lifetime, hereditary servitude, in the eighteenth century, the birth of the children did become "cost-effective," as the bourgeois term is.

121. Hening, 1:361 (1649); 3:256. Under a law passed in 1680, *imported* children of African origin were not to be tithable until they were twelve years of age, those coming from Europe not until they were fourteen years old (Hening, 2:479–80).

122. Hening, 2:168 (1662).

123. Ibid., 2:298 (1672).

124. Ibid., 2:170.

125. Hening, 3:87.

126. In the opinion of Whittington B. Johnson, "This course of action was probably forced upon slaveowners because there were so few African females in the colony"; it brought the owner "potential monetary gain" (Johnson, p. 242.)

127. This calculation was propounded in an opinion delivered by Judge Daniel Dulany, himself a slaveholder, in a historical appendix to a decision delivered by him on behalf of the Maryland Provincial Court on 16 December 1767. (Thomas Harris Jr and John McHenry, *Maryland Reports, being a Series of the Most Important Cases argued and determined in the Provincial Court and the Court of Appeals of the then province of Maryland from the Year 1700 down to the American Revolution* [New York, 1809], 2 vols., 1:559–64; 563.)

128. *Archives of Maryland*, 1:533 (1662); 13:546–9 (1692).

129. Hening, 2:170. Ballagh, *History of Slavery in Virginia*, p. 57.

130. Hening, 3:87.

131. *CSP, Col.*, 13:644 (Minutes of the General Assembly of Maryland, 21 May 1692).

132. *Elizabeth City County Records, 1684–99* (transcript), p. 83 (30 December 1695).

133. *Accomack County Records, 1703–9*, ff. 107–a, 118 (3 February and 2 June 1708).

134. Hening, 1:153–4; 2:195; 273. *Archives of Maryland*, 2:523–4. For some Virginia cases arising under such laws, see *Norfolk County Records, 1665–75*, p. 42 (1670), and ibid., *1675–86*; *Middlesex County Records, 1673–80*, f. 135 (1678); and *Accomack County Records, 1678–82*, p. 173 (1680).

135. Hening, 2:115–16 (1662).

136. The situation reported by an emissary of the London government in 1701 surely was not of recent origin. "A great many," he said, "choose to sit down loosers rather than go to the Law." (Report of George Larkin to the Lords of Trade and Plantations, CO 5/1312, 22 December 1701.)

137. Richard B. Morris, *Government and Labor in Early America* (New York, 1946), pp. 312–13.

138. *Charles City County Court Orders, 1655–1658*, in Beverley Fleet, comp., *Virginia Colonial Abstracts*, 34 vols., (Baltimore, 1961), vol. 10, p. 441 (8 February 1663/64).

139. McCormac, p. 44.

140. Ibid., p. 66. Ballagh, *White Servitude in the Colony of Virginia*, p. 59. Hening, 2:268 (1668).

141. *Archives of Maryland*, Vol. 60, *Proceedings of the County Court of Charles County, 1666–1674*, pp. xxxv–xxxvi.

142. Ibid., pp. 45–47. The matter is presented in fuller detail in the record.

143. Ibid., pp. 108–9.

144. *Northampton County [Wills] Order Book*, No. 10, 1674–1679, p. 270.

145. *Calendar of Virginia State Papers and Other Manuscripts ... Preserved in the Capitol at Richmond, 1652–1859* edited by W. P. Palmer, S. McRae, H. W. Flourney, et al., 11 vols. (Richmond, 1875–1893); 1:9–10.

146. *Journals of the House of Burgesses of Virginia*, H. R. McIlwaine, ed., 13 vols. (Richmond, 1915); 2:34–5. Library of Congress, Jefferson Papers, Series 8, Vol. 7 (Miscellaneous Documents), p. 232 (24 October 1666).

147. Smith, pp. 237–8. This was not so in Barbados in the late decades of the seventeenth century, where by law the European bond-laborers were guaranteed five pounds of meat a week and four pairs of shoes every year, along with corresponding quantities of other items of wearing apparel (Smith, p.237). This contrast is rooted in the relative difficulty of keeping European bond-laborers in the West Indies as compared with the continental plantation colonies. (See Chapter 12.)

148. *Accomack County Order Book I, 1632–1640*, p. 68 (1 February 1635/36); *Accomack County Deeds & Wills [Orders], 1666–1670*, p. 48 (17 February 1667/8). See also Smith, p. 250.

149. Gray, 1:366. Smith, p. 250.

150. For the customary diet in England, see E. H. Phelps-Brown and Sheila V. Hopkins, "Seven Centuries of the Prices of Consumables compared with Builders' Wage-rates," *Economica*, 23:296–307 (1956). Although the tabulation skips from the sixteenth to the eighteenth century, it indicates a trend of increase in the importance of meat and dairy products in the English diet. While the grains-and-peas proportion declined slightly, beef replaced herring in the diet, and by 1725, out of every 100 pence [the equivalent of less than ten days builders' wages] spent on "consumables" (food, drink, fuel and light, and textiles), the meat and dairy products portions accounted for 37½ pence and included 33 pounds of beef, 10 pounds of butter, and 10 pounds of cheese. (See ibid., Tables 1 and 2.) How nearly this approximated the wage worker's diet is not revealed, however.

See pp. 151–2 for bond-laborers' struggles over diet.

151. Aubrey C. Land, "The Planters of Colonial Maryland," *Maryland Historical Magazine*, 67:109–28 (1972); p. 124.

152. Bruce, 1:486. Gray, 1:209.

153. E. H. Phelps-Brown and Sheila V. Hopkins, "Wage-rates and Prices: Evidence for Population Pressure in the Sixteenth Century," *Economica*, 24:289–306 (1957); table 4, "England" column 1.

154. Bruce, 2:205–11.

155. Gray, 1:209.

156. Cf. Bruce, 2:8. Bruce cites York County records for 1657–1662 to argue that in 1661 bond-laborers were given meat three times a week. But he seems unable to find grounds for his speculation that, "It could not have been many years before this allowance was extended to each day in consequence of the enormous increase in the heads of hogs and horned cattle." Perhaps he might have cited from the same volume of York County records the rebellious complaint of bond-laborers that they were dieted on only corn and water, whereas they were supposed to get meat three times a week. (York County *Deeds, Orders, Wills, Etc*, f. 149 [6 January 1661/2]. Besides the folio number given here, there is page number 297 inscribed by the Virginia State Library, and a typescript page 384 of the same record. Bruce cites "p. 384." Could he have been using the typescript; and did he mean 1662 instead of 1661?) See references to this bond-laborers' plot in Chapter 8.

157. "Questions proposed by his Majestie and Councell for which I return this humble plain and true answer." [Henry] In *Coventry Papers Relating to Virginia, Barbados and other Colonies*, microfilm prepared by the British Manuscripts Project of the American Council of Learned Societies and available at the Library of Congress (originals at the estate of the Marquis of Bath, Longleat House, Wiltshire, England, hereafter to be cited as *Coventry Papers*.) The present citation is Vol. 77, f. 332. The report is not dated, but was obviously written in the fall of 1676. Henry Coventry was a Secretary of State with primary responsibility for the colonies.

158. Jasper Dankers and Peter Sluyter, *Journal of a Voyage to New York and a Tour in Several of the American Colonies in 1679–80*, translated and edited by Henry C. Murphy, Long Island Historical society Memoirs I (Brooklyn, 1867), p. 191.

The report of George Larkin to the Lords of trade and Plantations in December 1701 revealed that in Virginia and Maryland the owners still held to the principle of getting pennies by saving them at the expense of the bond-laborers' food allowance: ". . . a man had really better be hanged than come a servant into the Plantations, most of his food being homene and water. . . . I have been told by some of them that they have not tasted flesh meat in three months." (CO, 5/1312).

159. Gray, 1:365–6.

160. Using Menard's tabulations for the period 1660–79 inclusive for Maryland, the average output per worker was 1,603 pounds of tobacco, and the average price was 1.18*d*. In five years the labor of each bond-laborer would thus have brought to the owner an income of £39 8*s*. (See Menard, *Economy and Society in Early Colonial Maryland*, pp. 449 and 462.) In Virginia before 1660, according to Thomas J. Wertenbaker, "the average annual income from the labor of one able worker ... was not less than £12" (*The Planters of Colonial Virginia* [Princeton, 1922], p. 71). Morgan says that Virginia tobacco prices were "probably somewhat higher" than those in Maryland,

and he notes that in official transactions in Virginia in the last four decades of the seventeenth century, tobacco was rated at 10*s* per hundred pounds (1.2*d* per pound). (Morgan, p. 204 n. 20.) See also L. C. Gray's discussion of tobacco prices, 1:262–8.

Semmes states that an owner made an annual profit of "about fifty pounds sterling," citing, among other facts, the claim by a member of the Maryland Colony council that on average the bond-laborer "would produce to his master, at least fifty pounds sterling clear profit into purse, most commonly far more." (Semmes p. 80; the quoted phrase is cited from "Letters of Robert Wintour", unpublished manuscript in the collection of Dr Hugh H. Young, of Baltimore, Maryland.)

161. CO 5/1312. See notes 136 and 158 above. A quarter of a century before, the Virginia Assembly noted the practice among owners of pressuring bond-laborers who were nearing the end of their terms to agree to extend their servitude. (Hening 2:388–9.)

162. '. . . The observed increase in productivity probably resulted from making servants work harder" (Joseph Douglas Deal, *Race and Class in Colonial Virginia: Indians, Englishmen, and Africans on the Eastern Shore during the Seventeenth Century* (New York, 1993), p. 115).

163. Phillips, p. 126.

164. Robert, *Tobacco Kingdom*, p. 18.

165. Menard, *Economy and Society in Early Colonial Maryland*, p. 239.

166. George Fitzhugh in *De Bow's Review*, 30:89 (January 1861), cited in Phillips, p. 126.

167. Consequently, early in the season, when ready tobacco might not be available, exchanges were sometimes made completely or partially by direct barter, as in the following cases found in the Maryland court records. In April 1663, Elizabeth Holbrooke, a bond-laborer belonging to John Williams with four years to serve, was exchanged for "One yearling heyfer, with her encrease." In March 1667, John Godshall acquired a parcel of land called "Hogge Quarter" for "a Servant named Thomas Porch in hand paid." When Thomas King the following year bought five hundred acres of land on the north side of Nangemy Creek from Thomas and John Stone, he paid "Seven Thousand Pounds of Tobacco and Caske and two Servants" (*Archives of Maryland*, 49:7 [1663]; 60:147, 168–9 [1668]). The Lancaster County Virginia records for that same month reveal that Thomas Williamson had taken out a "mortgage" on a male bond-laborer, one Samuel Pen[?], on whom the mortgage holder, Thomas Williamson, was seeking foreclosure. (*Lancaster Orders, Etc., 1666–1680*, p. 34 [13 March 1666/7].)

168. Bruce, 1:447.

169. Land, p. 124.

170. Referring particularly to the 1660–80 period, when tobacco prices were much lower than in previous decades, Edmund S. Morgan writes that the small self-employed farmer was apt to be debt-ruined in times of especially low tobacco prices, but "a man with capital or credit to deal on a large scale" could thrive through it all by prudent market operations, and "by working his men [and women] a little harder" (Morgan, p. 191).

171. Bullock, p. 11. See also *A Perfect Description of Virginia, Being a Full and True Relation of the Present State of the Plantation, Their Health, Peace, and Plenty* . . . (London, 1649) in *Force Tracts*, II, No. 8, p. 6.

A century later the much-quoted William Eddis found that in Maryland, as a general rule, European bond-laborers were "strained to their uttermost to perform their allotted labor" under the watchful eye of the "rigid planter [who] exercises inflexible severity in matters of supervision."

172. *Accomack Court Orders, 1666–1670*, ff. 60–62 (16 June 1668). The name of this entrepreneur is notorious to the fellowship of scholars of the seventeenth-century Chesapeake.

173. Dankers and Sluyter, p. 216.

174. *Archives of Maryland*, 10:521 (22 September 1657).

175. *Archives of Maryland*, 1:21.

176. James Revel, "The Poor Unhappy Transported Felon's Sorrowful Account . . .," *VMHB*, 56:189–94 (1948). Reprinted in Billings, p. 140.

177. *Archives of Maryland*, 10:484–5 (10 March 1656/7).

178. Bruce, 2:33.

179. Revel, p. 140.

180. According to the author of *A Description of the Province of New Albion, And a Direction for Adventurers with small stock to get two for one, and good land freely*, written in 1649, only one out of nine Virginia immigrants was dying in the first critical year in the colony, but in the first three decades, five out of six died in the first year of bondage, called the "seasoning" time. (*Force Tracts*, II, No. 7, p. 5.) Governor Berkeley reported to the Lords of Trade and Plantations in 1671 that the bond-laborers then generally survived the first "seasoning" year, but that "heretofore not one of five escaped the first year" (CO 1/26, f. 198. Hening 2:515).

The Virginia records led Thomas J. Wertenbaker to conclude in 1922 that in the 1635–60 period one-third or more of the bond-laborers died in the first year of their servitude, but that conditions improved so much that by 1671 the proportion was only one out of five (Wertenbaker, pp. 40, 80). Abbot E. Smith, in 1947, without giving specific dates, wrote thus of the bond-servitude of European immigrants: "kill them it usually did, at least in the first years, when fifty over seventy-five of every hundred ... died without ever having a decent chance at survival" (Smith, p. 304). Walter Hart Blumenthal, in 1962, believed that of the bond-laborers coming to the tobacco colonies between 1620 and 1680, 35 percent of the women and 50 percent of the men died within five years after landing. (Blumenthal, p. 23). Wesley Frank Craven, in 1971, noted the high death rate among the earliest Virginia immigrants, but believed that subsequently the "first year ... was usually not fatal" (Craven, p. 26).

The odds against a chattel bond-laborer surviving the first year are indicated by the fact that a new laborer with five years to serve was commonly sold for less than a seasoned hand who had only three or four years to serve (Morgan, pp. 175–6). Russell Menard believes that the inflow of immigrant laborers did not rise steadily after 1644 as Morgan (p. 180) argues, but that it rose and fell in response to the rise or fall of tobacco prices (*Economy and Society in Early Colonial Maryland*, pp. 119–26). But, he says, "the mortality rate among new arrivals must have been frightening" (ibid;, p. 191; see also Table IV–4, p. 137).

Both Morgan and Menard call attention to the disparity between the mortality rates of New England and those in the tobacco colonies. That disparity explains why New England's population growth in the seventeenth century did not depend upon immigration, while in Maryland and Virginia population growth did. Among the factors making for the difference was that while some 80 percent of the immigrants to the Chesapeake were chattel bond-laborers, only a small percentage of New England immigrants were in that category. (Morgan, p. 180; Menard, pp. 129–30, 140, and Tables IV–3 and IV–5, pp. 135 and 141.)

181. Dankers and Sluyter, p. 217.

182. *Accomack County Wills, Deeds, & Orders, 1678–1682*, p. 260 (18 August 1881).

183. *Accomack County Order Book I (Orders, Deeds, Etc., No. 1), 1632–1640*, p. 104 (3 July 1637). *Norfolk County Wills & Deeds B, 1646–1651*, p. 117a (19 April and 31 July 1649).

In 1692 the Provincial Assembly of Maryland enacted a law providing that owners who grossly abused "any English Servant or Slave," or denied them provisions, or forced them to work beyond their strength, for the first and second offense were to be fined, and if the offense were then repeated, the bond-laborers were to be "free from their servitude." Accordingly, Thomas Courtney, who "most barbarously dismembered and cutt off both the Ears" of a "Molattoe girl," a limited-term bond-laborer, was merely ordered to set her free. There was no further "recompense" to the girl. Furthermore, that did not mean she was to be freed from servitude, but merely from servitude to Courtney. (*Archives of Maryland*, 13:451–7 [4 June 1692]).

184. Morris, pp. 485–7.

185. Hening, 2:53.

186. Although I am working directly with the colonial records as cited, almost all, or nearly all, of the cases mentioned here are also mentioned in Morris, pp. 485–8 and 491–96 (the Henry Smith case).

187. *Northampton County Orders, Deeds, Wills, Etc., No. 2, 1640–1645* (3 August 1640). I have had to interpolate somewhat in describing the indenture, because of damage to the manuscript.

188. But the inquest jury said,'how hee came by his death wee know not." (*Northampton County Order Book, 1654–1664*, pp. 21–2 [29 June 1658].) Burton may have had no reason to feign a headache. In a subsequent autopsy, a physician found that Burton's "heart [had been] very defective and ... his Lungs imperfect blacke and putrefied." (Ibid., p. 25 [same date].) For other examples, see: *Charles City County Records, 1655–1665*, p. 357 (3 February 1662/3; bond-laborer found starved to death, his body showing stripes from a whipping administered by the wife of his owner). *Northampton County Order Book, 1657–1564*, pp. 140, 142 (10 July and 24 August, 1662; owner posts "good behaviour" bond, which is returned to him three months later). *Lancaster County Orders, Etc., 1666–1680*, f. 10. (2 September 1666; bond-laborer dies "very shortly after" being "switched" by owner for "feigning" illness; court finds owner "innocent.") *Northampton County Order Book, 1664–1674*, p. 130. (28 June 1672; owner's agent kicks a young African-American boy to death, depositions are taken from fellow bond-laborers but no further court action is recorded.) See also: *Surry County Records, 1671–91*, p. 219. (12 September 1678; inquest finds owner to have caused the death of his woman bond-laborer; the court nullifies that finding.) *Middlesex County Order Book, 1694–1705*, pp. 234–42, 300, 458. (1 August and 2 October 1699; account of the whipping to death of a "Mulatto runaway boy" at the specific orders of his owner, Samuel Gray, a

minister; there is no record of any penalties.) The minister remained "one of the boys" of the county elite; he served as a member of the first Board of Visitors and of the Board of trustees of the College of William and Mary. (Richard L. Morton, *Colonial Virginia*, 2 vols. [Chapel Hill, 1960], 1:346 n. 15.)

189. *Archives of Maryland*, 3:146, 187–8; 10:522, 534–45. Seven years later, a member of the indicting grand jury, John Grammer, killed one of his bond-labors with a hundred lashes, but the grand jury declined to indict him. *Archives of Maryland*, 49:307–12.

190. Proceedings of the Provincial Court, 1663–1666 *Archives of Maryland*, 49:290, 304–7, 311–14. Fincher's last words before sentence of death was pronounced are a curiosity; after three months in jail he displayed none of the choler he had shown when in authority: "If I deserve it I must die" (p. 313).

191. *Archives of Maryland*, 54:390–91; 57:60–65. To be granted "benefit of clergy," a person found guilty was merely shown a bible and asked if he could read it "as a cleric." If the answer was "yes," the defendant was let go with a formalistic branding of the base of the thumb. This routine was a vestigial relic of medieval times when only persons of clerical status were able to read the Bible and when priests were to be tried only in ecclesiastical courts. Carpenter was assessed 2,998 pounds of tobacco for sheriff's fees, and 1,000 for the surgeon who "opened the skull" of the victim at inquest. (Ibid., 54:410.)

192. Smith appears in the record as a successful planter and as a thoroughgoing pathological brute. He scorned his wife, and beat her until she finally had to return to England to save her life. He sexually assaulted two of his women bond-laborers, so that they ran away. (Retaken, they were ordered to serve additional time double the days of their absence from Smith.) Another bond-laborer, mother of a child by him, charged that Smith had killed it. *Accomack County Orders, 1666–1670*, pp. 67 (December 1668); 112 (4 February 1668/9); 129, 131–7 (17 March and 2 April 1668/9); 168 (25 January 1669/70); 176–9 (3 February 1669/70). *MCGC*, p. 217 (1668–70), cited by Morris, p. 496 n. 145.

193. *Archives of Maryland*, 69:xvi–xvii, 413. Morris, p. 486.

194. *Archives of Maryland*, 41:478–80.

195. Ibid., p. 385.

196. Ibid., 49:166–8, 230, 233–5.

197. See Appendix II-D.

198. For cases in which special judicial consideration was given to psychopathic persons accused of crime, see Hening, 2:39 (1661) and *Northumberland County Records, 1678–98* (1 November 1683).

199. See p. 128.

200. "You may be a model citizen, perhaps a member of the Society for the Prevention of Cruelty to Animals, and in the odor of sanctity to boot; but the thing that you represent face to face with me has no heart in its breast. That which seems to throb there is my own heart-beating." Thus spake Marx's wage-worker in 1869. It was just as true for the relations of labor and capital in the plantation bond-labor system. (See Karl Marx, *Capital*, Vol. I, Chapter X, "The Working Day," Section 1.)

8 ... and Resisting

1. W. E. B. DuBois, in *Annual Report of the American Historical Association for the Year 1909* (1911), a forerunner of his *Black Reconstruction*, published in 1935.

2. Timothy H. Breen, "A Changing Labor Force and Race Relations in Virginia 1660–1710," *Journal of Social History*, Fall 1973, pp. 3–25.

3. Ibid., p. 7.

4. Ibid., p. 17. It will be apparent that this chapter draws on many of the same records cited by Breen. However, as I have indicated briefly in the Introduction of this work (*The Invention of the White Race*, Volume One, p. 20), I question Breen's attribution of the disappearance of solidarity of European-American and African-American laborers against the plantation bourgeoisie after 1676 to exclusively objective factors (such as tobacco prices and the arrival of non-English-speaking laborers directly from Africa). I also object to certain assertions requiring the reader to share his undocumented speculations about the attitudes of the European-American workers (he called them "whites") (pp. 7, 17). Finally, I attempt in this work to give some attention to the role of male supremacy and the resistance to it in the history of the period embraced in the title of Breen's article. This aspect appears to have been ignored, but not only by Breen.

5. "Servants responded to their lot in different ways. Some ran off at the first opportunity; other stole from their owners or attacked them; still others found momentary solace in drink or casual sexual liaisons. Planters viewed such behavior as a clear and constant danger to an orderly society and to their own economic well being. And why not? As a group the servile population accounted for half of Virginia's settlers." (Warren M. Billings, "The Law of Servants and Slaves in Seventeenth-Century Virginia," *Virginia Magazine of History and Biography*, 99:45–62 [January 1991]; p. 50.)

6. In the words of the Virginia Assembly in 1661 (Hening, 2:35).

7. *Northampton County Records, 1655–57*, p. 26. This first John Custis was the great-grand-father of Daniel Parke Custis, whose widow, Martha Dandridge Custis, married George Washington. (Edward Duffield Neill, *Virginia Carolorum, the Colony under the Rule of Charles the First and Second, AD 1625–1685* [Albany, NY, 1886], p. 209.)

8. See *The Invention of the White Race*, Volume One, p. 74, and Chapter 7, note 10 of this volume.

9. Hening, 1:411 (March 1655). After the restoration of the crypto-Catholic Charles II to the throne in England, the distinction was repealed in 1662, but the new law was not retroactive (Hening 2:113–14).

10. *Westmoreland County Records, 1661–62*, p. 52.

11. *York County Records, 1657–62*, f. 122. For other cases of bond-laborer suicide, see: *Archives of Maryland*, 53:501–2; *Northampton County Records*, p. 106 (1651); *York County Records, 1657–62*, f. 67. (1659); *York County Records, 1665–72*, p. 115 (1666); *Accomack County Records, 1676–78*, p. 29 (1677); *Accomack County Records, 1676–90*, f. 122 (1678).

Perhaps there was a class predisposition to "want of Grace"; I have found no seventeenth-century record of a suicide by a Chesapeake owner of bond-laborers.

12. *York County Records, 1657–62*, f. 46.

13. *Archives of Maryland*, 65:2–8. A second African-American bond-laborer was among the group of those originally charged, but the jury found him not guilty. Nevertheless, he was ordered to act as hangman of the other four.

The editorial definition of "petty treason" is "the killing of a master by his servants, of a husband by his wife, or of a high ecclesiastic by one of his inferiors" (p. xvii).

14. Hening, 2:118.

15. For a number of such Virginia "violent hands" cases, besides those detailed here, see: *Accomack County Records, 1666–70*, pp. 14, 38 (1666, 1667); *York County Records, 1665–72*, f. 52 (1666); *Northampton County Records, 1664–74*, pp. 69–70 (1669); *Northumberland County Records, 1666–78*, f. 93 (1670); *Lancaster County Records, 1666–80*, p. 200 (1671); *Middlesex County Records, 1673–80*, f. 6 (1674); *Northumberland County Records, 1666–78*, f. 197 (1674); *Accomack County Records, 1676–78*, pp. 20–21 (1676).

16. *Norfolk County Records, 1666–75*, p. 7 (1666).

17. *Lancaster County Records, 1666–80*, pp. 200–201.

18. *Northampton County Records, 1664–74*, pp. 133, 134, 137–8, 219, (1672, 1673).

19. *Surry County Records, 1671–84*, ff. 82, 97. You had to be there!

20. Hening 1:257 (March 1643).

21. *Norfolk County Records, 1651–56*, pp. 101, 105, 114. No reference is made to Bradley's age. The next law on this subject (Hening, 1:441–2) required non-indentured, "custom-of-the-country" bond-laborers who were under fifteen years old at the time of their arrival to serve until they were twenty-one. But that law was not enacted until 1658.

22. *Northumberland County Records, 1678–98*, p. 389.

23. *Northampton County Records, 1645–51*, ff. 132–3.

24. Hening, 1:244 (1643), 350 (1647); 2:129 (1662), 441 (1679). To kill a marked hog would logically make one subject to prosecution; but why did the ruling class insist on these severe penalties for killing and eating wild hogs? Was it a way of emphasizing to bond-laborers their general dependence on their owners for their "diet"? Was it aimed at discouraging runaways who might hope to maintain themselves on wild pork? Governor Francis Nicholson articulated that concern: the "stock of cattle and hogs" running "in the woods and about the frontiers," he said, "would supply them [runaways] with victuals." (*CSP, Col.*, 16:391, Nicholson to Commissioners of Trade and Plantations, 20 August 1698.)

25. For typical examples, see: *Northumberland County Records, 1652–65*, f. 351; ibid., *1666–78*, f. 151; ibid., *1678–98*, p. 6; *Lancaster County Records, 1666–80*, ff. 142, 215, 230, 352; *Middlesex County Records, 1673–80*, f. 36; ibid., *1680–94*, pp. 5, 31; ibid., *1694–1705*, p. 98, 289–90.

26. *Accomack County Records, 1676–90*, pp. 389–90 (7 November 1684).

27. *Archives of Maryland*, 49:8–10 (31 March 1663). The sentence of the court was that six suffer 30-lash whippings, to be administered by the other two.

28. *Lancaster County Records, 1666–80*, f. 158 (13 July 1670).

29. In regard to the components of the English diet at that time see page 321, n. 150.

30. *York County Records, 1657–62*, ff. 85 (24 July 1660); 143 (24 January 1661/2); 149 (25 January 1661/2); 150 (10 March 1661/2). A part of this record is printed in *VMHB*. 11:34–6 (1902–1903).

31. Library of Congress, Virginia (Colony) Collection microfilm, reel 4, depositions taken 13 September 1663. These materials have been printed in *VMHB*, 15:38–43 (1907–8). See also Robert Beverly, *History and Present State of Virginia* (1705); John Burk, *The History of Virginia from its First Settlement to the Commencement of the Revolution*, 3 vols. (Petersburg, Virginia, 1822), 1:135–7; and Charles Campbell, *History of the Colony and Ancient Dominion of Virginia* (Philadelphia, 1860).

32. Perhaps this was the Birkenhead mentioned in the Interregnum Record Book for 28 June 1653, who was scheduled to speak with a committee "concerning matters of importance" and to "give in names of such other persons as to be summoned before the Committee" (Great Britain Public Record Office, *Calendar of State Papers, Domestic*, 37:445).

33. Hening, 2:204 (16 September 1663).

34. Hening, 2:195.

35. Hening, 2:204.

36. A great portion, quite possibly half, of the seventeenth-century Virginia court records no longer exist. Of the lost seventeenth-century county records, a major part was destroyed by fires set when Robert E. Lee's Confederate army retreated from Richmond in the first days of April 1865. However, says an archival specialist, "an awful lot of [the] dates of destruction have nothing at all to do with the Civil War," many of the records having been lost in other wars, and in floods and non-wartime fires. Some few seem not to be accounted for at all. (Robert Clay, of the Virginia State Library Archives, in *The Callaway Family Association Journal, 1979*, pp. 48–56; see p. 51 for a list of Burned Record Counties.) This is simply a limitation to which historians must be reconciled, aware as they must ever be of the risks of attempting to generalize on the basis of incomplete information.

Of the approximately 1,675 total of all the years of existence of all the 27 Virginia counties that at some time existed in Virginia between 1634 (the beginning of county formation) to 1710, county court records of varying extents are available in photocopy and on microfilm as well as in abstracts from the records, at the Virginia State Archives in Richmond, comprising some 1,275 county-years. In the preparation of this study, I have examined the records covering some 885 of these county-years, including some made in four counties that were extinguished during that period: Accawmacke, Charles River, and Warrosquoake in 1643; Rappahannock in 1693. (See Martha W. Hiden, *How Justice Grew, Virginia Counties: An Abstract of Their Formation*, Jamestown 350th Anniversary Historical Booklet No. 19 [Richmond, 1957], especially charts 1–9, pp. 83–5.)

37. Billings, p. 50, J. Douglas Deal, *Race and Class in Colonial Virginia: Indians, Englishmen, and Africans on the Eastern Shore During the Seventeenth Century* (New York, 1993), p. 126.

38. There were paradoxical cases, as noted in Chapter 7, when the owners might find it to their advantage to "encourage" flight of bond-laborers in the last month or so of their bondage to avoid payment of the customary "corn and clothes" due at the end of their terms.

39. Due to "the late unhappy rebellion," the Assembly said in amending the statute of limitations in October 1677, "all judiciary proceedings were impeded and hindred for the greatest part of the last year." (Hening, 2:419–20). The records of the Provincial Court of Maryland tell of the flight of eight African-American bond-laborers from that province to Virginia during the time of Bacon's Rebellion. (*Archives of Maryland*, 49:355–6.)

40. Hening, 2:35.

41. Governor Berkeley to Lords of Trade and Plantations (Hening, 2:515): according to Berkeley there were bond-laborers in Virginia. 6,000 European-American and 2,000 African-American. Governor Culpeper's estimate, 12 December 1681, put the numbers at "fifteen thousand servants," of whom 3,000 were African-Americans (*CSP, Col.*, 11:157).

42. When "takers-up" of runaways applied to be certified by the General Assembly for compensation, the list of the captives gave no indication of whether two or more had acted in concert.

43. *MCGC*, p. 467 (17 October 1640). In the end the costs were to be repaid by extensions of the servitude of bond-laborers recaptured.

44. *MCGC*, p. 466. The owner would have preferred to dispose of them in Maryland.

45. *MCGC*, p. 468.

46. *MCGC*, p. 467 (22 July 1640).

47. *MCGC*, p. 467 (13 October 1640). By "The Dutch Plantation" they may have meant present-day Delaware.

48. Ibid.

49. *Northampton County Records, 1645–51*, f. 2 (11 November 1645). In this and subsequent notes, the dates given are those of the court proceedings; where the dates of the events described are significantly different from the date of the court record, those dates will be given.

50. *Accomack County Records, 1666–70*, ff. 31–3. Although the depositions in this case were taken in August 1663, they were not entered in the record until 16 July 1667.

51. Two, and possibly three, of the women were married, from which fact I infer that they were probably not chattel bond-laborers. By the same reasoning, I conclude that the conspirator husbands of two of them were not chattels. In all probability they were former bond-laborers.

52. They were, respectively, the son-in-law and daughter of Colonel Scarburgh (Deal, p. 119).

53. "Black James," was associated in the accounts with "Cornelius a dutchman's wife." James is not further identified. It is worth noting, however, that among the tithables of Lieutenant Colonel William Kendall in 1668 in neighbouring Northampton County were "Cornelius Arreale" and "James Negro." (*Northampton County Records, 1664–74*, p. 55.)

54. *Accomack County Records, 1671–73*, pp. 93–7. Although the depositions were taken in December 1670, they are entered in the record on 23 April 1672, more than two years later. Possibly they were used in evidence against one of the plotters, Isack Medcalfe, who at the later date was appealing for leniency in the matter of the extension of his time of servitude.

55. *Middlesex County Records, 1673–80*, f. 226 (4 October 1680).

56. *Accomack County Records, 1678–72*, p. 95 (16 July 1679).

57. *Lancaster County Records, 1666–80*, ff. 487–8 (10 September 1679).

58. *Northumberland County Records, 1678–98*, p. 176 (18 April 1683).

59. *Accomack County Records, 1682–97*, p. 131 (2 April 1688).

60. *Norfolk County Records, 1686–95*, p. 108 (17 February 1688).

61. *Middlesex County Records, 1680–94*, pp. 309–10 (14 October 1687).

62 *Middlesex County Records, 1680–94*, pp. 526–7 (9 October 1691); 535 (23 November 1691); 539 (4 January 1691/2. See also *Rappahannock County Orders, 1686–92*, p. 335 (3 February 1691/2).

63. *Northumberland County Records, 1678–98*, p. 443 (17 October 1688).

64. *York County Records, 1687–91*, p. 527 (26 January 1690/91; the date of their flight was 18 August 1690). One might speculate that these men had hoped for a better lot in Quaker country.

65. *Norfolk County Records, 1666–75*, f. 37 (18 August 1669).

66. *Lancaster County Records, 1666–80*, ff. 211–18 (10 March 1674/75).

67. *Norfolk County Orders, 1675–86*, f. 10 (15 December 1675). The Beverleys apparently represented the exceptional case of a bond-labor marriage.

68. *Accomack County Records, 1697–1703*, f. 67 (24 June 1699).

69. *Northampton County Records, 1664–74*, p. 123 (28 February 1671/2). A previous entry of the same date, concerning Rodriggus's wife, indicates that Rodriggus was employed by planter Mr John Eyre (or Eyres), though not as a bond-laborer.

70. *Norfolk County Orders, 1675–86*, p. 99 (16 August 1679).

71. *Northampton County Records, 1690–97*, p. 4 (19 November 1690), Presumably this is the same Crotofte of the clandestine feasts (see p. 151). Has he survived as a bond-laborer after all these six years? But who is this John Johnson? Presumably he is neither the son nor the grandson of Anthony Johnson, the patriarch of Pungoteague Creek. And what were the respective offenses for which they were in jail?

72. *Richmond County Records*, 1694–99 (4 August 1697). When Loyd sued Thacker for the long loss of Redman's services, Thacker, citing the 1662 Virginia law of descent through the mother, successfully contended that Redman was a free person, the child of an African-American father and a European-American woman.

73. *Henrico County Records, 1694–1701*, pp. 100–101 (1 April 1696).

74. In view of the fact that the woman was legally obligated to reveal the name of the father of the child, and in some instances was jailed until she complied, it is a mystery that the majority of the court records of such cases do not provide the name of the child's father. Does that mean that the owner was being protected? The person who paid the bond-laborer's "fornication" fine generally claimed the six months of servitude due from her on that account. Sometimes that claim

was not explicitly asserted in the record. Although it might be surmised that in some such cases the fine-payer was the father, I have left them out of account.

In some of these 140 cases where the identity has been given *only* as "a negro," the social status is assumed to be that of a bond-laborer. For the rest, when a person is not explicitly identified as a bond-laborer, it is assumed that he/she is a free person, because bond-laborers were identified as servants of an owner. It is possible to identify the male partner's social status in fewer than half the "fornication" case records; no conclusions can be drawn as to the free-to-bond proportions among the male partners in the other cases.

75. This inference is based on two facts. The overwhelming proportion of the seventeenth-century male inhabitants of the Chesapeake arrived as bond-laborers. Second, of these 121 men, only one is termed "Mr," the lowest order of honorific address.

76. Four of the women – three Europeans and one African-American – were free persons involved with male bond-laborers. Of the total of 139 women (one was involved with two different bond-laborers), eight were African-Americans, the rest were European-Americans.

77. *York County Records, 1657–62*, f. 148 (25 [?] January 1661/2).

78. See p. 131.

79. Two Middlesex County Court decisions applied this principle in declaring invalid two separate contracts executed by bond-laborers Rebecca Muns and of Martha Carroll (*Middlesex County Records, 1673–80*, ff. 54, 83 [10 April 1676, 19 November 1677).

80. Friedrich Engels dwells on this subject in relation to the proletariat, arguing that true monogamous relationships are best achieved where property considerations are absent (Friedrich Engels, *The Origin of the Family, Private Property and the State* [New York, n.d.], p. 59]).

81. Four of the women, including one African-American, were free persons.

82. *Accomack County Records, 1666–67*, pp. 59, 150.

83. *York County Records, 1677–84*, p. 535.

84. *Accomack County Records, 1682–97*, pp. 70, 95 (1 and 7 September 1685).

85. Hening, 2:114 (1662).

86. *Essex County Records, 1703–1708*, pp. 3, 10 (August and September 1703).

87. This point will be elaborated on in the discussion of Gernor Gooch's letter to the Commissioners of Trade and Plantations of 1736, in Chapter 13.

88. The general subject of the status of African-Americans in the Chesapeake colonies will be treated in Chapter 10.

89. Hening, 2:84 (March 1662); 170 (December 1662); 267 (September 1668).

90. *Accomack County Records, 1666–70*, p. 112 (4 February 1668/69).

91. *York County Records, 1694–97*, pp. 9–13.

92. *Accomack County Records, 1676–78*, pp. 54–5. (18 June 1677). Dun is identified as a bond-laborer of John David in the 1675 list of tithables.

93. *Accomack County Records, 1678–82*, pp. 271, 295–6. How much was Griffin's attitude different from that of two bond-laborers who nearly beat to death a James "a Scotchman" whom their owner had appointed to be their overseer? *Northampton County Records, 1664–74*, p. 61 (1 March 1668/9).

94. *York County Records, 1677–84*, pp. 360, 362–4 (2 December 1681). It is not absolutely clear whether the "he" in Wells's remark referred to himself or to Frank. What is not in doubt is that Wells and Frank were on the same side in the affair. All the persons mentioned in this account were European-Americans, except Frank.

95. Conway Robinson, "Notes from the Council and General Court Records, 1641–1672," p. 279, April 1669, in *VMHB*, 8:243 (1900–01).

96. "If, as Winthrop Jordan has remarked, the language of the laws against miscegenation was 'dripping with distaste and indignation,' it was the language of the most politically active of the planter class. We have no evidence that during most of the seventeenth century, most whites shared it. . . . The ideology of racism may have been present in the culture of the elite as early as 1600, but nonslaveowning whites in the Chesapeake seem to have absorbed it only gradually, with the growth of slave society in the late seventeenth and early eighteenth centuries" (Deal, p. 181.)

9 The Insubstantiality of the Intermediate Stratum

1. Warren M. Billings, "'Virginia's Deploured Condition,' 1660–1676: The Coming of Bacon's Rebellion," PhD thesis, University of Northern Illinois, June 1968, p. 128.

2. The county (originally "shire") form was adopted in August 1634 (Hening, 1:224). Martha W. Hiden, *How Justice Grew, Virginia Counties: An Abstract of Their Formation*, Jamestown 350th Anniversary Booklet No. 19 (Richmond, 1957).

3. Hening, 2:21 (March 1661).

4. Hening, 1:402 (March 1665/6). The county courts were courts of origin for all civil cases involving damages and costs amounting to less than 1,600 pounds of tobacco, and for all criminal cases except those in which the penalties included dismemberment or death (Hening, 2:66).

5. Hening, 2:280. The right of all freemen to vote had had its legislative ins and outs. In 1658, the last law on the matter (Hening, 1:475) enacted before that of 1670 had restored the right that had been taken away in 1655 (Hening, 1:411–12).

6. Hening, 2:59.

7. Hening, 1:483.

8. Hening, 2:21. As encouragement to the constables, they were to be rewarded by the owner of each runaway recaptured and returned.

9. Hening, 2:273–4.

10. Ibid. A year later the General Assembly, upon reflection on the prospective cost of the law and its susceptibility to local collusion, reduced the amount of the reward to 200 pounds of tobacco, payable for fugitives taken up more than ten miles from their owner (Hening, 2:277). See also Hening, 2:283–4, regarding fraudulent claims.

11. *Charles City County Records, 1655–65*, pp. 279–81, 284–8.

12. CO 1/30, pp. 114–15 (16 July 1673). This document may also be read in *VMHB*, 20:134–40 (1912).

13. Edmund S. Morgan, *American Slavery, American Freedom: The Ordeal of Colonial Virginia* (New York, 1975), pp. 247–8.

14. Sir Francis Bacon, Essay No. 15, "Of Seditions and Troubles" (1625) in *Works*, 6:406–12; p. 407. Bacon draws this reference from Isaiah, 45:1.

15. In the period 1660–76, seven out of ten of the colony elite had been in the country for no more than twelve years (*Billings*, p. 130).

16. Lionel Gatford, *Publick Good Without Private Interest* (London, 1657), p. 3.

17. John C. Rainbolt, *From Prescription to Persuasion: Manipulation of Eighteenth-century Virginia Economy* (Port Washington, NY, 1974), pp. 19–20. William S. Perry, ed., *Collections Relating to the American Colonial Church* (Hartford, 1870), 1:11, 15; Philip Alexander Bruce, *Institutional History of Virginia in the Seventeenth Century*, 2 vols. (New York and London, 1910), 1:131, 194–207; George M. Brydon, *Virginia's Mother Church and the Political Conditions under Which it Grew* (Richmond, 1947–52), 1:passim.

Apparently disregarding the mammonistic implication of the observation, one doctoral student commented in a footnote that "tobacco was to prove almost the coalescing factor in Virginia that religious fanaticism was to prove in New England" (Darrett B. Rutman, "The Virginia Company and Its Military Regime," in Darrett B. Rutman, ed., *The Old Dominion: Essays for Thomas Perkins Abernathy* [Charlottesville, 1964; Arno Press, 1979], p. 231). In justice to Rutman, it must be noted that the book and the author had "grown very far apart" in the interval between its writing and its publication (see the author's prefatory "Apologia," dated 1978).

18. Hening, 2:48, 180–83, 198; 3:298.

19. Rainbolt, p. 19. *Historical Statistics of the United States from Colonial Times to 1970*, p. 1168.

Yet in 1692, when Commissary James Blair, head of the Anglican Church in Virginia, requested funds to found a college in order to train up soul-savers for gospel-starved Virginia, English Attorney-General Hedges expostulated, "Damn your souls! Make tobacco!" (Charles Campbell, *History of the Colony and Ancient Dominion of Virginia* [Philadelphia, 1860], p. 346; Campbell cites "Franklin's correspondence"). This was reminiscent of the comment of a Barbadian slaveholder about 1680, that sugar planters "went not to those parts to save Souls, or propagate Religion, but to get money" (Morgan Godwyn, *The Negro's and Indians Advocate* [London, 1680], p. 39 marginal note). Godwyn repeated the observation five years later in his *Trade Preferr'd before Religion and Christ made to give place to Mammon* (London, 1685), p. 11. Nevertheless Blair's proposal for a college was given financial support by the English government, and when it opened its doors in 1697, it was named after the then reigning English monarchs, William and Mary.

20. Thomas Ludwell to John Lord Berkeley (Sir William Berkeley's brother), 24 June 1667 (Cited in Philip A. Bruce, *Economic History of Virginia in the Seventeenth Century*, 2 vols. [New York, 1895], 1:394.)

21. Rainbolt, p. 6. Rainbolt examines circumstantial factors that frustrated efforts at diversification of the Virginia economy. Although the title of his book (*From Prescription to Persuasion:*

Manipulation of Eighteenth Century Virginia Economy) refers to the eighteenth century, Rainbolt's main attention is directed to the 1650–1710 period, yet well after the commitment to tobacco had become a settled question in practical terms, and the guiding principle of colonial Virginia government had been firmly established: to secure the highest quickest profit for the Virginia planters, shippers, servant-trade merchants, English Crown interest, tax-and-customs farmers.

22. I fully accept the conclusion reached by Edmund S. Morgan, in a general note on tobacco prices, that "no reliable or regular series of annual prices current can be constructed for seventeenth-century Virginia" (Morgan, pp. 135–6, n. 7). Morgan refers to Russell R. Menard's work in assembling the available data. I have chosen to draw upon Menard's figures for present purposes, referring particularly to his summary of Chesapeake farm prices (Russell R. Menard, *Economy and Society in Early Colonial Maryland* [New York, 1985], pp. 448–9). I feel justified in this course because I have found much of the same data by my own research, and because Menard's picture of decade-to-decade trends is supported by other economic historians, such as Philip Alexander Bruce and Lewis C. Gray, and by Morgan himself.

23. Wilcomb E. Washburn is a dissenter from this generally accepted view. Washburn acknowledges the prevalence of desperate poverty among the people and their "unwillingness to accept their fate passively," but at the same time he considers poor planters' mutinies as insignificant (Wilcomb E. Washburn, *The Governor and the Rebel: A History of Bacon's Rebellion in Virginia* [New York, 1957], pp. 31, 187 n. 63). Moreover, Washburn denies that Bacon's Rebellion can be ascribed to the existence of class conflict within the colony. Rather, he regards the rebellion as merely a manifestation of "frontier" hostility to Indians (ibid., p. 235 n. 3).

Readers of Volume One of *The Invention of the White Race* will know how much I appreciate Dr Washburn's research and argument regarding the white-supremacist treachery toward, and repression of, American Indians under Anglo-American and United States "Indian policy." But his sensitivity to "racism" seems curiously limited in the dismissive terms with which he treats the participation by African-Americans in Bacon's Rebellion. As bond-laborers they were not motivated by anti-Indian interests, but by a determination to be freed form their bondage. (Ibid., p. 88. See Chapter 11.)

24. Bruce, *Economic History*, 1:391.

25. Accomack (for all the years except 1660, 1661, and 1662), Lancaster, Lower Norfolk, Northampton, Northumberland, and York (all years except 1663 and 1664). (Billings, pp. 168–73.)

26. Ibid., p. 159.

27. Edmund S. Morgan shows a total population of 3,628 in these six counties in 1674. (Morgan, pp. 412–13.)

28. The total of all debts was 51,870,000 pounds of tobacco; those owed *to* the elite amounted to 12,225,000 pounds; those owed *by* the elite totalled 6,227,000 pounds.

29. In three years the amount owed by the elite exceeded the amount owed to them, in the amount of 585,000 pounds; in the other thirteen years, the account stood the other way by 6,596,000 pounds.

30. Edmund S. Morgan, "Headrights and Head Counts," *VMHB*, 80:361–71 (1972); p. 366. The same information is largely recapitulated in Morgan, *American Slavery, American Freedom*, pp. 221–2.

31. Although Menard did not find a similar pattern of concentration of land ownership in three Maryland counties in the 1659–1706 period, he does not regard those findings as adequate for drawing a general conclusion regarding the matter. He comments on the rise in tenancy in this period, noting that an increasing number of people were falling into a landless status, a condition that would eliminate them from land ownership statistics altogether (Menard, pp. 309–12).

32. Kevin P. Kelly, "Economic and Social Development of Seventeenth-century Surry County, Virginia," PhD thesis, University of Washington, 1972, p. 137.

33. Thomas J. Wertenbaker, *The Planters of Colonial Virginia* (Princeton, 1922), p. 58.

34. CO 5/1539, pp. 20–22 (margin date, 6 October 1696). By way of remedy, Randolph recommended a strict collection of the one shilling per fifty acre quit-rent and the limiting of future land patents to 500 acres.

35. Wertenbaker, p. 59.

36. Menard, p. 316.

37. CO 1/30, pp. 114–15 (16 July 1673). This document may also be read in *VMHB*, 20:134–40 (1912).

38. Ibid.

39. *Surry County Records, 1671–84*, pp. 40–43 (3 and 20 January 1673/4); *1671–91*, pp. 41–2 (6 January 1673/4). Extensive excerpts from the record are printed in Warren M. Billings, ed., *The*

Old Dominion in the Seventeenth Century, A Documentary History of Virginia, 1606–1689 (Chapel Hill, 1975), pp. 263–7.

The proportion of propertyless freemen remained high. An exchange between the Surry County Court and Governor Effingham provides a rare example of precision regarding this economic differentiation among the free population. Surry County submitted the names of a total of 314 men for the militia at the end of 1687. Effingham returned the list and asked that the names of those who were "Free men [but] not free holders, or Housekeepers ... be struck out." As a result, the roll was reduced by 114, or 36 percent, presumably propertyless freemen. (*Surry County Records, 1671–91*, pp. 597–601; 619–23.)

40. Rainbolt, p. 12.

41. Sir William Berkeley, *A Discourse and View of Virginia* (London, 1663), p. 5.

42. Rainbolt, p. 46.

43. Historians have frequently taken note of the recurring enthusiams for diversification of the Virginia economy and of efforts to curtail tobacco production; the most thorough study of the subject is John C. Rainbolt's *From Prescription to Persuasion* (see note 17, and note 21 on the period mainly covered).

See also the special study of the subject by Sister Joan de Lourdes Leonard, "Operation Checkmate: The Birth and Death of a Virginia Blueprint for Progress," *WMQ.* ser. 3, 24:44–74 (1967).

44. Leo Francis Stock, ed., *Proceedings and Debates of the British Parliaments Respecting North America*, 5 vols., (Washington, DC, 1924); 1:374. House of Commons, 7 March 1671. *CSP, Col.*, 11:318. Petition of sundry merchants possessing estates in America to the Lords of Trade and Plantations, received 7 November 1682.

45. Rainbolt, pp. 154, 155, 159.

46. CO 324/9.

47. *Calendar of Virginia State Papers and Other Manuscripts, Vol I, 1651–1781* (Richmond, 1875), edited by William P. Palmer; pp. 137–8.

48. *Archives of Maryland*, 25:266–7.

49. "Representation of the Board of Trade relating to the Laws made, Manufactures set up, and Trade Carried on in His Majesty's Plantations in America," 1734; manuscript in the Rare Book Room of the New York Public Library, Research Libraries.

50. See, for example, the justification of "An Act for Ports" as a design to stop the "import or export [of] goods and merchandises, without entering or paying the duties and customes due thereupon." (Hening, 3:53–4 [1691]. In the end, the consequences of the prolonged struggle to achieve a diversified economy were thoroughly incongruous with the initial motives behind the effort. Designed as a solution to the economic ills of the tobacco economy, the various schemes often only disrupted the economy still more (Rainbolt, p. 171).

51. Eighteenth-century developments lie largely beyond the scope of the present work, but in the context of this discussion of diversification, brief mention is required of the increase in the relative importance of grain cultivations in the Chesapeake beginning in about 1740. This shift was not the result of any general diminution of demand for tobacco exports; indeed, tobacco exports to Britain, including that portion destined for re-export, followed a generally rising trend between 1740 and the War of Independence. (*Historical Statistics of the United States: Colonial Times to 1970* [Washington, DC, 1976], Series Z-441, Z-442, Z-449.) Rather, it resulted from two principal causes. The exhaustion of the soil under tobacco cultivation was such that under the custom of field rotation, twenty acres per hand was required to maintain tobacco production on three acres. That compelled either the acquisition and clearing of new land or a reduction of the size of the labor force, both of which tended to reduce the rate of profit. Second, there was a rise in demand for grains, particularly wheat, in Europe, as well as in northern colonies and the West Indies. This shift hardly qualified, however, as significant diversification of the economy of the region. Despite the limited increase in the value of grains in total exports, tobacco still accounted for three times as much as wheat and corn together in the period 1768–72 (Klingaman, "Significance of Grain", pp. 274–5, cited in full below); and the profits of the Chesapeake bourgeoisie remained absolutely dependent on exports of one major and one or two minor crops. (This paragraph is based on the following sources: Lewis Cecil Gray, assisted by Esther K. Thompson, *History of Agriculture in the Southern United States to 1860*, 2 vols., [Washington, DC, 1932], pp. 166–9; David Klingaman, "The Development of the Coastwise Trade of Virginia in the Late Colonial Period," *VMHB*, 77:26–45 [1969], especially pp. 30–31; idem, "The Significance of Grain in the Development of the Tobacco Colonies," *Journal of Economic History*, 29:268–78 [1969] especially pp. 270–75; Allan Kulikoff,

"The Economic Growth of the Eighteenth-century Chesapeake Colonies," *Journal of Economic History*, 39:275–88 [1979], especially pp. 284–6.)

Yet instead of promoting the rise of a domestic market by investing in developing improved instruments of production and raising the productivity of labor, the plantation bourgeoisie spent their revenues "to increase their standard of living, improve their land, and expand the size of their labor force" (Allan Kulikoff, *Tobacco and Slaves: The Development of Southern Cultures in the Chesapeake, 1680–1800* [Chapel Hill, 1986], p. 118).

The capitalist exploiters of bond-labor seemed to sense their dilemma before Marx and Engels made it manifest: "The bourgeoisie cannot exist without constantly revolutionizing the instruments of production and thereby the relations of production ..." In 1690, Dalby Thomas pointed out that diversification of production in the colonies would lead the plantation bourgeoisie to "part with their black slaves" (Dalby Thomas, *An Historical Account. Rise and Growth of the West Indies Colonies and great Advantages they are to England in Respect to Trade* [London, 1690], in Harleian Miscellany, 12 vols., 9:432.) Obversely, among reasons cited by General James Oglethorpe in the eighteenth century for excluding slavery from the projected colony of Georgia was his conviction that it would result in a market-glutting monocultural economy rather than a diversified one (*Diary of the Earl of Egmont*, entry for 17 January 1739, cited in Elizabeth Donnan, *Documents Illustrative of the History of the Slave Trade* [Washington, DC, 1931], 4 vols; 4:592.)

52. Rainbolt, p. 169.

53. In 1663, the English seized a number of labor-exporting locations in West Africa. The Dutch made a generally successful counterattack later that year, but the English did manage to maintain their hold on one major fort there, at Cape Corso, or Cape Coast Castle, and their position there was confirmed by the Treaty of Breda. (Sir George Clark, *The Later Stuarts, 1660–1714*, 2nd edn. [Oxford, 1956], p. 332.) Those disposed to deal with the almost arcane diplomatic language of the relevant documents may read them in Frances Gardiner Davenport, ed., *European Treaties bearing on the History of the United States*, 5 vols. (Washington, DC, 1929; volume 2, documents 53 and 57.

54. See Appendix II-E.

55. CO 5/1356, p. 47 (King in Council to Culpeper, 27 January 1681/82). The Royal African Company was headed by the Duke of York, Charles's brother, who reigned as James II from 1685 to 1688. But a number of the leading shareholders had a dual interest as employers of plantation bond-labor. (Kenneth L. Davies, *The Royal African Company* [London, 1957], pp. 64–6.)

56. CO 5/1356, p. 138 (Culpeper to the Lords of Trade and Plantations, 20 September 1683).

57. See Gray, 1:369–71. I apologize for the tone of these lines, but that is how the bourgeoisie weighs investment choices. The Royal African Company in 1672 posted a price of £18 each for bond-laborers to be delivered in Virginia (Davies, p. 294).

58. CO 5/1356, p. 138. In the years 1680 to 1688, capitalists in both commerce and agriculture were naturally concerned that nearly one-fourth (23.5 percent) of their investment was lost in the Middle Passage. A half-century later they could congratulate themselves that these losses were down to 10 percent. (Davies, p. 292).

59. Reference has been made in Chapter 6 to Bruce's exposition of the question, and to his conclusion that the Virginia colony was destined by nature for tobacco monoculture.

60. Sir Francis Bacon advised historians to leave observations and conclusions to others (*Advancement of Learning*, Book II, in *Works*, 3:339), but he himself could not forgo the opportunity, as when he interpreted the events of the reign of Henry VII.

61. Bacon, Essay Number 33, "Of Plantations," in *Works*, 6:457–9; p. 458.

62. See p. 109.

63. Philip Alexander Bruce, A. E. Smith and Wesley Frank Craven are among those who propound this thesis. See Chapter 6, pp. 103–6, and p. 312 note 53 for full citations.

64. New England's genocidal policy with regard to the native population, however, was far from that advocated by Bacon in his essay.

65. Michael G. Kammen, ed., "Virginia at the Close of the Seventeenth Century: An Appraisal by James Blair and John Locke," *VMHB*, 74:141–69 (1966); p. 155. Kammen says that while the opening lines were written by John Locke, the most influential member of the Commission of Trade and Plantation and a strong support of Blair, this work "has to be Blair's composition" (p. 147).

66. See p. 69.

67. Herbert Moller, "Sex Composition and Correlated Culture: Patterns of Colonial America," *WMQ*, 3d ser., 2:113–53 (1945) p. 118.

68. Melville Egleston, *The Land System of the New England Colonies*, Johns Hopkins University Studies in History and Political Science, Vol. 4 (Baltimore, 1886), pp. 15, 21–2, 26.

This practice was the basis of the six-mile square "township" form of allotment of "public" land established by the Continental Congress in 1785 that prevailed in states formed out of the Northwest Territory. It is relevant to note that, "The southern members ... did not believe in the township system of settlement." (Payson Jackson Treat, "Origin of the National Land System under the Confederation," in Vernon Carstensen, ed., *The Public Lands; Studies in the History of the Public Domain* [Madison, Wisconsin, 1968], pp. 11–12.)

69. Egleston, pp. 44–5.

70. Percy Wells Bidwell and John L. Falconer, *History of Agriculture in the Northern United States, 1620–1860* (Washington, 1925; 1941 reprint), pp. 49–50.

71. Ibid., p. 54.

72. In the first three decades of the Massachusetts colony, before individual royal land grants were discontinued in favor of community land grants, just over one hundred individual land grants were made. Six were extremely large, ranging from 2,000 to 3,200 acres each; the rest averaged less than 400 acres each. But the greatest part of New England land distribution throughout the colonial period was made out of community land grants by the communities themselves. (Egleston, pp. 19–20.)

73. Gary B. Nash, "Colonial Development," in Jack P. Greene and J. R. Pole, *Colonial British America: Essays in the New History of the Modern Era* (Baltimore, 1984), p. 238. An economic historian, referring to "the northern colonies" generally throughout the colonial period, writes: "In the absence of a market strong enough to enforce specialization and necessitate acquiring anything by purchase, people produced for themselves." (Robert E. Mutch, "Yeoman and Merchant in Pre-industrial America: Eighteenth-century Massachusetts as a Case Study," *Societas*, 7:279–302; 282.

74. Recent academic discussions of the subject of "the transition to capitalism" in continental Anglo-America have directly and indirectly shed important light upon this aspect of the question. The discussion centers on the extent to which households in non-plantation areas were engaged in exchange of products, even to the extent of interregional exchanges. The time period that gets most attention begins about the middle of the eighteenth century. Regardless of how one may view the controversies that arise in this regard, for our present purpose all of these studies serve to show that communities of family households, largely independent of export/import exchanges, were characteristic of these areas. For a bibliography on this discussion see Allan Kulikoff, "The Transition to Capitalism in Rural America," *WMQ* 46:120–144 (1989).

This debate seems to have been induced by the long-running debate on the transition from feudalism to capitalism as it occurred in Europe. I find discussion conducted under this heading useful for drawing conclusions regarding the degree of dependence on, or independence of, the New England colonial economy with respect to the export/import trade. But as Kulikoff points out (pp. 126–7), there is a fundamentally different significance to be attached to the class struggle interpretation of the revolutionary transition from feudalism to capitalism in Europe, on the one hand, and the evolution from subsistence farming to capitalist production (neither the producer nor the consumer being the owner) in non-plantation areas of rural continental Anglo-America.

75. Bidwell and Falconer, pp. 82–3.

76. One informative narrative of this transition is Hannah Josephson, *The Golden Threads: New England's Mill Girls and Magnates* (New York, 1949).

77. Gary B. Nash, "Social Development," in Greene and Pole, eds., pp. 236, 243.

78. Ibid., pp. 236, 247.

79. Francis Bacon, "Of Plantations."

80. Governor William Berkeley to Thomas Ludwell, 1 July 1676. In *Coventry Papers*, microfilm reel no. 63.

The outbreak of Bacon's Rebellion, says Thomas J. Wertenbaker, was the outcome of policies that "practically eliminated the middle class" (Thomas J. Wertenbaker, *Bacon's Rebellion, 1676*, Jamestown 350th Anniversary Historical Booklet No. 8 [Williamsburg, 1957], p. 55. Cf. Charles M. Andrews, *Narratives of the Insurrections, 1675–1690* [New York, 1915], pp. 11–12.)

10 The Status of African-Americans

1. Works particularly concerned with this aspect of seventeenth-century Chesapeake history include: Philip Alexander Bruce, *Economic History of Virginia in the Seventeenth Century*, 2 vols. (New York, 1895), especially 2:121–9; James Curtis Ballagh, *A History of Slavery in Virginia*

(Baltimore, 1920; reprinted 1968); John H. Russell, *The Free Negro in Virginia, 1619–1865* (Baltimore, 1913); Susie M. Ames, *Studies of the Virginia Eastern Shore in the Seventeenth Century* (New York, 1940); James H. Brewer, "Negro Property Owners in Seventeenth Century Virginia," *WMQ*, vol. 12 (1955); Ross M. Kimmel, "Free Blacks in Seventeenth-century Maryland," *Maryland Historical Magazine*, 71:19–25 (1976); Whittington B. Johnson, "The Origin and Nature of African Slavery in Seventeenth Century Maryland," *Maryland Historical Magazine*, 73:236–45 (1978); Tomothy H. Breen and Stephen Innes, *"Myne Owne Ground": Race and Freedom on Virginia's Eastern Shore in the Seventeenth Century* (New York, 1980); Douglas Deal, "A Constricted World: Free Blacks on Virginia's Eastern Shore," in Lois Greene Carr, Philip D. Morgan and Jean B. Russo, *Colonial Chesapeake Society* (Chapel Hill, 1988); Joseph Douglas Deal, *Race and Class in Colonial Virginia: Indians, Englishmen, and Africans on the Eastern Shore During the Seventeenth Century* (New York, 1993).

2. See pp. 32 and 34 of *The Invention of the White Race*, Volume One.

3. "[E]xcluded from many civil privileges which the humblest white man enjoyes" – that was the contemptuous description of free Negroes as expressed by a meeting of white men in Northampton County, Virginia, in December 1831. (Luther Porter Jackson, *Free Negro Labor and Property Holding in Virginia, 1830–1860* [New York, 1942] p. 13.)

4. Winthrop D. Jordan, *White over Black: American Attitudes Toward the Negro, 1550–1812* (Chapel, Hill, 1968), p. 44.

5. Oscar Handlin and Mary F. Handlin, "Origins of the Southern Labor System," *WMQ*, 3d series, No. 7:199–222 (1950), pp. 211–12.

6. "Freedom, like slavery, acquired social meaning not through statute law or intellectual treatises, but through countless human transactions that first defined and then redefined the limits of that [the African-American condition]." (Breen and Innes, pp. 31–2.) I merely wish to stress that the essential character of those "human transactions" was the struggle between the contending social classes.

7. See pp. 19–22.

8. See Edmund S. Morgan, *American Slavery, American Freedom: The Ordeal of Colonial Virginia* (New York, 1975) Chapter 8, "Living With Death," especially pp. 158–63.

9. ". . . it was easier to incorporate the negroes in [the existing] system than to put them in a class apart." (Helen Tunncliff Catterall, ed., *Judicial Cases Concerning Slavery and the Negro*, 5 vols. [Washington, DC, 1926–37], 1:55.)

10. See p. 154.

11. Each of the three was to receive a whipping of thirty lashes. The terms of servitude of each of the two European-Americans were to be extended by four years.

12. Jordan, p. 75. For a criticism of Jordan's views, see the Introduction to Volume One of *The Invention of the White Race*.

13. See *The Invention of the White Race*, Volume One, pp. 80, 346 n. 34. But as pointed out, there was a sharp difference among the officers of the Providence Island venture regarding the enslavability or non-enslavability of Christians by Christians.

14. Breen and Innes, pp. 70–72.

15. The first Negroes who arrived in Virginia, says Phillips, "were . . . not fully slaves in the hands of their Virginia buyers, for there was neither law or custom establishing the institution of slavery" (Ulrich Bonnell Phillips, *American Negro Slavery: A Slavery of the Supply, Employment and Control of Negro Labor as Determined by the Plantation Regime* [New York, 1918], p. 75.)

16. Hening, 1:257; 2:113.

17. See *The Invention of the White Race*, Volume One, pp. 73–5. Recall Sir William Petty's assessment made in 1672 of the values of human chattels: Irish men and Negro men at £15 each. *Economic Writings of Sir William Petty*, 2 vols. (London, 1691; Augustus Kelley reprint; New York, 1963); 1:152.

In 1653 a license was granted to one Richard Netherway of Bristol, England, to export one hundred Irish men to be sold as slaves in Virginia. (Great Britain. Public Record Office. Calendar of State Papers, Domestic, vol. IV; Interregnum Entry Book, Vol. 98, p. 405. Cited by Bruce, 1:609).

18. Hening, 1:411. Although this law was enacted in 1655, its provisions were made to apply to such surviving Irish bond-laborers as had arrived since the beginning of 1653. Recaptured runaway bond-laborer Walter Hind was ordered, "according to the act for Irish servants," to "serve continue and complete the term of six yeares from the time of arriveall, and make good the time neglected." (*Charles City County Deeds, Wills, Orders, Etc., 1655–1665*, p. 223. [3 February 1659/60].)

19. Hening 1:538–9.

20. See *The Invention of the White Race*, Volume One, Appendix H.

21. The one brief, wavering exception was Anthony Johnson, as is noted below, p. 183.

22. The Accomack and Northampton records have been treated in great detail by other historians, most recently by Breen and Innes, and by Joseph Douglas Deal (*Race and Class in Colonial Virginia*). For that reason I shall select only a few individual cases recorded in those two counties for brief elaboration; I will attempt to cover the rest by suitable generalizations accompanied by full footnote references for the convenience of those who may desire to study the records directly.

23. *MCGC*, p. 33.

24. *MCGC*, pp. 66–8, 71–2, 73.

25. *Accomack County Records, 1663–66*, p. 54. The Northampton County Court found for Francis Payne in a suit arising out of his contract to build a house for Richard Haney. (*Northampton Country Records, 1657–64*, p. 173, 28 August 1663.)

26. *Northampton County Records, 1651–54*, p. 215 (3 January 1653/4). "Speciality" meant a bond or a contract. In August 1647, Mr Stephen Charlton was awarded a judgment for a debt against Tony Longo, to be paid out of the next crop. (*Northampton County Records, 1645–51*, p. 111.)

27. The name (variously rendered in the records as Manuel and Rodriguez, Rodriggus, Drigges, Drigs, etcetera) suggests a personal history with the Iberians or with the Dutch leaving Brazil.

28. Susie M. Ames, *Studies of the Virginia Eastern Shore in the Seventeenth Century* (Richmond, 1940), p. 97.

29. *Northampton County Records, 1651–54*, p. 148; court record dated 12 September 1653.

30. Since all the entries listed in this note are from *Northampton County Records*, the volume years will serve to locate the citations. *1645–51*, p. 26: sale of calf by John Pott to John Johnson, 6 May 1647. Ibid., p. 38: sale of a heifer by Francis Payne to slow-paying Marylander Jospeh Edlowe, 28 July 1651. *1651–54*, p. 133: 8 February 1652/3. *1657–66*, p. 30: sale of a cow and a heifer by John Johnson to Edward Marten, 30 May 1659. Ibid., pp. 49–50: gift of a heifer by Emanuel Driggs to Sande, son of a bond-laborer, 28 May 1659. Ibid., p. 47: signing over by Anthony Johnson of five calves to his son John, 30 May 1659. Ibid., p. 62: sale of a mare colt by Francis Payne (the name is variously spelled) to Anthony Johnson, 31 January 1659/60. Ibid., p. 88: sale by Emanuell Drigges of a gray colt to Alexander Wilson, 15 May 1661. Ibid., pp. 137–8: sale of a mare by Manuel Rodrigues to Willim Kendall, 11 March 1661/62, *1664–1674*, p. 146: dispute in court between John Francisco and John Alworth over the sale of a filly, 19 September 1672.

31. The gift was recorded January 1657/8. *Northampton County Records, 1657–64*, pp. 2, 7.

32. Nell Nugent, *Cavaliers and Pioneers; Abstracts of Virginia Land Patents and Grants, 1623–1666*, 2nd edn. (Baltimore, 1963), 2:11 18 April 1667.

33. *York County Records, 1665–72*, p. 237–8 (28 August 1669); the court record is dated 12 April 1670.

34. *Northampton County Records, 1657–66*, p. 116, 236 (4 June 1662, 28 December 1665); and *Northampton County Records, 1668–80*, pp. 3, 34 (4 December 1668; 28 December 1672).

35. See Morgan's discussion in *American Slavery, American Freedom*, pp. 166–72.

36. Mongum first appears in the record in July 1650 when he and two other men – Demigo Matthews[?] and a European-American plantation overseer, Robert Berry – are said to have reported a plot of the Nanticoke Indians to attack the Eastern Shore settlements (*Northampton County Records, 1645–51*, f. 217). See also *Northampton County Order Book, 1674–79*, p. 273. For the joint tenancy, see Ralph T. Whitelaw, *Virginia's Eastern Shore*, 2 vols. (Richmond, 1951), 1:228; 2:216. The name is variously spelled; I have decided to use the "Mongum" form throughout, except when direct quotations have an alternate spelling.

37. *Northampton Country Records, 1651–54*, pp. 32–3. The agreement was witnessed by Thomas Gilbert and Richard Buckland on 5 March 1650/1; it was entered in the court record on 22 December 1651. Joseph Douglas Deal reads the name as "Merris" and notes that she does not again appear in the records. She is not to be confused with the African-American named Mary, a second[?] wife of Mongum, who is listed in available Northampton tithable records beginning in 1665 and on through 1674. It seems that Breen and Innes confuse the two "Marys." (see Breen and Innes, p. 83.)

Another such disclaimer in contemplation of marriage was subscribed by parish minister Francis Doughty of Northampton County Court before his marriage to Ann Eaton, whereby he did "disowne and discharge all right, to her estate and to her children." (Richard Duffield Neill, *Virginia Carolorum: The Colony under the Rule of Charles the First and Second, AD 1625–1685* [Albany, NY, 1986], p. 407.)

38. *Northampton County Records, 1664–74*, pp. 220–21. The will was dated 9 May 1673 and probated 29 September 1673.

39. *Northampton County Records, 1674–79*, p. 59 (29 August 1675). See also ibid., pp. 58, 70, 72.

40. The couple came to the notice of the court when Skipper (Cooper) was ordered to pay "levies tythes for his wife (shee being a negro)"; and again when they were suspected of shielding the father of her child from the hue and cry. (*Norfolk County Wills and Deeds "E" 1665–75, Part 2, Orders*, ff. 75, 76–7.) See *Norfolk County Deed Book, No. 4, 1675–86*, pp. 14 and 30, regarding the times of their deaths. See Nugent, 2:232, for the landholding of Skipper (Cooper).

With regard to other intermarriages of African-Americans and European-Americans, it is to be inferred that the Mary Longo who married John Goldsmith in Hungary parish on 13 October 1660 was an African-American, since the only Longos found in Northampton County records at that time were African-Americans; and that Emannuel Driggus's first wife, Elizabeth, the mother of Thomas Driggus, was a European-American. (See Stratton Nottingham, *Accomack*, p. 452; and ibid., cited by Deal, *Race and Class in Colonial Virginia*, pp. 271, 284.) See also the marriage of Elizabeth Key and William Greenstead, below.

41. Lerone Bennett Jr, *The Shaping of Black America* (Chicago, 1975), pp. 14–16, 24–7.

42. Breen and Innes make this point in relation to Anthony Johnson's patent, saying that none of the names, except Richard Johnson, appear on subsequent Northampton tithables lists. They identify this Richard Johnson as the same Richard Johnson who later appears as Anthony Johnson's son. But how could Anthony's son, presumably born in Virginia, qualify for a headright? Was Richard Johnson, Negro, Anthony's biological son, or possibly a Negro from England whom Anthony adopted?

43. *Northampton County Records, 1651–54*, f. 226; 8 March 1653/4. Some doubt remains, however, about Johnson's final decision, since his original signed agreement to free Casar was entered in the record of 26 September 1654. (Ibid., *1654–1655/6*, f. 35-b) *Archives of Maryland*, 54:760–61. See also Clayton Torrence, *Old Somerset on the Eastern Shore* (Richmond, 1935), pp. 75–7.)

In 1638, George Menefie, a member of the Virginia Colony Council, laid claim to 3,000 acres of land for the importation of sixty bond-laborers, including twenty-three unnamed "Negroes I brought out of England with me." (Virginia Land Patent Book, No. 1, 1623–34, abstracted in Nugent, 1:118.) Possibly Casar was one of that number.

44. See p. 326, note 36.

45. See Morgan, pp. 412–13, Table 3, "Population Growth by County."

46. Deal is one who emphasizes that "a larger proportion of Eastern Shore blacks were free than was probably the case elsewhere in Virginia" (*Race and Class in Colonial Virginia*, p. xi).

47. *Northampton County Records, 1651–54*, ff. 118–19, 174–5 (13 May 1649). Court record date 30 December 1652. Estimates of tobacco production per capita in the Chesapeake at mid-century range between 1,500 and 2,000 pounds. See: *A Perfect [or New] Description of Virginia*, in *Force Tracts*, II, No. 8, p. 4, "two thousand waight a year"; William Bullock, *Virginia Impartially Examined*, (London, 1649), p. 9; Russell R. Menard, "From Servant to Freeholder: Status Mobility and Property Accumulation in Seventeenth-century Maryland," *WMQ*, 30:37–64 (1973); p. 51.

48. *Northampton County Records, 1651–54*, ff. 118–19, 174–5. Note that Payne and the Eltonheads were all literate. Breen and Innes appear to have misread the year of the deal with Walker (Breen and Innes, p. 74).

49. *Northampton County Records, 1654–55/6*, p. 100-b. *Northampton County Orders, No. 7, 1655–57*, p. 19. A bond of £200 was pledged by Mrs Eltonhead to insure the Payne family against any challenge that might be made to their free status. At the current price of about 2*d.*, this would be the equivalent of 24,000 pounds of tobacco.

50. *Northampton County Records, 1651–54*, f. 178.

51. Hening 2:26. The same phrase was used in a law on runaways passed a year later. (Hening 2:116–17).

52. Hening, 2:267.

53. Hening, 2:270.

54. Hening, 2:239.

55. *Norfolk County Records, 1646–51*, pp. 115–16. A year earlier the term "forever" was used in referring to the "conveyance" of three bond-laborers from the widow of George Menefie to Stephen Charlton. But since the phrase "heirs and assigns" is missing, the term may merely refer to the conveyor's relinquishment "forever" of all claims to these workers. (*Northampton County Records, 1651–54*, p. 28.)

Argoll was the son of Francis Yeardley, the Governor of Virginia mentioned in Chapters 4 and 5.

56. *Northampton County Records, 1651–54*, pp. 165–6.

57. *Lancaster County Records, 1654–1702*, pp. 46–9.

58. *Northampton County Records, 1645–51*, p. 120.

59. *Northampton County Records, 1655–57*, p. 8.

60. *Lancaster County Records, 1654–1702*, pp. 46–9.

61. *Northampton County Records, 1655–57*, f. 78. At his death three years later, Pannell bequeathed Ann Driggus "and her increase" to his daughter. (Ibid., *1657–66*, pp. 82–4.) Ann Driggus was the daughter of Emannuel Driggus (see note 27).

62. *Northampton County Records, 1654–1655/6*. ff. 25-b, 54-a. Some time before 29 August 1654, Phillip and Mingo did pay off the 1,700 pound obligation. (Ibid., f. 27-a.) For an earlier event involving Phillip, see p. 155.

63. *Northampton County Records, 1645–51*, p. 82.

64. He was so described at the Virginia General Court on 10 March 1653/4, the record of which is preserved apparently only in the record of the Baptista case as it was continued before the Maryland Provincial Court in 1661. (*Archives of Maryland*, 41:499.)

65. *Norfolk County Records, 1651–56*, ff. 8, 68, 75, 137, *Archives of Maryland*, 41:499. For further information on Baptista's involvement with courts see: *Norfolk County Records, 1656–66*, pp. 226–7, 233, 244; *Archives of Maryland*, 41:460, 485, 499–500; and Beverley Fleet, *Virginia Colonial Abstracts, No. 31, Lower Norfolk County, 1651–54*, pp. 12–13.

66. *Lancaster County Records, 1655–66*, f. 370.

67. *Charles City County Records, 1655–65*, pp. 601–5, 617–18. Beverley Fleet, *Virginia Colonial Abstracts*, 34 vols. (Baltimore, 1961; originally published in 1942); 13:54–7, 65–6.

68. *Northampton County Records, 1640–45*, p. 16 (3 August 1640). Littleton himself was a member of the court.

69. *Northampton County Records, 1654–55/6*, ff. 60b–61a (1 November 1654.)

70. *Accomack County Records, 1666–67*, p. 151.

71. Ibid.

72. Ibid. p. 154 (26 August 1669).

73. *Robinson Transcripts, Virginia (Colony) General Court Records*, Virginia Historical Society, Mss. No. 4/v 81935/a 2, p. 161. Printed in *MCGC*, p. 354.

74. In 1658 John Bland, a rich London merchant, recruited bond-laborers for his Virginia plantation from among inmates of Chelsea College jail; "two mulattoes offered to go rather than remain eternally in prison." (Neill, p. 365 n. 1.)

75. *Archives of Maryland*, 66:294.

76. But it was apparently assumed that the Virginia law of 1662 (see p. 197) was sufficient guarantee that no claim could be made on the grounds of having been baptized a Christian, and that therefore Scarburgh did not need to post any bond against that contingency. (*Accomack County Records, 1676–78*, p. 7.)

77. Winthrop D. Jordan's chapter titled "The Souls of Men: The Negro's Spiritual Nature" is a mine of informative bibliographic references on the relation between Christian principles and racial oppression, as revealed in the opinion of English and Anglo-American preachers and theologians during the colonial period. The works cited are with three or four exceptions products of the eighteenth century. (Jordan, pp. 179–215.) The chapter is made an integral part of his history of "American attitudes," which, as is noted in the Introduction to the present work, is anchored in Jordan's presumption of a psychological need for Anglo-Americans to know they were "white." (Jordan, p. xiv. The page citation in *The Invention of the White Race*, Volume One, p. 236 n. 41, was erroneously given as p. ix.)

78. Morgan Godwyn, *The Negro's and Indians Advocate, Suing for their Admission into the Church, or a Persuasive to the Instructing and Baptizing of the Negro's and Indians in our Plantations, That as the Compliance therewith can prejudice no Mans just Interest, So the wilful Neglecting and Opposing of it, is no less than a manifest Apostacy from the Christian Faith. To which is added, A brief Account of Religion in Virginia* (London, 1680); idem, *A Supplement to The Negro's and Indians Advocate: or, Some Further Considerations and Proposals for the Effectual amd Speedy Carrying on of the Negro's Christianity in Our Plantations (Notwithstanding the Late Pretended Impossibilities) without any Prejudice to their Owners* (London, 1681); idem, *Trade preffer'd before Religion, and Christ made to give place to Mammon: Represented in a Sermon Relating to the Plantations. First Preached at Westminster Abby, And afterwards in divers Churches in London* (London, 1681). For Godwyn in Virginia, see Neill, pp. 342–5.

79. George Fox, *Gospel of Family-Order, Being a Short Discourse Concerning the Ordering of Families, Both of White, Blacks and Indians* (London, 1676); idem, *A Journal or Historical Account of the Life, Travels, Sufferings, Christian Experiences, and Labour of Love in the Work of the Ministry of that ancient, Eminent and Faithful servant of Jesus Christ*, 2 vols. (London, 1694).

80. Richard Baxter, *A Christian Directory, or, a Summ of Practical Theologie and Cases of Conscience* (London, 1673).

81. Thomas E. Drake, *Quakers and Slavery in America* (New Haven, 1950), p. 3.

82. It is not my intention to undertake a treatment of this historical phenomenon, but merely to point to it as one of the elements of the institutional inertia that obstructed the imposition of lifetime hereditary bondage on Africans and African-Americans. It seems only fair to note that Quaker slaveholders late in the eighteenth century finally acceded to the logic of their doctrine and stopped owning or dealing in lifetime bond-laborers. (See Drake, pp. 68–84. In this way they were following the leadership of the Mennonites who had refused to engage in such traffic and exploitation from the beginning of their settlement in the colonies.

83. Godwyn, *Trade preferr's before Religion*, p. 11.

84. Drake, *Quakers and Slavery*, p. 6

85. George Fox, *Journal*, 2:131. Cf. Drake, *Quakers and Slavery*, p. 6.

86. A century later, English enemies of the African slave trade such as James Ramsay and William Wilberforce were pointing to the possibility that ending that inhuman traffic would be of benefit to the bond-laborer already at work in the West Indies. (Elsa V. Goveia, *Slave Society in the British Leeward Islands* [New Haven, 1965], p. 25.)

87. Godwyn, *The Negro's and Indians Advocate*, pp. 3, 12.

88. Ibid., pp. 13–14.

89. Joseph Bess, *A Collection of the Sufferings of the People Called Quakers for the Testimony of a Good Conscience . . .*, 2 vols. (London, 1753); see the section on Barbados, especially pp. 305–8.

90. Hening, 2:48 (1662), 180–83 (1663). Under the terms of the 1663 law, Quaker Meeting was outlawed altogether, and violators were to be fined 200 pounds of tobacco for the first offense and 500 for the second offense, to be satisfied by seizure and sale of the offender's assets, with the Quaker community made collectively responsible for any unsatisfied amount. For the third offense, the penalty was to be banishment from the colony to a place chosen by the Governor and Colony Council. Other provisions were aimed at preventing Quaker preachers from coming into Virginia by imposing a fine of 5,000 pounds of tobacco upon householders who hosted those preachers.

91. ". . . the freedom and equality of man [was] involved in the true profession of Christ." (Ballagh, p. 46.)

92. See p. 21.

93. See Chapter 2, n. 65; Leviticus, 25:8–10.

94. The Virginia General Court ruled in 1772 that Indians were free by virtue of the 1691 "Act for a free trade with Indians." (Hening 3:69.) The court, relying on ancient English legal precedent, held that allowing the right of free trade carried with it "all incidents necessary to the exercise of that right, as protection of their persons, properties, &c, and consequently takes from every other the right of making them slaves." (Thomas Jefferson, *Reports of Cases Determined in the General Court of Virginia, From 1730 to 1740, and from 1668–1772* [Charlottesville, 1829].) The ruling was made in relation of Robin, an Indian being held as a slave, who sued for his freedom. The opinion was written by George Mason.

95. *Northampton County Records, 1651–54*, f. 114 (12 January 1652/3). The clerk noted in the margin that the statement, which was dated two weeks earlier, had been signed by Pott but not Charlton.

96. *Northampton Country Records, 1645–51*, ff. 150–51. "Hardly rejecting slavery outright," notes Douglas Deal, "Charlton nevertheless displayed some uneasiness about the custom of owning and selling Africans for life." (Deal, *Race and Class in Colonial Virginia*, p. 254.)

97. *Northampton County Records, 1645–51*, f. 205. Richard Vaughan, Stephen Charlton's brother-in-law, "seems to have been wholeheartedly opposed to owning Africans and slaves for life." (Deal, *Race and Class in Colonial Virginia*, p. 254.)

98. *Northampton County Records, 1654–55/6*, f. 54-b. Yet as noted above (p. 188), Charlton specified hereditary bondage for Sisley in a transaction in 1647.

99. *York County Records, 1657–62*, f. 16.

100. *Northampton County Records, 1657–66*, f. 47.

101. *York County Records, 1657–62*, ff. 82, 85, 89.

102. *Northampton County Records, Deeds and Wills, No. 8 (1666–68)*, p. 17. Although the fact is

not noted in this document, Driggus is elsewhere identified as a "Negro"; whether Williams may have been one of England's Negro seamen is not indicated.

103. The facts presented here regarding the Key case are drawn from *Northumberland County Court Records, 1652–58*, ff. 66–7, 85, 87 and 124–5; *1652–65*, ff. 40, 41, 46, 49; *1658–66*, f. 28; and from *MCGC*, p. 504. Credit for bringing this case into the discussion on the origin of racial slavery is due to Warren M. Billings for "The Cases of Fernando and Elizabeth Key: A Note on the Status of Blacks in the Seventeenth Century," *WMQ*, 30:467–74 (1973), and for his presentation of material from the record of the Key case in his edited work *The Old Dominion in the Seventeenth Century: A Documentary History of Virginia, 1606–1698* (Chapel Hill, 1975); pp. 165–9. All the documents cited here by me, except one, are to be found in the latter work, though with certain errors of transcription. In Anthony Lenton's deposition (p. 146), a passage is made unintelligible by the inadvertent omission of fifteen words, and the name "Mottrom" is given where it should have been "Key." On the same page, a June and a July record entry are presented as if they were one entry and for a single day.

Regrettable as these editor's errors may be, they do not detract from the force of the evidence he presents, evidence that led him to challenge Winthrop D. Jordan's argument that racial slavery was the result of an "unthinking decision." To the contrary, says Billings in "The Cases of Fernando and Elizabeth Keys," the laws passed by the Virginia Assembly in 1662 and 1667 (for descent through the mother, and uncoupling freedom from Christian conversion – see p. 197) "were deliberately calculated to undercut the meager rights of black laborers" (*WMQ*, 30:473–4).

However, his concluding allusion to "white alarm" as the motive for the course of events that ended in racial slavery seems too facile, and not based on his evidence. Furthermore, it would seem to undermine his own challenge to Jordan's entire thesis, which is based on the presumption of an immemorial "white alarm."

104. As indicated by the fact that he had paid the fine for "getting her Mother with Child."

105. "The planters," writes Billings, "were beginning to look upon slavery as a viable alternative to indentured servitude." (Billings, "The Cases of Fernando and Elizabeth Key," 30:471.) I belong with Billings in favoring the economic interpretation of history. But his phrase "the planters" suggests a unanimity among the plantation owners, whereas the great significance of the Elizabeth Key case is precisely that at that moment some "planters" had basic reservations that, had they prevailed, would have prevented the eventual imposition of racial oppression in Anglo-America.

106. From the brief of the appellant in the case of Eleanor Toogood v. Dr Upton Scott, held in October 1782 in the Maryland Provincial Court. (Thomas Harris Jr and John McHenry, *Maryland Reports, being a series of the Most Important Cases argued and determined in the Provincial Court and the Court of Appeals of the then Province of Maryland from the Year 1700 down to the American Revolution* [New York, 1809, 1812] vol. 2; 26–38; p. 37.) One shrinks from the callousness of this language, but it proceeded in the circumstances of the time from the same "market principles" that still, today, leave "no other nexus between man and man than naked self-interest, than callous 'cash payment.'" (Marx and Engels, *The Communist Manifesto*, in Karl Marx and Frederick Engels, *Selected Works in Two Volumes* (Moscow, 1955), 1:36.

107. See *The Invention of the White Race*, Volume One, pp. 86–7.

108. See ibid., pp. 8, 80, 236, n. 34.

109. See ibid., p. 80, 81.

110. Hening, 2:170.

111. Hening, 2:260.

112. Kenneth G. Davies, *The Royal African Company* (London, 1957), p. 41.

113. Hening, 2:280–81.

114. See p. 172.

115. Hening, 2:299.

116. Susan Westbury, "Slaves of Colonial Virginia: Where They Came From," *WMQ*,, 42:228–48 (1985); pp. 229–30. In the absence of further records, Westbury makes this conjecture based on bills of exchange and the price prevailing at that time. These workers may be among those referred to in the following record: "A List of Ships freighted by the Royal African Company Since January 1673/4." The account shows a total of 5,200 persons taken from Africa, of whom 300 on the *Swallow* and 350 on the *Prosperous* were supposed to be being sent to Virginia, the others being destined for Jamaica, Barbados and Nevis. (CO 1/31, f. 32.)

117. CO 324/1. "Certain Instructions and Additional Instructions to Colonial Governors, Comissions and Orders in Council." The date is between 1662 and 1774, according to Charles. M. Andrews, *Guide to the Materials for American History to 1783, in the Public Record Office of Great Britain*, 2 vols. (Washington, DC, 1912–14); 1:226.

118. Bruce, 2:59. This comment, however, was made in the context of Bruce's opinion that in general African-American bond-laborers were not defiant or rebellious.

119. Sir John Knight to the Earl of Shaftesbury, 29 October 1673 (*CSP, Col.*, 7:530).

120. Sir Henry Chicheley to Sir Thomas Chicheley, 16 July 1673 (*CSP, Col.*, 7:508).

121. See Appendix 2-A. That was precisely the prospect that concerned William Byrd II "of Westover." Byrd noted that "On the back of the British Colonys on the Continent of America about 250 miles from the ocean, runs a chain of High Mountains." He urged that steps be taken to "prevent the Negroes taking Refuge there as they do in the mountains of Jamaica" and making allies with the French against the English as did many of the Indian Tribes. (William Byrd II of Westover to Mr Ochs, ca. 1735, *VMHB*, 9:225–8 [1902]; 226.)

11 Rebellion – and Its Aftermath

1. See Chapter 6, note 80.

2. The reader is referred to: (1) the excellent bibliographic essay done by the late Jane Carson for the Jamestown Foundation, *Bacon's Rebellion, 1676–1976* (Jamestown, Virginia, 1976); (2) John B. Frantz, ed., *Bacon's Rebellion: Prologue to the Revolution?* (Lexington, Massachusetts, 1969), a volume of extensive excerpts from source documents, supplemented by selections from the writings of ten of the principal historians of the colonial period, analyzing the causes and assessing the significance of the rebellion; (3) the entries for Nathaniel Bacon, the rebel, and Bacon's Rebellion in *The Virginia Historical Index*, compiled by Earl G. Swem, an exhaustive bibliography compiled of materials published in the *Calendar of Virginia State Papers*, Hening's *Virginia Statutes*, and five principal historical magazines published between 1809 and 1930. Finally, an indispensable guide to primary source materials is John Davenport Neville, *Bacon's Rebellion: Abstracts of Materials in the Colonial Records Project* (Jamestown, 1976).

3. See Bernard Bailyn, "Politics and Social Structure in Virginia," in James Morton Smith, ed., *Seventeenth-century America, Essays in Colonial History* (Chapel Hill, 1959).

4. Wilcomb E. Washburn, *The Governor and the Rebel* (Chapel Hill, 1957). The quoted phrase is at p. 162.

Washburn's challenge to the uncritical glorification of Bacon's Rebellion supplied an overdue corrective to the white-chauvinist "frontier democracy" myth, but he made the case in the form of an uncritical assessment of Governor Berkeley. As a result, there seems to be no room in Washburn's account for the mass of poor freemen, freedmen and bond-laborers, relief of whose sufferings was of no more concern to Berkeley than it was to his peers, despite his invocation of those sufferings to pursue easement of the rigors of the Navigation Act. So far as any self-activation on their part is concerned, Washburn sees only "frontier aggression." It is regrettable that Washburn, in his laudable purpose of exposing the counterfeit of "frontier democracy," did not so much as look at the Virginia County Records. If he had done so, he might not have canonized Berkeley as he did, and he might not have so completely ignored the bond-laborers and their own independent cue and motive for rebellion unrelated to "Indian policy." He particularly failed to give any historical significance to the bond-laborers' participation in the rebellion. He mentions Negroes being among the rebels, for which he deserves credit; but he attaches no thematic significance to the fact. (See ibid., pp. 80–81; 88; 209 n. 23.) Francis Jennings's research into the records regarding the Indians of the eastern section of the continent and his forceful, sympathetic treatment of them are a truly seminal contribution. (See particularly his *The Invasion of America: Indians, Colonialism, and the Cant of Conquest* [Chapel Hill, 1975].) In an earlier article, Jennings defended Washburn's *The Governor and the Rebel* as the best work on Bacon's Rebellion, free of the common fault of relying on Virginians' "self-serving depositions." Apparently he, too, did not interest himself in a study of the Virginia County Records and he certainly takes no account of the bond-laborers; he is content to characterize the rebellion as nothing other than an action of "militant back settlers" led by a demagogue for the sole purpose of seizing "attractive real estate" from Indians. (Francis Jennings, "Glory, Death and Transfiguration: The Susquehannock Indians in the Seventeenth Century," *Proceedings of the American Philosophical Society*, 102:15–53 [1968]; pp. 34–5.)

5. Craven believes it is an anachronistic error to interpret that event in terms of democratic principles that are standards of a much later time: "Bacon's Rebellion belongs to the seventeenth century …," he writes, and historians should leave it there (Wesley Frank Craven, *The Colonies in Transition, 1660–1713* [New York, 1968], p. 142).

6. John B. Fiske, writing in the populist era at the end of the nineteenth century, presented a class-struggle interpretation of Bacon's Rebellion, but one short on equalitarianism. He draws the line at the "rabble ... who [had] little or nothing to lose, ... [and who] entertained communistic notions" typical of the "socialist tomfoolery" of such times. His single reference to the bond-laborers is as "servile labor," without any political personality of their own. (John B. Fiske, *Old Virginia and Her Neighbors*, 2 vols. [Boston and New York, 1900], 106.)

7. I am, of course, indebted to Edmund S. Morgan, Timothy H. Breen, and Lerone Bennett Jr, who before me ventured somewhat along this line. See my Introduction to Volume One of *The Invention of the White Race*, pp. 16–21.

8. Those who are interested in the details as they are presented by English and Anglo-American chroniclers will want to follow the bibliographies and sources as listed in note 1. Among works noted there, a good selection for the reader with a critical eye would surely include: the section on Bacon's Rebellion in Charles M. Andrews, *Narratives of the Insurrections, 1675–1690* (New York, 1915) pp. 16–28, 47–59; Richard L. Morton, *Colonial Virginia*, 2 vols. (Chapel Hill, 1960) particularly Chapter 13 of Volume One, "Indian War – The Background of Rebellion"; and Washburn, particularly Chapter 2, "Background to Rebellion," and Chapter 3, "The Occaneechee Campaign."

9. Alden T. Vaughan writes: "[C]olor prejudice ... happened to Indians ... though not until two centuries of culture contact had altered Anglo-American perceptions ... The perceptual shift from Indians as white men to Indians as tawnies or redskins was neither sudden not universally accepted" until the eighteenth century. (Alden T. Vaughan, "From White Man to Redskin: Changing Anglo-American Perceptions of the American Indian," *American Historical Review*. 87:917–53 (October 1982); pp. 918, 930.)

10. In July 1676 a petition apparently initiated by the local Gloucester County elite and asking Governor Berkeley for protection against Bacon, invoked the specter of "their wives & Children being exposed to the cruelty of the merciless Indians." (Sherwood, *Virginia's Deploured Condition, Or an Impartiall Narrative of the Murders comitted by the Indians there, and of the Sufferings of his Majesties Loyall Subjects under the Rebellious outrages of Mr Nathaniell Bacon Junior*, dated August 1676, Massachusetts Historical Society *Collections* 4th ser. 9:162–76 (Boston, 1871); p. 173. The text of the petition and Berkeley's reply are printed in the same volume, pp. 181–4.)

11. Andrews, p. 110–11.

12. Jerry A. O'Callaghan, "The War Veteran and the Public Lands," in Vernon Carstensen, *The Public Lands: Studies in the History of the Public Domain* (Madison, Wisconsin, 1968), p. 112.

A similar analogy is presented by the English Revolution which began in a fury at the massacre of Protestants in an uprising of the Irish in the fall of 1641, but ended with the overthrow of the monarchy in England. (Brian Manning, "The Outbreak of the English Civil War," in R. H. Parry, ed., *The English Civil War and after, 1642–1658* [Berkeley, 1970], p. 4.)

13. Bailyn, p. 99. In this paragraph I have followed Bailyn's impressive treatment of the etiology of the division in the ranks of the Virginia colony elite.

14. As already mentioned (see note 4), however, that the Navigation Act was not an issue as such in Bacon's Rebellion, although Nathaniel Bacon did speak of the Dutch trade as an alternative to dependence on England. (Dialogue with John Good, around 2 September 1676, CO 5/1371, ff. 121vo–122. It appears at this location on reel 32 of the microfilm prepared by the Virginia Colonial Records Project. Thomas J. Wertenbaker [*The Planters of Colonial Virginia* (Princeton, 1922) p. 17, n. 22] and Washburn [*Governor and the Rebel*, p. 235 n. 22] both cite CO 5/1371, pp. 233–40. I cannot account for this confusion of page or folio numbers. In the *Coventry Papers*, I found it at 77:347–8, as did Washburn. The text is printed in Fiske, 82–6. Ever since 1663, Governor Berkeley had complained of the unfairness of the Navigation Act under which "40,000 people [were] impoverished to enrich little more than 40 [English] merchants, who being the whole buyers of our tobacco, give us what they please for it." (Sir William Berkeley, *A Discourse and View of Virginia* (London, 1663), p. 6. Berkeley to the Lords of Trade and Plantations, 1671, CO 1/26, f. 77, cited in Wertenbaker, pp. 95–6.)

15. So called after the name of Berkeley's home plantation.

16. In 1645, the Virginia General Assembly declared that taxation exclusively by the poll, or head, had "become insupportable for the poorer sort to bear," and enacted that all levies were to be paid on "visible estates," in which the poll tax was to constitute only 30 percent of a composite list of such taxable properties (Hening, 1:305–6). Meeting as a committee of the whole, the General Assembly adopted a resolution favoring the enactment of legislation providing for taxation on landholdings rather than by the poll (Hening, 2:204). Though this sentiment was regularly expressed, taxation continued to be by the poll throughout the seventeenth century.

In 1656, on the no-taxation-without-representation principle, all freemen, propertyless as well as propertied, were given the right to vote (Hening, 1:403), but in 1670 the Assembly repealed the 1656 provision and restricted the suffrage to landholders or "householders" because former bond-laborers were judged not to have "interest enough to tye them to endeavour of the public good" (Hening, 2:280). In 1661 and 1662, in the name of reducing the costs of government, the Governor and Colony Council were authorized for a period of three years to impose annual levies without consulting the House of Burgesses (Hening, 2:24, 85).

17. These "frontier" plantation owners were the vanguard of the emerging "county family" faction. The flare-up was in the context of English aggression and Indian defensive response. The particular incident, according to English accounts, was the result of a barter between an English planter named Mathews and some Doeg Indians, residents of Maryland on the other side of the Potomac. The Indians fulfilled their end of the bargain on time but Mathews did not, and the Indians acted to settle the account by taking some of Mathews's hogs. The Susquehannock Indians (who had moved from Pennsylvania to Maryland on Maryland's invitation, or else because of pressure from the Iroquois Seneca) became involved when five of their chieftains were murdered while parleying with the English under a flag of truce, an act of treachery that was condemned formally even by the Maryland and Virginia officials. (Andrews, pp. 16–19, 47–8, 105–6. Jennings, "Glory, Death, and Transfiguration," pp. 27, 34.)

18. Bacon is sometimes called Nathaniel Bacon Junior to distinguish him from his older cousin of the same name who was also a member of the Colony Council. The birth year of Bacon the rebel, 1674, is inferred from the date of the death of his mother, Elizabeth. (*New England Historical and Genealogical Register*, 37:191 [1883].) Wertenbaker so interprets the record (Thomas J. Wertenbaker, *The Torchbearer of the Revolution: The Story of Bacon's Rebellion and Its Leader* [Princeton, 1940] p. 215). June Carson apparently accepts 1647 also, since she says Bacon was twenty-seven when he arrived in Virginia in 1674. Carson, p. 24.

19. Bacon arrived in Virginia in the spring of 1674; he was appointed to the Colony Council on 3 March 1675; and he assumed the role of leader of the anti-Indian campaign in April 1676, and was for the first time declared a rebel by Governor Berkeley. (Jane Carson, *Bacon's Rebellion, 1676–1976* [Jamestown, 1976], "Chronology," pp. 4, 6.)

20. Wilcomb E. Washburn, "Governor Berkeley and King Philip's War," *New England Quarterly*, 30:363–77 (1957); p. 377. But Washburn cites Berkeley's assertion that the English who were driving the Indians out of their land had "this privilege by his Majesties Grant." (Ibid., p. 375, Berkeley to Secretary Joseph Williamson, 1 April 1676.)

21. Hening, 1:323–4, 353–4.

22. *Rappahannock County Records, 1663–68*, pp. 57–8. When Berkeley himself came into possession of a thirteen-year-old Indian girl as an item of booty from the estate of a Bacon rebel, he gave her "to the Master of a ship who hath caryed her for England." (CO 5/1371, f. 243.) Cf. Warren M. Billings, "Sir William Berkeley – Portrait By Fischer: A Critique," *WMO*, 3d ser., 48:598–607 (1991), p. 602; and "David Hackett Fischer's Rejoinder," ibid., 608–11; p. 610.

23. "... all but five which were restored to the Queen by Ingram who was Bacon's Generall." (Andrews, p. 127.) Andrews cites CO 5/1371, "A True Narrative of the Rise, Progress, and Cessation of the Late Rebellion in Virginia, Most Humbly and Impartially Reported by His Majestyes Commissioners appointed to Enquire into the Affaires of the Said Colony" (July 1677).

24. Andrews, pp. 123–7.

25. Sherwood, p. 168.

26. See also p. 43.

27. *Rappahannock County Records, 1656–64*, p. 13. The date of the agreement is missing, but by interpolation it appears to have been in 1656 or 1657. Roanoake (or Wampompeake) was a medium of exchange made by the Indians. It was made of polished shell beads strung or woven together, and was sometimes exchanged as the equivalent of English money at the rate of five shillings per six feet (*Encyclopedia Britannica*, "Wampum or Wampum-Peage"). See also Hening 1:397.

28. Assistant Colony Secretary Philip Ludwell to Secretary of State Williamson, 28 June 1676, *VMHB* 1:180 (1893).

29. Hening, 2:20, 114, 140. See also p. 60.

30. Bailyn, p. 103.

31. County Grievances, CO 5/1371, ff. 149–9. Sixteen counties and one parish submitted a total of 204 grievances. Only two counties called for the enslavement of Indian war captives. Surry County requested "that the Indians taken in the late Warr may be made Slaves" (f. 156), and James

City County asked that "Indian slaves that were taken in the late Indian Warr ... be disposed to a Publick use and Profitt" (f. 150vo).

The names of the authors of the "grievances" are not supplied. It is certain that none of them were bond-laborers.

32. Sherwood, p. 164.

33. Thomas Ludwell and Robert Smith, Virginia representatives in England, writing to the king, 18 June 1676, *Coventry Papers*, 77:128. Cited in Edmund S. Morgan, *American Slavery, American Freedom: The Ordeal of Colonial Virginia* (New York, 1975), p. 221.

"Few of the indentured servants, coming over after 1660," writes Wertenbaker, "succeeded in establishing themselves in the Virginia yeomanry." "[P]robably less than fifty per cent [of the bond-laborers] could hope even in the most favorable times [i.e. prior to 1650] to become freeholders," he concludes, and by the time of Bacon's Rebellion, the probability was reduced to about one out of twenty. (Wertenbaker, *Planters of Colonial Virginia*, pp. 80–83, 97–98.) Menard finds a parallel experience in Maryland where "Opportunities declined after 1660," when, the indications are, only 22 to 29 percent of the freemen became landowners. (Russell R. Menard, "From Servant to Freeholder: Status Mobility and Property Accumulation in Seventeenth-Century Maryland," *WMO*, 30:374 [1973]; pp. 57, 62–3.)

34. County Grievances, CO 5/1371, ff. 150vo–151. James City County grievance number 10.

35. The grievances of three counties (Lancaster, Isle of Wight, and Nansemond) expressed a desire for a general anti-Indian war. Every list of grievances included at least one complaint about taxes, the amount, the manner of their imposition, and their misappropriation, and the exemptions granted to some favored few. James City, Warwick and Isle of Wight wanted land taxes be imposed instead of poll taxes. The request by Rappahannock County and Cittenborne Parish that landholders be forced to pay their quitrents was, in terms of logic, linked with the desire for a break-up of the large landholdings. (CO 5/1371, County Grievances, ff. 150vo–151, 151vo, 153, 156vo, 157, 161vo.)

36. Ibid. In replying to each separate proposal of this tenor, the commissioners acknowledged that the "unlimited liberty of taking up such vast tracts of Lande is an apparent cause of many mischiefs," and that the proposed remedy was desirable. But, they said that such a radical step was impractical because of the certain opposition of the great landholders. They proposed a more modest revision, whereby the poll tax would be retained but for every 100 acres over a thousand the owner would pay an added levy equal to that for one tithable. (CO 5/1371, ff. 150vo–151, 160, 161vo.)

37. Sherwood, p. 164.

38. CO 1/36. Received in England in June 1676 by English Secretary of State Joseph Williamson. See note 49.

39. Hening, 2:85. See also note 15.

40. Morgan, pp. 244–5. Hening, 2:518–43, 569–83. The second of these two grants, covering all of Virginia south of the Rappahannock, was limited to thirty-one years. (Hening, 2:571–2.) In 1684, Thomas Lord Culpeper sold his rights back to the king. (Ibid., 2:521.)

41. Noted by Francis Moryson and Thomas Ludwell in their urgent appeals to the king for a revocation of the massive grants he had made to his friends. (Hening, 2:539.)

42. From 1661 until the declaration of war against the Indians in March 1676, the Governor had the licensing of traders dealing with the Indians, authority that Berkeley could exploit for his own enrichment. Then all those licenses were revoked, and each of the counties was authorized to designate five or fewer traders, with the provision that no powder, shot, or arms might be sold to Indians. Under a law passed in 1677, all restrictions on trade with Indians were removed. (Hening, 2:20, 124, 140, 336–8, 402.)

43. Washburn, *Governor and the Rebel*, p. 29, citing *Coventry papers*, Vol. 77, ff. 6, 8.

44. Sir John Berry, Francis Moryson and Herbert Jeffreys, *A True Narrative of the Rise, Progress, and Cessation of the Late Rebellion in Virginia, Most Humbly and Impartially Reported by His Majesty's Commissioners Appointed to Inquire into the Affaires of the Said Colony* (October 1677), *VMHB*, 4:117–54 (1896); p. 121.

This suspicion was voiced in popular irony: "Bullets would never pierce Bever Skins." (Thomas Mathew, *The Beginning, Progress and Conclusion of Bacon's Rebellion in Virginia in the Years 1675 and 1676*, in Andrews, p. 20.)

45. Lee to Secretary Coventry, 4 August 1676 (*Coventry Papers*, 77:161).

46. *VMHB*, 1:433 (1893).

47. I take the formation of new counties as a rough index of colony expansion. Counties were first established in Virginia in 1634. In the nineteen-year period 1651 to 1669, ten new counties

were formed. It was twenty-two years before the next county, King and Queen, was formed in 1691. (Martha W. Hiden, *How Justice Grew – Virginia Counties: An Abstract of Their Formation*, Jamestown 350th Anniversary Historical Booklet No. 19, [Richmond, 1957], pp. 83–5.)

48. Bailyn, p. 105.

49. CO 1/36, ff. 111–12. The only date recorded is that of the receipt of the letter, June 1676; the time of transatlantic transmittal was usually over a month.

50. Major Isaac Allerton, one of the coerced burgesses, to Secretary Coventry 4 August 1676 (*Coventry Papers* 77:160–61). Hening, 2:380.

51. "A Review, Breviary and Conclusion drawn from the narrative of the Rebellion in Virginia" by Royal Commissioners John Berry and Francis Moryson, 20 July 1677, in Samuel Wiseman's Book of Record, 1676–1677 Pepysian Library ms. no. 2582. In Neville, pp. 318–24. Wiseman was the clerk to the Royal Commission sent to investigate the rebellion and to suggest remedies.

52. Wilcomb E. Washburn, "The Effect of Bacon's Rebellion on Government in England and Virginia," United States National Museum *Bulletin* 225 (1962), pp. 137–40; p. 139.

53. Samuel Wiseman's Book of Record, p. 107 (16 July 1677). In Neville, p. 332.

54. CO 5/1371, Proceedings and Reports of the Commissioners for Enquiring Into Virginian Affairs and Settling the Virginian Grievances, f. 180 (15 October 1677).

55. Moryson to Secretary of State William Jones, October 1676 (CO 5/1371, ff. 8vo–13vo). Francis Moryson was a royalist veteran of the English Civil War and the son of Richard Moryson and nephew of Fynes Moryson who were engaged in the Tyrone War under Mountjoy in Ireland. (See *The Invention of the White Race*, Volume One, especially pp. 61–5 and Appendix F.)

56. Berry and Morsyon to Thomas Watkins, Secretary to the Duke of York, 10 February 1676/7. Samuel Wiseman's Book of Record. See Virginia Colonial Records Project, Survey Report 6618, for microfilm number. The letter is also printed in *Coventry Papers*, 77:389.

57. Hening, 2:515. In Virginia in 1676, at age sixteen or over, all men, African-American women, and Indian women bond-laborers were tithable. There seems to have been no intersection of the two sets – all possible combatants and tithables – in which bond-laborers were not the majority.

58. Eric Williams stressed the bond-laborers' struggle as the key factor in the general history of the British West Indies. (Eric Williams, *Capitalism and Slavery* [Chapel Hill, 1944], pp. 201–2.) C. L. R. James does the same in *Black Jacobins*, his full-blown history of the Haitian Revolution. Morgan, in his main work on colonial Virginia, does not ignore the bond-laborers, but in effect disparages their aptitude for rebellion, especially so far as African-Americans are concerned. (*American Slavery, American Freedom*, pp. 296–7, 309.) Breen alone has, in passing, noted the bond-laborers' role in Bacon's Rebellion. (Timothy H. Breen, "A Changing Labor Force and Race Relations in Virginia, 1660–1710," *Journal of Social History*, Fall 1973, pp. 10–12, 17.) See the fuller discussion of this aspect in *The Invention of the White Race*, Volume One, pp. 15–21.

59. See, for example, the pioneering works done for Johns Hopkins University on "white servitude" in continental Anglo-America, including: James C. Ballagh, *White Servitude in the Colony of Virginia* (Baltimore, 1895); and Eugene Irving McCormac, *White Servitude in Maryland, 1634–1824* (Baltimore, 1904).

60. See, for example, Russell R. Menard, *Economy and Society in Early Colonial Maryland* (New York, 1985) and David Galenson, *White Servitude in Colonial America: An Economic Analysis* (New York, 1981).

61. In the Royal Commissioners' report, the Lancaster County Grievances nos. 11 and 12 call for laws for "the encouragement of servants." However, no particulars are supplied and the Royal Commissioners simply say the petitioners should seek remedy by the Assembly. (CO 5/1371, f. 156vo.)

62. CO 1/3, ff. 35–62/8/6 (October 1676), "Proposals most humbly offered to his most sacred Majestie by Thomas Ludwell and Robert Smith for Reducing the Rebells in Virginia to their obedience." Printed in *VMHB* 1:433–5.

63. CO 1/37, f. 37 (Ludwell to Williamson, 28 June 1676).

64. *Northampton County Records, 1168–80*, p. 11, in a proclamation concerning the apprehension of runaway bond-laborers dated 30 December 1669.

65. G. N. Clarke, *The Later Stuarts, 1660–1714* (Oxford, 1934), pp. 5–8, 82–3. David Ogg, *England Under the Reign of Charles II*, 2 vols. (Oxford, 1934), 1:74–5; 2:342, 346, 446, 449.

66. CO 1/34, f. 200 (Petition of Virginia's representatives to the King, June [?] 1675). CO 1/36, ff. 111–12 (letter from the collector of customs, Giles Bland, in Virginia to Secretary of State Sir Joseph Williamson, received in England in June 1676).

Besides the loss of tobacco revenues, the government spent £80,000 in quelling the rebellion.

(Governor Alexander Spotswood to the Board of Trade, 4 June 1715, referring to "Journals of this Colony in 1676" [*CSP, Col.*, pp. 199–201].)

67. So one might conclude from a letter from Mr William Harbord to the Earl of Essex, dated 17 December 1676, in which reference is made to revenue losses due to both Bacon's Rebellion and King Philip's War in New England: "[I]ll news from Virginia and New England doth not only alarm us but extreamly abates the customs so that notwithstanding all the shifts Treasurer can make this Parliament or another must sitt." (Clements Edwards Pike, ed., *Selections from the Correspondence of Arthur Capel, Earl of Essex, 1675–1677*, Camden Society Publications, 3rd ser. [London, 1913], p. 87. My attention was directed to this letter by Washburn's citation of it in *Governor and the Rebel*, p. 214, n. 5.) This crisis, to which the rebellion in Virginia so materially contributed, marked the beginning of party politics that was to lead to the so-called Glorious Revolution and the end of the Stuart monarchy. For the tobacco fleet number, see Ogg, 1:75.

68. *Coventry Papers*, 77:332. The document, which was apparently addressed to Secretary of State Williamson, is not dated, but it was probably written in October 1676 during preparations for sending troops to Virginia.

69. *Charles City Records (Order Book) 1677–79*, 9 August 1677.

70. *The Vestry Book of Christ Church Parish, 1663–1767* (in Middlesex County), edited by C. G. Chambelayne (Richmond, 1927), p. 25.

71. *Westmoreland County Records, 1675–89*, p. 68.

72. *Petsworth Parish Vestry Book, 1677-1795* (Gloucester County), edited by C. G. Chamberlayne (Richmond, 1933), p. 17. Chamberlayne suggestively noted that Nathaniel Bacon's death occurred at the home of Thomas Pate, the churchwarden of Petsworth Parish.

73. Such conjecture would not suit John Finley, apparently. He steadfastly refused to be freed from servitude by the rebels, preferring to remain their close prisoner for the space of twelve weeks. That's what he said, in support of his owner's action for trespass against a rebel officer. His faithfulness presumably exempted him from the added year of servitude imposed on bond-laborers absent from their owners during the rebellion. (*Charles City Order Book, 1677–79*, pp. 179–80 [13 September 1677].)

74. *Charles City County Records, 1655–66*, p. 5234 (18 October 1664).

75. See p. 135.

76. *Middlesex County Records, 1673–80*, f. 135 (2 September 1678).

77. *Middlesex County Order Book, 1694–1705*, pp. 234–42 (1 August and 2 October 1699).

78. See p. 154.

79. See p. 149.

80. "The Names and short Characters of those that have bin executed for Rebellion" submitted by Berkeley to the Royal Commissioners, in Samuel Wiseman's Book of Record. (See Neville, pp. 274–75.)

81. Neill identifies Wilson as a "servant," and says the death sentence was passed on him on 11 January. (Richard Duffield Neill, *Virginia Carolorum: The Colony under the Rule of Charles the First and Second, AD 1625–1685* [Albany, NY, 1886] pp. 373, 377.) *York County Records, 1677–84*, f. 88 (24 April 1679). *Accomack County Records 1678–82*, p. 158 (17 March 1679/80).

82. Fletcher was in court on four occasions between 17 February and 9 July 1677, and it appears that the beatings and kicking she suffered from her owner(s) followed her return from several months as a rebel. Even though she was sentenced on 4 July to two added years for bearing a child, and another five months for the time she was with the rebels, she embarked on a campaign of "wearying" her owner until he should sell her to someone else. As part of this wearying process, she resisted a whipping in the following manner, "when (her owner) began to strike her shee layd hold of him and flung him downe." (*Surry County Records, 1671–84*, ff. 121, 131; ibid., *1671–91*, 133, 152.)

83. Manscript of a letter from Andrew Marvell, poet and member of Parliament, to his friend Henry Thompson, 14 November 1676. I am grateful to the Henry E. Huntington Library and Art Gallery, San Marino, California, for supplying me with a photocopy of the letter.

84. New York Public Library, George Chalmers Collection, I, folio 49. The Bacon forces burned Jamestown on 19 September 1676. The letter was dated 19 October.

Why would Bacon want to free bond-laborers? Of 25 condemned rebels whose estates were inventoried, 14 were listed as owners of bond-laborers. The largest individual holding was that of Bacon's own 11 bond-laborers – 1 Irishman, 2 African-American men, 1 African-American woman and her one-year-old "mulatto" daughter, and 5 Indians, ranging in age from four to sixteen years of age. (CO 5/1371, f. 219vo-246ro; Bacon's list, 227vo-230vo.) Neither Bacon nor anyone else has left a record concerning his motives in this respect. One obvious reason is that he was fighting for his life – it was indeed victory, or death by drawing and quartering – that he needed the bond-laborers on his side, and that they would not go along without a promise of freedom.

85. Thomas Holden(?) to Secretary Joseph Williamson, 1 February 1677, at the end of a three-month return voyage from Virginia. (*CSP, Dom.*, 18:530.)

86. Hening 2:395 (February 1677).

87. Samuel Wiseman's Book of Record, entry for 11 March 1676/7. For an abstract of this document see Neville, p. 328; or Virginia Colonial Records Project Survey Report 6618 (old designation C-7) at Virginia State Archives.

By royal proclamation dated 26 October 1676 regarding the bond-laborers of rebel owners who failed to accept the king's offer of pardon and surrender by the middle of November, those bond-laborers, if they enlisted in Berkeley's forces, were to be freed from "the Said offenders." (*Coventry Papers*, 77:263.) Berkeley's offer was limited and did not promise liberty, but only liberty from Baconite owners.

88. *Coventry Papers*, 77:301–2. Unless otherwise explicitly noted my section on Grantham's encounters with the rebels is based on this document.

89. *CSP, Dom*, 19:115.

90. "This History of Bacon's and Ingram's Rebellion," Massachusetts Historical Society *Proceedings*, 9 (1867), pp. 299–342. Reprinted in Andrews, pp. 47–104; pp. 93.4.

91. Berkeley wrote a letter to Walklett on 1 January thanking him for his "letters . . . so full and discreet and your Actings so judicious," urging Walkett to go further and try to capture another rebel leader especially hated by Berkeley. He closed by saying that "Mr Ingram and Capt. Langston are with mee and wee shall dine togther within this quarter of an hour, where wee will drinke your health and happy success." (*Coventry Papers*, 78:177.) Walklett and Langston had been commanders of horse troops under Bacon. (Andrews, pp. 34–5, 87.) Herbert Jeffreys, one of the Royal Commission to Virginia and successor to Berkeley as Governor there, declared that the rebels would not have been "so easily reduced had not the said Walklett and one Ingram then general, surrendred their armes to Sir William Berkeley and disbanded their forces whereby the country came to a speedy settlement." (*Coventry Papers*, 78:175.)

92. Their bitterness was no doubt particularly caused by loss of West Point as a strategic location almost impregnable to heavily armed merchantmen or English naval attack by virtue of "the difficulty of the Channell and the Shoaliness of the water [that would] prevent any Great Shipps from pursuing . . . and where alsoe the Narrowness of the River and Commodiousness of the place Contribute soe much to our Advantage that we may with the Greatest facility given an effectuall Repulse to all the force that can their [there] Attack us." Such was the assessment submitted by experts whose opinions were sought by the Virginia Governor and Colony Council regarding defense against a possible French invasion in 1706. I have assumed that at the time of Bacon's Rebellion thirty years earlier both the rebels and Grantham similarly appreciated its strategic advantage. (See "Colonial Papers," Virginia State Archives, Richmond, folder 17, item 29.) "Bacon, with the instinct of the true strategist, had already selected West Point . . . as his headquarters and his main point of concentration." (Wertenbaker, *Torchbearer of the Revolution*, p. 184.)

93. Grantham said that most of these four hundred rebels accepted his terms, "except about eighty Negroes and twenty English which would not deliver their Armes." Grantham tricked these one hundred men on board a sloop with the promise of taking them to a rebel fort a few miles down the York River. Instead, towing them behind his own sloop, he brought them under the guns of another ship and thus forced their surrender, although "they yielded with a great deal of discontent, saying had they known my resolution, they would have destroyed me."

94. CO 1/38, f. 31. Andrews gives the number as "more than 1,100 officers and men." (Andrews, p. 102.)

95. CO 5/1371, ff. 119vo–a23. Report submitted to Governor Berkeley, ca. 30 January 1676/7, by John Good, a Henrico plantation owner on or about 2 September 1676. See note 14.

96. Thomas Wentworth, Earl of Strafford, sentenced for treason and beheaded 12 May 1641.

97. Aside from the garrison at West Point, and two others near West Point (the Brick House at King's Creek, under William Drummond and Richard Lawrence, chief co-leaders of the Bacon movement, and the four hundred at the chief garrison at Colonel West's house, scene of Grantham's most historic encounter, three miles north from West Point), they were located at: Green Spring (now Williamsburg), on the north side of the James River; Arthur Allen's expropriated house (since known as Bacon's Castle), further down and on the south shore of the James, about twenty-five miles northeast of the scene of Nat Turner's Rebellion in 1831; the expropriated house of Bacon's cousin, a Berkeley adherent, at King's Creek on York River; and further down at the place later made famous as Yorktown, scene of Cornwallis's surrender; and two other locations

expropriated from prominent Berkeleyites, one in Gloucester County and another in Westmoreland. (Locations as given in Wertenbaker, *Torchbearer of the Revolution*, pp. 184–6). The total number in all those places is not known; it appears that the one thousand in and around West Point comprised the majority of the rebel troops.

98. Andrews, p. 140. The Royal Commissioners' narrative was dated 20 July 1677. (Neville, p. 220). The cessation of fighting on one river is noted laconically in the 29 January entry in the journal of the *Young Prince*: "Blowing, 'thick weather.' Wind at SW. The cundry being reduced so went about our owne businesse as per the Governor['s] Proclamation." (CO 1/37.)

99. Neill, pp. 373, 374. CO 5/1371, ff. 219vo–246ro. CO 1/39, ff. 64–5. Two other condemned rebels cheated the gallows by dying in prison before they could be executed.

100. Francis Moryson was the son of Sir Richard Moryson and the nephew of the chronicler Fynes Moryson. The uncle and the father are mentioned in Volume One in connection with the Mountjoy conquest of Ireland. (See *The Invention of the White Race* Volume One, pp. 62–5 and Appendix F.) However, the view taken there differs from that of Charles M. Andrews, who unreflectingly credits Sir Richard with "a long and honorable career in Ireland." (Andrews, p. 102.)

101. *Coventry Papers*, 77:263. This proclamation is also to be found at Hening, 2:423–4, where the date is given as 10 October. But the defeated rebels were given no chance to swear such an oath.

102. Hening, 2:280 (1670), 356 (1676), 380 (February 1676/7). The "Bacon Assembly's extension of suffrage to freemen was strongly condemned by the Royal Commissioners in response to a Grievance of Rappahannock County and by the Colony officials in Maryland" (5/1371, f. 152vo; "Remonstrance by the Governor and Council of Maryland," *Maryland Archives*, 15:137–8).

103. For a defense of Berkeley in his quarrels with the Royal Commissioners, see Washburn, *Governor and the Rebel*, Chapter 8.

Excepting Washburn, historians have customarily characterized Berkeley's demeanor as simple vindictive fury linked with the spoils-to-the-victors program. Some of them add references to the old Governor's notorious irascibility, and to a possible sensibility about the great age disparity between Berkeley and Lady Frances, his wife. Paradoxical though it may seem, perhaps his attitude is better understood as foreshadowing the ultimately ascendant colony-centered, rather than "empire-centered," position on which the Virginia ruling elite eventually united.

104. Charles II is reported to have reacted to news of Berkeley's vendetta by noting that "that old fool has hanged more men in that naked country than I did for the Murther of my father." (Andrews, p. 40.) The same point was made by Royal Commissioners Berry and Moryson. Letter to Mr Watkins, 10 February 1676/7, abstracted in Neville, p. 246.

The reliability of the attribution is not established, but the accuracy of the observation is. Charles II hanged a total of thirteen, not counting Cromwell and Ireton, whose dead bodies were exhumed for hanging. ("Regicide," *Encyclopedia Britannica*, 15th edition, [Chicago, 1997], 26:1035.

105. Samuel Wiseman's Record Book, abstracted in Neville, pp. 245–6.

106. *CSP, Col.*, 11:134 (31 October 1681).

107. CO 5/1356, f. 71, Spenser to Sir Leolin Jenkins, 8 May 1682.

108. Blathwayt Papers, ca. 1675–1715, 41 vols. on microfilm at Colonial Williamsburg; vol. 15, Spencer to Blathwayt, 29 May 1682. William Blathwayt was Secretary to the Lords of Trade and Plantations. I am indebted to the New York Historical Society Manuscripts Library for the use of its microfilm set of the Blathwayt Papers.

109. *VMHB*, 2:16, 136–7, 141, 142 cited in Morton 1:327.

110. Culpeper to Blathwayt, 20 March 1682/3 (Blathwayt Papers, Vol. 17).

111. Spencer to Blathwayt, 1 March 1688/9 (Blathwayt Papers, Vol. 15).

112. Dudley Digges to Blathwayt, 23 October 1710 Blathwayt Papers, Vol. 18.

113. Allan Kulikoff, *Tobacco and Slaves: The Development of Southern Cultures in the Chesapeake, 1680–1800* (Chapel Hill and London, 1986), p. 79.

114. *CSP Col.*, 11:130 (Culpeper to the Lords of Trade and Plantations, 25 October 1681).

115. Dalby Thomas, *An Historical Account, Rise and Growth of the West Indies Colonies and great Advantages they are to England in Respect to Trade* (London, 1690), in Harleian Miscellany, 12 vols.; 9:425.

116. "It was evident," says Professor Richard L. Morton, "that diversification of industry as a remedy for overproduction of tobacco would take years ... But a remedy was needed at once" (Morton, p. 300). But I would respectfully suggest that, of all the Anglo-American colonies, none had had more time than Virginia; time was not the problem, but rather the plantation system based on bond-labor.

117. In 1708, Virginia Colony Secretary Edmund Jennings said that of a total of 30,000 tithables,

there were slightly more than 12,000 bond-laborers, although the number of European-American bond-laborers was "inconsiderable" because "so few have been imported since the beginning of the war" (*CSP Col.*, 24:156). But the Virginia and Maryland laws and official records show that in subsequent years their presence was anything but "inconsiderable."

118. See p. 119.

119. Hening, 2:515.

120. Kulikoff (p. 39.)

121. Ibid., p. 40.

122. Menard, *Economy and Society in Early Colonial Maryland*, p. 433.

123. Kulikoff, p. 42. Menard, *Economy and Society in Early Colonial Maryland* Appendix II.

124. In Virginia in 1699 there were 21,888 tithables in a total population of 57,339, a ratio of 1:2.62, or 38 percent (*CSP, Col.*, 19:635–6; Cf. Morgan p. 414). In Maryland in 1712 the total population was 46,073. Of that number, European-American men werre 11,025, and the number of "Negroes" was 8,830, making a total of 19,855. On that basis, the ratio of tithables to total population in Maryland would be 1:2.42, or 43.1 percent. An uncertain number of European-American women in Maryland worked in the crop and were therefore tithable. (See CO 5/717 [15 July 1712] and 5/716, Governor Seymour to Board of Trade, 21 August 1706). These total population figures from the records correspond closely with the figures for 1700 and 1710 for Virginia and Maryland respectively as presented in *Historical Statistics of the United States, Colonial Period to 1970*, series Z 13, 14.

125. *CSP, Col.*, 16:390–91 (20 August 1698).

126. *CSP, Col.*, 17:liv, 261.

127. *CSP, Col.*, 25:83 (24 April 1710).

128. *CSP, Col.*, 27:70 (15 October 1715).

129. *CSP, Col.*, 36:414–15 (29 June 1729).

130. Louis B. Wright, ed., *The History and Present State of Virginia*, (Chapel Hill, 1947), p. 92. This edited work is a revised edition of the 1705 work, published in 1722.

131. "Culpeper Report on Virginia in 1683," *VMHB* 3:222–38; p. 222. A hogshead at this time probably contained 475 to 500 pounds of tobacco. Cutting as many plants in an hour "as well would have imployed twenty men a Summers tendance to have perfected," in Gloucester alone these plant-cutting rioters destroyed 200 plantations in the first week of their campaign. (CO 5/1356, p. 70, Colony Secretary Spencer to Secretary Leoline Jenkins, 8 May 1682.)

132. Perhaps Governor Culpeper was exaggerating somewhat in saying, "scarce one of them was worth a Farthing" ("Report on Virginia in 1683," *VMHB*, 3:231).

133. Morgan, p. 286, citing CO 1/48, ff. 261, 263, 275, and CO 1/49, f. 56.

134. Morgan, pp. 291–2.

135. Ibid., pp. 308–9. See also my comment on Morgan's book in the Introduction to Volume One of the present work.

136. *VMHB*, 3:222–38; p. 230.

137. See the discussion of Sir Francis Bacon's essay on the history of the reign of Henry VII in Chapter 2, pp. 17–18.

138. The Colony Council had roughly estimated that one-third of free men in 1673 were either unable to make a living or were else mired in debt (see pp. 168–9).

139. Samuel Pepys, Secretary to the Admiralty, to Secretary of State Henry Coventry, 7 October 1676 (*Coventry Papers*, 77:233–4).

140. Admiralty Papers, 51/134, Log of HMS *Bristol*, entry for 15 February 1676/7.

141. CO 389/6, p. 200.

142. CO 5/1355. Culpeper's request, 13 December 1677; Lords of Trade and Plantations reply, August 1678.

143. CO 5/1355, p. 408. Culpeper to the Lords of Trade and Plantations, 25 October 1681.

144. CO 5/1356, ff. 2–3, 22 November 1681.

145. CO 5/1356, 8 May 1682.

146. *CSP, Col*, 11:498.

147. CO 5/1356, pp. 183–4.

148. CO 5/1356, pp. 247–8.

149. *Archives Maryland*, 5:152–4. *Proceedings of the Council 1671–1681*. Governor Notley to [name not given in the record], 22 January 1676/77.

150. CO 1/40, f. 186, Notley to Charles Calvert, Lord Baltimore, Proprietary of the Province of Maryland, 22 May 1677. It appears from the copy of this document made by the Virginia Colonial Records Project that this folio once was numbered "88," by which number Wertenbaker refers to

it. (Thomas J. Wertenbaker, *Virginia Under the Stuarts* [Princeton, 1914], p. 137, n. 58.) I thank Cecily J. Peeples for last-minute checking of the records relating to this and half a dozen other facts at the Virginia State Archives.

12 The Abortion of the "White Race" Social Control System in The Anglo-Caribbean

1. Speaking of those forms of the bourgeoisie whom he had studied most closely, Professor Dunn renders this documented judgement: "The sugar planters were always businessmen first and foremost, and from a business standpoint it was more efficient to import new slaves of prime working age from Africa than to breed up a creole generation of Negroes in the Caribbean.... Some of the slave masters found it hard to resist the temptation to get rid of the young and old by systematic neglect and underfeeding." (Richard S. Dunn, *Sugar and Slaves: The Rise of the Planter Class in the English West Indies, 1624–1712* [Chapel Hill, 1972; W. W. Norton reprint, 1973] p. 321.

2. Strictly speaking, it is only after the formation of Great Britain by the Act of Union of England and Scotland in 1707 that the Anglo-Caribbean islands are referred to as the British West Indies. But aside from the effect of the opening of trade between Scotland and the English islands, this is a distinction that may generally be ignored in the present discussion.

The British West Indies comprised a dozen island colonies, annexed over a period of 178 years: from Barbados (1625) to St Lucia (1803); from the Bahamas (1718[?], 1729[?]; see Michael Craton, *A History of the Bahamas* [London, 1962], p. 120) in the northwest to Trinidad (1797) in the southeast; from formerly Spanish Jamaica captured by the English (1655) with its 4,470 square miles, to Nevis (1628), with 50 square miles. Some were captured from Britain one or more times by the French: for example, Nevis, St Kitts (St Christopher), Antigua, Montserrat, Grenada, and Dominica. Though I generalize regarding certain common characteristics of these colonies, I am aware that each has its own distinctive history and traditions. At the same time I believe that the Anglo-Caribbean colonies were characterized by a common history of a ruling-class social control policy that led to the establishment of a tripartite social structure that included persons of some degree of African ancestry in the intermediate buffer social control stratum, a social structure that differed fundamentally from that established in continental Anglo-America at the beginning of the eighteenth century.

3. Almost simultaneously, English colonies were begun on St Kitts (St Christopher), St Eustatius, Tobago, Antigua, and Montserrat. In 1655 the English began settling in Jamaica, which they had captured from Spain. All were essentially monocultural enterprises; the principal product was sugar; minor products were tobacco, cotton, aloes and indigo. The main labor force was made up of chattel bond-laborers.

4. *Coventry Papers*, 85:11 cited in Dunn, p. 74. See the testimony of Captain Henry Powell regarding his efforts to employ Indians in his Barbados plantation. "Papers relating to the early History of Barbados," *Timehri*, new ser., 5:53–5 (1891) (cited in Dunn, p. 227). *The Laws of Jamaica, Comprehending all the Acts in Force Passed between the Thirty Second Year of the Reign of Charles the Second and the Thirty-third Year of the Reign of King George the Third ... Published under the Direction of Commissioners appointed for that Purpose*, 2 vols. (St Jago de la Vega, Jamaica, 1792), pp. 129–30. 8 Geo. I, c. 1 (1721), "An Act to encourage the settling the north-east part of this island," refers to "every free mulatto, Indian or negro."

5. When Dunn says p. 74 that "Indians could not be turned into acceptable agricultural laborers" I take him to mean *bond*-laborers. Dunn himself cites the record of Guiana Indians who in 1627 voluntarily came to Barbados with Captain Henry Powell to cultivate land as "free people" there and to help to promote trade with the mainland. (Ibid., p. 227.) Twenty years later, Powell returned to Barbados and found that those Indians and their families had been involuntarily integrated into the chattel bond-labor system. He petitioned the Barbados Assembly "to set these poor people free that have been kept thus long in bondage." (*Timehri* [1891], 5:53–5.)

6. Historical Manuscripts Commission, Vol. xiv, part 2, Portland Manuscripts, III, p. 268; and CO 1/22, no. 55. (cited in Vincent T. Harlow, *A History of Barbados 1625–1685*, [Oxford, 1926; Negro Universities Press reprint, 1969] pp. 152, 192).

7. Dunn, p. 74.

8. "A Briefe Relation of the Voyage Unto Maryland," in the *Calvert Papers*, Number Three (Baltimore, 1899) p. 32. This account, of which there are two slightly differing versions, one in

Latin, the other in English, is credited to Father Andrew White. A translation of the Latin version is found in Peter Force, *Tracts and Other Papers Relating Principally to the Origin, Settlement and Progress of the Colonies in North America From the Discovery of the Country to the Year 1776* (Washington, 1836, 1947 reprint), vol. 4, no. XII (referred to throughout as *Force Tracts*). The *Force Tracts* version uses the word "slaves" instead of "servants."

9. The Dutch invaded Brazil in 1624, and by 1637 had seized half of the Portuguese administrative areas of settlement (*capteaneos*) there. Dutch-held Pernambuco alone accounted for one-third of Brazil's plantation and sugar mill enterprises, and imported more than half the African bond-laborers brought to Brazil. A rebellion of Portuguese, in which free Afro-Brazilians played a major part, succeeded in finally ousting the Dutch in 1654. Already for the better part of a decade before that final evacuation, Dutch plantation owners had been liquidating their Brazilian operations and leaving the country. A significant number of them settled in Barbados with their capital and technology, and with access to credit and markets in Holland. (Johannes M. Postma, *The Dutch in the Atlantic Slave Trade, 1600–1815*, [Cambridge, 1990] pp. 14, 16, 17, 19–20. R. K. Kent, "Palmares, An African State in Brazil," in Richard Price, ed., *Maroon Societies: Rebel Slave Communities in the Americas*, pp. 170, 171, 174. E. E. Rich and C. H. Wilson, eds., *The Economy of Expanding Europe in the Sixteenth and Seventeenth Centuries* [Cambridge, 1967], [Volume IV of the *Cambridge Economic History of Europe*], p. 334. Harlow, p. 84.)

10. Harlow, p. 325.

11. Ibid., p. 305.

12. Barbados governor Daniel Searle to John Thurloe, Secretary of the Council of State, 18 September 1655 (*A Collection of the State Papers of John Thurloe...*, 7 vols. [London, 1742], 4:39–40.)

13. *CSP, Col.*, 12:155 (Minutes of the Barbados Colony Council, 16 February 1686).

14. *CSP, Col.*, 13:733–4 (Barbados Governor Kendall to the Lords of Trade and Plantations, 3 November 1692). The investigation found that "the ringleaders" were mainly "overseers, artisans and domestic servants," who could exploit their relatively greater freedom of movement for organizing the revolt.

15. Dunn, p. 256.

16. Orlando Patterson, *The Sociology of Slavery: An Analysis of the Origins, Development and Structure of Negro Slave Society* (London, 1967), pp. 266, 271–3.

17. R. C. Dallas, *History of the Maroons*, 2 vols. (London, 1803), pp. 23–4.

18. Bryan Edwards, *The History, Civil and Commercial, of the British Colonies in the West Indies* 3 vols. (West Indies, 4th edition, 3 vols. London 1807) 1:522–35, and 537–45 reprinted in Price, ed., pp. 230–32.

19. Dallas (*History of the Maroons* p. 60) says "fifteen hundred" acres, less than two and a half square miles, but such an area would seem absurdly small to provide farming land sufficient for even the one section of the maroons signing this particular treaty. I have substituted the figure given by Patterson: 15,000 acres. (Patterson, pp. 279–71, citing the Jamaica *Journal of the House of Assembly*, 3:458.)

20. Dallas, pp. 58–65.

21. The basic economic, demographic and sociological facts on which the following five points of differentiation rely are long established and are well known to every student of the history of the West Indies. The original colonial-period sources are familiar to all, and the vast bibliography of secondary works, although they differ in interpretation and emphasis, presents a general consensus regarding those facts.

22. I have used Morgan's estimate of the total population, but excluded Henrico County (partially above the Fall Line) and the Eastern Shore counties of Northampton and Accomack. (See Edmund S. Morgan, *American Slavery, American Freedom: The Ordeal of Colonial Virginia* (New York, 1975), Table 3, pp. 412–13.) The Tidewater area is given in standard encyclopedias.

23. The 11,000 squares miles of the Tidewater area is equal to 7,040,000 acres. The quitrent rolls for Virginia's twenty counties in 1704 show an area of some 2,780,000 acres. (Thomas J. Wertenbaker, *The Planters of Colonial Virginia* [New York 1922], Appendix, "Rent Rolls of Virginia 1704–1705.")

24. See pp. 164, 170. See also Virginia laws (Hening, 2:53–69 (1691), and 404–19 (1705), aimed at centralizing customs collections in specific port locations because otherwise royal "customes and revenues [were] impossible to be secured" (2:53). See also John C. Rainbolt, *From Prescription to Persuasion* (Port Washington, NY, 1974), pp. 6, 113.

25. For seventeenth-century Barbados population figures, see Harlow, p. 338; and Sheppard, p. 33. I have used Harlow's figure here. I have made no attempt to investigate the decline of the

total Barbados population suggested by the estimate of only 62,324 in 1748 contained in Jerome S. Handler and Arnold A. Sio, "Barbados," in David W. Cohen and Jack P. Greene, eds., *Neither Slave Nor Free: The Freedman of African Descent in the Slave Societies of the New World* (Baltimore, 1972), p. 338.

26. Hilary Beckles, *Black Rebellion in Barbados: The Struggle Against Slavery, 1627–1838* (Bridgetown, Barbados, 1984), p. 62.

27. The 1698 population of Jamaica is given as 47,400 in Cohen and Greene, eds., p. 338.

28. Philip D. Curtin, *Two Jamaicas: The Role of Ideas in a Tropical Country* (Cambridge, Massachusetts, 1955), p. 69. "Unlike Barbados and the Leewards, where all the land suitable for sugar cane was soon taken up and overproduction exhausted the soil, Jamaica was never quite fully exploited before sugar and slavery declined." (Michael Craton, *Sinews of Empire: A Short History of British Slavery* [Garden City, New York, 1974] p. 46.)

29. Dallas, p. 1xix. Dallas's proportion of unused land is consistent with Curtin's, but his absolute number of acres exceeds the area of Jamaica by some 40 percent.

30. Patterson, p. 270 (citing CO 137/18).

31. Dunn, pp. 170–71, 197, 266–7. Hilary Beckles, *White Servitude and Black Slavery in Barbados, 1627–1715*, pp. 157–58.

32. Dunn, pp. 171 (Table 18), 197, 266 (Table 24), 267 (Table 25).

33. According to Beckles, it was less than 3 percent in Barbados. Wertenbaker puts the Virginia proportion at between 5 and 6 percent. (Beckles, *White Servitude and Black Slavery*, p. 158; Wertenbaker, p. 98.)

34. Sheppard, p. 33.

35. "Lacking means of sustenance, 30,000 Europeans streamed out of Barbados alone during the latter half of the seventeenth century . . . but the majority remained in the Caribbean relocating over and over again in Jamaica, Guiana, the Windwards, and Trinidad." (David Lowenthal, *West Indian Societies* [London, 1972], pp. 29–30.)

In February 1679, however, only a minority appeared to have chosen other West Indies islands. Of 593 persons granted leave to depart Barbados in 1679, 233 were going to North America, 205 to England, 154 to other Caribbean islands, and 1 to Holland. It appears that somewhat over half of these were former bond-laborers. (Dunn, pp. 110–11.)

36. Dunn, p. 312.

37. Craton, p. 44.

38. Harlow, 174–5.

39. The novelty of this form of social identity is to be noted in the comments of George Fox and Morgan Godwyn. During a visit to Barbados in 1671, Fox, founder of the Quaker religion, addressed some members of a Barbados audience as "you that are called white." (George Fox, *Gospel of Family-Order* . . . [London, 1675], p. 38.) About the same time, Godwyn found it necessary to explain to his readers that in Barbados "white" was "the general name for Europeans." (*The Negro's and Indians Advocate* . . . [London, 1680], p. 83.) Even a century later a historian, writing in Jamaica for readers in Britain, felt it necessary to supply a parenthetical clarification: "white people (as they are called here)." (Edward Long, *The History of Jamaica, or, General Survey of the Antient and Modern State of the Island, with Reflections on its Situation, Settlements, Inhabitants, Climate, Products, Commerce, Laws, and Government*, 3 vols. [London, 1774], 2:289.)

40. See *The Invention of the White Race*, Volume One, p. 80.

41. In ordering the forced exile of 1,500 to 2,000 Irish boys to Jamaica to serve as bond-laborers, Henry Cromwell, Oliver's son and deputy in Ireland, wrote to Secretary Johne Thurloe, "who knows, but that it may be a measure to make them Englishmen, I meane rather, Christians." (H. Cromwell to John Thurloe, Secretary of the Council of State, 11 and 18 September 1655. *Papers of John Thurloe* 4:23–4, 40.)

The free persons of color in Barbados made known their determination that "Christian" should not be regarded as a mere euphemism for "white." When the "slave consolidation act" of 1826 was passed making it a crime for a slave to assault "any white person," the free persons of color protested that it deprived them of a protection that they had had as Christians since 1688. (Jerome S. Handler, *The Unappropriated People: Freedmen in the Slave Society of Barbados* [Baltimore, 1974], p. 98.)

42. English Attorney-General Edward Northey, in the normal course of his duty of reviewing laws passed in the colonies, objected to a Nevis Assembly enactment providing for punishment by death or dismemberment for slaves who attempted to escape their bondage. In particular he argued that "white slaves" who had been kidnapped and sent to bondage in the West Indies, should not be so treated merely for trying to regain the freedom of which they had been unjustly deprived. Joseph

Jory, representative of Nevis in London, clarified matters by saying that "white servants are not to be taken as slaves." Whereupon Northey withdrew his objection (though he did say that the application of such penalties against Africans should be approved for only a limited time, and then be subject to review as to their effects.) (*CSP, Col.*, 23:126 [1 May 1706].)

43. A reminder given by the Commissioners of Trade and Plantations in 1709. (*CSP Col.*, 24:454.)

44. *CSP, Col.*, 17:423.

45. *Acts of Assembly Passed in the Island of Nevis from 1664, to 1739, inclusive* ([London?], 1740) pp. 37–9. Alan Burns (*History of the British West Indies* [London, 1954], p. 217) says that the general rule was one European man to every ten Africans.

46. *CSP, Col.*, 13:348 (Lords of Trade and Plantations to Barbaros governor Kendall, 20 November 1690). This provision apparently was designed to prevent a repetition of the exodus of pardoned rebels from Jamaica that had been followed by a rebellion of five hundred African bond-laborers there on 29 July 1690. (*CSP Col.*, 13:315–17 [31 August 1690].)

47. Harlow says that after 1660 in Barbados the former five-to-seven years of servitude required of English bond-laborers was reduced to three or four years. The motive was the plantation owners' fear of "the slave menace." (Harlow, p. 301.) Representatives of the Barbados plantation bourgeoisie asked the king to allow one or two thousand English bond-laborers, "though but for 2 yeares service for the charge of their passage." (Irish Manuscripts Commission, *Analecta Hibernia*, No. 4 [October 1932], "Documents Relating to the Irish in the West Indies," Aubrey Gwynne SJ, collector, p. 266 [16 September 1667]. Hereafter these materials will be referred to as "Gwynne, *Analecta Hibernia*, No. 4.")

48. Dunn, p. 242, citing CO 30/2/114–25 (Barbados MSS Laws, 1645–82).

49. *CSP, Col.*, 14:446–7.

50. *Journal of the Commissioners of Trade and Plantations*, 2:63–4 (17 August 1709). *CSP, Col.*, 24:450–52 (24 August 1709).

51. *CSP, Col.*, 28:154–5.

52. Sheppard, p. 38. Philip Rowell of Christ Church Parish in Barbados was an exception; sometime around 1680 he gave five of his time-expired bond-laborers six acres of land and two lifetime bond-laborers each in order that they might avoid the common fate of beggary or dependency on parish charity. (Beckles, *White Servitude and Black Slavery*, p. 159.)

53. Sheppard, pp. 38–9, 44, 63. This unique slim volume is indispensable for the study of the subject of "race" in Anglo-America. In Barbados, where the "poor whites" were the majority of the European population, the story of the "military tenants" epitomized the marginalization of that entire class in the system of social control. If our American sociologists were to examine this phenomenon, they might find a new application for their term "underclass." An order of the Jamaica Colony Council Assembly provided that a European bond-laborer disabled in military service "shall have an able negro delivered to him forever, for his maintenance." (*CSP, Col.*, 7:474 21 March 1673.)

54. See *The Invention of the White Race*, Volume One, points 1 and 2 of "operative principles of social control in a stable civil society constituted on the basis of racial oppression," pp. 134–5.

55. Europeans made up a higher proportion of the population in Barbados than in any other British West Indies colony. For the specific reference to the majority being "poor whites" in 1680 and a century and a half later, see Sheppard, pp. 31, 63, 68. Follow the declining social career of the "poor white" majority through Sheppard's Chapter 4, "From Indentured Servants to Poor Whites (1704–1839)"; Chapter 5, "Disbandment of the Military Tenants (1839)"; and Chapter 6, "The Problems of Degeneration." Beckles's study of Barbados parishes found that "From the mid-1680s on [through 1715, the terminal year of his study] the majority of freemen were categorized by vestries as 'very poore'." (Beckles, *White Servitude and Black Slavery*, p. 159.)

Concluding her study of the "Redlegs" of Barbados, Professor Sheppard supplies a comment that may yet prove to have a wider application: "As soon also as poor whites were forced, through the removal of any special status, to mix on equal terms with their black peers, then much of their former arrogance began, albeit slowly, to disappear." (Sheppard, p. 120.)

56. The Nevis Assembly showed sensitivity to this challenge. In 1675 it made it a crime for "servants and slaves to company or drink together." (*CSP, Col.*, 9:236. Also cited by C. S. Higham, *The Development of the Leeward Islands Under the Restoration, 1660–1688: A Study of the Foundations of the Old Colonial System* [Cambridge, 1921], pp. 174–5.) Another Nevis law, passed in 1700, made it a crime for "any white Person to converse or keep Company with" "Negroes or other slaves." (*Acts of Assembly Passed in the Island of Nevis from 1664 to 1739, inclusive* [London, 1740], p. 28.) A marginal note here says "Obsolete, but re-enacted in 1717."

57. The Barbados Colony Council felt this Irish "whiteness gap" so keenly that in 1690, while urgently asking for "white servants," they excluded "Irish rebels . . .; for we want not labourers of that Colour to work for us; but men in whom we may confide, to strengthen us." (*CSP, Col.*, Vol. 13, Item 1108, cited in Sheppard, p. 35.) Perhaps they meant green.

58. The War of Devolution, 1667–68; the War of the League of Augsburg (known in England as King Billy's War), 1689–1697; the War of the Spanish Succession (known in England as Queen Anne's War), 1701–1713; and the War of the Austrian succession, 1740–48, for which England's War of Jenkin's Ear, against Spain, was a prelude.

59. See *The Invention of the White Race*, Volume One.

60. Gwynne, *Analecta Hibernia*, No. 4, p. 233.

61. Ibid., pp. 236–7.

62. Ibid., pp. 243, 245. According to an English eyewitness, during one engagement on St Kitts, the Irish in the rear of the English forces fired into the ranks of the English ahead of them. (Ibid., p. 244.) Compare this with Mountjoy's policy of putting the Irish allies in the front ranks. (*The Invention of the White Race*, 1:64.)

63. Gwynne, *Analecta Hibernia*, pp. 265–6.

64. Ibid., p. 267.

65. Ibid., pp. 278–9.

66. *CSP, Col.*, 9:236 (26 May 1675). See note 56.

67. *CSP, Col.*, 13:733 (Governor Kendal to the Lords of Trade and Plantations, 3 November 1692).

68. *Acts of Assembly Passed in the Island of Nevis from 1664, to 1739 inclusive*, pp. 35–9.

69. Gwynne, *Analecta Hibernia*, No. 4, p. 282.

70. See ibid., pp. 282–5.

71. See Fortescue's Preface to *CSP, Col.*, Sol. 16 (27 October 1697 31 December 1698), p. viii.

72. Sir John Davies, *A Discovery of the True Causes why Ireland was never entirely Subdued nor brought under Obedience of the Crowne of England, Until the Beginning of his Majesties happie Reign* (London, 1612), pp. 6–7. Cited in *The Invention of the White Race*, Volume One, p. 65.

73. Roger Norman Buckley, *Slaves in Redcoats: The British West India Regiments, 1795–1815* (New Haven, 1979), p. 124, citing Great Britain Public Record Office, WO [War Office] 1/95, Brigadier General Thomas Hislop, "Remarks" enclosed to the Duke of York, 22 July 1804.

74. Dunn, p. 181.

75. Ibid., p. 4.

76. Patterson, p. 49.

77. Ibid., p. 282, citing CO 137/19, Governor Hunter to the Board of Trade.

78. Ibid., citing CO 137/20, ff. 165, 184, 192–3.

79. Dallas pp. 9–10.

80. Long, 1:147–8.

81. Dallas, 1:1xvii.

82. Ibid., 1:19–20. Buckley, p. 9 (citing C. L. R. James, *Black Jacobins Toussaint L'Ouverture and the San Domingo Revolution*, [New York, 1963] pp. 128–9, 139–142; and Thomas O. Ott, *The Haitian Revolution, 1789–1804* [Knoxville, Tennessee, 1973], pp. 65–72, 82–3).

83. Buckley, p. 8.

84. *CSP, Col.*, 16:vii–viii.

85. Sheppard, p. 42.

86. John Luffman, *A Brief Account of Antiqua, together with the Customs and Manners of its Inhabitants, as well White as Black* (London, 1789), pp. 15, 87, 172. This work is a series of letters addressed by Luffman in Antigua to a correspondent in London during the period 1786–88.

87. The 1700 total is for Virginia, Maryland, South Carolina, and North Carolina; the 1780 total includes Georgia, which was founded as a colony in 1732. Taking the continental plantation colonies/states as a whole, from 1700 to 1860 European-Americans were never less than 60 percent of the total population. (*Historical Statistics of the United States, Colonial Times to 1970* US Department of Commerce, Bureau of the Census [Washington, DC, 1975], p. 1168, Series Z 1–19. Cohen and Greene, eds., p. 339, Table A-9 "United States, Upper and Lower South, 1790–1860.")

88. Dunn, p. 312 (Table 26). In Barbados by 1768 they were fewer than one out of six. (Sheppard, p. 43.)

89. *CSP, Col.*, 7:141 (Barbados planters in London, 14 December 1670). p. 71.

90. Dunn, pp. 198, 319. On Barbados sugar estates already in 1667, an English observer noted that skilled Negro bond-laborers were being substituted for European tradesmen, while European

workers were toiling at field work. (Harlow, *History of Barbados, 1625–1685*, p. 309, citing CO 1/21, No. 170.)

91. Douglas Hall, "Jamaica," in Cohen and Greene, eds., pp. 202–3. Hilary Beckles devotes an entire absorbing chapter to Afro-Barbadian women bond-laborers in retail trade, "Marketeers: The Right to Trade." Again and again laws were enacted designed to deny these women trading rights, but the laws proved ineffective. (Hilary McD. Beckles, *Natural Rebels: A Social History of Enslaved Black Women in Barbados* [New Brunswick, 1989] Recurring references to the ineffectiveness of the prohibitory laws are found at pp. 77, 79, 84, 86–7.) For the same activity by black women bond-laborers in Antigua, see Luffman pp. 138–41, Letter XXII, 28 March 1788.

92. Cohen and Greene, p. 339.

93. Gad J. Heuman, *Between Black and White: Race, Politics and the Free Coloreds in Jamaica, 1792–1865* (Westport, Connecticut, 1981). p. 7.

94. Handler and Sio, pp. 218–19.

95. Elsa V. Goveia, *Slave Society in the British Leeward Islands at the End of the Eighteenth Century* (New Haven, 1965), p. 312.

96. Handler and Sio, pp. 240–41. In the West Indies, the terms "freedman" or "freedwoman" strictly speaking implied that the person had once been a bond-laborer. "Free black," or Negro, was reserved for persons of presumed undiluted African descent. "Free colored," or sometimes "mulatto," was used to describe a person of mixed African and European ancestry. Such terminological differences implied important social distinctions in the West Indies. In continental Anglo-America they were not important. Except where the context requires a distinction, or where a quotation must be preserved intact, I shall feel free to use the term "freeman" or "freedwoman" to mean any non-bond-laborer in the West Indies who is of one degree or another of African ancestry.

97. Sheppard, p. 44. In continental Anglo-American colonies, by contrast, free African-Americans were excluded from trades by "white" workers, but they could do little to discourage the employers from employing African-American bond-laborers in skilled occupations. See Charles H. Wesley, *Negro Labor in the United States* (New York, 1927), pp. 69–73. See also Frederick Douglass's eloquent analysis of this peculiarity. (Frederick Douglass, *Life and Times of Frederick Douglass* [1892; New York, 1962], pp. 179–80.)

98. Heuman, p. 9. The quoted phrase is intended to apply to the British West Indies generally. (Hall, p. 202.)

99. Handler, pp. 129–30. George Pinckard, *Notes on the West Indies: Written during the Expeditions under the Command of the late General Sir Ralph Abercromby*, 3 vols., 2nd ed (London, 1803), 1:369–70.

100. See *The Invention of the White Race*, Volume One, pp. 93, 260 n. 52, and the references there to Lecky and Sullivan.

101. Hall, pp. 202–3. Handler, 126–7.

102. Heuman, p. 28.

103. There was a discrimination in favor of "whites," who were offered thirty acres. *Laws of Jamaica* (8 Geo. I, c. 1, 1:129–30.) This combination of concession and discrimination parallels the Bogland Act of 1772 in Ireland granting Catholics expanded rights to lease, but not to purchase land; and the Southern Homestead Act of 1866 in the United States allowing African-Americans only half the 160 acres allowed to whites under the Homestead Law of 1862. (See *The Invention of the White Race*, Volume One, pp. 93, 140–41.)

104. Burns, *History of the British West Indies*, p. 441.

105. Heuman, p. 84. For the total number of slaves, see Hall, p. 194.

106. Handler, pp. 68–72.

107. Buckley, pp. 11, 17–18.

108. Buckley, pp. 13, 53–5. Between 1795 and 1808 the British army in the West Indies purchased 13,400 Africans for military service, of whom 8,924 were purchased in Africa.

109. Buckley, pp. 13, 30–31, 41, 127.

110. In 1673, the Barbados authorities had tried to have the best of both possibilities. While increasing the exploitation of the African bond-laborers unrelentingly, even as they reduced their rations, the authorities sought to strengthen the militia by recruiting and arming militiamen from among these same bond-laborers. But that proved a prelude to a plot for a general African rebellion in 1675. (Dunn, pp. 257–8. Sheppard, p. 34.)

111. Buckley, p. 124. Of the African-born soldiers, who generally did not want to return to Africa, some were settled in Trinidad and Honduras, the others, willingly or otherwise, were sent

to Sierra Leone. Those who had been inducted from the West Indies, along with the youngest of those brought from Africa, remained in the West Indies. (Ibid., p. 35, citing CO 318/55.)

112. Edmund Burke, *An Account of European Settlements in America*, 2 vols. (London, 1758), 2:118, 130–31.

113. Long, 2:333–4.

114. James Ramsay, *An Essay on the Treatment and Conversion of Slaves in the British Sugar Colonies* (London, 1784), pp. 288–9. Ramsay (1733–89) served as an Episcopal priest in the West Indies on two separate occasions, but his espousal of Christian charity toward the bond-laborers earned the hostility of the planters. On his final return to England he published the *Essay*, and became associated with the abolitionist movement. (*Dictionary of National Biography*.)

115. See *The Invention of the White Race*, Volume one, p. 112.

116. Pinckard, 2:532 (emphasis in original). Pinckard's design seem to have worked out very satisfactorily for the British ruling class, at least as late as the second decade of the twentieth century. Sir Sidney Olivier, after serving as Governor of Jamaica from 1907 to 1913, was convinced that "this [mulatto] class as it at present exists is a valuable and indispensable part of any West Indies community, and that a colony of black, coloured, and whites has a far more organic efficiency and far more promise in it than a colony of black and white alone. . . . The graded mixed class in Jamaica helps to make an organic whole of the community and saves it from this distinct cleavage." (Sir Sidney Olivier, *White Capital and Coloured Labour* new edition, rewritten and revised [London, 1928], pp. 65–6.)

117. Beckles, *Black Rebellion in Barbados*, p. 83, citing Minutes of the Council, 1 November 1803, Barbados Archives.

118. Handler and Sio, pp. 218–19. Table 7–1. Heuman, p. 7.

119. Sheppard, p. 61.

120. Long, 2:335. See also A. E. Furness, "The Maroon War of 1795" *Jamaican Historical Review*, 5:30–45 (1965).

121. Handler, p. 205. Handler was writing about Barbados.

122. The Jamaica figures are from Heuman, p. 7. Handler and Sio, pp. 218–19, Table 7–1.

123. Heuman, p. 30.

124. Handler, pp. 148, 150. These were not merely normal "owners" of members of their own families, as might be the case in the United States. See Carter G. Woodson, *Free Negro Owners of Slaves in the United States in 1830* (Washington, 1935); Luther Porter Jackson, *Free Negro Labor and Property-Holding in Virginia, 1830–1860* (New York, 1942), p. 22.

125. Heuman, p. 29.

126. See Robin Blackburn, *The Overthrow of Colonial Slavery* (London, 1988), Chapter XI, "The Struggle for British Slave Emancipation, 1823–38,," especially pp. 421–8, 432–7, 439, 447–8, 451–2, and 454–9.

127. Hall, "Jamaica," pp. 207–8.

128. See *The Invention of the White Race*, Volume One, Chapter 4.

129. Handler and Sio, p. 238. "The event that tipped the scales in favor of ameliorative legislation was a slave revolt which broke out on the night of April 14, 1816." (Ibid., p. 234.)

"In the late eighteenth and early nineteenth centuries the Jamaican legislature passed hundreds of bills granting well-educated and well-to-do coloured individuals the perquisites of whites." (Foreword by Philip Mason to David Lowenthal, *West Indies Societies* [London, 1972], p. vi.)

13 The Invention of the White Race – and the Ordeal of America

1. Edmund Burke, *An Account of European Settlements in America*, 2 vols. (London, 1758); 2:118.

2. CO 5/1371, 150vo–151 (James City County Grievance No. 10).

3. John C. Rainbolt, "The Alteration in the Relationship between Leadership and Constitutents in Virginia, 1660–1720," *WMO*, 27:411–34 (October 1970); p. 412.

4. John C. Rainbolt, *From Prescription to Persuasion* (Port Washington, NY, 1974), p. 97.

5. Edmund S. Morgan, *American Slavery, American Freedom: The Ordeal of Colonial Virginia* (New York, 1975), chapters 15–18, the closing section of the book.

6. ". . . social peace gradually arrived, according to several studies, as race, not class, separated the privileged from the unprivileged." (A. Roger Ekirch, "Exiles in the Promised Land: Convict

Labor in the Eighteenth Century Chesapeake," *Maryland Historical Magazine*, 82:95–122 [Summer 1987]; p. 96).

7. Lyon G. Tyler, "Virginians Voting in the Colonial Period," *WMQ*, ser. 1, 6:7–8 (1897–98). Tyler may also have been the author of a piece by "Lafayette," "No Feudalism in the South," in which it is stated that, "The great distinction in Virginia was color not class." *Tyler's Quarterly Historical and Genealogical Magazine*, 10:73–5, p. 74.

8. Gary B. Nash, "Colonial Development," in Jack P. Greene and J. R. Pole, eds., *Colonial British America: Essays in the New History of the Modern Era (London, 1984), pp. 244–5.*

9. Nash says that this all-class "white" unity was the result of the plantation bourgeoisie "relocating their reservoir of servile labor from . . . England and Ireland to . . . West Africa." (Nash, p. 244).

10. Russel R. Menard, *Economy and Society in Early Colonial Maryland* (New York, 1985) and David W. Galenson, *White Servitude in Colonial America: An Economic Analysis* (New York, 1981) are of particular interest in this regard. Neither seems to have taken into account the "racial quotas," deficiency laws, and laws passed in the plantation colonies to bar Negroes from skilled trades – enactments that had nothing to do with a "free market" search for skilled workers, but everything to do with maintaining "the southern labor system." See Galenson's generalization of the argument (pp. 166–8). Menard combines the assertion that "African slaves could not compete with indentured servants for the few good jobs that did exist," with a reference to "cultural barriers and the depth of racial prejudice" (p. 269). This seems at best redundant to the argument that the skilled labor shortage was the determinant of the transformation of "the labor system"; or tautological, if it is meant to explain racial discrimination in employment by reference to racially discriminatory ideas in employers' heads; and at worst it is a reversion to the "natural racism" rationale for racial slavery. A very recent review by Menard, however, seems to indicate a readiness to take a new look at the "white race." (Menard's comments appeared in *Journal of American Ethnic History*, spring 1996, pp. 57–8.) Incidentally, while my point of view and interpretation differ from those of Menard regarding historical subjects of common interest, I have never presumed to characterize his work as "tendentious,"; and I am at a loss to know why Menard thinks I have done so.

11. "Slaves . . . had none of the rising expectations that have often prompted rebellions in human history." (Morgan, p. 309.)

12. Orlando Patterson finds that the newly arriving Africans, who had been born free, were especially difficult to control. Though displaced from their native lands, their tribal stems retained a marked degree of vitality. In Jamaica in the last quarter of the seventeenth century, it was precisely they who were the most resistant, as shown in insurrections mounted by them in 1673, 1682, 1685 and 1690. Orlando Patterson, "Slavery and Slave Revolts: A Historical Analysis of the First Maroon War, 1665–1740," *Social and Economic Studies*, 19:289–325 [1970], reprinted in Richard Price, ed., *Maroon Societies: Rebel Slave Communities in the Americas* [Garden City, NY, 1973], pp. 246–92; 255–8.)

13. Thomas Roderick Dew (1802–46), Professor of History and Political Law at William and Mary College and the thirteenth president of that institution, set forth this inversion of the cause and effect of "white solidarity" and racial slavery. Because of the imposition of lifetime hereditary bondage on African-Americans, he said, "there is at once taken away the greatest cause for distinction and separation of the ranks of ["white"] society." (Thomas Roderick Dew, *The Pro-Slavery Argument* [Charleston, South Carolina, 1852; Negro Universities reprint, 1968], p. 461.)

14. See p. 235.

15. Thomas N. Ingersoll, ed., "'Releese us out of this Cruell Bondegg': An appeal from Virginia in 1723," *WMQ*, 3d ser., 51:777–82. The author of this letter did not reveal his or her name for fear of being put to death if identified. There is some reason to believe, as Ingersoll points out, that the letter was a collective effort. The date of the letter is 8 September 1723, but there are indications that it may have been composed over a period of days.

16. West served as counsel to the Board of Trade from 1718 to 1725. Soon thereafter he assumed the office of Chancellor of Ireland, but survived there only a year. George Chalmers, comp. and ed., *Opinions of Eminent Lawyers on Various Points of English Jurisprudence chiefly concerning the Colonies, Fisheries, and Commerce*, 2 vols. (London, 1814; Burt Franklin Reprint, 1971, from the original edition in the Brooklyn Public Library), p. xxxiii.

17. Hening, 4: 133–4.

18. Chalmers, 2:113–14.

19. Alured Popple, Secretary to the Board of Trade, to Governor William Gooch of Virginia, 18 December 1735 (CO 5/1366, pp. 134–5). Although West made his report in January 1724, it was

eleven years later that the objection came to the attention of the Board of Trade, who then instructed Popple to ask for an explanartion from Gooch. There is as yet no accounting for the board's long delay in taking up the matter with the Virginia government. (See Emory G. Evans, ed., "A Question of Complexion," *VMHB*, 71:411–13 [1963].) Is it possible that Bishop Edmund Gibson played some part in getting particular attention paid to the question after receiving the African-American appeal for freedom sent from Virginia in 1723? (See p. 241, n. 15).

20. CO 5/1324, ff. 19, 22. The Gooch quotations in the following paragraph are from this same document.

21. Along with Catholics who refused to conform to the Protestant way, "and others not being Christians," Negroes were "incapable of in law, to be witnesses in any cases whatsoever" under terms of the Virginia code of 1795 (Hening, 3:298). It may be speculated that Gooch's choice of words here implicitly referred to that law. But Gooch must have been aware that in 1723, and again in 1732, this loophole was closed by making it possible for African-Americans to give evidence in trials of other African-Americans for rebellion or other capital offenses. (Hening, 4:127 [1723], 327 [1732]).

22. The contrast between the denial of middle-class status to persons of any degree of African descent and the middle-class role of mulattos and free blacks in the Caribbean was occasionally dramatized in the Virginia courts. In 1688, on the cusp of King Billy's War, John Servele (the name is variously spelled), a "molatto" born in St Kitts of a French father and a free Negro mother and duly baptized there, through a series of misadventures was sold into Virginia where he was claimed as a lifetime bond-laborer by a succession of owners. In consideration of testimonials from the Governor of St Kitts and a Jesuit priest there, and the fact that Servele had already served more than seven years, the Governor and Council ordered that Servele be released and given his "corn and cloathes" freedom dues. (*Norfolk County Records, 1686–95, (Orders)*, pp. 107, 115, 17 September and 15 November 1688.) Another man, Michael Roderigo, a native of St Domingue, likewise a victim of misadventures that ended with him being sold as a lifetime bond-laborer in Virginia, took advantage of a lull in the Anglo-French warring to petition the Virginia Colony Council for his freedom. In support of his claim as "a Christian and a free subject of France," he proposed to call as a witness a Virginia plantation owner "who hath bought slaves" from him in Petit Guaves, St Domingue. (Virginia Colony Council proceedings, 22 February 1699/1700. Library of Congress, Virginia [Colony] Collection, 80–75775.)

23. It would be another half-century before James Madison, speaking as a member of the Virginia Council of State, would propose, though unpersuasively, that freedmen were readily absorbed into the system of control over bond-laborers. Replying to the idea of inducing "whites" to join the "fight for freedom" by giving each one an African-American lifetime bond-laborer, Madison suggested a more direct approach to recruitment: "would it not be as well," he said, "to liberate and make soldiers at once of [those] blacks themselves as to make them instruments for enlisting white Soldiers?" He reassured doubters that this course would constitute no danger to the institution of slavery, "experience having shown that a freedman immediately loses all attachment & sympathy for his former fellow slaves." (William T. Hutchinson and William M. E. Rachle, eds., *The Papers of James Madison*, 9 vols. [Chicago, 1962]; 2:198–201, 209–11; the cited passage is at page 209 [Correspondence with Joseph Jones, 24 and 28 November 1780]. See also *Journal of the [Virginia] House of Delegates, 1777–1780* [Richmond, 1827], pp. 56, 64, 65, 67, 98, 100, 105, 113, 116, 119, cited by Robert E. Brown and B. Katherine Brown, *Virginia 1705–1786, Democracy or Aristocracy?* [East Lansing, 1964], p. 68).

24. "Instead of creating problems, the union of a white man and a Negro woman was sometimes considered a judicious mingling of business with pleasure." (Brown and Brown, p. 68). Thomas Jefferson's considered opinion on the subject of "breeding women" was that "a child raised every 2 years is of more profit than the crop of the best laboring man." "What [such a] mother produces," he wrote, "is an addition to capital, while his labors disappear in mere consumption." (Jefferson, letters to William Yancey, 17 January 1819, and to W. Eppes, 30 June 1820; cited in William Cohen, "Thomas Jefferson and the Problem of Slavery," *Journal of American History*, 16:518 [1969].)

25. Hening, 3:87–8 (1691).

26. See Appendix II-F.

27. "In regard to the Reasons you have offered in behalf of the Act we shall let that Act lie by." (Board of Trade to Gooch, 15 October 1736 CO 5/1366, p. 137.)

28. *CSP, Col.*, 16:390–91.

29. CO 5/1363 Jennings to Commissioners for Trade and Plantations, 24 April 1710. See also Virginia State Archives, "Colonial Papers' collection, folder 20, items 11, 13, 14.

30. *Journals of the House of Burgesses of Virginia, 1619–1777*, edited by H. R. McIlwaine and J.

P. Kennedy, 13 vols. (Richmond, 1905–15); volume for 1702 to 1712, p. 240. Cited by Brown and Brown, p. 70.

31. See p. 581.

32. *CSP, Col.* 36:114, Gooch to the Board of Trade, 29 June 1729.

33. *American Historical Review*, 1:88–90 (1895, "Documents" [No.1]). Byrd to Lord Egmont. One may speculate that his reference to a man of "desperate fortune" was in memory of Nathaniel Bacon, whose rebellion Byrd's father had first urged on, and then abandoned when the English and Negro bond-laborers enlisted in it.

34. *Legislative Journal of the Council of Colonial Virginia*, 3 vols., edited by H. R. McIlwaine (Richmond, 1918), 2:1034–35 (11 April 1749). An estimated 30,000 convict bond-laborers were sent to America in 190 shiploads between 1717 and 1772. Of these cargoes, 100 went to the Chesapeake, 53 to Maryland and 47 to Virginia. (Arthur Price Middleton, *Tobacco Coast: A Maritime History of Chesapeake Bay in the Colonial Era* [Newport News, 1953], p. 152.)

35. Thomas J. Wertenbaker, *Patrician and Plebeian in Virginia, or the Origin and Development of the Social Classes of the Old Dominion* (New York, 1910, 1958, 1959). Idem, *The Planters of Colonial Virginia* (Princeton, 1922; New York, 1959). The "Middle Class," to whom Wertenbaker devotes Part Two of the former work, is called "the Virginia yeomanry" in the latter (pp. 137, 160). See Chapter 2 above for a discussion of the "forty-shilling freeholder."

36. One historian drew the line between those who inherited any wealth at all and those who inherited none: "Herein lay the contrast between the two classes often but erroneously confused, the "poor whites" and the yeomen." (Ulrich Bonnell Phillips, *Life and Labor in the Old South* (Boston, 1929), p. 346). Another, Edmund S. Morgan, states that a man qualified as a yeoman if he owned land. (Morgan, p. 377.)

37. Robert E. and B. Katherine Brown reject such a definition of interests. After observing unselfconsciously that, "Slavery was profitable, it enabled a man to live with a minimum of physical labor," they conclude with the self-standing assertion that: "Protection of slave property was of constant and vital concern to all classes of the white population.... [Slavery] definitely set off the white man as the master in society, and it did create a lower class – which could be exploited by the master race." (Brown and Brown, p. 77).

38. Allan Kulikoff, *Tobacco and Slaves: The Development of Southern Cultures in the Chesapeake, 1680–1800* (Chapel Hill, 1986), p. 262. Taking estates in personalty as the index, Aubrey Land says that the "great planters ... never formed more than a fraction of the total community of planters, something like 2.5 percent in the decade 1690–1699 and about 6.5 percent half a century later." (Aubrey C. Land, "Economic Behavior in a Planting Society: The Eighteenth-century Chesapeake," *Journal of Southern History*, 33:469–85; pp. 472–3.

39. These latter constituted the self-perpetuating ruling bourgeois elite. "The wealthiest planters and planter-merchants," writes Kulikoff, "dominated local [County Court] benches and provincial legislatures from the 1650s to the Revolution.... By 1705, three-fifths of Virginians who owned two thousand or more acres of land were justices or burgesses." (Kulikoff, p. 268.)

In Virginia over the period 1720 to 1776, 630 men held seats in the House of Burgesses. Of this number, 110 dominated the proceedings of the House by virtue of their committee positions in that body. Of that 110, three out of four each owned more than 10,000 acres of land. With regard to the extent of their holdings of lifetime bond-laborers, eleven held more than 300 each; 25 held from 50 to 300; 25 held from 50 to 300 each; and 22 others held more than ten. (Jack P. Greene, "Foundations of Political Power in the Virginia House of Burgesses," *WMQ*, ser. 3, 16:485–506; pp. 485–8.) A tabulation of the population and the voting in seven Virginia counties in the period 1783–90 shows a total population of 80,893, including 45,111 "whites". Free "white" males sixteen years of age and over numbered 11,084, of whom 4,242 were owners of the 25 acres required of qualified voters. (Charles S. Sydnor, *Gentlemen Freeholders: Political Practices in Washington's Virginia*, Chapel Hill, 1952, pp. 141–3.)

40. Kulikoff, p. 268. While this definition of "yeoman" is more elastic than my standard for "middle class", and Kulikoff's "above half" may be on the high side of the estimates by Land and Main given below, it has the virtue of being related to ownership of lifetime bond-laborers.

41. Ibid., p. 262. See also the half-dozen authorities cited by Kulikoff there. With regard to the yeomen's credit dependency on the gentry, see ibid., pp. 288–9.

42. Aubrey C. Land, "Economic Base and Social Structure; The Northern Chesapeake in the Eighteenth Century," *Journal of Economic History*, 25:639–54 (1965); p. 641. Although this study is limited to Maryland, Land believes that "differences between the areas [of the Chesapeake] are not very great" in respect to the thesis he presents.

43. Ibid., pp. 642–3.

44. Ibid., p. 648. See also my comments on eighteenth-century tenancy on pp. 104–5.

45. See *The Invention of the White Race*, Volume One, pp. 122–3.

46. Land, "Economic Base and Social Structure," p. 653.

47. Ibid., pp. 643–4.

48. Ibid., p. 644.

49. Ibid., pp. 644, 654.

50. Jackson Turner Main, "The Distribution of Property in Post-Revolutionary Virginia," *Mississippi Valley Historical Review*, 41:241–58 (1954–55). (The name of this publication was later changed to *The Journal of American History*.) See also Jackson T. Main, *The Social Structure of Revolutionary America* (Princeton, 1965), esp Chapter II, "The Economic Class Structure of the South."

51. Main, "Distribution of Property," p. 258.

52. Jackson Turner Main, "Distribution of Property," pp. 241, 242–3, 248. The "Northern Neck," the area between the Potomac and the Rappahannock rivers, had double the proportion of landless, and of these most were laborers, not tenants. (Ibid., p. 248.) See also Gloria L. Main's study of probate records of Virginia and Maryland, "Inequality in Early America: The Evidence from Probate Records of Massachusetts and Maryland," *Journal of Interdisciplinary History*, 7:559–81; 570–2, 580.

Brown and Brown, p. 31 n. 142, refer to the contrast between their view and that of Jackson T. Main with regard to laboring-class expectations. However, they do not make any effort to challenge Main's thesis. But also compare D. Alan Williams, "The Small Farmer in Eighteenth-century Virginia Politics," *Agricultural History*, 43:91–101 (1969).

53. Not more than 49 percent of the total adult white male population were landowners. The large-owner one-fifth, plus three-fourths of the middle-size landowners' two-thirds share of the total number of landowners, would make up a total of 70 percent as the approximate proportion of landowners who were also owners of lifetime bond-laborers, and that would represent less than 35 percent of the total adult white male population. Main does not even suggest any statistically significant employment of bond-labor by owners of one hundred acres or less. Taking into account Main's mention of the ownership of bond-laborers by non-landowners, I have attempted to make a generous discount for that factor in setting the proportion of non-owners of bond-labor at around 60 percent of the total adult white male population.

54. Kulikoff, p. 262.

55. Governor Notley's words of advice. See pp. 221–2.

56. The coincidence of names is not accidental. This Nathaniel Bacon and Sir Francis had a common ancestor; Nathaniel's great-grandfather and Sir Francis were first cousins. It is also interesting to note that Nathaniel Bacon's grandfather, also named Nathaniel, was an artist and a republican writer during the time of Cromwell. ("The Bacons of Virginia," *New England Historical and Genealogical Register*, 37:189–98 [1883]; p. 197.)

57. Francis Bacon, Essay No. 15, "Of Seditions and Troubles," in *Works*, 6:406–12. The slavocracy's most eminent "theoretician" well understood the premise of that strategy. "The dominant party," he said, "can only be overturned by concert and harmony among the subject party." (Thomas Roderick Dew, *An Essay on Slavery* [Richmond, 1849], p. 103.)

58. Morgan, p. 328. Ira Berlin appears to endorse Morgan on this point. "Chesapeake planters," he writes, "consolidated their class position by asserting white racial unity." (Ira Berlin, "Time, Space, and the Evolution of Afro-American Society on British Mainland North America," *American Historical Review*, 85:44–78 [1980]; p. 72.)

59. Philip Alexander Bruce, *Social Life in Virginia in the Seventeenth Century, An Inquiry into the Origin of the Higher Plantation Class, Together with an Account of the Habits, Customs and Diversions of the People* (Richmond, 1902), pp. 137–8.

60. H. M. Henry, *Police Control in South Carolina* (Emory, 1914), pp. 190–91. Henry asks rhetorically whether the poor whites cooperated with the slaveholders because they perceived that a threat was posed by African-Americans to "their personal security and that of their families." (Ibid.) He does not attempt to sustain this speculation. If they were worried on that score why would they encourage the expansion of the system by providing security for the large planters?

61. Hening 3:87–8. In such cases the emancipator was required to pay for the exiling of the freed person within six months, or else to pay a £10 fine which would be used to pay for the freed person's transportation out of Virginia as arranged by the church wardens of the parish.

62. *Norfolk County Wills*, p. 26. *Executive Journals of the Council of Colonial Virginia,* edited by H. R. McIlwaine (Richmond, 1928), 3:332. The Colony Council justified this unprecedented

infringement of testamentary rights on the grounds that the increase in the number of free Negroes would "endanger the peace of this Colony" by encouraging the freedom aspirations of others held in bondage.

63. Hening, 2:117–18 (1662). In Maryland, also in 1705, laws were passed to guarantee "white" servants against abuse and against being detained in servitude beyond their time, and declaring that "Negroes [were] Slaves during their Naturall Lives nor freed by Baptisme." (CO 7/15, pp. 14, 15. Report of Governor John Seymour, 3 July 1705, to the Board of Trade on laws passed in Maryland that year.) Bond-laborer Margaret Godfrey sought in vain to claim the protection of her "white" status by defiantly telling her overseer, "If you whip me it will be worse for you for I am not a Slave." The overseer, with the express leave of the mistress, cut Godfrey's clothes from her body and beat her severely two successive times. Her offense had been to plead for humane treatment for her severely injured husband. The Godfreys' petition for relief was rejected by the Court. (*St George's County Records*, HH, pp. 165–8 [June 1748]. Maryland State Archives, Annapolis.)

64. Hening, 3:448 (1705).

65. Hening, 3:449

66. Hening, 4:351.

67. Hening, 3:103, 459–60. As noted in Chapter 12, throughout the British West Indies it was customary for even bond-laborers to earn money by marketing goods produced on plots of land allowed them whereby they might buy themselves out of bondage. Hilliard d'Auberville proposed, among other measures to control the bond-laborers of St Domingue, "to give them wives, encourage them to raise cattle, hold them with ties of property." (Hilliard d'Auberville, *Considérations sur l'état présent de la colonie française de St Domingue*, 2 vols. [Paris, 1776–77]; 2:59–62. Cited in Gwen Midlo Hall, *Social Control in Slave Plantation Societies: A Comparison of St Domingue and Cuba*, [Baltimore, 1971], p. 83.)

68. Hening, 2:267 (1668).

69. Hening, 2:280–81 (1670).

70. Hening, 3:251 (1705).

71. Hening, 3:298 (1705); 4:327 (1732).

72. Hening, 3:459 (1705).

73. Hening, 4:119 (1723).

74. Hening, 4:130 (1723). A provision was made for free African-American "householders", and any free African-American who lived on a "frontier plantation" and was able to secure a license from a justice of the peace, to keep one gun and the powder and shot needed for it.

75. See *The Invention of the White Race*, Volume One, p. 89. "The white man's pursuit of black women frequently destroyed any possibility that comely black girls could remain chaste for long," writes Blassingame. According to autobiographies of former bond-laborers, the home of a bond-laborer was "considered by many white men ... as a house of ill-fame." (John W. Blassingame, *Plantation Life in the Ante-Bellum South* [New York, 1972], p. 82.)

76. Philip J. Schwarz, *Twice Condemned: Slaves and the Criminal Laws of Virginia, 1705–1865* (Baton Rouge, 1988), p. 159.

77. "A white man may go to the house of a free black, maltreat and abuse him, and commit any outrage upon his family, for all of which the law cannot reach him, unless some white person saw the act committed." Thus observed Mr Wilson of Perquimon County, speaking at the 1835 North Carolina State Constitutional Convention of 1835. (John S. Bassett, *Slavery in the State of North Carolina* [Baltimore, 1899], bound as one of a number of studies in Bassett, *Slavery in the United States, Selected Essays* [New York: Negro Universities Press, 1969], p. 42.)

78. Hening, 3:447–62, 4:126–34 (emphasis added). The citations of these laws that follow are from Hening.

79. Ulrich Bonnell Phillips spoke of "the methods of life which controlled the history of Virginia through the following centuries and of the many colonies and states which borrowed her plantation system." This was "Dixie," where, he said, "the white folk [are] a people with a common resolve indomitably maintained – that it shall be and remain a white man's country." (Ulrich Bonnell Phillips, *The Slave Economy of the Old South: Selected Essays in Economic and Social History*, edited by Eugene D. Genovese [Baton Rouge, 1968], pp. 8, 274. The dates of these pronouncements were 1910–11 and 1918, respectively.)

80. Winthrop D. Jordan, *White Over Black: American Attitudes Toward the Negro, 1550–1812* (Chapel Hill, 1968), p. 123. I find Jordan's observation accurate and very pertinent, but I have appropriated it for an argument that he does not support. His "unthinking decision" approach to the origin of racial slavery rejects Morgan's (and my) attribution of deliberate ruling-class manipulation for social control purposes.

81. Wertenbaker, *Patrician and Plebeian*, p. 212.

82. Hening, 4:202.

83. Schwarz, p. 13.

84. Brown and Brown, p. 48.

85. Warren B. Smith, *White Servitude in the Colony of South Carolina* (Columbia, 1961), p. 30.
The American Revolution wrought no difference in this respect. Seventy-five years later "[p]oor
white men habitually kept their eyes open for strange Negroes without passes, for the apprehension
of a fugitive was a financial windfall ... [W]hite workingmen on the Baltimore and Susquehanna
Railroad caught several Maryland bondsmen who had escaped to within five miles of the
Pennsylvania border. The workingmen returned them to their owners and collected the reward."
(Kenneth M. Stampp, *The Peculiar Institution: Slavery in the Ante-Bellum South* [New York, 1956],
p. 153.)

86. Basset, *Slavery in the State of North Carolina*, pp. 29–30.

87. Smith, pp. 30–31. Other variations of the same quota principle were enacted.

88. Ibid., p. 35.

89. Elizabeth Donnan, ed., *Documents Illustrative of the Slave Trade to America*, 4 vols.
(Washington, DC, 1935), 4:595 (1739), 605 (1742).

90. Ibid., 4:610. See also Klaus G. Loewald, Beverley Starika and Paul S. Taylor, eds., "Johann
Martin Bolzius Answers a Questionnaire on Carolina and Georgia," *WMQ*, ser. 3, 14:218–261
(1957); pp. 227, 242.

91. "Irish-Americans [arriving in the United States in the ante-bellum period] were not the
originators of white supremacy; they adapted to and were adopted into an already existing 'white'
American social order." (*The Invention of the White Race*, Volume One, p. 199.)

92. Ulrich Bonnell Phillips, "The Slave Labor Problem in the Charleston District," *Political
Science Quarterly*, 22:416–39 (1907); reprinted in Phillips, *Slave Economy of the Old South*, p. 198.

93. Richard B. Morris, *Government and Labor in Early America* (New York, 1946), p. 182.

94. James Hugo Johnston, *Race Relations in Virginia and Miscegenation in the South, 1776–1860*
(Amherst, Massachusetts, 1970), p. 58, citing *Archives of Virginia, Legislative Papers*, petitions:
9789, Culpeper, 9 December 1831; 9860, Dinwiddie, 20 December 1831; 177707, Norfolk, 12
November 1851). It would seem relevant to note that the first two of these petitions were submitted
in the wake of Nat Turner's Rebellion and during the Virginia House of Delegates' debate on
slavery. (See Theodore William Allen, "'... They Would Have Destroyed Me': Slavery and the
Origins of Racism," *Radical America*, 9:41–63 (1975); pp. 58–9.)

95. For this aspect of the question, see the Introduction in Volume One of *The Invention of the
White Race*, pp. 4–14, "The Psycho-cultural Argument."

96. Edmund Burke, *Writings and Speeches*, 12 vols. (London, 1803). 2:123–4.

97. Dew, *Essay on Slavery*, p. 99.

98. Morgan, p. 376. The general term "Virginians" is used by Morgan to mean "white" people
in Virginia. In the concluding Chapter 18 the term appears some twenty-two times, but only twice
is it modified by "white". Morgan's imposition of this "white" assumption on the reader,
objectionable in itself, more importantly conforms with his treatment of the African-Americans as
mere background to the rise of "liberty and equality."

99. Ibid., p. 380.

100. Ibid., p. 364.

101. Ibid., pp. 366, 369.

102. Ibid., p. 386.

103. See page 240.

104. Hutchinson and Rachle, eds., 2:209.

105. Letter from "Civis," an eastern Virginia slaveholder, in the *Richmond Enquirer*, 4 May 1832.

106. Edmund S. Morgan, "Slavery and Freedom, The American Paradox," *Journal of American
History*, June 1972, pp. 5–6.

107. Morgan, *American Slavery, American Freedom*, pp. 386, 387.

108. Wertenbaker, *Planters of Colonial Virginia*, p. 160.

109. See pp. 245–7, particularly the summary on p. 247.

110. Marquis de Chastellux, *Travels in North-America in the Years 1780, 1781, and 1782*,
translated by an English gentleman who resided in America at that period, 2 vols., 2nd edn.
(London 1787; 1968 reprint), 2:190.

111. See p. 255.

112. Wertenbaker, *Patrician and Plebeian*, p. 211.

113. "[T]here existed a numerous supply of potential tenants ... from that group of small planters

who, in consequence of the trifling quantity of poor tobacco produced on their overworked land in the east, could not successfully compete with a large amount of excellent tobacco grown on the fresh land of the great planters. Faced with impoverishment they looked to the more fertile lands of the Piedmont and Valley as a means of bettering their condition." (Willard F. Bliss, "The Rise of Tenancy in Virginia,"*VMHB* 58:427–442 (1950).

114. Kulikoff, pp. 150, 152, 153, 296, 297–8. See also pp. 104–5.

115. George W. Summers of Kanawha County, speaking in the Virginia House of Delegates, during the debate on slavery, following Nat Turner's Rebellion (*Richmond Enquirer*, 2 February 1832).

116. "[T]he 'warlike Christian men' recruited by Virginia to defend its borders in 1701 were the direct ancestors of the dragoons whose Colts and Winchesters subdued the Sioux of the Great Plains a century and a half later." (Ray Allen Billington, *America's Frontier Heritage* [New York, 1966], p. 40.) The interior quotation is from an Act passed by the Virginia Assembly in August 1701, designed to encourage English frontier settlers (Hening, 3:207).

117. Frederick Jackson Turner, *The Frontier in American History* (New York, 1920; 1947), p. 38.

118. Ibid., p. 1. A century has passed since that first essay, and Turner's frontier thesis continues to be meat and drink for historiographical evaluation and disputation. But a marked tendency has been apparent to limit the "frontier" concept, reducing it to a Western regional subject, which of course risks "abandonment of the cross-regional and national emphasis he [Turner] sought to establish for the field" (William Cronon, cited in John Mack Farragher, "The Frontier Trail: Rethinking Turner and Reimagining the American West," *American Historical Review*, 98:106–17 [1993], p. 117). Since the 1960s, critics have shown a welcome sensitivity to Turner's neglect of Indians, Mexicans and Chinese or, worse, his chauvinistic attitude toward them. Finally, in 1995, a reference was made to Turner's pervasive "whiteness," the significant fact that "his own racial identity was a completely foreign concept to him" (Patricia Nelson Limerick, "Turnerians All: The Dream of a Helpful History in an Intelligible World," *American Historical Review*, 100:697–716 [1995], p. 715).

119. Turner, p. 38.

120. Ibid., pp. 280–81.

121. Ibid., p. 321.

122. James C. Malin, *Essays on Historiography* (Lawrence, Kansas, 1946, p. 38, cited in Harry Nash Smith, *Virgin Land* (Cambridge, 1950), p. 302.

123. The free-land "safety valve" theory at one time was the subject of extensive debate among economic, labor and land historians. Its limitations, even in its own white-blind terms, as an explanation of the low level of proletarian class-consciousness were forcefully pointed out decades ago by such historians as Carter Goodrich, Sol Davison, Murray Kane, and Fred A. Shannon, whose names are prominent in the extensive bibliography of the "safety valve" controversy. Subsequently it could only be defended in a greatly watered-down form of the original Turner formulation. See Ray Allen Billington, *The American Frontier Thesis: Attack and Defense* (Washington, DC, 1971, pp. 20–25, and idem, *America's Frontier Heritage*, pp. 31–8, 292–3.

124. I borrow here the title of a well-known work of William Appleman Williams, *The Contours of American History* (New York, 1988; originally published in 1966).

125. See *The Invention of the White Race*, Volume One, pp. 145–7, 152–7, 184–6, 195–7, 198–9.

Appendix II-A

1. Richard Price, ed., *Maroon Societies: Rebel Slave Communities in the Americas* (New York, 1973), pp. 1, 3.

2. Jose L. Franco, "Maroons and Slave Rebellions in the Spanish Territories," in Price, ed., p. 47, 48.

3. David M. Davidson, "Negro Slave Control and Resistance in Colonial Mexico, 1519–1659," in Price, ed., p. 91.

4. Ibid., pp. 96–7.

5. Aquiles Escalante, "Palenques in Colombia," in Price, ed., pp. 77–9.

6. Price, ed., pp. 20, 33; Franco, p. 41.

7. Roger Bastide, "The Other Quilombos," in Price, ed., pp. 191–2.

8. R. K. Kent, "Palmares: An African State in Brazil," in Price, ed., p. 172.

9. Ibid., pp. 179, 185, 187.
10. Ibid., pp. 177, 178–80, 183, 185.
11. Ibid., pp. 180–81.
12. Price, ed., "Introduction," p. 20.
13. Kent, p. 172.

Appendix II-B

1. No one, then or since, could know within any great degree of exactitude the proportion of the English population destroyed by the plague. The lowest estimate seems to be 20 percent. (Josiah Cox Russell, "Demographic Patterns in History," Population Studies, No. 1, 1948; cited in Cambridge Economic History of Europe, 4:612.) The same economic historians say the toll was one-third to half of the population. James E. Rogers, in The Economic Interpretation of History (London, 1889), says it was one-third (p. 263). George M. Trevelyan says three-eighths of the people perished (A Shortened History of England [New York, 1942] p. 192).
2. Rogers, p. 22.
3. H. S. Bennett says that, even before 1348, "once the serf made up his mind to run away, it was difficult to restrain him." (H. S. Bennett, Life on the English Manor [London, 1948], p. 306.) See also Charles Oman, The Great Revolt of 1381 (Oxford, 1906), pp. 8–9.
4. This discussion of the revolt of 1381 is based mainly on Oman, The Great Revolt and R. B. Dobson, The Peasants Revolt of 1381 (London, 1970).
5. Oman, p. 1.
6. Ibid., p. 56.
7. Ibid., p. 64.
8. "Anonimal Chronical"; cited by Oman, pp. 200–201.
9. Dobson, p. 25.
10. Ibid., p. 30.
11. Rogers, p. 82.

Appendix II-D

1. Philip A. Bruce, Economic History of Virginia in the Seventeenth Century, 2 vols. (New York, 1895; reprint, 1935), 2:15.
2. James C. Ballagh, White Servitude in the Colony of Virginia, A Study of the System of Indentured Labor in the American Colonies (Baltimore, 1895; 1969 reprint), pp. 75–6.
3. Eugene I. McCormac, White Servitude in Maryland, 1634–1824 (Baltimore, 1904) p. 75.
4. Lewis C. Gray, assisted by Esther K. Thompson, History of Agriculture in the Southern United States to 1860, 2 vols. (Washington, DC, 1932) 1:506.
5. Richard B. Morris, Government and Labor in Early America, (New York, 1946), p. 484.
6. McCormac, pp. 61, 72–5.
7. A. E. Smith, Colonists in Bondage: White Servitude and Convict Labor in America, 1607–1776, p. 204. In considering Smith's conclusions cited here, one must keep in mind that his book dealt with bond-servitude in all Anglo-American colonies during the entire colonial period of the seventeenth and eighteenth centuries, whereas the present work is concerned with bond-servitude in the continental colonies, and particularly the seventeenth-century tobacco colonies, Virginia and Maryland.
8. Ibid., pp. 254, 258–60.
9. Russel R. Menard, Economy and Society in Early Colonial Maryland (New York, 1985), pp. 190–91. David W. Galenson, a University of Chicago economics professor, brings "bottom-line" logic to bear: "it would be surprising if severe physical abuse had been very common, for it would have interfered with the servants' work capacity, to the detriment of their masters' profits." "The Rise and Fall of Indentured Servitude in the Americas: An Economic Analysis," Journal of Economic History, 44:1–126 [1984]; p. 8. Galenson's argument on this point is essentially the same as that made by South Carolina governor Hammond and by George Fitzhugh in justification of slavery in the ante-bellum period. (See Volume One, p. 163.)

10. Edmund S. Morgan, *American Slavery, American Freedom: The Ordeal of Colonial Virginia* (New York, 1975) pp. 63–8.

11. Russell R. Menard, commenting on his own finding of a wide gap between life expectancy of immigrant Marylanders and men born in New England in the seventeenth century, does suggest that "This wide regional variation in mortality might prove a useful reference point for scholars concerned with differences in the social history of New England and the Chesapeake colonies." (*Economy and Society in Early Colonial Maryland*, p. 140.)

See Chapter 9 for further discussion of the New England contrast.

12. See Gloria L. Main, "Inequality in Early America: The Evidence from Probate Records of Massachusetts and Maryland, "*Journal of Interdisciplinary History*, 7:559–81 (1977),

13. Morris, pp. 282–3.

14. Ibid., p. 482.

Appendix II-E

1. Leslie A. Clarkson, *The Pre-industrial Economy of England, 1500*, New York, 1972, pp. 26–7.

2. Eleanora Mary Carus-Wilson, ed., *Essays in Economic History*, 3 vols. (London, 1962), 2:299.

3. Clarkson, pp. 26–7.

4. George M. Trevelyan, *Blenheim*, pp. 113, 216, 218.

5. Ibid., pp. 216–18.

6. Leo Francis Stock, ed., *Proceedings and Debates of the British Parliaments Respecting North America*, 5 vols. (Washington, DC, 1924), 1:343, n.

7. Cited in Klaus E. Knorr, *British Colonial Theories, 1570–1850* (Toronto, 1944), p. 72.

8. Roger Coke, *A Treatise Wherein is demonstrated that the Church and State of England are in equal danger with the trade of it,* p. 16. Cited in C. H. Hull, ed., *The Economic Writings of Sir William Petty* (London, 1899; 1963 reprint), 1:242, n.

9. William Petty, *Political Arithmetick,* in Hull, ed., pp. 293, 301–2.

Appendix II-F

1. Hening, 3:181.

2. Hening, 3:229–481.

3. CO 5/1356 (emphasis added). These instructions were addressed to Governor Effingham in 1684.

4. Hening, 2:117–18 (1662); 3:448 (1705).

5. Hening, 3:449.

6. Virginia State Archives, "Colonial Papers," folder 17, item 13. "Amendments proposed by the Council to the Bill entituled and concerning Servants and Slaves." [17 May 1706].

7. Hening, 3:459.

8. CO 391/16, f. 357, 1–2 March 1703/4.

9. CO 391/8.

10. Virginia State Archives, "Colonial Papers," folder 15, item 17. See also CO 5/1361, f. 46, 28 November 1704.

11. CO 391/7.

12. See CO 5/1312, Part 1, ff. 303, 305–11; and part 2, ff. 1–4, 202, 205–6, 228; and CO 5/1313, ff. 83, 249–55.

Index

abolition of slavery 237, 253
Accomack County 155, 157, 161, 166, 180, 184
acquisition costs 121
Act of Assembly (1661) 163
Act concerning Servants and Slaves (1705) 250, 251, 253
Act directing the trial of Slaves (1723) 250, 251
Act repealing ban on slavery (1750) 253
Adventurers 53–4, 63–4, 109, 206
African-Americans, status of 177–99
  challenging hereditary bondage 188–91
  Elizabeth Key case 194–9
  evangelical questions and objections 191–2
  labor time, unpaid 187–8
  landholding, historical significance of 182–6
  marriage and social mobility 181–2
  opposition by propertied classes to racial oppression 193–6
  owners of European-American bond-laborers 186–7
Afro-Caribbeans 41, 232–8
Agrarian Revolution 17–18, 24, 26
Albemarle see North Carolina
Amaru, Tupac 33
Amelia County 257
American Revolution 203, 205
American War of Independence 169
Andros, Governor 273
Anglo-Caribbean 38–9, 40, 41, 240, 242–3, 244
  see also social control
Anglo-Dutch Wars 168–9, 170
  Second (1665–67) 168, 197
  Third (1672–74) 168, 199, 209
Anglo-French wars 170
Angolans, enslavement of 34
anti-Indian war see Bacon's Rebellion
anti-vagabond laws 20–22, 24

Antigua 232
apprentices 23
  see also Duty boys
Aptheker, Herbert 148
Argall, Governor Samuel 56–8, 81–2
Asiento de negras 8
Azores 40
Aztecs 32

Bacon Assembly 216
Bacon, Sir Francis 11, 16–18, 28–9, 164, 173, 248; "Of Plantations" 105–6
Bacon, Nathaniel 176, 205, 206–7, 209, 210, 212, 213, 215
Bacon's Rebellion (1676) 37, 119, 123, 147, 148, 153, 169, 203–22, 239
  African-American/European-American collaboration in 248
  aftermath 216–17
  anti-Indian phase 204–7, 210
  civil war phase (1676–77) 204, 205
  destabilizing factors 217–22
  enslaving Indian war captives 204
  ruling, deficiency of during 240
  status of African-Americans 178
  see also under tobacco
Bailyn, Bernard 205–6, 208, 210
Ball, John 264
Ballagh, James C. 50, 267
Barbados 3, 63, 224, 242
  Afro-Caribbean majorities 233
  Afro-Caribbeans as middle class 235, 237
  Brown Privilege Bill 238
  Colony Council 230
  emigration of freemen 228, 229
  free coloreds 234
  General Assembly 230
  land area limits and capital costs 227
  Quakers and Christianity 191–2, 197
  revolt (1816) 237
  Sunday markets 234
  unfitness rationale 38

THE HAYMARKET SERIES

Recent and Forthcoming Titles

ANYTHING BUT MEXICAN: Chicanos in Contemporary Los Angeles *by Rudi Acuña*

THE INVENTION OF THE WHITE RACE, VOLUME I: Racial Oppression and Social Control *by Theodore Allen*

LABOR AND THE COURSE OF AMERICAN DEMOCRACY: US History in Latin American Perspective *by Charles Bergquist*

MIAMI *by John Beverley and David Houston*

CORRUPTIONS OF EMPIRE: Life Studies and the Reagan Era *by Alexander Cockburn*

ROLL OVER CHE GUEVARA: Travels of a Radical Reporter *by Marc Cooper*

BUILDING THE WORKINGMAN'S PARADISE: The Design of American Company Towns *by Margaret Crawford*

THE CULTURAL FRONT: The Laboring of American Culture in the Twentieth Century *by Michael Denning*

NOTES FROM UNDERGROUND: The Politics of Zine Culture *by Stephen Duncombe*

NO CRYSTAL STAIR: African Americans in the City of Angels *by Lynell George*

THE WAY THE WIND BLEW: A History of the Weather Underground *by Ron Jacobs*

POWER MISSES: Essays Across (Un)Popular Culture *by David James*

RACE AND POLITICS IN THE UNITED STATES: New Challenges and Responses for Black Activism *edited by James Jennings*

WHITE SAVAGES IN THE SOUTH SEAS *by Mel Kernahan*

THE HISTORY OF FORGETTING: Los Angeles and the Erasure of Memory *by Norman M. Klein*

THE PUBLIC BROADCASTING SERVICE *by James Ledbetter*

IMAGINING HOME: Class, Culture and Nationalism in the African Diaspora *by Sidney Lemelle and Robin D. G. Kelley*